ADDISON-WESLEY

WESTERN CANADIAN EDITION

Applied Mathematics 10

SOURCE BOOK

Robert Alexander
Mathematics Teacher
and Consultant
Richmond Hill, Ontario

Ron Coleborn
Burnaby South
Secondary School
Burnaby, British Columbia

Garry Davis
Saskatoon Public Board
of Education
Saskatoon, Saskatchewan

Florence Glanfield
Professor of Mathematics
Education
University of Saskatchewan
Saskatoon, Saskatchewan

Stephen Khan
Mathematics Education
Consultant
Winnipeg, Manitoba

Jim Nakamoto
Sir Winston Churchill
Secondary School
Vancouver, British Columbia

David Sufrin
Ballenas Secondary School
Parksville, British Columbia

Paul Williams
Red Deer College
Red Deer, Alberta

Elizabeth Wood
National Sport School
Calgary Board of Education
Calgary, Alberta

Rick Wunderlich
Shuswap Junior
Secondary School
Salmon Arm, British Columbia

Leanne Zorn
Mount Boucherie
Secondary School
Kelowna, British Columbia

Addison Wesley

Don Mills, Ontario • Reading, Massachusetts
Harlow, England • Glenview, Illinois
Melbourne, Australia

DEVELOPMENTAL EDITORS
Claire Burnett
Enid Haley

EDITORS
Mei Lin Cheung
Santo D'Agostino
John Yip-Chuck

RESEARCHER
Louise MacKenzie

DESIGN/PRODUCTION
Pronk&Associates

ART DIRECTION
Pronk&Associates

ELECTRONIC ASSEMBLY/TECHNICAL ART
Pronk&Associates

ISBN 0–201–39585–1

This book contains recycled product and is acid free.

4 5 – BP – 03 02

Pilot Teacher Reviewers

The authors and publishers would like to extend special acknowledgment to the pilot teachers and their students who worked with this resource before it was in final form.

André Favreau
Fort Richmond Collegiate
Winnipeg, Manitoba

Steven Hardy,
Darwin Holt,
Matthew Walker
Harry Ainlay High School
Edmonton, Alberta

Sheeva Harrysingh
J. H. Bruns Collegiate
Winnipeg, Manitoba

Carol Besteck Hope
Elmwood High School
Winnipeg, Manitoba

B. Maureen Mills
Dr. E. P. Scarlett Senior High School
Calgary, Alberta

Mark Mortenson
John G. Diefenbaker High School
Calgary, Alberta

Angie O'Brien,
Jacquie Karch
Lord Beaverbrook High School
Calgary, Alberta

Kelly Paul
W. P. Wagner Secondary School
Edmonton, Alberta

Bruce Podetz
Cedar Secondary School
Nanaimo, British Columbia

Bruce Waters
Miles MacDonell Collegiate
Winnipeg, Manitoba

Kevin Weimer
Lester B. Pearson High School
Calgary, Alberta

Reviewers

Carole Bilyk
Dakota Collegiate Institute
Winnipeg, Manitoba

Ron Flaig
Henry Wise Wood High School
Calgary, Alberta

Liliane Gauthier
Saskatoon Board of Education
Saskatoon, Saskatchewan

Doug Halladay
Fraser Academy
Vancouver, British Columbia

R. Bruce Kabaroff
Edmonton Public Schools
Edmonton, Alberta

Kathy McCabe
Universtiy of Alberta
Edmonton, Alberta

Fred Pauls
Mennonite Brethren Collegiate
Winnipeg, Manitoba

Louis Robitaille
Nova Scotia Community College
Lunenberg Campus, Nova Scotia

Marg Warren
Program Coordinator
Peel District School Board
Mississauga, Ontario

CONTENTS

Addison-Wesley Applied Mathematics 10 Source Book

Welcome

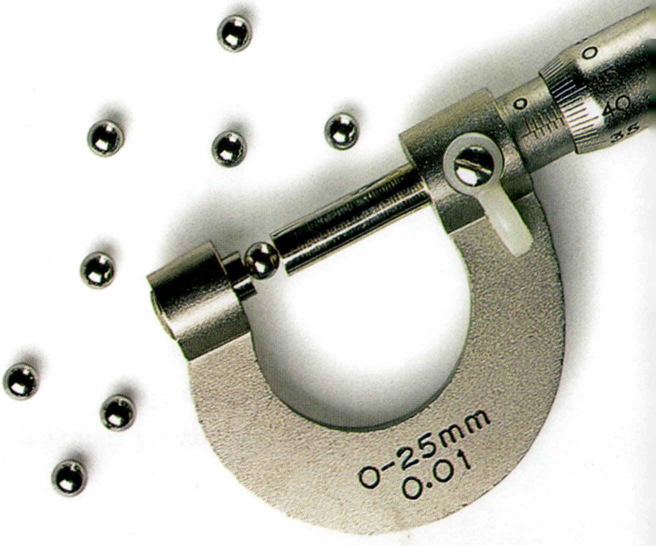

CONTENTS

CONTENTS

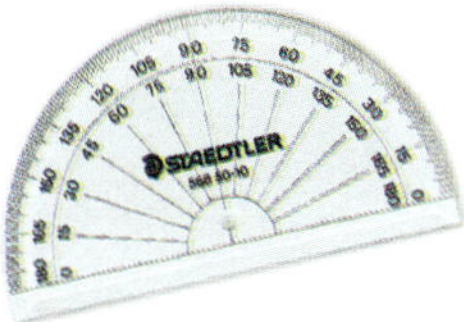

7 Trigonometry 319

Welcome to Addison-Wesley Applied Mathematics 10

Western Canadian Edition

Addison-Wesley Applied Mathematics presents mathematics as an essential tool in everyday life and in many careers. In this course, you will develop new mathematical concepts and skills by examining authentic situations and investigating solutions.

To meet the requirements of the Applied Mathematics course, you need to work from both the Project Book, and the Source Book. These introductory pages illustrate how your student books work.

Source Book

The Source Book has 7 chapters and three reference sections.

Each chapter starts with an Overview. This table tells you what mathematics you'll be learning.

Each chapter presents a Chapter Project, and a series of Tutorials.

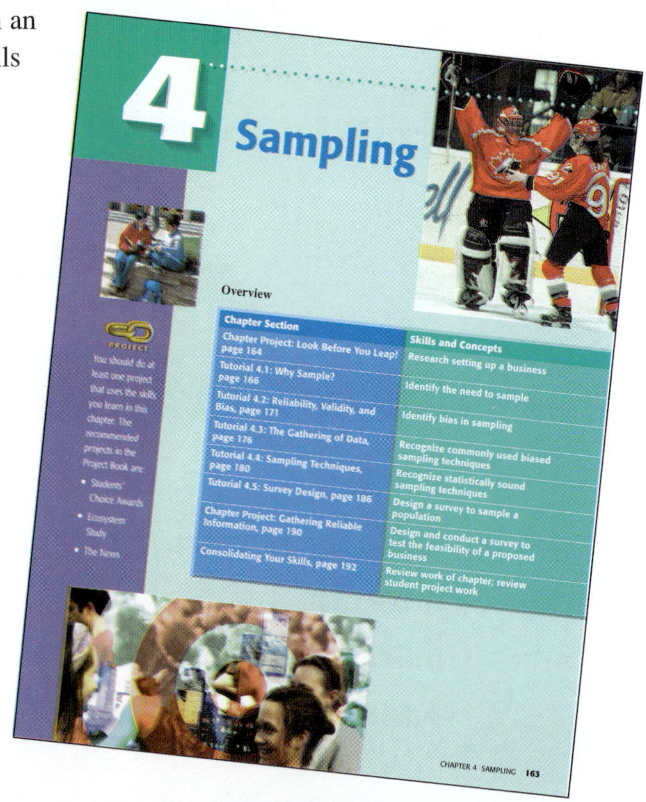

4 Sampling

PROJECT

You should do at least one project that uses the skills you learn in this chapter. The recommended projects in the Project Book are:

- Students' Choice Awards
- Ecosystem Study
- The News

Overview

Chapter Section	Skills and Concepts
Chapter Project: Look Before You Leap! page 164	Research setting up a business
Tutorial 4.1: Why Sample? page 166	Identify the need to sample
Tutorial 4.2: Reliability, Validity, and Bias, page 171	Identify bias in sampling
Tutorial 4.3: The Gathering of Data, page 176	Recognize commonly used biased sampling techniques
Tutorial 4.4: Sampling Techniques, page 180	Recognize statistically sound sampling techniques
Tutorial 4.5: Survey Design, page 186	Design a survey to sample a population
Chapter Project: Gathering Reliable Information, page 190	Design and conduct a survey to test the feasibility of a proposed business
Consolidating Your Skills, page 192	Review work of chapter; review student project work

CHAPTER 4 SAMPLING 163

Chapter Project

Two pages introduce the Chapter Project at the start of the chapter.

The Project Link tells you what mathematical concepts and skills you need for the project, and the Tutorials you might complete to develop those concepts and skills.

FYI Visit refers you to our web site, where you can connect to other sites to research the Chapter Project.

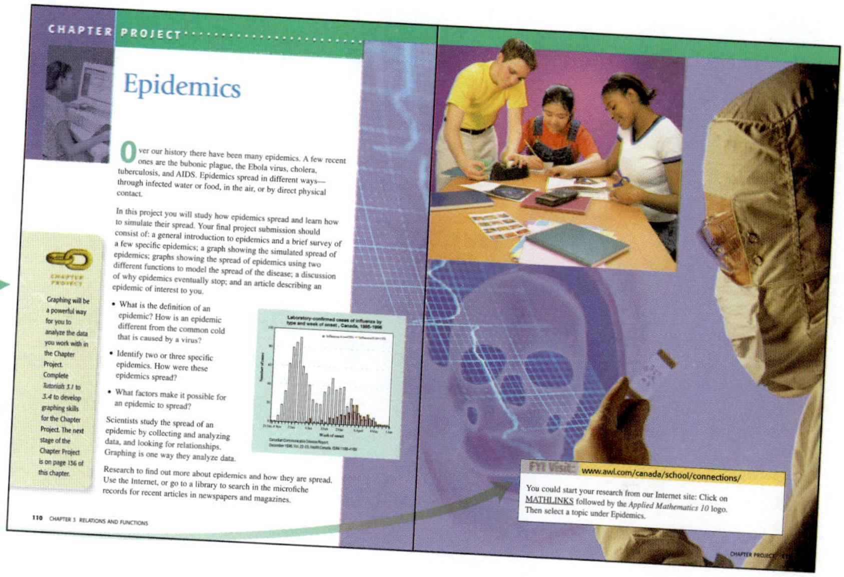

CHAPTER PROJECT

Epidemics

Over our history there have been many epidemics. A few recent ones are the bubonic plague, the Ebola virus, cholera, tuberculosis, and AIDS. Epidemics spread in different ways—through infected water or food, in the air, or by direct physical contact.

In this project you will study how epidemics spread and learn how to simulate their spread. Your final project submission should consist of: a general introduction to epidemics and a brief survey of a few specific epidemics; a graph showing the simulated spread of epidemics; graphs showing the spread of epidemics using two different functions to model the spread of the disease; a discussion of why epidemics eventually stop; and an article describing an epidemic of interest to you.

- What is the definition of an epidemic? How is an epidemic different from the common cold that is caused by a virus?
- Identify two or three specific epidemics. How were these epidemics spread?
- What factors make it possible for an epidemic to spread?

Scientists study the spread of an epidemic by collecting and analyzing data, and looking for relationships. Graphing is one way they analyze data.

Research to find out more about epidemics and how they are spread. Use the Internet, or go to a library to search in the microfiche records for recent articles in newspapers and magazines.

CHAPTER PROJECT

Graphing will be a powerful way for you to analyze the data you work with in the Chapter Project. Complete *Tutorials 3.1* to *3.4* to develop graphing skills for the Chapter Project. The next stage of the Chapter Project is on page 136 of this chapter.

FYI Visit: www.awl.com/canada/school/connections/

You could start your research from our Internet site: Click on MATHLINKS followed by the *Applied Mathematics 10* logo. Then select a topic under Epidemics.

110 CHAPTER 3 RELATIONS AND FUNCTIONS

CHAPTER PROJECT

You return to the Chapter Project after completing relevant Tutorials.

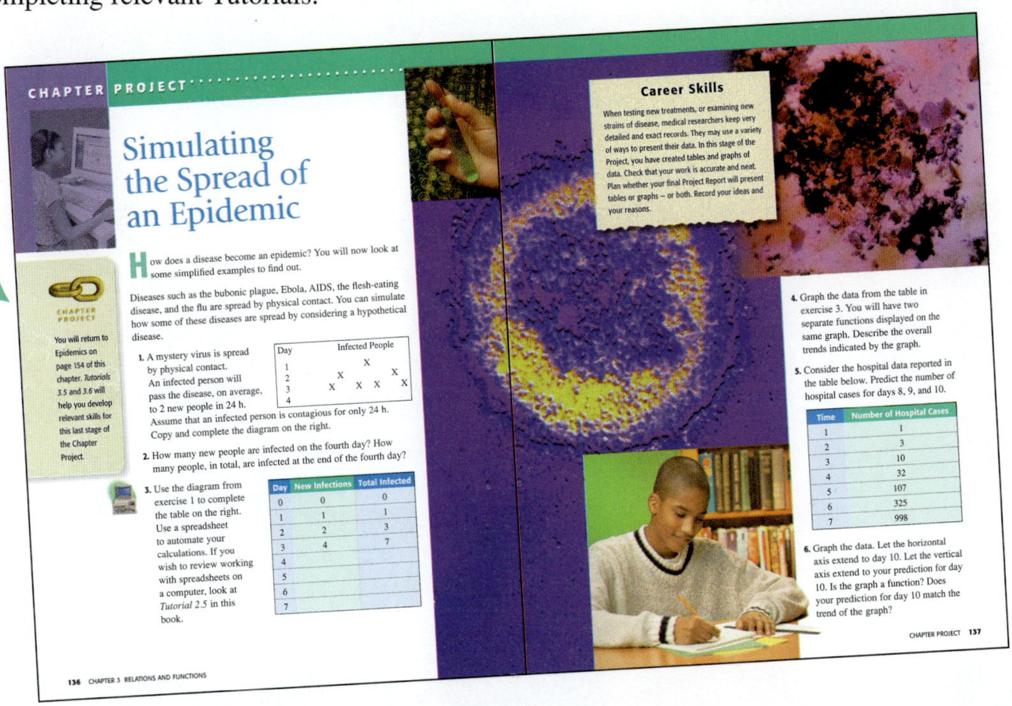

CHAPTER PROJECT

Simulating the Spread of an Epidemic

How does a disease become an epidemic? You will now look at some simplified examples to find out.

Diseases such as the bubonic plague, Ebola, AIDS, the flesh-eating disease, and the flu are spread by physical contact. You can simulate how some of these diseases are spread by considering a hypothetical disease.

1. A mystery virus is spread by physical contact. An infected person will pass the disease, on average, to 2 new people in 24 h. Assume that an infected person is contagious for only 24 h. Copy and complete the diagram on the right.

2. How many new people are infected on the fourth day? How many people, in total, are infected at the end of the fourth day?

3. Use the diagram from exercise 1 to complete the table on the right. Use a spreadsheet to automate your calculations. If you wish to review working with spreadsheets on a computer, look at *Tutorial 2.5* in this book.

Day	New Infections	Total Infected
0	0	0
1	1	1
2	2	3
3	4	7
4		
5		
6		
7		

CHAPTER PROJECT

You will return to Epidemics on page 154 of this chapter. *Tutorials 3.5* and *3.6* will help you develop relevant skills for this last stage of the Chapter Project.

Career Skills

When testing new treatments, or examining new strains of disease, medical researchers keep very detailed and exact records. They may use a variety of ways to present their data. In this stage of the Project, you have created tables and graphs of data. Check that your work is accurate and neat. Plan whether your final Project Report will present tables or graphs – or both. Record your ideas and your reasons.

4. Graph the data from the table in exercise 3. You will have two separate functions displayed on the same graph. Describe the overall trends indicated by the graph.

5. Consider the hospital data reported in the table below. Predict the number of hospital cases for days 8, 9, and 10.

Time	Number of Hospital Cases
1	1
2	3
3	10
4	32
5	107
6	325
7	998

6. Graph the data. Let the horizontal axis extend to day 10. Let the vertical axis extend to your prediction for day 10. Is the graph a function? Does your prediction for day 10 match the trend of the graph?

136 CHAPTER 3 RELATIONS AND FUNCTIONS

CHAPTER PROJECT 137

Tutorials

Each Tutorial develops a specific mathematical concept or result.

Here is how a typical Tutorial works.

- **Practise Your Prior Skills** provides a chance to review previous work.
- **Investigations** lead you to explore important mathematical concepts.

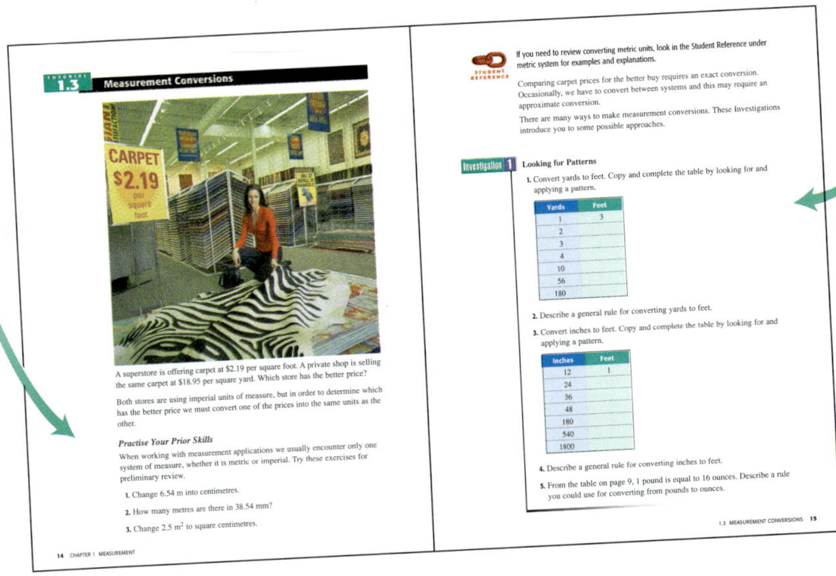
TUTORIAL 1.3 Measurement Conversions

CARPET $2.19 per square foot

A superstore is offering carpet at $2.19 per square foot. A private shop is selling the same carpet at $18.95 per square yard. Which store has the better price?

Both stores are using imperial units of measure, but in order to determine which has the better price we must convert one of the prices into the same units as the other.

Practise Your Prior Skills

When working with measurement applications we usually encounter only one system of measure, whether it is metric or imperial. Try these exercises for preliminary review.

1. Change 6.54 m into centimetres.
2. How many metres are there in 38.54 mm?
3. Change 2.5 m^2 to square centimetres.

14 CHAPTER 1 MEASUREMENT

STUDENT REFERENCE If you need to review converting metric units, look in the Student Reference under metric system for examples and explanations.

Comparing carpet prices for the better buy requires an exact conversion. Occasionally, we have to convert between systems and this may require an approximate conversion.

There are many ways to make measurement conversions. These Investigations introduce you to some possible approaches.

Investigation 1 Looking for Patterns

1. Convert yards to feet. Copy and complete the table by looking for and applying a pattern.

Yards	Feet
1	3
2	
3	
4	
10	
56	
180	

2. Describe a general rule for converting yards to feet.
3. Convert inches to feet. Copy and complete the table by looking for and applying a pattern.

Inches	Feet
12	1
24	
36	
48	
180	
540	
1800	

4. Describe a general rule for converting inches to feet.
5. From the table on page 9, 1 pound is equal to 16 ounces. Describe a rule you could use for converting from pounds to ounces.

1.3 MEASUREMENT CONVERSIONS 15

- **Examples** illustrate how to use the new mathematical methods.

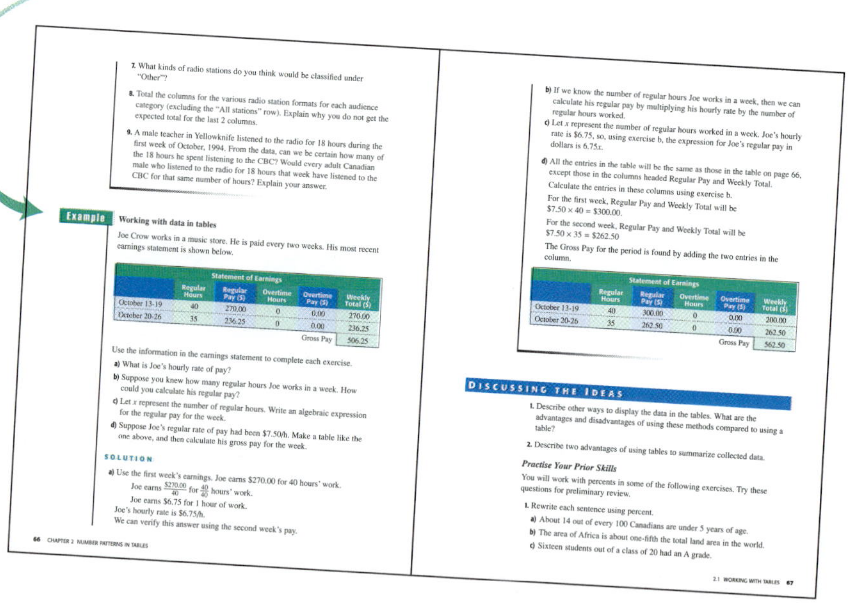
7. What kinds of radio stations do you think would be classified under "Other"?
8. Total the columns for the various radio station formats for each audience category (excluding the "All stations" row). Explain why you do not get the expected total for the last 2 columns.
9. A male teacher in Yellowknife listened to the radio for 18 hours during the first week of October, 1994. From the data, can we be certain how many of the 18 hours he spent listening to the CBC? Would every adult Canadian male who listened to the radio for 18 hours that week have listened to the CBC for that same number of hours? Explain your answer.

Example Working with data in tables

Joe Crow works in a music store. He is paid every two weeks. His most recent earnings statement is shown below.

Statement of Earnings

	Regular Hours	Regular Pay ($)	Overtime Hours	Overtime Pay ($)	Weekly Total ($)
October 13-19	40	270.00	0	0.00	270.00
October 20-26	35	236.25	0	0.00	236.25
				Gross Pay	506.25

Use the information in the earnings statement to complete each exercise.

a) What is Joe's hourly rate of pay?
b) Suppose you knew how many regular hours Joe works in a week. How could you calculate his regular pay?
c) Let x represent the number of regular hours. Write an algebraic expression for the regular pay for the week.
d) Suppose Joe's regular rate of pay had been $7.50/h. Make a table like the one above, and then calculate his gross pay for the week.

SOLUTION

a) Use the first week's earnings. Joe earns $270.00 for 40 hours' work.
Joe earns $\frac{\$270.00}{40}$ for $\frac{40}{40}$ hours' work.
Joe earns $6.75 for 1 hour of work.
Joe's hourly rate is $6.75/h.
We can verify this answer using the second week's pay.

66 CHAPTER 2 NUMBER PATTERNS IN TABLES

b) If we know the number of regular hours Joe works in a week, then we can calculate his regular pay by multiplying his hourly rate by the number of regular hours worked.
c) Let x represent the number of regular hours worked in a week. Joe's hourly rate is $6.75, so, using exercise b, the expression for Joe's regular pay in dollars is $6.75x$.
d) All the entries in the table will be the same as those in the table on page 66, except those in the columns headed Regular Pay and Weekly Total.
Calculate the entries in these columns using exercise b.
For the first week, Regular Pay and Weekly Total will be $7.50 × 40 = $300.00.
For the second week, Regular Pay and Weekly Total will be $7.50 × 35 = $262.50
The Gross Pay for the period is found by adding the two entries in the column.

Statement of Earnings

	Regular Hours	Regular Pay ($)	Overtime Hours	Overtime Pay ($)	Weekly Total ($)
October 13-19	40	300.00	0	0.00	300.00
October 20-26	35	262.50	0	0.00	262.50
				Gross Pay	562.50

DISCUSSING THE IDEAS

1. Describe other ways to display the data in the tables. What are the advantages and disadvantages of using these methods compared to using a table?
2. Describe two advantages of using tables to summarize collected data.

Practise Your Prior Skills

You will work with percents in some of the following exercises. Try these questions for preliminary review.

1. Rewrite each sentence using percent.
a) About 14 out of every 100 Canadians are under 5 years of age.
b) The area of Africa is about one-fifth the total land area in the world.
c) Sixteen students out of a class of 20 had an A grade.

2.1 WORKING WITH TABLES 67

- **Discussing the Ideas** helps you clarify your understanding by talking about the concepts in the Investigations and Examples.
- **Exercises** give you opportunities to apply the mathematical concepts and skills in different contexts.

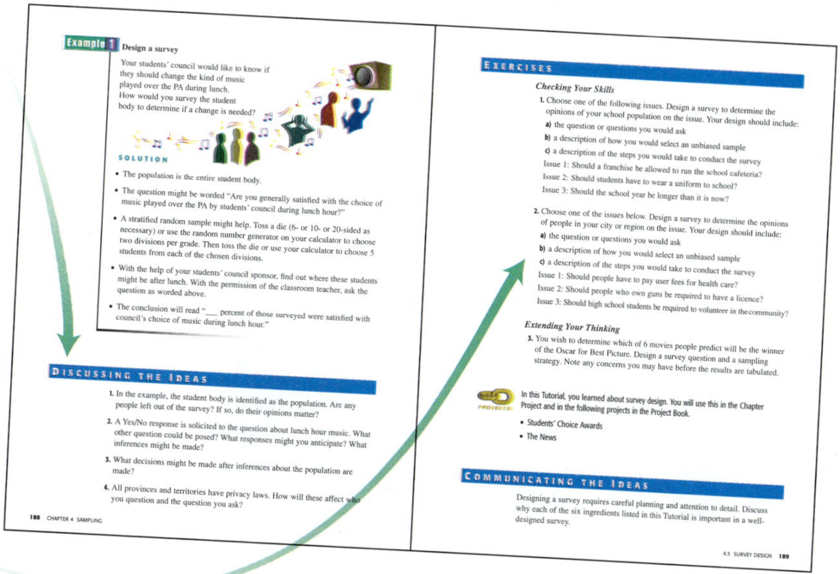

Example 1 Design a survey

Your students' council would like to know if they should change the kind of music played over the PA during lunch. How would you survey the student body to determine if a change is needed?

SOLUTION

- The population is the entire student body.
- The question might be worded "Are you generally satisfied with the choice of music played over the PA by students' council during lunch hour?"
- A stratified random sample might help. Toss a die (6- or 10- or 20-sided as necessary) or use the random number generator on your calculator to choose two divisions per grade. Then toss the die or use your calculator to choose 5 students from each of the chosen divisions.
- With the help of your students' council sponsor, find out where these students might be after lunch. With the permission of the classroom teacher, ask the question as worded above.
- The conclusion will read "__ percent of those surveyed were satisfied with council's choice of music during lunch hour."

DISCUSSING THE IDEAS

1. In the example, the student body is identified as the population. Are any people left out of the survey? If so, do their opinions matter?
2. A Yes/No response is solicited to the question about lunch hour music. What other question could be posed? What responses might you anticipate? What inferences might be made?
3. What decisions might be made after inferences about the population are made?
4. All provinces and territories have privacy laws. How will these affect who you question and the question you ask?

188 CHAPTER 4 SAMPLING

EXERCISES

Checking Your Skills

1. Choose one of the following issues. Design a survey to determine the opinions of your school population on the issue. Your design should include:
a) the question or questions you would ask
b) a description of how you would select an unbiased sample
c) a description of the steps you would take to conduct the survey
Issue 1: Should a franchise be allowed to run the school cafeteria?
Issue 2: Should students have to wear a uniform to school?
Issue 3: Should the school year be longer than it is now?
2. Choose one of the issues below. Design a survey to determine the opinions of people in your city or region on the issue. Your design should include:
a) the question or questions you would ask
b) a description of how you would select an unbiased sample
c) a description of the steps you would take to conduct the survey
Issue 1: Should people have to pay user fees for health care?
Issue 2: Should people who own guns be required to have a licence?
Issue 3: Should high school students be required to volunteer in the community?

Extending Your Thinking

3. You wish to determine which of 6 movies people predict will be the winner of the Oscar for Best Picture. Design a survey question and a sampling strategy. Note any concerns you may have before the results are tabulated.

In this Tutorial, you learned about survey design. You will use this in the Chapter Project and in the following projects in the Project Book.
- Students' Choice Awards
- The News

COMMUNICATING THE IDEAS

Designing a survey requires careful planning and attention to detail. Discuss why each of the six ingredients listed in this Tutorial is important in a well-designed survey.

4.5 SURVEY DESIGN 189

- **Project Link** identifies the focus for the Tutorial, and highlights the projects that involve the same concepts and skills.

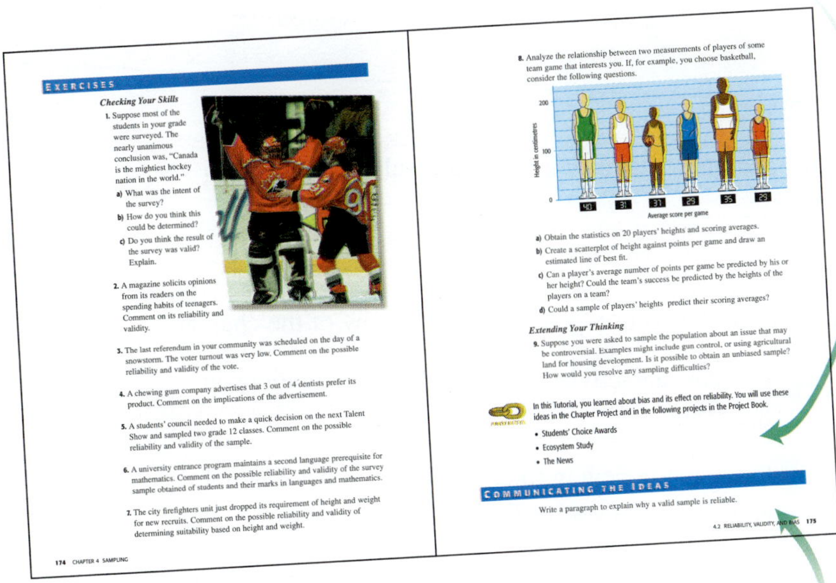

EXERCISES

Checking Your Skills

1. Suppose most of the students in your grade were surveyed. The nearly unanimous conclusion was, "Canada is the mightiest hockey nation in the world."
a) What was the intent of the survey?
b) How do you think this could be determined?
c) Do you think the result of the survey was valid? Explain.
2. A magazine solicits opinions from its readers on the spending habits of teenagers. Comment on its reliability and validity.
3. The last referendum in your community was scheduled on the day of a snowstorm. The voter turnout was very low. Comment on the possible reliability and validity of the vote.
4. A chewing gum company advertises that 3 out of 4 dentists prefer its product. Comment on the implications of the advertisement.
5. A students' council needed to make a quick decision on the next Talent Show and sampled two grade 12 classes. Comment on the possible reliability and validity of the sample.
6. A university entrance program maintains a second language prerequisite for mathematics. Comment on the possible reliability and validity of the survey sample obtained of students and their marks in languages and mathematics.
7. The city firefighters unit just dropped its requirement of height and weight for new recruits. Comment on the possible reliability and validity of determining suitability based on height and weight.

174 CHAPTER 4 SAMPLING

8. Analyze the relationship between two measurements of players of some team game that interests you. If, for example, you choose basketball, consider the following questions.

a) Obtain the statistics on 20 players' heights and scoring averages.
b) Create a scatterplot of height against points per game and draw an estimated line of best fit.
c) Can a player's average number of points per game be predicted by his or her height? Could the team's success be predicted by the heights of the players on a team?
d) Could a sample of players' heights predict their scoring averages?

Extending Your Thinking

9. Suppose you were asked to sample the population about an issue that may be controversial. Examples might include gun control, or using agricultural land for housing development. Is it possible to obtain an unbiased sample? How would you resolve any sampling difficulties?

In this Tutorial, you learned about bias and its effect on reliability. You will use these ideas in the Chapter Project and in the following projects in the Project Book.
- Students' Choice Awards
- Ecosystem Study
- The News

COMMUNICATING THE IDEAS

Write a paragraph to explain why a valid sample is reliable.

4.2 RELIABILITY, VALIDITY, AND BIAS 175

- **Communicating the Ideas** suggests a writing or drawing activity in which you summarize the key learning for the Tutorial.

Consolidating Your Skills

Each chapter ends with a Consolidating Your Skills section. This starts with a table that summarizes the work of the chapter.

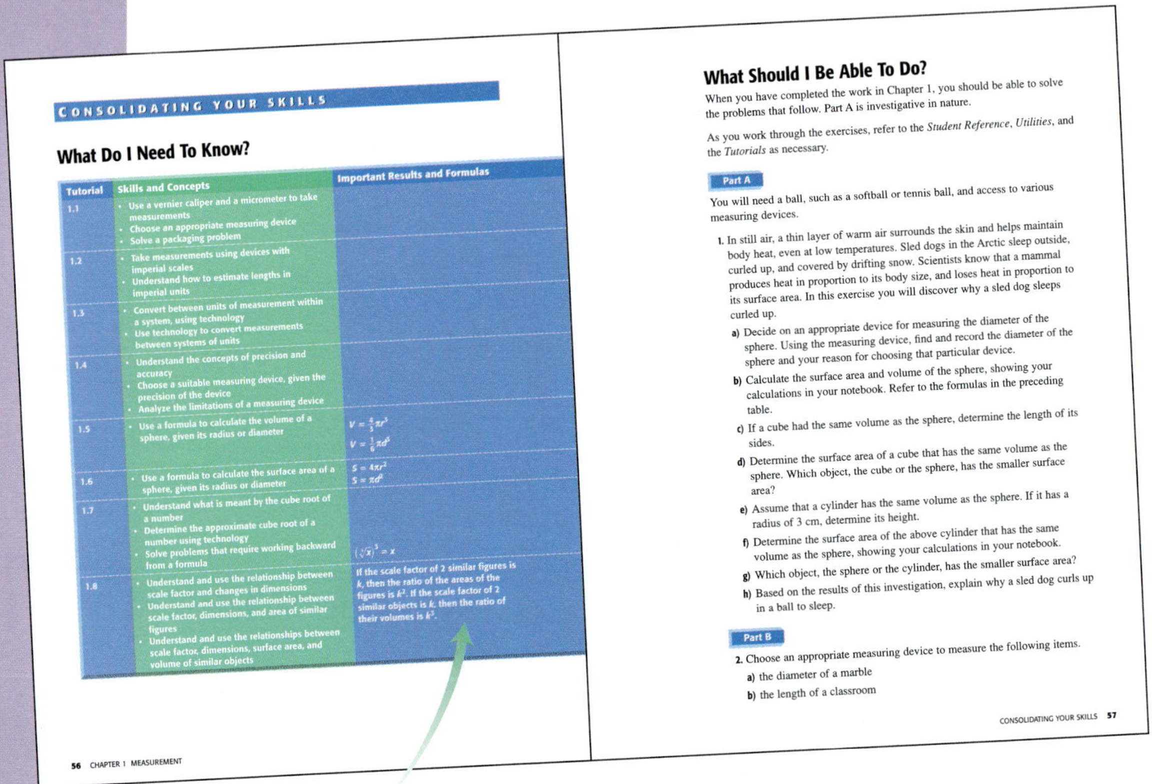

CONSOLIDATING YOUR SKILLS

What Do I Need To Know?

Tutorial	Skills and Concepts	Important Results and Formulas
1.1	• Use a vernier caliper and a micrometer to take measurements • Choose an appropriate measuring device • Solve a packaging problem	
1.2	• Take measurements using devices with imperial scales • Understand how to estimate lengths in imperial units	
1.3	• Convert between units of measurement within a system, using technology • Use technology to convert measurements between systems of units	
1.4	• Understand the concepts of precision and accuracy • Choose a suitable measuring device, given the precision of the device • Analyze the limitations of a measuring device	
1.5	• Use a formula to calculate the volume of a sphere, given its radius or diameter	$V = \frac{4}{3}\pi r^3$ $V = \frac{1}{6}\pi d^3$
1.6	• Use a formula to calculate the surface area of a sphere, given its radius or diameter	$S = 4\pi r^2$ $S = \pi d^2$
1.7	• Understand what is meant by the cube root of a number • Determine the approximate cube root of a number using technology • Solve problems that require working backward from a formula	$(\sqrt[3]{x})^3 = x$
1.8	• Understand and use the relationship between scale factor and changes in dimensions • Understand and use the relationship between scale factor, dimensions, and area of similar figures • Understand and use the relationships between scale factor, dimensions, surface area, and volume of similar objects	If the scale factor of 2 similar figures is k, then the ratio of the areas of the figures is k^2. If the scale factor of 2 similar objects is k, then the ratio of their volumes is k^3.

56 CHAPTER 1 MEASUREMENT

What Should I Be Able To Do?

When you have completed the work in Chapter 1, you should be able to solve the problems that follow. Part A is investigative in nature.

As you work through the exercises, refer to the *Student Reference*, *Utilities*, and the *Tutorials* as necessary.

Part A

You will need a ball, such as a softball or tennis ball, and access to various measuring devices.

1. In still air, a thin layer of warm air surrounds the skin and helps maintain body heat, even at low temperatures. Sled dogs in the Arctic sleep outside, curled up, and covered by drifting snow. Scientists know that a mammal produces heat in proportion to its body size, and loses heat in proportion to its surface area. In this exercise you will discover why a sled dog sleeps curled up.
   a) Decide on an appropriate device for measuring the diameter of the sphere. Using the measuring device, find and record the diameter of the sphere and your reason for choosing that particular device.
   b) Calculate the surface area and volume of the sphere, showing your calculations in your notebook. Refer to the formulas in the preceding table.
   c) If a cube had the same volume as the sphere, determine the length of its sides.
   d) Determine the surface area of a cube that has the same volume as the sphere. Which object, the cube or the sphere, has the smaller surface area?
   e) Assume that a cylinder has the same volume as the sphere. If it has a radius of 3 cm, determine its height.
   f) Determine the surface area of the above cylinder that has the same volume as the sphere, showing your calculations in your notebook.
   g) Which object, the sphere or the cylinder, has the smaller surface area?
   h) Based on the results of this investigation, explain why a sled dog curls up in a ball to sleep.

Part B

2. Choose an appropriate measuring device to measure the following items.
   a) the diameter of a marble
   b) the length of a classroom

CONSOLIDATING YOUR SKILLS 57

Review this column to identify important results and formulas.

The remainder of the section gives a 3-part review of the chapter.

Part A involves an activity, just like the Investigations in the chapter.

Part B has some review problems, similar to the Examples and Exercises you've done in the Tutorials.

Part C focuses on the Chapter Project.

These photographs show you some actual student work.

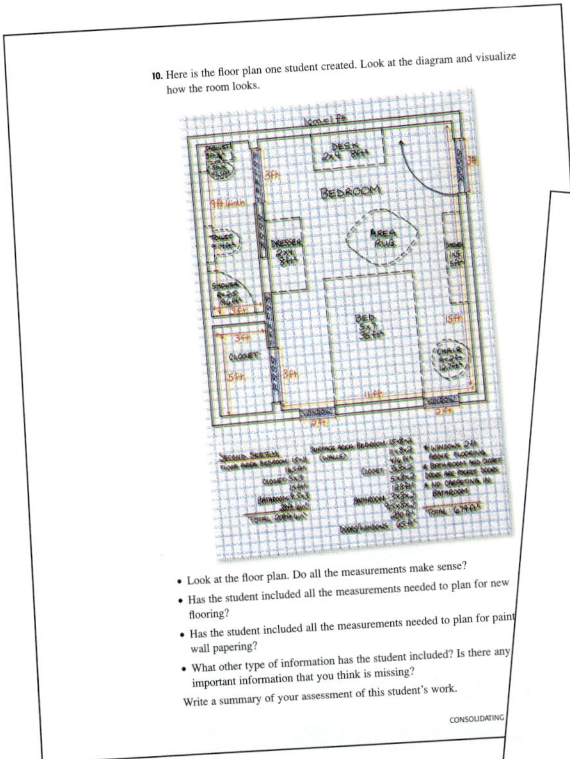

10. Here is the floor plan one student created. Look at the diagram and visualize how the room looks.

- Look at the floor plan. Do all the measurements make sense?
- Has the student included all the measurements needed to plan for new flooring?
- Has the student included all the measurements needed to plan for paint wall papering?
- What other type of information has the student included? Is there any important information that you think is missing?

Write a summary of your assessment of this student's work.

CONSOLIDATING

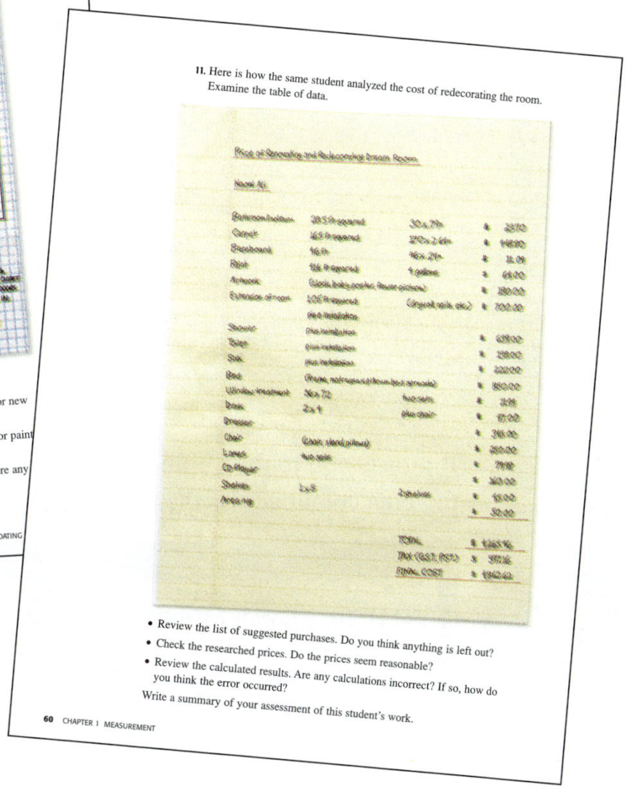

11. Here is how the same student analyzed the cost of redecorating the room. Examine the table of data.

- Review the list of suggested purchases. Do you think anything is left out?
- Check the researched prices. Do the prices seem reasonable?
- Review the calculated results. Are any calculations incorrect? If so, how do you think the error occurred?

Write a summary of your assessment of this student's work.

60 CHAPTER 1 MEASUREMENT

Follow-up questions develop your skills at assessing project work.

Use Part C for inspiration with your own project, and to learn how to examine your own work critically.

Reference Sections

People at work use many reference materials: building codes; interest tables; sales policies.

This book can help you develop your skills with using reference materials. It contains three important reference sections: Utilities, Student Reference, and Answers.

Utilities

Watch for this blue link symbol in Tutorials or Projects in the Project Book.

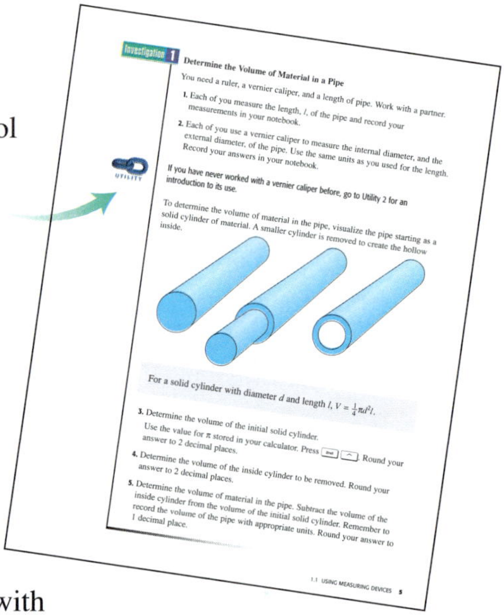
Investigation 1 **Determine the Volume of Material in a Pipe**

You need a ruler, a vernier caliper, and a length of pipe. Work with a partner.

1. Each of you measure the length, l, of the pipe and record your measurements in your notebook.
2. Each of you use a vernier caliper to measure the internal diameter, and the external diameter, of the pipe. Use the same units as you used for the length. Record your answers in your notebook.

UTILITY If you have never worked with a vernier caliper before, go to Utility 2 for an introduction to its use.

To determine the volume of material in the pipe, visualize the pipe starting as a solid cylinder of material. A smaller cylinder is removed to create the hollow inside.

For a solid cylinder with diameter d and length l, $V = \frac{1}{4}\pi d^2 l$.

3. Determine the volume of the initial solid cylinder. Use the value for π stored in your calculator. Press [2nd] [^]. Round your answer to 2 decimal places.
4. Determine the volume of the inside cylinder to be removed. Round your answer to 2 decimal places.
5. Determine the volume of material in the pipe. Subtract the volume of the inside cylinder from the volume of the initial solid cylinder. Remember to record the volume of the pipe with appropriate units. Round your answer to 1 decimal place.

1.1 USING MEASURING DEVICES 5

It directs you to the Utilities, with the blue colour across the top of each page.

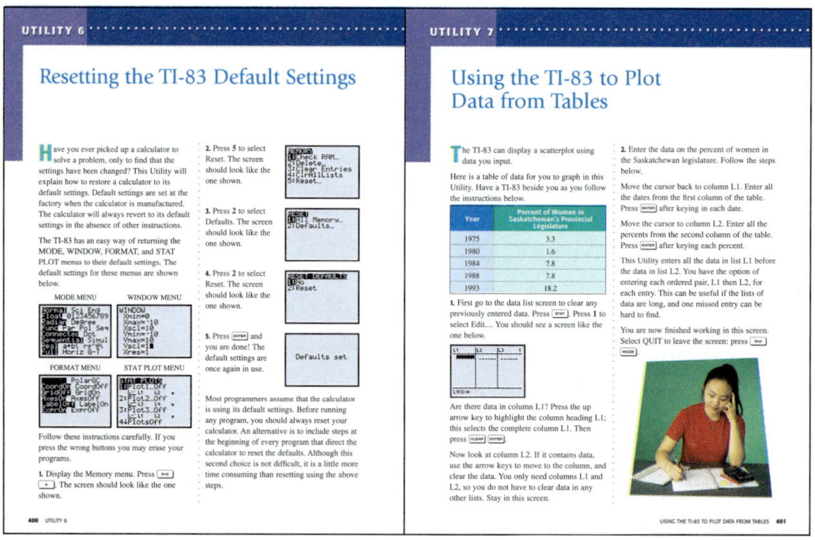
UTILITY 6

Resetting the TI-83 Default Settings

Have you ever picked up a calculator to solve a problem, only to find that the settings have been changed? This Utility will explain how to restore a calculator to its default settings. Default settings are set at the factory when the calculator is manufactured. The calculator will always revert to its default settings in the absence of other instructions.

The TI-83 has an easy way of returning the MODE, WINDOW, FORMAT, and STAT PLOT menus to their default settings. The default settings for these menus are shown below.

MODE MENU WINDOW MENU

FORMAT MENU STAT PLOT MENU

Follow these instructions carefully. If you press the wrong buttons you may erase your programs.

1. Display the Memory menu. Press [2nd] [+]. The screen should look like the one shown.
2. Press **5** to select Reset. The screen should look like the one shown.
3. Press **2** to select Defaults. The screen should look like the one shown.
4. Press **2** to select Reset. The screen should look like the one shown.
5. Press [ENTER] and you are done! The default settings are once again in use.

Most programmers assume that the calculator is using its default settings. Before running any program, you should always reset your calculator. An alternative is to include steps at the beginning of every program that direct the calculator to reset the defaults. Although this second choice is not difficult, it is a little more time consuming than resetting using the above steps.

400 UTILITY 6

UTILITY 7

Using the TI-83 to Plot Data from Tables

The TI-83 can display a scatterplot using data you input.

Here is a table of data for you to graph in this Utility. Have a TI-83 beside you as you follow the instructions below.

Year	Percent of Women in Saskatchewan's Provincial Legislature
1975	3.3
1980	1.6
1984	7.8
1988	7.8
1993	18.2

1. First go to the data list screen to clear any previously entered data. Press [STAT]. Press **1** to select Edit.... You should see a screen like the one below.

Are there data in column L1? Press the up arrow key to highlight the column heading L1; this selects the complete column L1. Then press [CLEAR] [ENTER].

Now look at column L2. If it contains data, use the arrow keys to move to the column, and clear the data. You only need columns L1 and L2, so you do not have to clear data in any other lists. Stay in this screen.

2. Enter the data on the percent of women in the Saskatchewan legislature. Follow the steps below.

Move the cursor back to column L1. Enter all the dates from the first column of the table. Press [ENTER] after keying in each date.

Move the cursor to column L2. Enter all the percents from the second column of the table. Press [ENTER] after keying each percent.

This Utility enters all the data in list L1 before the data in list L2. You have the option of entering each ordered pair, L1 then L2, for each entry. This can be useful if the lists of data are long, and one missed entry can be hard to find.

You are now finished working in this screen. Select QUIT to leave the screen: press [2nd] [MODE].

USING THE TI-83 TO PLOT DATA FROM TABLES 401

These Utilities teach you how to use specific tools for this course. Read the Utility while you work with the tool you are learning. If you're reading a Utility about the graphing calculator, key in the instructions as you read. Check that your results match the results shown in the Utility.

Student Reference

Watch for this red link symbol in Tutorials or Projects in the Project Book.

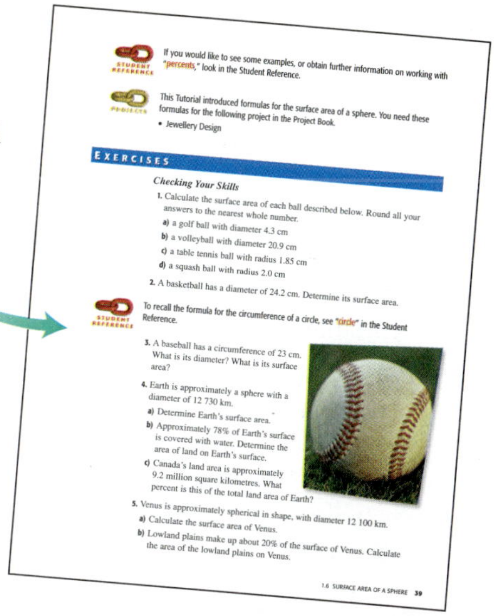

STUDENT REFERENCE If you would like to see some examples, or obtain further information on working with "percents," look in the Student Reference.

PROJECTS This Tutorial introduced formulas for the surface area of a sphere. You need these formulas for the following project in the Project Book.

- Jewellery Design

EXERCISES

Checking Your Skills

1. Calculate the surface area of each ball described below. Round all your answers to the nearest whole number.
   a) a golf ball with diameter 4.3 cm
   b) a volleyball with diameter 20.9 cm
   c) a table tennis ball with radius 1.85 cm
   d) a squash ball with radius 2.0 cm
2. A basketball has a diameter of 24.2 cm. Determine its surface area.

STUDENT REFERENCE To recall the formula for the circumference of a circle, see "circle" in the Student Reference.

3. A baseball has a circumference of 23 cm. What is its diameter? What is its surface area?
4. Earth is approximately a sphere with a diameter of 12 730 km.
   a) Determine Earth's surface area.
   b) Approximately 78% of Earth's surface is covered with water. Determine the area of land on Earth's surface.
   c) Canada's land area is approximately 9.2 million square kilometres. What percent is this of the total land area of Earth?
5. Venus is approximately spherical in shape, with diameter 12 100 km.
   a) Calculate the surface area of Venus.
   b) Lowland plains make up about 20% of the surface of Venus. Calculate the area of the lowland plains on Venus.

1.6 SURFACE AREA OF A SPHERE 39

It directs you to the Student Reference. Look for the pages with the red colour across the top.

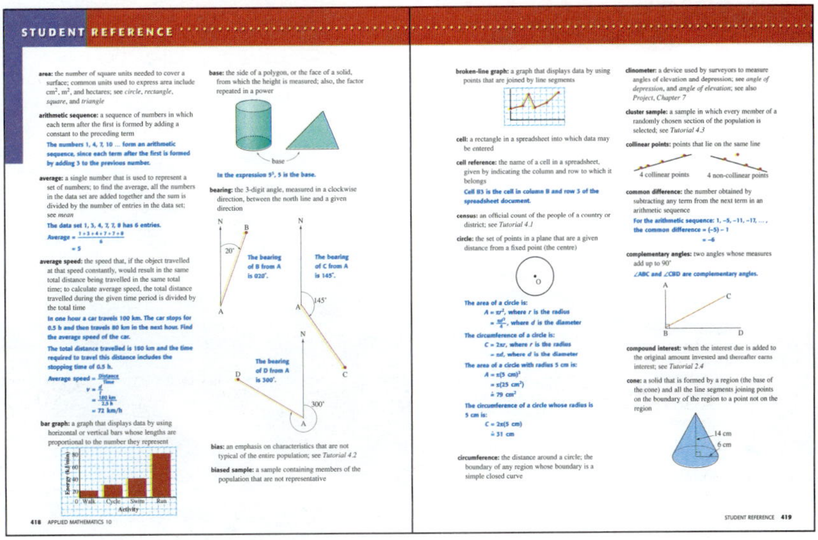

STUDENT REFERENCE

area: the number of square units needed to cover a surface; common units used to express area include cm^2, m^2, and hectares; see *circle*, *rectangle*, *square*, and *triangle*

arithmetic sequence: a sequence of numbers in which each term after the first is formed by adding a constant to the preceding term

The numbers 1, 4, 7, 10 ... form an arithmetic sequence, since each term after the first is formed by adding 3 to the previous number.

average: a single number that is used to represent a set of numbers; to find the average, all the numbers in the data set are added together and the sum is divided by the number of entries in the data set; see *mean*

The data set 1, 3, 4, 7, 7, 8 has 6 entries.

$$\text{Average} = \frac{1+3+4+7+7+8}{6} = 5$$

average speed: the speed that, if the object travelled at that speed constantly, would result in the same total distance being travelled in the same total time; to calculate average speed, the total distance travelled during the given time period is divided by the total time

In one hour a car travels 100 km. The car stops for 0.5 h and then travels 80 km in the next hour. Find the average speed of the car.

The total distance travelled is 180 km and the time required to travel this distance includes the stopping time of 0.5 h.

$$\text{Average speed} = \frac{\text{Distance}}{\text{Time}}$$
$$v = \frac{d}{t} = \frac{180\text{ km}}{2.5\text{ h}} = 72\text{ km/h}$$

bar graph: a graph that displays data by using horizontal or vertical bars whose lengths are proportional to the number they represent

base: the side of a polygon, or the face of a solid, from which the height is measured; also, the factor repeated in a power

In the expression 5^3, 5 is the base.

bearing: the 3-digit angle, measured in a clockwise direction, between the north line and a given direction

The bearing of B from A is 020°. **The bearing of C from A is 145°.** **The bearing of D from A is 300°.**

bias: an emphasis on characteristics that are not typical of the entire population; see *Tutorial 4.2*

biased sample: a sample containing members of the population that are not representative

418 APPLIED MATHEMATICS 10

broken-line graph: a graph that displays data by using points that are joined by line segments

cell: a rectangle in a spreadsheet into which data may be entered

cell reference: the name of a cell in a spreadsheet, given by indicating the column and row to which it belongs

Cell B3 is the cell in column B and row 3 of the spreadsheet document.

census: an official count of the people of a country or district; see *Tutorial 4.1*

circle: the set of points in a plane that are a given distance from a fixed point (the centre)

The area of a circle is:
$A = \pi r^2$, **where r is the radius**
$= \frac{\pi d^2}{4}$, **where d is the diameter**

The circumference of a circle is:
$C = 2\pi r$, **where r is the radius**
$= \pi d$, **where d is the diameter**

The area of a circle with radius 5 cm is:
$$A = \pi(5\text{ cm})^2 = \pi(25\text{ cm}^2) \doteq 79\text{ cm}^2$$

The circumference of a circle whose radius is 5 cm is:
$$C = 2\pi(5\text{ cm}) \doteq 31\text{ cm}$$

circumference: the distance around a circle; the boundary of any region whose boundary is a simple closed curve

clinometer: a device used by surveyors to measure angles of elevation and depression; see *angle of depression*, and *angle of elevation*; see also *Project, Chapter 7*

cluster sample: a sample in which every member of a randomly chosen section of the population is selected; see *Tutorial 4.3*

collinear points: points that lie on the same line

4 collinear points   4 non-collinear points

common difference: the number obtained by subtracting any term from the next term in an arithmetic sequence

For the arithmetic sequence: 1, −5, −11, −17, ..., the common difference = (−5) − 1 = −6

complementary angles: two angles whose measures add up to 90°

∠ABC and ∠CBD are complementary angles.

compound interest: when the interest due is added to the original amount invested and thereafter earns interest; see *Tutorial 2.4*

cone: a solid that is formed by a region (the base of the cone) and all the line segments joining points on the boundary of the region to a point not on the region

STUDENT REFERENCE 419

The Student Reference provides:

- definitions for key terms
- general results, such as the Pythagorean Theorem
- brief review of concepts from previous grades
- examples when relevant
- references to Source Book tutorials when relevant

Answers

Check your answers after completing a set of Investigations or Exercises to see how well you understood the material.

By using the Answers responsibly, you can improve your mathematical learning and develop good study habits.

Project Book

The Project Book contains 20 projects. Each project relates to a specific career area, and ties to one or more chapters from the Source Book.

You do not have to complete all the projects, but you may be interested in pursuing several of them. To cover all of the grade 10 Applied Mathematics curriculum, you will need to complete one compulsory project, which you select from a choice of four.

Here is how a typical project works.

Jewellery DESIGN

THE TASK

In this project, you will work in a group of three to design your own line of jewellery. The members of your group will include two jewellery designers and one marketing manager. You will work with area, surface area, volume, scale factors, and metric units of measurement.

Suggested Group Size: 3

Materials: Various pieces of jewellery, a micrometer, calipers, and compasses

BACKGROUND

The history of jewellery is as old as the history of humanity. Jewellery has been made and worn by people of all ages, both male and female, from all cultures, in all parts of the world. Jewellery can be inexpensive, made of plastics and common metals like copper; or jewellery can be very expensive, made of precious metals like silver and gold, and gemstones like diamonds.

- Why do you think people wear jewellery?
- Why do you think people make jewellery? What skills are involved in the art of jewellery-making?
- What materials are used to make jewellery? Think of present-day jewellery and jewellery that has been worn throughout history.
- What jewellery is popular with your age group? Does this jewellery convey any specific message?
- What jewellery do you wear or like? Why?

SOURCE LINK

- If you need to review the concepts of *area*, *surface area*, or *volume*, see the Student Reference in the Source Book.
- For metric units of measurement, the volume and surface area of a sphere, and scale factors, refer to the Source Book, Chapter 1: Measurement.

2 PROJECT 1 JEWELLERY DESIGN

PROJECT 1 JEWELLERY DESIGN 3

- **The Task** explains the purpose of the project, and a specific application you will investigate.
- **Materials** describes the supplies you need to complete the project.
- **Source Link** points you to required skills in the Source Book, if you need them.

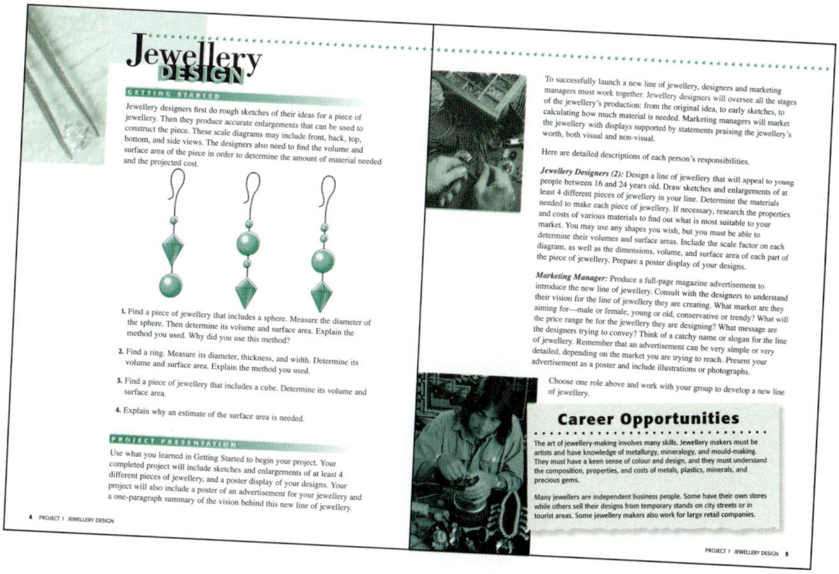

Jewellery DESIGN

GETTING STARTED

Jewellery designers first do rough sketches of their ideas for a piece of jewellery. Then they produce accurate enlargements that can be used to construct the piece. These scale diagrams may include front, back, top, bottom, and side views. The designers also need to find the volume and surface area of the piece in order to determine the amount of material needed and the projected cost.

1. Find a piece of jewellery that includes a sphere. Measure the diameter of the sphere. Then determine its volume and surface area. Explain the method you used. Why did you use this method?
2. Find a ring. Measure its diameter, thickness, and width. Determine its volume and surface area. Explain the method you used.
3. Find a piece of jewellery that includes a cube. Determine its volume and surface area.
4. Explain why an estimate of the surface area is needed.

PROJECT PRESENTATION

Use what you learned in Getting Started to begin your project. Your completed project will include sketches and enlargements of at least 4 different pieces of jewellery, and a poster display of your designs. Your project will also include a poster of an advertisement for your jewellery and a one-paragraph summary of the vision behind this new line of jewellery.

4 PROJECT 1 JEWELLERY DESIGN

To successfully launch a new line of jewellery, designers and marketing managers must work together. Jewellery designers will oversee all the stages of the jewellery's production: from the original idea, to early sketches, to calculating how much material is needed. Marketing managers will market the jewellery with displays supported by statements praising the jewellery's worth, both visual and non-visual.

Here are detailed descriptions of each person's responsibilities.

Jewellery Designers (2): Design a line of jewellery that will appeal to young people between 16 and 24 years old. Draw sketches and enlargements of at least 4 different pieces of jewellery in your line. Determine the materials needed to make each piece of jewellery. If necessary, research the properties and costs of various materials to find out what is most suitable to your market. You may use any shapes you wish, but you must be able to determine their volumes and surface areas. Include the scale factor on each diagram, as well as the dimensions, volume, and surface area of each part of the piece of jewellery. Prepare a poster display of your designs.

Marketing Manager: Produce a full-page magazine advertisement to introduce the new line of jewellery. Consult with the designers to understand their vision for the line of jewellery they are creating. What market are they aiming for—male or female, young or old, conservative or trendy? What will the price range be for the jewellery they are designing? What message are the designers trying to convey? Think of a catchy name or slogan for the line of jewellery. Remember that an advertisement can be very simple or very detailed, depending on the market you are trying to reach. Present your advertisement as a poster and include illustrations or photographs.

Choose one role above and work with your group to develop a new line of jewellery.

Career Opportunities

The art of jewellery-making involves many skills. Jewellery makers must be artists and have knowledge of metallurgy, mineralogy, and mould-making. They must have a keen sense of colour and design, and they must understand the composition, properties, and costs of metals, plastics, minerals, and precious gems.

Many jewellers are independent business people. Some have their own stores while others sell their designs from temporary stands on city streets or in tourist areas. Some jewellery makers also work for large retail companies.

PROJECT 1 JEWELLERY DESIGN 5

- **Getting Started** leads you to explore some of the basic mathematical concepts underlying the application.
- **Project Presentation** lets you pursue a variety of extensions of the work done in Getting Started, and suggests ways to present your project report.

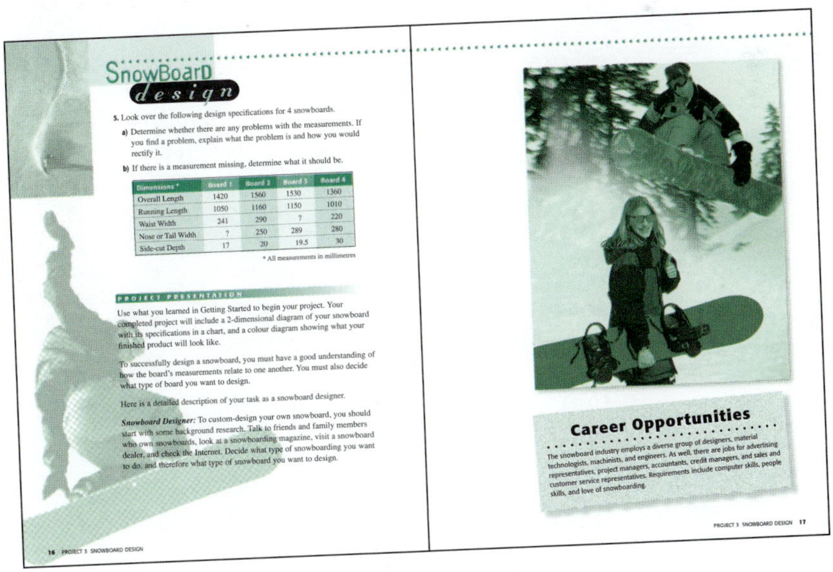

SnowBoarD design

5. Look over the following design specifications for 4 snowboards.
   a) Determine whether there are any problems with the measurements. If you find a problem, explain what the problem is and how you would rectify it.
   b) If there is a measurement missing, determine what it should be.

Dimensions*	Board 1	Board 2	Board 3	Board 4
Overall Length	1420	1560	1530	1360
Running Length	1050	1160	1150	1010
Waist Width	241	290	?	220
Nose or Tail Width	?	250	289	280
Side-cut Depth	17	20	19.5	30

* All measurements in millimetres

PROJECT PRESENTATION

Use what you learned in Getting Started to begin your project. Your completed project will include a 2-dimensional diagram of your snowboard with its specifications in a chart, and a colour diagram showing what your finished product will look like.

To successfully design a snowboard, you must have a good understanding of how the board's measurements relate to one another. You must also decide what type of board you want to design.

Here is a detailed description of your task as a snowboard designer.

Snowboard Designer: To custom-design your own snowboard, you should start with some background research. Talk to friends and family members who own snowboards, look at a snowboarding magazine, visit a snowboard dealer, and check the Internet. Decide what type of snowboarding you want to do, and therefore what type of snowboard you want to design.

16 PROJECT 3 SNOWBOARD DESIGN

Career Opportunities

The snowboard industry employs a diverse group of designers, material technologists, machinists, and engineers. As well, there are jobs for advertising representatives, project managers, accountants, credit managers, and sales and customer service representatives. Requirements include computer skills, people skills, and love of snowboarding.

PROJECT 3 SNOWBOARD DESIGN 17

- **Career Opportunities** describes how the mathematical skills of the project relate to careers.

1 Measurement

PROJECT

You should do at least one project that uses the skills you learn in this chapter. The recommended projects in the Project Book are:

- Jewellery Design
- Candy Boxes

Overview

Chapter Section	Skills and Concepts
Chapter Project: Dream Room, page 2	Design and research the redecoration of a room
Tutorial 1.1: Using Measuring Devices, page 4	Use direct measurement to solve problems
Tutorial 1.2: Taking and Estimating Measurements, page 9	Take measurements using imperial units; estimate measurements using imperial units
Tutorial 1.3: Measurement Conversions, page 14	Use technology to convert measurements
Tutorial 1.4: Precision and Accuracy in Measurement, page 22	Describe the limitations of measuring tools
Chapter Project: Planning Your Dream Room, page 28	Take measurements of a room and create an accurate plan; calculate the costs of redecoration
Tutorial 1.5: Volume of a Sphere, page 30	Determine the volume of a sphere
Tutorial 1.6: Surface Area of a Sphere, page 36	Determine the surface area of a sphere
Tutorial 1.7: Square Roots and Cube Roots, page 41	Solve area and volume problems involving unknown dimensions; describe a set of instructions for finding the cube root of a number
Tutorial 1.8: Enlarging and Reducing Figures, page 46	Describe the relationship between the scale factor, and changes in dimension, area, surface area, or volume
Chapter Project: Modelling Your Dream Room, page 54	Create a three-dimensional model of the room, to scale
Consolidating Your Skills, page 56	Review work of chapter

CHAPTER PROJECT

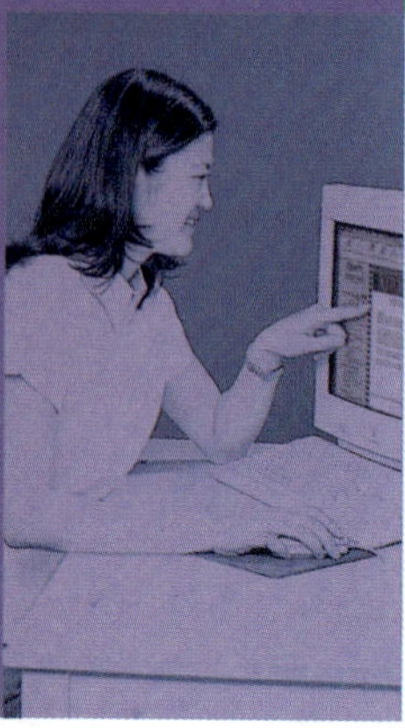

Dream Room

Have you ever wished you could redecorate your bedroom? This is your project for Chapter 1. You will create a detailed plan for your bedroom and estimate how much it will cost to redecorate. Your final project will consist of: a written description of your room; a scale drawing of your room; an itemized list of furniture, with suppliers, cost estimates, and calculations; and a model of your room. Here are some initial questions to consider.

- What colour do you want the walls to be? Will you use paint or wallpaper?
- What kind of flooring do you want?
- What furniture will you include?
- What kind of lighting do you want?
- What will you put on the walls?
- Use your responses from the questions above. List the things you need to redecorate your room.
- How much do you think it will cost to turn your room into a dream room? Record your assumptions about who will do the work.

Research decorating ideas and prices. Sources of information include the Internet, decorating magazines, catalogues, and decorating stores. If you need help searching the Internet, see Utility 1.

CHAPTER PROJECT

To do this Chapter Project, you need to take measurements using the conventions that apply in the field of decorating. Complete *Tutorials 1.1 to 1.4* to develop an understanding of the related skills. You will return to this Chapter Project on page 28 of the chapter.

FYI Visit: www.awl.com/canada/school/connections/

You can start your research from our Internet site: Click on MATHLINKS, followed by the *Applied Mathematics 10* logo. Then select a topic under Dream Room.

TUTORIAL 1.1

Using Measuring Devices

Canada adopted the metric system of measurement in 1976, but construction and manufacturing industries continue to use the imperial system of measurement. Many Canadians still remember their height and weight in imperial units. Your ruler may be marked in centimetres and millimetres along one edge, and inches and fractions of an inch along the other. In this chapter you will learn to work with both systems.

It is important to choose an appropriate measuring device whenever you take a measurement. One consideration is the size of the object to be measured. Another is the unit of measurement to use. A ruler is not very helpful if you must measure the thickness of a human hair, or the distance from your home to school, but it is suitable for measuring the dimensions of your textbook. This Tutorial will introduce you to two measuring devices that can be used to measure small objects.

Practise Your Prior Skills

In the following Investigation, you must substitute values into an expression. Try these exercises for preliminary review.

1. Find the value of $2x^2 + 5x$ if $x = 3.5$.

2. Evaluate the expression $\pi r^2 h$ when $r = 2.4$ and $h = 6$. Round your answer to 1 decimal place.

STUDENT REFERENCE

If you need more information, or would like to see some examples, refer to the Student Reference under "substituting values into expressions."

A manufacturer is considering a new product that will require the production of a pipe. As part of the evaluation and costing process, the volume of material in the pipe must be determined. *Investigation 1* shows one way to do this using a vernier caliper. This is an instrument that can be used to measure inside and outside dimensions of an object.

Investigation 1

Determine the Volume of Material in a Pipe

You need a ruler, a vernier caliper, and a length of pipe. Work with a partner.

1. Each of you measure the length, l, of the pipe and record your measurements in your notebook.

2. Each of you use a vernier caliper to measure the internal diameter, and the external diameter, of the pipe. Use the same units as you used for the length. Record your answers in your notebook.

UTILITY

If you have never worked with a vernier caliper before, go to Utility 2 for an introduction to its use.

To determine the volume of material in the pipe, visualize the pipe starting as a solid cylinder of material. A smaller cylinder is removed to create the hollow inside.

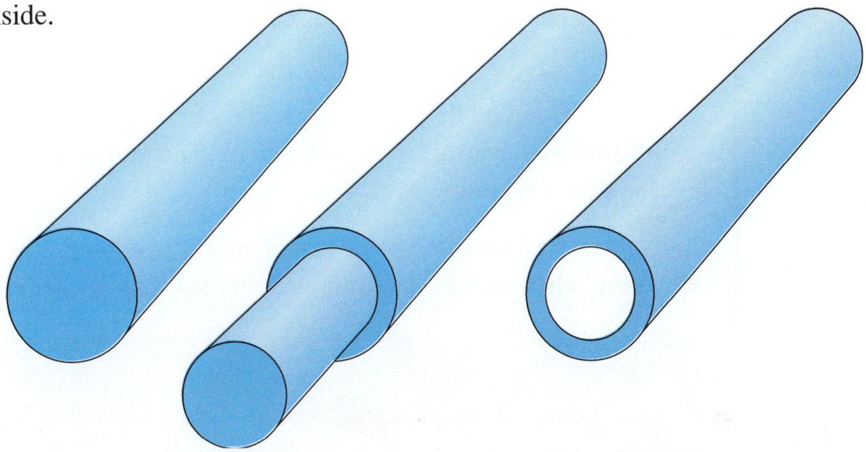

For a solid cylinder with diameter d and length l, $V = \frac{1}{4}\pi d^2 l$.

3. Determine the volume of the initial solid cylinder.

Use the value for π stored in your calculator. Press [2nd] [^]. Round your answer to 2 decimal places.

4. Determine the volume of the inside cylinder to be removed. Round your answer to 2 decimal places.

5. Determine the volume of material in the pipe. Subtract the volume of the inside cylinder from the volume of the initial solid cylinder. Remember to record the volume of the pipe with appropriate units. Round your answer to 1 decimal place.

A paper company decides to make its printer paper available in packages of 200 sheets. It will ship the paper in boxes of 12 packages each. Complete this Investigation to determine possible dimensions of each box.

Investigation 2 Designing a Box

You will need a metric ruler, a micrometer, and 10 sheets of paper. Work with a partner.

1. Each of you find the length and width of one sheet of paper by measuring. Record your answers in your notebook. Did you both report the same answers in the same way?

In mathematics, we often work with numbers assuming they are exact. However, when taking a measurement, there is always some degree of error.

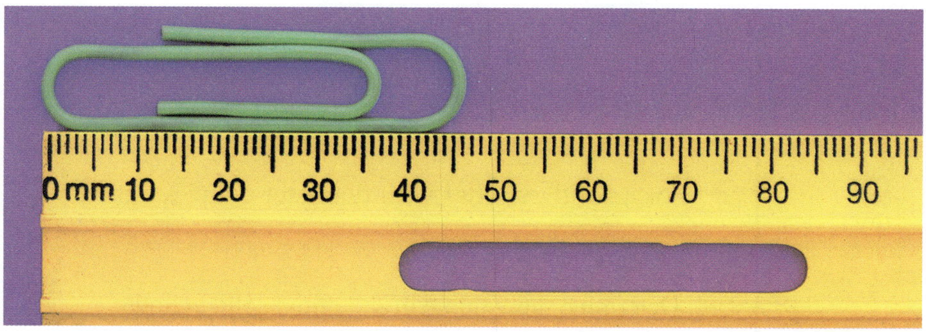

Look at the paper clip above. Its length is more than 4.6 cm but less than 4.7 cm. Since its length is closer to 4.6 cm than to 4.7 cm, its length would be recorded as 4.6 cm.

> Record measurements using the smallest scale division on the measuring instrument.

If the length of the paper clip were 5 cm, it should be recorded as 5.0 cm to indicate that the smallest scale division of the ruler is 0.1 cm, not 1 cm.

2. Use a micrometer to measure the thickness of 10 sheets of copy paper.

UTILITY

If you have never used a micrometer before, see Utility 3.

3. Use your measurements to predict the dimensions of one package of 200 sheets of paper.

4. Design a box to hold 12 packages of this copy paper. The box must be rectangular and have a lid. As part of your design, include a sketch of your box with its dimensions.

STUDENT REFERENCE

If you need to review the "net of a rectangular box," look in the Student Reference.

5. Determine the amount of cardboard needed to construct the box you have designed. Include any additional cardboard for construction tabs on the box.

DISCUSSING THE IDEAS

1. Consider the three measurements you took in *Investigation 2*. If you only had access to a ruler, which measurement would you be least confident about?

2. Describe how a slight error in determining the thickness of the paper would affect the dimensions of the box.

3. Describe any assumptions you made when designing a box to hold 12 packages of 200 sheets each. How might your assumptions affect the way in which the 12 packages would really fit in the box? How could you modify your calculations to ensure that the 12 packages would actually fit?

4. The Greek mathematician Archimedes, 287-212 B.C., discovered that a body, when completely immersed in a liquid, will displace an amount of liquid equal to its own volume. Describe another method of determining the volume of a pipe.

5. Discuss which device is appropriate to use, and why, when determining:

   a) the thickness of a book cover

   b) the diameter of a pencil

   c) the length of your Project Book

   d) your height

6. Discuss the metric and imperial units of measurement that would be appropriate for measuring the quantities in exercise 5.

PROJECTS

In this Tutorial you used direct measurement to determine the volume of a pipe and to investigate the dimensions of paper packages. You will need these skills when you do the Chapter Project and the following project in the Project Book.

- **Candy Boxes**

COMMUNICATING THE IDEAS

A millimetre ruler is suitable to make some measurements but not others. Explain why. What limitations are there for a balance that measures mass to the nearest 0.1 g?

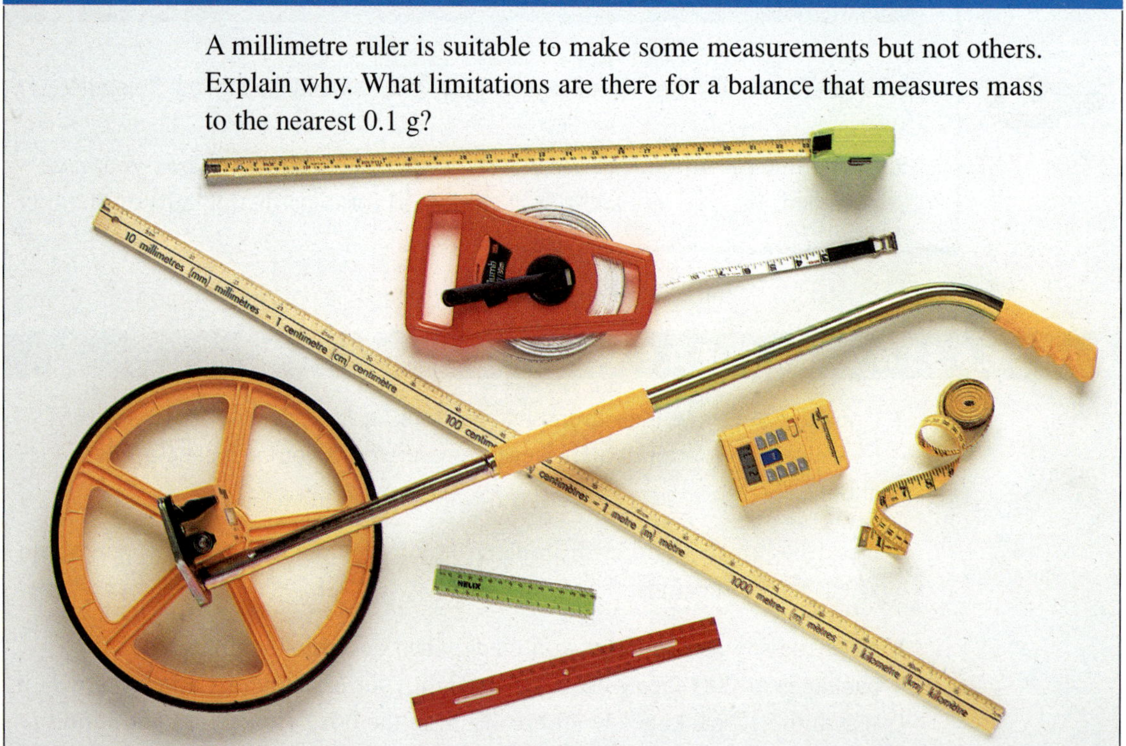

TUTORIAL 1.2

Taking and Estimating Measurements

In 1954, Roger Bannister became the first person to run the 1-mile race in under 4 min. Today, the 1-mile race has been replaced by the 1500-m race. The current men's world record time for this distance is considerably less than 4 min. Are the athletes really much faster than they were in 1954, or is the distance less? We live in a world that uses two systems of measurement: we must be able to work in both systems.

Relationships between Common Imperial Units	Relationships between Common Imperial Units and Metric Units	Relationship between Common Metric Units
Length		
1 mile = 1760 yards = 5280 feet	1 mile $\doteq$ 1.609 km	1 km = 1000 m
1 yard = 3 feet = 36 inches	1 yard = 0.9144 m	1 m = 100 cm
1 foot = 12 inches	1 foot = 0.3048 m	1 cm = 10 mm
	1 inch = 2.54 cm	
Capacity (Volume)		
1 gallon = 4 quarts = 8 pints	1 gallon $\doteq$ 4.546 L	1 L = 1000 mL
1 quart = 2 pints		
Mass (Weight)		
1 ton = 2000 pounds	1 pound $\doteq$ 0.454 kg	1 t = 1000 kg
1 pound = 16 ounces	1 ounce $\doteq$ 28.35 g	1 kg = 1000 g

So which *is* longer, 1500 m or 1 mile?

From the table, 1 mile = 1.609 km. So the 1-mile race is longer than the 1.5-km race. We would expect the record time to be less, even if athletes' performances had not improved.

Many imperial rulers show an inch divided into eighths, sixteenths, or sometimes even thirty-seconds. To take a measurement using such a ruler, you must first determine the smallest indicated unit, possibly by counting the number of divisions between two inch markers. The ruler on page 10 has 16 divisions between the 3- and 4-inch marks, so the smallest indicated unit is $\frac{1}{16}$ of an inch.

The pencil in the diagram has a length that is closest to the 7th division marker from 3, so the length is reported as $3\frac{7}{16}$ inches.

If your imperial ruler has 10 divisions between the inch markers, you can read it as you would a metric ruler, and use decimal numbers when reporting measurements.

The Investigations will help you develop familiarity with imperial units. They focus on linear and area measurement, since these applications relate to the Chapter Project.

You should complete both *Investigations 1* and *2*, then work on either *Investigation 3* or *4* with a partner. Plan how you will report your third Investigation to the class.

Investigation 1 Measuring in the Classroom

You will need a variety of measuring tools: imperial rulers, yard sticks, tape measures, and trundle wheels if they are available. You will also need a selection of items from your backpack and from within the classroom. Work with a partner.

1. Some imperial rulers are marked in tenths of an inch; some are marked in eighths or even sixteenths of an inch. Look at your rulers. Before you start any measuring, identify the smallest indicated unit. Repeat this step when you switch from the rulers to tape measures, yardsticks, or trundle wheels.

2. Select some items to measure. You should have at least:

- 3 items that fit on the palm of your hand
- 3 items that fit on a desk top
- 3 items that are larger than your desk

3. Each of you measure the items in each of the three categories. Take as many measurements as you think are necessary to accurately describe the item. Record and compare your measurements.

Investigation 2 Visualizing Measurement

1. Which units of imperial measurement are appropriate for measuring each of the following?
   - **a)** your height
   - **b)** a wallet photograph
   - **c)** the distance between towns
   - **d)** the length of a driveway
   - **e)** a computer screen
   - **f)** the thickness of a book

2. Which units of metric measurement would you select for measuring each item in exercise 1?

3. Your answers to exercises 1 and 2, for each object, show pairs of corresponding units in the imperial and metric systems of measurement. For example, you probably indicated inches and centimetres for exercise 1b. For each pair of corresponding units, describe a way to estimate a metric equivalent of the imperial unit.

4. Create a table of approximate measurement conversions, working from the table on page 9.

Investigation 3 Measuring Beyond the Classroom

You will need tape measures or trundle wheels. Work with a partner.

1. Familiarize yourself with the measurement tool you are using. What is the smallest unit of measurement it shows?

2. Select some distances to measure within the school grounds. You should have at least:
   - 1 in-class distance
   - 1 straight hallway distance
   - 1 outdoor distance
   - 1 path joining 2 places within the school (for example, the path from your locker to your home room)

   Record a description of each distance you plan to measure.

3. What is the most reasonable unit to use for each of the distances you described? Explain each choice.

4. Work with your partner to measure each distance you described in exercise 2. Record your measurements.

5. What was the longest distance you measured in this Investigation? How many times would you have to walk that distance in order to walk a mile? How long do you think it would take you to walk a mile?

Investigation 4 Working with Area

You will need sheets of newspaper, tape, scissors, a metre stick, a yardstick, and an imperial tape measure or trundle wheel. Work with a partner.

1. Measure, cut, and tape the newspaper to create a square 1 m by 1 m.

2. What is the side length of the square in centimetres? How many square centimetres are there in 1 m^2?

3. Use the yardstick to mark off 1-foot measures along each side of the square metre. Extend the 1-foot marks to create a grid of 1-foot squares that almost fills the square metre.

4. About how many square feet are there in 1 m^2? About how many square yards are there in 1 m^2? How many square feet are there in 1 square yard?

5. Measure, or count tiles, to determine the area of your classroom floor in square feet. How many square yards is your classroom floor? Approximately how many square metres is that?

6. Measure, or count tiles, to determine the floor area of one hallway in your school. How many square yards is your hallway floor? Approximately how many square metres is that?

Discussing the Ideas

1. One way to estimate measurement is to have a reference that approximately represents one unit of measurement. Even if you don't have any measuring tools with you, you can still use the reference to estimate. Identify a reference that will approximately relate to each of the following units:

   a) inch   **b)** foot   **c)** yard

2. You have been working with the metric system of measurement in all your previous mathematics classes. What references did you develop for approximating each of the following metric units? How do these references compare to the ones from exercise 1?

   a) metre   **b)** centimetre   **c)** millimetre

3. Describe how you might estimate the distance from your desk to the front of the classroom. Compare your estimate to those of the rest of your class.

4. Describe how you might estimate the distance from your classroom to the end of the hall. Compare your estimate to those of the rest of your class.

5. Describe how you would estimate the distance you travelled to come to school today. How could you check this estimate?

6. When contractors advertise new homes under construction, they include information about the square footage of each home. The measure they give reflects the floor area covered on all levels. If you saw an advertised house size of 1500 square feet, explain how you might interpret the information.

PROJECTS

In this Tutorial you developed skills in measuring and estimating with imperial units of measurement. You will need these skills to complete the Chapter Project and the following projects in the Project Book.

- Candy Boxes
- Jewellery Design

Communicating the Ideas

Describe some of the strategies you developed for estimating measurements in imperial units. Include a description of strategies for both small measurements and large distances. Provide some examples that demonstrate how your estimation strategies will work in specific cases.

TUTORIAL

1.3 Measurement Conversions

A superstore is offering carpet at $2.19 per square foot. A private shop is selling the same carpet at $18.95 per square yard. Which store has the better price?

Both stores are using imperial units of measure, but in order to determine which has the better price we must convert one of the prices into the same units as the other.

Practise Your Prior Skills

When working with measurement applications we usually encounter only one system of measure, whether it is metric or imperial. Try these exercises for preliminary review.

1. Change 6.54 m into centimetres.

2. How many metres are there in 38.54 mm?

3. Change 2.5 m^2 to square centimetres.

STUDENT REFERENCE

If you need to review converting metric units, look in the Student Reference under metric system for examples and explanations.

Comparing carpet prices for the better buy requires an exact conversion. Occasionally, we have to convert between systems and this may require an approximate conversion.

There are many ways to make measurement conversions. These Investigations introduce you to some possible approaches.

Investigation 1 Looking for Patterns

1. Convert yards to feet. Copy and complete the table by looking for and applying a pattern.

Yards	Feet
1	3
2	
3	
4	
10	
56	
180	

2. Describe a general rule for converting yards to feet.

3. Convert inches to feet. Copy and complete the table by looking for and applying a pattern.

Inches	Feet
12	1
24	
36	
48	
180	
540	
1800	

4. Describe a general rule for converting inches to feet.

5. From the table on page 9, 1 pound is equal to 16 ounces. Describe a rule you could use for converting from pounds to ounces.

If you have access to a computer with a spreadsheet program installed, you could create a spreadsheet that would perform conversions.

Investigation 2 Using Technology

Many inexpensive calculators have built-in functions to perform measurement conversions. Although the TI-83 does not have built-in conversion functions, a program called CONVERT will perform common measurement conversions within or between the metric and imperial systems of measure. Ask your teacher for this program. In order to load the program into your calculator, you will need to use the LINK feature on the TI-83.

For additional information on using the LINK feature on the TI-83, refer to Utility 4.

Running this program will allow you to complete the measurement conversions between common units of length, area, volume, and mass within a system and between systems of units.

For additional information on running programs, refer to Utility 5.

1. Using the CONVERT program, convert 5 miles into yards by following these steps.
   - Choose 1:LENGTH in order to convert units of length.
   - Since we want to convert from miles to yards, we must choose to convert "length from" miles. The unit "miles" does not appear on the first menu screen, so choose 6:MORE>. The unit "miles" is the second choice on this menu, so choose 2:MILES.
   - The unit we want to convert "length to" is yards, so choose 5:YARDS.
   - Now input the number of miles you wish to convert and press ENTER. The equivalent unit in yards will appear on the screen.
   - To restart the program, press ENTER.

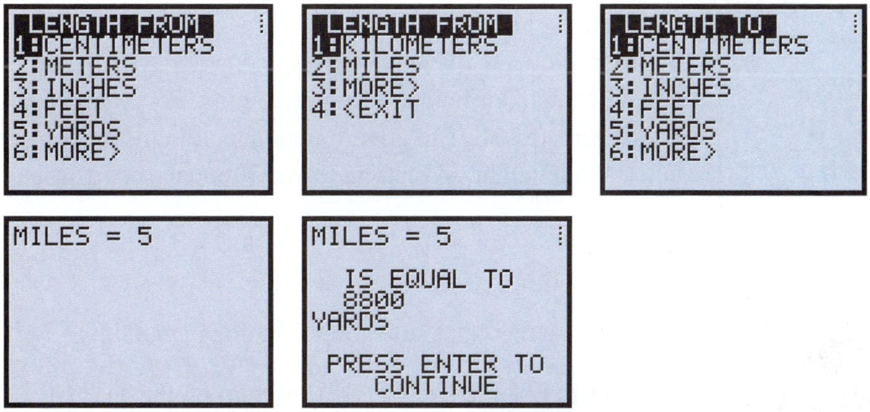

2. Using the CONVERT program, fill in the following table.

3. What rule is used by the calculator to find the number of yards in a mile?

4. Use the TI-83 and a similar table to discover the relationship between feet and metres.

Miles	Yards
5	
10	
15	
20	
25	
30	

Example 1 **Compare prices**

Return to the opening problem for this Tutorial. The superstore offers carpet at \$2.19 per square foot. The private store sells the same carpet at \$18.95 per square yard. Which is the better buy?

SOLUTION

Express 1 square yard in square feet. Use technology, as in this Investigation, or a conversion table.

1 square yard = 9 square feet

Now, 1 square foot costs \$2.19, so 9 × 1 square foot costs 9 × \$2.19.

9 square feet cost \$19.71.

Thus, the superstore is charging \$19.71 per square yard. The private store offers the better buy.

Example 2 Converting units

In order to obtain a Canadian passport, you have to give your height. Most people know their height in imperial units. For example, Brendan Shanahan is 6 feet 3 inches tall. But government departments prefer measurements in metric units. What height, in metres, would Brendan report when he applies for a passport?

SOLUTION

Choose a method that suits the technology available.

Method 1: Use the CONVERT program on the TI-83.

First, we must convert the imperial units either to inches or feet. Choose inches.

Run the program and choose 1:LENGTH. Select 4:FEET from the LENGTH FROM menu, followed by 3:INCHES from the LENGTH TO menu. Enter **6** and press [ENTER] to obtain the statement that 6 feet = 72 inches.

So, 6 feet 3 inches = 72 inches + 3 inches.
= 75 inches

Run CONVERT again to convert the length 75 inches into metres. Choose 1:LENGTH, then select 3:INCHES from the LENGTH FROM menu. Select 2:METERS from the LENGTH TO menu, and enter **75** at the prompt.

The calculator reports that 75 inches = 1.905 m.

Brendan Shanahan would report his height as 1.91 m.

Method 2: Use a conversion table, such as the one on page 9 of this resource. It contains an equation that relates feet to metres, so choose to convert the height to feet.

From the table:

$$1 \text{ foot} = 12 \text{ inches}$$
$$\text{so } 1 \text{ foot} \div 12 = 12 \text{ inches} \div 12$$
$$0.083333333 \text{ foot} = 1 \text{ inch}$$

Multiplying both sides by 3:

$$3 \times 0.083333333 \text{ foot} = 3 \times 1 \text{ inch}$$
$$0.25 \text{ foot} = 3 \text{ inches}$$

Brendan Shanahan is 6 feet + 0.25 feet tall, or 6.25 feet.

The passport office requires the height in metres, so we must now convert from feet to metres. Choose the suitable equation from the table:

$$1 \text{ foot} = 0.3048 \text{ m}$$
$$\text{so } 6.25 \times 1 \text{ foot} = 6.25 \times 0.3048 \text{ m}$$
$$6.25 \text{ feet} = 1.905 \text{ m}$$

Brendan Shanahan would report his height as 1.91 m.

DISCUSSING THE IDEAS

1. What part did patterns play in the measurement conversions you worked with in the Investigations?
2. Suppose you wanted to convert a measurement from a smaller unit to a larger unit, for example, changing centimetres to metres or inches to feet. Would you expect your answer to be a larger or smaller number than the original measurement? Explain.
3. Another way to solve the carpet problem would be to convert 1 square foot to square yards first. Try solving the problem this way. Which method do you prefer? Why?
4. The Investigations and Examples demonstrated different strategies for converting measurements. What are the advantages of each? When would you use them?

PROJECTS

In this Tutorial you developed skills with measurement conversions. You will need these skills to complete the Chapter Project and the following projects in the Project Book.

- Candy Boxes
- Jewellery Design

EXERCISES

Checking Your Skills

1. For each of the following celebrities, determine:

a) their height in inches

b) the height in metres they would report on their passport form

Wayne Gretzky – 6 feet

Silken Laumann – 5 feet 11 inches

Joanne Malar – 5 feet 8 inches

Michael J. Fox – 5 feet 4 inches

Theoren Fleury – 5 feet 6 inches

Celine Dion – 5 feet 7 inches

2. In basketball, the three-point field goal line is 23 feet 9 inches from the centre of the basket. How far is this in metres?

3. In the past, track athletes ran the 100-yard dash. Now competitors run the 100-m dash. Which one is farther and by how much?

4. The West Edmonton Mall in Alberta is one of the largest shopping malls in the world. It covers 5.2 million square feet.

a) How many square yards does the mall cover?

b) How many square metres does the mall cover?

5. The official 1-mile land speed record is 763.04 miles per hour. It was set by Andy Green on October 16, 1997, in the *Thrust SCC*. Green's car was powered by 2 Rolls Royce jet engines, which are normally found in British Phantom fighter planes. How fast is Green's speed record in kilometres per hour?

Extending Your Thinking

6. The fuel consumption for a car in Canada is given in terms of how many litres of fuel it will consume for every 100 km travelled. In the United States, the fuel consumption for a car is given in terms of how many miles it can travel using a gallon of gasoline. The U.S. gallon is equivalent to 3.785 L.

a) Copy the following table into your notebook.

b) Convert each fuel consumption from miles per gallon to kilometres per litre. Record your answers in your table.

Miles per U.S. Gallon	Kilometres per Litre	Litres per 100 km
5		
10		
20		
30		
40		
50		

c) Use a ratio to determine how many litres it takes to travel 100 km for each given fuel consumption. Record your answers in the table.

d) Draw a scatterplot of the data. Plot fuel consumption in miles per gallon on the horizontal axis and fuel consumption in litres per 100 km on the vertical axis. Draw in a line or a smooth curve to best represent this relationship.

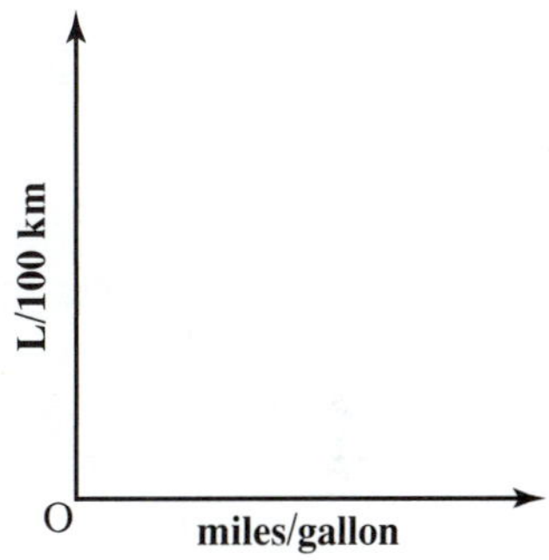

e) Use your graph to convert a fuel consumption of 9 L/100 km into miles per U.S. gallon.

f) Use your graph to convert a fuel consumption of 35 miles per U.S. gallon into litres per 100 km.

g) Research fuel consumption for a car you would like to own and for a car of an adult you know.

COMMUNICATING THE IDEAS

Select one of the strategies you developed for making measurement conversions. Describe how you would apply the strategy in a specific example. Explain how you would check your answer for reasonableness.

TUTORIAL 1.4

Precision and Accuracy in Measurement

A carpenter has a ruler that has become slightly bowed over the years. She is making a bookcase 5 feet long, with 4 shelves. She uses the same ruler in all her measurements.

- Will the shelves fit into the bookcase?
- Will she meet the specification of a 5-foot length?

Cover up the remainder of this page. Discuss the two questions above before reading further.

If the carpenter works carefully, her bookcase should fit together. The length of the bookcase will be less than 5 feet, however, since the bowed ruler will affect each measurement.

The carpenter's measurements will not be accurate. The term *accuracy* indicates how close a measurement comes to its true value. The difference between a measurement and its true value is the *measurement error*. The closer to the target, the more accurate the measurement, the lower the error.

Because the carpenter is experienced and careful, her measurements will be precise. If we were to get close to the same measurement each time we used a device, we would have *precision* in our measurements.

The *uncertainty* of a measurement device is related to its smallest scale division. The greater the number of divisions in a measuring device, the lower the uncertainty, and the greater the precision.

Look at the ruler below. To use this ruler to compare two lengths, they would have to differ by more than 0.1 inch. The ruler has a precision of 0.1 inch.

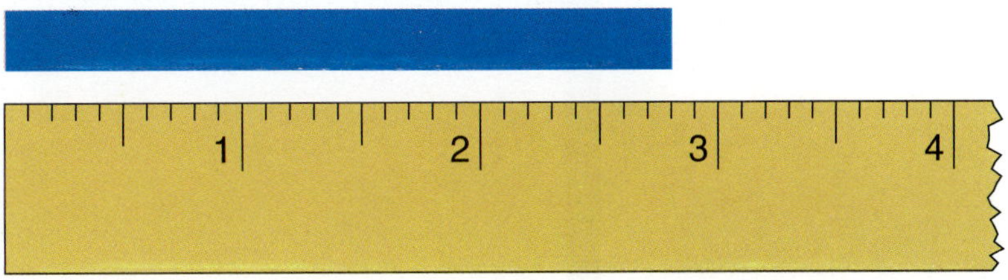

The rectangle has a length of 2.8 inches, within 0.05 inch. Its actual length lies somewhere between 2.75 inches and 2.85 inches. If you needed a more precise measurement, you would need a ruler with greater precision. If you needed a more accurate measurement, you would need to have an instrument that has been recently calibrated.

Example 1 **Determining precision and accuracy of a measurement**

An interior decorator recommends a shatterproof coating for a large rectangular picture window. He measures the window to be 2.23 m long and 1.47 m high.

a) What measuring device do you think he used?

b) What is the precision of the measuring device?

c) What is the uncertainty of the measurements?

d) What is the area of glass to be coated?

SOLUTION

a) A suitable measuring device would be a tape measure marked in metres and centimetres.

b) The decorator's measurements show two decimal places. The tape measure has a precision of 0.01 m or 1 cm.

c) The uncertainty of each measurement is ±0.005 m or ±0.5 cm. The length is between 2.225 m and 2.235 m. The width is between 1.465 m and 1.475 m.

d)
$$\text{Area} = 2.23 \text{ m} \times 1.47 \text{ m} = 3.2781 \text{ m}^2$$

Consider the result for *Example 1d*, obtained by multiplying length by width. Since the length and width are measurements, they are not exact. We cannot say for certain that the area is 3.2781 m^2.

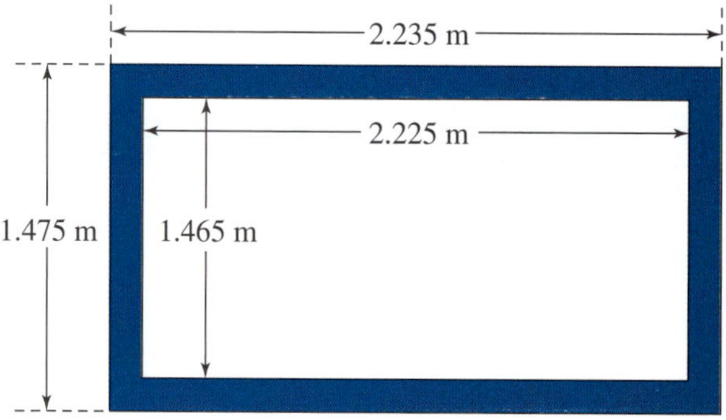

The length could be as short as 2.225 m and the width as short as 1.465 m. With these measurements, the area would be 3.259 625 m^2. Rounding this to three digits, the area could be as small as 3.26 m^2.

The length could be as long as 2.235 m and the width as long as 1.475 m. With these measurements, the area would be 3.296 625 m^2. Rounding this to three digits, the area could be as large as 3.30 m^2.

We could round 3.2781 m^2 to 3.28 m^2, which gives the same number of decimal places as the original measurements. This convention seems reasonable, since 3.28 m^2 falls within the range of areas calculated for the diagram above, 3.26 m^2 and 3.30 m^2 or 3.28 $m^2 \pm 0.02$ m^2.

The uncertainty has gone from ±0.005 m for the length and width measurements to ±0.02 m^2 for area calculation.

Example 2 **Using the concepts of precision and accuracy**

A bathroom scale consistently gives masses that are 3 kg below the true mass. Does this scale have poor precision or poor accuracy?

SOLUTION

Since the bathroom scale gives masses that are consistently 3 kg too low, it is able to discriminate between masses and, therefore, has good precision. However, since all masses are 3 kg too low, the scale has poor accuracy.

Example 3 **Analyzing the limitations of measuring instruments**

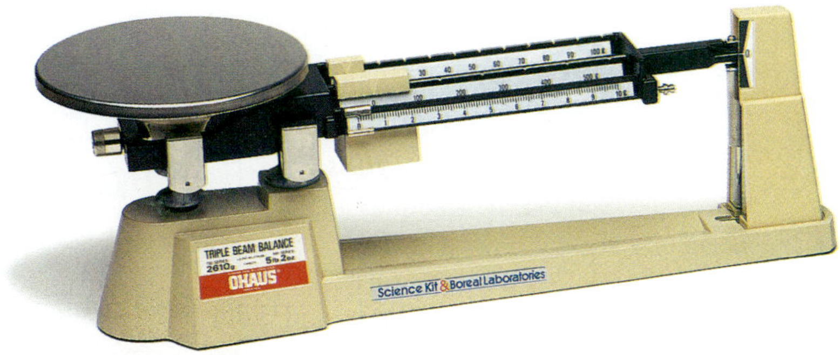

A decigram balance has a precision of 0.1 g. Indicate if this instrument is appropriate for finding the mass of each of the following items.

a) a graphing calculator

b) one paper clip

SOLUTION

Since the scale has a precision of 0.1 g, every measurement will have an uncertainty of ±0.05 g. Given this uncertainty, the scale should only be used to determine masses that are larger than 0.1 g.

a) Estimate the mass of a graphing calculator to be greater than 50 g. The balance would be well suited to finding the mass of the calculator.

b) Estimate the mass of a paper clip to be less than 1 g. The balance is not well suited to finding the mass of one paper clip, since the precision of the balance is only 0.1 g.

DISCUSSING THE IDEAS

1. Generally, any number of zeros can be placed to the right of the decimal point in a whole number without changing the value of the number. For example, 25 = 25.00. This is not true when recording measurements. Why?

2. You can use a centimetre vernier caliper to measure objects to the nearest 0.01 cm. You can use a micrometer to measure small objects to the nearest 0.01 mm. If both these devices are available, which one would you choose to determine the thickness of 8 sheets of copy paper? Explain your choice.

3. Explain why a ruler is not an appropriate instrument for measuring the thickness of 8 sheets of copy paper.

4. Explain why increasing the precision of a measuring instrument should decrease the difference between successive measurements of the same quantity.

5. In *Example 1*, the interior decorator measured the dimensions of the glass. Suppose he also measured the window to order draperies. Explain why these measurements would be greater than those given in the Example.

PROJECTS

In this Tutorial you worked with concepts of precision and accuracy, and you described how to distinguish between them. You will use these concepts in the Chapter Project and the following projects in the Project Book.

- Candy Boxes
- Jewellery Design

EXERCISES

Checking Your Skills

1. Explain whether it is reasonable to use each of the following measuring instruments for the given measurement.

a) a balance with a precision of 0.01 g for a mass of 182.48 g

b) a balance with a precision of 0.01 g for a mass of 0.04 g

c) a clock with a precision of 1 s to measure the duration of a math class

d) a clock with a precision of 1 s to time a runner in a 100-m race

e) a bathroom scale with a precision of 0.5 kg to find the mass of an adult

f) a bathroom scale with a precision of 0.5 kg to find the mass of a baby

g) a ruler with a precision of $\frac{1}{8}$ of an inch to measure a football field

2. A carpenter is using a tape measure to determine the length of baseboard required for a room.

a) Is it important that the tape measure be accurate? Why, or why not?

b) The carpenter decides to use a metre stick to measure the board and determine where he should make his cut. Explain why this could result in the baseboard not fitting when put into the room.

3. These four diagrams represent shots at a target.

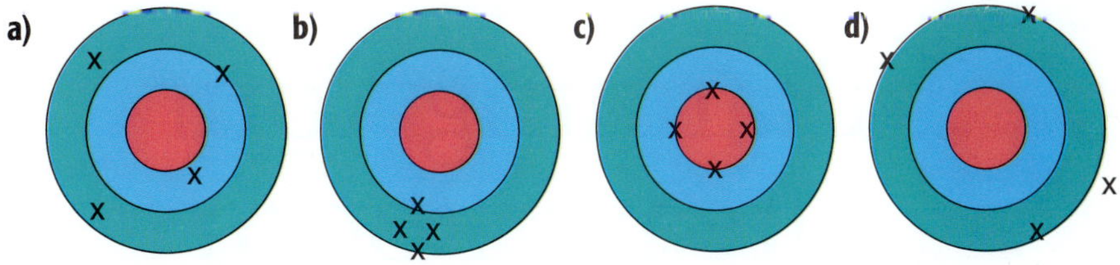

Which diagram represents the best precision and accuracy? Explain.

4. A student wishes to find out whether there is significant variation in the thickness of a quarter. He measures the thickness of 1 quarter, then the thickness of 100 quarters stacked on top of one another. Is a vernier caliper, whose smallest scale division is 0.01 cm, an appropriate measuring instrument for this experiment? Explain your answer.

5. When two students determined the mass of an object, a measurement error of 0.4 g occurred. The students were arguing about whether this would be considered a significant error. How would you respond if you were asked to give your opinion?

6. Look at rulers with both metric and imperial scales. Which is more precise: a ruler divided into tenths of an inch, a ruler divided into eighths of an inch, or a ruler divided into millimetres? Explain your answer.

Extending Your Thinking

7. Using a micrometer, a student determined the thickness of a piece of paper to be 0.09 mm. Using a ruler, she found the length of the paper to be 27.6 cm.

   a) What is the precision associated with each measurement?

   b) If the true measurements are known to be 0.10 mm and 27.8 cm respectively, explain which measurement is more accurate.

COMMUNICATING THE IDEAS

Use an example to explain the importance of precision and accuracy when taking measurements.

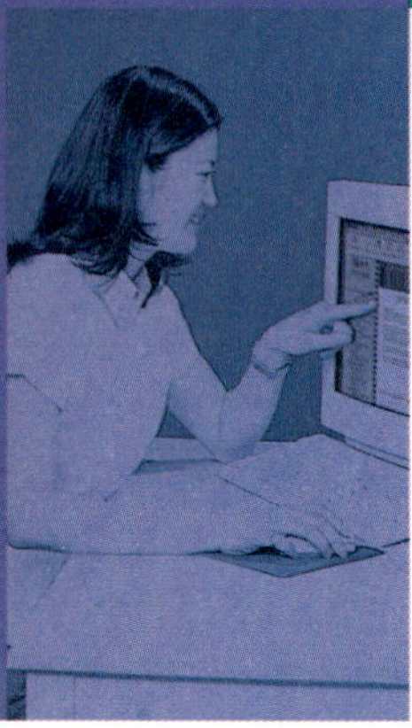

Planning Your Dream Room

At the beginning of this project, on page 2, you started making plans for a dream room. Now you need to put your plans on paper and estimate costs.

- Write a description of your dream room. Include details of the flooring, walls, artwork, furniture, and so on.
- Sketch a floor plan of your room. Take all the measurements you will need to create an accurate plan, and record them on your sketch. Measure the height of the room, and the size of the windows and doors. Provide a reason for the units you used in your recorded measurements, and the degree of precision.
- Create an accurate floor plan from your sketch. Show all measurements. Indicate the position and size of windows and doors.
- Calculate the floor area of your room.
- Calculate the surface area of walls and ceiling to be painted or papered. If you plan to use wallpaper, find out about wastage for the pattern you select.
- Work out the cost of your decorating. Use catalogues or the Internet, or go to some stores to obtain prices. Look for prices of decorating equipment too, such as paint brushes and rollers. Organize and record your cost estimates. If you are familiar with spreadsheet programs, and have access to one, you may find it helpful to create your own cost spreadsheet.
- Keep copies of your drawings, calculations, and cost estimates to form part of your project report.
- Investigating costs may lead you to refine your original plan. If this happens, redo your plan and recalculate the costs. Keep a record of both plans. Include a summary of your reasons for changing.

CHAPTER PROJECT

In the next stage of this Chapter Project, you create a cardboard model of your dream room. *Tutorial 1.8* will help you develop an understanding of the related skills.

You will return to this Chapter Project on page 54.

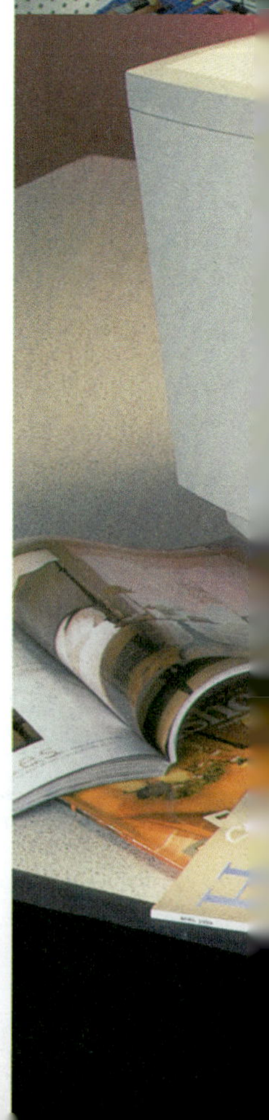

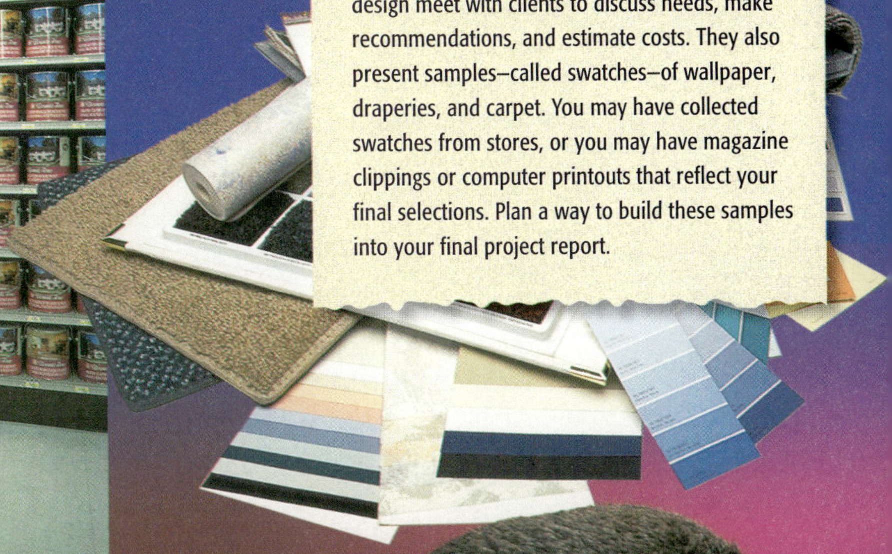

Career Skills

People who work in architectural and interior design meet with clients to discuss needs, make recommendations, and estimate costs. They also present samples–called swatches–of wallpaper, draperies, and carpet. You may have collected swatches from stores, or you may have magazine clippings or computer printouts that reflect your final selections. Plan a way to build these samples into your final project report.

TUTORIAL 1.5

Volume of a Sphere

We live in a three-dimensional world where many of the objects around us do not have flat surfaces. A common three-dimensional object, suggested by the tennis ball, is the sphere.

The greatest distance across a sphere, measured through the centre, is its *diameter*. The *radius* of a sphere is half its diameter.

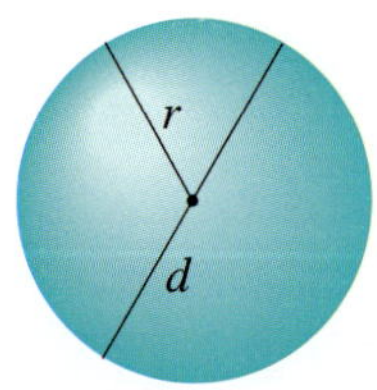

Investigation

The Volume of a Sphere

You will need an empty 355-mL frozen juice can, a millimetre ruler, a vernier caliper, an old tennis ball, a sharp knife or pair of scissors, some water, and an overflow container.

UTILITY

If you have not worked with a vernier caliper before, go to Utility 2 for an introduction to its use.

Work with a partner.

1. Each of you use the vernier caliper to measure the diameter of the tennis ball. Repeat the measurement in 5 different places on the ball. Record your answers.

2. Discard the highest and lowest value for the diameter. Average the 6 remaining values to determine the diameter of the tennis ball.

STUDENT REFERENCE

If you need to review averaging a set of numbers, look in the Student Reference under "average."

3. Complete the following steps.

- Place the tennis ball in water and allow it to soak.
- Carefully cut the can so that its inside height is equal to the diameter of the ball.
- Place the can in the overflow container and carefully fill the can to the top with water, but do not allow it to overflow.
- Slowly place the tennis ball in the can. Allow the water to overflow into the container. Gently push the ball right down to the bottom of the can.
- Take the can out of the overflow container, empty the water from the can, and remove the ball.
- Pour the water from the overflow container into the can.
- Using the millimetre ruler, measure the depth of the water.

4. How does the volume of the water that was made to overflow from the can compare with the volume of the ball? Explain your answer.

5. At the end of exercise 3, what fraction of the can was filled with water?

6. In this Investigation, the diameter of the cylinder is equal to its height. The sphere has the same diameter as the cylinder. What probable conclusion can you make about the volume of the sphere compared with the volume of the cylinder?

7. Calculate the volume of the can used in this experiment.

STUDENT REFERENCE

If you need to review volume of a cylinder, see "cylinder" in the Student Reference.

8. Use your results from exercises 6 and 7 to estimate the volume of the ball.

9. Suppose the can and the ball both had radius r. Use your result from exercise 6 to write formulas for the volumes of the can and the sphere.

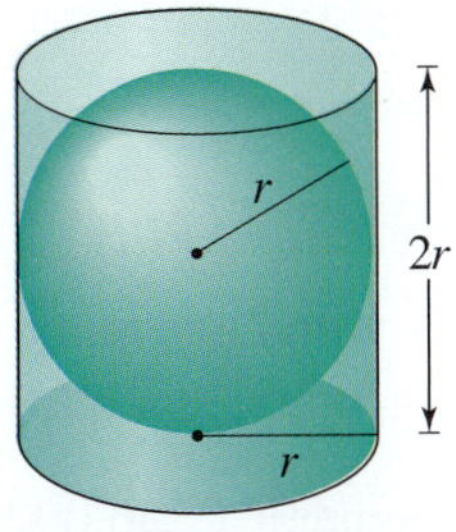

In the *Investigation*, you determined a volume relationship between a particular sphere and a cylinder that just holds the sphere. This relationship is true, in general, for any sphere.

The volume V of a sphere with radius r is $V = \frac{4}{3}\pi r^3$.

The volume V of a sphere with diameter d is $V = \frac{1}{6}\pi d^3$.

STUDENT REFERENCE

When using formulas such as the ones given above, you have to review "substituting values into expressions." If you need to review this topic, look in the Student Reference.

Example 1 **Calculate the volume of a sphere, given its diameter**

A machine builder needs a ball bearing with a diameter of 0.54 cm. What volume of steel does it contain?

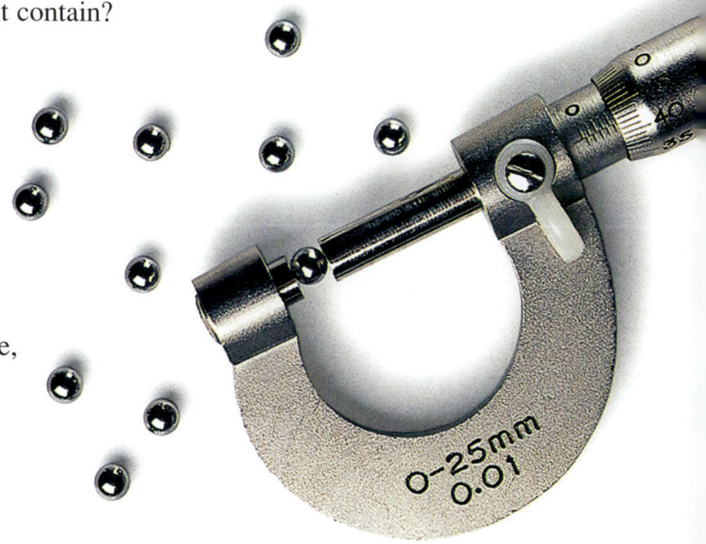

SOLUTION

The ball bearing is spherical and the volume of steel is the volume of the sphere.

You are given a value for the diameter, d, of the sphere, so choose the formula for volume of a sphere in terms of the diameter.

$$\text{Volume} = \frac{1}{6}\pi d^3$$

Substitute $d = 0.54$.

$$\begin{aligned}\text{Volume} &= \frac{1}{6}\pi(0.54)^3 \\ &= 0.082\ 447\ 957\ 6\end{aligned}$$

The volume of steel is approximately 0.082 cm^3.

Practise Your Prior Skills

When working with large numbers, calculators report answers in scientific notation. Try these exercises for preliminary review.

1. Write the numeral 1 250 000 in scientific notation.

2. Write 3.078×10^4 in decimal notation.

STUDENT REFERENCE

If you need more information, or would like to see some examples, look in the Student Reference for "scientific notation."

Example 2 Calculate the volume of a sphere, given its radius

Visualize Earth. Although Earth is not exactly spherical, it is approximately so. The mean radius of Earth is 6365 km. Using this figure, calculate its volume.

SOLUTION

Visualize Earth as a sphere. We are given its mean radius, so choose the formula for the volume of a sphere in terms of its radius.

$$\text{Volume} = \frac{4}{3}\pi r^3$$

Substitute $r = 6365$.

$$\begin{aligned}\text{Volume} &= \frac{4}{3}\pi(6365)^3 \\ &= 1.080\ 149\ 411 \times 10^{12}\end{aligned}$$

Earth has a volume of approximately 1.1×10^{12} km^3.

STUDENT REFERENCE

If you need to review "*substituting values into expressions*," look in the Student Reference.

DISCUSSING THE IDEAS

1. In this *Investigation* you measured the diameter of the tennis ball 5 times, then you discarded the highest and lowest measurements. Explain why we discard the highest and lowest measurement.

2. Why did you soak the tennis ball before placing it into the can of water?

3. In this *Investigation* you used a can with approximately the same radius as the tennis ball. If you had used a can with a different radius, you would not have been able to find the volume of the ball in terms of its radius. Explain why not.

4. The formula for the volume, V, of a sphere with radius r is $V = \frac{4}{3}\pi r^3$. Explain where the $\frac{4}{3}$ comes from.

5. Suppose you can remember the formula $V = \frac{4}{3}\pi r^3$. Visualize the relationship between the radius, r, and the diameter, d, of the sphere. Explain how you would determine the formula, $V = \frac{1}{6}\pi d^3$, for the volume in relation to the diameter. You may wish to use algebra in your explanation.

PROJECTS

This Tutorial introduced formulas for the volume of a sphere. You need these formulas for the following projects in the Project Book.

- Candy Boxes
- Jewellery Design

EXERCISES

Checking Your Skills

1. Find the volume of each ball described below.

a) a golf ball with diameter 4.3 cm

b) a volleyball with diameter 20.9 cm

c) a table tennis ball with radius 1.85 cm

d) a squash ball with radius 2.0 cm

2. The sun is made of gases and has a diameter of 1.392 million kilometres. Find the volume of the sun in cubic kilometres.

STUDENT REFERENCE

If you need to review the circumference of a circle, look under "circle" in the Student Reference.

3. Often the size of a ball used in a sport is specified not by its radius or diameter, but by its circumference. A basketball has a circumference of 76 cm.

a) Use the formula for the circumference of a circle. Determine the radius of the basketball.

b) Determine the volume of the basketball.

4. A spherical balloon is blown up from a diameter of 20 cm to a diameter of 60 cm. Calculate its original volume and its new volume. By how many times has its volume increased?

5. The radius of Uranus is almost 4 times as great as the radius of Earth. The mean radius of Earth is 6365 km. Calculate

a) the radius of Uranus.

b) the volume of Uranus.

Extending Your Thinking

6. Raindrops are almost spherical. Their diameters rarely exceed 6 mm. Calculate the number of raindrops that would be required to fill a cylindrical pop can with volume 355 mL.

7. A spherical soap bubble contains a fixed volume of air. When it lands on a flat surface, its shape changes to that of a *hemisphere*. Find the ratio of the radius of the hemisphere to the radius of the sphere.

COMMUNICATING THE IDEAS

When you calculate the volume of a sphere, you use an approximation for the irrational number π. You should always use the value of π stored in your calculator to ensure that you can report a reasonable and appropriate answer.

Give an example which demonstrates that using 3.14 as an approximation for π does not allow you to round your answer appropriately.

TUTORIAL 1.6

Surface Area of a Sphere

Lacrosse balls are made of a very hard rubber, coated with a layer of sealant. When they are being manufactured, one question that must be answered is:

- What surface area needs to be coated for each ball?

This leads us to ask:

- Is it possible to generalize a method for determining the surface area of a sphere?

Do the following Investigation to examine the underlying ideas behind these questions.

Investigation

Surface Area of a Sphere

You will need an orange, a vernier caliper, and graph paper. Try to choose an orange that is nearly spherical and one that has a thin skin.

UTILITY

If you have not worked with a vernier caliper before, go to Utility 2 for an introduction to its use.

Work with a partner.

1. Use the vernier caliper to measure the diameter in 5 different places on the orange. Record your measurements.

2. Discard the highest and lowest value for the diameter of your orange. Average the 3 remaining values to determine the diameter of your orange.

3. Peel the orange carefully and arrange the peels on the graph paper. Press them down to make them as flat as possible, and trace around them. By counting full squares and part squares, estimate the area of the orange peel in square centimetres.

4. Divide your estimate of the area of the peel by the square of the diameter of the orange. Record this result.

5. Share your results with your classmates. Create a table like the one below to show all the results obtained by your class.

Diameter, d	Surface Area, A	$\frac{A}{d^2}$

6. Consider the ratio of the surface area of a sphere to the square of its diameter. What probable conclusion can you make about this ratio? What special mathematical number does the ratio almost equal?

7. Suppose a sphere has diameter d. If we conclude that generally $\frac{A}{d^2} = \pi$, state a formula for the surface area of a sphere if we know the diameter of the sphere.

8. Recall that the relationship between the diameter, d, and the radius, r, of a sphere is $d = 2r$. Substitute this expression for d into the formula you wrote in exercise 7.

In the *Investigation*, you examined a possible relationship for one particular sphere. This relationship is true, in general, for all spheres.

The surface area A of a sphere with diameter d is $A = \pi d^2$.

The surface area A of a sphere with radius r is $A = 4\pi r^2$.

Example Determine the surface area of a sphere, given its diameter

A lacrosse ball has a diameter of 5.4 cm. What is the surface area to be coated?

SOLUTION

Visualize the lacrosse ball as a sphere. You are given the diameter of the ball, so use the formula for the surface area of a sphere in terms of its diameter.

Surface area = πd^2.

Substitute 5.4 for d.

$$\text{Surface area} = \pi(5.4)^2$$
$$\doteq 92$$

The surface area of the lacrosse ball is approximately 92 cm^2.

DISCUSSING THE IDEAS

1. Examine the diameter measurements you took in exercise 1 of the *Investigation*. Was your orange a perfect sphere? Explain.

2. In the *Investigation* you took two sets of measurements: one set to find the surface area of the orange and the other set to find its diameter. Which set do you think was more accurate and why?

3. How could you increase the precision of the measuring device used to find the surface area of the orange? Would this make the surface area easier to find, or more difficult? Explain.

4. In exercise 5 of the *Investigation*, how close was the value you obtained to the accepted value of π? List some reasons to account for any differences.

Practise Your Prior Skills

In the exercises that follow, you need to work with percents. Try these exercises for preliminary review.

1. Determine 35% of 842.

2. Determine 15% of $2.35.

STUDENT REFERENCE

If you would like to see some examples, or obtain further information on working with "percents," look in the Student Reference.

PROJECTS

This Tutorial introduced formulas for the surface area of a sphere. You need these formulas for the following project in the Project Book.

- Jewellery Design

EXERCISES

Checking Your Skills

1. Calculate the surface area of each ball described below. Round all your answers to the nearest whole number.

a) a golf ball with diameter 4.3 cm

b) a volleyball with diameter 20.9 cm

c) a table tennis ball with radius 1.85 cm

d) a squash ball with radius 2.0 cm

2. A basketball has a diameter of 24.2 cm. Determine its surface area.

STUDENT REFERENCE

To recall the formula for the circumference of a circle, see "circle" in the Student Reference.

3. A baseball has a circumference of 23 cm. What is its diameter? What is its surface area?

4. Earth is approximately a sphere with a diameter of 12 730 km.

a) Determine Earth's surface area.

b) Approximately 78% of Earth's surface is covered with water. Determine the area of land on Earth's surface.

c) Canada's land area is approximately 9.2 million square kilometres. What percent is this of the total land area of Earth?

5. Venus is approximately spherical in shape, with diameter 12 100 km.

a) Calculate the surface area of Venus.

b) Lowland plains make up about 20% of the surface of Venus. Calculate the area of the lowland plains on Venus.

6. A balloonist plans to construct an approximately spherical hot air balloon with diameter 10 m.

a) Calculate the amount of material necessary to construct the balloon.

b) The material costs \$35.95 per square metre. Calculate its cost.

c) Suppose the diameter of the balloon is increased to 14.2 m. Calculate the cost of the material needed to construct this new balloon.

7. When we see a full moon in the night sky, it looks like a circle. Compare the visible surface area of a full moon with the area of the circle that it appears to be.

STUDENT REFERENCE

To recall the formula for the area of a circle, see "circle" in the Student Reference.

Extending Your Thinking

8. Find a formula for the surface area of a sphere in terms of its circumference, C.

9. A light source emits light in all directions. At a given distance, r, the light can be thought of as illuminating a sphere with radius r.

The relationship between light intensity and distance can be explored using the CBL and the light probe. Go to experiment P6 in the *Experimental Workbook* for the CBL. The instructions there will guide you through an investigation involving light intensity and distance.

COMMUNICATING THE IDEAS

In this chapter, you worked with surface areas and volumes of various objects. How can you tell, just by looking at a formula, whether it applies to area or volume? How can you tell by looking at a measurement whether it represents an area or a volume?

TUTORIAL 1.7

Square Roots and Cube Roots

We often have to work backward to solve a problem. For example, the volume of a spherical ball is known to be 2 cm^3. By working backward from the formula for the volume of a sphere, we can calculate its diameter.

Practise Your Prior Skills

In the *Investigation* that follows, you will work with the square root of a number and use the laws of exponents. Try these exercises for preliminary review.

1. Determine $\sqrt{10}$ correct to 3 decimal places.

2. State the value of $(\sqrt{5})^2$.

3. Write a statement without a root that has the same meaning as $\sqrt{25} = 5$.

4. Write $(2^2)^3$ as a single power of 2.

5. Simplify: **a)** 5^0 **b)** 4^1

STUDENT REFERENCE

If you would like to see examples of square roots and exponents, or an explanation of these topics, look in the Student Reference under "square roots" or "laws of exponents".

Investigation

Going Backward

We often have to work backward to solve problems. This *Investigation* leads you to consider ways of going backward to solve some types of measurement problems.

1. The circumference of a circle is 20 cm. Explain how to find its radius.

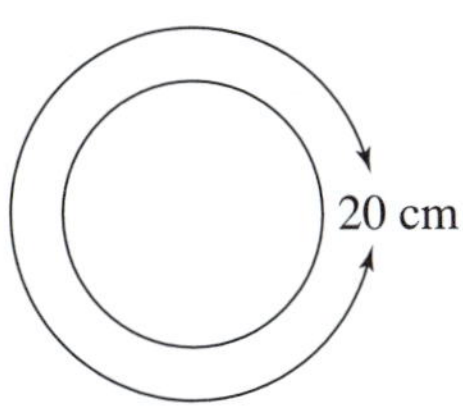

2. The area of a circle is 100 cm^2. Write a set of instructions explaining how you would use your calculator to find the radius of the circle.

3. The volume of a cube is 8 cm^3. Write a set of instructions explaining how you would find the length of the side of the cube. Cover up the rest of this page.

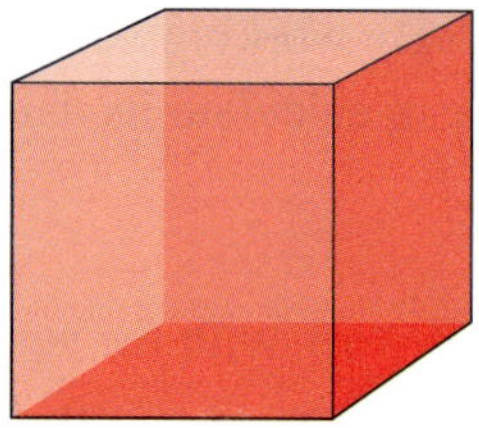

You may have started exercise 3 by thinking of the formula for the volume of a cube with side length x.

$$\begin{aligned}\text{Volume} &= x \times x \times x \\ &= x^3\end{aligned}$$

Since the volume is 8 cm^3, you must find the number that, when multiplied by itself 3 times, gives 8. The number is 2, since $2^3 = 8$.

We say that 2 is the *cube root* of 8, and write this $2 = \sqrt[3]{8}$.

Notice that $\quad (\sqrt[3]{8})^3 = 2^3$
$\qquad\qquad\qquad\quad = 8$

Just as with square roots of numbers, not all cube roots can be found exactly. Some calculators have a cube root key that can be used directly.

To use the cube root function on the TI-83 calculator, press [MATH]. If you are using a different graphing calculator, refer to the user's handbook.

To determine an approximate value for $\sqrt[3]{2}$ on the TI-83, press [MATH], **4 2** [ENTER].

$$\sqrt[3]{2} \doteq 1.259\,921\,05.$$

The cube root of many numbers, such as $\sqrt[3]{2}$, cannot be found exactly. They are *irrational numbers.*

STUDENT REFERENCE

For a description of "irrational numbers" and other "number systems," look in the Student Reference.

Example 1 Evaluate cube roots using a calculator

Determine an approximate value for each of the following expressions. Round your answers to 3 decimal places.

a) $\sqrt[3]{7}$ **b)** $\sqrt[3]{342}$

SOLUTION

a) Press MATH **4 7** ENTER to get the answer 1.912931183.

$\sqrt[3]{7} = 1.913$, correct to 3 decimal places.

b) Press MATH **4 342** ENTER to get the answer 6.993190657 in the display.

$\sqrt[3]{342} = 6.993$, correct to 3 decimal places.

Now return to the problem at the beginning of this Tutorial.

Example 2 Solve problems using cube roots

The volume of a spherical ball is known to be 2 cm^3. Calculate its diameter.

SOLUTION

The formula for the volume of a sphere with diameter d can be obtained either in *Tutorial 1.5*, or the Student Reference.

Volume $= \frac{1}{6}\pi d^3$

Substituting the value given for the volume, $V = 2$:

$$2 = \frac{1}{6}\pi d^3$$

To solve this equation, first isolate d^3 by multiplying both sides of the equation by $\frac{6}{\pi}$.

$$\frac{6}{\pi} \times 2 = \frac{6}{\pi} \times \frac{1}{6}\pi d^3$$

$$\frac{12}{\pi} = d^3$$

Taking the cube root of both sides:

$$\sqrt[3]{\frac{12}{\pi}} = \sqrt[3]{d^3}$$

$$\text{so } \sqrt[3]{\frac{12}{\pi}} = d$$

Use the calculator.

Press MATH **4 12** ÷ 2nd ^ ENTER to obtain 1.563185284 in the display.

The diameter of the ball is approximately 1.6 cm.

DISCUSSING THE IDEAS

1. A calculator shows that the cube root of 2 is approximately 1.259 921 05. Describe a way to check this result.
2. There may be other ways to find a cube root on your calculator. Investigate your calculator. Describe a way to use your calculator to find $\sqrt[3]{5}$.

PROJECTS

This Tutorial establishes calculator procedures for determining the square root or the cube root of a number. You need to use these procedures in *Tutorial 1.8,* and for the following project in the Project Book.

- Candy Boxes

EXERCISES

Checking Your Skills

1. Use a calculator to determine the approximate value of each of the following numbers. Round your answers to 2 decimal places.

   a) $\sqrt[3]{4}$ **b)** $\sqrt[3]{0.02}$

2. The surface area of a glass ball is 30 cm^2. What is its radius?

3. A building block in the shape of a cube has a volume of 24 cm^3. What is the length of the side of the cube?

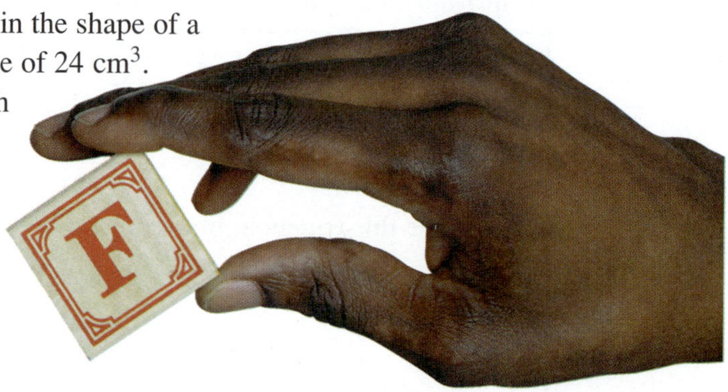

4. A spherical hot air balloon has a volume of 40 m^3. Calculate its diameter.

5. In one day, a gold mine produces approximately 1600 cm^3 of gold. If five days' gold production is cast into a cube, how long is its edge?

6. A child's building brick, in the shape of a cube, has a surface area of 28 cm^2. Calculate its volume.

7. A spherical hot air balloon has a volume of 24 cm^3. We pump 20 additional cubic centimetres of air into the balloon.

   a) What is the new diameter? **b)** What is the new surface area?

Extending Your Thinking

8. A hot air balloon has a spherical shape and a diameter of 4 m. Suppose 30 additional cubic metres of air are pumped into the balloon. What is each new value?

a) for the diameter **b)** for the volume **c)** for the surface area

COMMUNICATING THE IDEAS

Finding the cube root of a number comes up regularly in measurement problems involving volumes of solids. Write to explain why this is so.

TUTORIAL 1.8

Enlarging and Reducing Figures

Suppose you want to make an accurate representation of a region: a floor plan, a map, or a craft design. You can reduce or enlarge the region, proportionally, by multiplying all dimensions by the same *scale factor*. The *scale drawing* will have the same shape as the original.

Mathematically, we say the two figures are *similar*. For example, the two illustrations, that provide patterns for stained-glass designs, represent similar figures.

Each dimension in the larger diagram can be obtained by multiplying the corresponding dimension in the smaller diagram by 1.5.

Investigation 1

The Relationship between Scale Factor and Area

1. Copy and complete the table below for similar rectangles. Sketch each rectangle on grid paper as you work through your calculations.

Rectangle	Length (cm)	Width (cm)	Perimeter (cm)	Area (cm^2)
A	1	3		
B	2	6		
C	5	15		

2. Copy the table below into your notebook. Use your results from exercise 1 to complete the table.

Rectangle	Scale Factor	Ratio of Perimeters	Ratio of Areas
B to A			
C to A			
C to B			

3. a) What is the relationship between the scale factor and the ratio of the perimeters?

   b) What is the relationship between the scale factor and the ratio of the areas?

Investigation 2

The Relationship between Scale Factor, Surface Area, and Volume

Enlargements and reductions can also take place in three dimensions. If we enlarge or reduce an object by multiplying all dimensions by the same scale factor, the new object will be similar to the original.

Spheres

1. Copy and complete the following table.

Sphere	Radius (cm)	Surface Area (cm^2)	Volume (cm^3)
A	1		
B	3		
C	5		

2. Use the data from exercise 1. Copy and complete this table.

Sphere	Scale Factor	Ratio of Surface Areas	Ratio of Volumes
B to A			
C to A			
C to B			

3. a) What is the relationship between the scale factor and the ratio of the surface areas of two spheres?

   b) What is the relationship between the scale factor and the ratio of the volumes of two spheres?

4. Use the relationships from exercise 3, and information from the table in exercise 1, to predict each of the following.

   a) the surface area of a sphere whose radius is 6 cm

   b) the volume of a sphere whose radius is 6 cm

   Use the formulas from *Tutorials 1.5* and *1.6* to check your results in exercises a and b.

Cylinders

5. Copy and complete the following table for cylinders.

Cylinder	Radius (inches)	Height (inches)	Surface Area (square inches)	Volume (cubic inches)
A	1	3		
B	2	6		
C	5	15		

6. Copy the table below. Use the data in exercise 5 to complete the table.

Cylinder	Scale Factor	Ratio of Surface Areas	Ratio of Volumes
B to A			
C to A			
C to B			

7. a) What is the relationship between the scale factor and the ratio of the surface areas of two similar cylinders?

b) What is the relationship between the scale factor and the ratio of the volumes of two similar cylinders?

c) How do these results compare to the equivalent results for spheres?

8. In exercise 5, you calculated the volume and the surface area of a cylinder with a radius of 1 inch and a height of 3 inches. Use your results from exercise 5, together with your results from exercise 7, to predict the following measurements.

a) the surface area of a cylinder whose dimensions are 3 times as large

b) the volume of a cylinder whose dimensions are 3 times as large

Use formulas to check your results.

9. Explain what you think is the relation between the scale factor and ratios of the surface areas and volumes of two cubes. Use examples in your explanation.

10. Suppose you have two similar solids whose scale factor is k. What is the ratio of the following measurements?

a) surface areas

b) volumes

Example 1 **Use the relationship among linear scale factor, perimeter, and area**

A picture measuring 2 cm by 3 cm is enlarged to 8 cm by 12 cm.

a) What is the scale factor of the enlargement?

b) How many times as great as the perimeter of the original picture is the perimeter of the enlargement?

c) How many times as great as the area of the original picture is the area of the enlargement?

SOLUTION

Use the results from *Investigation 1*.

a) The scale factor is the ratio of the new length to the corresponding old length.
Scale factor $= \frac{8 \text{ cm}}{2 \text{ cm}} = \frac{4}{1} = 4$

b) The perimeter of the enlargement is the scale factor times the original perimeter.
The enlarged perimeter is 4 times as long as the original perimeter.

c) The ratio of the area of the enlargement to the area of the original picture is the square of the scale factor.
The area of the enlargement is 4^2 times as great as the area of the original picture.
The area of the enlargement is 16 times as great as the area of the original picture.

Example 2 **Use the relationships among the linear scale factor, surface area, and volume of similar solids**

The planets are all approximately spheres. The radius of Uranus is about 4 times that of Earth. For these two planets, what is the relationship between

a) the surface areas? **b)** the volumes?

SOLUTION

The planets can be visualized as spheres.

The scale factor is the ratio of the radius of Uranus to the radius of Earth, so it has a value of 4.

a) The ratio of the surface area of Uranus to that of Earth is the square of the scale factor to 1. This is 4^2:1.
Uranus has 16 times the surface area of Earth.

b) The ratio of the volume of Uranus to that of Earth is the cube of the scale factor to 1. This is 4^3:1.
Uranus has 64 times the volume of Earth.

DISCUSSING THE IDEAS

1. Use a diagram to explain why doubling the dimensions of a room does not simply double the area of the room.

2. In earlier Tutorials, you converted between different metric units for area and volume. Compare the procedures used to convert square centimetres into square millimetres, and cubic centimetres into cubic millimetres to the relationship you discovered in the Investigation. Explain why this relationship exists.

PROJECTS

In this Tutorial you worked with scale and you investigated relationships between linear scale factors, linear dimensions, areas, surface areas, and volumes. You will use these relationships for the following projects in the Project Book.

- Candy Boxes
- Safety Technology

EXERCISES

Checking Your Skills

1. The Eiffel tower was built in Paris in 1889. It has a height of about 300 m. An architectural technician makes a scale drawing of the tower using a scale factor of 0.0001.

a) How tall is the tower in her drawing?

b) If, in her drawing, the tower were 4 cm high, what would the scale factor be?

2. The moon has a radius of about one quarter of that of Earth. How many times smaller is its volume than that of Earth?

3. A quilt pattern book offers a selection of traditional designs. After selecting a design, a quilter enlarges the 3-unit square pattern to create a 12-unit block. Select one of the designs below, and enlarge it to a 12-unit square. How many times larger than the original area is the area of your enlarged design?

4. Suppose that two solids are similar. Copy and complete the table below.

Scale Factor	Ratio of Edges	Ratio of Surface Areas	Ratio of Volumes
2:5			
4:3			
1:4			
	5:6		
	3:2		
		25:9	
		16:49	
			1:216
			27:125

5. Examine the graph shown.
Suppose that Rapid Realty outsells their competitor 2 to 1.
Explain why this graph is misleading.

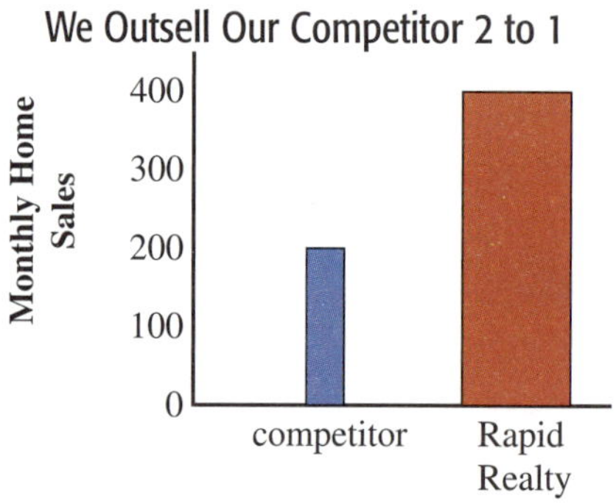

6. The area of a rectangle is 10 cm^2.

   a) The sides of the rectangle are doubled. By what factor does the area increase?

   b) By what factor must each dimension be multiplied to increase the area by 20 cm^2? Express your answer to 3 decimal places.

7. A model engine is built to a scale of 1:50. The length of the model engine is 20 cm. An area of 180 cm^2 of sheet metal is used to cover the outside of the model.

   a) Determine the actual length of the engine, in metres.

   b) Determine the area of sheet metal that would be needed to cover the actual engine, in square metres.

   c) The volume displaced by the model engine is 126 cm^3. What is the volume displaced by the real engine, in cubic metres?

8. A ball of string is 10 cm in diameter. It sells for $1.99. Another ball of the same string is 15 cm in diameter. It sells for $5.99.

   a) What is the scale factor for these two balls of string?

   b) What is the ratio of the surface areas of these two balls of string?

   c) What is the ratio of the volumes of these two balls of string?

   d) Which ball of string is the better buy? Explain why.

Extending Your Thinking

9. Could a giant survive? In the movie *Honey, I Blew Up the Kid!*, an inventor accidentally enlarges his 2-year-old boy. The child eventually grows from 1 m to 32 m tall, terrorizing Las Vegas until the change is reversed. Choose one or more of the biological systems described below. What health problems are implied for the giant child?

Transpiration system: Your body generates heat according to its volume. But the rate of cooling depends on the area of your skin, since an important cooling mechanism is perspiration. As the water on your skin evaporates, it helps keep you cool.

Respiratory system: All the cells in your body require oxygen. The number of cells depends on volume, but the amount of oxygen processed by your respiratory system depends on the surface area of your lungs.

Skeletal system: Your mass depends on volume, but the strength of your bones depends on the area of their cross-section.

COMMUNICATING THE IDEAS

Many people believe that in order to double the volume of a box its dimensions have to be doubled. Write a paragraph to explain how the surface area and volume of a rectangular box would be affected by doubling each of its dimensions. Use an example in your explanation.

CHAPTER PROJECT

Modelling Your Dream Room

A three-dimensional model of your dream room will help you visualize how it will look. A simple way to construct a model is to make an extended floor plan, like a net of the room, that includes the walls on every side. By folding up the walls, you create a three-dimensional model of your room, with the ceiling left out so that you can see inside.

- Use the floor plan you made earlier. Transfer the floor plan to a piece of Bristol board, enlarging it as you do so. Remember to leave enough space to include the fold-up walls.
- Use the same scale factor to create cardboard cutouts representing each piece of furniture you want in your dream room. Having furniture cutouts will enable you to position the furniture many different ways, until you determine the best arrangement for you.
- If you obtained swatches of flooring or wall covering, you may want to glue them in your model, or you may want to display them beside your model.

Complete your project by checking your report and finishing your model. In your report include your drawings, lists of furniture and equipment, cost estimates, and the three-dimensional model.

Career Skills

People who work in architectural design often present their design ideas to large groups of people, such as a company's Board of Directors. They use a scale model to convey a realistic sense of how their final design will appear.

Plan how you will present your scale model in a report to the class.

CONSOLIDATING YOUR SKILLS

What Do I Need To Know?

Tutorial	Skills and Concepts	Important Results and Formulas
1.1	• Use a vernier caliper and a micrometer to take measurements • Choose an appropriate measuring device • Solve a packaging problem	
1.2	• Take measurements using devices with imperial scales • Understand how to estimate lengths in imperial units	
1.3	• Convert between units of measurement within a system, using technology • Use technology to convert measurements between systems of units	
1.4	• Understand the concepts of precision and accuracy • Choose a suitable measuring device, given the precision of the device • Analyze the limitations of a measuring device	
1.5	• Use a formula to calculate the volume of a sphere, given its radius or diameter	$V = \frac{4}{3}\pi r^3$ $V = \frac{1}{6}\pi d^3$
1.6	• Use a formula to calculate the surface area of a sphere, given its radius or diameter	$S = 4\pi r^2$ $S = \pi d^2$
1.7	• Understand what is meant by the cube root of a number • Determine the approximate cube root of a number using technology • Solve problems that require working backward from a formula	$(\sqrt[3]{x})^3 = x$
1.8	• Understand and use the relationship between scale factor and changes in dimensions • Understand and use the relationship between scale factor, dimensions, and area of similar figures • Understand and use the relationships between scale factor, dimensions, surface area, and volume of similar objects	If the scale factor of 2 similar figures is k, then the ratio of the areas of the figures is k^2. If the scale factor of 2 similar objects is k, then the ratio of their volumes is k^3.

What Should I Be Able To Do?

When you have completed the work in Chapter 1, you should be able to solve the problems that follow. Part A is investigative in nature.

As you work through the exercises, refer to the *Student Reference*, *Utilities*, and the *Tutorials* as necessary.

Part A

You will need a ball, such as a softball or tennis ball, and access to various measuring devices.

1. In still air, a thin layer of warm air surrounds the skin and helps maintain body heat, even at low temperatures. Sled dogs in the Arctic sleep outside, curled up, and covered by drifting snow. Scientists know that a mammal produces heat in proportion to its body size, and loses heat in proportion to its surface area. In this exercise you will discover why a sled dog sleeps curled up.

a) Decide on an appropriate device for measuring the diameter of the sphere. Using the measuring device, find and record the diameter of the sphere and your reason for choosing that particular device.

b) Calculate the surface area and volume of the sphere, showing your calculations in your notebook. Refer to the formulas in the preceding table.

c) If a cube had the same volume as the sphere, determine the length of its sides.

d) Determine the surface area of a cube that has the same volume as the sphere. Which object, the cube or the sphere, has the smaller surface area?

e) Assume that a cylinder has the same volume as the sphere. If it has a radius of 3 cm, determine its height.

f) Determine the surface area of the above cylinder that has the same volume as the sphere, showing your calculations in your notebook.

g) Which object, the sphere or the cylinder, has the smaller surface area?

h) Based on the results of this investigation, explain why a sled dog curls up in a ball to sleep.

Part B

2. Choose an appropriate measuring device to measure the following items.

a) the diameter of a marble

b) the length of a classroom

c) the interior diameter of a pipe

d) the thickness of a piece of paper

3. An object was measured with a ruler, a vernier caliper, and a micrometer. The lengths were 2.12 cm, 21.232 mm, and 21.2 cm.

   a) Which measurement is most precise? Explain your answer.

   b) Which measurement do you think is inaccurate? Explain your answer.

   c) Identify the device used to produce each of the three lengths given.

4. A plane going from Calgary to Toronto flew at an altitude of 41 000 feet. Use technology, or a conversion table, to determine the altitude in metres.

5. Angey's bedroom is being repainted. Her choice of paint costs $7.99 for a can that will cover approximately 9.5 m^2. When estimating how much paint to purchase, visualize the room without windows. The room measures 4 m by 3.4 m and the walls are 2.5 m high. How many cans of paint should Angey buy?

6. A spherical beach ball has a radius of 1 foot.

   a) Use an appropriate formula to determine the volume of air in the ball.

   b) Use the appropriate formula to determine the surface area of the ball.

7. Use your calculator to determine $\sqrt[3]{5.06}$.

8. A cube has a volume of 70 mm^3.

   a) What is the length of the side of the cube?

   b) What is the surface area of the cube?

   c) If the volume is doubled to 140 mm^3, how does this affect the length of the side of the cube? How does it affect the surface area of the cube?

9. The scale factor used to build a model of a car is $\frac{1}{20}$. The area of sheet metal used to cover the outside of the model is 56 square inches. If the length of the model car is 7.2 inches, what is the actual length of the car? What is the actual area of the metal sheeting used to cover the car?

Part C

The Chapter Project combines many skills and concepts in a single problem. Here is a sampling of possible student work from different stages of the Project. Review these samples to gain insights into your own project work.

10. Here is the floor plan one student created. Look at the diagram and visualize how the room looks.

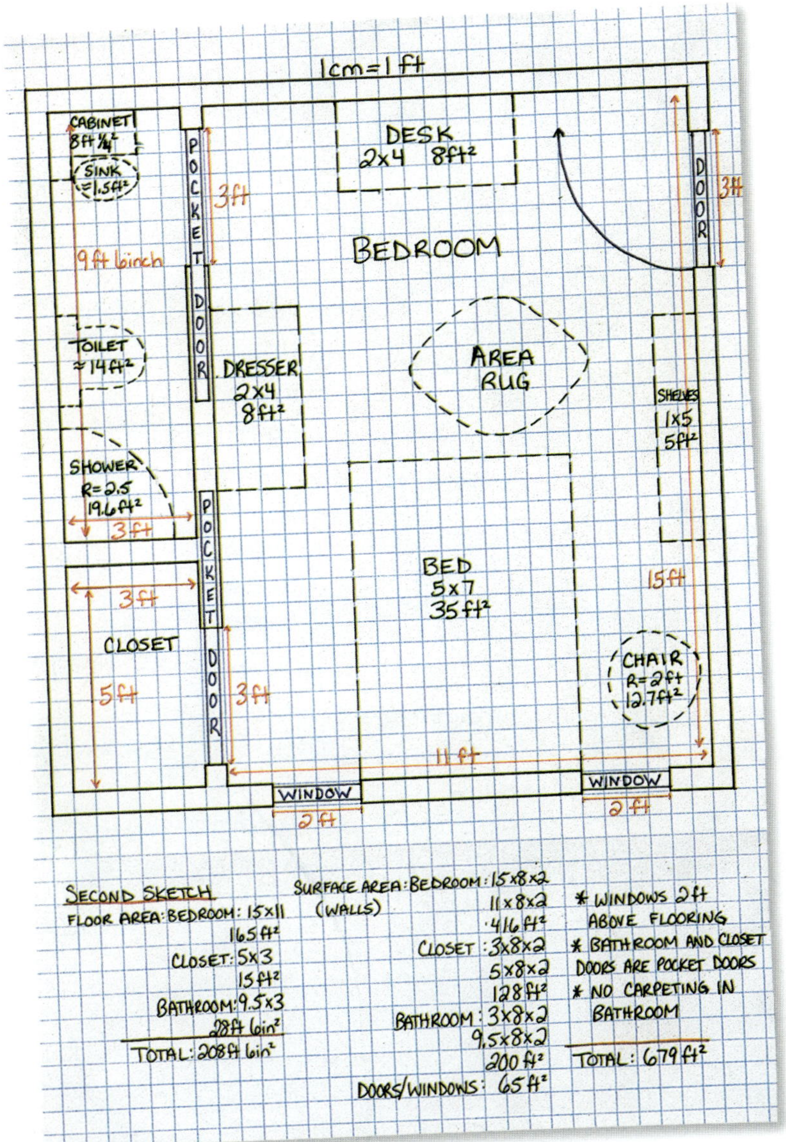

- Look at the floor plan. Do all the measurements make sense?
- Has the student included all the measurements needed to plan for new flooring?
- Has the student included all the measurements needed to plan for painting or wall papering?
- What other type of information has the student included? Is there any important information that you think is missing?

Write a summary of your assessment of this student's work.

11. Here is how the same student analyzed the cost of redecorating the room. Examine the table of data.

Price of Renovating and Redecorating Dream Room

Naomi Ali

Bathroom linoleum	28.5 ft squared	30 x .79=	$ 23.70
Carpet	165 ft squared	170 x 2.64=	$ 448.80
Baseboard	46 ft	46 x .24=	$ 11.04
Paint	416 ft squared	4 gallons	$ 64.00
Artwork	(clock, baby poster, flower picture)		$ 180.00
Extension of room	105 ft squared	(drywall, nails, etc.)	$ 700.00
	pipe installation		
Shower	plus installation		$ 639.00
Toilet	plus installation		$ 138.00
Sink	plus installation		$ 222.00
Bed	(frame, matresses, pillows, bed spreads)		$ 850.00
Window treatment	36 x 72	two sets	$ 11.99
Desk	2 x 4	plus chair	$ 47.00
Dresser			$ 345.00
Chair	(chair, stand, pillows)		$ 250.00
Lamps	two sets		$ 79.98
CD Player			$ 160.00
Shelves	1 x 5	2 shelves	$ 45.00
Area rug			$ 50.00
		TOTAL	$ 4,265.46
		TAX (GST, PST)	$ 597.16
		FINAL COST	$ 4,862.62

- Review the list of suggested purchases. Do you think anything is left out?
- Check the researched prices. Do the prices seem reasonable?
- Review the calculated results. Are any calculations incorrect? If so, how do you think the error occurred?

Write a summary of your assessment of this student's work.

2 Number Patterns in Tables

Overview

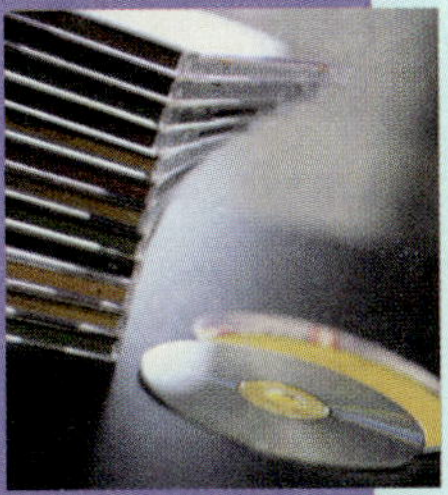

PROJECT

You should do at least one project that uses the skills you learn in this chapter. The recommended projects in the Project Book are:

- The Hockey Pool
- The Sawmill
- Sports Statistics
- Health-Care Planning
- Cross-Canada Tours

CHAPTER PROJECT

Opening a Store

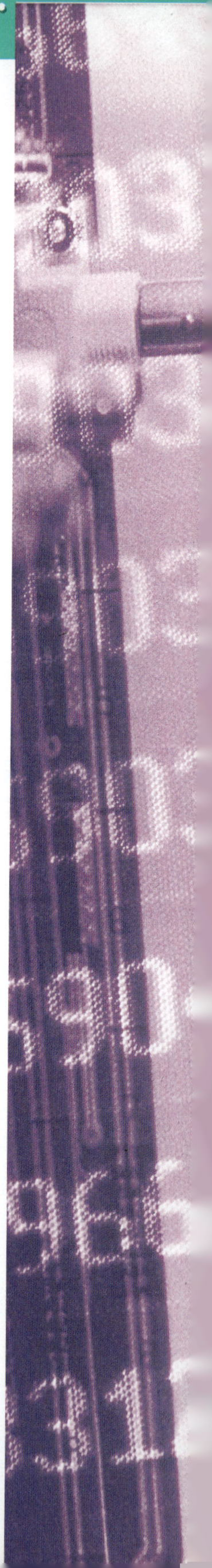

Many people dream about running their own business. For some people, the dream is about opening a new store.

Work with a partner to plan for opening your own store. This activity outlines some of the first steps you could follow.

- If you could open your own store, what type of store would it be? You may wish to consider the kinds of stores needed in your area, what products may be fads, and what products will bring repeat business.
- Would you go into business on your own, or with partners? Explain your choice.
- One thing you will have to plan is staffing your store. What other things will you have to plan?
- What information will you need to help you plan? Where might you get that information?
- Opening a new store requires a considerable amount of money. You may have to borrow some money from a bank. What kind of research will you have to do in order to produce a plan to take to the business loans officer?

Record your present plans for a store. As you progress through the chapter you will develop your plans. Your final project will consist of: a written description of your store; an inventory table; and a table showing expected costs, sales, and profits.

CHAPTER PROJECT

To complete this Chapter Project, you will need to record and use information stored in tables. Complete *Tutorials 2.1*, *2.2*, *2.3*, and *2.4*, and then return to this Project on page 94.

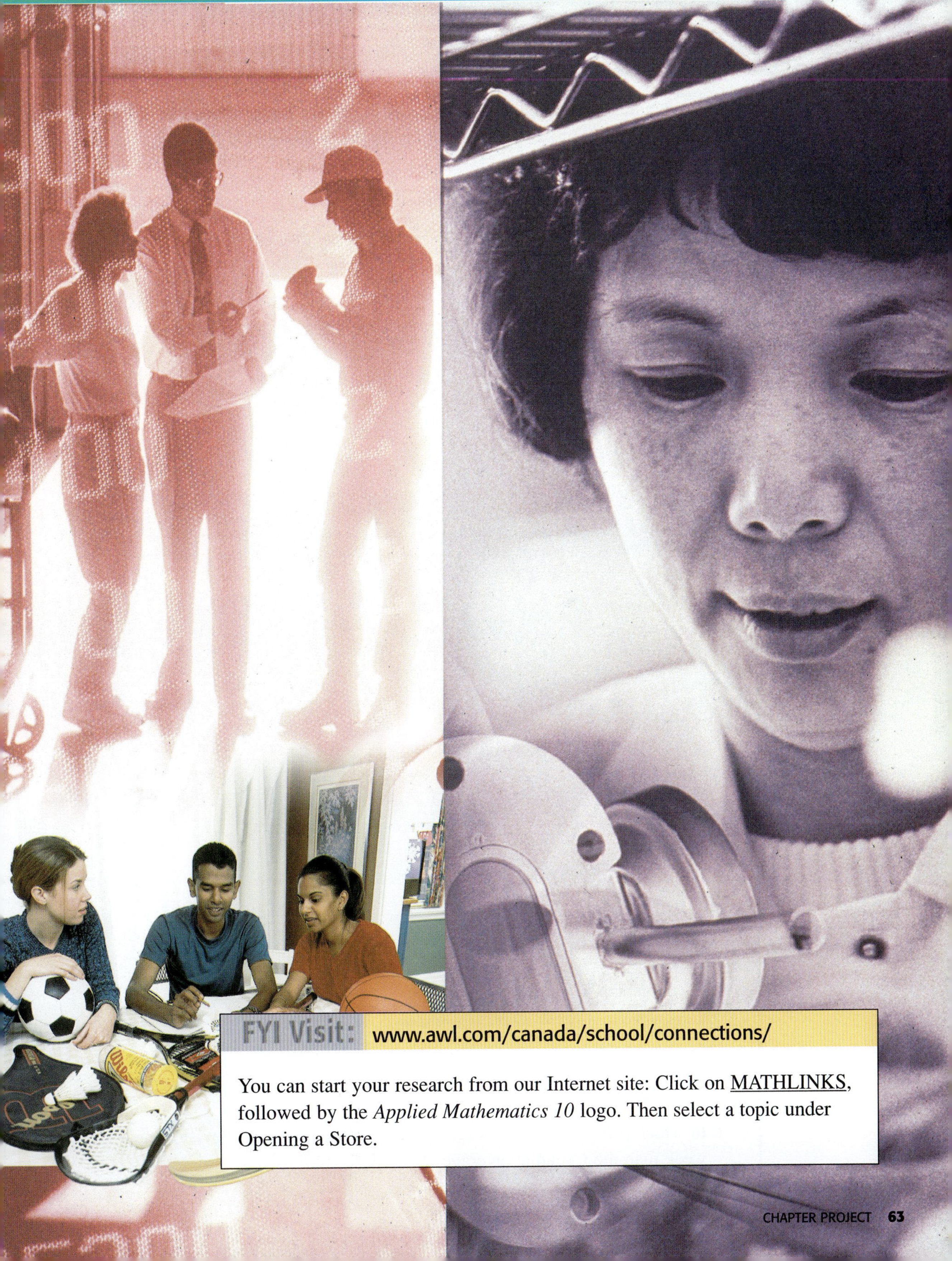

FYI Visit: www.awl.com/canada/school/connections/

You can start your research from our Internet site: Click on MATHLINKS, followed by the *Applied Mathematics 10* logo. Then select a topic under Opening a Store.

TUTORIAL 2.1

Working with Tables

Tables are a convenient and efficient way to present large amounts of data. Tables can highlight patterns and trends. In the Investigation below, you will study and interpret tables.

Investigation

Television Viewing and Radio Listening Habits of Canadians, Fall 1994

Statistics Canada publishes much of its data in table form. The following are examples of such tables.

Average hours per week of television viewing, by age and sex – Canada and the provinces, fall 1994

	Total Population	Children 2–11 Years	Adolescents 12–17	Men 18 Years or Older	Women 18 Years or Older
Canada	22.7	17.7	17.1	21.5	26.8
Newfoundland	24.1	23.8	18.9	21.8	27.8
Prince Edward Island	22.3	19.8	16.6	22.5	24.5
Nova Scotia	24.1	19.9	19.9	22.5	27.9
New Brunswick	23.7	18.3	15.5	22.6	28.2
Quebec					
Total*	25.7	19.9	18.8	24.0	30.8
English**	22.8	17.1	17.3	22.3	25.8
French**	26.3	20.1	19.0	24.3	31.8
Ontario	21.8	17.0	16.8	20.6	25.7
Manitoba	22.1	17.3	15.8	21.4	25.9
Saskatchewan	21.9	17.2	17.1	21.4	25.5
Alberta	20.5	16.8	17.6	19.3	23.9
British Columbia	20.6	15.2	13.9	20.3	24.2

*Includes respondents who did not indicate a language spoken at home or who indicated a language other than English or French.
**Language spoken at home.
Source: Statistics Canada, http://www.statcan.ca/english/Pgdb/People/Culture/arts23.htm, received 04/08/98

1. In which provinces do adolescents watch more hours of television each week than the Canadian average for adolescents?

2. In which provinces do men 18 years and older watch less television each week than the Canadian average for men over 18?

3. Look at the column for adolescents. Compare each entry with the other entries in the same row. How do the viewing habits of adolescents compare with those of other Canadians?

4. Calculate the average of the entries for children, adolescents, men, and women in the first row. Compare the answer with the entry for the total population of Canada. Explain why they are not the same.

Percentage share of radio listening time by format and audience category, fall 1994

	All Ages	Adolescents 12–17 Years	Men 18 Years and Over	Women 18 Years and Over
	% of Listening Time			
All stations	100.0	100.0	100.0	100.0
Adult-contemporary/ golden/rock	34.4	31.2	34.6	34.6
Middle of the road	6.9	2.6	6.0	8.3
Country	13.7	8.9	13.6	14.3
Canadian Broadcasting Corporation (CBC)	9.2	1.5	9.0	10.1
Album-oriented rock	5.6	8.8	7.1	3.9
Contemporary	4.9	21.7	4.3	3.9
Easy listening	1.1	0.2	0.9	1.3
Talk	12.1	1.7	12.0	13.2
Sports	0.5	0.4	0.9	0.1
Dance	4.7	13.6	4.8	3.6
U.S. stations	3.2	6.6	3.1	3.0
Other	3.7	2.8	3.9	3.6

Source: Statistics Canada,
http://www.statcan.ca/english/Pgdb/People/Culture/arts17.htm, received 04/08/98

5. Which kinds of radio stations are more popular with adolescents than with adults 18 years and over?

6. What are the 2 least popular radio station formats for all 3 audience categories?

7. What kinds of radio stations do you think would be classified under "Other"?

8. Total the columns for the various radio station formats for each audience category (excluding the "All stations" row). Explain why you do not get the expected total for the last 2 columns.

9. A male teacher in Yellowknife listened to the radio for 18 hours during the first week of October, 1994. From the data, can we be certain how many of the 18 hours he spent listening to the CBC? Would every adult Canadian male who listened to the radio for 18 hours that week have listened to the CBC for that same number of hours? Explain your answer.

Example

Working with data in tables

Joe Crow works in a music store. He is paid every two weeks. His most recent earnings statement is shown below.

Statement of Earnings						
	Regular Hours	Regular Pay ($)	Overtime Hours	Overtime Pay ($)	Weekly Total ($)
October 13-19	40	270.00	0	0.00	270.00
October 20-26	35	236.25	0	0.00	236.25
				Gross Pay	506.25

Use the information in the earnings statement to complete each exercise.

a) What is Joe's hourly rate of pay?

b) Suppose you knew how many regular hours Joe works in a week. How could you calculate his regular pay?

c) Let x represent the number of regular hours. Write an algebraic expression for the regular pay for the week.

d) Suppose Joe's regular rate of pay had been \$7.50/h. Make a table like the one above, and then calculate his gross pay for the week.

SOLUTION

a) Use the first week's earnings. Joe earns \$270.00 for 40 hours' work.

Joe earns $\frac{\$270.00}{40}$ for $\frac{40}{40}$ hours' work.

Joe earns \$6.75 for 1 hour of work.

Joe's hourly rate is \$6.75/h.

We can verify this answer using the second week's pay.

b) If we know the number of regular hours Joe works in a week, then we can calculate his regular pay by multiplying his hourly rate by the number of regular hours worked.

c) Let x represent the number of regular hours worked in a week. Joe's hourly rate is \$6.75, so, using exercise b, the expression for Joe's regular pay in dollars is $6.75x$.

d) All the entries in the table will be the same as those in the table on page 66, except those in the columns headed Regular Pay and Weekly Total.

Calculate the entries in these columns using exercise b.

For the first week, Regular Pay and Weekly Total will be
$\$7.50 \times 40 = \$300.00$.

For the second week, Regular Pay and Weekly Total will be
$\$7.50 \times 35 = \$262.50$

The Gross Pay for the period is found by adding the two entries in the column.

Statement of Earnings						
	Regular Hours	Regular Pay ($)	Overtime Hours	Overtime Pay ($)	Weekly Total ($)
October 13-19	40	300.00	0	0.00	200.00
October 20-26	35	262.50	0	0.00	262.50
				Gross Pay	562.50

DISCUSSING THE IDEAS

1. Describe other ways to display the data in the tables. What are the advantages and disadvantages of using these methods compared to using a table?

2. Describe two advantages of using tables to summarize collected data.

Practise Your Prior Skills

You will work with percents in some of the following exercises. Try these questions for preliminary review.

1. Rewrite each sentence using percent.

   a) About 14 out of every 100 Canadians are under 5 years of age.

   b) The area of Africa is about one-fifth the total land area in the world.

   c) Sixteen students out of a class of 20 had an A grade.

2. Write 6% as a decimal.

3. According to a survey, 6% of garbage collected is metal. How much metal is there in a 250-kg load of garbage?

STUDENT REFERENCE

If you need to review "percent," or would like to see some examples using percent, look in the Student Reference.

EXERCISES

Checking Your Skills

1. Here are the final standings for the Western Conference of the National Hockey League at the end of a recent season.

	Games Played	Wins	Losses	Ties	Points
Colorado	82	49	24	9	107
Dallas	82	48	26	8	104
Detroit	82	38	26	18	94
Anaheim	82	36	33	13	85
Phoenix	82	38	37	7	83
St. Louis	82	36	35	11	83
Edmonton	82	36	37	9	81
Chicago	82	34	35	13	81
Vancouver	82	35	40	7	77
Calgary	82	32	41	9	73
Toronto	82	30	44	8	68
Los Angeles	82	28	43	11	67
San Jose	82	27	47	8	62

The entries in this table are calculated by awarding 2 points for a win and 1 point for a tie.

a) Let x represent the number of games a team won, and y the number of games the team tied. Write an expression to represent the total points earned as shown in this table.

b) What if wins were worth 3 points, ties 1 point, and losses 0 points? Calculate the points for each team. Do the standings change?

c) What if teams were awarded 1 point for a win, no points for a tie, and –1 point for a loss? Calculate the points for each team. Do the standings change?

Stores are responsible for collecting the sales taxes on all the goods and services they sell. They must then send the collected taxes to a government agency. The federal government collects a goods and services tax (GST). Except for Alberta, all provincial governments collect provincial sales tax (PST). Unless stated otherwise, the taxes are collected on the selling price of the item. The table below shows the sales tax rates in 1997.

Province or Territory	GST (%)	PST (%)
Alberta	7	no tax
British Columbia	7	7
Manitoba	7	7
Northwest Territories	7	no tax
Ontario	7	8
Prince Edward Island*	7	10
Quebec*	7	6.5
Saskatchewan	7	7
Yukon	7	no tax

New Brunswick, Nova Scotia, and Newfoundland and Labrador each have a "harmonized sales tax" of 15%, which is included in the selling price and not added separately at the cash register. This tax is split between the federal and provincial governments and replaces GST and PST.

* In Prince Edward Island and Quebec, PST is calculated after the GST has been added to the price of an item.

2. A visitor to Calgary bought a picture as a souvenir of her visit. The picture was priced at $125.
   a) How much did the visitor pay at the cash register for the picture?
   b) The visitor's home province was Ontario. How much would she have had to pay for the same picture if she had bought it at home?

3. A store in Saskatoon advertises a "No GST" sale. It gives the customer a discount equal to the GST, and then adds taxes in the usual way. Use the information given before exercise 2. Copy and complete the table below.

Price ($)	7% Discount ($)	Discounted Price ($)	PST ($)	GST ($)	Total Price ($)
100.00					

a) What would the price be if only PST was paid on the regular price?

b) Is the sale equivalent to "No GST"? Explain your answer.

4. In a certain province, costs and taxes for two items are detailed in the table below.

Price ($)	GST ($)	PST ($)	Total ($)
80.00	5.60	8.56	94.16
124.75	8.73	13.35	146.83

For the table above:

a) What is the rate of GST? How is the GST calculated?

b) What is the rate of PST? How is the PST calculated?

c) What province might be reflected in this particular case?

5. Use the information given before exercise 2. Write an algebraic expression to represent the total cost of an item in each of the following provinces and territories.

a) Alberta, Northwest Territories, or Yukon

b) Ontario

c) Prince Edward Island

d) Quebec

6. The stopping distance for a car depends on many factors: road surface, weather conditions, and driver reactions being some of them. The table below relates the stopping distance of a car to the speed of the car at the moment when the driver sees a hazard.

Speed		Reaction Time Distance		Braking Distance		Total Stopping Distance	
mph	km/h	Feet	Metres	Feet	Metres	Feet	Metres
10	16	11	3.4	9	2.7	20	6.1
20	32	22	6.7	23	7.0	45	13.7
30	48	33	10.1	45	13.7	78	23.8
40	64	44	13.4	81	24.7	125	38.1
50	80	55	16.8	133	40.5	188	57.3
60	96	66	20.1	206	62.8	272	82.9
70	113	77	23.5	304	92.7	381	116.1

a) How is the total stopping distance related to the reaction time distance and the braking distance?

b) A car is travelling at 60 mph when the driver sees a hazard. How far will the car travel before the brakes are applied?

c) To avoid a collision with a deer, a driver applies the brakes firmly and comes to a stop leaving tire marks 24.7 m long. How fast was the vehicle travelling when its driver spotted the deer?

d) Under the conditions described in exercise c, suppose the vehicle stopped 3 m in front of the deer. How far away was the deer when the driver spotted it?

7. Newspapers regularly print Foreign Exchange tables similar to the one below. To convert money from one currency to another, follow these steps:
- Find the column for the currency you have.
- Go down that column to the row of the currency you require.
- Multiply that number by the amount of the original currency.

Foreign Exchange

	Canadian dollar, $	U.S. dollar, $	British pound, £	German mark, DM	Japanese yen, ¥	French franc, F	Italian lira, L.
Canadian dollar, $	1	1.3672	2.2117	0.8054	0.011280	0.2386	.000807
U.S. dollar, $	0.7314	1	1.6177	0.5891	0.008250	0.1745	.000590
British pound, £	0.4521	0.6182	1	0.3642	0.005100	0.1079	.000365
German mark, DM	1.2416	1.6975	2.7461	1	.014005	0.2963	.001002
Japanese yen, ¥	88.6500	121.2100	196.0700	71.4000	1	21.1500	.071543
French franc, F	4.1911	5.7301	9.2695	3.3755	.047276	1	.003382
Italian lira, L.	1239.1600	1694.1800	2740.6400	998.0200	13.977695	295.6600	1

a) Use the table to convert $100 Canadian to:
  i) U.S. dollars ii) German marks iii) Japanese yen

b) Convert $450 Canadian to:
  i) U.S. dollars ii) British pounds iii) Italian lira

c) Convert 10 000 Japanese yen to:
  i) Canadian dollars ii) French francs iii) German marks

8. Use the table in exercise 7.

a) Write the steps to convert from one currency to another. Start with the currency you require and the amount of that currency you need.

b) Assume you require \$200 Canadian. How much do you need in these currencies?

i) British pounds **ii)** French francs **iii)** Japanese yen

c) Assume you require \$250 U.S. How much do you need in these currencies?

i) Canadian dollars **ii)** German marks **iii)** Italian lira

d) Assume you require 500 British pounds. How much do you need in these currencies?

i) Canadian dollars **ii)** U.S. dollars **iii)** Japanese yen

Extending Your Thinking

9. Suppose you live in either British Columbia, Manitoba, or Saskatchewan. You buy two CDs at regular prices of \$15.99 and \$12.99, respectively. They are both on sale for 20% off. Using the tax rates table before exercise 2:

a) Calculate the amount of discount, sales taxes, and total cost. Copy and complete the table below.

	Price ($)	Discount ($)	Price After Discount ($)	GST ($)	PST ($)	Final Price ($)
CD1	15.99					
CD2	12.99					
Total						

b) Repeat exercise a, calculating the sales taxes before the discount. Complete the table below.

	Price ($)	GST ($)	PST ($)	Price After Taxes ($)	Discount ($)	Price After Discount ($)
CD1	15.99					
CD2	12.99					
Total						

c) Compare your answers to exercises a and b. Explain why the amount the customer pays is the same regardless of whether the discount is applied before or after the taxes are added.

d) Are the amounts the store receives in the two situations the same?

e) Are the amounts the government collects in the two situations the same?

10. Refer to exercise 9. Let x dollars represent the price of a CD. Use algebra to explain the answers to exercises c, d, and e.

COMMUNICATING THE IDEAS

Your friend missed class today. He wants to know why he needs to work with tables. Write a note to explain to him why using a table is sometimes a better way to display data than drawing a graph.

PROJECTS

This Tutorial introduced you to interpreting tables and applying the information they display. These skills relate to the Chapter Project and to the following projects in the Project Book.

- The Sawmill
- The Hockey Pool
- Health-Care Planning
- Sports Statistics

TUTORIAL 2.2

Computer Lab: Creating a Number Pattern in a Spreadsheet

You can think of a spreadsheet as a calculator that can perform many calculations simultaneously. Spreadsheets are excellent tools for exploring patterns in tables, from simple to complex. In this Tutorial, you will use a spreadsheet to create tables of number patterns.

A spreadsheet is made up of small rectangles, called *cells*, arranged in rows and columns. In most spreadsheets, the rows are numbered from top to bottom while the columns are lettered, beginning with A on the left. Cells are identified using the column letter and row number. This is its *cell reference*. For example, cell reference C3 refers to the cell in column C, row 3.

The *active cell* in a spreadsheet is the cell currently selected, in which the cursor is active. The data entry bar shows the contents of the active cell. Whatever you type is displayed in the data entry bar until you press the **Enter**, **Return**, or **Tab** key. It is then displayed in the cell.

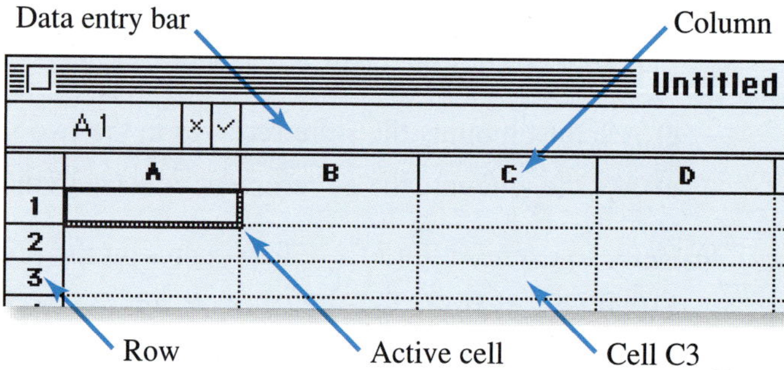

If you get ####### in a cell, this indicates that the column is not wide enough to display the number. You can make the column wider by placing the mouse pointer on the right edge of the column heading cell. When the mouse pointer changes to a double arrow, drag to the right.

Numbers, text, or a formula can be entered into a cell. Numbers (including special kinds of numbers like dates and times) can be used in calculations, but text cannot. A formula may contain numbers, cell names, and mathematical operators or functions. In most spreadsheet programs, a formula must begin with an equals sign, "=". A cell that contains a formula usually displays the number that is the result of the mathematical calculation. To see the formula that produced the number, click on the cell and look at the data entry bar.

Start the spreadsheet application on your computer and begin a new spreadsheet document. Save the document using a name such as PATTERNS1. Remember to save frequently during this Tutorial. This way, if your computer crashes while you are working, you will not lose much of your work.

These exercises are set up for Microsoft Office. You may need to make some changes. Check with your teacher before you begin.

1. If the cursor is not in cell A1, click on A1 now. Type **1** and press **Enter** or **Return**. The cursor should be in cell A2. If it is not, use the arrow keys to move to A2. Type **=A1+1** and press **Enter** or **Return**. The equals sign indicates that a formula is being entered.

a) What number is displayed in cell A2?

b) What did the formula tell the spreadsheet to do?

c) Enter **A1+1** in cell A2 and press **Enter** or **Return**. Describe what happens if you forget to enter the = sign in front of the formula. Now correct the formula to read =A1+1.

2. Select cells A2 to A15. To do this, place the cursor in cell A2. Click and hold down the mouse button while you drag down to cell A15. Let go of the mouse button when the cursor reaches cell A15. Cells A2 to A15 should be highlighted to show they are selected (with some spreadsheet applications, the original cell will not be entirely highlighted, only its border will be highlighted). From the menus at the top of the screen, find and select the **Fill** or**Fill Down** command.

a) Describe the number pattern in column A.

b) What happened when you used the Fill or Fill Down command to copy the formula in cell A2? Click on the cells in column A and look at the formula in each data entry bar to confirm your answer.

c) Change the number in cell A1 to **10** and press **Enter** or **Return**. Describe what happens, then change it back to 1.

d) Change the formula in cell A2 to **=A1+2**. Did the formulas in cells A3 to A15 change automatically? If not, change them so that the first 15 odd numbers are displayed in column A.

3. Clear the data from column A. To do this, select all the cells that contain data. When the cells are selected, choose the **Cut** or **Clear** command from the menus at the top of your screen.

a) Leave cell A1 blank. In cell A2, enter **1**. Use formulas to display the numbers from 2 to 15 in cells A3 to A16. In cell B1, enter **0.25**.

b) In cell B2, enter **=A2+$B$1**. Copy the formula in B2 down to B16. A cell reference containing a dollar sign before the column and row name is an *absolute reference*.

c) In cell C2, enter **=A2+B1**. Copy the formula in C2 down to C16. A cell reference with no dollar signs is a *relative reference*.

d) Compare the numbers in columns B and C. Try to determine which numbers are being added by each formula. To check your answer, click on a cell and look at the formula in the data entry bar.

Clear the data from columns B and C. To do this, select all the cells in these columns that contain data. When the cells are selected, choose the **Cut** or **Clear** command from the menus at the top of your screen, or press the **Delete** key.

4. Click on cell B2. Type **=A2*5** and press **Enter**.Select all cells from B2 to B16 and use the **Fill Down** command to copy the formula from cell B2. Describe the number pattern in column B.

   a) Follow a similar procedure to display the first 15 multiples of 3 in column C. What formula did you enter in cell C2?

   b) In cell D2, enter a formula to display the sum of the numbers in cells B2 and C2. Use the **Fill Down** command to copy the formula to cells D3 to D16. Describe the number pattern in column D and explain why this pattern occurs.

DISCUSSING THE IDEAS

Based on your observations, what is the difference between an absolute and a relative reference?

EXERCISES

Checking Your Skills

1. How are rows labelled on a spreadsheet document? How are columns labelled?

2. Explain the meaning of cell reference.

3. What is the active cell?

4. What type of information can you store in a cell?

5. What must you do to move information displayed in the data entry bar to the cell?

6. A formula must begin with which symbol?

7. What type of information can you use in a formula?

8. A formula was used to produce a number in cell A3 of a certain spreadsheet document. How can you see the formula?

9. Explain the meaning of absolute cell reference.

10. Explain the meaning of relative cell reference.

If you have access to a computer with a spreadsheet program installed, try the following exercises.

11. Start a new spreadsheet document. Use a method similar to the one you used in the Lab to place the numbers 1 to 15 in rows 2 to 16 of column A. Make B2 the active cell. Type **=A2*5** in cell B2 and press **Enter**. Copy the formula from cell B2 to all the cells down to B16. Describe the number pattern in column B.

12. Use the spreadsheet from exercise 11. Clear the data from columns B, C, and D. Create a table that uses formulas to display the first 15 square numbers in column B and the first 15 cubic numbers in column C.

Extending Your Thinking

13. Begin a new spreadsheet document.
    a) Type **1** in cell A2. Find a way to put the natural numbers from 1 to 12 in rows 2 to 13 of column A.
    b) Type **1** in cell B1. Find a way to put the natural numbers from 1 to 12 in columns 2 to 13 of row B.
    c) Use absolute cell references to create a 12 by 12 multiplication table in rows 2 to 13 and columns B to M.

PROJECTS

In this Tutorial you learned the fundamentals of spreadsheet use while creating number patterns. Spreadsheets will help you complete the Chapter Project and the following projects in the Project Book.

- Students' Choice Awards
- The Sawmill

COMMUNICATING THE IDEAS

Explain how to modify the procedure in exercise 4a, on page 76, so that it uses an absolute cell reference to create the same number pattern in column B.

TUTORIAL

2.3 Building Tables 1

Investigation 1

A Ready Reckoner

In the exercises of *Tutorial 2.1*, you worked with provincial sales tax (PST). Many retail businesses use a point-of-sale machine that calculates taxes at the touch of a key. Such machines are expensive, however, and many new small businesses need to keep their expenses low. In this *Investigation* you will build a table that, together with mental mathematics, can be used to determine PST.

Consider a province with 7% PST.

1. Calculate the PST on items with the following costs.

a) \$0.09 **b)** \$0.12 **c)** \$1.00 **d)** \$1.09 **e)** \$1.12

2. What is the appropriate rounding to use when working out sales taxes?

3. Sales taxes are not paid on very low cost items. What is the lowest price of an item on which sales taxes must be paid?

4. Many items with differing prices end up having the same sales tax assessed on them. Use your calculator to investigate this.

5. Create a table that shows the sales taxes to be charged on items that cost up to \$1. Use the results of your investigation from exercise 4 to make your table short, so that it is easy for a sales clerk to use.

If you have access to a computer with a spreadsheet program, you may wish to create the table as a spreadsheet document.

6. A customer buys goods that cost \$1.66. Use the table from exercise 5, and mental mathematics, to determine the sales tax.

7. Modify your table from exercise 5 for use in a province with 8% PST.

Investigation 2 Regular Interest Canada Savings Bonds

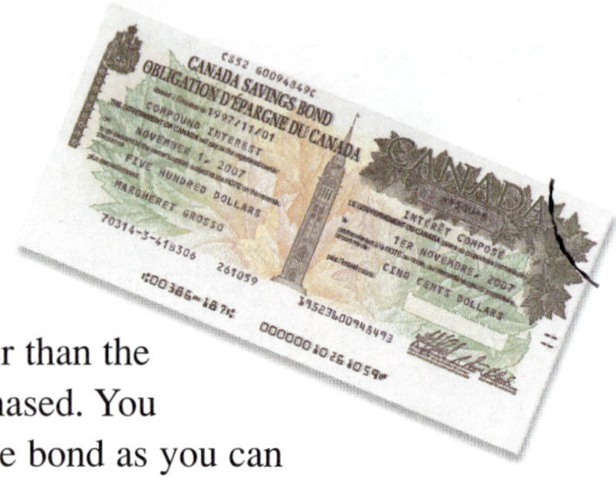

Each November, the federal government sells a new issue of Canada Savings Bonds. These bonds usually offer a higher interest rate than a savings account, and the rate is guaranteed never to be lower than the interest rate at the time the bond was purchased. You cannot deposit or withdraw money from the bond as you can with a savings account. Once you have the bond, however, it can be redeemed for cash at any time.

One type of Canada Savings Bond issued is a Regular Interest Bond. The interest earned each year by the bond is paid to the owner by cheque, or is deposited into the owner's bank account.

The following interest rates were offered for a Canada Savings Bond purchased in November 1997 and invested for 3 years.

Year	Annual Interest Rate (%)
1998	3.00
1999	4.00
2000	5.00

1. To keep track of the investment and interest to be paid, create a table like the one below.

Year	Opening Value of Bond ($)	Annual Interest Rate (%)	Interest Payment ($)	Closing Value of Bond ($)
1998	1000.00	3.00	30.00	1000.00
1999	1000.00			
2000	1000.00			

2. Verify that the 1998 figures in the table are correct.

3. Complete the table. Use the interest rate table given above.

4. Explain why the value of the bond does not change from year to year.

5. Is it possible to complete the third row of this table before the second row? Explain your answer.

6. Explain how to find the total interest earned by this bond.

DISCUSSING THE IDEAS

1. How would you use a Ready Reckoner for amounts greater than those in the table you created in exercise 5 of *Investigation 1*?
2. Which other amounts would you add to your Ready Reckoner? Explain.
3. Why do you think the table is called a Ready Reckoner?
4. In each of the *Investigations*, did you need to calculate the entries in any particular order? Explain.

Example

Creating a table to solve a problem

Sacha has a rectangular sheet of cardboard, 26 cm by 20 cm, available to make an open rectangular box. She decides to make the box by cutting out squares with integer lengths from each corner, folding up the sides, and taping the edges.

She wants the box to have as great a volume as possible.

a) What is the largest length of the cut-out square Sacha could use?

b) Create a table with the headings shown below. Complete the entries in the table.

Length of Cut-Out Square (cm)	Length of Box (cm)	Width of Box (cm)	Height of Box (cm)	Volume of Box (cm^3)

c) What length of cut-out square should Sacha use to produce a box with the greatest volume? What is this greatest volume?

SOLUTION

a) The paper is 20 cm wide. If the square has a length of 1 cm, this length is removed from each end of the width.

To have a box, the largest length of the cut-out square is 9 cm.

b) If the cut-out square has a length of 1 cm, the length of the box is 24 cm, the width of the box is 18 cm, and its height is 1 cm.
The volume is 24 cm × 18 cm × 1 cm = 432 cm^3.

If the length of the cut-out square is 2 cm, then the dimensions of the open box will be 22 cm by 16 cm by 2 cm.
The volume is 22 cm × 16 cm × 2 cm = 704 cm^3.

Calculate the other rows similarly to produce the completed table shown below.

Length of Cut-Out Square (cm)	Length of Box (cm)	Width of Box (cm)	Height of Box (cm)	Volume of Box (cm^3)
1	24	18	1	432
2	22	16	2	704
3	20	14	3	840
4	18	12	4	864
5	16	10	5	800
6	14	8	6	672
7	12	6	7	504
8	10	4	8	320
9	8	2	9	144

c) Look down the column on the right for the greatest value. This is 864. It occurs when the length of the cut-out square is 4 cm.

To maximize the volume of the box, Sacha should cut out squares of length 4 cm. The greatest volume is 864 cm^3.

EXERCISES

Checking Your Skills

1. a) Use the table below to determine the total interest earned on a Regular Interest Canada Savings Bond with an initial value of $5000.

Year	Opening Value of Bond ($)	Annual Interest Rate (%)	Interest Payment ($)	Closing Value of Bond ($)
1998	5000.00	3.00		
1999		4.00		
2000		5.00		

b) Compare the interest earned by this \$5000 bond to the interest earned by a \$1000 Regular Interest Bond.

c) Describe a way to predict the total interest earned on a comparable bond of any value.

2. a) Suppose you went to a store in Ontario where PST is 8%. Copy and complete the following table.

Item	Price (\$)	GST (\$)	PST (\$)	Total (\$)
Cassette tape	5.99			
CD	16.75			

b) Write algebraic expressions for GST, PST, and total cost.

c) Modify the table to allow for PST of 7% of the price before taxes.

3. Use the table below.

Price	GST	PST	Total
\$120.00	\$8.40	\$12.84	\$141.24
\$275.00	\$19.25	\$29.43	\$323.68

a) What is the rate of PST?

b) Modify the table to allow for a PST of 6.5% of the price before taxes.

c) If the price after both taxes is \$138 and PST is charged on the \$120 price before taxes, what is the rate of PST?

4. Chai Kim works full time at a video store. She is paid \$8.50/h, plus double time for overtime. Overtime is any time over 40 hours a week. Here is her entry in the payroll table for one week in November.

	Su	M	Tu	W	Th	F	Sa	Total Hours
Chai Kim	5	8.5	7.25	8.75	8.25	3.5	0	

Reg. Rate (\$)	Reg. Earnings (\$)	OT Earnings (\$)	Total Earnings (\$)
8.5/h			

Copy and complete the table to calculate her total earnings for the week.

Extending Your Thinking

5. Ben Singh works in a bookstore. His regular rate of pay is \$7.80/h. He is paid time-and-a-half for time worked over 8 hours on a given day. Create a table to calculate his total earnings for one week in which he worked the following hours.

Monday: 9.5; Tuesday: 7; Wednesday: 10.75; Thursday: 4.5; Friday: 8.75.

6. Use the information given in exercise 5.

a) Write down the formulas you used to make each calculation in exercise 5.

b) Create a spreadsheet to calculate total earnings.

PROJECTS

In this Tutorial you built tables by calculating unknown values in each row. You will need to know how to create tables to complete the Chapter Project, and for the following projects in the Project Book.

- The Sawmill
- Students' Choice Awards
- Safety Technology
- Candy Boxes

COMMUNICATING THE IDEAS

Write a note to a new clerk to explain how to use a Ready Reckoner to determine the sales tax on items costing more than \$1. Use examples in your explanation.

TUTORIAL 2.4

Building Tables 2

Tables where the entries in one row are calculated from data in previous rows can be entered readily into a spreadsheet. In this *Tutorial*, you will create and modify such tables. *Investigation 1* shows that tables can often be created using different methods.

Investigation 1

Cutting Paper

For this *Investigation* you will need paper and a micrometer.

1. Determine the thickness of a sheet of paper.
2. Cut the piece of paper in half once and place the pieces in a stack. The paper stack has 2 layers and has the same thickness as 2 sheets of paper. Cut the stack in half again and restack. Count how many layers of paper you have now. Create a table in your notebook similar to the one below and enter your data.

Number of Cuts	Number of Layers	Thickness (mm)
0	1	
1	2	
2		
3		
4		
5		

   Continue the process of cutting the paper, stacking, counting layers, and entering the data in the table, until you have made 3 more cuts.

3. Describe any patterns in the table. Predict the value in the next 3 rows.
4. Explain how the number of layers after n cuts can be calculated in each of the following cases.
   a) using values from the previous row
   b) using the number of cuts

In the table above, the entries in each row can be calculated from data in previous rows. Such a table has its rows related *recursively*.

5. Which of the methods you described in exercise 4 is a recursive method?
6. Create algebraic expressions for your results in exercise 3.

7. Measure your own height. How many layers of paper would you need to match your height? If you had a very large piece of paper, how many times would you have to cut and stack it? Do you think this would be possible? Explain your answer.

Tables that have rows related recursively are used frequently in finance and business.

Investigation 2

Compound Interest Canada Savings Bonds

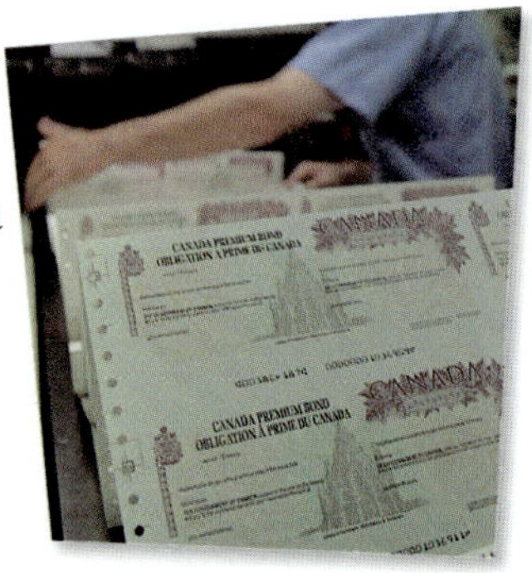

In an earlier *Investigation* you worked with Regular Interest Canada Savings Bonds. Another type of Canada Savings Bond is the Compound Interest Bond. These bonds earn an interest payment each year; however, the interest is added to the value of the bond. The following year, this interest also earns interest. Interest calculated in this manner is called *compound interest*.

1. A bank customer buys a $1000 Compound Interest Bond in November, 1997. Make a table like the one below.

Year	Opening Value of Bond ($)	Annual Interest Rate (%)	Interest Payment ($)	Closing Value of Bond ($)
1998	1000.00	3.00	30.00	1030.00
1999	1030.00	4.00		
2000		5.00		

2. Verify that the 1998 figures in the table are correct.
3. Explain how the closing value of the bond is determined.
4. Complete the table.
5. Could the third row of this table be completed before the second row? Explain your answer.
6. Describe two methods you could use to find the total interest earned by this bond.
7. Look at your results for *Tutorial 2.3*, *Investigation 2*, where you studied Regular Interest Canada Savings Bonds. Which type of Canada Savings Bond earns more interest?
8. Explain why some people might prefer Regular Interest Bonds.

Example **Create and modify a table generated by a recursive situation**

In 1998, the sales of a particular video game doubled every month. The game was released in May 1998 and sales that month totalled 32 000 units.

a) Prepare a table to illustrate the 1998 monthly sales figures.

b) How many video games were sold in December 1998?

c) Starting in January 1999, and every month thereafter, sales were cut to one-quarter of what they were in the previous month. Create a new table or modify the table you prepared in exercise a to show the sales during 1999.

d) How many video games were sold in April 1999?

e) Because of declining demand, the video game was withdrawn from the market at the end of April 1999. How many video games were sold during the time it was on the market?

SOLUTION

a) The sales double each month that the video game is available during 1998. To calculate the sales in June, multiply the sales for May by 2. To calculate the sales for July, multiply the sales in June by 2. The table of sales for 1998 is shown here.

Year	Month	Sales (in thousands)
1998	May	32
	June	64
	July	128
	August	256
	September	512
	October	1024
	November	2048
	December	4096

b) From the table prepared in exercise a, the December sales were 4 096 000 games.

c) Modify the table prepared in exercise a by adding additional rows for sales for the first four months of 1999. The entry in the sales column for these rows is obtained by multiplying the entry in the previous row by $\frac{1}{4}$. This is the same as multiplying each entry by 0.25, or dividing the previous entry by 4.

The entry for January 1999 is $4096 \div 4 = 1024$.

Complete the modified table similarly.

Year	Month	Sales (in thousands)
1998	May	32
	June	64
	July	128
	August	256
	September	512
	October	1024
	November	2048
	December	4096
1999	January	1024
	February	256
	March	64
	April	16

d) From the table in exercise c, the sales in April 1999 were 16 000 games.

e) To obtain the total sales of the video game, the numbers in the sales column have to be added up.

The total sales of the video game were 9 264 000 units.

Note: This exercise could be completed using a spreadsheet program.

DISCUSSING THE IDEAS

1. Explain what condition a table must satisfy in order for its rows to be related recursively.

2. Could the jobs on an automobile assembly line be considered to be related recursively? Explain your answer.

Practise Your Prior Skills

You will work with percents in the exercises that follow. Try these exercises for preliminary review.

1. Express 40% as a decimal.

2. Calculate 60% of 5890.

STUDENT REFERENCE

If you need to review working with "percent," look in the Student Reference for examples and explanation.

EXERCISES

Checking Your Skills

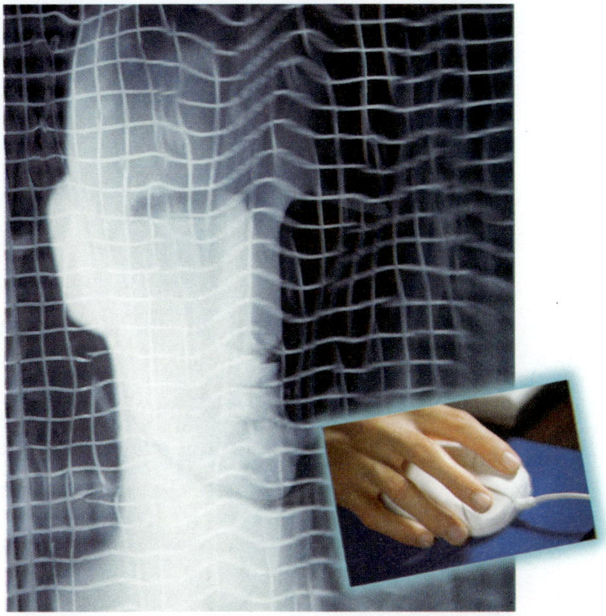

1. In 1997, sales of a particular computer game approximately doubled every month. The game was released in April 1997 with sales of 28 000 units. In December 1997, sales peaked. For the next 6 months sales were about 60% of the previous month's sales.

a) Create a table to illustrate the sales of this computer game in 1997.

b) How many games were sold in December 1997?

c) Complete the table for the first 3 months of 1998. Determine how many games were sold in total during the first year of sales.

d) If sales continue to drop to 60% of the previous month's sales, will they ever reach zero sales in a month? Explain.

2. An employment contract includes a pay increase of 2% in the first year of the contract, 3% in the second year, and 1% in the final year. An employee has a salary of $38 750 when the contract begins.

Year	Previous Year's Salary ($)	Rate of Increase (%)	Pay Increase ($)	Salary for the Year ($)
1	38 750.00	2.00		
2		3.00		
3		1.00		

a) Use a table like the one above to determine the salary of the employee in the coming years.

b) Are the rows in this table related recursively? Justify your answer.

c) Some union members argued that a pay increase of 2% in the first year of the contract, 2% in the second year, and 2% in the final year would have been more beneficial. Create a table to determine if this is in fact the case.

3. a) Consider a Compound Interest Canada Savings Bond that has an initial value of $5000. Annual interest rates are 3% in the first year, 4% in the second year, and 5% in the third year. Use the table below to determine the total interest earned in 3 years.

Year	Opening Value of Bond ($)	Annual Interest Rate (%)	Interest Payment ($)	Closing Value of Bond ($)
1997				
1998				
1999				

b) Explain why the interest earned by this $5000 bond is 5 times the interest earned by a $1000 Compound Interest Savings Bond.

4. Consider a compound interest savings account with an opening balance of $1000, earning 4% interest each year.

Year	Opening Balance ($)	Annual Interest Rate (%)	Interest Earned ($)	Closing Balance ($)
1				
2				
3				

a) Make a table to determine the interest earned and closing balances each year for three years.

b) What is the value of the investment at the end of 3 years?

c) How much interest did the investment earn?

5. Suppose the money in exercise 4 had been invested at an annual interest rate of 8%.

a) Predict how the interest earned by this investment would change.

b) Recalculate the investment results.

c) How much interest was earned by the investment? Was your prediction in exercise a correct or incorrect?

6. Use the table you completed in exercise 4.

a) Describe how to calculate the interest earned in a year.

b) Describe how each row is related to the row above it.

7. The annual inflation rate measures the general increase in the price of goods and services. If the inflation rate is 5% for a year, goods that cost $100 at the beginning of the year will increase by $5 to $105 at the end of the year.

a) Suppose an item cost $500 at the beginning of 1989. Create a table to determine how much it would have cost at the end of 1991.

Year	Cost of Item Jan. 1 ($)	Inflation Rate (%)	Price Increase ($)	Cost of Item Dec. 31 ($)
1989	500.00	4.02		
1990		4.82		
1991		5.61		

b) Create a second table to determine how the cost of an $80 000 home would change due to inflation over this time period.

Year	Cost of Item Jan. 1 ($)	Inflation Rate (%)	Price Increase ($)	Cost of Item Dec. 31 ($)
1989	80 000	4.02		
1990		4.82		
1991		5.61		

c) What would you expect a movie ticket costing \$3.50 in 1989 to cost at the beginning of 1992?

Year	Cost of Item Jan. 1 (\$)	Inflation Rate (%)	Price Increase (\$)	Cost of Item Dec. 31 (\$)
1989	3.50	4.02		
1990		4.82		
1991		5.61		

8. A store is having a sale; the price of each item is discounted by 10% of its previous day's price for 5 consecutive days.

a) Create a table to determine the price of a \$249-item for each day of the 5-day sale.

b) At the end of the 5 days, is the price discounted by 50%? Explain.

9. A snail is at the bottom of a 30-m well. Each day it can climb 3 m up the side of the well. During the night, it slides 1 m back down. Create a recursive table to determine how many days it will take the snail to climb out of the well.

Extending Your Thinking

10. Open the file BONDS from the Template Disk. This spreadsheet gives the details of a bond that could have been purchased in 1997. The interest rates for each year are listed.

a) Explain why a column has not been included to determine the value of a Regular Interest Bond.

b) Use the Fill Down command to complete all columns for Interest Earned and Value of Bond.

c) Explain how the Interest Earned for each type of bond changes as the years progress.

d) Enter the following formula into cell D13:
=Sum(D6..D12) or **=Sum(D6:D12)**, depending on your software program. Explain why this formula will give the total interest earned by the Regular Interest Bond during its 9-year term.

e) Enter a similar formula to determine the total interest earned by the Compound Interest Bond during its 9-year term. What is the difference in the interest earned by the two bonds?

f) Explain the advantages and disadvantages of each of these bonds.

g) Research the interest rates currently offered by Canada Savings Bonds. Modify the spreadsheet to determine the value of \$10 000 using current interest rates.

11. One story of the invention of chess attributes its development to a mathematician who worked for an ancient king. As a reward for his invention, the mathematician asked for a quantity of wheat, determined as follows: one grain of wheat for the first square of the chess board, two for the second square, four for the third, and so on.

a) Use a spreadsheet to determine how many grains of wheat should be given for each of the squares of the chess board (remember there are 64 squares in total). If you get ####### in any of your cells, this indicates that the column is not wide enough to display the number. Make the column wider.

b) If you have access to some wheat, use a balance and appropriate techniques to determine the mass of one grain of wheat. Explain what procedure can be used to increase the accuracy of this measurement.

c) Add a third column to your spreadsheet to determine the mass of the wheat given for each of the squares of the chess board.

d) Canada's annual wheat production was approximately 30 million tonnes in 1996. For which square of the chess board would Canada's annual wheat production be needed?

e) How many years of Canada's wheat production would be needed for the next three squares after this one?

f) The world's annual wheat production was 581 million tonnes in 1996. On which square of the chess board would the world's annual production of wheat be needed?

PROJECTS

In this Tutorial you created tables in which rows were related recursively. You will use related skills for the Chapter Project and the following project in the Project Book.

- Students' Choice Awards

COMMUNICATING THE IDEAS

Write a message to a friend explaining the difference between recursive and non-recursive tables. Give examples of each type in your explanation.

Creating an Inventory

On page 62, you and your partner decided on the type of store you want to open. You discussed the need for extra staff, and the information required in a business plan.

In this stage of the project, you will research the items you will sell. Your *inventory* is the collection of all your sale items, both on the shelves and in storage.

1. Use a catalogue, flyer, or newspaper.

a) Select up to 20 items to sell.

b) Record the items. Start an inventory table like the one below.

Item	Cost Price/ Item ($)	Quantity	Cost to Purchase Stock ($)	Calculated Markup/ Item ($)	Retail Price ($)	Gross Profit/ Item ($)	Total Gross Profit ($)

The *cost price, or wholesale price*, is the price you pay the manufacturer for the item. The *retail price* is the price your customer will pay for the item. The difference between the cost price and the retail price of an item is called the *markup*.

2. Decide how many of each item you think you should stock. Enter your numbers in the table.

3. Estimate the cost price of the items you have chosen. One way to do this is to deduct 40% from the prices you saw in the flyer, catalogue, or newspaper. You may wish to research inventory and markup by talking to a retailer in your community.

Do you think a store is likely to use a higher markup on "big-ticket" items like computers, or on "small-ticket" items like T-shirts? Discuss this with your partner and record your ideas.

CHAPTER PROJECT

To complete the Chapter Project you must gain skill working with spreadsheets. Complete *Tutorial 2.5*, and then return to the Project on page 102.

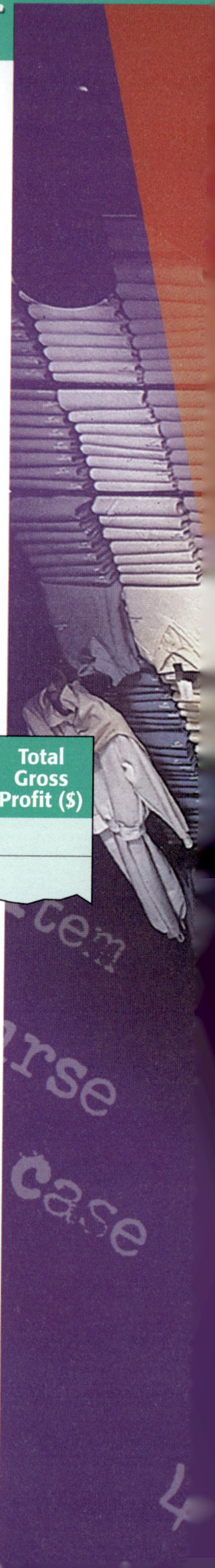

Career Skills

Budgeting your time is a critical skill for jobs that involve many tasks. Some examples are office assistants, commercial designers, journalists, and store managers. How long did it take you to create your inventory table for 20 items? How many items do you think you would really have to stock? How often would you have to check inventory?

Use your answers to decide how much time you would have to spend on inventory, and how frequently. Record your ideas.

4. Decide how you will mark up the items on your list. It might make sense to apply one markup to all the inventory, if every item has approximately equal value. Or, you might decide to apply different markup rates depending on the item.

5. Calculate the markup on each item. Add the markup to the wholesale cost to get the retail price. Decide whether to adjust the retail price. For example, a calculated retail price of $50.78 may appeal more to customers if you adjust it to $49.99. Record your prices in your table.

6. Determine your gross profit on each item by calculating the difference between your retail price and the cost price. Determine your total gross profit on the items.

TUTORIAL 2.5

Computer Lab: Using Spreadsheets to Explore Loans

Many businesses borrow money from banks or other financial institutions in order to start up or to expand. The amount borrowed is called the *principal*.

When a business obtains a loan from a financial institution, it must repay the amount of the loan plus interest. Usually, the loan is repaid in equal payments at regular time intervals. Often the payments are made monthly, but with some businesses, for example a seasonal operation, the payments may be made each year.

Most spreadsheets, as well as some calculators, have built-in financial features that calculate the regular payments for loans.

Consider a \$25 000 business loan at an interest rate of 9% per annum, to be repaid over 5 years with annual payments of \$6427.31.

1. Make a table like the one below in your notebook. Include the information shown, with rows down to Year 5.

Year	Opening Balance (\$)	Interest Rate (%)	Interest Charged (\$)	Regular Payment (\$)	Closing Balance (\$)
1	25 000.00	9.00	2250.00	6427.31	20 822.69
2	20 822.69	9.00	1874.04	6427.31	16 269.42
3				6427.31	
4					
5					

a) Explain how the closing balance is calculated at the end of the first year.

b) Verify the figures in the table.

c) Complete the next three rows of the table.

d) Calculate the total interest for the loan.

e) Describe two methods of determining the total interest for the loan.

2. Suppose the loan was for $50 000 instead of $25 000.

a) What would the annual payment be?

b) How much interest would be paid over the 5 years?

3. If the $25 000 loan were paid back over 10 years instead of 5 years, the annual payment would be $3895.50. The table below shows how the loan is repaid.

Year	Opening Balance ($)	Interest Rate (%)	Interest Charged ($)	Regular Payment ($)	Closing Balance ($)
1	25 000.00	9	2250.00	3895.50	23 354.50
2	23 354.50	9	2101.91	3895.50	21 560.91
3	21 560.91	9	1940.48	3895.50	19 605.89
4	19 605.89	9	1764.53	3895.50	17 474.92
5	17 474.93	9	1572.74	3895.50	15 152.16
6	15 152.16	9	1363.69	3895.50	12 620.35
7	12 620.35	9	1135.83	3895.50	9860.68
8	9860.68	9	887.46	3895.50	6852.64
9	6852.64	9	616.74	3895.50	3573.88
10	3573.88	9	321.65	3895.50	0.03

a) Compare the annual payments in this situation to the annual payments from exercise 1, over 5 years. Explain why you think it is not half the payment for a 5-year loan.

b) Determine the total interest that would be paid over 10 years.

c) Compare the amount of interest paid over 10 years to the amount of interest paid over 5 years.

The loan repayment table above is a table whose rows are related recursively. To investigate loan repayments further, a spreadsheet is an ideal tool.

AT THE COMPUTER: Open the file LOANPYMTS from the Template Disk. A spreadsheet will appear that contains the same information as the table on page 98.

Calculating Loan Payments

	A	B	C	D	E	F
1						
2						
3	Principal		$25 000.00			
4	Annual interest rate (%)		9			
5	Number of years		10			
6						
7	Payment	Opening	Interest	Interest	Regular	Closing
8	number	balance	rate (%)	charged	payment	balance
9	1	$25 000.00	9	$2250.00	$3895.50	$23 354.50
10	2	$23 354.50	9	$2101.91	$3895.50	$21 560.91
11	3	$21 560.91	9	$1940.48	$3895.50	$19 605.89
12	4	$19 605.89	9	$1764.53	$3895.50	$17 474.92
13	5	$17 474.92	9	$1572.74	$3895.50	$15 152.16
14	6	$15 152.16	9	$1363.69	$3895.50	$12 620.35
15	7	$12 620.35	9	$1135.83	$3895.50	$9860.68
16	8	$9860.68	9	$887.46	$3895.50	$6852.65
17	9	$6852.65	9	$616.74	$3895.50	$3573.88
18	10	$3573.88	9	$321.65	$3895.50	$0.03

You can use the program to calculate the annual payments for any loan by entering the principal, the interest rate, and the number of years in cells C3, C4, and C5, respectively.

4. Predict whether the annual payment for the loans below will be greater than or less than the annual payment above. Use the computer to confirm this.

a) Borrow $25 000 at 7%, and repay over 10 years.

b) Borrow $25 000 at 9% and repay over 8 years.

5. Use the spreadsheet to calculate the annual payment required for each of the following loans.

a) Borrow $5000 at 6.5% and repay over 5 years.

b) Borrow $29 000 at 11.25% and repay over 9 years.

Modify the spreadsheet to accommodate periods up to 25 years. To do this, copy the formulas in row 18 down to row 33. A quick way to do this is to select a block of cells starting with row 18 and use the Fill or Fill Down option.

6. Use the spreadsheet to calculate the annual payment required for each of the following loans.

   a) Borrow \$25 000 at 9% and repay over 25 years.

   b) Borrow \$100 000 at 8.25% and repay over 20 years.

   Modify the spreadsheet to calculate the total interest paid. To do this, enter the following in the indicated cells:

   G7: **Total** G8: **Interest**

   G9: **=D9** G10: **=G9+D10**

   Copy the formula in cell G10 down column G to row 33.

7. Calculate the total interest paid for each of the following loans.

   a) Borrow \$25 000 at 9% and repay over 25 years.

   b) Borrow \$100 000 at 8.25% and repay over 20 years.

   Modify the spreadsheet to accommodate extra payments by inserting a new column between columns E and F, and labelling it "Extra Payment."

   Click on cell G9 and change the formula to:

   =B9+D9–E9–F9

   Copy this formula down column G to row 33.

8. Consider a loan agreement for \$25 000 at 9% over 10 years, which allows the borrower to make an extra payment in any year.

   a) Suppose an additional payment of \$1000 was made at the end of Year 3. Adjust the spreadsheet to reflect this payment.

   b) Describe how this would affect the loan.

   c) How would this affect the total interest repaid?

9. The loan for \$25 000 at 9% over 25 years is to be paid off early.

   a) What extra payment would pay off the loan at the end of Year 3?

   b) What extra payment at the end of Year 3 would pay off the loan at the end of Year 7?

DISCUSSING THE IDEAS

Refer to the spreadsheet shown in this section.

1. Why are the numbers in the Interest Charged column decreasing?

2. Why is the closing balance at the end of Year 10 not 0? What simple adjustment would make it 0?

PROJECTS

In this Tutorial you modified spreadsheets. You will use this skill in the Chapter Project and in the following projects in the Project Book.

- The Sawmill
- Scuba-Diving Tours
- Students' Choice Awards

EXERCISES

Checking Your Skills

The following table provides data on the repayment of a $100 000 farm loan. The farmer has negotiated for one annual payment to be made each year after the harvest. Use the table below to answer exercises 1 to 4.

Year	Opening Balance ($)	Interest Rate	Interest Charged ($)	Regular Payment ($)	Closing Balance ($)
1	100 000.00	7.50%	7500.00	17 072.70	90 427.30
2	90 427.30	7.50%	6782.05	17 072.70	80 136.64
3	80 136.64	7.50%	6010.25	17 072.70	69 074.19
4	69 074.19	7.50%	5180.56	17 072.70	57 182.05
5	57 182.05	7.50%	4288.65	17 072.70	44 398.00
6	44 398.00	7.50%		17 072.70	
7		7.50%		17 072.70	
8		7.50%		17 072.70	0.00

1. a) How long does it take to repay this loan?

b) What is the amount of the annual payment?

c) What is the annual interest rate?

2. a) Complete the last three rows of this table.

b) What is the total amount of money the farmer must pay for the loan?

c) How much interest must be paid?

3. What percentage of the annual payment was used to pay interest in each of the following years?

a) Year 1 **b)** Year 2 **c)** Year 5

4. **a)** How much would be owing at the end of Year 8 if the interest rate increased to 9.25% during this year only?

   b) Explain how you found the solution for exercise a.

5. Consider the farm loan described in exercise 1. Suppose the farmer makes an extra payment of $20 000 at the end of Year 4.

   a) Show how this affects the loan.

   b) Calculate the total interest paid.

   c) How much interest does the farmer save by making this extra payment?

6. What extra payment at the end of Year 3 would pay off the farm loan in exercise 1 at the end of each of the following years?

   a) Year 7 **b)** Year 6 **c)** Year 5

Open the file LOANPYMTS from the Template Disk to solve the following exercises.

7. Consider a $50 000 loan with an annual interest rate of 8%. Determine the annual payment and the total interest repaid if the loan is paid off over each length of time.

   a) 5 years **b)** 10 years **c)** 15 years **d)** 20 years **e)** 25 years

   f) Describe how changing the term of a loan affects the annual payment and the total interest repaid.

8. Consider a $100 000 loan paid off over 10 years. Determine the annual payment and the total interest repaid for each annual interest rate.

   a) 4% **b)** 6% **c)** 8% **d)** 12% **e)** 16%

Extending Your Thinking

9. Consider an $80 000 loan at 8% with a term of 20 years. An extra payment of $4000 can be made at the end of one year. Describe the effect of this extra payment if it is made at the end of the indicated year.

   a) Year 16 **b)** Year 10 **c)** Year 4 **d)** Year 1

   e) If an extra payment can be made on a loan, when does it have the greatest effect? Explain why this is so.

COMMUNICATING THE IDEAS

Write a paragraph explaining the advantages of using a spreadsheet to carry out calculations involving loans rather than using a table and calculator.

Establishing Daily Costs and Daily Sales

This section represents the culminating activity for the Chapter Project. As you progress through this activity, record your cost estimates in a table like the one started below. If you can, use a spreadsheet so that you can revise estimates quickly and efficiently.

	A	B	C	D
1	*Projected Daily Costs for Year 1*			
2	**Type of Cost**	**Monthly Cost**	**Annual Cost**	**Daily Cost**
3	Inventory loan/interest	not needed		0.00
4	Rent		0.00	0.00
5	Utilities	0.00	0.00	0.00
6	Staff		0.00	0.00
7	Totals	n/a	0.00	0.00

1. Refer to the Creating an Inventory activity on page 94. Determine the total cost of your inventory. Assume you can pay 25% of the cost, but need a loan for the rest. You obtain a bank loan at 8% interest; all you pay in the first year is the interest payments.

a) What are your interest charges for the first year?

b) What are your daily interest charges during your first year?

2. Real estate rentals typically involve measurements in square feet. Estimate the size of your store in square feet.

a) A typical retail rental is $1.20 per square foot per month. What is your monthly rent?

b) What are your rental costs for your first year?

c) What is your daily rental cost?

3. Utilities, such as electricity, usually cost about 10% of the rent. Add utilities to the daily costs of running your store.

4. What will be your store hours? Assume you need an average of 2 staff on duty at any time. Assume it costs an average of $10/h for wages and benefits for each staff member. Calculate the average daily cost of staffing your store.

Career Skills

The days of mechanical, repetitive jobs are disappearing. Today's workers usually have many diverse tasks that they have to prioritize, plan, and organize. Think about the work you did in this activity. What strategies helped you organize your work? How could you apply those strategies in other areas? Record your ideas in your journal.

5. Calculate the total daily cost of operating your store, based on your estimates above. How much gross profit must the store make in order to cover these costs?

6. Go to your inventory list from Creating an Inventory. Estimate the average number of each item you will sell each day. Calculate the gross profit you would make from sales each day.

7. Your gross profit must be used to pay for costs. Subtract daily fixed costs from daily profit to determine daily net profit. Extend the table started on page 102, and add information about predicted daily sales and net profit.

8. Estimate the number of hours that you will work in the store each day. What will be your average hourly earnings?

9. Your final project should consist of a business plan—the written description of your store, your inventory table, and projected daily cost for Year 1.

CONSOLIDATING YOUR SKILLS

What Do I Need To Know?

Tutorial	Skills and Concepts	Important Results and Formulas
2.1	• Use words and algebraic expressions to describe data in a table with rows that are not related recursively • Read and modify tables	
2.2	• Know the basic parts of a spreadsheet • Know how to modify a spreadsheet to produce a given result	• The terminology of a spreadsheet: cell, active cell, absolute reference, relative reference
2.3	• Understand Regular Interest Canada Savings Bonds • Explain how to use a Ready Reckoner • Create, read, and modify a table for non-recursive situations	• A table with rows that are not related recursively has rows that are not obtained from data in previous rows.
2.4	• Use words and algebraic expressions to describe data in a table with rows that are related recursively • Describe patterns in the rows • Understand and explain the meaning of recursive and non-recursive tables; explain the difference between the two • Understand Compound Interest Canada Savings Bonds • Create, read, and modify a table for recursive situations	• A table with rows that are related recursively has rows that are obtained from data in previous rows.
2.5	• Read and use tables generated by a spreadsheet • Create and modify tables using a spreadsheet • Predict what will happen to a spreadsheet	

What Should I Be Able To Do?

When you have completed the work in Chapter 2, you should be able to solve the problems that follow. Part A is investigative in nature and requires access to a computer with the LOANPYMTS program. You may wish to use spreadsheets when answering Part B.

As you work through the exercises, refer to the *Student Reference*, the *Utilities*, and the *Tutorials* as necessary.

Part A

At the computer, open the LOANPYMTS file from the Template Disk.

1. Which cells contain the following information?

a) the amount of money borrowed

b) the rate of interest to be charged

c) the number of years over which the loan will be repaid

2. Modify the spreadsheet to calculate the annual payment required for the following loans.

a) borrow \$50 000 at 9% per annum and repay over 10 years

b) borrow \$25 000 at 7.25% per annum and repay over 15 years

c) borrow \$30 000 at 8.75% per annum and repay over 20 years

3. Determine the total interest paid on a loan of \$100 000 at 6% per annum repaid over 10 years. Investigate the effect of doubling the repayment time. If the repayment time is doubled, does the total interest paid double?

Part B

4. Natural gas has less energy value at higher altitudes than it does at lower altitudes. Domestic Gas split the area that it serves into 5 zones. It assigned each zone a number. The average altitude above sea level of an area was used to designate its zone.

Zone	1	2	3	4	5
Zone number	1.00973	1.00566	0.99749	0.99749	0.99308

Cost of gas for the consumer =
Amount of gas used (m^3) × Zone number × Rate(\$/m^3)
The rate is the cost in dollars for 1 m^3 of gas.

Calculate the cost of gas for the consumer if:

a) 1000 m^3 was used in zone 2 and the rate is \$0.19/m^3.

b) 3578 m^3 was used in zone 5 and the rate is \$0.18/m^3.

5.

Price (\$)	GST (\$)	PST (\$)	Total (\$)
50.00	3.50	3.50	57.00
243.29	17.03	17.03	277.35

a) What is the PST rate?

b) Modify the table to provide for a PST of 8.5%.

c) Suppose the total cost of the first item after both taxes is \$59.75. What is the PST rate?

6. Naomi was offered a job as a salesperson. She was given the choice of 3 different salary plans.

A: \$1500 per month

B: \$750 per month + 10% of all her monthly sales

C: 15% of her monthly sales

Create a table to show the monthly pay for each plan when monthly sales are:

a) \$5000 **b)** \$7500 **c)** \$10 000 **d)** \$12 500 **e)** \$15 000

7. From 1975 to 1995, the population of Alberta increased by approximately 11% every 5 years. Assume this trend continues. Copy and complete the table to predict the population of Alberta in 2000, 2005, and 2010.

Year	Population	5-year growth rate (%)	Increase in population	Population 5 years later
1965	2 747 000	11		
2000				
2005				
2010				

8. A store is going out of business and decides to hold a sale. There are two pricing methods to consider.

a) The price of every item in the store is discounted by 15% of its price on the previous day. Create a table to determine the price of an item that originally cost \$356 over each of 6 consecutive days during the sale.

b) The store reduces the price of the item by 15% of its original price on each consecutive day over 6 days.

Which method of pricing results in a better return for the store?

Part C

The Chapter Project combines many skills and concepts in a single problem. Here is a sampling of possible student work from different stages of the project. Review these samples to gain insights into your own project work.

9. Here is the inventory table two students created. Examine the data.

Mystique Computer Services

We sell more than products – we sell innovation.

Inventory Spreadsheet:

Item	Wholesale Price	Quantity	Cost of stock
Intel Pentium II 450Mhz Processor	$ 410.00	45	$ 18,450.00
128MB PC100 8ns CAS2 SDRAM	135.00	45	6,075.00
Abit BH6 100mhz Motherboard	90.00	45	4,050.00
Matrox Millenium G200 16MB	95.00	25	2,375.00
Diamond Monster 3D II 12MB	125.00	35	4,375.00
Diamond Viper 550 TNT	162.00	20	3,240.00
Diamond Monster Fusion	75.00	17	1,275.00
Creative Labs Sound Blaster Live	81.00	45	3,645.00
NEC MultiSync E700 17" 0.25 Monitor	504.00	15	7,560.00
ViewSonic Optiquest Q71 17" Monitor	380.00	30	11,400.00
Panasonic 40x CDROM	78.00	45	3,510.00
Maxtor 8.4GB 7500rpm UDMA HD	150.00	30	4,500.00
Western Digital 11.4GB SCSI HD	450.00	15	6,750.00
3Com FastEtherlink 10Base T NIC	90.00	14	1,260.00
USR Sportster v.90 56k Modem	78.00	16	1,248.00
Syquest 1.5GB Syjet Drive	99.00	11	1,089.00
Imation LS-120 Drive	60.00	45	2,700.00
Act Labs FF Steering Wheel	74.00	8	592.00
Microsoft Sidewinder Gamepads	36.00	20	720.00
		Total Cost of Stock	$ 84,814.00

Markup	Retail Price	Ticketed Price	Gross Profit
140%	$ 574.00	$ 574.00	$ 7,380.00
120%	162.00	162.00	1,215.00
133%	119.70	120.00	1,350.00
137%	130.15	129.95	873.75
130%	162.50	162.50	1,312.50
135%	218.70	219.00	1,140.00
146%	109.50	109.50	586.50
132%	106.92	106.99	1,169.55
167%	841.68	840.00	5,040.00
160%	608.00	608.98	6,869.40
120%	93.60	93.60	702.00
117%	175.50	175.50	765.00
137%	616.50	616.50	2,497.50
141%	126.90	126.90	516.60
125%	97.50	99.00	336.00
165%	163.35	164.00	715.00
145%	87.00	88.00	1,260.00
139%	102.86	102.99	231.92
139%	50.04	50.00	280.00
		Total Gross Profit	34,240.72

- Look at the list of products. Are the products appropriate for the type of store the students plan to open? Would you include any other products?
- Check the wholesale costs. Are they calculated correctly?
- Look at the quantities the students plan to stock. Are they reasonable?
- Examine the markup rates and the markup on each item. Are the rates appropriate? Is the markup on each item calculated correctly?
- Check the retail price and gross profit for each item. Are any of the calculations incorrect? How do you think the error occurred?

Write a summary of your assessment of these students' work.

10. Here is the cost spreadsheet the same students created. Examine it carefully.

Mystique
Computer Services
We sell more than products – we sell innovation.

Annual Costs Spreadsheet:

Area (m^3)	Annual Cost of Renting	Utilities	Total Cost of Stock	Loan Cost	Annual Payment on Loan
14	$21,700.75	$2,170.08	$84,814.00	$63,610.50	$5,088.84

Number of Staff	Staff Salary	Hours Per Week	Annual Total Staff Cost	Total Annual Costs	Total Gross Profit
1	$6.50	20	$5,200.00	$34,159.67	$34,240.72
				Net Gain	$81.05

- Is the spreadsheet set up correctly? Would you make any changes to the way it is set up?
- Check the interest charges for the first year. Are the calculations correct?
- Look at the cost of rental, utilities, and staff. Do these costs seem appropriate? Do you think any are too low or too high?
- Check the gross profit from sales. Do the estimated sales seem reasonable? Would you make any changes?
- Check the net profit. Is it correct?
- Based on the spreadsheet, will the store be a success?

Write a summary of your assessment of these students' work.

3 Relations and Functions

Overview

Chapter Section	Skills and Concepts
Chapter Project: Epidemics, page 109	Research epidemics
Tutorial 3.1: Interpreting and Creating Graphs, page 112	Describe situations that match a given graph; sketch a graph to represent a given situation
Tutorial 3.2: Graphing from Tables of Data, page 117	Record data in tables and graph the data in scatterplots
Tutorial 3.3: Graphing from Equations, page 122	Construct a graph of an equation using technology, or by creating a table of values
Tutorial 3.4: Representing Functions in Many Ways, page 130	Interpret functions presented by equations, graphs, tables of values, or mapping diagrams; present functions in different forms
Chapter Project: Simulating the Spread of an Epidemic, page 136	Use simplified examples to investigate how a disease becomes an epidemic
Tutorial 3.5: Domain and Range, page 138	Identify the domain and range of a function, and describe the significance of each
Tutorial 3.6: Function Notation, page 146	Interpret information given using function notation, and create graphs and tables of values from equations given in function notation form
Chapter Project: Researching an Epidemic, page 154	Model the spread of epidemics using functions; research an epidemic
Consolidating Your Skills, page 156	Review work of chapter; review student project work

PROJECT

You should do at least one project that uses the skills you develop in this chapter. A recommended project in the Project Book is:

- Safety Technology

Epidemics

Over our history there have been many epidemics. A few recent ones are the bubonic plague, the Ebola virus, cholera, tuberculosis, and AIDS. Epidemics spread in different ways—through infected water or food, in the air, or by direct physical contact.

In this project you will study how epidemics spread and learn how to simulate their spread. Your final project submission should consist of: a general introduction to epidemics and a brief survey of a few specific epidemics; a graph showing the simulated spread of epidemics; graphs showing the spread of epidemics using two different functions to model the spread of the disease; a discussion of why epidemics eventually stop; and an article describing an epidemic of interest to you.

CHAPTER PROJECT

Graphing will be a powerful way for you to analyze the data you work with in the Chapter Project. Complete *Tutorials 3.1* to *3.4* to develop graphing skills for the Chapter Project. The next stage of the Chapter Project is on page 136 of this chapter.

- What is the definition of an epidemic? How is an epidemic different from the common cold that is caused by a virus?
- Identify two or three specific epidemics. How were these epidemics spread?
- What factors make it possible for an epidemic to spread?

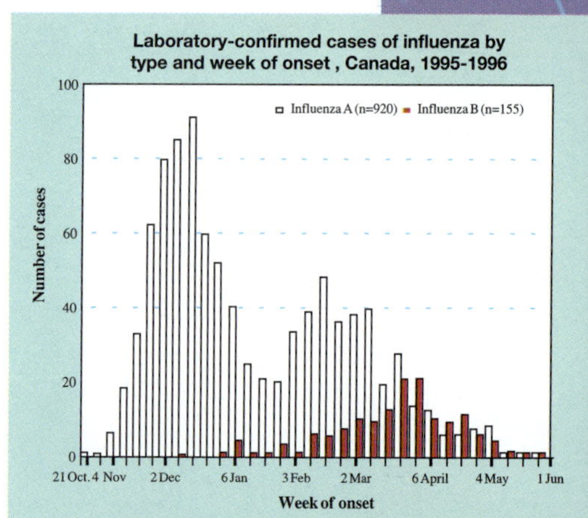

Canadian Communicable Disease Report, December 1996, Vol. 22-23, Health Canada, ISBN 1188-4169

Scientists study the spread of an epidemic by collecting and analyzing data, and looking for relationships. Graphing is one way they analyze data.

Research to find out more about epidemics and how they are spread. Use the Internet, or go to a library to search in the microfiche records for recent articles in newspapers and magazines.

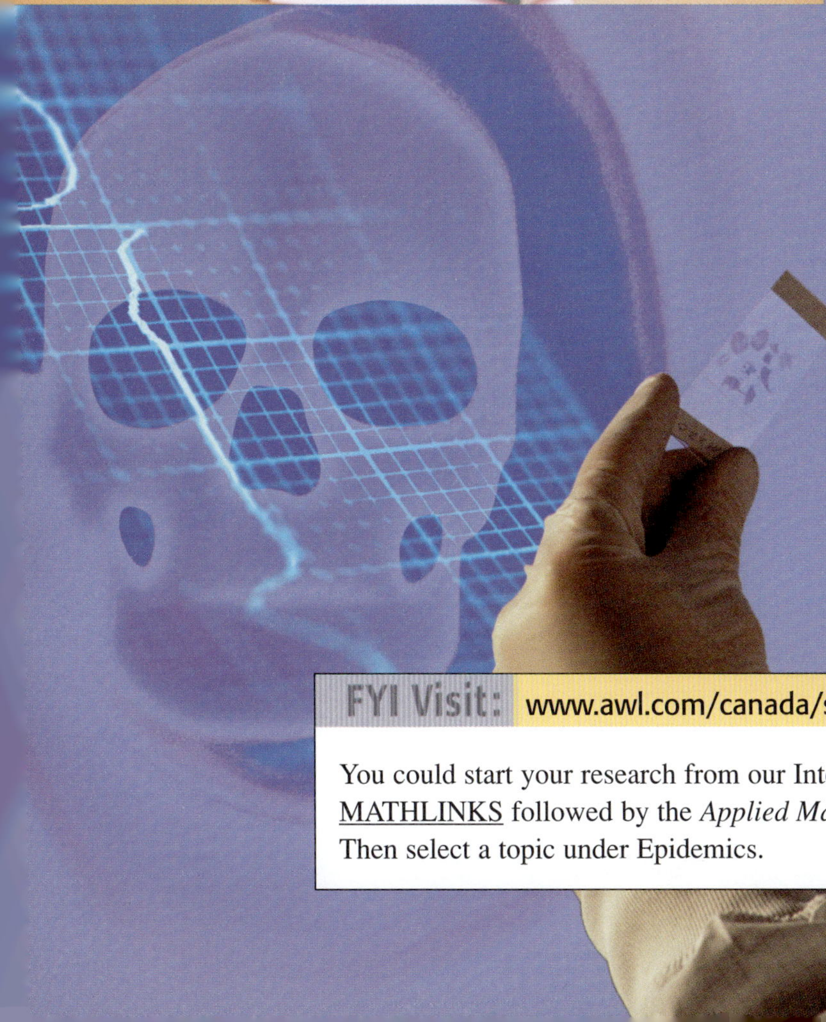

FYI Visit: www.awl.com/canada/school/connections/

You could start your research from our Internet site: Click on MATHLINKS followed by the *Applied Mathematics 10* logo. Then select a topic under Epidemics.

TUTORIAL 3.1

Interpreting and Creating Graphs

Have you ever heard the saying, "A picture is worth a thousand words"? A graph is a picture of a relationship between 2 quantities. When we draw a graph, we show how one quantity changes with respect to the other.

For example, we could draw a graph to illustrate the relationship between the volume of a cube and the length of the side of the cube. The volume of the cube depends on the length of the side, so we call volume the *dependent variable*. The length of the side of the cube is the *independent variable*.

Changes in the value of the independent variable produce changes in the dependent variable. Usually, we represent the independent variable along the horizontal axis and the dependent variable along the vertical axis.

Example 1

Creating a scenario to match a graph

The following graph shows the height of water in a bathtub over a period of time. Do not look at the Solution and write a scenario (story) that could describe the graph.
Think about the name on each axis and the points where the graph crosses the axes, as well as possible reasons for changes at the key points indicated.

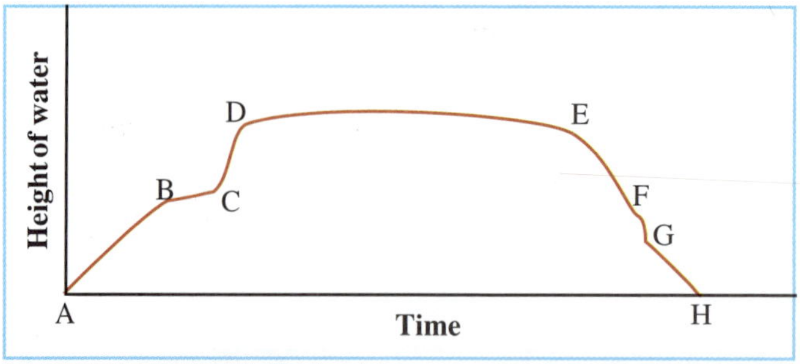

SOLUTION

Check with your classmates. How many of you have the same scenario? How many of you have different scenarios? Could all the scenarios be correct?

Here are 2 possible scenarios for the graph.

Scenario 1

At point A the tub is empty. A person puts in the plug and turns on the water. At point B he turns off the water. At point C he gets into the tub and sits there for a while. At point E he pulls out the plug and the water starts to drain. At point F he gets out and the water continues to drain. At point H the tub is empty again.

Scenario 2

At point A a person sitting in the tub turns on the water. At point B she turns off the water. At point C she adds hot water to the tub because the water is getting cold. At point E she pulls out the plug and the water starts to drain. At point F she gets out and the water continues to drain. At point H the tub is empty again.

Both scenarios describe possible ways in which the graph shows the relationship between the height of the water and the time. At point A, where the axes meet, the height of the water and the time are both zero. At point H the height of the water is zero but the time is not zero.

From point A to point B, the water level is rising more slowly than from C to D. From point E to point F, the height of the water drops more quickly than from F to G.

Example 2 Creating a graph to illustrate a scenario

As the days change through the year, the number of hours of daylight changes. For example, on January 15 in Vancouver there are about 9 hours of daylight, while on July 15, there are about 16 hours of daylight. In the High Arctic on the same days there are 0 and 24 hours of daylight, respectively. For your locality, draw a graph to represent the relationship between the hours of daylight per day and the time of year.

SOLUTION

The hours of daylight at different times of the year are affected by latitude. Places at higher latitudes have greater extremes in the hours of daylight than places at lower latitudes.

Graph 1

If we choose Lethbridge, Alberta, the graph might look like this.

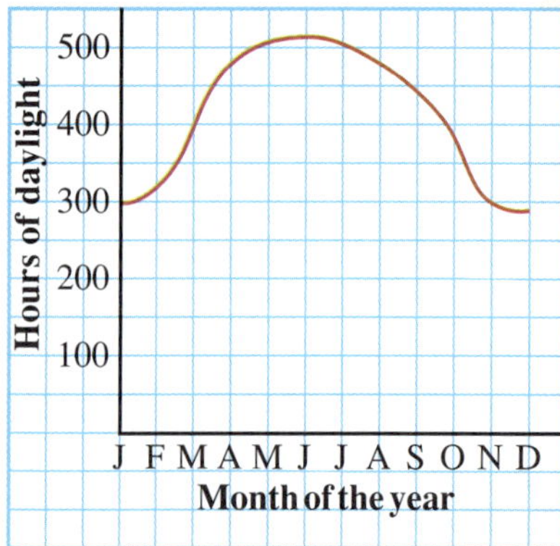

Graph 2

If we choose Whitehorse in the Yukon Territory, the graph might look like this.

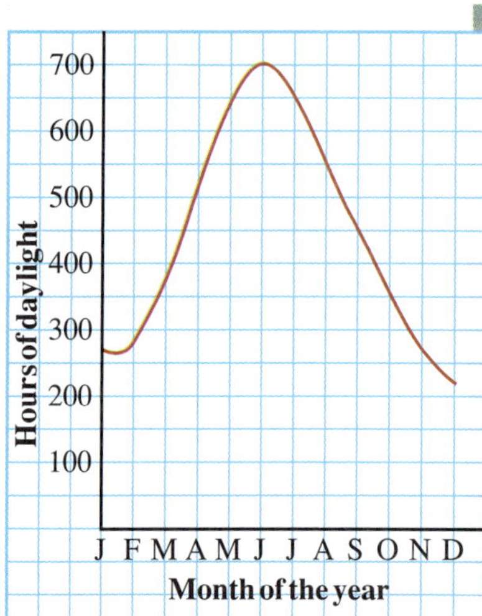

DISCUSSING THE IDEAS

1. How many different scenarios did your class create for *Example 1*? Can a picture tell more than one story? Explain.

2. As a class, revise the scenario to give the best possible explanation.

3. Think of another possible graph for the scenario in *Example 2*.

4. In *Example 1* you described a scenario to fit a graph. In *Example 2* you sketched a graph to fit a scenario. What factors did you need to consider?

PROJECTS

In this Tutorial you interpreted given graphs, or created graphs to fit a given situation. The skills you used relate to the Chapter Project, and to the following projects in the Project Book.

- **Safety Technology**
- **Space Technology**

EXERCISES

Checking Your Skills

1. Even though it can be very important to show graphs to scale, it is not essential. Decide which of the following graphs might represent each of the following scenarios.

   a) the height of a tree over time

   b) the height of a chair on a Ferris wheel as the ride is running

   c) the number of hours of sleep required per day over a person's lifetime

   d) the number of computers sold, compared to the selling price

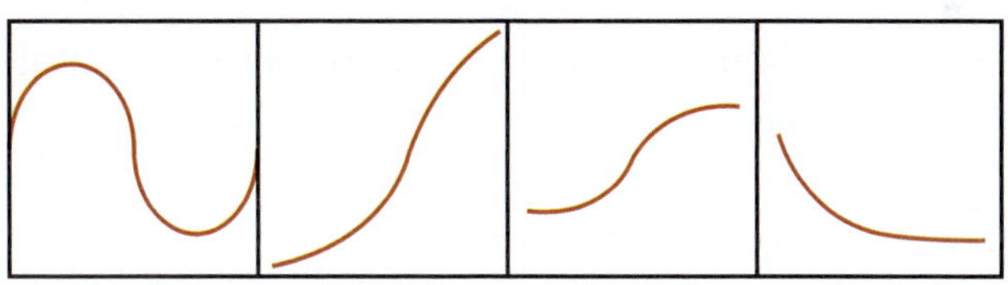

Graph 1 Graph 2 Graph 3 Graph 4

2. Suggest a possible scenario for each of the following graphs. Describe the significance of any key points or changes in the graph.

a)

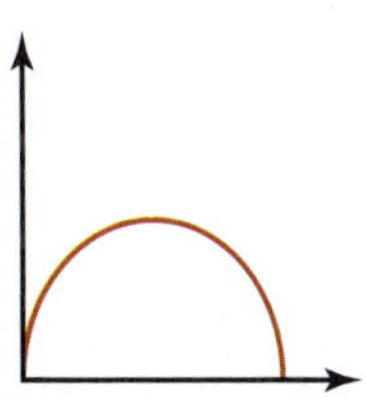

b)

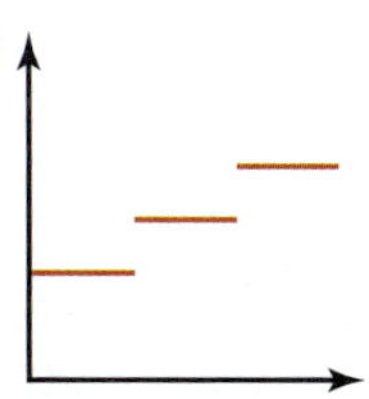

c)

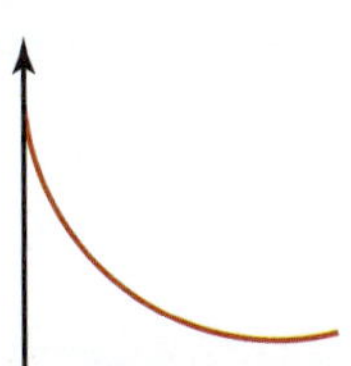

d)

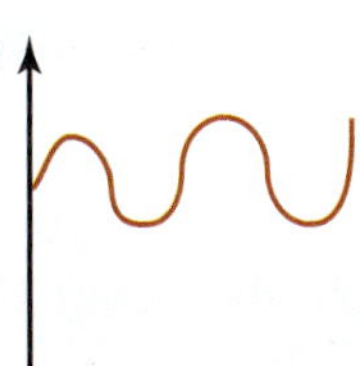

3. The graph shows the speed of Raoul's bike as he rides from home to school. Write a possible description of this portion of Raoul's journey.

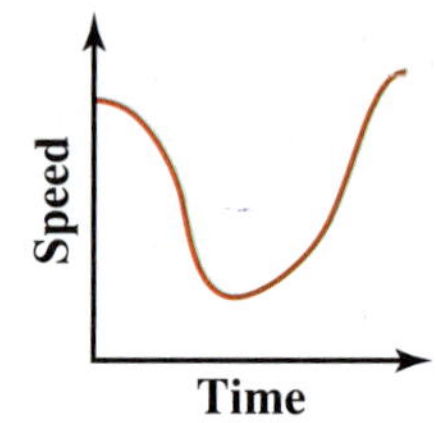

4. Shakira walks to exercise. The graph shows her distance from home during one of her walks. Write a scenario to describe her walk.

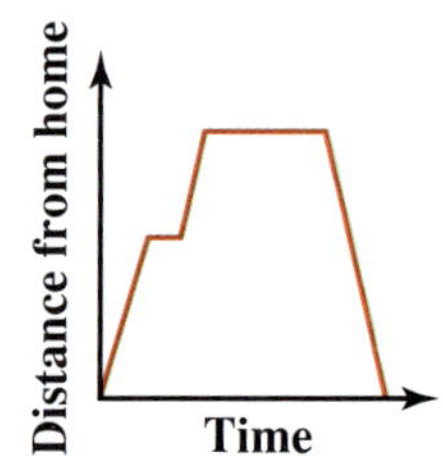

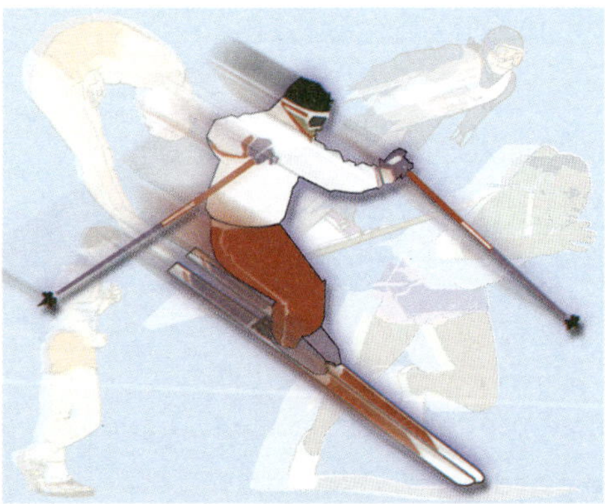

5. Create a graph, with clearly labelled axes, to fit the scenario.
   a) a person running the 3000-m race around a track
   b) a person walking along a level road, climbing a hill, stopping to rest at the top, and then coming back down the hill
   c) person diving off a diving board
   d) a ski jumper jumping during a competition
   e) an alpine skier skiing in a slalom race

6. Select one of the graphs you drew in exercise 5. Write to describe how your graph fits the scenario.

Extending Your Thinking

7. Select one of the following to research and graph.
   a) changes in your height from the time you were born until now
   b) changes in your school population from the year the school opened until now
   c) changes in the numbers of Internet subscribers over the years
   d) a topic of your choice

COMMUNICATING THE IDEAS

Create a scenario and draw a graph to represent it. Give your scenario to a friend, and ask your friend to draw a graph for your scenario. How are your two graphs the same? How are they different?

TUTORIAL 3.2

Graphing from Tables of Data

In Chapter 2, you worked with tables of data. Graphing from a table often provides a powerful new perspective that highlights patterns.

Practise Your Prior Skills

In this Tutorial, you will investigate relationships by generating and plotting data. You will draw scatterplots of your results. Try this exercise as preliminary review

Make a scatterplot of these data.

Height (cm)	156	163	166	170	157	160	169	161	178	154
Shoe size	6	7.5	8	10	7	8.5	9	7.5	10	5.5

STUDENT REFERENCE

If you need to review "scatterplots," look in the Student Reference.

A graphing calculator can be used to record your data and draw the scatterplot.

UTILITY

If you have never used a graphing calculator before, Utility 6 shows you how to reset a TI-83 calculator. If you have never used a graphing calculator to graph scatterplots, Utility 7 shows you how to do this on the TI-83. If you are working with a different calculator, check the user's guide that came with it.

You should work on at least one of the following Investigations. Do *Investigation 4* only if you have a Computer Based Laboratory (CBL). Be prepared to report your results to the rest of the class when you are done.

Investigation 1

Length and Frequency of a Pendulum

Is there a predictable relationship between the length of a pendulum and the number of times it swings back and forth per second?

You will need to make 5 simple pendulums: 100-cm, 80-cm, 60-cm, 40-cm, and 20-cm long. You can make a pendulum by tying a weight to the end of a piece of string. Work in groups of 3.

1. Set up a table to record the length of a pendulum and the time it takes to swing back and forth 5 times.
2. For your first trial, use a pendulum that is 100-cm long. Do a test swing to ensure the pendulum swings freely. Pull the weight to an angle of approximately 30° from the rest position. Release the weight. Allow 1 swing before starting to time. Measure and record the time the pendulum takes to swing back and forth 5 times. Repeat this with each pendulum length.
3. Plot the data on a scatterplot. Use appropriate scales.
4. Would it make sense for the points on the scatterplot to be connected? Explain.
5. From the graph, predict how many seconds it will take for a 50-cm pendulum to swing 5 times. How many seconds per swing is this? This is the *period* of the pendulum.
6. The *frequency* of a pendulum is the number of complete back-and-forth cycles it makes per second. From your graph, predict the frequency of a pendulum that is 50-cm long. Test your prediction.
7. Describe how you made your prediction in exercise 6. How would you predict the frequency for other pendulum lengths?

Investigation 2 Circumference of the Wrist and Neck

Is there a predictable relationship between people's wrist and neck measurements?

You will need a vinyl or cloth measuring tape or a ribbon and a metre stick. Work in groups of 5.

1. Make up a table to record the circumference of the wrist and the circumference of the neck for 10 people.
2. Measure the circumference of your wrist and the circumference of your neck. Record your measurements in the table, along with the measurements of everyone else in your group. Obtain additional data from other groups, until you have data for 10 people.
3. Plot the data on a scatterplot. Use appropriate scales.
4. Would it make sense for the points to be connected? Explain.

5. Describe any relationship you see between the circumference of the wrist and the circumference of the neck.

6. Find someone who was not included in your original data. Measure her or his wrist. Predict the size of her or his neck, and then measure to check your prediction. Record whether the new data support the relationship you described in exercise 5.

Investigation 3 Tallying Dice Sums

What patterns are there in the numbers of times that different sums come up when someone rolls a pair of dice?

You will need a pair of dice for each pair of students in your group. Work in groups of 4 to 6.

1. List all the possible sums that can result from the roll of a pair of dice.
2. From the list, create a table that will let you tally experiment results, and total the result for each possible sum.
3. Your group needs to obtain results for 100 rolls of the dice. Discuss how your group can make these trials most efficiently.
4. Conduct the 100 trials and determine the total number of times each sum appeared.
5. Plot the data on a scatterplot. Would it make sense for the points on the scatterplot to be connected? Explain.
6. Interpret and discuss your graph. What does it tell you about the chance of rolling a particular sum?

Investigation 4 Tracking Temperature Changes

What relationship is there between temperature and time, as a hot drink cools down to room temperature?

You will need a CBL unit with a thermometer probe, and a mug holding a hot drink. If your classroom is close to the school cafeteria or staff room, you may be able to bring a hot drink from there. Get permission from your teacher first.

1. Set up the thermometer probe and the CBL to track the temperature of the hot drink over a 20-min time period.
2. Graph the data that the CBL gathers.
3. The graph displays a smooth curve. Why is it appropriate to represent the situation with a smooth curve?
4. Describe the graph. What does the graph tell you about the rate at which the hot drink cools down?
5. Suppose the hot drink were in a taller, narrower mug. How do you predict the graph might change? If you can, test your hypothesis by using a taller, narrower mug.

DISCUSSING THE IDEAS

1. Each Investigation in this Tutorial illustrates a relation. Describe what you think is meant by a relation.
2. Summarize how you generated the data for each Investigation. How was the process the same in each Investigation? How was it different?
3. What decisions do you need to make when setting up a graph? How do you choose axes?
4. What factors do you need to consider when deciding whether or not the points on a scatterplot should be connected?

PROJECTS

In this Tutorial you collected and graphed data. You used the graph to identify patterns and relationships. The skills and concepts you used relate to the Chapter Project, and to the following projects in the Project Book.

- Safety Technology
- Space Technology

COMMUNICATING THE IDEAS

In your journal, describe what is meant by a relation. Explain how you would decide when to connect the points in the graph of a relation.

Write up one of the Investigations as an experiment for inclusion in your journal or portfolio. Include the data in table form, the graph, and any conclusions you reached.

TUTORIAL 3.3

Graphing from Equations

In *Tutorial 3.2* you graphed relations from tables of data. Chapter 2 demonstrates that many tables can be set up as spreadsheets. In this Tutorial, you will look at some spreadsheet formulas, and other equations, to see how they might lead to graphs.

Here are some simple spreadsheet formulas. Each formula relies on a single cell reference.

=A1+1 =A1^2

Every time the input value, A1, changes, the formula recalculates the output value. Here are some possibilities.

=A1+1

Input	Output
−3	−2
−2	−1
−1	0
0	1
1	2
2	3
3	4

=A1^2

Input	Output
−3	9
−2	4
−1	1
0	0
1	1
2	4
3	9

No matter what the input number, you can be confident of obtaining exactly one output number.

A relation for which each input has a unique output is a *function*.

The input/output table for each spreadsheet formula yields a graph.

=A1+1

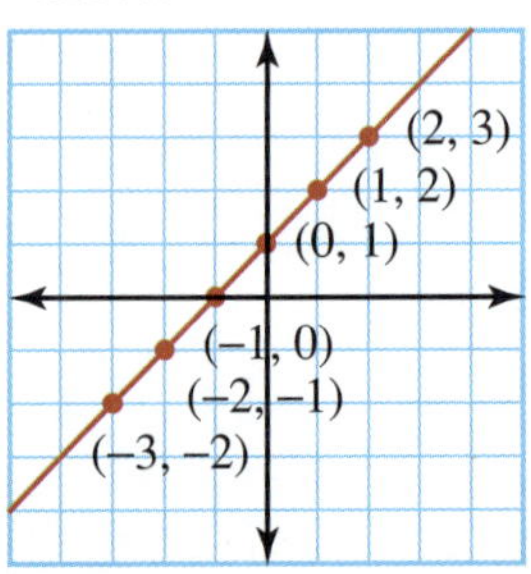

=A1^2

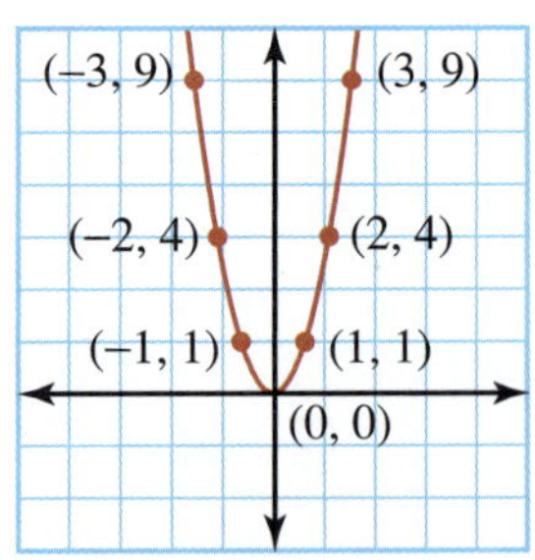

Functions derived from equations, such as the ones graphed from the spreadsheet formulas, are well suited for graphing on computers or graphing calculators. By convention, the [Y=] key on a graphing calculator uses the variable x to represent the input value, and the variable y to represent the output value. The two equations below, written with x and y, correspond to the spreadsheet formulas graphed on page 122.

$$y = x + 1 \qquad , \qquad y = x^2$$

UTILITY

If you have never graphed an equation using the [Y=] key on a graphing calculator, Utility 8 shows you how to do this on the TI-83. If you have a different graphing calculator, check the user's guide that came with it.

Example 1 Graphing equations in x and y

Graph each equation.

a) $y = 2x - 1$ **b)** $y = 2^x$

SOLUTION

Method 1

Create a table of values to produce a paper-and-pencil graph.

a) $y = 2x - 1$

x	y
−2	−5
−1	−3
0	−1
1	1
2	3

b) $y = 2^x$

x	y
−1	0.5
0	1
1	2
2	4
3	8

a)

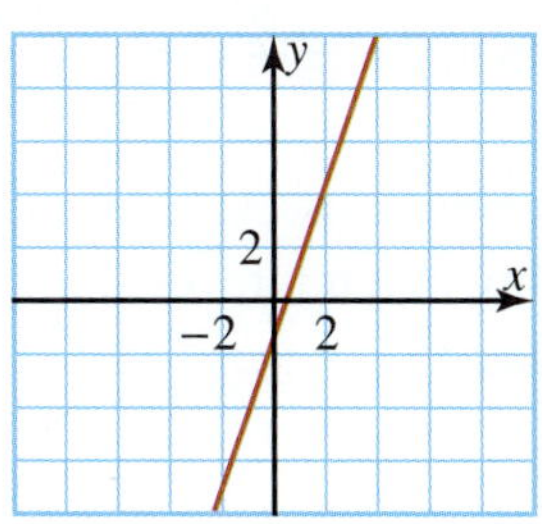

b)

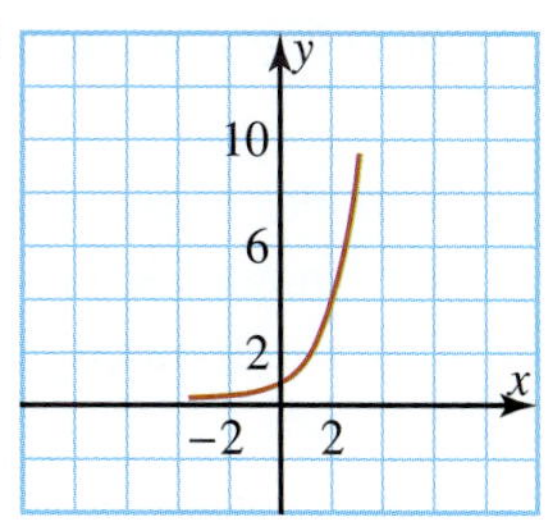

In the graph of $y = 2x - 1$, the points lie along a line.
In the graph of $y = 2^x$, the points lie along a curve.

Method 2

Use technology to display the graph of each equation.

The technology could be a spreadsheet program or a graphing calculator. Choose to use a graphing calculator.

Initialize the calculator. Clear any other Y= equations and turn off any statplots.

a) Set the window. A suitable window is shown below.

On the graphing calculator, press

[Y=] 2 [X,T,θ,n] [–] 1 [ENTER] [GRAPH] to enter $y = 2x - 1$ and display:

```
WINDOW
 Xmin=-5
 Xmax=5
 Xscl=1
 Ymin=-5
 Ymax=5
 Yscl=1
 Xres=1
```

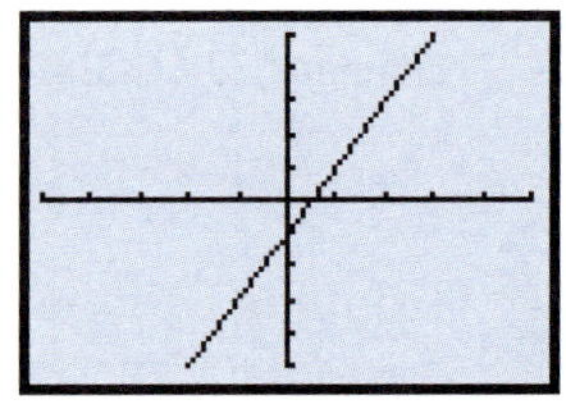

b) Set the window. A suitable window is shown below. On the graphing calculator, press [Y=] [CLEAR] to clear the first function.

Then press 2 [^] [X,T,θ,n] [ENTER] [GRAPH] to enter the function $y = 2^x$ and display:

```
WINDOW
 Xmin=-5
 Xmax=5
 Xscl=1
 Ymin=-5
 Ymax=5
 Yscl=1
 Xres=1
```

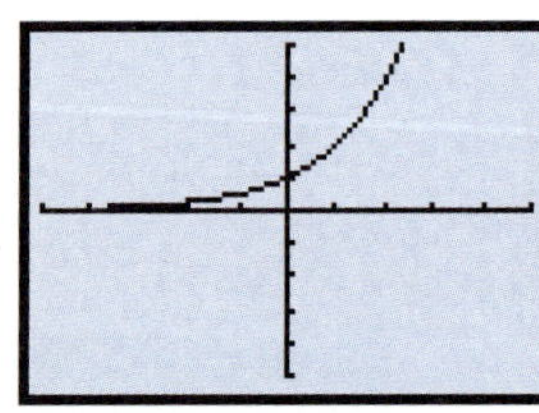

The graphing calculator will also display the table of values that corresponds to a graph display. Before clearing the function from *Example 1b*, press [2nd] [GRAPH] to display a table of values. By scrolling up and down the table, you can view as many x and y values as you wish.

UTILITY

Utility 9 explains how to set the "x" values in the table view.

Formulas arise in many situations: business, investments, science, construction, and nursing. A formula may not convey much information by itself; its graph may reveal much more about the situation.

Example 2 **Graphing and interpreting formulas**

A ball is kicked upward with an initial speed of 19.5 m/s. After t seconds, the ball's height in metres is approximately $h = 19.5t - 4.9t^2$.

Graph the formula. Describe what the graph reveals about the relationship represented by the formula.

What is the maximum height reached by the ball?

SOLUTION

To graph the formula on a graphing calculator, rewrite it using x and y variables.

$$y = 19.5x - 4.9x^2$$

Press [Y=] and enter the expression on the right side of the equation. We must choose suitable window and scale settings to display the graph, or pressing [GRAPH] may result in a blank screen.

The equation gives the height, y metres, of a ball after a time, x seconds. Time is measured from the instant the ball is kicked, so we should not consider negative values of x.

The minimum value for x is 0. Start by choosing 0 as the minimum value for y. To choose the maximum values for x and for y, make an initial guess after looking at the numbers in the equation. Try 5 as the maximum value for x and 20 as the maximum value for y. If these values do not result in a complete curve in the display, we must adjust them, using trial and error. With these values, suitable scales are 1 division for 1 unit on the x-axis and 1 division for 2 units on the y-axis.

Press [WINDOW] to adjust the values to those shown on the screen below left. Then press [GRAPH] to obtain the graph shown below right.

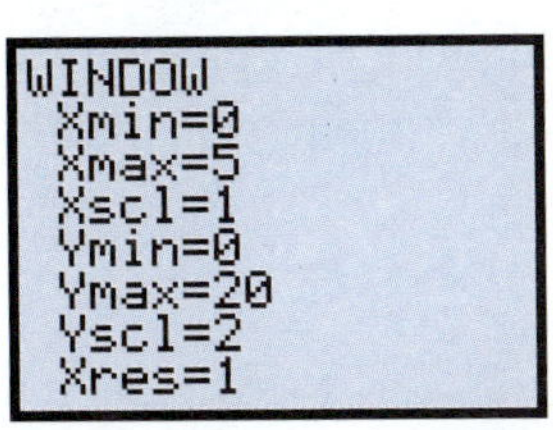

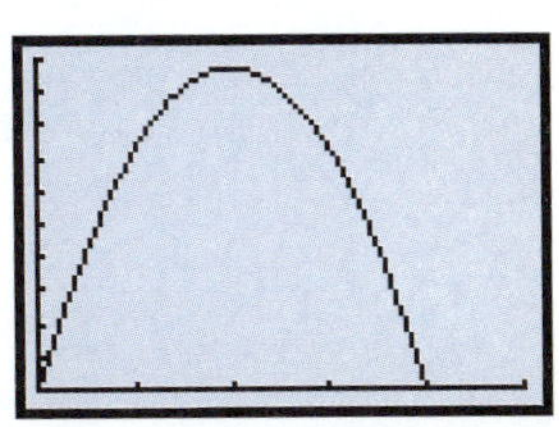

The graph does not show the path of the ball. This would be a vertical line since the ball is kicked straight up.

The graph on page 125 demonstrates that the height of the ball increases, reaches a maximum, and then decreases. Interesting points would be the points where the curve meets the axes, and the point with the highest y-value.

You could use the TRACE feature to look for key points. Use it to confirm the following:

UTILITY

If you have never used the TRACE feature of a graphing calculator, go to Utility 10 to see how.

- The curve passes through (0, 0), indicating that the ball is on the ground when it is first kicked.
- The highest y-value, as you trace along the curve, is about 19.4. This indicates that the ball reaches a height of about 19.4 m before it starts to fall.
- The curve meets the x-axis at about (4, 0). This indicates that the ball is in the air for about 4 s before it lands.

DISCUSSING THE IDEAS

1. For the spreadsheet formula =A1+1, it is possible to have input values that are not integers, such as 1.5 or 2.25. Describe the types of output values you would expect from non-integer input values. Explain how these examples support the statement that the points in the corresponding graph can be joined with a straight line.

2. Select a point from the graph in *Example 1a* that is not in the corresponding table of values. Explain why the (x, y) values from this point should satisfy the equation of the function.

3. *Example 1* demonstrated two ways to graph a function from its equation. What are some advantages of using technology to graph a function? What might be some advantages of using paper and pencil?

4. Suppose you have graphed an equation using a graphing calculator or computer software. How could you check the reasonableness of the graph displayed?

5. *Example 2* presented $h = 19.5t - 4.9t^2$ as a formula for the *approximate* height of the ball. Describe some conditions that you think would affect the relative accuracy of the formula.

6. A rule relating two quantities is a function if every possible input value has only one output value. Visualize the graph of a circle with centre (0, 0) and radius 5 units. Explain, using examples, why this cannot be the graph of a function.

PROJECTS

In this Tutorial you graphed functions from given equations, and interpreted graphs of equations. The skills and concepts you used relate to the Chapter Project, and to the following projects in the Project Book.

- Safety Technology
- Space Technology

EXERCISES

Checking Your Skills

1. Graph the function represented by each equation below. If you cannot print out a graphed display, record each graph by sketching it in your notebook. For each function, determine the value of y when $x = 0$.

a) $y = 5x - 3$ **b)** $y = 2x^2 + 3x - 1$

c) $y = 2 + 0.5x$ **d)** $y = x^3 - 3x - 4$

e) $y = x - 7$ **f)** $y = 0.25x^2 + 3$

g) $y = 0.5x$ **h)** $y = x^2 + x$

2. The cost, C dollars, of holding a party in a local hall is represented by the formula $C = 100 + 10n$, where n is the number of people attending the party.

a) Use a graphing calculator to graph the situation represented by this formula. Use values of n from 0 to 100 and values of C from 0 to 1200. Choose suitable scales.

b) The *fixed cost* of holding the party is the cost incurred even if no one attends the party. Determine the fixed cost of this party. Explain what you think this fixed cost represents.

c) Use the TRACE feature of the calculator to estimate the cost of holding the party if 50 people attend.

3. Look at the graphs you drew in exercise 1.

a) Examine the equations whose graphs are straight lines. How are they similar?

b) Examine the equations whose graphs are curves. How are they similar?

c) Explain why all the graphs represent functions.

4. Suppose an object falls from a resting position. The distance the object travels, d metres, and the time it takes, t seconds, are related by the formula $d = 4.9t^2$.

a) Graph the situation represented by the formula. Use the graph to describe as much information as you can about an object falling from a resting position.

b) How long would it take an object to hit the ground when dropped from a height of 20 m? What about 30 m?

c) The formula implies that any object, regardless of its mass, will fall a given distance in the same time. Do you think this is true? What factors, aside from gravity, affect the time an object falls a given distance?

5. A computer salesperson earns a monthly salary of \$2083.33, plus 3% commission on all sales. Here is a formula for her monthly income, I dollars, when she has sales totalling s dollars for the month.

$$I = 2083.33 + 0.03s$$

a) Use a graphing calculator to graph the situation represented by this formula. Use window settings similar to those shown in the screen below.

Use the graph to describe as much as you can about the salesperson's earnings.

b) How much must her sales total for her to earn \$2500 in a month?

c) Suppose the salesperson has a personal goal of earning \$40 000 in a year. How much is this each month? What would her sales have to be? Do you think it is realistic for a computer salesperson to sell that much?

d) Did you use the graph, the formula, or another approach to solve part c of this exercise? Write to explain your work.

Extending Your Thinking

6. In 1994 the United Nations held a world summit on world population issues. The world population had just surpassed 6 billion. Scientists, trying to predict future populations, worked out a number of possible formulas for different scenarios.

- Assuming an average 0.5% annual increase in population:
  $P = 6\,000\,000\,000(1.005)^{t-1994}$
- Assuming an average 1% annual increase in population:
  $P = 6\,000\,000\,000(1.01)^{t-1994}$
- Assuming an average 3% annual increase in population:
  $P = 6\,000\,000\,000(1.03)^{t-1994}$

a) Graph each of these possible scenarios. Since the graphing calculator cannot accommodate x and y values in the billions, you will need to use another approach, or modify the formulas.

b) In each case, determine the predicted population in the year 2010; in the year 2050.

c) Some scientists believe that Earth will not be able to support the world's population if it exceeds 12 billion. For each of the possible formulas above, in what year does the population exceed 12 billion?

d) None of the formulas above really describes how our world population will grow over the next 50 years. Describe possible factors that might cause significant changes in the rate of growth over time.

Communicating the Ideas

Describe how it is possible to obtain a graph from an equation. Explain the significance of each point that lies on the graph of a function.

TUTORIAL 3.4

Representing Functions in Many Ways

In *Tutorial 3.3*, you used graphing calculators and other methods to look at functions in three important ways:

- Symbolically, as an equation $y = 2^n$
- Numerically, in a table

n	y
0	1
1	2
2	4
3	8
4	16

- Visually, in a graph

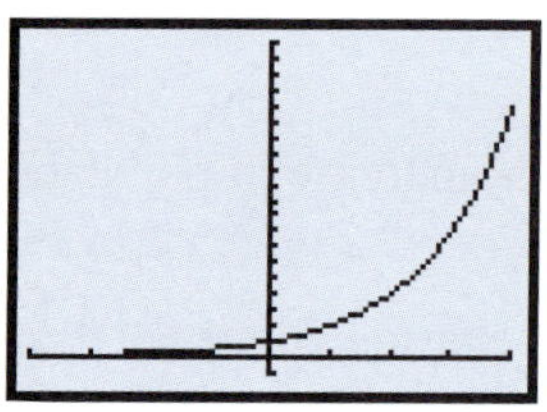

Other ways to represent functions include input/output diagrams and word descriptions. An input/output diagram, often called a *mapping diagram*, is an alternative to a table of values, where we indicate a relationship between numbers by an arrow. The arrow shows the direction of the relationship: from the independent variable (the input) to the dependent variable (the output).

Having one representation of a function often enables you to find alternative ways to represent the same function.

Example 1 **Interpreting a mapping diagram**

Each mapping diagram represents a function.

a) Describe a rule for each function.

b) Give a table of values for each function.

i)
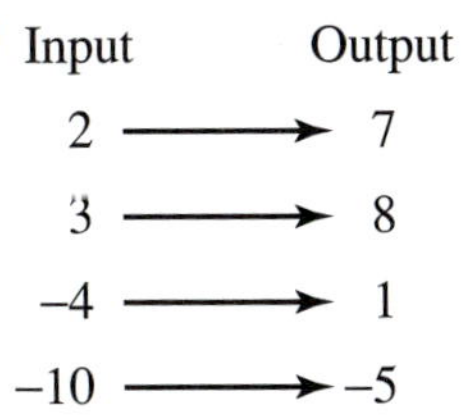

ii)
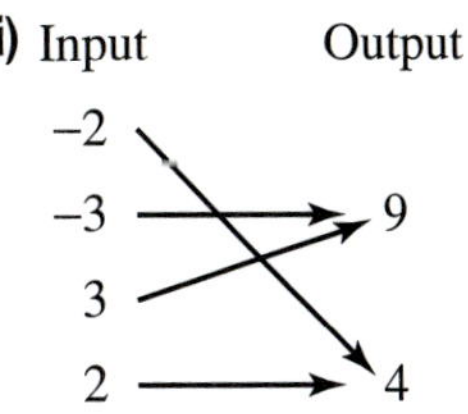

SOLUTION

a) Look for a pattern in the pairs of related numbers. A rule for finding the output in table i is *add 5* to the *input*. A rule for finding the output in table ii is *square the input*.

b) Reorder the input values to increasing order and label the input value x and the output value y.

x	y
−10	−5
−4	1
2	7
3	8

x	y
−3	9
−2	4
2	4
3	9

Example 2 Deriving an equation from a table of values

The following table of values represents a function.

Time (hours)	Distance (kilometres)
1	30
2	60
3	90
4	120

a) Describe the function in words.

b) Write an equation that represents the function.

SOLUTION

a) Every hour, the distance increases by another 30 km. The distance equals the time multiplied by 30.

b) Use the variable d to represent distance in kilometres; use the variable t to represent time in hours: $d = 30t$.

DISCUSSING THE IDEAS

1. Give an example of an input/output table that represents a function.

2. Give an example of an input/output table that represents a relation that is not a function.

3. You are shown a mapping diagram. How can you tell by looking at where the arrows start whether it represents a function or a relation that is not a function?

4. So far you have seen functions represented in different ways: in words, as a graph, as a table of values, as a mapping diagram, and as an equation. Find an example of each representation in this chapter.

PROJECTS

In this Tutorial you learned to describe functions in multiple ways. The skills and concepts you used relate to the Chapter Project, and to the following projects in the Project Book.

- Safety Technology
- Space Technology

EXERCISES

Checking Your Skills

1. a) Finish the input/output tables below.

i)

A	B
1	−1
2	0
3	1
4	
5	
6	

ii)

H	K
−4	−8
−1	−2
0	0
3	
5	
9	

iii)

J	$J + 2$
−6	−4
−2	
0	
1	
2	
5	

iv)

R	R^2
−3	
−1	
0	
1	
2	
6	

b) Which of the input/output tables represent functions? Explain.

c) In words, describe how to find the output from the given input in each table.

d) Write an equation that corresponds to the function in each of tables i and ii.

2. A car dealership states in its advertisement that leasing and driving a new compact car will cost about $400 per month for 24 months.

   a) Create a table of values relating the cost of leasing and driving a compact car to the number of months for which it is driven.

   b) Draw a graph of the cost against the number of months for which it is driven.

   c) Let C represent the cost, and n the number of months. Write an equation that represents the relationship between the cost of leasing and driving a new compact car and the number of months for which it is driven.

3. On the right is a graph of the cost of parking in a parking lot versus the time.

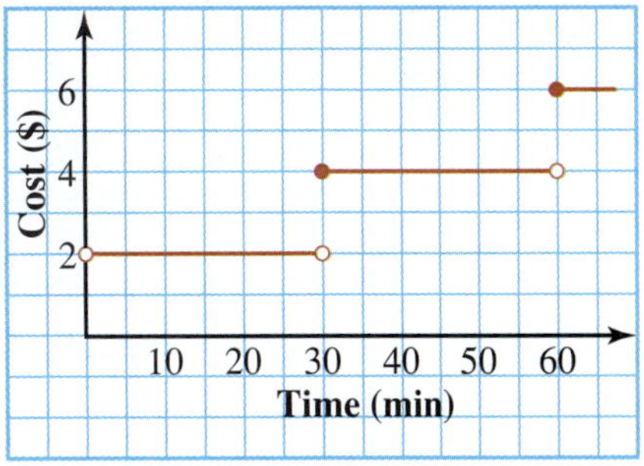

   The graph uses an open dot to indicate that the point circled is not included in the line segment and a full dot to indicate that it is included in the line segment. For example, the graph shows that the cost of parking for 30 min is $4, while the cost of parking for any time period less than 30 min is $2.

   a) Use the graph to complete the table of values given.

Time (in min)	0	1	10	20	29	30	40	50	59	60
Cost (in $)										

   b) In words, describe the relationship between the number of minutes parked and the cost.

4. Make up a table like the one below. Complete the table to show the different representations of each function. The first one has been done for you.

Table of Values	Equation	Words	Graph
Fuel consumption (miles/gallon) (L/100 km) 10 28.30 20 14.15 30 9.43	$F = \frac{283}{M}$	The fuel consumption in L/100 km is 283 divided by the fuel consumption in miles/gallon.	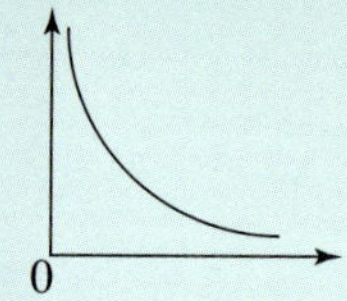
40 7.08 Monthly Sales ($) Earnings($) 0 0 1000 100 2000 200 3000 300			
		A & B Records has CDs on sale for $8 each.	
			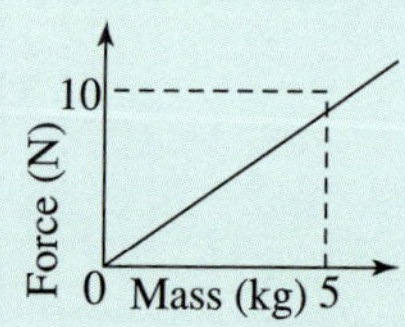
	$V = \frac{4}{3}\pi r^3$		

5. The World Wildlife Federation has stated that every hour Canada loses approximately 240 acres of wilderness.

a) Copy and complete this table.

Time in hours	0	1	2	3	4	5	6	7	8
Total area lost (acres)									

b) Draw a graph of the total area lost against the time.

c) Let A represent the total area lost, t the time in hours. Write an equation that represents the relationship between the total area of wilderness lost in Canada and the time in hours.

Extending Your Thinking

6. a) Find a formula that is used in science. You may need to ask your science teacher or look in a science book. Is this formula a function?

   b) Express the formula in 4 different ways. Identify the variables used.

   c) Can you isolate a different variable in the formula? Is the formula still a function when you do this?

COMMUNICATING THE IDEAS

Write an explanation of the different representations of a function. Create an example that will let you demonstrate all the possible ways to represent a function.

Simulating the Spread of an Epidemic

CHAPTER PROJECT

You will return to Epidemics on page 154 of this chapter. *Tutorials 3.5* and *3.6* will help you develop relevant skills for this last stage of the Chapter Project.

How does a disease become an epidemic? You will now look at some simplified examples to find out.

Diseases such as the bubonic plague, Ebola, AIDS, the flesh-eating disease, and the flu are spread by physical contact. You can simulate how some of these diseases are spread by considering a hypothetical disease.

1. A mystery virus is spread by physical contact. An infected person will pass the disease, on average, to 2 new people in 24 h. Assume that an infected person is contagious for only 24 h. Copy and complete the diagram on the right.

Day	Infected People					
1				X		
2		X				X
3	X		X		X	X
4						

2. How many new people are infected on the fourth day? How many people, in total, are infected at the end of the fourth day?

3. Use the diagram from exercise 1 to complete the table on the right. Use a spreadsheet to automate your calculations. If you wish to review working with spreadsheets on a computer, look at *Tutorial 2.5* in this book.

Day	New Infections	Total Infected
0	0	0
1	1	1
2	2	3
3	4	7
4		
5		
6		
7		

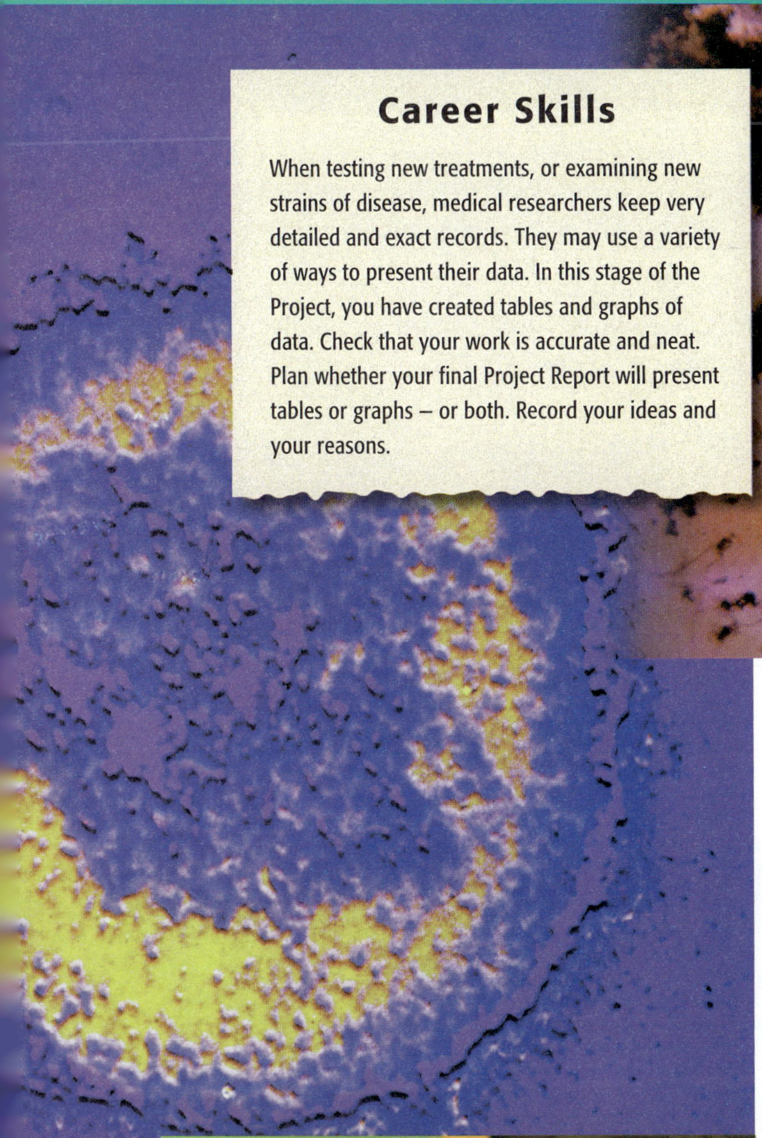

Career Skills

When testing new treatments, or examining new strains of disease, medical researchers keep very detailed and exact records. They may use a variety of ways to present their data. In this stage of the Project, you have created tables and graphs of data. Check that your work is accurate and neat. Plan whether your final Project Report will present tables or graphs – or both. Record your ideas and your reasons.

4. Graph the data from the table in exercise 3. You will have two separate functions displayed on the same graph. Describe the overall trends indicated by the graph.

5. Consider the hospital data reported in the table below. Predict the number of hospital cases for days 8, 9, and 10.

Time	Number of Hospital Cases
1	1
2	3
3	10
4	32
5	107
6	325
7	998

6. Graph the data. Let the horizontal axis extend to day 10. Let the vertical axis extend to your prediction for day 10. Is the graph a function? Does your prediction for day 10 match the trend of the graph?

TUTORIAL 3.5

Domain and Range

When you graphed the pendulum data, there were certain reasonable values for both the first and second quantities you graphed. When you graphed equations written with the variables x and y, there were certain possible values for each of the two variables.

In this Tutorial, you will look more closely at the coordinates of the possible points in the graph of a function.

Investigation

Decay Simulation

You will need an empty container and one holding 100 M&M candies. Work in groups of 5.

Allergy alert: Please read the label on the candies. If you have food allergies, let your teacher know.

1. Make up a table like the one below. "Group X" refers to your group.

Trial	1	2	3	4	5	6	7	8
Group A								
Group B								
Group C								
Group D								
Group E								
Average Number Remaining								

2. Shake the candies and pour them onto a flat, clean surface. Remove all the candies that have the M facing up and put them into the other empty container. In the column for Trial 1, record the number of candies that remain.

3. Put the remaining candies back into the original container and repeat the process. Continue until you've removed all the candies.

4. Collect the data from the other groups in your class. Calculate to fill in the last row of the table.

5. Plot the averaged data for the class on a scatterplot. Display Trials along the horizontal axis, and Average Number Remaining along the vertical axis.

6. Would it make sense to connect the points in the scatterplot? Explain.

7. What are all the values along the horizontal axis, for the trials?

8. What are all the possible values along the vertical axis, for the average number of candies that remain?

The values along the horizontal axis of the graph are called the *domain* of the function. The values along the vertical axis are called the *range* of the function.

DISCUSSING THE IDEAS

1. Go to the scatterplot you graphed in the Investigation.
   a) What factors do you need to consider when determining the domain and range of a function?
   b) How would the domain and range change if the points were connected?
   c) How might the domain and range change if the class repeated the Investigation?

2. Another way to describe a function is to use an input/output table. Explain how to determine the domain and range of the function in this case.

3. Use a graphing calculator to graph $y = \sqrt{x} + 2$.

```
WINDOW
 Xmin=0
 Xmax=16
 Xscl=1
 Ymin=0
 Ymax=8
 Yscl=1
 Xres=1
```

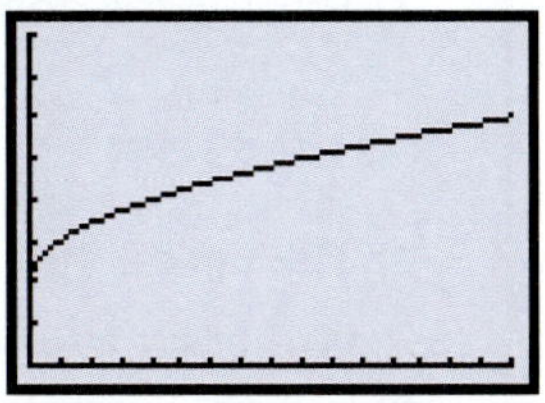

a) Visualize a light shining along the paper from directly above the graph. The graph shadows a portion of the x-axis. What are the values of x that are in the shadow? Explain why the domain of the function is given by all the values of x that fall in the shadow of the graph.

b) Visualize a light shining along the paper from the right of the graph, with a shadow falling on the y-axis. What are the values of y that are in the shadow? Explain why the range of the function is given by all the values of y that fall in the shadow of the graph.

c) What are the domain and range of the function?

4. The previous question involves the concept of shadows to determine domain and range. Describe how to use the shadow concept to determine the domain and range of the function represented by $y = (x - 3)^2$. What are the domain and range?

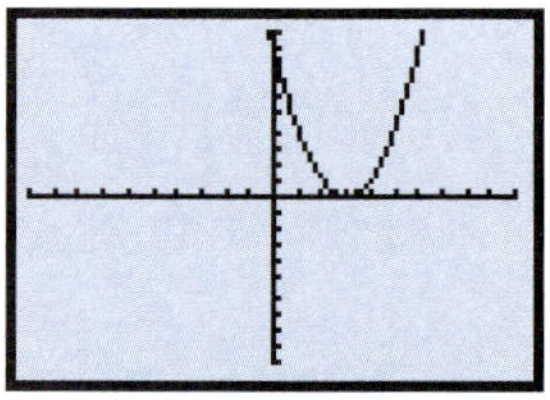

Example 1 **Determine the domain and range of a function from a graph**

The graph describes the amount of fuel in pounds in a helicopter's fuel tank. To begin, the tank is full.

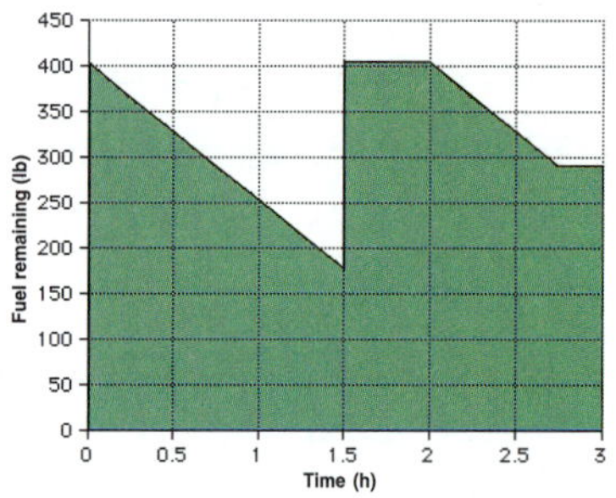

a) What is the fuel capacity of this helicopter?

b) Explain why this cannot be the graph of a function.

c) What is the domain and range of this relation?

SOLUTION

a) The tank is full to begin, so the fuel capacity of the helicopter is the amount of fuel remaining at time 0. The capacity is 400 pounds.

b) For a relation to be a function, every input value must be related to just one output value. From the graph, the input value 1.5 is related to all the numbers from about 180 to 400. The graph is not the graph of a function.

c) To determine the domain, visualize the shadow of the graph on the horizontal axis.

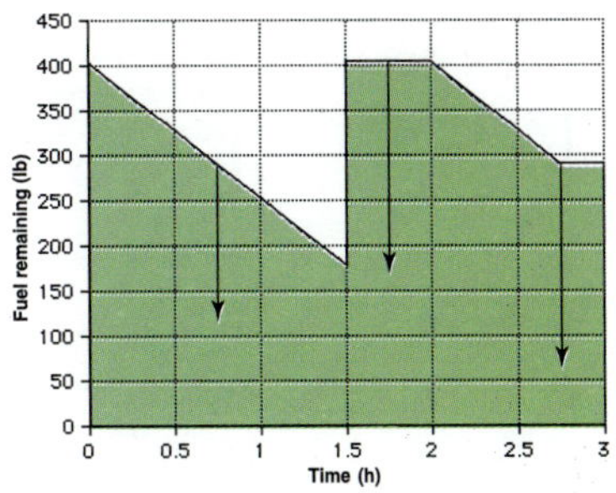

The domain of the relation is the set of all numbers from 0 to 3 inclusive.

To determine the range, visualize the shadow of the graph on the vertical axis.

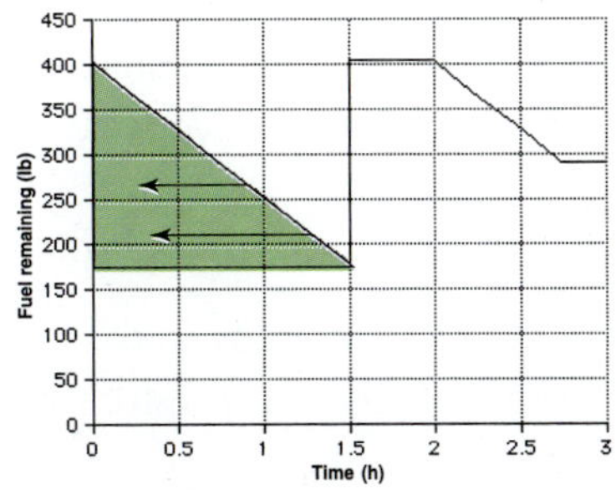

The range of the relation is all the numbers from 175 to 400 inclusive.

Example 2 **Determine the domain and range of a function using the TRACE feature of a graphing calculator**

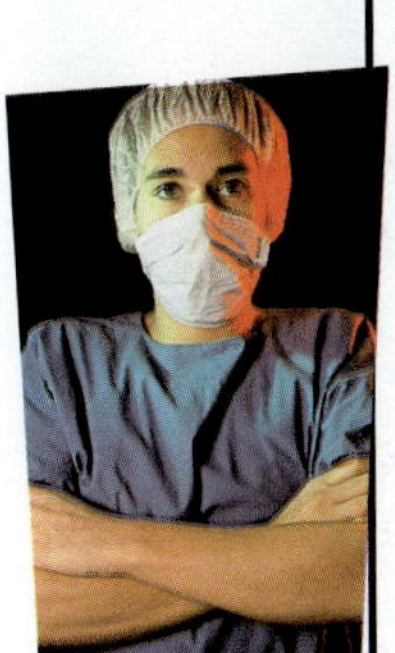

Nurses monitor their patients' medication, liquids, and foods. Their daily routine includes work with formulas to interpret and predict patients' daily needs. The formula $A = 15(0.84^t)$ gives the amount, A, of a 15-mg dose of antibiotic remaining in a patient's bloodstream after t hours.

a) Graph the function over a 24-h period.

b) What are the domain and range of the function?

c) If the antibiotic must be re-administered before the amount of antibiotic remaining in the bloodstream falls below 1.5 mg, should it be administered every 8 h, 12 h, or 24 h? Explain your answer.

SOLUTION

a) Use a graphing calculator. Using the window settings shown below on the left, we obtain the graph shown below on the right.

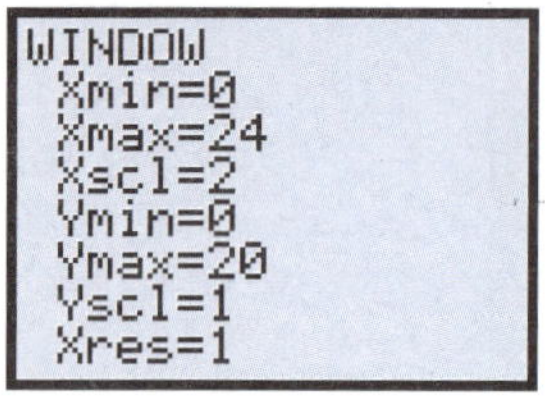

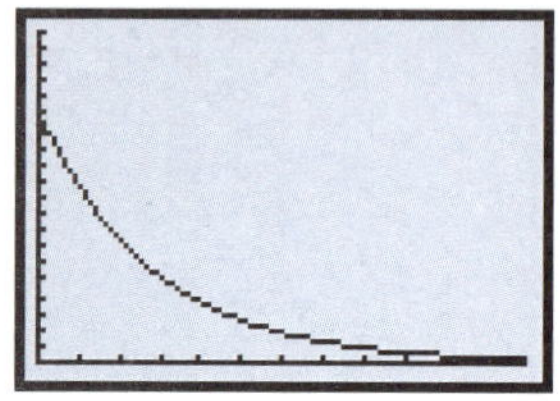

b) Visualize the shadow cast by the graph on the x-axis. The domain is all the numbers from 0 to 24.

Visualize the shadow cast by the graph on the y-axis. The graph is very close to the x-axis when x approaches 24. Use the TRACE feature to determine the values of y.

UTILITY

If you have never used the TRACE feature of a graphing calculator to determine the domain and range of a function, Utility 10 shows you how to do this using a TI-83.

The range of the function is all the numbers from about 0.23 to 15.

c) Calculate the level of antibiotic remaining in the bloodstream after 8 h, 12 h, and 24 h by substituting these values in turn for t in the formula:

If $t = 8$, $A = 15(0.84^8) \doteq 3.7$ mg.

If $t = 12$, $A = 15(0.84^{12}) \doteq 1.9$ mg.

If $t = 24$, $A = 15(0.84^{24}) \doteq 0.23$ mg.

Most medical practitioners prefer to give as little antibiotic as possible. The antibiotic is probably administered every 12 h, but it could also be administered every 8 h.

PROJECTS

In this Tutorial you learned to identify the domain and range of a function. You will need to determine meaningful x and y values for a function in the Chapter Project, and in the following projects in the Project Book.

- **Safety Technology**
- **Space Technology**

EXERCISES

Checking Your Skills

1. The graph of the function $y = \sqrt{(4 - x^2)}$ is shown in the diagram below.

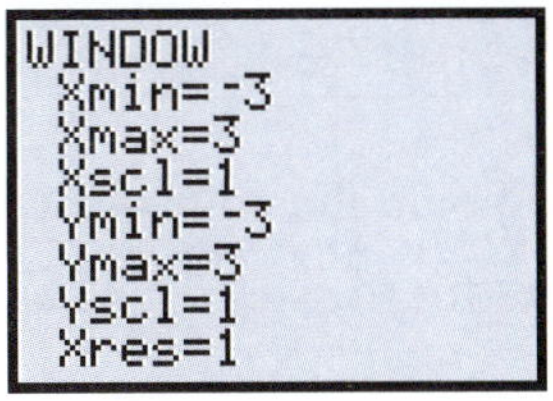

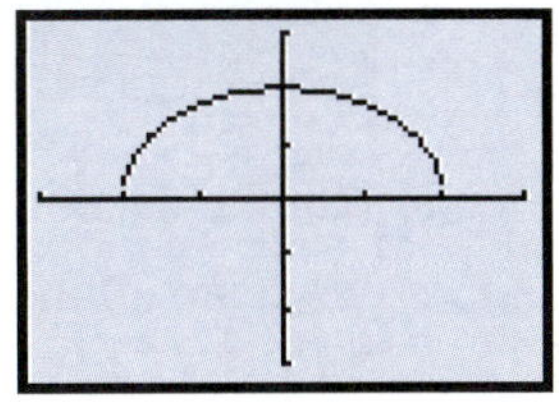

Use the shadow method to determine the domain and range of the function.

2. The graph illustrates the number of similar pages, n, printed by an ink jet printer as a function of time, T minutes.

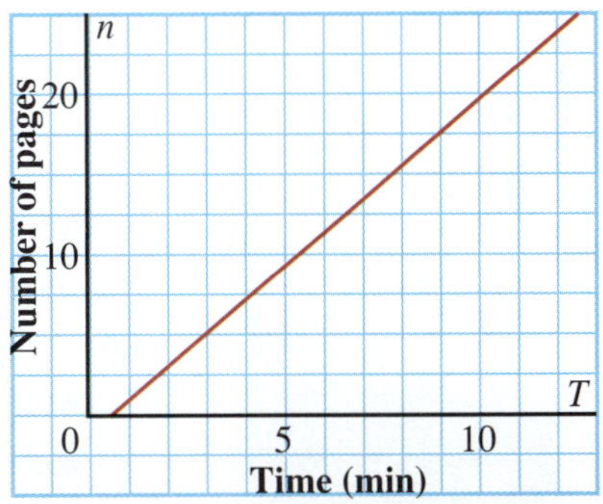

a) Use the shadow method to determine the domain of the function. What is the range?

b) Determine the value of T when $n = 0$. Explain what this represents.

3. A high school basketball team is planning an 80-km drive to the provincial tournament. The team bus will drive no slower than 40 km/h and no faster than 100 km/h and will maintain a constant speed.

STUDENT REFERENCE

If you need to review "speed," see the Student Reference.

a) Make up a table of values like the one below. Complete the table by calculating the time it will take to drive to the tournament at each speed listed.

Average Speed (km/h)	40	50	64	80	100
Time (h)					

b) Plot the data on a scatterplot. Should the points be connected? Explain.

c) What are all the possible values for the speed? What are these numbers called?

d) What are all the possible values for the time? What are these numbers called?

4. Madison baby-sits for \$3/h. Her baby-sitting jobs last up to 6 h each. All her clients calculate the amount they owe by rounding up to the nearest half-hour.

a) Create a graph to show Madison's possible earnings on a single baby-sitting job.

b) Identify the domain and range of the graph. Write to explain the significance of each.

5. Consider the sequence of numbers 2^1, 2^2, 2^3, 2^4, and so on.

a) Complete a table of values like the one below for this sequence.

Term of the sequence	1	2	3	4	5	6	7	8	9	10	11
Value of the term	2	4	8	16	32						
Units digit of the term	2	4	8	6							

b) Plot the data from the second and third rows of your table. Should the points be connected? Explain.

c) What are the domain and range of the graph?

d) What pattern do you notice about the units digit of the term?

e) Using your pattern, predict the units digit of 2^{113}.

6. The circle below touches each of the x-axis and the y-axis at a single point. What are the domain and range of the relation?

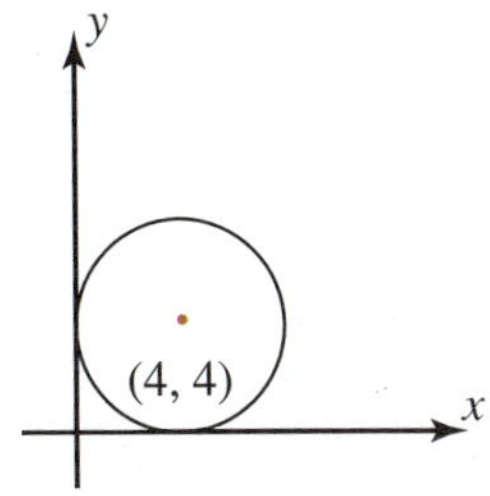

Extending Your Thinking

7. Consider the right triangle below. The hypotenuse is 5 units long. What are all the possible values for the other two sides?

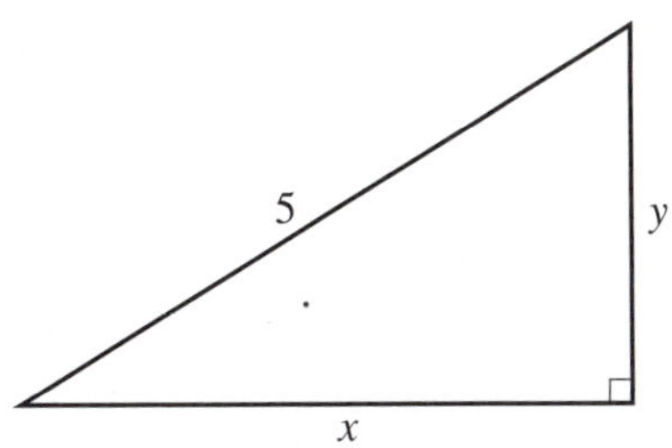

COMMUNICATING THE IDEAS

Think of an experiment in which the domain would be different depending on the conditions. Write a description of your experiment. Include a description of the domain in each case. Write down why you think the domain would change under different conditions.

TUTORIAL 3.6

Function Notation

Use the graph below to answer the following questions.

1. What was the maximum temperature on February 3, 1996?
2. For what date(s) was the temperature −18°C?
3. For what date(s) was the temperature greater than 0°C?
4. During what time spans was the temperature rising?
5. On what days was the maximum daily temperature 0°C?

Calgary's Daily Maximum Temperature for February 1996

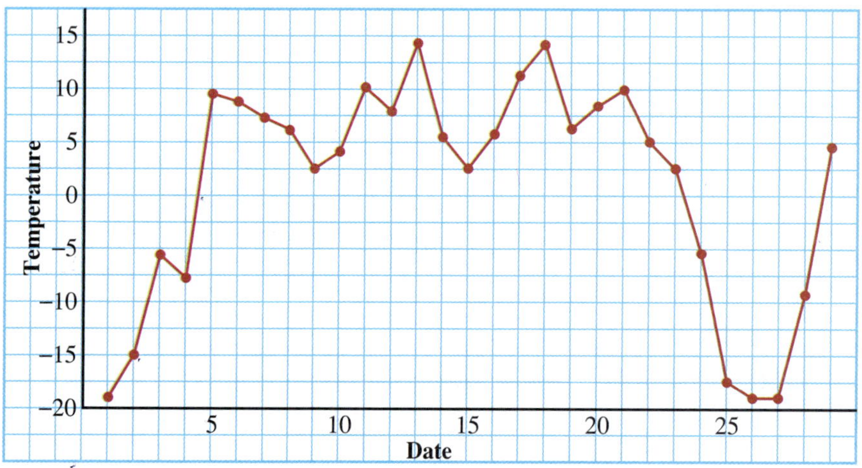

Another way of asking these questions is with a shorthand called *function notation*. Match the following questions to the first set of questions.

Let T represent temperature, and d the date.

A. On what intervals is $T(d)$ increasing?

B. What is $T(3)$?

C. What is the solution set to $T(d) > 0$?

D. What is the solution set to $T(d) = 0$?

E. For what value(s) is $T(d) = -18$?

Confirm and discuss the following matches.

A. 4 B. 1 C. 3 D. 5 E. 2

The phrase "the maximum daily temperature in Calgary on February 3, 1996" has the same meaning as the mathematical phrase $T(3)$. From the graph, $T(3) = -6$.

"What is $T(d)$?" is a compact way of asking "What is the maximum daily temperature for a given date?" Read $T(d)$ as "T of d" or "T at d." For input d, $T(d)$ is the output.

An equation that represents a function can be written in function notation. The area of a circle, for example, is given by $A = \pi r^2$. In function notation this becomes $A(r) = \pi r^2$.

A(2) indicates the area of a circle with radius 2 units, and $A(2) = 4\pi$.

Example 1 Interpreting a cost equation

The total cost for printing a school notice includes a *fixed* cost of $25 and a cost of 1¢ for each notice printed. The cost, C, in dollars, as a function of printing n notices is given by the equation:

$$C(n) = 25 + 0.01n$$

a) Describe a reasonable domain for this function. Define an appropriate window setting for graphing the function on a graphing calculator.

b) Graph the function. Is it possible to interpret all the points in the display?

c) What is the fixed cost and what is the variable cost? Where is this information found on the graph?

d) Determine the value of $C(200)$, and explain its significance.

e) Determine the value of n for which $C(n) = 40$. Interpret the significance of this value.

SOLUTION

a) The domain is all positive integers. However, it is unlikely that a school would order fewer than 100 notices. It makes sense to graph the equation for values of n ranging from 0 to 2000.

On a graphing calculator, the given equation needs to be rewritten in x and y.

$$y = 25 + 0.01x$$

Set the window to display x-values from 0 to 2000. Display y-values from 0 to 50.

Using mental math, $C(2000) = 25 + 0.01(2000)$, or $25 + 20$. So displaying y-values up to 50 will accommodate the function display.

STUDENT REFERENCE

If you need to review evaluating an expression by substitution, see evaluate in the Student Reference.

b) Using the window setting shown below left, a graphing calculator will display the graph below right.

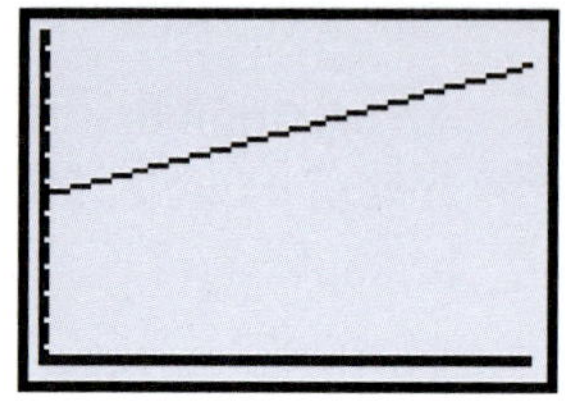

Use TRACE to view some of the points on the graph. As you trace along the line, you will see decimal values for x and y. In the context of printing flyers, the only points that are meaningful are those with whole-number values for x. Move to the Table view: the calculator displays whole-number x-values; all the corresponding values of y are money values to the nearest cent.

UTILITY

If you have never changed the Table Setup on a graphing calculator, Utility 9 shows how to do this on a TI-83.

c) The fixed cost is \$25, and the variable cost is represented by the expression $0.01n$. On the graph, the fixed cost is the y-value where the graph crosses the vertical axis. The point (0, 25) is not really meaningful in this situation, however, since you would never pay for printing 0 notices. The point is included in order to view the graph with both axes also displayed.

d) Use TABLE to view the function. Changing the Table setup will allow you to display x-values increasing by 100s, or any multiple.

$C(200) = 27$

This means it would cost \$27 to print 200 flyers.

e) Use the TABLE view. Look for a y-value of 40, and find the corresponding x-value.

$C(1500) = 40$. Interpret the significance of this value.

This means you could have 1500 notices printed for \$40.

Example 2 Using algebra with function notation

Two variables are connected by the equation $t^2 + w = 25$.

a) Express w as a function of t so that $w = w(t)$.

b) Determine the value of $w(3)$.

c) Determine the value of t for which $w(t) = 9$.

STUDENT REFERENCE

SOLUTION

a) To express w as a function of t, solve the equation for w.

If you need to review "solving an equation," see the Student Reference.

$$t^2 + w = 25$$
$$w = 25 - t^2$$

This equation gives the rule for finding w as a function of t. Replace w with $w(t)$.

$$w(t) = 25 - t^2$$

b) Substitute $t = 3$ into $w(t) = 25 - t^2$.

$$\begin{aligned} w(3) &= 25 - (3)^2 \\ &= 25 - 9 \\ &= 16 \end{aligned}$$

c) Substitute $w(t) = 9$ into $w(t) = 25 - t^2$, and solve for t.

If $w(t) = 9$, then

$$\begin{aligned} 25 - t^2 &= 9 \\ -t^2 &= 9 - 25 \\ -t^2 &= -16 \\ t^2 &= 16 \\ t &= \sqrt{16} \text{ or } -\sqrt{16} \\ t &= 4, -4 \end{aligned}$$

We often write this as $t = \pm 4$.

DISCUSSING THE IDEAS

1. Look at the graph for the function $C(n) = 25 + 0.01n$ in *Example 1*. What does $C(500) = 30$ mean? What are at least two other mathematical ways to represent this relationship?

2. Describe how you could use graphing to solve *Example 2b* and *2c*. Which approach do you prefer? Why?

3. Explain what additional information you can derive from the graph of the function in *Example 2*.

CHAPTER PROJECT

In this Tutorial you learned to represent a function using function notation, and to interpret information given using function notation. You will need to understand function notation to complete the Chapter Project.

EXERCISES

Checking Your Skills

1. The temperature gauge of an old oven is in Fahrenheit degrees. To convert to degrees Celsius C from degrees Fahrenheit F, you could apply the function C below.

$$C(F) = \frac{5}{9}(F - 32)$$

a) What does $C(50) = 10$ mean?

b) At sea level, pure water freezes at 0°C, and boils at 100°C. What are the freezing and boiling temperatures of water in Fahrenheit degrees?

c) A cookie recipe indicates that the oven should be pre-heated to 180°C. At what temperature should you set the oven in Fahrenheit degrees?

d) The chef using the oven bakes muffins at a temperature of 425°F. What is the temperature of the oven in degrees Celsius?

2. A scientist was studying the growth of a population of small marsupials. She used N to represent the number of animals in the population, and t to represent the number of months since she began the study.

a) The scientist began by writing $N = N(t)$. Explain what this means.

b) The scientist determined that a suitable model of the population growth is given by the formula $N(t) = 0.2t^2 + 4t + 50$. Determine the values for $N(0)$, $N(1)$, and $N(-1)$. Explain how you would interpret these values.

3. a) When we use mathematics to model results, we often wish to use a function in the description. You did this when you drew an estimated line of best fit for a scatterplot in earlier grades. A function used to model results need not have a graph that is a line.

Draw the graph of one function that satisfies the following conditions: $f(-7) = 8, f(3) = 4$, and $f(5) = -2$.

b) 3 is a value in the domain of the function in part a. What is the corresponding value in the range?

4. A triangle has sides x, $x + 5$, and y. Its perimeter is 16 units. Express y as a function of x. What is the domain and range of the function?

5. Refer to the graph below.

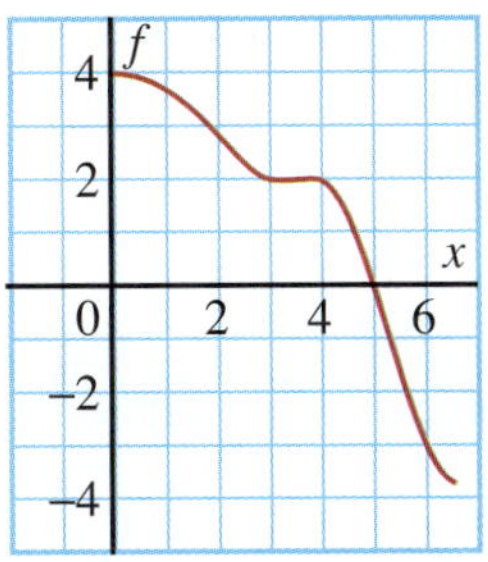

a) Determine the value of $f(4)$.

b) Determine the values of x for which $f(x) = -3$.

c) Create a possible scenario that could be represented by this graph. Describe the scenario, and identify and explain significant points on the graph.

Extending Your Thinking

6. In this chapter you have examined relations and functions. In further courses you will look at systematic ways to classify the functions you have worked with throughout this chapter. This exercise will give you some insights into the work to come. Work with a partner.

a) Make 4 copies of the table on page 152. This will give you one table for each group of functions you are going to examine.

b) Use a graphing calculator to graph all the functions in each group. For each graph, fill in the first 4 rows of the corresponding table.

Group A: $y = x$ $\qquad$ $y = 2x + 3$

$x + 3y = 6$ $\qquad$ $y = 2$

Group B: $y = x^2$ $\qquad$ $x^2 + y = 3$

$2x^2 - y - 5 = 0$ $\qquad$ $y = x(x - 2)$

Group C: $y = x^3$ $\qquad$ $y = x^3 - 2$

$y = 0.5x^3 + 3$ $\qquad$ $y = x(x - 2)^2$

Group D: $y = 2^x$ $\qquad$ $y = 1.5^x$

$y = 1.5^{3x}$ $\qquad$ $y = 4^{-3x}$

c) Discuss how the graphs in each group are similar. How are the equations in each group similar? Record your observations in the table for the corresponding group.

Functions Group ____________________

Equation				
Sketch				
Domain				
Range				
Similarities of graph				
Similarities of equations				

d) Each group of functions has a different name.

Group A: linear functions

Group B: quadratic functions

Group C: cubic functions

Group D: exponential functions

Group A

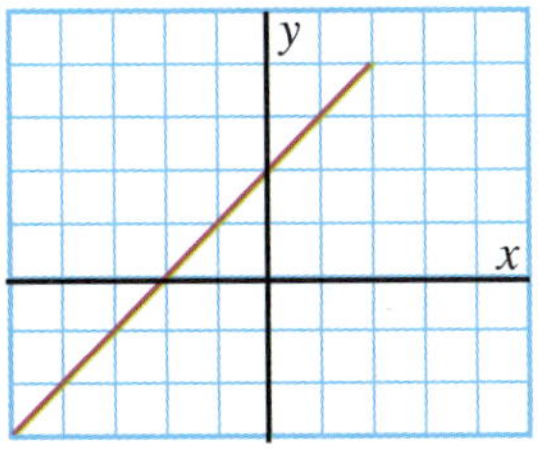

Group B

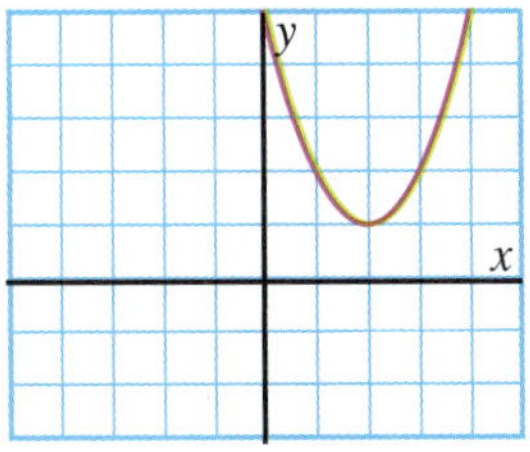

Group C

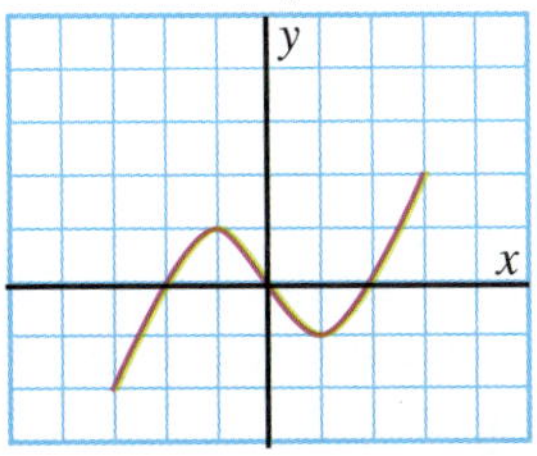

Group D

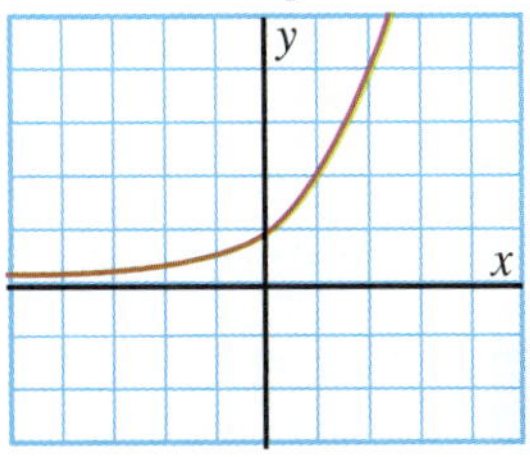

You can use these names, and the similarities and differences you observed, to classify functions. Review the functions you graphed in this chapter. Look for examples in both your notebook and this Source Book. Select one or more examples of each type of function above. Compare your selections with those of another student.

COMMUNICATING THE IDEAS

Explain the relationship between function notation and a graph. Use an example to illustrate your explanation.

Researching an Epidemic

On pages 136 and 137 you examined some simplified models of a disease. You produced tables and graphs to demonstrate how an epidemic might spread.

Scientists working with disease data look for relationships that they can express in equation form. This use of functions enables them to predict what the future may hold. The following exercises will give you an opportunity to graph equations of the type that come up in epidemic analyses.

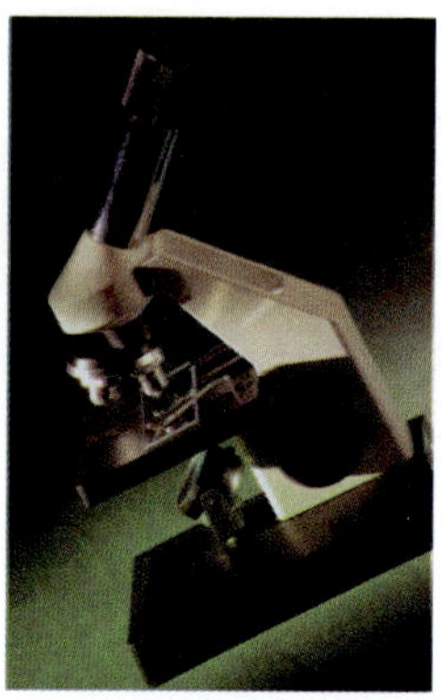

1. Graph the function $f(x) = 2^x - 1$. Compare this graph to the one you created for exercise 6 on page 137.

2. Suppose the equation $y = 2^x - 1$ represents the spread of a disease. How many people would be infected in 20 days? in 30 days? in 40 days?

3. Find out the population of your community, town, or city. Based on your graph for the spread of the disease, how long would it take for your community, town, or city to be completely infected?

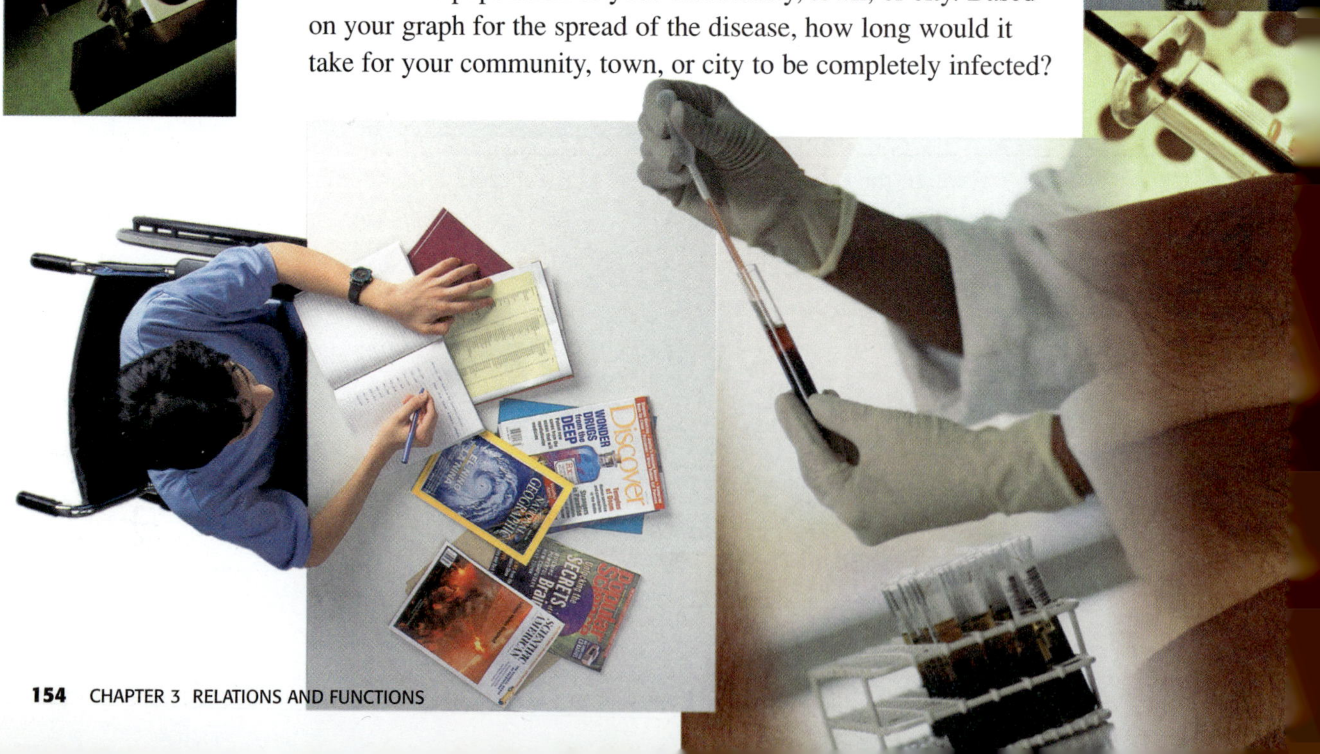

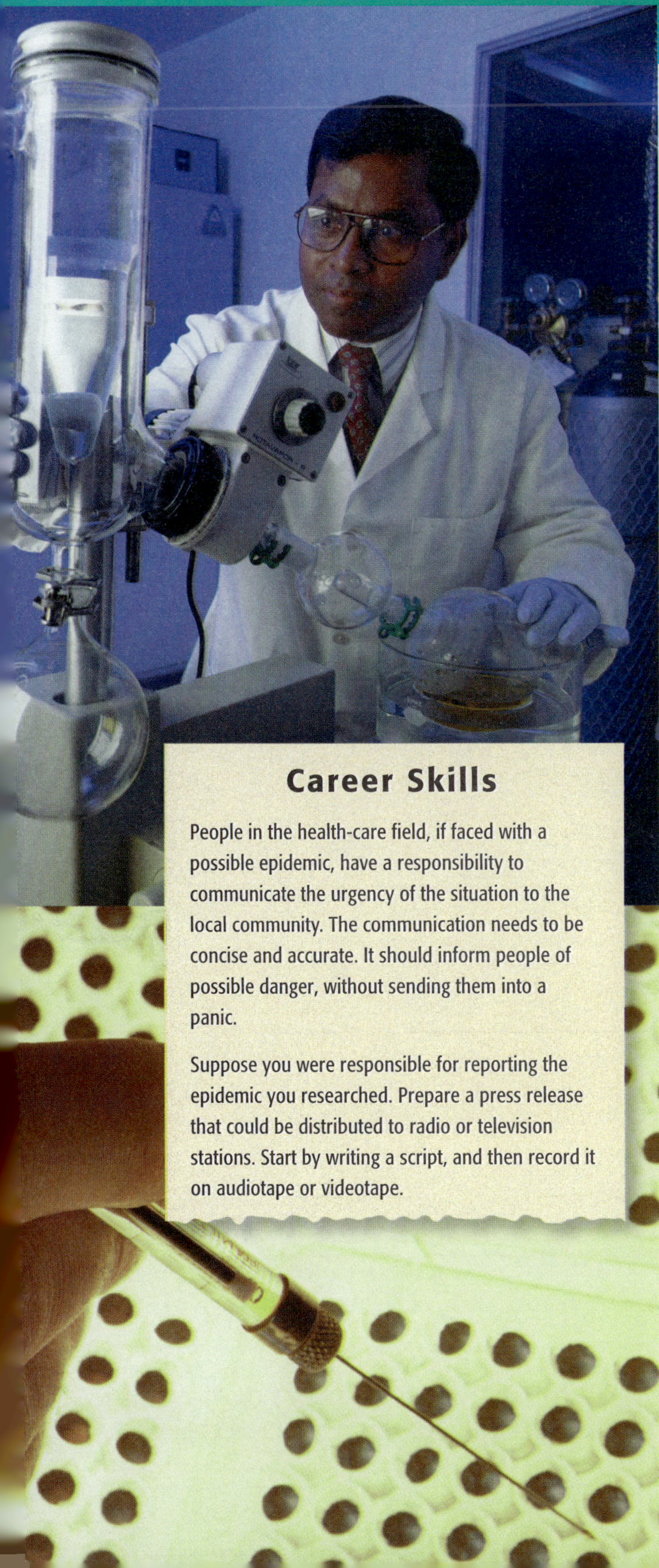

Career Skills

People in the health-care field, if faced with a possible epidemic, have a responsibility to communicate the urgency of the situation to the local community. The communication needs to be concise and accurate. It should inform people of possible danger, without sending them into a panic.

Suppose you were responsible for reporting the epidemic you researched. Prepare a press release that could be distributed to radio or television stations. Start by writing a script, and then record it on audiotape or videotape.

4. What if the disease were spreading at a different rate? Graph the function $f(x) = 1.4^x - 1$, which could also represent the spread of a disease. Compare this graph to the one you did in exercise 1.

5. Suppose the disease was spreading at a faster rate. How would the equation representing the epidemic probably change? Explain.

6. The functions you graphed in exercises 1 and 4 imply that an epidemic continues indefinitely. In reality, even with a fatal disease, an epidemic probably would not wipe out an entire population. Why do you think epidemics eventually stop? Give as many different reasons as you can.

By completing the exercises above, and those on pages 136 and 137, you demonstrated the mathematical patterns that lead to epidemics. Extend your hypothetical work by researching an actual disease.

Choose an epidemic that you would like to learn more about. It could be an epidemic that you've read about recently, such as cholera, tuberculosis, or AIDS.

Write up your research as an article. If the epidemic you researched is a current epidemic, you may want to submit your article to your school newspaper for publication. Include graphs that indicate the rate of growth. Can you and your fellow students do anything to help the people affected by this epidemic?

CONSOLIDATING YOUR SKILLS

What Do I Need To Know?

Tutorial	Skills and Concepts	Important Results and Formulas
3.1	• Describe a possible situation represented by a graph • Sketch a graph to represent a situation	
3.2	• Generate data and record them in tables on the graphing calculator • Create a scatterplot of data from tables using a graphing calculator • Understand what is meant by a relation	• A relation between two sets of numbers is a rule that connects numbers in the first set (input) with numbers in the second set (output).
3.3	• Understand the difference between a relation and a function • Create a graph of an equation using a table of values • Use a graphing calculator to create a graph of an equation • Use the TRACE feature of a graphing calculator to determine the coordinates of points on a graph	• A function is a relation for which each input value has exactly one output value.
3.4	• Be able to interpret the different methods of representing a function • Understand how to interpret a mapping diagram or an input/output table	
3.5	• Understand what is meant by the domain and range of a relation • Determine the domain and range of a relation using the shadow method and the TRACE feature of a graphing calculator	• The domain of a relation is the set of input values. • The range of a relation is the set of output values.
3.6	• Understand and use function notation • Know how to change the equation of a function into function notation	• To write an equation in function notation, first rearrange the equation to isolate y. Write $y = f(x)$.

What Should I Be Able To Do?

After you have completed the work in Chapter 3, you should be able to solve the problems that follow. Part A is investigative in nature.

As you work through the exercises, refer to the *Student Reference*, the *Utilities*, and the *Tutorials* as necessary.

Part A

You will need a supply of 55 marbles or counters.

1. The picture shows 6 balls arranged to form a triangle.

Six is a triangular number.

a) Arrange your counters or marbles in a square-based pyramid with 2 layers. How many counters have you used?

If you use marbles you will need to prevent them from rolling by using books at the base of the pyramid.

Use your graphing calculator, or paper and pencil, to start a table of values for the number of layers and the corresponding pyramidal number. Explain why it is reasonable to consider the number 1 as a pyramidal number. Build pyramids with the counters and fill in the table until you have built a pyramid with 5 layers.

b) Graph the table of values you have produced. Should the dots be connected?

c) Look at the patterns in the table. Visualize how you can add to a pyramid to construct the next. What is the rule for generating one pyramidal number from the previous one?

d) Determine the domain and range of the relation.

e) Explain why the relation is a function.

f) If P represents the value of the 6th pyramidal number, write an expression for P as a sum of numbers.

Part B

2. Suggest a possible scenario for each of the following graphs.

a)

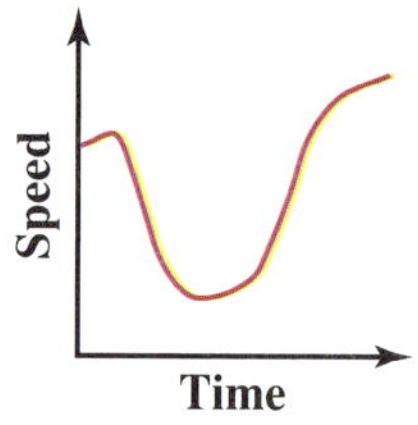

b)

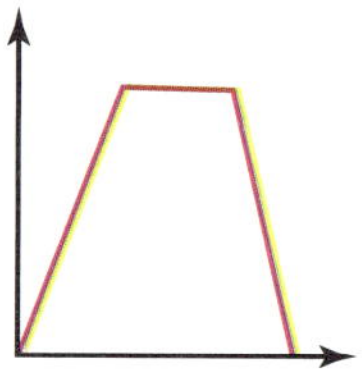

3. A roast of meat is taken from the refrigerator and put into a hot oven. The temperature of the meat depends on the time for which it has been in the oven.

a) What is the independent variable in the relationship? What is the dependent variable?

b) Sketch a graph that illustrates the temperature of the roast of meat from the time when it is put into the oven.

4. Does the following input/output table represent a function? Why or why not?

Input	Output
9	3 or −3
1	1
16	4
25	−5
49	7

5. For each of the following tables of values:

a) Draw a graph of the function.

b) Determine the rule that expresses y in terms of x.

x	y
0	0
1	4
2	8
3	12
4	16

x	y
0	−1
1	0
2	3
3	8
4	15

x	y
0	−1
1	1
2	3
3	5
4	7

6. The cost of printing newsletters consists of a fixed cost of \$35 and a cost per newsletter of 3¢. The function relating the cost, C dollars, of printing n newsletters is

$$C(n) = 35 + 0.03n.$$

a) Draw a graph of the function.

b) What is the domain and range of the function?

c) Determine the cost of printing 1000 newsletters.

d) Explain what is meant by $C(250)$.

7. A helicopter 100 m from an observer takes off vertically. It is not allowed to fly higher than 2000 m.

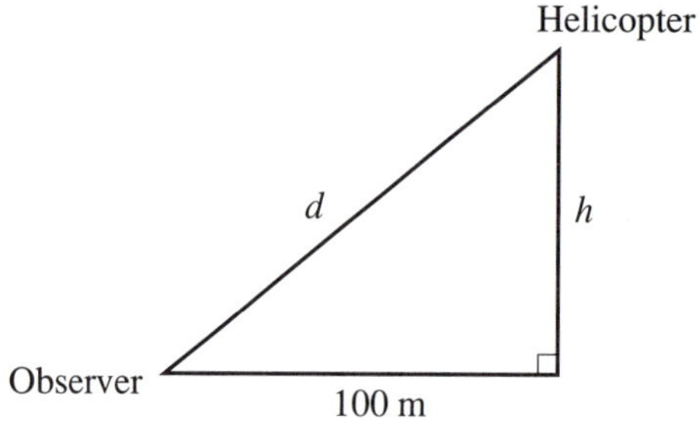

Assume that the helicopter and the observer are standing on level ground.

a) Use the Pythagorean Theorem to express the distance, d metres, of the person from the helicopter as a function of the height, h metres, of the helicopter.

b) Draw a graph of the function.

c) What are the domain and range of the function?

d) Explain the meaning of $d(50)$.

Part C

The Chapter Project combines many skills and concepts in a single problem. Here is a sampling of possible student work from different stages of the Project. Review these samples to gain insights into your own project work.

8. Here are the results of a student's completed spreadsheet and graph for the epidemic simulation on page 136.

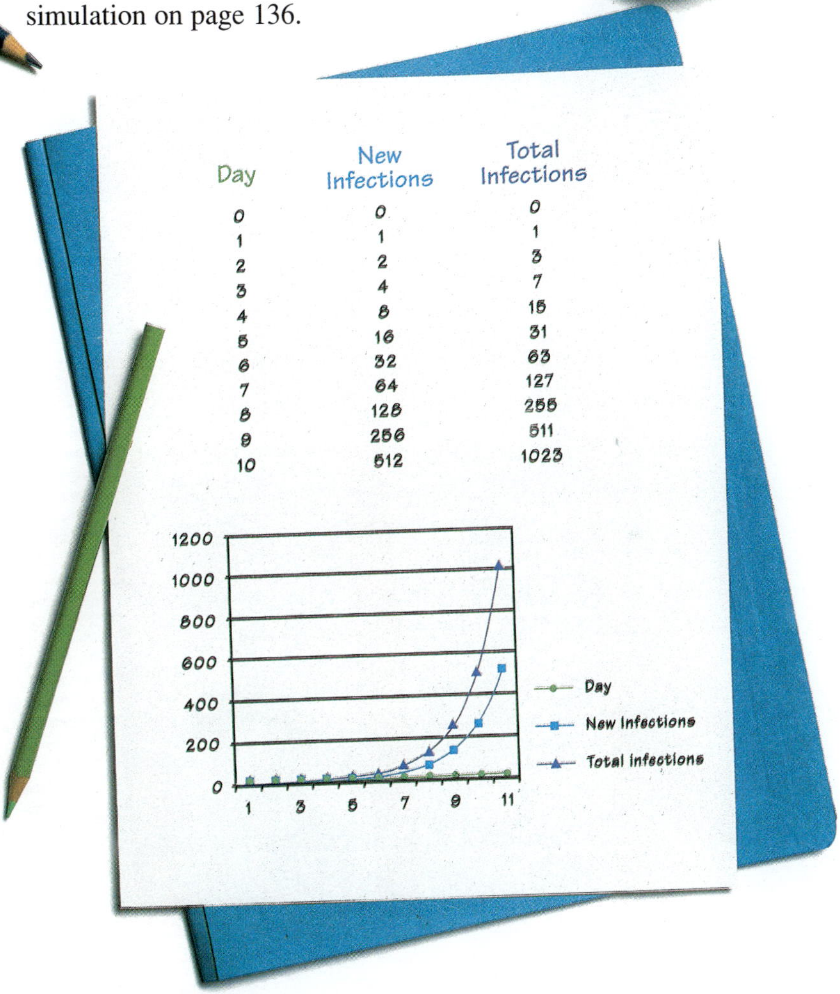

- Was the spreadsheet set up correctly? Explain.
- Check whether the student has used appropriate formulas. Are all the numerical results correct?
- Is the graph clear and easy to read? Does it accurately reflect the results in the spreadsheet?

Write a summary of your assessment of this student's work.

9. Here is the same student's final article, on Ebola.

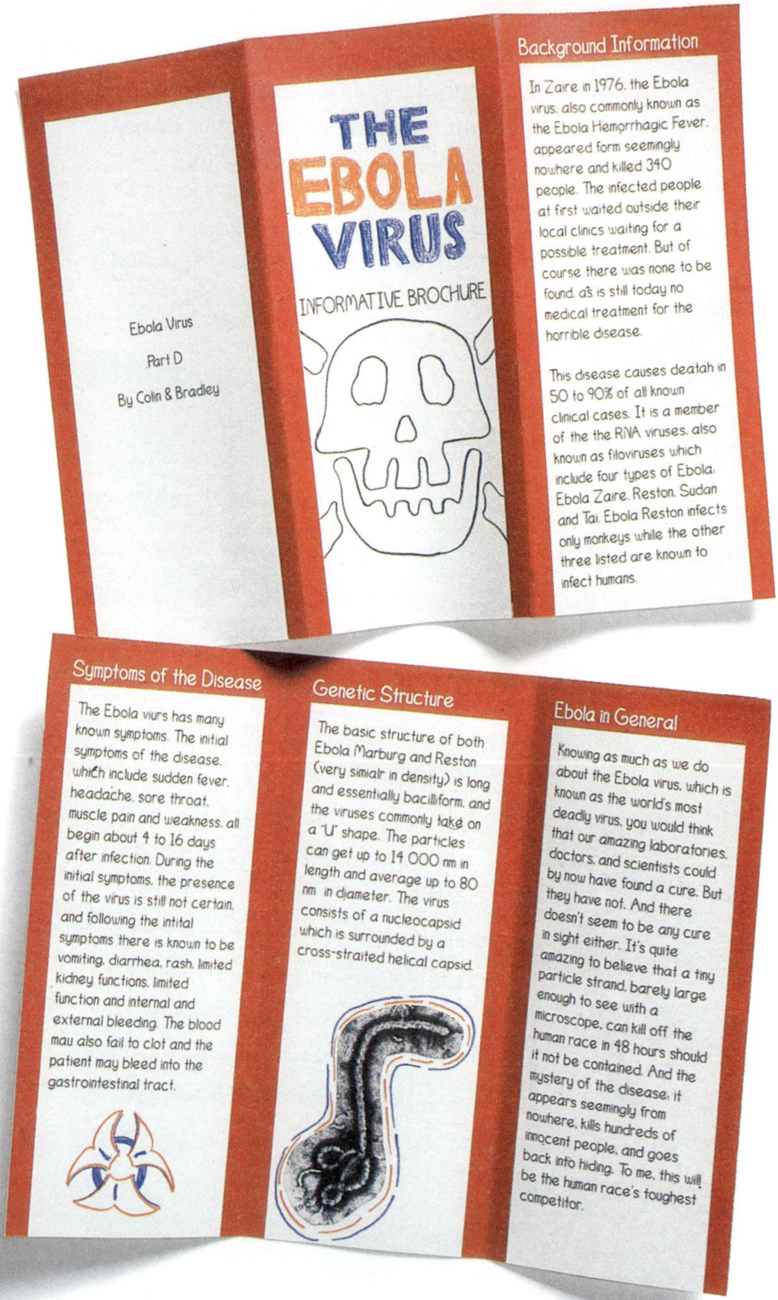

THE EBOLA VIRUS

INFORMATIVE BROCHURE

Ebola Virus

Part D

By Colin & Bradley

Background Information

In Zaire in 1976, the Ebola virus, also commonly known as the Ebola Hemorrhagic Fever, appeared form seemingly nowhere and killed 340 people. The infected people at first waited outside their local clinics waiting for a possible treatment. But of course there was none to be found, as is still today no medical treatment for the horrible disease.

This disease causes deatah in 50 to 90% of all known clinical cases. It is a member of the the RNA viruses, also known as filoviruses which include four types of Ebola: Ebola Zaire, Reston, Sudan and Tai. Ebola Reston infects only monkeys while the other three listed are known to infect humans.

Symptoms of the Disease

The Ebola viurs has many known symptoms. The initial symptoms of the disease, which include sudden fever, headache, sore throat, muscle pain and weakness, all begin about 4 to 16 days after infection. During the initial symptoms, the presence of the virus is still not certain, and following the intital symptoms there is known to be vomiting, diarrhea, rash, limited kidney functions, limited function and internal and external bleeding. The blood mau also fail to clot and the patient may bleed into the gastrointestinal tract.

Genetic Structure

The basic structure of both Ebola Marburg and Reston (very simialr in density) is long and essentially bacilliform, and the viruses commonly take on a 'U' shape. The particles can get up to 14 000 nm in length and average up to 80 nm in diameter. The virus consists of a nucleocapsid which is surrounded by a cross-straited helical capsid.

Ebola in General

Knowing as much as we do about the Ebola virus, which is known as the world's most deadly virus, you would think that our amazing laboratories, doctors, and scientists could by now have found a cure. But they have not. And there doesn't seem to be any cure in sight either. It's quite amazing to believe that a tiny particle strand, barely large enough to see with a microscope, can kill off the human race in 48 hours should it not be contained. And the mystery of the disease, it appears seemingly from nowhere, kills hundreds of innocent people, and goes back into hiding. To me, this will be the human race's toughest competitor.

- Read the article. Are the statements accurate? Is there a logical flow in the ideas?
- Has the student clearly conveyed the mathematical patterning underlying the gravity of the epidemic?
- How do the student's graphic displays help to support the written work?

Write a summary of your assessment of this student's work.

4 Sampling

PROJECT

You should do at least one project that uses the skills you learn in this chapter. The recommended projects in the Project Book are:

- Students' Choice Awards
- Ecosystem Study
- The News

Overview

Chapter Section	Skills and Concepts
Chapter Project: Look Before You Leap! page 164	Research setting up a business
Tutorial 4.1: Why Sample? page 166	Identify the need to sample
Tutorial 4.2: Reliability, Validity, and Bias, page 171	Identify bias in sampling
Tutorial 4.3: The Gathering of Data, page 176	Recognize commonly used biased sampling techniques
Tutorial 4.4: Sampling Techniques, page 180	Recognize statistically sound sampling techniques
Tutorial 4.5: Survey Design, page 186	Design a survey to sample a population
Chapter Project: Gathering Reliable Information, page 190	Design and conduct a survey to test the feasibility of a proposed business
Consolidating Your Skills, page 192	Review work of chapter; review student project work

Look Before You Leap!

Would you like to make money *your* way? Many students become entrepreneurs entirely on their own or through a program like Junior Achievement.

In Chapter 2 you planned to open your own store. In this chapter you'll be introduced to *how* you might plan ahead to undertake a project such as starting a business, coordinating a fundraising project, or proposing new activities for your students' council.

To make money in business, you need to plan ahead to provide the products and services that interest people. Here are some questions for you to consider.

- How would you determine the potential customers' interest in your particular business or service?
- How would you decide what range of products or services to offer? What should your prices be?
- How would you describe the typical client or customer for your business? What is the age or income group?
- How would you monitor your customers' satisfaction with your product and service to help you improve your business?

Conduct some research on sampling the target population. Sources of information include the Internet and the library.

You will return to this Chapter Project on page 190 of this chapter.

CHAPTER PROJECT

To do this Chapter Project, you need to use reliable and valid sampling procedures that will enable you to make critical business decisions. Complete *Tutorials 4.1* to *4.4* to develop an understanding of the necessary concepts. You will return to this Chapter Project on page 190.

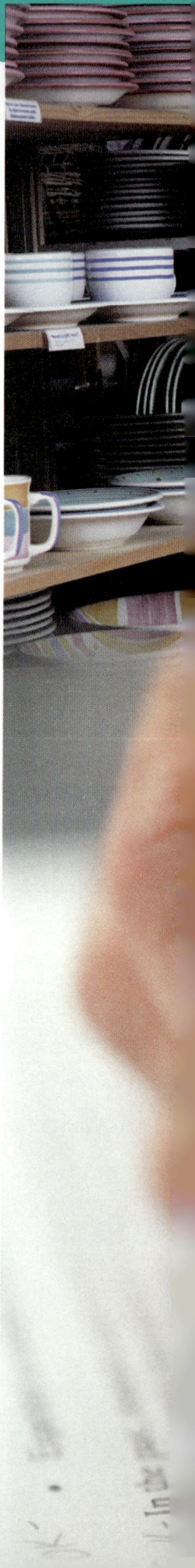

FYI Visit: www.awl.com/canada/school/connections/

You can start your research from our Internet site: Click on MATHLINKS, followed by the *Applied Mathematics 10* logo. Then select a topic under Sampling.

TUTORIAL 4.1

Why Sample?

Frequently, a business, an organization, or a political party wishes to find out what people think about an idea. To do this, a *sample* of people are consulted. That is, only a small number of those who could have been asked are consulted. All of the people who could have been consulted make up the *population*.

Sampling is used to gain information about a very large body of people or things by testing or observing only a portion of it. For example, a company that conducts a national survey to identify trends in Canada may interview 1000 of the 18 000 000 people in Canada who are over 18 years of age.

Think of some of your community's organizations and what information they like to have about people.

Investigation 1 Being One and Only

What percent of the population grew up as "an ONLY child"? With a partner, consider how this question can be answered.

1. Identify the population. You are certainly not about to say something about the entire population of this planet. Perhaps you could comment on the population of Canada … , British Columbia … , Victoria ... , or simply My Secondary School.

2. There are too many people to ask, even in a school. How else can you obtain this information for this population?

3. Consider for the moment that the population is your class. Choose a small sample of 6 or 7 people from your class. Determine the percentage of "only children" in the sample. How well do you think this value compares to the actual percentage in the class? Check your answers by surveying your class.

4. Determine the true percentage of "only children" within your class. Describe how well your sample result compares to this actual percentage.

5. Now consider the whole class to be a sample. Describe how well this sample compares to the true population percentage for the school.

Investigation 2

Home, but not Alone

What is the average number of children in a family? Again, we should limit our population, since the figures vary widely in different parts of the world.

1. Draw a sample from your class. Determine the percentage of students with no siblings, 1 sibling , 2 siblings, 3 siblings, ... How well would these estimates compare to the true population percentages?

2. Determine the average number of children in the sample.

3. Determine the average number of children in a family in your class. Check your answer by taking a class survey.

4. Compare the results of exercises 2 and 3.

Example

Identify a possible population

For each study described, what is the population about which the information is sought?

a) To assess the opinions of Canadians regarding which team will win the Grey Cup, researchers conducted telephone surveys of 1000 people selected from the Winnipeg telephone book.

b) To assess the support of the Canadian people for an increase in funding for health care, the researchers counted the number of callers for and against to a radio call-in show.

c) To determine what legal driving age is preferred by Canadian teenagers, researchers interviewed 2000 high school students from across Canada.

SOLUTION

Many different answers are possible for each part of this question. Each sample may be considered as a subgroup of many different groups. Some possible answers are:

a) The people who live in Winnipeg, or the people who live in Manitoba, or all Canadians.

b) Radio listeners, or people with access to a telephone on the evening the show aired, or all Canadians.

c) High school students, or all Canadian teenagers, or all Canadians.

DISCUSSING THE IDEAS

1. Discuss what the problems and limitations might be in getting and using population data.

2. A *census* is an official count of the people living in a region or country. Describe how the federal or a provincial government collects census data. How much might such a project cost? How often do you think such information about the entire population is gathered? Check your answers by researching these subjects on the Internet or at the library.

3. Based on *Investigation 1*, what percent of your school population are "only children"? Discuss whether your conclusion is reasonable.

4. What is the most common number of children in a family? Discuss the difference between finding the number of siblings, and the average number of children in a family.

EXERCISES

Checking Your Skills

1. Identify the population you would sample for an opinion on each topic.

a) public transit fares

b) minimum driving age

c) the GST

d) the legal drinking age for Canadian teenagers

e) who will win the Stanley Cup this year

2. Identify the segment of the school population you would sample for an opinion on each topic.

   a) student parking spaces
   b) cafeteria food
   c) fees for athletic teams

3. Give an example of sampling as a technique for gathering information

   a) at home.
   b) at school.
   c) at the workplace.
   d) for a medical test.

4. Find census data in the library or by using the Internet that would summarize population information for your province or territory, and for Canada. What are the problems associated with gathering such information?

5. Many newspaper articles contain reports of surveys. An example is given on page 186. Find a newspaper article containing a report of a survey. What data are given as evidence for a conclusion? Do you find this information believable?

6. Many provincial and national polls gather information from 500 to 1000 respondents. Do you feel these numbers are adequate? Explain why or why not.

Extending Your Thinking

7. In each situation, why would data be collected from a sample and not from the population?

a) To find the average age of drivers when they get their drivers' licences.

b) To find the number of hours a high-efficiency light bulb will burn.

c) To find the average volume of milk in a 2-L carton.

8. Refer to exercise 6. Suppose you are able to sample a larger portion of the population. Would this give better estimates? Explain why or why not.

9. Collect a few survey results from a newspaper and keep a record of the number of respondents and the "margin of error" in each article. Describe what you think is the relationship between the two. Create a display for a bulletin board.

PROJECTS

In this Tutorial, you learned what is meant by sampling. You will use this knowledge in the Chapter Project and for the following projects in the Project Book.

- Students' Choice Awards
- Ecosystem Study
- The News

COMMUNICATING THE IDEAS

Describe the difference between a population and a sample, and the pros and cons of sampling instead of taking a census.

TUTORIAL 4.2

Reliability, Validity, and Bias

When a sample is not representative of a population, we say that it is *biased*. Nothing invalidates a conclusion faster than bias. In statistics, bias is one component of *reliability*, the measure of whether a sample statistic can be duplicated in another survey. A *sample statistic* is a numerical value that describes a characteristic of a sample. Naturally, with a biased or non-representative sample, it is likely that the measure of reliability will be low.

Investigation 1 Just Like You

1. Choose a new CD or movie that you like. Ask 5 friends in your class what they think of the CD or movie. Gauging from their responses, predict what the population of your school might say.
2. Ask the same question of 5 students in your class whom you do not know as well. Describe any differences in their responses compared to what your friends thought of the CD or movie.
3. Choose 5 students at random and ask the same question.

Practise Your Prior Skills

In the Investigation that follows, you must draw a scatterplot and consider the appropriateness of drawing a line of best fit for the data. Try the following exercise for preliminary review.

1. The following data represent the sales of a store in millions of dollars for a 10-year period.

Year	1	2	3	4	5	6	7	8	9	10
Sales ($)	1.36	1.44	1.69	1.84	2.14	2.59	2.75	2.89	2.95	3.15

a) Draw a scatterplot of the data. Represent the year along the x-axis and the sales on the y-axis. Choose suitable scales.

b) Use a clear ruler to draw an estimated line of best fit for the data.

STUDENT REFERENCE

If you need to see an explanation of a "line of best fit," look in the Student Reference section.

Investigation 2

Validity

Validity is an indicator of how well a test measures what it's meant to measure. A sample statistic is valid if it closely approximates the same quantity for the whole population.

In this Investigation, you will collect data in your class relating to the number of concerts attended last year and the number of recordings owned. Choose to survey either CDs or cassette tapes.

1. Do you expect there to be a relationship between these two?

2. In your notebook, on a computer spreadsheet, or on your graphing calculator, create a table like the one below.

Student	Number of concerts attended last year (x)	Number of recordings owned (y)
1		
2		
3		

3. Obtain a random sample of 10 students from your class. Ask each student the number of concerts attended last year and the number of recordings owned. Enter your results in the table.

4. Create a scatterplot of x against y.

5. Look at your scatterplot. Would drawing a line of best fit be reasonable? Can the number of recordings owned be predicted by the number of concerts attended?

6. Instead of sampling students to find the number of recordings owned, would using the graph and the number of concerts attended be as valid?

Example **Determine the validity of a survey result**

A phone-in survey conducted in Calgary indicates that "...80% of Calgarians favour a Formula One race in the middle of the city." Explain why this result may not be valid.

SOLUTION

The quotation makes a claim about Calgarians. For the result to be valid this must be an accurate indication of the views of all Calgarians.

The sample of the population surveyed should be representative of the people of Calgary in all ages, areas of residence, interests, and so on. This may not be the case with a phone-in survey. Only people who are really interested in the race will respond by phone. The result may not be valid if the number of people surveyed was too small. For example, the results from a sample of size 5 may be unreliable and not an accurate indication of the result for the whole population of Calgary.

DISCUSSING THE IDEAS

1. Discuss whether your friends' preferences in *Investigation 1* were typical of the entire class. What might that say about you?

2. Discuss some statistics often used to predict performance in sports and the validity of the survey measurements.

3. Describe how a poorly selected sample can be biased.

4. Explain how a biased sample is not reliable, yet an unbiased sample may not be valid.

EXERCISES

Checking Your Skills

1. Suppose most of the students in your grade were surveyed. The nearly unanimous conclusion was, "Canada is the mightiest hockey nation in the world."

a) What was the intent of the survey?

b) How do you think this could be determined?

c) Do you think the result of the survey was valid? Explain.

2. A magazine solicits opinions from its readers on the spending habits of teenagers. Comment on its reliability and validity.

3. The last referendum in your community was scheduled on the day of a snowstorm. The voter turnout was very low. Comment on the possible reliability and validity of the vote.

4. A chewing gum company advertises that 3 out of 4 dentists prefer its product. Comment on the implications of the advertisement.

5. A students' council needed to make a quick decision on the next Talent Show and sampled two grade 12 classes. Comment on the possible reliability and validity of the sample.

6. A university entrance program maintains a second language prerequisite for mathematics. Comment on the possible reliability and validity of the survey sample obtained of students and their marks in languages and mathematics.

7. The city firefighters unit just dropped its requirement of height and weight for new recruits. Comment on the possible reliability and validity of determining suitability based on height and weight.

8. Analyze the relationship between two measurements of players of some team game that interests you. If, for example, you choose basketball, consider the following questions.

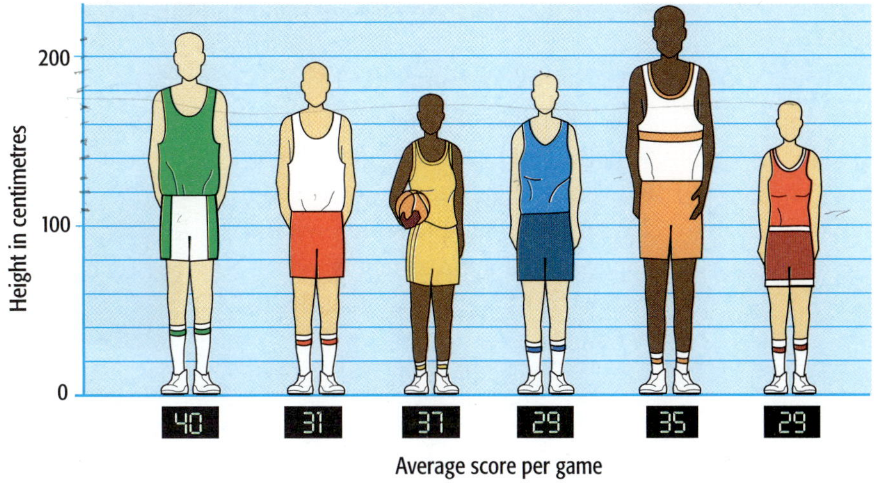

a) Obtain the statistics on 20 players' heights and scoring averages.

b) Create a scatterplot of height against points per game and draw an estimated line of best fit.

c) Can a player's average number of points per game be predicted by his or her height? Could the team's success be predicted by the heights of the players on a team?

d) Could a sample of players' heights predict their scoring averages?

Extending Your Thinking

9. Suppose you were asked to sample the population about an issue that may be controversial. Examples might include gun control, or using agricultural land for housing development. Is it possible to obtain an unbiased sample? How would you resolve any sampling difficulties?

PROJECTS

In this Tutorial, you learned about bias and its effect on reliability. You will use these ideas in the Chapter Project and in the following projects in the Project Book.

- Students' Choice Awards
- Ecosystem Study
- The News

COMMUNICATING THE IDEAS

Write a paragraph to explain why a valid sample is reliable.

TUTORIAL **4.3**

The Gathering of Data

Various companies use sampling to survey the Canadian population. They take great care that their samples are valid and reliable. Here are two examples.

- A.C. Neilsen monitors the TV viewing habits of Canadians. It samples 1500 Canadian households by installing monitoring devices on TV sets. This sample represents the population of approximately 10 500 000 TV viewing households in Canada.
- The Society of Composers, Authors, and Music Publishers of Canada (SOCAN) samples, in one year, about two weeks of air time on every Canadian radio station to decide how much royalties should be paid to each recording artist whose songs are played on the radio.

In order to obtain a survey with the least amount of work or planning, many organizations gather data in the most convenient or expedient way. Unfortunately, many of the problems associated with poor sampling are due to a lack of advance planning. Here are two biased, yet common, sampling methods you should recognize and avoid.

A. Convenience Sample

A convenient member or subgroup of the population is chosen. For example, your friends, teammates, or "approachable people" are sampled.

B. Self-Selected Sample

Only volunteers are sampled to represent the population. For example, the responses to a questionnaire available only to the subscribers of a magazine are considered a sample.

Example 1 **Identify the sampling method**

A shoe store conducts a survey of the most popular brands of athletic shoes before ordering for the new season. It asks the first 200 people in the mall who are wearing athletic shoes to respond.

a) What sampling method is used?

b) Are the data obtained likely to be valid? Explain.

SOLUTION

a) This is convenience sampling.

b) The data obtained are unlikely to be valid. For example, the age group of the people in the mall may depend on the day and the time of day. Further, the person wearing the athletic shoe may not be the one who decided which type of shoe to buy.

Example 2 **Identify the sampling method**

You intend to survey your school population to determine whether the students would attend another dance this month. Identify each sampling technique below. Comment on the validity of the data you would get.

a) You distribute a questionnaire to each student and wait for responses.

b) You ask your friends.

SOLUTION

a) This is a self-selected sample. The data may not be valid because only those interested would respond.

b) This is a convenience sample. The data may not be valid because your friends may agree with you, or they may not want to offend you.

Example 3 **Identify the sampling method**

An Edmonton company is hired by a newspaper to find out which team Canadians think will win the Stanley Cup later in the season. To collect data, the company considers sampling Canadians in one of the following ways.

a) Poll 1000 people in Alberta by visiting 10 NHL games and asking the first 100 people entering the stadium their opinion.

b) Put an advertisement in the newspaper asking people to mail in their preferences.

c) Send out questionnaires to 100 companies chosen randomly from a listing of Canadian businesses, to be completed by anyone at all in the company.

SOLUTION

a) Preferences in sports are often regional. A sample of people attending NHL games in Alberta is not likely to be representative of the opinions of all Canadians. This is a convenience sample.

b) Generally, only ardent hockey fans would take the trouble to mail in a response to this advertisement. This is a self-selected sample.

c) This sample would be likely to exclude many groups of the population, such as farmers, homemakers, or senior citizens. This is a convenience sample.

DISCUSSING THE IDEAS

1. Why is a sample obtained from "approachable" people not representative of the population?

2. Consider the segment of the population who typically do not respond to questionnaires. Discuss if and how their responses may be different from those who feel they need to respond.

EXERCISES

Checking Your Skills

1. A suggestion box is left in the school hallway to obtain students' reactions to a new school policy. Comment on the reliability of the sample.

2. A gardening magazine publishes photographs of the 3 gardens that the editors have pre-selected in the annual search for the best garden and invites its readers to vote for the grand prize winner. Comment on the reliability of the sample.

3. In a chili cook-off, the general public attending the contest are allowed to sample as many of the recipes of the 20 contestants as they wish, and then cast their votes for the Best Chili award. Comment on the sampling method.

4. What questions could you ask about the reliability or validity of an automobile owner's satisfaction survey?

5. A TV program chooses its Movie of the Week according to the votes cast by viewers phoning one of two 1-900 phone numbers. Comment on the sampling technique.

6. In order to provide quality control, the foreman inspects a random sample from the batch of items assembled by 9:30 a.m. each morning. Comment on the sampling technique.

Extending Your Thinking

7. Each summer, major league baseball holds an All-Star Game that pits the American League against the National League. The players in the starting lineups are chosen by baseball fans. For a few weeks prior to the All-Star Game, voting cards are distributed to people who attend all major league games. People punch holes in these cards to register their choices. Give some reasons why this method may not result in the best players playing in the All-Star Game.

Communicating the Ideas

Think of the problems that may arise with a convenience sample or a self-selected sample. Organize your thoughts and create an outline or web.

TUTORIAL

4.4 Sampling Techniques

In order to minimize bias, several reliable sampling techniques are commonly used. Many of the statistically sound methods use a list of random numbers. This is a list of digits selected in such a way that each digit has an equal chance of occurring. There are many ways of obtaining random numbers, such as:

1. Use a spinner. Place a circular object such as a pop can on a piece of card and draw round the base. Cut out the circular disc and divide it into 10 equal sectors as shown. Label the sectors from 0 to 9. To make a spinner, use a paper clip as shown. Spin it about a pencil. Write down the number on which it lands.

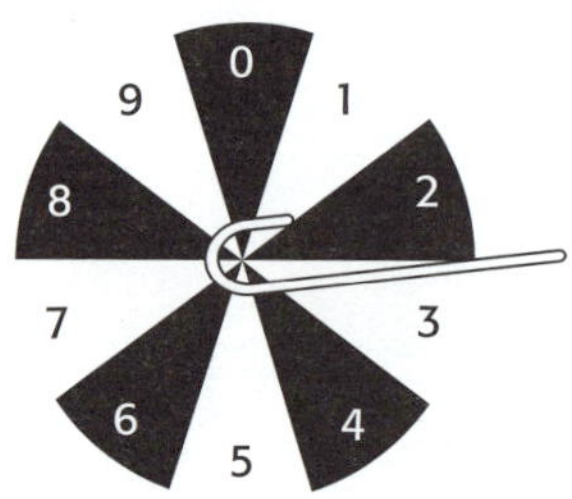

Use the spinner to generate as many digits as you need. These are random numbers.

2. Use a telephone directory. Turn to any white page of a telephone directory. Without looking, put a pencil point on a number. Write down the last digit of this number. Repeat until you have as many random numbers as you want.

3. Use a graphing calculator.

UTILITY

If you have never used a graphing calculator to generate random numbers, Utility 11 shows you how to do this.

4. Use a spreadsheet program on a computer. Start a new spreadsheet document. Enter the text and numbers shown in the first and third rows.

	A	B	C	D	E
1	Random Number Generator				
2					
3	Lowest:	0	Highest:	9	
4					
5	9	6	8	5	5
6	0	5	2	0	4
7	5	0	4	7	2
8	3	3	4	8	7
9	3	5	3	1	1

In cell A5, enter this formula:

- for Microsoft Works and Microsoft Excel
  =INT(RAND()*($D$3–$B$3+1))+$B$3
- for ClarisWorks
  =INT(($D$3–$B$3+1)*RAND())+$B$3

Copy this formula down and to the right block of cells to generate a set of random numbers. These will be random numbers in which the lowest digit is the number in cell B3 and the highest in cell D3. You can change these numbers to generate sets of random numbers between any two digits you want.

Here are some statistically sound sampling methods. These can be effectively incorporated into your projects.

A. Simple Random Sample

If every member of the population has an equal chance of being selected, a sample drawn is called a *simple random sample*. For example, if a sample of 5 students is required to test a new candy, then these can be obtained using a "names in a hat" method if the population is small, such as a class of 30. Each person writes her or his name on an identical piece of paper. All the pieces of paper are put into a large bowl. The pieces are thoroughly mixed, and a piece drawn. This is repeated until 5 pieces of paper are obtained.

To draw names from a bowl would be unmanageable for a large population, such as the whole school. A better way is to use random numbers to produce the random sampling. Assign a number to each student in the school. If there are less than 1000 students in the school (for example, if there are 432), we need to generate 3-digit random numbers. This can be done from a list by grouping the digits in threes, then discarding any numbers, such as 653, that are too large to correspond to the number of a student. Technology will give random integers within a given range.

Although theoretically the most reliable sampling method, logistically, it may not be possible: for example, in situations when testing an item destroys it.

B. Systematic Sample

If every *n*th member of the population is selected, it is called a *systematic sample*. For example, to select a sample from your class the teacher chooses every 4th student entering the room. This technique assumes that students enter a room in random order — this may or may not be true.

Systematic sampling is often used in industry for quality control purposes. A company may decide to test an item from a production line every 5 minutes, or perhaps every 10th item, to ensure that the quality of the product is acceptable.

C. Cluster Sample

The population is subdivided into non-overlapping subgroups or clusters, and every member of a randomly chosen subgroup is part of the sample. For example, in order to randomly draw some grade 10 students from the eight divisions in the grade (10A, 10B, …), a division is randomly chosen. Then every student in that entire division is in the sample. This method assumes that each cluster contains members who were randomly selected.

D. Stratified Random Sample

When sampling very large populations, we can sometimes divide the population into subgroups on the basis of some characteristic. For example, a school population can be subdivided into grade levels. These subgroups are called *strata*.

The population is subdivided into subgroups, and a predetermined number of members are chosen from each subgroup. For example, three students are sampled from each of the eight divisions in the grade.

Stratified random sampling allows us to take a number of samples from each segment proportional to the size of the segment. For example, suppose a school has a student body where there are 500 students in grade 10, 400 students in grade 11, and 450 students in grade 12. When sampling the school, we might choose to randomly select 10 students from grade 10, 8 students from grade 11, and 9 from grade 12, to reflect the number of students in each grade.

Example **Identify the sampling method**

You intend to survey your school population to determine whether the students would attend another dance this month. Identify each sampling technique below. Comment on the validity of the data you would get.

a) You ask every third person passing through the hall.

b) You obtain all the class lists and generate random numbers to identify who should be in your sample. Then you ask those students.

c) You use numbers to select one class from each grade at random, then use random numbers again to pick names from each class. Then you ask those students.

SOLUTION

a) This is a systematic sample. The data may not be valid if only certain students are likely to be in the hall at that particular time.

b) This is a simple random sample. The data should be valid because every student in the school has an equal chance of being selected.

c) This is a stratified sample. Although every student does not have an equal chance of being selected, the data should be valid.

DISCUSSING THE IDEAS

1. For a simple random sample, how would you ensure that every member would have an equal chance of being selected?

2. Why should you always ignore the first three digits when you generate random numbers using a telephone directory?

3. A small sample is obtained systematically. If you come to a conclusion, how valid will it be for the large population?

4. You plan to conduct a survey of your community or city. Explain the difference between a cluster sample and a stratified random sample in this context.

EXERCISES

Checking Your Skills

1. A television program conducts a regular survey by asking viewers to call one of two 1-900 phone numbers to cast a vote. Is the sample obtained in this way a random sample? Explain.

2. The computer system of a large hospital contains the records for 60 000 patients. The records are numbered sequentially from 1 to 60 000. The hospital administrator wishes to determine the level of satisfaction of patients with hospital food. She sampled the records by choosing the records numbered 100, 200, 300, and so on. What type of sampling did she use?

3. Describe how you might obtain

a) a simple random sample from the school population.

b) a systematic sample of cars in a parking lot.

c) a cluster sample of residents in a city.

d) a stratified random sample of strawberries in a field.

4. The school cafeteria would like to introduce a new vegetarian pizza. How should the population be sampled to determine which of 3 possible toppings should be introduced?

5. Purchasing decisions by wine purchasing agents often involve a ritual in which a small amount of wine is examined for bouquet, flavour, and taste. Is a mouthful a suitable random sample? Explain.

6. Your mother probably engages in random sampling as she tests a cake with a toothpick. Is this a reliable random sample?

7. A manufacturer of widgets would like to maintain quality control through random sampling. How might this be done?

Extending Your Thinking

8. A school population comprises grades 8 through 12, distributed approximately as follows.

Grade	8	9	10	11	12
Students	300	400	450	450	400

The school council wishes to conduct a survey of the number of hours of extracurricular activities in which students are involved. How would you advise them to choose a sample of the school population? Explain why you chose that method rather than any other.

PROJECTS

In this Tutorial, you learned some sampling methods. You will use these in the Chapter Project and in the following projects in the Project Book.

- Students' Choice Awards
- Ecosystem Study
- The News

COMMUNICATING THE IDEAS

Describe in your journal the basic ideas behind effective and reliable sampling methods and the basic flaw behind the unreliable ones.

TUTORIAL 4.5

Survey Design

The details that accompany various surveys often distinguish how accurate and believable they are. Compare the following samples.

People near route strongly in favor of expanded skytrain, poll says

SCOTT SIMPSON
VANCOUVER SUN

People living within walking distance of the new SkyTrain route are over-whelmingly in favour of building more rapid transit in the Lower Mainland, says a new Angus Reid poll released Monday by the Rapid Transit project office.

By contacting more than 3,500 residents and business people in Coquitlam, New Westminster and Burnaby between Sept. 21 and Oct. 22, pollsters found that 91 per cent want more rapid transit.

Pollsters went door-to-door along the SkyTrain route proposed to link New Westminster, through Coquitlam, to Burnaby's Lougheed Mall – a 6.5-kilometre line that could be operational within two years.

However, concern about potential negative impacts of the project remains strong – 40 per cent of those in favour are worried that SkyTrain will lead to an increase in crime.

Project director Lecia Stewart, referring to a Canadian Facts poll last summer that pegged support for SkyTrain at 71 per cent across the region, noted that the level of support for the new line appears to be climbing – in spite of opposition that has emerged in some neighbourhoods along the route.

"We thought we would run into diminishing support as we got closer," Stewart said. "In fact, our support is higher, which shows that people understand the benefits of rapid transit and they believe it will help their lives."

Stewart said the most encouraging part of the poll was an indication by almost half of all respondents that they would leave their cars at home and use SkyTrain once the line is built.

"Those are new customers to transit," she said. "When was the last time we made that kind of a modal shift from the automobile to a rapid transit system?

"In this business, let me tell you, if you shift one or two per cent of market share, that's huge, because it's a mass product."

However, the survey is being criticized as too general by a spokesman for a coalition of ratepayers in New Westminster who feel the line will intrude on their community.

Although the project office will not announce until later this month its plans for a section of the route along East Columbia Street, residents of the Fraserview – Jamieson Court area doubt the government will accede to their wishes and put the line in a tunnel.

A tunnel would eliminate noise and protect their views of the Fraser River – but would boost construction costs by $100 million, according to the project office.

Ratepayers coalition leader Jerry Kielmann said he is not surprised by the survey results, describing rapid transit as a motherhood issue that enjoys almost universal support.

But he said the Rapid Transit project office is using surveys to mask its own lack of attention to critical details of the project, and its determination to over-ride neighbourhood concerns in its haste to get the line built.

Keilmann said: "It's not about SkyTrain per se, it's about the lack of process. Our rights as taxpayers and voters are being violated and trampled on. We have not had a process."

Half of respondents to the Angus Reid survey cited the possibility that the system will reduce traffic congestion as the main reason for their support.

The poll is considered accurate within plus or minus 1.6 percentage points 19 times out of 20.

Nov. 10'98

KARMA & DOGMA

The Weekend Sun,
Saturday, May 3, 1997

A miscellany of fascinating facts and factoids, prosaic and profound

STATS QUO

More Internet numbers we refuse to stand behind

- 13 per cent (mostly men) have spent a night in jail.
- 70 per cent of us drink orange juice daily.
- Snickers is the most popular candy.
- 22 per cent of us skip lunch daily. Nine per cent of us skip breakfast daily.
- 66 per cent of us eat cereal regularly.
- 22 per cent of all restaurant meals include french fries.
- 14 per cent of us eat the watermelon seeds.
- Only 13 per cent brush our teeth from side to side
- 45 per cent use mouthwash every day.

KIDSDAY POLL

Hold that door – Survey finds older people are more polite

BILLY ARCHER and STEVEN CARALE
Kidsday staff Reporters

Are people polite? Do they take the time to say thank you anymore, or are they just too busy? We wanted to find out so we conducted a test at a local shopping mall.

We spent an hour just holding the door for people going in and out of the mall. We wanted to see if people still had manners, and were kind enough to say thank you. Here is what we found out:

MALE, SAID THANK YOU, SAID NOTHING

Men, 69, 23.
Teens, 4, 5.
Younger boys, 3, 10.

FEMALE, SAID THANK YOU, SAID NOTHING

Women, 94, 17.
Teens, 35, 8.
Younger Girls, 4, 6.

Most people were polite, but we did find that older people were more polite than younger people. We appreciate it when someone says thank you when we are being courteous.

Los Angeles Times•Washington Post

The first is accompanied by a disclaimer about its reliability. The second shows some results but no indication of the sampling method. The third seems more technical in detail.

In order to conduct a reliable survey, some key components have to be considered.

1. the *identification* of the population
2. a clear and precise *wording* of the question
3. a reliable *sampling method*
4. a detailed plan including *where* and *how* the question will be posed
5. a calculation of the *statistic*
6. a *conclusion* with an inference about the population

An *inference* is a conclusion about a population based on data from a sample.

Example 1 **Design a survey**

Your students' council would like to know if they should change the kind of music played over the PA during lunch. How would you survey the student body to determine if a change is needed?

SOLUTION

- The population is the entire student body.
- The question might be worded "Are you generally satisfied with the choice of music played over the PA by students' council during lunch hour?"
- A stratified random sample might help. Toss a die (6- or 10- or 20-sided as necessary) or use the random number generator on your calculator to choose two divisions per grade. Then toss the die or use your calculator to choose 5 students from each of the chosen divisions.
- With the help of your students' council sponsor, find out where these students might be after lunch. With the permission of the classroom teacher, ask the question as worded above.
- The conclusion will read "___ percent of those surveyed were satisfied with council's choice of music during lunch hour."

DISCUSSING THE IDEAS

1. In the example, the student body is identified as the population. Are any people left out of the survey? If so, do their opinions matter?
2. A Yes/No response is solicited to the question about lunch hour music. What other question could be posed? What responses might you anticipate? What inferences might be made?
3. What decisions might be made after inferences about the population are made?
4. All provinces and territories have privacy laws. How will these affect who you question and the question you ask?

EXERCISES

Checking Your Skills

1. Choose one of the following issues. Design a survey to determine the opinions of your school population on the issue. Your design should include:

a) the question or questions you would ask

b) a description of how you would select an unbiased sample

c) a description of the steps you would take to conduct the survey

Issue 1: Should a franchise be allowed to run the school cafeteria?

Issue 2: Should students have to wear a uniform to school?

Issue 3: Should the school year be longer than it is now?

2. Choose one of the issues below. Design a survey to determine the opinions of people in your city or region on the issue. Your design should include:

a) the question or questions you would ask

b) a description of how you would select an unbiased sample

c) a description of the steps you would take to conduct the survey

Issue 1: Should people have to pay user fees for health care?

Issue 2: Should people who own guns be required to have a licence?

Issue 3: Should high school students be required to volunteer in the community?

Extending Your Thinking

3. You wish to determine which of 6 movies people predict will be the winner of the Oscar for Best Picture. Design a survey question and a sampling strategy. Note any concerns you may have before the results are tabulated.

PROJECTS

In this Tutorial, you learned about survey design. You will use this in the Chapter Project and in the following projects in the Project Book.

- Students' Choice Awards
- The News

COMMUNICATING THE IDEAS

Designing a survey requires careful planning and attention to detail. Discuss why each of the six ingredients listed in this Tutorial is important in a well-designed survey.

Gathering Reliable Information

At the beginning of this chapter, you considered questions about how you might plan for a successful business venture. Choose a type of business you would like to develop, for example, the store you worked with in Chapter 2.

Use the skills from this chapter to conduct a survey of the community in which your business will be located. Refer to page 188.

- Determine the population that will be sampled. You need to determine the feasibility of your venture in terms of business hours, the price structure, and the new product or service that will be offered.
- Determine the precise wording of the question(s) that will be posed. Avoid words and phrases that may be misunderstood and take into account privacy laws. Define terms if necessary.
- Select a reliable method of sampling.
- Conduct the survey.
- Analyze the results.
- Prepare your report. Include a description of the venture planned, your survey, and the results of your analysis.

Career Skills

Several polling firms focus on meeting the needs of businesses, organizations, and individuals that desire to know what the public is thinking. Many newspaper articles now contain excellent reports of such surveys. The strategies that you have considered so far are part of the career skills of the employees of such firms.

What Do I Need To Know?

Tutorial	Skills and Concepts	Important Results and Formulas
4.1	• Identify the need to sample a population	• A population is all people or things being considered. • A sample is a representative portion of the population.
4.2	• Understand reliability • Identify bias in a sample • Understand validity of a survey	• Reliability is a measure of whether a sample statistic can be duplicated in another survey. • Bias indicates whether the sample is representative of the population. • Validity indicates how well a test measures what it is meant to measure.
4.3	• Identify convenience and self-selected samples as statistically unsound sampling methods	• A convenience sample is a sample chosen for the convenience of the pollster. • A self-selected sample consists only of volunteers from the population.
4.4	• Generate random numbers with and without technology • Understand and identify statistically sound sampling methods	• In a simple random sample, each member of the population has an equal chance of being selected. • In a systematic sample, every *n*th member of the population is chosen. • In a cluster sample, every member of a randomly selected segment of the population is chosen. • In a stratified random sample, the population is divided into subgroups and a predetermined number of each subgroup is chosen.
4.5	• Understand how to design a survey	

What Should I Be Able To Do?

After completing the work of the chapter, you should be able to answer the following questions. Use any source of information you need.

Part A

1. Design a survey to determine the average number of letters in the words of a particular book.
   a) What is the population you will sample?
   b) What kind of sampling method will you use? Justify your choice.
   c) Collect the data.
   d) Draw a graph of the data.
   e) Calculate the average for your sample.

Part B

2. Identify the population you would sample for an opinion on
   a) school cafeteria food.
   b) mathematics competition fees.
   c) the minimum driving age.
   d) free public transportation.

3. Identify the segment(s) of the population who would strongly bias a survey about each topic.
   a) gun control
   b) pit bull terriers as household pets
   c) gay rights

4. Professional pollsters take great care with the wording of a survey question to avoid bias.
   a) Write a biased survey question about the rating of a TV show.
   b) Reword the question to eliminate the bias.

5. The draft copy of the new course for grades 10 to 12 is sent to all mathematics teachers in the province or territory to solicit their comments. From the responses, the level of satisfaction with the course is determined and changes are made.
   a) Who do you think is most likely to respond to the survey?
   b) Do you think the data obtained would be valid? Explain.
   c) What kind of sampling method is being used?

6. Suppose you have to choose a simple random sample of 6 students from your class. List as many different ways as you can to choose 6 students at random.

7. Design a survey to determine the opinion of your school population on the issue of inline skaters being required to wear knee, elbow, and wrist protectors. Include:
   a) the question or questions you would ask
   b) a description of how you would select an unbiased sample
   c) a description of the steps you would take to conduct the survey

Part C

The Chapter Project combines many skills and concepts in a single problem. Here is a sampling of possible students' work from different stages of the Project. Review these samples to gain insight into your own project work.

8. Here is a sample of how one student designed his survey as required on page 190 .

Survey for "The Lid" Date: ____________________

1. Do you own any of the following types of hats?

A. Baseball cap with a team logo on it (i.e. Maple Leafs)	Yes	No
B. Baseball cap with a designer logo on it (i.e. Nike)	Yes	No
C. Baseball cap with another type of logo on it (i.e. Bands)	Yes	No
D. Normal Ski Toque	Yes	No
E. Designer Ski toque (Jester, Dr. Seuss)	Yes	No
F. Bandanas	Yes	No
G. Other: ____________		

2. How many hats do you buy a year? 0 1 2 3 4 more than 4

3. Which kind of hat woul.d you most likely buy in the near future?

A. Baseball cap with a team logo on it	Yes	No
B. Baseball cap with a designer logo on it	Yes	No
C. Baseball cap with another type of logo on it	Yes	No
D. Normal Ski toque	Yes	No
E. Designer Ski toque (Jester, Dr. Seuss)	Yes	No
F. Bandanas	Yes	No
G. Other: ____________		

4. What is the maximum price range you are willing to pay for the following:

	Dollars			
A. Baseball cap with a team logo on it	0-5	5-10	10-15	15-20
B. Baseball cap with a designer logo on it	0-5	5-10	10-15	15-20
C. Baseball cap with another type of logo on it	0-5	5-10	10-15	15-20
D. Normal Ski toque	0-5	5-10	10-15	15-20
E. Designer Ski toque (Jester, Dr. Seuss)	0-5	5-10	10-15	15-20
F. Bandanas	0-5	5-10	10-15	15-20

5. When do you normally shop at the mall?

Weekdays	9am - noon	noon - 3pm	3pm - 6pm	6pm - close
Weekends	9am - noon	noon - 3pm	3pm - 6 pm	6pm - close

Thank you for your time.

- Is the survey method reliable?
- Are the questions clear?

Write a summary of your assessment of this student's work.

9. Here is the same student's final calculations.

Survey results

Q1. Percentage that answered yes

A. 84% B. 42% C. 35%
D. 93% E. 33% F. 27%
G. 18%

Q2. Hats bought in a year

Hats bought in a year	Percentage
0	21%
1	48%
2	6%
3	8%
4	5%
More than 4	2%

Q3. Percentage that answered Yes

A. 34% B. 22% C. 12%
D. 6% E. 39% F. 16%
G. 8%

Q4. Percentage that chose the price range

	$0-5	$5-10	$10-15	$15-20
A.	5%	10%	30%	55%
B.	4%	15%	39%	42%
C.	12%	24%	38%	26%
D.	10%	54%	27%	9%
E.	14%	25%	48%	13%
F.	38%	32%	22%	8%

Q5. Percentage that spent the times at the mall

	9am-Noon	Noon-3pm	3pm -6pm	6pm - close
Weekdays	16%	27%	75%	81%
Weekends	30%	69%	54%	25%

Summary of Results

The survey was conducted at the local mall both on the weekend and during the weekday. A total of 200 people completed the survey, and they included teenagers right up to retired people. Both males and females were asked as well.

This venture would be successful if the store specialized in baseball caps and ski hats. 84% of the people surveyed owned a baseball cap with a team logo on it, and 93% own a ski toque. Close to half of those surveyed (48%) buy a hat every year, so there is quite a large market for them.

The price range for each type of hat would depend on the wholesale price, baseball caps could sell for $15.00 - $20.00.

With regards to staffing the store, the busiest times are on weekdays after 3pm and on weekends it is between noon and 6pm. It would require most staff at this time, and minimal staff at the other times.

- Did he make the correct interpretations of the results displayed by his calculator?
- Were his conclusions about the viability of the venture appropriate?

5 Line Segments

Overview

PROJECT

You should do at least one project that uses the skills you learn in this chapter. A recommended project in the Project Book is:

- Skiing in San Diego

Chapter Section	Skills and Concepts
Chapter Project: Designing a Water Ride, page 198	Research the design of a water ride
Tutorial 5.1: Distance, page 200	Understand the distance formula for line segments on a coordinate grid; solve problems using the distance formula on the coordinate plane
Tutorial 5.2: Slope, page 213	Understand the slope formula for line segments on a coordinate grid
Tutorial 5.3: Positive and Negative Slope, page 220	Understand and use positive and negative slopes
Chapter Project: Investigating Water Rides, page 230	Investigate the effect of change of slope on the distance travelled uphill
Tutorial 5.4: Slopes of Parallel and Perpendicular Line Segments, page 232	Understand the relationships between the slopes of parallel and perpendicular line segments on a coordinate grid
Tutorial 5.5: Midpoints, page 238	Understand the formula for the coordinates of the midpoint of a line segment on a coordinate grid
Chapter Project: Modelling a Water Ride, page 246	Design a water ride
Consolidating Your Skills, page 248	Review work of chapter; review student project work

Designing a Water Ride

A water ride combines the ideas of a water slide and roller coaster. Like a water slide, stairs are climbed at the start of a water ride, passengers sit on a rubber raft, and the riders end up splashing into a pool of water. There are both downhill and uphill sections on a water ride, just like a roller coaster.

Safety and fun are the primary concerns in designing a water ride. Mathematics, physics, and engineering concepts are all considered in the design.

You have been commissioned by Way-Cool Water Park to design a ride that gives the rider a choice of three water rides that vary in thrill level. Here are some initial questions to consider.

- How long should the water rides be?
- At what height above the ground should the riders start?
- Is there a minimum length or a maximum steepness for each uphill or downhill section?
- How do the length and steepness of the sections relate to the time and speed of each ride?
- Where should the supports be under each section of the ride?

Research water rides by using the Internet and the library.

CHAPTER PROJECT

To complete this Chapter Project, you will need to understand slope, and the relationship between slope and distance. Complete *Tutorials 5.1* to *5.3* to develop your skills. You will return to the Chapter Project on page 230.

FYI Visit: www.awl.com/canada/school/connections/

You can start your research from our Internet site: Click on MATHLINKS followed by the *Applied Mathematics 10* logo. Then select a topic under Designing a Water Ride.

TUTORIAL 5.1

Distance

Did you ever use a city map to locate a building downtown? If you did, you probably used a coordinate system to identify locations. Coordinate systems are used to locate the position of stars in the sky, cities on Earth's surface, and a cell on a spreadsheet document. The Cartesian coordinate system is useful to describe the position of points in a plane.

Practise Your Prior Skills

In this chapter, you will study *line segments*. A line segment is the part of a line joining two points. You will work with Cartesian coordinate grids. Try these exercises as preliminary review.

1. List the coordinates of the points A, B, C on the diagram below.

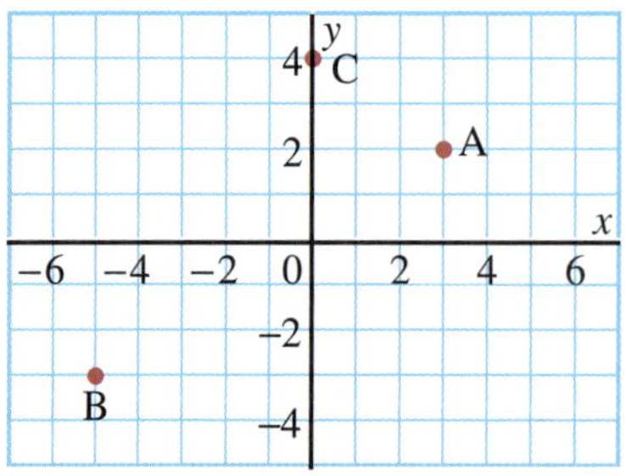

2. The coordinate axes divide the plane into 4 quadrants. Write mathematical statements about the coordinates of all points in quadrant IV.

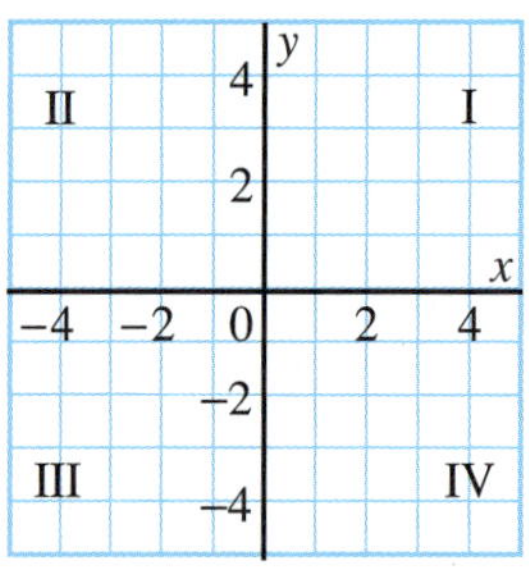

STUDENT REFERENCE

If you need further explanation of Cartesian coordinates, look up "coordinates" in the Student Reference.

When an oil-bearing formation is found under the earth's surface, data are taken to calculate the volume of oil in the formation. Data are collected on the thickness and area of the formation as well as the porosity (percentage of pore space in the rock). The thickness is found by sending special measurement tools down the oil well; the data are recorded as coordinates.

An interesting thing happens when drilling for oil: the well bends as it is being drilled and will end up being perpendicular to the plane of the formation.

horizontal oil-bearing formation

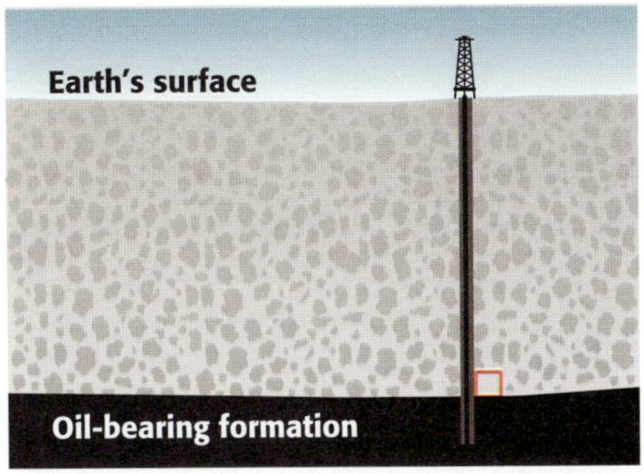

oblique oil-bearing formation

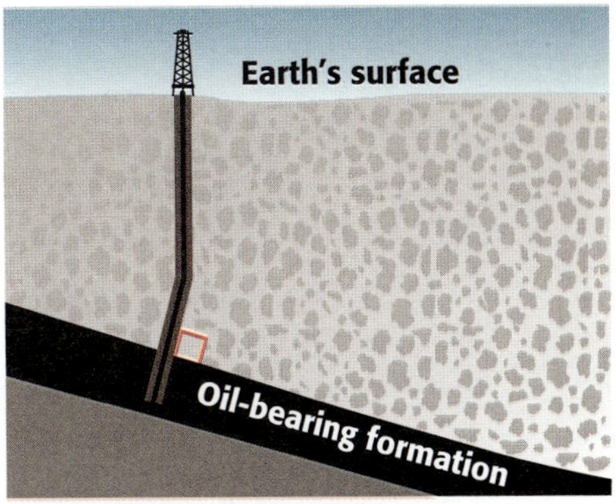

In mathematics, coordinate axes are drawn vertically and horizontally in the plane. In real life, this may not be the natural positions for the number lines used for axes, so we change their positions and label them accordingly.

Investigation 1

The Length of Vertical and Horizontal Line Segments

A well is drilled to a horizontal oil-bearing formation. The coordinates that are recorded for the top and bottom of the formation are (0, 800) and (0, 950). These numbers are in metres.

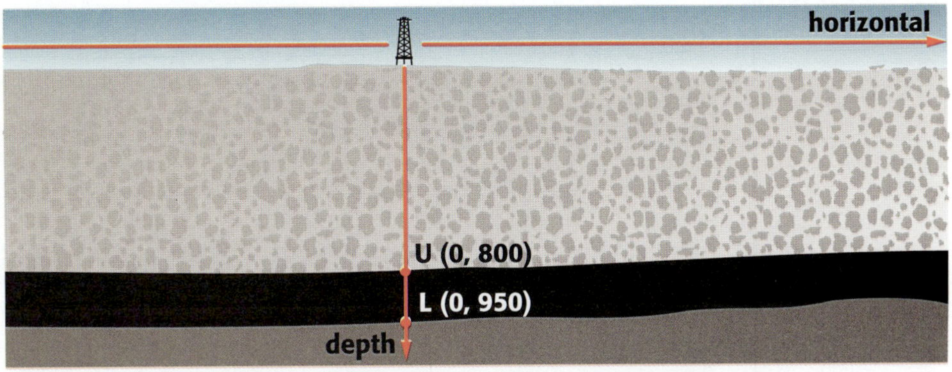

1. Look at the diagram. What is the length of the line segment UL?

2. How did you find the length of UL?

3. If you now consider points C(10, 800) and D(10, 950), how could you find the length of CD using only the numbers 800 and 950?

4. Is the order important when you work with the numbers in exercises 1 and 3? Explain.

5. How can you determine the vertical distance between two points from their coordinates without graphing?
6. Visualize the situation where two points are located on a horizontal line segment instead of a vertical line segment. How could the length of the line segment be found from the coordinates without graphing?

Practise Your Prior Skills

You will use the Pythagorean Theorem in *Investigation* 2. Try this exercise as preliminary review.

Use the Pythagorean Theorem to calculate x in the diagrams below. Give your answer to one decimal place.

1.

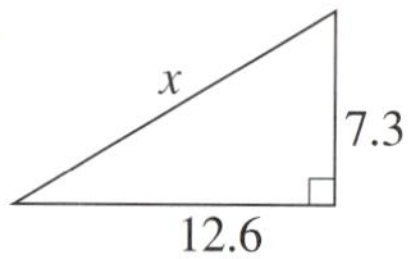

2.

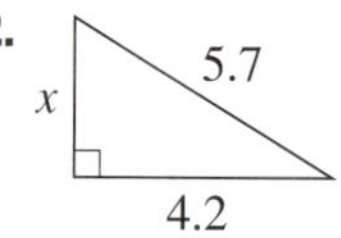

Investigation 2 The Distance between Two Points

You will need grid paper and a ruler.

Many cities in North America were built on a grid system, with the origin at some important building or feature.

Instead of using NE and so on to describe location, we can set up number lines as axes along Centre Avenue and Centre Street. If we choose scales, we have a coordinate system that we can use to describe location.

1. Use grid paper. Draw coordinate axes and mark the points A(–3, 3) and B(4, –2).

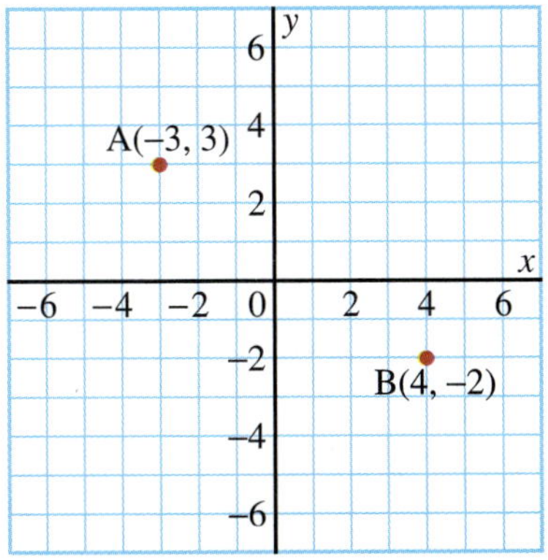

2. Draw a right △ABC for which AB is the hypotenuse.

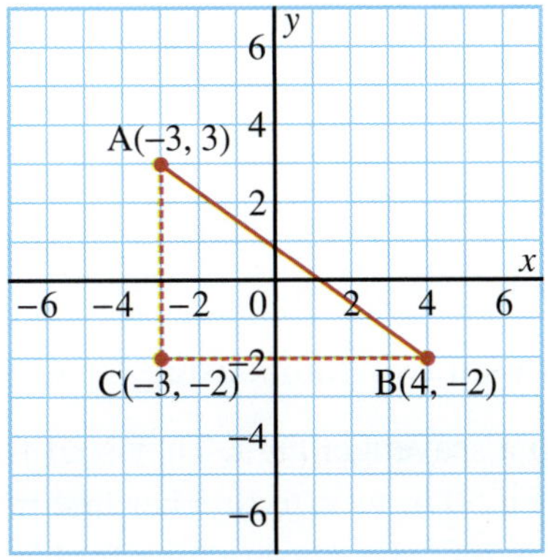

3. Use the results of *Investigation 1* to calculate the lengths of AC and CB.

4. Use the Pythagorean Theorem to write down an expression for the length of AB^2 in terms of AC and CB.

5. Use your results from exercises 3 and 4 to calculate the length of AB.

Develop a formula for the distance between any two points $A(x_A, y_A)$ and $B(x_B, y_B)$.

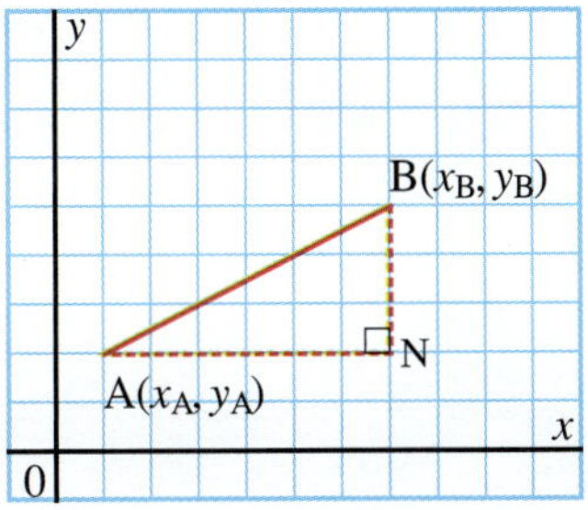

In the diagram, $\triangle$ABN is a right triangle. Recall from *Investigation 1*, the coordinates of N are (x_B, y_A) and

$$AN = x_B - x_A \text{ or } x_A - x_B, \text{ whichever is positive}$$
$$NB = y_B - y_A \text{ or } y_A - y_B, \text{ whichever is positive}$$

Use the Pythagorean Theorem.

$$\begin{aligned} AB^2 &= AN^2 + NB^2 \\ &= (x_B - x_A)^2 + (y_B - y_A)^2 \\ AB &= \sqrt{(x_B - x_A)^2 + (y_B - y_A)^2} \end{aligned}$$

The distance between any two points $A(x_A, y_A)$ and $B(x_B, y_B)$ is given by the formula:

$$AB = \sqrt{(x_B - x_A)^2 + (y_B - y_A)^2}$$

Example 1

Calculate the distance between two points using the distance formula

Silema and Kim take part in a scavenger hunt. They start from the same point. Silema walks 30 m north then 50 m west to find her first treasure. Kim walks 70 m south then 30 m west before she stops to look for her first treasure. How far are the girls from each other?

SOLUTION

Construct a coordinate grid with the origin at the starting point of the scavenger hunt and the *x*-axis to the east, the *y*-axis to the north.

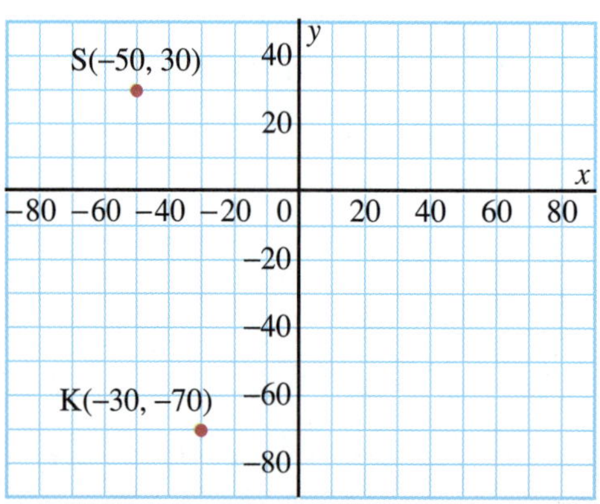

Let one unit on the grid represent 1 m. Silema stops at S(–50, 30) and Kim stops at K(–30, –70).

Use the distance formula. Replace A with K and B with S to calculate KS, the girls' distance apart.

$KS = \sqrt{(x_S - x_K)^2 + (y_S - y_K)^2}$

Substitute the values for the coordinates.

$= \sqrt{(-50 - (-30))^2 + (30 - (-70))^2}$

Simplify within the brackets.*

$= \sqrt{(-20)^2 + (100)^2}$ Calculate the exponents

$= \sqrt{400 + 10\,000}$ Perform the addition

$= \sqrt{10\,400}$ Determine the square root

$\doteq 102$

Silema and Kim are approximately 102 m apart.

Note: The expression * for KS can be keyed directly into a graphing calculator. Care must be taken to enter the negative integer using the (–) key, and not the [–] operation key.

Example 2 Determine the yield of an oil well

Refer to the information on oil wells before *Investigation 1*.

An oil well is drilled to an oil-bearing formation, situated at an angle to Earth's surface. The points of intersection of the well and the oil-bearing formation are A(6, 1500) and B(47, 1566), related to the axes shown in the diagram below. All measurements are in metres. For this particular oil-bearing formation, the porosity is calculated to be 12% and its area 5.2 km^2.

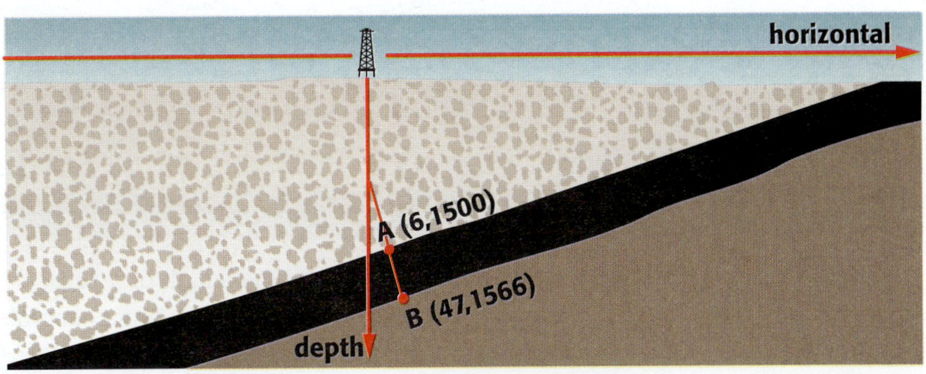

a) Calculate the thickness of the oil-bearing formation.

b) The volume of oil in a formation can be calculated using the formula:

Volume = (Thickness)(Area)(Porosity)

Calculate the volume of oil, in cubic metres, in this formation.

c) One barrel of oil represents a volume of approximately 0.159 m^3 of oil. How many barrels of oil might this formation yield?

SOLUTION

a) The thickness is the length of the line segment AB.

Use the distance formula substituting A(6, 1500) and B(47, 1566).

$$\begin{aligned} AB &= \sqrt{(x_B - x_A)^2 + (y_B - y_A)^2} \\ &= \sqrt{(47 - 6)^2 + (1566 - 1500)^2} \\ &= \sqrt{41^2 + 66^2} \\ &= \sqrt{6037} \\ &\doteq 77.7 \end{aligned}$$

The formation is approximately 77.7 m thick.

b) Volume = (Thickness)(Area)(Porosity), where

thickness = 77.7 m

area = 5.2 km^2, or 5 200 000 m^2 by using the CONVERT program from Chapter 1

porosity = 12 %, or 0.12

$$\begin{aligned} \text{Volume of oil} &= (77.7 \text{ m})(5\ 200\ 000 \text{ m}^2)(0.12) \\ &= 48\ 484\ 800 \text{ m}^3 \end{aligned}$$

The volume of oil in the formation is approximately 48 500 000 m^3.

c) One barrel of oil has a volume of 0.159 m^3, so

$\frac{1}{0.159}$ barrels have a volume of 1 m^3.

$48\ 500\ 000 \times \frac{1}{0.159}$ barrels have a volume of 48 500 000 m^3.

The formation should yield about 305 000 000 barrels of oil.

DISCUSSING THE IDEAS

1. In *Investigation 1*, you determined the length of a vertical line segment. Suppose you work out the difference of the vertical coordinates and the answer was a negative number. How would you report the length of the line segment and why?

2. In *Investigation 2*, is there another right triangle you could draw to use to calculate the length of AB? If so, would the calculations be the same as, or different from those for the triangle you drew? Explain.

3. In the distance formula derived on page 205, does it matter which x-coordinate you subtract from which to determine the difference in the x-coordinates? Is it the same for the y-coordinates?

4. The distance formula involves the square root sign, which indicates the positive square root of a number. Why is this appropriate here?

EXERCISES

Checking Your Skills

1. A city is built on a grid pattern. Buildings are located at A(–4, 3) and B(7, 3). Calculate the shortest distance between them.

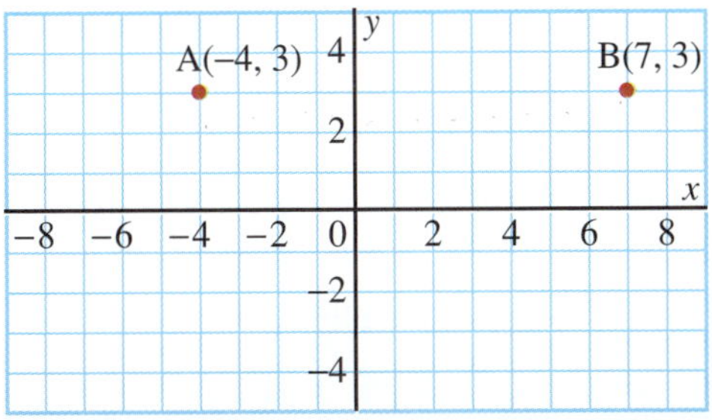

2. Bob and Christine want to meet; see the map below. Each block has dimensions of 120 m by 120 m. Assuming that the roads are of negligible width, how far does Bob have to travel to get to Christine? Find two separate answers, one for a path along roads and one for a direct path.

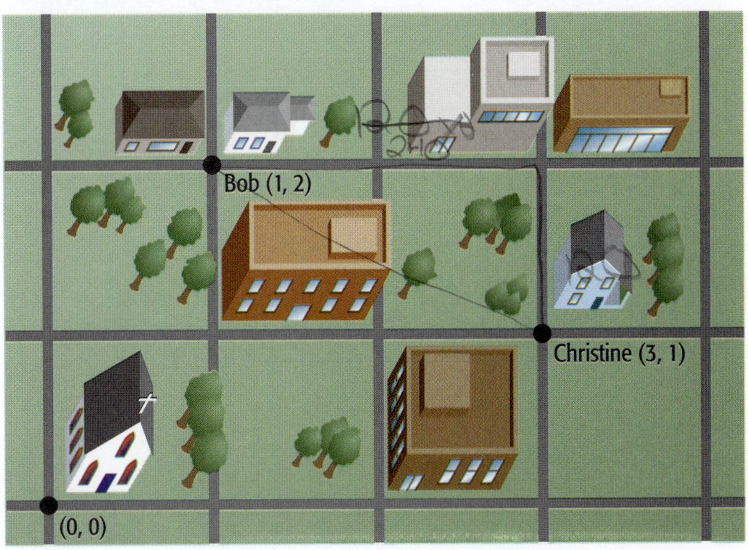

3. In a game of "Flags," one team's flag is at A(8, 3), and the other at B(2, 9).

a) Determine the distance between the flags.

b) Determine the perimeter of the playing field if it is a rectangle with vertices at

i) P(0, 0), Q(9, 0), R(9, 10), S(0, 10)

ii) T(0, 7), U(10, 1), V(13, 6), W(3, 12)

4. In the Bell telephone system, each exchange in North America is given a set of coordinates called V-H coordinates. This system is based on a grid that has its origin somewhere in the Atlantic Ocean. The rules for a coordinate plane also apply to this system.

What is the straight-line distance between Lethbridge and Winnipeg if the phone system coordinates for each place are (5696, 7592) and (5034, 5473) respectively?

5. A person in a lighthouse gives the location of a ship as an ordered pair. The first coordinate is the distance, in nautical miles, measured due east from the lighthouse to the north-south line that passes through the ship. The second coordinate is the distance, in nautical miles, measured due north from the lighthouse to the east-west line that passes through the ship. An ocean freighter sends a distress signal from a location F(240, 160). A second freighter at S(50, 420) and a coast guard cutter at C(520, 100) hear the distress call.

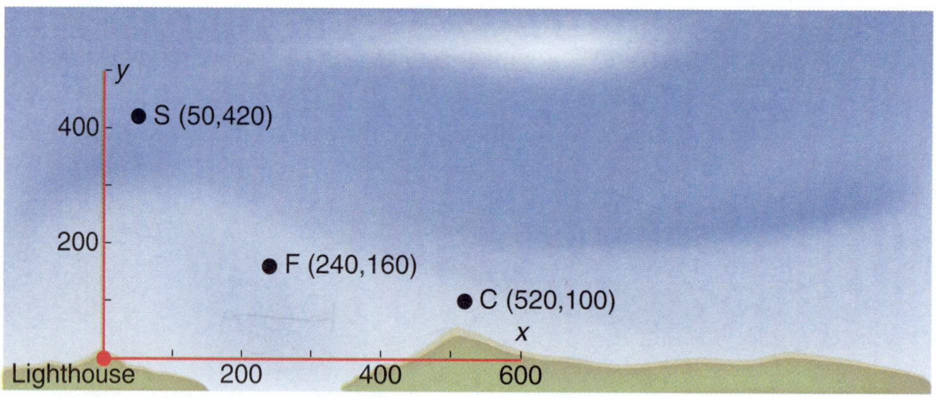

a) Determine the distances FS and FC. Which vessel is closer to the ship in distress?

b) Are there factors other than distance that should come into play when determining which vessel should come to the rescue?

6. Below is a photograph of Nose Hill Park in Calgary with a coordinate grid overlaid.

What is the straight-line distance from point A to point B? Is this the actual distance you would walk if you went from A to B? Explain.

7. Shown below is a partially completed side view of a water ride. The sections will never be straight lines, but for purposes of analysis, we will assume them to be straight. Estimate the length of the water ride. Check your answer by determining the lengths of each section of the water ride and adding these lengths together.

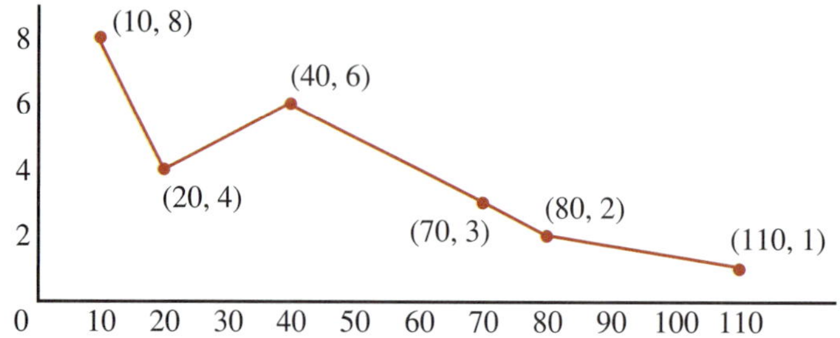

Extending Your Thinking

8. In order to determine the area of a section of land, surveyors collect data on the coordinates of key points. A surveyor wishes to determine the area of a triangular section of land. On a map with numerical coordinates in kilometres, the coordinates of the vertices of the triangle are: A(0, 0), B(12.3, 17.1), and C(32.7, 2.5).

a) Determine the distances between the points A and B, B and C, and C and A.

b) To determine the area of the triangle, the surveyor uses Heron's formula, named for a first century A.D. Greek mathematician. Heron's formula gives the area of a triangle in terms of the lengths of the sides.

$A = \sqrt{s(s-a)(s-b)(s-c)}$ where a, b, and c are the lengths of the sides of the triangle, and the semi-perimeter $s = \frac{1}{2}(a + b + c)$. What is the area of the triangular section of land?

9. When designing networks of railways, roads, and power lines, an important objective is to use the least amount of materials. Architect Frei Otto used soap-film models to help him design structures that used the least amount of construction materials.

Whether the motive is minimizing distance or area, soap-film models have proven invaluable.

You are responsible for deciding where underground power lines will be placed in a new development consisting of 4 houses at the vertices of a 100-m square. You would like to place the power lines so that the total length of cable joining the four homes is minimized. You could begin by modelling this with Plexiglas and four rods to represent the homes. The result of dipping the Plexiglas model into a soap solution is shown below.

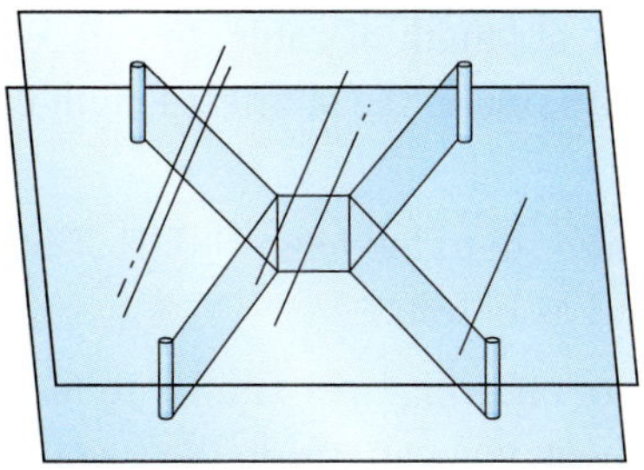

You can use a computer to solve the problem. You will also need a sheet of grid paper.

a) On a sheet of grid paper, draw a diagram similar to this. The soap-film model has given us a big hint about what shape the power lines should be in.

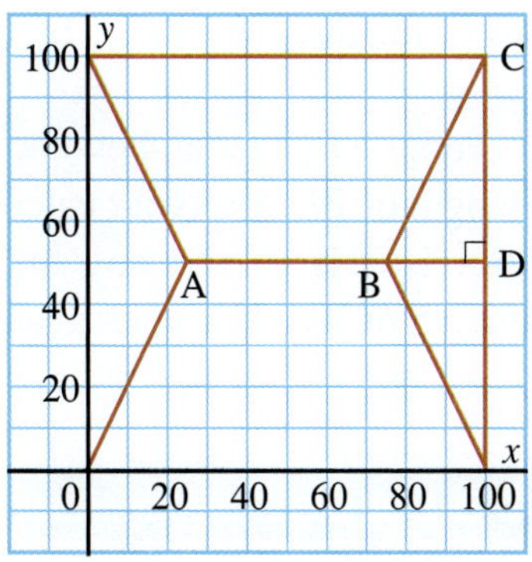

b) **i)** Visualize how the diagram changes if point B starts at the centre of the square and moves to the right. As it does so, point A also moves to the left so that the diagram is symmetrical at all times.

ii) How do the coordinates of point B change as point B moves to the right from the centre of the square?

c) This spreadsheet will display the total length of the cable for any position of point B.

	A	B	C	D
1	SHORTEST NETWORK PROBLEM			
2	x-coordinate of B	Length of AB	Length of BC	Length of cable
3	55	=2*(A3-50)	=SQRT((100-A3)^2+50^2)	=B3+4*C3
4	=A3+0.1			

d) Now drag and fill down all the formulas. Find the shortest cable length. Now zoom in! In cell A3, enter the x-coordinate of B for the cable length one cell above the shortest length of cable. In cell A4, enter the formula **=A3+0.1**. Drag and fill to obtain the shortest length of cable, accurate to one decimal place.

Repeat, this time zooming in to the nearest 0.01. Change cell A4 to **=A3+0.01**. Drag and fill as before.

e) i) Draw a large diagram on grid paper similar to the one above. Plot point B as accurately as you can, using the x-coordinate corresponding to the minimum network length that you calculated.

ii) Plot point A the same distance to the left of the centre of the square as point B is to the right. Use a ruler to draw the network and $\triangle$BCD.

iii) Use a protractor. Measure the angles at which the three segments meeting at point B intersect. What do you notice?

iv) What are the measures of the angles in $\triangle$BCD?

f) i) Calculate the lengths of the three sides of $\triangle$BCD as accurately as you can.

ii) Use your result in exercise e iv. Predict how the length of BD compares with the length of BC. Use your calculator to check.

iii) Use your result in exercise e iv. Predict how the length of CD compares with the length of BD. Use your calculator to check.

COMMUNICATING THE IDEAS

Write the distance formula in a way that will be easy to remember.

PROJECTS

In this Tutorial you developed the distance formula and solved problems involving distance. You will need these skills when you work on the Chapter Project and on the following projects in the Project Book.

- Jet Propulsion
- Skiing in San Diego

TUTORIAL 5.2

Slope

The concept of *slope* provides a numerical measure of the steepness of a line. In this Tutorial, slope is defined and you will learn how to calculate the slope of a line segment.

Complete *Investigations 1*, *2*, and *4*, or *Investigations 1*, *3*, and *4* if you have access to a CBR. *Investigation 5* requires computer access with a geometry investigative program.

Investigation 1

Modelling a Machine

Some machines perform the same steps over and over. In this Investigation, you are going to model a machine. Work with two other students. If you are not wearing shoes with laces, you need a piece of string to tie around your foot.

1. While one person times, the other two tie and untie their left shoe lace as many times as possible in 30 s. If you do not have a lacing shoe, tie a cord or a shoelace around your foot and follow the instructions above. Repeat this process two more times so that each person is the timer once. Using all the data from your group, determine the average number of times a person can tie and untie a shoe lace in 30 s.
2. Repeat the experiment for 1 min, then again for 2 min.
3. Plot the data on a grid, using appropriate scales. Plot the independent variable, time, on the horizontal axis and the dependent variable, the average number of shoe ties/unties, on the vertical axis.
4. The data should be close to linear. Draw a line of best fit and choose two points on it. Make the line segment joining the points the hypotenuse of a right triangle. Complete the triangle, making the other sides parallel to the coordinate axes.
5. What is the length of the horizontal line segment? This represents the change in time.

6. What is the length of the vertical line segment? This represents the change in the average number of shoe ties.

The slope of a line segment is equal to the change of the vertical component divided by the change of the horizontal component. This can be written:

$$\text{Slope} = \frac{\text{Change of the vertical component}}{\text{Change of the horizontal component}} = \frac{\text{Rise}}{\text{Run}}$$

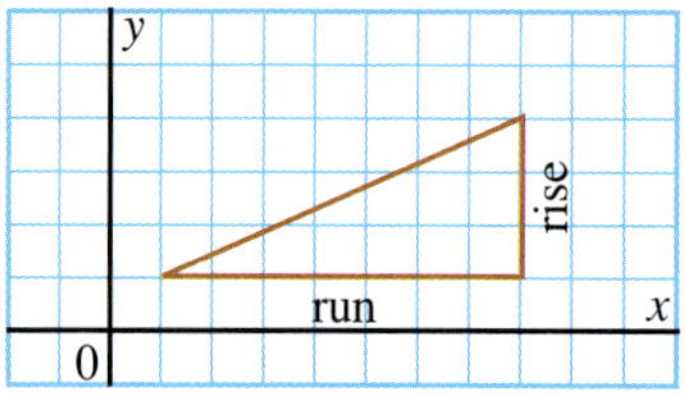

7. What is the slope of the hypotenuse of the right triangle?

8. How does your group's result for the slope compare with other groups' results?

Investigation 2 A Car Journey

You will need 3 sheets of 8.5" × 14" paper and a model car.

1. Tape the paper together lengthwise. Down the middle of the paper, draw a straight roadway. Make marks every 2 cm. The space between two neighbouring marks represents 10 km on the actual road. Put the town of Ici on the left-most point of the roadway. Ici is at distance zero.

2. Your model car travels at 60 km/h.

   a) Put your car on Ici.

   b) Copy this table into your notebook. Complete the first line of the table.

Time	Distance from Ici (*km*)
0	
1	
2	
3	
4	

c) Move your car to where it would be after one hour. Complete the second line of the table. Repeat this process until you have completed the table.

d) Plot the data on a grid, using appropriate scales. Plot the independent variable, time, on the horizontal axis and the dependent variable, distance, on the vertical axis. Note that the points are collinear.

e) Connect the points.

f) What is the slope of this line segment? What are the units of slope? What does the slope of this line segment tell you about the car?

g) On a real car journey, would you expect to produce the same results? Explain.

3. Your model car travels at 100 km/h.

a) Put your car on the point that is 30 km from Ici.

b) Repeat exercises 2a to 2f.

4. You have two model cars. The first (car A) starts at Ici and its speed is 50 km/h. The second (car B) starts at a distance of 40 km from Ici and its speed is 30 km/h.

a) Put the cars at their respective points on the roadway.

b) Copy this table into your notebook. Complete the first line of the table.

Time (*h*)	Distance from Ici (km) for model car A	Distance from Ici (km) for model car B
0		
1		
2		
3		
4		

c) Move your cars to where they would be after one hour. Complete the second line of the table. Repeat this process until you have completed the table.

d) Plot the data on a grid, using appropriate scales. Plot times on the horizontal axis and distances on the vertical axis. Use different colours for each set of data.

e) Connect the points for each set of data.

f) What are the slopes of these line segments? What do the slopes of the line segments tell you about the cars?

g) What is the significance of the point where the graphs cross?

Investigation 3 **Walking**

You will need a CBR, or CBL and motion detector, and a compatible graphing calculator. Run the RANGER program on the calculator. If you need to download this program, consult the manual that came with the CBR.

Select 1:SETUP/SAMPLE from the MAIN MENU. Press ENTER. Change the options on the screen to look like the ones below.

REALTIME:	**NO**
TIME(S):	**5**
DISPLAY:	**DIST**
BEGIN ON:	**[TRIGGER]**
SMOOTHING:	**MEDIUM**
UNITS:	**METERS**

To toggle to different settings use the ENTER key; to move to the next line use the arrow keys. Once all of the settings have been changed, move the cursor to the top of the screen, highlight START NOW, and press ENTER. Follow the instructions on the screen.

1. Once you have detached the CBR, stand at the back of the class and point the head of the CBR at the front wall. Press the TRIGGER button and walk slowly and steadily to the front of the class.

   When the CBR stops making noise, it has finished recording the data. Connect the CBR and the graphing calculator together and press ENTER on the calculator. A distance-time graph will appear on the calculator screen. If you are not satisfied with the graph (it should be fairly smooth), press ENTER and select 5:REPEAT SAMPLE and try again. When you have a graph that you like, press ENTER and select 7:QUIT.

2. Using TRACE on your calculator, determine the coordinates of two points on the graph. Transfer these points to paper on which a coordinate grid has been drawn.

3. Connect these points. This line segment is to be the hypotenuse of a right triangle. Finish drawing the triangle, making the other sides parallel to the coordinate axes.

4. Determine the slope of the line segment.

5. Repeat exercises 1 to 4, but walk quickly instead of slowly.

6. Given that the graph is a distance-time graph, what do you think the slope might tell you about your movement?

7. Repeat exercises 1 to 4, but instead of walking slowly the entire distance, run the first half and walk slowly for the second half.

   a) You should notice on your graph two different segments, one steeper than the other. Explain these in terms of the experiment.

   b) Using the TRACE button on your calculator, determine the coordinates of two points on *each* segment. Determine the slope of each line segment.

   c) The graph is a distance-time graph. How do the slopes relate to your movement?

Slope indicates how fast one quantity changes with respect to another. It gives the rate of change of one variable with respect to another.

In *Investigations 2* and *3*, slope represented the change in distance per unit of time; this is called speed. Sometimes, distance is measured positively in one direction and negatively in the opposite direction. A positive slope then indicates motion in the positive direction, a negative slope indicates motion in the negative direction. In *Investigation 4*, the formula for calculating the slope of line segments in a coordinate plane will be developed.

Investigation 4 Slope Using a Coordinate Grid

1. On a grid, draw *x*- and *y*-coordinate axes and mark the scale.

2. Plot the points A(–2, –3) and B(11, 7). Connect these points.

3. Using this line segment as the hypotenuse of a right triangle, construct a vertical line segment from B and a horizontal line segment from A to make a right triangle. Label the third vertex of the triangle C.

4. Calculate the length of AC and label it on the triangle.

5. Calculate the length of BC and label it on the triangle.

6. Complete one row of the following table.

x-coordinate of A	y-coordinate of A	x-coordinate of B	y-coordinate of B	Rise (change in vertical component)	Rise (change in horizontal component)	Slope of AB

7. Repeat exercises 2 to 6 with points A(1, 4) and B(9, –15).

8. Complete the table with another three sets of points.

9. Examine the rise and run columns in the chart. How could these numbers be found using some of the numbers in the first four columns?

10. Using the words in the first four columns of the table, complete the following:

$$\text{Slope} = \frac{\text{Rise}}{\text{Run}} = \frac{\text{Change in vertical component}}{\text{Change in horizontal component}} =$$

Investigation 5 Slope Using Technology

This Investigation is written for Geometer's Sketchpad. If you are using a different investigative geometry program, consult your manual for the appropriate commands.

1. Choose New Sketch from the File menu.

2. Choose Create Axes from the Graph menu.

3. Choose Plot Points from the Graph menu. Check off Free Points.

4. Input the following values for the x- and y-coordinates of two points: (–1, 2), (3, 5).

5. Label the points. Select both points.

6. Choose Segment from the Construct menu.

7. Choose Slope from the Measure menu.

8. Grab and move the point (3, 5) around the plane. What happens to the slope? What does the line segment look like when the slope is positive, negative, zero?

9. Select Snap to Grid from the Graph menu. What is the slope of a vertical line? What is the slope of a horizontal line?

UTILITY

Many graphing calculators can be programmed to calculate the slope of a line segment. Utility 13 shows you how to program a TI-83 calculator.

DISCUSSING THE IDEAS

1. In *Investigations 1*, *2*, and *3*, what did the slope represent?
2. In general, what does a slope represent?
3. State two different ways to calculate a slope.
4. Visualize the line segment AB, where (2, 3) are the coordinates for A, and (6, 11) are the coordinates for B. Describe in words how the line segment would look. How would your description differ for line segments that have a negative slope or a slope of zero?
5. Visualize a horizontal line segment. What must be its slope?

PROJECTS

In this Tutorial you calculated slopes and determined the slope formula. You will use these skills and concepts when you return to the Chapter Project, and for the following projects in the Project Book.

- Jet Propulsion
- Skiing in San Diego

COMMUNICATING THE IDEAS

Draw a diagram showing a coordinate grid with line segments having slopes 0.25, –0.5, 0, and undefined. Label each line segment with its slope and the endpoints with their coordinates.

TUTORIAL 5.3 Positive and Negative Slope

In *Tutorial 5.2, Investigation 4*, you determined the formula for slope as:

$$\text{Slope} = \frac{\text{Rise}}{\text{Run}}$$
$$= \frac{\text{Difference between the } y\text{-coordinates}}{\text{Difference between the } x\text{-coordinates}}$$

Another way of representing this is:

Given two points $A(x_A, y_A)$ and $B(x_B, y_B)$, the slope of the line segment AB is:

$$\text{Slope} = \frac{y_B - y_A}{x_B - x_A}, x_A > x_B$$

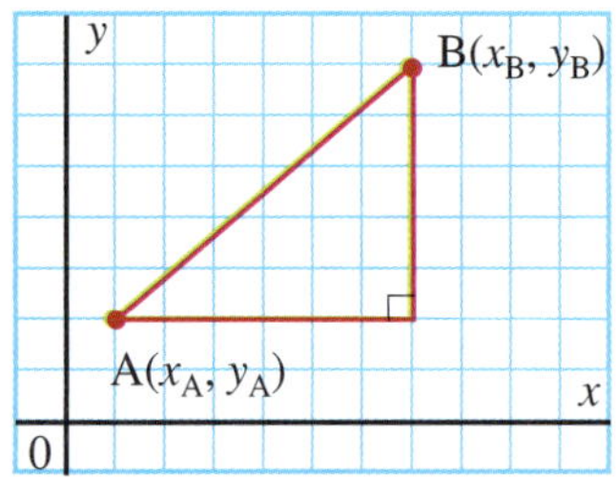

Example 1 Calculate the slope of line segments in the coordinate plane

This is a simplified side view of a section of a water ride.

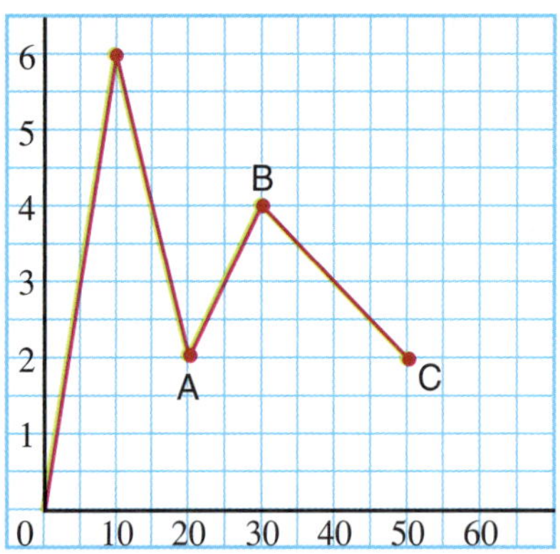

Determine the slope of the two labelled sections.

SOLUTION

The first section has endpoints at A(20, 2) and B(30, 4).

$$\text{Slope} = \frac{4 - 2}{30 - 20}$$
$$= \frac{2}{10}$$
$$= \frac{1}{5}$$
$$= 0.2$$

The second section has endpoints of B(30, 4) and C(50, 2).

$$\begin{aligned}\text{Slope} &= \frac{2 - 4}{50 - 30} \\ &= \frac{-2}{20} \\ &= -\frac{1}{10} \\ &= -0.1\end{aligned}$$

Notice that in *Example 1* the segment AB, which has a positive slope, is an uphill part of the water ride. Segment BC, which has a negative slope, is a downhill part of the water ride.

You can use these observations to quickly tell whether a line segment has a positive or negative slope. Pretend that the line segment is part of a hill (or water ride) and imagine that you are walking (or sliding) along it. Always walk from left to right, just as we read from left to right, since the x-coordinates increase from left to right. If you go uphill, the slope is positive; if you go downhill, the slope is negative; if you move on level ground, the slope is zero; if you climb up or down a vertical cliff the slope is not defined.

Example 2 **Calculate the slope of a line segment by drawing a right triangle**

Builders refer to the pitch of a roof when they talk about its slope. Determine the slope of the roof of this house.

SOLUTION

Use the roof line as the hypotenuse of a right triangle.

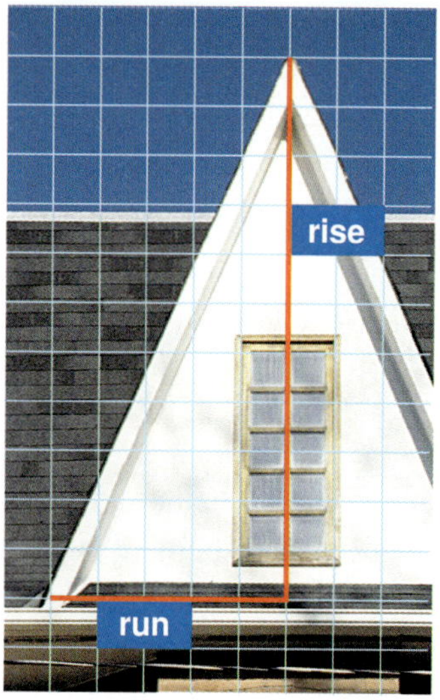

The rise of the right triangle is 7 and the run is 6.

$$\text{Slope} = \frac{\text{Rise}}{\text{Run}} = \frac{7}{6}$$

Example 3 **Solve a problem involving rise, run, and slope of a line segment**

One safety standard for a ladder is that the distance from the wall to the base of the ladder should be one-quarter of the distance up the wall to the top of the ladder.

a) What is the slope of a ladder that is leaning safely?

b) A ladder is 2.6 m long. The top of the ladder touches a window 2.5 m above the ground. What is the slope of the ladder? Is the ladder safe?

SOLUTION

a) Draw a diagram to model the ladder.

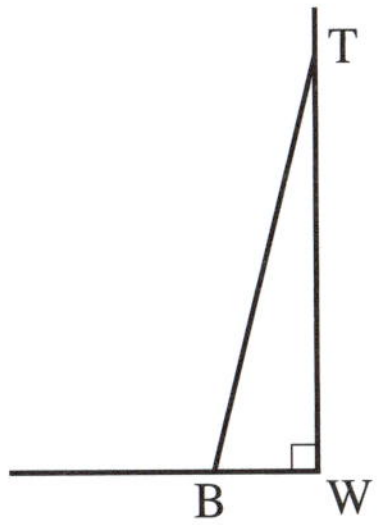

BW is to be one-quarter of WT for safety.

$BW = \frac{1}{4}WT$, so $\frac{BW}{WT} = \frac{1}{4}$

Slope of line segment FT $= \frac{WT}{BW}$

$= 1 \div \frac{BW}{WT}$

$= 1 \div \frac{1}{4}$

$= 4$

The slope of a ladder that is leaning safely is 4.

b) Draw a diagram. Mark the sides with the known lengths.

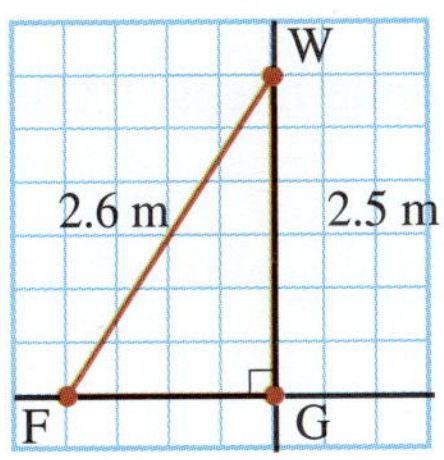

From part a, to lean safely, the slope of the ladder must be 4.

To calculate the slope of the ladder, we must determine the run FG.

Use the Pythagorean Theorem in the right triangle FGW.

$$FW^2 = FG^2 + GW^2$$

Isolate FG^2: subtract GW^2 from both sides of the equation.

$$FW^2 - GW^2 = FG^2$$

Take the square root of both sides.

$$FG = \sqrt{FW^2 - GW^2}$$

Substitute the known values for FW and GW.

$$FG = \sqrt{2.6^2 - 2.5^2}$$

The slope of the line segment $FW = \frac{\text{rise}}{\text{run}}$

$$= \frac{GW}{FG}$$

$$= \frac{2.5}{\sqrt{2.6^2 - 2.5^2}}$$

$$\doteq 3.5$$

The slope of the ladder is $\doteq 3.5$. It is not leaning safely, since this is not equal to 4.

DISCUSSING THE IDEAS

1. When is the formula Slope $= \frac{y_B - y_A}{x_B - x_A}$ used? Could the formula Slope $= \frac{\text{Rise}}{\text{Run}}$ be used in these cases?

2. Recalculate the slopes in Example 1 using the formula Slope $= \frac{y_A - y_B}{x_A - x_B}$. Why does this formula give the same value? Why does the formula $\frac{y_B - y_A}{x_A - x_B}$ not work?

3. Explain why the slope of every horizontal line is 0. Use the slope formula in your explanation.

4. Explain why vertical lines have an undefined slope.

EXERCISES

Checking Your Skills

1. A section of a roller coaster track falls 25 m in a horizontal distance of 15 m. What is the slope of this section of track?

2. A graphic designer decides to start the creation of a certain design on grid paper. She sets up a coordinate system and marks the following points: A(–4, –4), B(–2, –1), C(–2, 1), D(–4, 4), E(4, 4), F(2, 1), G(2, –1), H(4, –4)

Draw a coordinate grid and mark the above points. Join the points in order, then A to H. Calculate the slope of each line segment in the design.

3. The diagram shown represents a roof. Determine its slope.

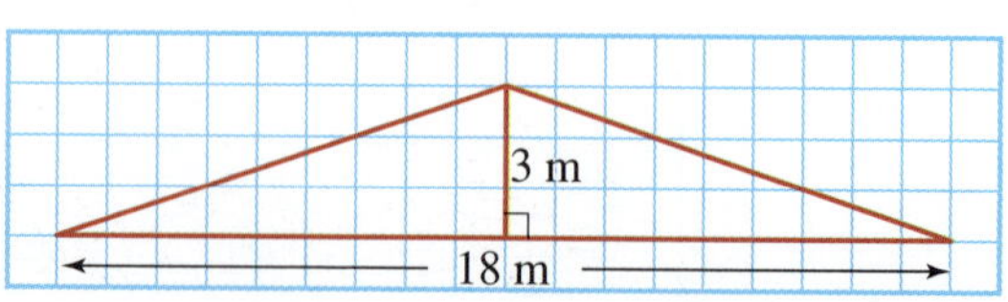

4. Working backwards is a skill that designers often use. A designer needs to draw a line of slope 6 that passes through the points A(2, 5) and B(1, k). Use the slope formula to determine the value of k.

5. Below is a scale drawing showing the side view of part of a small roller coaster. Each square represents one square metre. The roller coaster will travel from left to right as shown on the page.

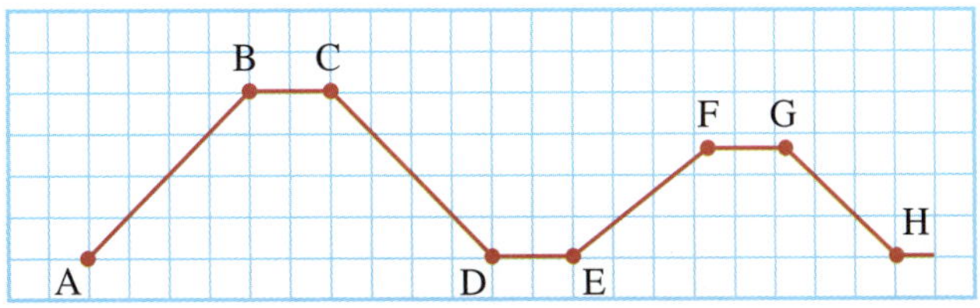

   a) Create a simplified version of the roller coaster on a coordinate grid. List the portions of the track where the roller coaster will be climbing and where it will be dropping.
   b) Calculate the height of the two hills. Which hill is the highest?
   c) Which of the two hills has the steepest climb? Explain.
   d) Which of the two hills has the steepest drop? Explain.
   e) Explain how two hills can have the same height and yet may not have the same steepness.
   f) How will the steepness of the track affect the speed of the roller coaster?

6. The following photograph shows part of a roller coaster. Measure to determine the slope of sections AB and CD of the roller coaster.

7. Below is a series of time lapse photographs of a plant. Each photograph is labelled with the height of the plant and the time.

a) Plot this data using appropriate scales, with the time in weeks plotted on the horizontal axis and the height of the plant in centimetres on the vertical axis. Can the points be connected?

b) What is the slope of the line segment?

c) How much did the plant grow in one week? This is called the rate of change of the plant's height.

d) Compare your answers to b and c. What can you conclude?

8. If the slopes of the line segments joining any pair of a series of points are the same, the points are *collinear*. When interpreting data, we often want to approximate the data with a function. Before doing this, the type of function must first be determined.

Perform the following experiment.

Put a piece of paper on your desk and shine a flashlight straight down onto the paper. Measure the diameter of a beam of light when the flashlight is held at various heights. Plot the data on a grid where the height of the flashlight above the paper is plotted on the horizontal axis and the diameter of the beam is plotted on the vertical axis. Use appropriate scales.

a) Do the points lie on the same line segment?

b) If the slopes between the points are constant or almost constant, then the data can be approximated by a function whose graph is a line. Can this relationship be approximated by such a function?

9. You have learned that slope represents rate of change. In the situations we have considered, the slope has been constant—this corresponds to a straight-line graph. There are many situations for which the rate of change of a quantity itself changes.

A model car moves along a track. There are markers on the track every metre, rather like a giant number line. The data in the table give the position of the car on the track (in metres) at various times, t (measured in seconds).

t(s)	d(m)
0	4
1	5
2	7
3	10
4	15
5	19

a) Plot a graph of d against t. If the car moves smoothly along the track, we should join the points with a smooth curve. For simplicity, join neighbouring points with straight line segments.

b) Calculate the slopes of the line segments you drew in exercise a, including units. What do these slopes mean in terms of the car?

c) Plot the values from exercises b against time, t, on a different grid. Label the axes of the new graph with the correct units.

d) Again, join neighbouring points with line segments for simplicity. Calculate the slope of these line segments, including units. What do these slopes represent in terms of the car? Is there a common word used to describe this concept?

e) Some of the values calculated for the slope in part d are negative. Explain what the positive and negative values indicate about the car.

10. This is an elevation profile of a railway line.

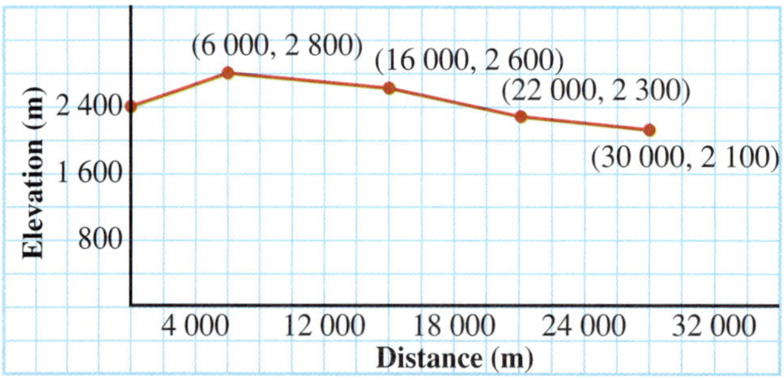

a) What is the slope of each section of the railway line?

b) When railways are constructed, the maximum slope is kept to 2.2% (a rise of 2.2 m in 100 m). If the slope is greater than this, extra locomotives are required to pull trains. In what sections of the above railway line would extra locomotives be required?

Extending Your Thinking

11. Shown below is a partially completed plan of a water ride. Determine the coordinates of each point and the length of each section of the water ride. The slope is indicated by m.

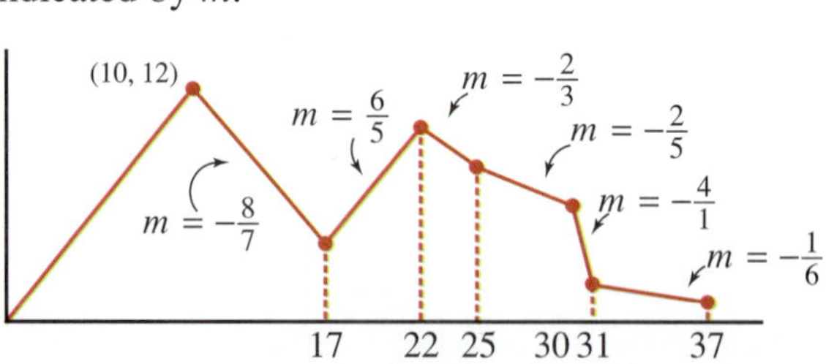

12. Certain specifications must be met when building a staircase. The Canadian Mortgage and Housing Corporation (CMHC) recommends that staircases have a maximum rise of 200 mm and a minimum run of 250 mm.

In the 17th century, Francois Blondel was the director of the Royal Academy of Architecture in Paris. Blondel proposed the ideal staircase: the measurements of the run plus twice the rise equalled 620 mm. He determined that 620 mm was the average length of a person's normal walking stride on horizontal ground.

a) Given the criteria listed above, create a list of possible rise and run values, in centimetres, for staircases. Set up a spreadsheet to determine the values.

	A	B	C
1	Length of the run	Height of the rise	Slope of the staircase
2			

b) Given a vertical distance of 2.65 m between floors, what is the minimum horizontal space needed to install the staircase?

c) Given a vertical distance of 2.95 m between floors, what is the minimum horizontal space needed to install the staircase?

CHAPTER PROJECT

In this Tutorial you solved problems involving positive and negative slopes. You will use these skills and concepts when you return to the Chapter Project on page 246.

COMMUNICATING THE IDEAS

You have learned a number of different definitions of slope. In your journal, explain each definition in your own words. Include the characteristics of line segments with positive, negative, and zero slopes and also line segments that do not have slopes.

Investigating Water Rides

At the start of this Chapter Project, you researched the design of a water ride. It is important to determine what length and slope of a downhill section will allow a rider to make it through a subsequent uphill slope of a given length.

Work in a group. You need a cardboard tube, cut in half lengthwise, a marble, wide tape, and a tape measure. Alternative equipment is clear polyethylene tubing, a small ball bearing, and a tape measure.

- Create a model of a downhill and an uphill section of a water ride. Tape the two sections of cardboard together at their ends. Keep the joint on the floor. Make the joint as smooth as possible. If you are using clear tubing, tape it to the floor or desktop to create a bend. Make sure the ball bearing is not obstructed at the bend.
- Support your sections with V-notched Bristol board if necessary.
- Copy the following table into your notebook.

Distance marble travels downhill	Slope of downhill section	Slope of uphill section	Distance marble travels uphill			
			trial 1	trial 2	trial 3	average

Career Skills

People who work in roller coaster, water slide, and water ride design meet with clients to discuss needs, make recommendations, and estimate costs. They also present examples of designs of other projects. In your reasearch, you may have found examples of designs of water rides. Plan a way to build these examples into your final project report.

- Using your model, place the uphill and downhill sections of the water ride at definite slopes. Secure the sections so that they cannot move. Measure the slopes. Release the marble from a certain distance and measure the distance the marble travels uphill. Repeat for two more trials. Enter the data in the table. Calculate the average distance that the marble travels uphill.
- Keep the slope of the downhill section the same but change the slope of the uphill section. Collect data for five different uphill slopes.
- Repeat the third step for five different downhill slopes.
- For each downhill slope, plot the data on its own grid, using appropriate scales. Plot the slope of the uphill section on the horizontal axis and the average distance the marble travels uphill on the vertical axis. Connect the points with a smooth curve.

TUTORIAL 5.4

Slopes of Parallel and Perpendicular Line Segments

In this Tutorial you will explore the relationship between the slopes of parallel lines and between the slopes of perpendicular lines.

Do either *Investigations 1*, *2*, and *4* or *Investigations 3* and *4*.

Investigation 1

Slopes of Parallel Lines

1. Draw a coordinate grid.
2. The edges of a ruler are parallel. Place your ruler on the coordinate plane and draw two line segments using each edge of the ruler.

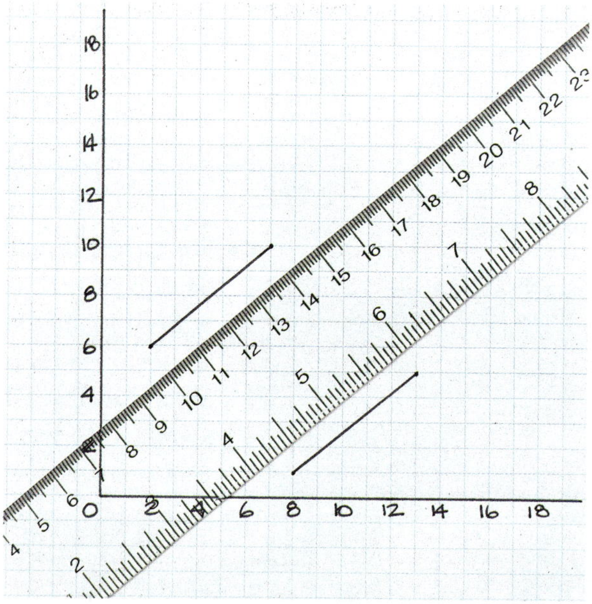

3. These line segments are parallel. Determine the slopes of the line segments. What do you notice about the values for the slopes of these line segments?
4. Move your ruler to another spot on the coordinate plane. Angle the ruler differently, and again draw line segments using both edges of the ruler. What do you notice about the values for the slopes of these lines?
5. Move your ruler one more time and determine the slopes of the parallel line segments.
6. Write a rule concerning the slopes of parallel line segments.
7. Does the rule make sense? Why or why not?

Investigation 2

Slopes of Perpendicular Line Segments

1. Using grid paper, draw a coordinate grid.
2. On the coordinate grid, place an object (such as a framing square, a plastic right triangle called a set square, or a piece of paper) that has at least two edges that are *perpendicular*.
3. Draw two line segments using the perpendicular edges. Calculate the slopes of the perpendicular lines. Express the slopes of these line segments as fractions.
4. Move the object to a new location on the coordinate plane, angle it differently, and repeat the Investigation.
5. Move the object again to another new location and repeat the Investigation one more time.
6. Look at the 3 pairs of fractions you have written. What mathematical operation(s) must be performed on one fraction to get the other in the pair?
7. What can you conclude about the slopes of perpendicular line segments?
8. Does this result make sense? Why or why not?

Investigation 3

Slopes of Parallel and Perpendicular Lines Using Technology

You need a computer with Geometer's Sketchpad loaded, or another investigative geometry program. If you are using software other than Geometer's Sketchpad, consult your manual for the appropriate commands.

1. Choose New Sketch from the File menu.
2. Choose Create Axes from the Graph menu.
3. Draw a line segment and plot a point not on the line segment.
4. Select both the line segment and point.
5. Choose Parallel Line from the Construct menu.
6. Select both the line and line segment.
7. Choose Slope from the Measure menu.
8. What do you notice about the slopes?

9. Grab and move one of the end points of one line segment. What can you conclude about the slopes of parallel line segments?

10. Choose New Sketch from the File menu.

11. Choose Create Axes from the Graph menu.

12. Draw a line segment and plot a point not on the line segment.

13. Select both the line segment and point.

14. Choose Perpendicular Line from the Construct menu.

15. Select both the line and line segment.

16. Choose Slope from the Measure menu.

17. Choose Calculate from the Measure menu. Select one slope then multiply by the other slope. What do you notice about the slopes?

18. Grab and move one of the end points. What can you conclude about the slopes of perpendicular line segments?

To design pictures that will be displayed on a computer screen, the mathematics of line segments can be used. The computer screen has its origin at the top left-hand corner of the screen, so, as in *Tutorial 5.1*, it is natural to place the number lines for the axes as shown in the diagram below.

The next Investigation uses a coordinate plane like the one shown above.

Investigation 4 Working with a Computer Screen

1. On grid paper, draw axes to replicate a computer's coordinate plane.
2. Plot and connect points A(3, 2) and B(1, 7).
3. Construct a rectangle where AB is one of the sides of the rectangle.
4. Use your knowledge of slope to explain why the quadrilateral constructed is a rectangle.
5. On the same set of axes, draw a line segment with a slope of $-\frac{2}{3}$.
6. Construct a right triangle where this line segment is one of the legs of the triangle.
7. Explain your method of construction.

Example Determine whether line segments are perpendicular

A triangle has vertices at A(–2, 3), B(8, –2), and C(4, 6). Determine whether it is a right triangle.

SOLUTION

Draw a coordinate grid and plot the points A, B, and C.

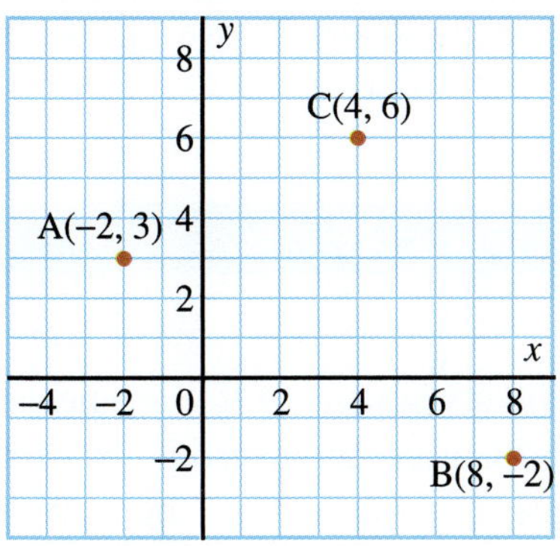

From the diagram, ∠C appears to be a right angle.

Calculate the slopes of line segments AC and BC.

Slope of AC $= \frac{6-3}{4-(-2)}$ Slope of BC $= \frac{6-(-2)}{4-8}$

$= \frac{3}{6}$ $= \frac{8}{-4}$

$= \frac{1}{2}$ $= -2$

Since $\frac{1}{2}(-2) = -1$, AC is perpendicular to BC and $\triangle$ABC is a right triangle.

DISCUSSING THE IDEAS

1. What do you know about the slopes of parallel line segments? Is this result true if the line segments are vertical, horizontal, rise to the left, or rise to the right?

2. What do you know about the slopes of perpendicular line segments? Is the result true if one of the line segments is vertical, or horizontal, or rises from left to right, or falls from left to right?

3. Do the properties regarding the slopes of line segments also apply to lines?

CHAPTER PROJECT

In this Tutorial you discovered the relationship between the slopes of parallel and perpendicular line segments. These skills and concepts will be helpful when you return to the Chapter Project on page 246.

EXERCISES

Checking Your Skills

1. The coordinates of the end points of pairs of line segments are given. Plot the points on a coordinate grid, or use an investigative geometry package on a computer if this is available. Determine their slopes. Which line segments are parallel?

   a) A(–2, –1), B(1, 5) and C(2, –1), D(4, 3)

   b) E(–3, 2), F(5, 5) and O(0, 0), H(5, 2)

   c) R(–1, 4), S(7, –2) and T(3, 4), U(9, 0)

2. Determine the slope of a line segment perpendicular to a segment with each given slope.

   a) $\frac{2}{3}$ **b)** $\frac{5}{8}$ **c)** $-\frac{1}{3}$ **d)** -2

3. Graph each pair of line segments on a coordinate grid, or use an investigative geometry program on a computer. Determine the slopes only for the pairs of line segments that are perpendicular.

a) A(–4, 12), B(–2, 2) and C(7, 3), D(–11, 1)

b) E(3, 0), F(9, 9) and G(13, 0), H(4, 9)

c) J(2, 10), K(–7, –2) and L(7, 0), M(–5, 9)

d) N(–5, –8), P(8, –7) and P(8, –7), R(7, –5)

Extending Your Thinking

4. In the 1996 Olympic summer games, Canadian sprinter Donovan Bailey won the 100-m sprint in a world-record time of 9.84 s. Five days later, American sprinter Michael Johnson won the 200-m sprint in a world-record time of 19.32 s.

a) On graph paper, draw coordinate axes with time in seconds along the horizontal axis and distance in metres along the vertical axis.

b) Plot point D to represent Donovan Bailey's time for the 100-m sprint. Join OD. Calculate the slope of OD. What does this slope represent?

c) Plot point M to represent Michael Johnson's time for the 200-m sprint. Join OM. Calculate the slope of OM. What does this slope represent?

d) From your graph, who do you think was faster in the 1996 Olympics?

e) At the start of a race, it takes a certain time for runners to react to the sound of a starter's pistol. Suppose this is subtracted from the runners' time for the two races. Estimate what this reaction time might be. Modify the graphs you drew in parts b and c. Repeat the slope calculations. Now who do you think is faster?

f) What would the reaction time have to be for the two runners to have run equally fast?

COMMUNICATING THE IDEAS

The slope of a line segment is $\frac{12}{7}$. Prepare a poster presentation that explains how to find the slopes of line segments parallel and perpendicular to it. Include diagrams in your presentation.

TUTORIAL 5.5

Midpoints

In this Tutorial you will develop a formula to enable you to determine coordinates of the midpoint of a line segment.

Do either *Investigation 1* or *2*, then *Investigation 3*. *Investigation 2* requires access to a computer with investigative software.

Investigation 1

Midpoint of a Line Segment Using a Coordinate Grid

You need grid paper and a ruler.

1. On grid paper, draw a coordinate grid showing all 4 quadrants.

2. Copy the following two charts into your notebook.

x-coordinate of the first point	x-coordinate of the second point	x-coordinate of the midpoint

y-coordinate of the first point	y-coordinate of the second point	y-coordinate of the midpoint

3. Mark two points, A(1, 5) and B(5, –3), on the coordinate plane.

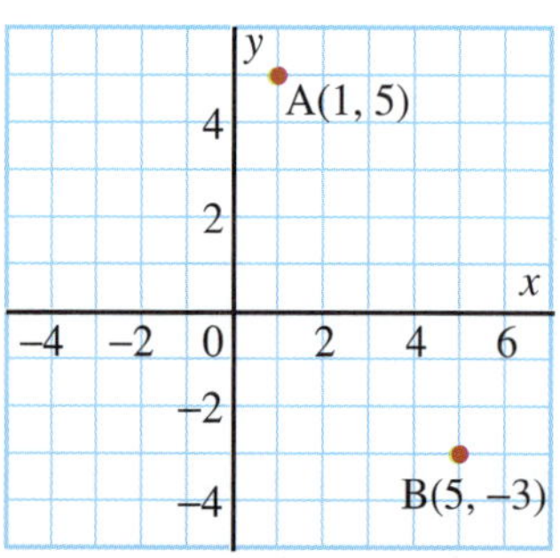

4. Connect these two points.
5. Using a ruler, determine the midpoint of this line segment.
6. Fill in the charts for these points.
7. Repeat exercises 3 to 6 for at least four more different pairs of points. Choose points in all 4 quadrants.
8. Look at the values for the x-coordinates for the first and second points. What mathematical operations yield the x-coordinate for the midpoint?
9. Look at the values for the y-coordinates for the first and second point. What mathematical operations yield the y-coordinate for the midpoint?
10. Write a formula for determining the midpoint of a line segment, given the endpoints of the line segment.
11. Use the formula you developed in exercise 10. Determine the midpoint of line segment AB, where (2, 3) are the coordinates for A and (10, 5) are the coordinates for B. Check this by drawing the line segment AB and measuring with a ruler.
12. Use your new formula to calculate the midpoints of line segments CD, EF, and GH, for the following points.

    C(1, 5), D(–1, 6), E(5, –3), F(–2, –10), G(–1, 0), H(–4, 7)

Investigation 2

Midpoint of a Line Segment Using Technology

You need access to a computer with Geometer's Sketchpad, or another investigative geometry program. If you are using some investigative geometry software other than the Geometer's Sketchpad, consult your manual for the appropriate commands.

1. Choose New Sketch from the File menu.
2. Choose Create Axes from the Graph menu.
3. Choose Plot Points from the Graph menu.
4. Input values for the x- and y-coordinates of two points.
5. Label the points. Select both points.
6. Choose Coordinates from the Measure menu.
7. Choose Segment from the Construct menu.

8. Select the line segment and choose Point at Midpoint from the Construct menu.

9. Choose Coordinates from the Measure menu.

10. Copy the following two charts into your notebook.

x-coordinate of the first point	*x*-coordinate of the second point	*x*-coordinate of the midpoint

y-coordinate of the first point	*y*-coordinate of the second point	*y*-coordinate of the midpoint

11. Fill in the charts for these points.

12. Repeat exercises 3 to 11 at least four more times.

13. Look at the values for the x-coordinates for the first and second point. What mathematical operations yield the x-coordinate for the midpoint?

14. Look at the values for the y-coordinates for the first and second point. What mathematical operations yield the y-coordinate for the midpoint?

15. Write a formula for calculating the midpoint of a line segment, given the endpoints of the line segment.

One way to express the midpoint formula is as follows.

> The x-coordinate of the midpoint is the average of the x-coordinates of the endpoints.
> The y-coordinate of the midpoint is the average of the y-coordinates of the endpoints.

Investigation 3 Playing Pool

The object of pool is to knock a target ball into a pocket by hitting it with the cue ball. If a ball hits the side of the pool table without spinning, it will rebound at the same angle that it strikes the side. For example, if the ball's path makes a 30° angle as it hits the side of the table, the ball's exit path also makes a 30° angle with the side of the table. From physics we know that the angle of incidence is equal to the angle of reflection.

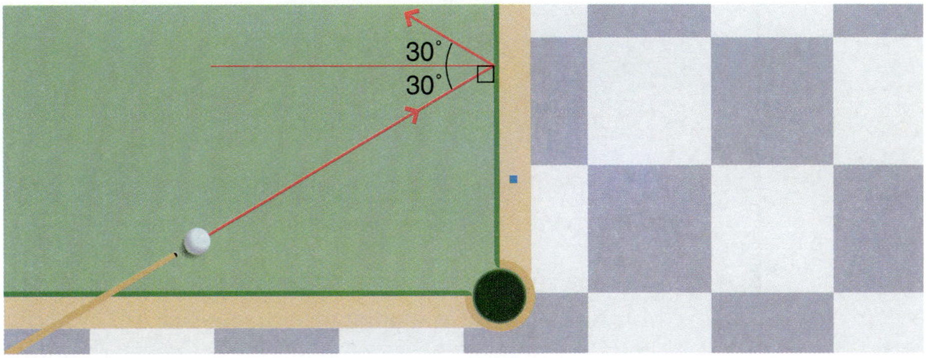

Consider the following scenario. You wish to hit the orange ball with the cue ball, but the path is blocked. You must *bank* the shot. This means shoot the cue ball so that it rebounds off the side of the table and hits the other ball.

How do you determine the spot on the side of the table where you should aim the cue ball? Imagine that the side of the table is a mirror, and aim at the imaginary mirror image of the orange ball. Look at the illustration below.

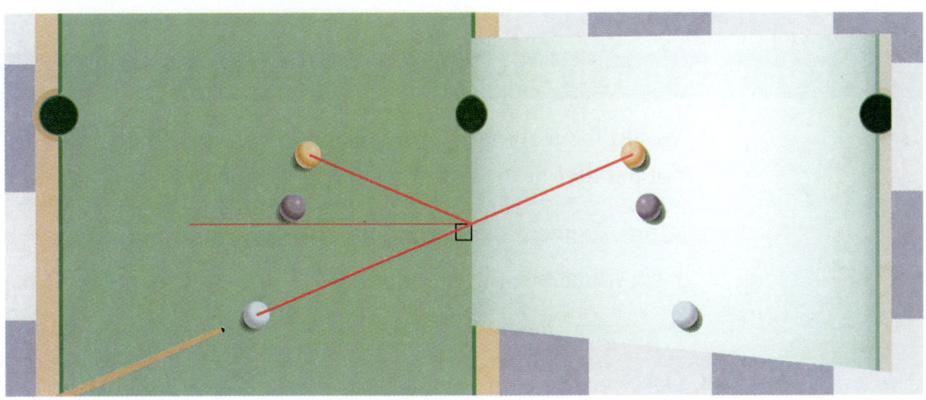

Follow these steps to go through the mathematics of this procedure.

1. Transfer the pool table to a coordinate plane. Label the orange ball A, the cue ball B, and the right edge of the pool table l.

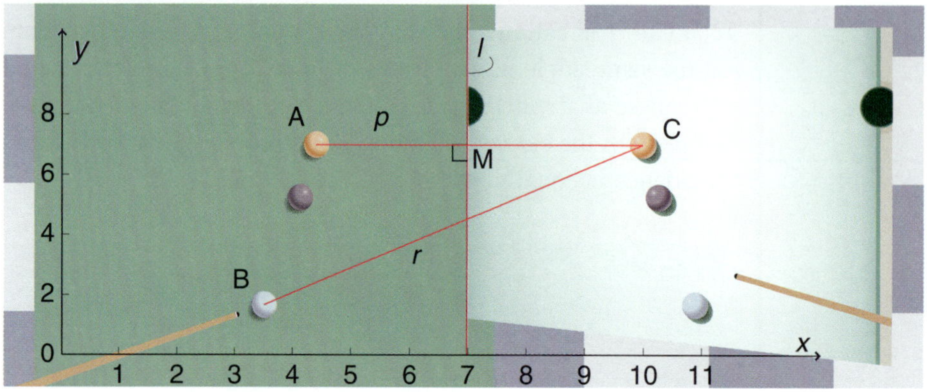

2. Draw a line through A that is perpendicular to line l. Label this line p. Use the label M for the intersection point of l and p.

3. Determine a point C, on line p, the same distance from M as A is from M. CM = AM. M is the midpoint of line segment AC. Determine the coordinates of C. (C is the location of the imaginary mirror image of the orange ball.)

4. Draw a line r joining B and C. What are the coordinates of the point of intersection of lines l and r? This is the target point for the cue ball.

5. Determine the target point for the cue ball for striking each of the other balls.

DISCUSSING THE IDEAS

1. Would the technique in *Investigation 3* work if the billiards table sides were not parallel to the coordinate axes? Explain.

2. A line segment has end points $A(x_A, y_A)$ and $B(x_B, y_B)$. Why is the x-coordinate of the midpoint $\frac{x_A + x_B}{2}$? Could the y-coordinate of the midpoint be $\frac{y_A + y_B}{2}$? Explain.

3. Describe the formulas for the coordinates of the midpoint of a line segment.

CHAPTER PROJECT

In this Tutorial you developed the formula for the coordinates of the midpoint of a line segment. These skills and concepts will be helpful when you return to the Chapter Project on page 246.

Example

Use the midpoint of a line segment

A map's numerical coordinates are in kilometres. The town of Plimville is at (4.5, 6.1) and Valley View is at (13.3, 2.7). A road is to be constructed on a direct line joining Plimville and Valley View. Each community is responsible for the cost of construction of the road to the midpoint. The cost of construction is $23 000 per kilometre.

a) Determine the coordinate of the midpoint of the road.

b) Determine the cost of the construction for Valley View.

c) What is the total cost of the road?

SOLUTION

a) Draw a diagram of the map on a coordinate grid and mark the location of Plimville with P(4.5, 6.1) and Valley View V(13.3, 2.7)

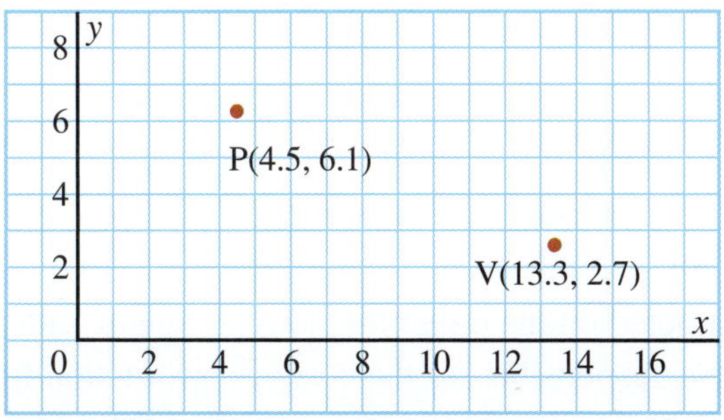

The midpoint of PV is the point M, whose coordinates (x_M, y_M) are the means of the coordinates of P and V.

$$x_M = \frac{4.5 + 13.3}{2} \qquad y_M = \frac{6.1 + 2.7}{2}$$

$$= 8.9 \qquad = 4.4$$

b) The length of road whose construction must be paid for by Valley View is represented by VM.

Use the distance formula.

$$VM = \sqrt{(x_M - x_V)^2 + (y_M - y_V)^2}$$
$$= \sqrt{(8.9 - 13.3)^2 + (4.4 - 2.7)^2}$$
$$\doteq 4.7$$

Valley View must pay for approximately 4.7 km of road construction at $23 000 per kilometre.

The cost for Valley View = 4.7 × $23 000
= $108 100

The cost of construction for Valley View is $108 100.

c) The total cost of constructing the road is twice the cost for Valley View, since M is the midpoint of PV.

The total cost of construction is \$216 200.

EXERCISES

Checking Your Skills

1. An engineer has to design a highway so that it is the same distance from two towns located at (7824, 3012) and (7790, 2994). Give the coordinates of at least one point on the highway and a description of the highway's location.

2. Many people say that Red Deer is half-way between Edmonton and Calgary. The telephone coordinates for Edmonton are (4887, 7824), and for Calgary (5438, 7811). Check the validity of this statement if the coordinates of Red Deer are (5168, 7820).

3. On a map with numerical coordinates in kilometres, the village of Sundown is at (6.3, 2.9), and the town of Sunup is at (4.7, 13.2). A water main is being constructed on the direct line joining Sunup with Sundown. Each community is responsible for the cost of construction from the community to the midpoint. Determine the coordinates of the midpoint. Sundown spends \$63 475 per kilometre for construction. Determine Sundown's costs.

4. The following is the elevation profile for a hiking trail. Determine the midway point of each segment of the trail.

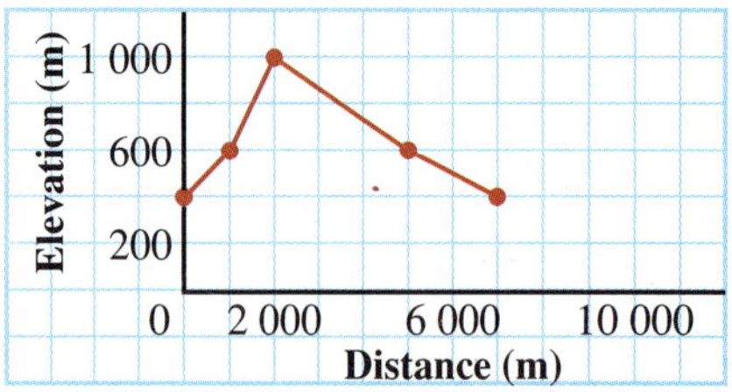

5. **a)** Draw a quadrilateral on a coordinate grid.

b) Determine the midpoints of all of the sides of the quadrilateral.

c) Connect the midpoints to form a new quadrilateral.

d) Determine the lengths and slopes of each of the sides of the new quadrilateral. What do you notice?

e) Repeat exercises a to d for two different irregular quadrilaterals. What can you conclude?

6. a) Draw a triangle on a coordinate grid.

b) Determine the midpoints of two of the sides.

c) Connect the midpoints. Determine the length and slope of this new line segment.

d) Determine the length and slope of the third side of the triangle.

e) What do you notice?

f) Repeat exercises a to e for two different triangles. What can you conclude?

Extending Your Thinking

7. A computer designer wishes to draw a triangle with a circle passing through all the vertices of the triangle. The designer knows that the point where the perpendicular bisectors of the sides of the triangle meet is the centre of such a circle.

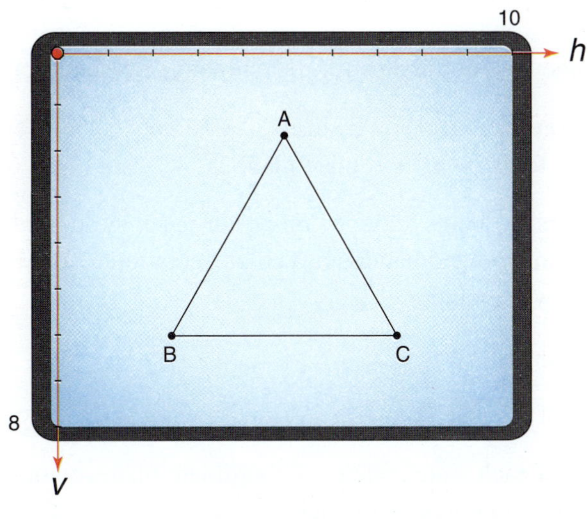

Determine the coordinate of the centre of the circumscribed circle.

COMMUNICATING THE IDEAS

Write a definition of the midpoint of a line segment. You must not use the word "midpoint" in your definition. Read your definition to a partner. Once your definition is clear and concise, write the definition in your journal.

CHAPTER PROJECT

Modelling a Water Ride

You are now ready to design your water rides. Use the results of the Investigation of water rides.

- Sketch the three water rides; include the length and slope of each section. In your design, you must adhere to the building restrictions of stairways given in *Tutorial 5.3*, exercise 3.
- A designer needs the coordinates of all key points on the water ride to draw the water ride using a computer-aided design program (CAD). Sketch a profile for each of the rides. On each sketch draw in coordinate axes so that the bottom of the stairs is at the origin.
- Determine the coordinates for the endpoints of each section.
- Draw coordinate grids on 3 sheets of grid paper. Transfer each side view to its own coordinate plane.

Presentations to clients are done on poster paper supported by a verbal explanation and handouts. The presentation to Way-Cool Water Park will include:

- a theme for the ride;
- a sketch of the ride;
- a profile of each water ride on a coordinate plane, complete with coordinates at endpoints of each section;
- the calculations of the coordinates of the endpoints of each section; and
- the data from the Investigation.

Career Skills

Technicians with skills in Computer Aided Design (CAD) find employment with architectural, engineering, and design companies. Precision and accuracy are extremely important since any errors in the plans could have serious consequences.

CONSOLIDATING YOUR SKILLS

What Do I Need To Know?

Tutorial	Skills and Concepts	Important Results and Formulas
5.1	• Determine the distance between two points in a vertical or horizontal line in the coordinate plane • Calculate the distance between two points in the coordinate plane	• Vertical distance between two points is the positive difference between the *y*-coordinates • Horizontal distance between two points is the positive difference between the x-coordinates • If $A(x_A, y_A)$ and $B(x_B, y_B)$, then $AB = \sqrt{(x_B - x_A)^2 + (y_B - y_A)^2}$
5.2	• The slope of a line segment = $\frac{\text{Rise}}{\text{Run}}$	• If $A(x_A, y_A)$ and $B(x_B, y_B)$, then Slope of AB $= \frac{y_B - y_A}{x_B - x_A}$
5.3	• Use the slope of a line segment to solve problems	• Horizontal line segments have slope 0. • Vertical line segments have slope undefined. • If the value of the slope is a positive number, the line rises from left to right. • If the value of the slope is a negative number, the line falls from left to right.
5.4	• Investigate the slope of parallel line segments • Investigate the slope of perpendicular line segments	• Parallel line segments have equal slopes. • Perpendicular line segments have slopes whose product is −1.
5.5	• Investigate the midpoint of a line segment on the coordinate plane	• If $A(x_A, y_A)$ and $B(x_B, y_B)$, the coordinates of the midpoint of AB are: $(\frac{x_A + x_B}{2}, \frac{y_A + y_B}{2})$

What Should I Be Able To Do?

When you have completed the work in Chapter 5, you should be able to solve the problems that follow. Part A is investigative in nature.

As you work through the exercises, refer to the *Student Reference*, *Utilities*, and *Tutorials* as necessary.

Part A

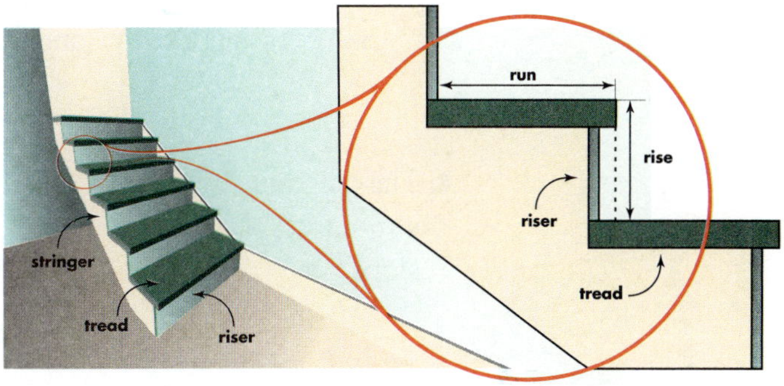

You will need a measuring tape, ruler, and grid paper.

Staircases come in many shapes and sizes, but all staircases have three main parts.

The run or *tread* is the horizontal part of a stair.

The rise or *riser* is the vertical part of a stair.

The *stringers* are the sloping boards running diagonally between floors, on either side of the treads. They support and stabilize the staircase. Their slope determines the steepness of the staircase.

1. Choose one of the staircases in your school. Measure the rise and run of a step.

2. Draw a sketch of the step, showing the measurements you took.

3. As mentioned in *Tutorial 5.3*, François Blondel proposed that, for an ideal staircase, the measurements of the run plus twice the rise should equal 620 mm. Does the staircase you chose fit Blondel's rule? Explain.

4. The Canadian Mortgage and Housing Corporation (CMHC) recommends that staircases have a maximum rise of 200 mm and a minimum run of 250 mm.

Does the staircase you chose fit the CMHC recommendation? Explain.

5. Use Blondel's rule. Calculate the run that corresponds to the maximum rise recommended by the CMHC. What is the slope of the stringer?

6. Your classroom is to be used by a kindergarten class over the vacation. They will need a set of stairs that will reach from the floor to the top of your teacher's table. Make the necessary measurement. Draw an accurate diagram on grid paper of the stairs you would design. Your design must fit Blondel's rule.

Part B

7. Comina at C wants to travel to her brother Dan at D. Each block is 30 m by 30 m.

a) How many direct paths can Comina take if she uses the roads?

b) How far must Comina travel if she uses the roads?

c) What is the length of the straight-line path between Comina and Dan?

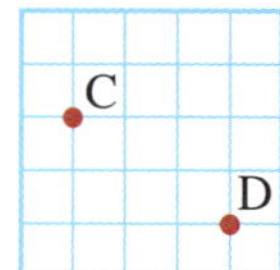

8. The diagram shown represents a roof truss. Determine its slope.

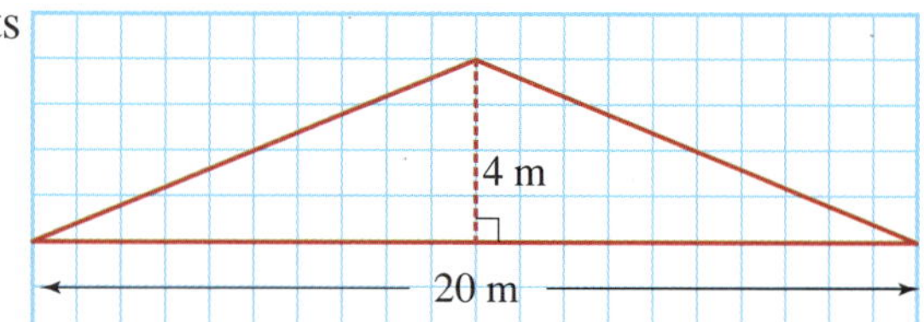

9. A triangle has vertices A(–4, 4), B(2, –2), and C(4, 6).

a) Determine the slope of each side.

b) Determine the coordinates of the midpoint of each side.

c) Show that the triangle formed by joining the midpoints has sides parallel to those of $\triangle ABC$.

10. A quadrilateral has vertices P(–2, 0), Q(1, 1), R(2, 4), and S(–1, 3). Show that the diagonals of this quadrilateral are perpendicular.

11. John and Lee are playing pool on a table that measures 1.4 m by 2.6 m. To establish the position of a ball, consider a coordinate system on a square grid, where each square has side length 0.2 m. The origin, O(0, 0), is at the bottom left corner of the table. The cue ball is at C(3, 10), and the target ball is at T(5, 1).

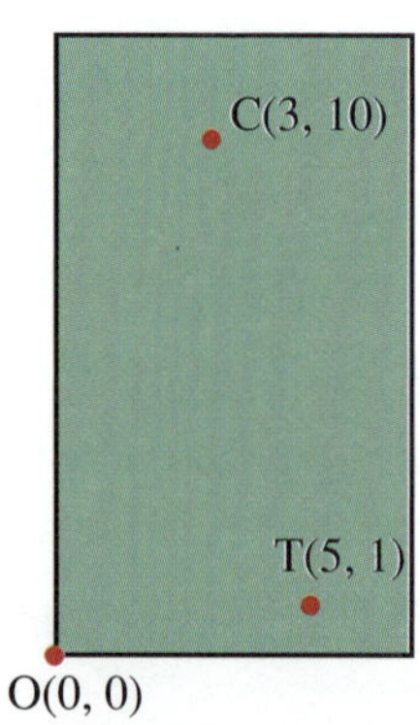

a) What are the coordinates of the other three corners of the table?

b) If Lee hits the cue ball directly at the target ball, how far must the cue ball travel before it hits the target ball?

12. In exercise 11, Lee decides to aim the cue ball so that it will hit the target ball after reflecting from the side cushion of the table. What are the coordinates of a point on the side cushion at which Lee should aim the cue ball to hit the target ball?

13. How many answers to exercise 12 are possible? Determine which of the possible paths is shortest.

Part C

The Chapter Project combines many skills and concepts in a single problem. Here is a sampling of possible student work from different stages of the Chapter Project. Review these samples to gain insights into your own project work.

14. Here is the data a student collected in the investigation on distance and slope.

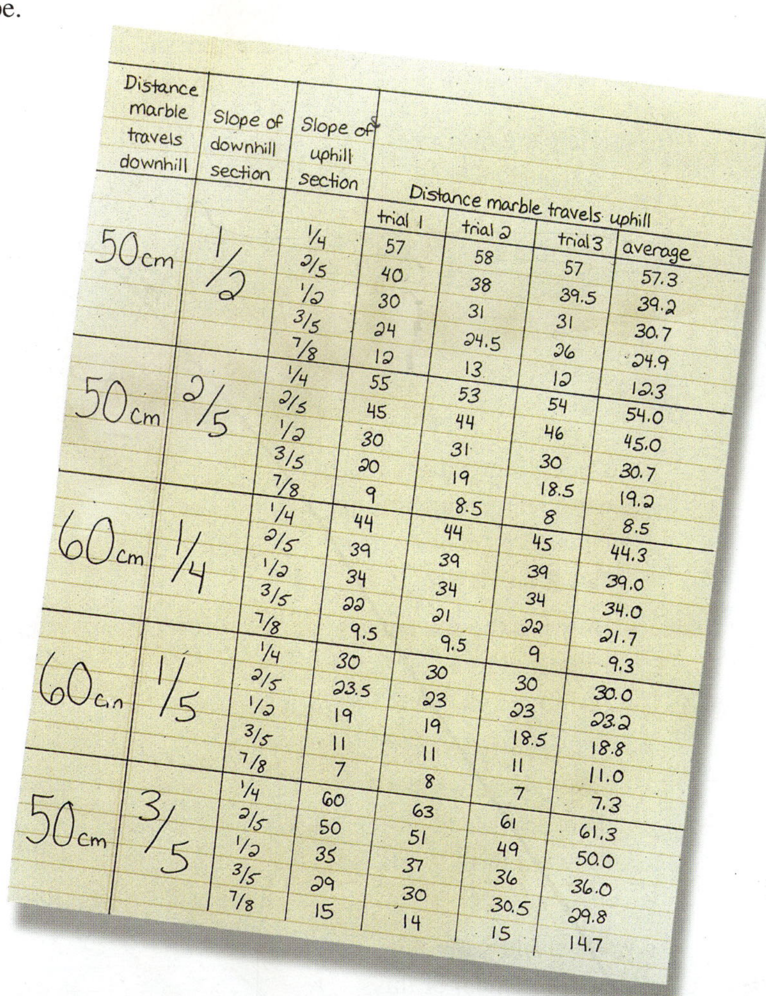

Distance marble travels downhill	Slope of downhill section	Slope of uphill section	Distance marble travels uphill: trial 1	trial 2	trial 3	average
50cm	1/2	1/4	57	58	57	57.3
		2/5	40	38	39.5	39.2
		1/2	30	31	31	30.7
		3/5	24	24.5	26	24.9
		7/8	12	13	12	12.3
50cm	2/5	1/4	55	53	54	54.0
		2/5	45	44	46	45.0
		1/2	30	31	30	30.7
		3/5	20	19	18.5	19.2
		7/8	9	8.5	8	8.5
60cm	1/4	1/4	44	44	45	44.3
		2/5	39	39	39	39.0
		1/2	34	34	34	34.0
		3/5	22	21	22	21.7
		7/8	9.5	9.5	9	9.3
60cm	1/5	1/4	30	30	30	30.0
		2/5	23.5	23	23	23.2
		1/2	19	19	18.5	18.8
		3/5	11	11	11	11.0
		7/8	7	8	7	7.3
50cm	3/5	1/4	60	63	61	61.3
		2/5	50	51	49	50.0
		1/2	35	37	36	36.0
		3/5	29	30	30.5	29.8
		7/8	15	14	15	14.7

Here is the elevation profile of one of the water rides the student designed using the data on the previous page.

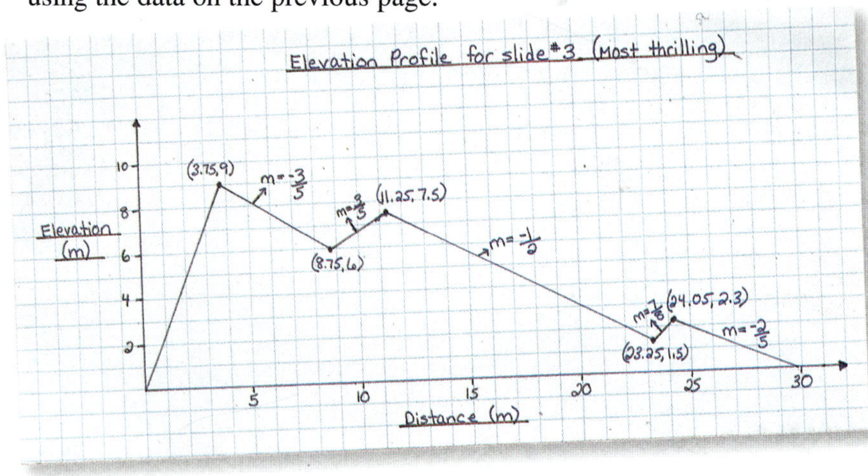

Examine the lengths and slopes of each uphill and downhill section in the elevation profile. Does the data from the Investigation support this design? Write a summary of your assessment of this student's work.

15. Here are the three-dimensional and elevation views of the ride one student created.

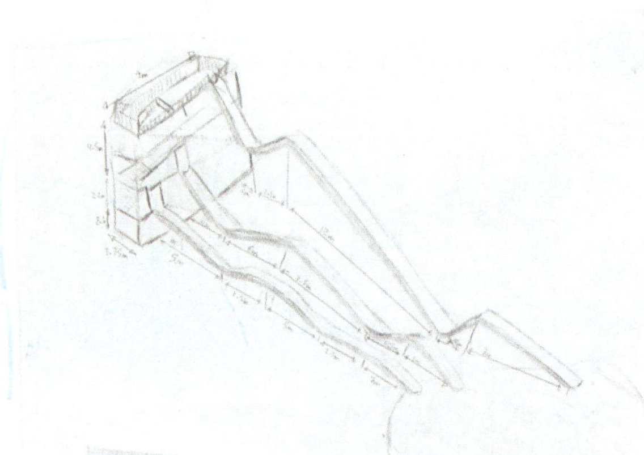

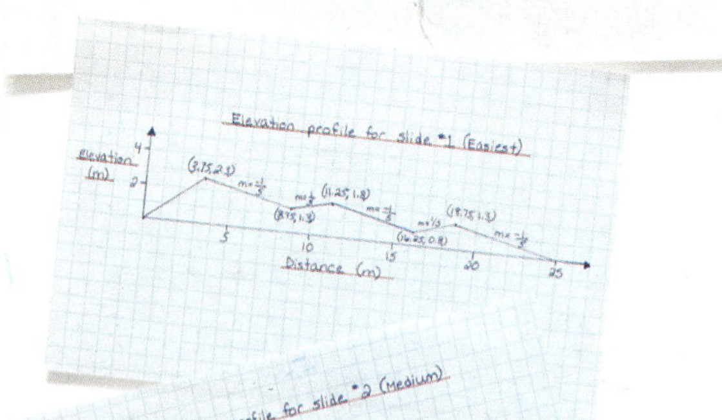

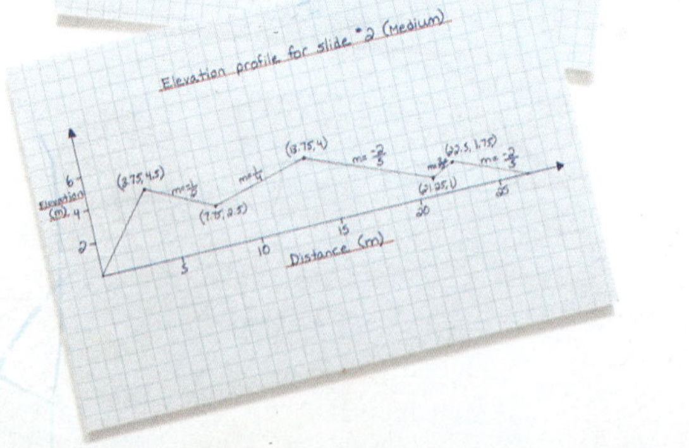

- Does all the information on the three-dimensional view correspond to the elevation views?
- How has the student addressed turns on the ride in the elevation view?
- Is it clear from the elevation views that there are three different thrill levels of water rides?

Write a summary of your assessment of this student's work.

6 Linear Functions

Overview

PROJECT

You should complete at least one project that uses the skills of this chapter. Recommended projects in the Project Book are:

- Scuba-Diving Tours
- Hair Products Research
- Anthropology
- Space Technology

Form and Function

The relationship between form and function is important in biology. The physical structure of an animal is related to its behaviour and adaptation to its environment.

In this Chapter Project you will investigate characteristics of two species: *Gorilla gorilla* and *Homo sapiens*. You will compare their structures and how they relate to function. One interesting characteristic they share is that both species walk upright. Here are some initial questions to consider.

- What do you know about gorillas?
- List some differences in the structures of gorillas and humans.
- How do their environments differ?

Research gorillas in encyclopedias, the Internet, biology textbooks, and zoos.

CHAPTER PROJECT

To do this Chapter Project, you need to plot and interpret data. Complete *Tutorials 6.1* to *6.5* to develop an understanding of the related skills. You will return to this Chapter Project on page 292.

FYI Visit: www.awl.com/canada/school/connections/

You can start your research from our Internet site: Click on MATHLINKS, followed by the *Applied Mathematics 10* logo. Then select a topic under Form and Function.

TUTORIAL 6.1

The Characteristics of Linear Functions

In this *Tutorial*, you will begin the study of a special type of function called a linear function. It is so called because its graph is a line. It is used often to produce a mathematical model of the relationship between two variables. Work with a partner to complete the following Investigations.

Investigation 1

Relationship between Arm Span and Height

You will need a measuring tape and grid paper.

1. Measure and record your arm spans, from fingertip to fingertip, with your arms stretched out. Measure and record your heights without shoes. Record your data in a table of values or as a set of ordered pairs.
2. Share the data with the rest of your class or group.
3. Obtain data from as many people as possible by making measurements at lunch time and after school.
4. Draw a scatterplot of the data with the arm span measurements represented on the horizontal axis and the heights on the vertical axis.
5. Estimate and draw a line of best fit for the data. Use a clear ruler.
6. The line you drew in exercise 5 represents a function. Explain why a line provides an appropriate model for your data.
7. Record your data and graph in your notebook. You will need them in the Chapter Project.

In the *Investigation* above you found a line of best fit for data. It is useful for predicting unknown values. Knowing this can help to ensure such predictions are as reasonable as the data allow.

In this chapter you will examine various ways to obtain an equation to represent a given line. You will look at characteristics of equations that represent a straight line in *Investigation 2*.

Practise Your Prior Skills

In the following Investigation, you will need to rearrange equations in order to use your calculator to graph them. Try the following exercises as preliminary review.

Rearrange each of the following to isolate y.

1. $y + 6 = 5x$

2. $5 - y = 4 + 3x$

3. $5y = 25x - 15$

4. $2 - 4y = 6x$

STUDENT REFERENCE

If you would like to see some examples of equation rearrangement, look in the Student Reference under "formula rearrangement."

Investigations 2 and *3* use a graphing calculator with the viewing window set as shown below. This is a "friendly window" that allows you to read values easily when using the TRACE function.

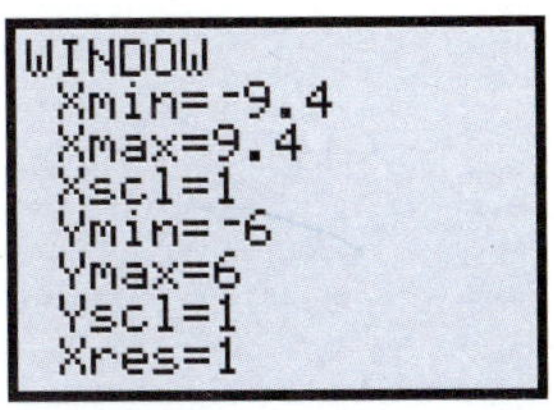

UTILITY

If you are using a TI-83 calculator and need to review window setting, refer to Utility 8. If your calculator is a different model, consult your owner's manual.

You may wish to store this window setting in the memory of your TI-83 calculator. Utility 16 shows you how.

Investigation 2 Linear Functions

1. Graph the function defined by the first equation in the list below. Sketch the graph in your notebook and write its equation. Clear the screen.

$y = 2x + 3$ $\qquad$ $y = x^2 - 4$ $\qquad$ $y - 3 = 2x$ $\qquad$ $y = x^3$

$y = -x + 3$ $\qquad$ $y + 5 = x$ $\qquad$ $y = 0.75x + 4$

$y = \frac{1}{x}$, $x \neq 0$

UTILITY

If you need to review using a TI-83 to graph with the Y= list, refer to Utility 8.

2. Repeat exercise 1 for each of the functions in the list above.

3. List the equations of the functions that have a straight-line graph.

4. Describe the similarities between the equations you listed in exercise 3.

A *linear function* can be represented by an equation written in the form $y = mx + b$, where m and b are constants. Its graph is a straight line.

When we work with linear functions and their graphs, points that have special importance are those where the graph intersects the axes. For example, when you graphed the function representing the total cost of printing a school flyer in Chapter 3, *Tutorial 3.6*, the point of intersection of the graph with the vertical axis represented the fixed cost.

Investigation 3

Find the Intercepts

1. Graph the function $y = 5x + 4$.

2. Determine the coordinates of the point where the graph intersects the y-axis. Use the TRACE feature of your calculator.

UTILITY

If you need to review the use of the TRACE feature on the TI-83, refer to Utility 10.

3. Determine the coordinates of the point of intersection of the graph with the x-axis. Write the coordinates as an ordered pair.

4. Repeat exercises 1 to 3 for these functions.

$y = x - 3$ $\qquad$ $y = 5x + 6$ $\qquad$ $y = 3x + 4$

$y - 2x = 1$ $\qquad$ $2y + x = 2$

5. What are the x-coordinates of the points where the lines intersect the y-axis? Write a rule that is true for all points on the y-axis.

6. What are the y-coordinates of the points where the lines intersect the x-axis? Write a rule that is true for all points on the x-axis.

The *x-intercept* of a line is the x-coordinate of the point where the line intersects the x-axis. Similarly, the *y-intercept* is the y-coordinate of the point where the line intersects the y-axis.

DISCUSSING THE IDEAS

1. When is it useful to draw a line of best fit when working with data on a scatterplot?

2. Explain how you drew the line of best fit in *Investigation 1*.

3. Is it necessary that any of the data points lie on a line of best fit? Explain.

4. How can we use a line of best fit to estimate a value for y given a value for x?

5. The graph of a certain function is a straight line. What do you know about the equation of the graph?

6. In *Investigation 3*, you wrote rules regarding points on the x and y axis. Describe how you could use these rules to determine the intercepts of a line using algebra.

PROJECTS

In this Tutorial you drew a line of best fit to investigate the relationship between arm span and height, and investigated the equation of a linear relationship. You will need these skills when you do the Chapter Project, and for the folowing projects in the Project Book.

- Hair Products Research
- Anthropology

COMMUNICATING THE IDEAS

Write a set of instructions to determine the y-intercept of a linear function. Show that your instructions are correct by using them to determine the y-intercept of $y = 0.5x + 0.25$.

TUTORIAL 6.2

The Equation of a Line

You discovered in *Tutorial 6.1* that a linear function has an equation $y = mx + b$, where m and b are constants. If you are to use the *equation* and its graph when solving problems, it would be useful to interpret, the numbers m and b in terms of the graph. In the following *Investigations*, use a graphing calculator with the window set to the "friendly window" given in *Tutorial 6.1*.

In *Investigation 1* you will discover what happens to the graph of $y = mx + b$ when m changes, by looking at the graphs of several linear functions whose equations differ only in the value of m.

Investigation 1 Changing *m*

1. Clear the Y= list of your calculator. Enter the functions in the list below in the Y= list as functions Y1 to Y6.

$y = 2x + 2$	$y = x + 2$
$y = 0.5x + 2$	$y = 0x + 2$
$y = -x + 2$	$y = -3x + 2$
$y = -5x + 2$	

2. On the same screen, graph the equations. The TI-83 calculator will pause after drawing each graph if you press ENTER. Press ENTER to resume graphing.
3. Describe any similarities in the graphs.
4. What is the same about each of the equations?
5. How do the graphs differ?
6. What is different about each of the equations?
7. What are the y-intercepts for each of the lines?
8. Visualize how the graph of $y = mx + 2$ changes as m varies.
9. What does m represent in exercise 8?
10. Predict what the graph of $y = 4x + 2$ would look like. Sketch the graph in your notebook. Use your graphing calculator to check your prediction.

In *Investigation 2* you will discover what happens to the graph of $y = mx + b$ when b changes, by looking at the graphs of several linear functions whose equations differ only in the value of b.

Investigation 2 Changing *b*

1. Clear the Y= list of your calculator. Enter the functions in the list below in the Y= list as functions Y1 to Y6.

   $y = 2x + 5$ $y = 2x + 3$ $y = 2x + 1$

   $y = 2x + 0$ $y = 2x - 2$ $y = 2x - 4$

2. Graph the functions on the same screen. Pause after each graph.
3. Describe any similarities in the graphs.
4. What is the same about each of the equations?
5. How do the graphs differ?
6. What is different about each of the equations?
7. Visualize how the graph of $y = 2x + b$ changes as b varies.
8. What does b represent in exercise 7?
9. Predict what the graph of $y = 2x - 4$ would look like. Sketch the graph in your notebook and then use your calculator to check your answer.

The graph of the equation $y = mx + b$ is a straight line with slope m and y-intercept b. This equation is called the slope y-intercept form of the equation of a line.

In *Investigation 3* you will review the slope of a horizontal line and a vertical line and relate these to the equation of a linear function.

Investigation 3 Horizontal and Vertical Lines

1. Clear the Y= list of your calculator.
2. On the same screen, graph the lines with the equations below.

   $y = 0x + 5$ $y = 0x + 2$ $y = 0x - 4$

3. Describe the slope and y-intercept of each graph.
4. Visualize how the line $y = b$ changes as b varies. Describe the slope and y-intercept of a line $y = b$.

5. Think of a way to graph the equation $x = 3$. Explain why you cannot use the Y= list on your graphing calculator to graph this equation.

6. What is the slope of the line $x = 3$? What is its y-intercept?

7. Visualize how the line $x = a$ changes as a varies.

8. What is the slope and y-intercept of a line $x = a$?

Example **Determine the slope and intercepts of the function defined by a linear equation**

Graph each of the following equations. Determine the slope and y-intercept of each line.

a) $x - y + 6 = 0$ **b)** $x - 2y - 8 = 0$

SOLUTION

There are several different methods that can be used to solve this problem. Some methods are more appropriate when the graph is to be drawn using paper and pencil. A computer with the appropriate geometry software could be used. The solutions presented below use the graphing calculator.

a) Rearrange the equation to enter it into the Y= list of the calculator.

Isolate the term in y by adding y to both sides of the equation.

$$y + x - y + 6 = 0 + y$$
$$x + 6 = y$$

Interchange the sides.

$$y = x + 6$$

Use the "friendly window" setting to produce the graph shown below.

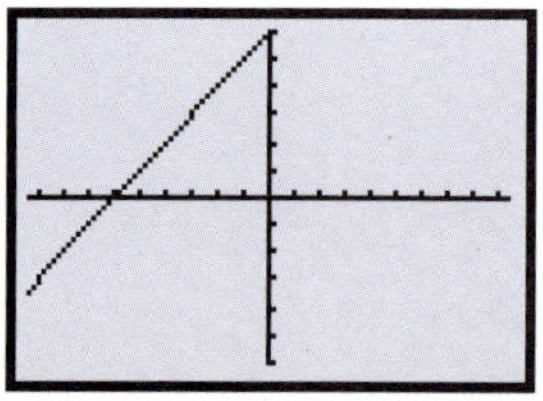

To determine the slope and y-intercept, the simplest method is to compare the equation with $y = mx + b$. The value for m is the coefficient of x (the number multiplying x) and b is the constant.

$$m = 1 \text{ and } b = 6$$

The line has a slope of 1 and a y-intercept of 6.

b) Rearrange the equation so that it can be entered in the Y= list of the graphing calculator. Isolate the term in y by adding $2y$ to both sides of the equation.

$2y + x - 2y - 8 = 2y$

Simplify by collecting like terms.

$$x - 8 = 2y$$

Isolate y by multiplying both sides by $\frac{1}{2}$.

$$\frac{1}{2}(x - 8) = \frac{1}{2}2y$$

Simplify.

$$\frac{1}{2}x - 4 = y$$

Interchange the sides.

$$y = \frac{1}{2}x - 4$$

Clear the Y= list on the graphing calculator, then enter this as Y1.

Use the friendly window to produce the graph shown.

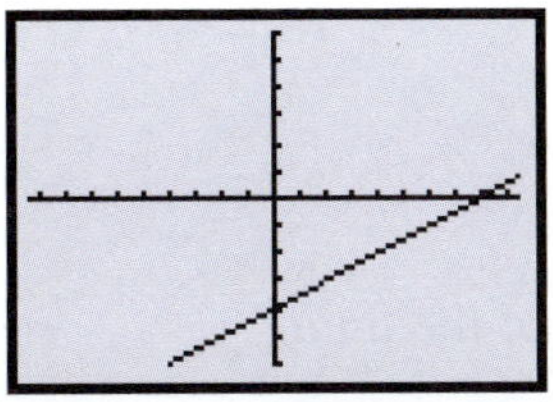

Compare the equation with $y = mx + b$.

$m = \frac{1}{2}$, $b = -4$

The slope of the line is $\frac{1}{2}$ and the y-intercept is -4.

DISCUSSING THE IDEAS

1. Based on *Investigation 1*, describe how the value of m affects the graph of the equation $y = mx + b$.

2. Based on *Investigation* 2, describe how the value of b affects the graph of $y = mx + b$.

3. Describe the line with equation $y = b$.

4. Describe the line with equation $y = mx$.

5. What will be the equation of a vertical line with x-intercept a?

6. Does the equation of a straight line always define a function? Explain your answer using examples.

7. Describe a method you could use to solve the example above that is different from the one given and that would be appropriate if you were to graph the lines using paper and pencil.

8. Describe the characteristics of a line with equation $y = mx + b$, for x which is a real number.

EXERCISES

Checking Your Skills

1. Graph each of the following equations. Determine the slope and y-intercept of each line.

a) $y = 2x + 3$

b) $y + x - 5 = 0$

c) $3x - 2y + 6 = 0$

2. Graph the equation $y = x$.

a) What is m? What is the slope of the line?

b) What is b? What are the intercepts?

3. Express the following equations in slope y-intercept form. State the slope and the y-intercept of each line.

a) $12x + 3y - 6 = 0$

b) $-4x - 2y + 16 = 0$

c) $-5x + 2y - 7 = 0$

d) $5x + 3y + 1 = 0$

e) $3x + 5y + 30 = 0$

f) $-2x + 6y + 10 = 0$

4. Graph each of the following equations. For each, determine the intercepts, slope, domain, and range of the function.

a) $y = -\frac{1}{3}x$

b) $y = 3$

c) $x = 4$

d) $y = \frac{1}{3}x + 5$

5. Equations produce pictures. Draw a coordinate grid. To produce the letter A, graph the following equations on the same grid.

$y = x + 5$; x is a real number between -4 and -2

$y = -x + 1$; x is a real number between -2 and 0

$y = 2$; x is a real number between -3 and -1

6. List the equations needed to produce a square with its centre at the point (0, 0), and side of length 4 units.

7. Graph the following equations. For each, determine the intercepts, slope, domain, and range of the function.

   a) $y = 2x$; for $x = 0, 1, 2, 3, 4, 5, 6$

   b) $y = -x$; for $x = -3, -2, -1, 0, 1, 2, 3$

Extending Your Thinking

8. Manipulate the standard form of the equation of a line

   $Ax + By + C = 0$

   into the slope and y-intercept form. Determine the rules that connect A, B, and C to the slope, m, and to the intercepts.

PROJECTS

In this Tutorial you investigated the interpretation of the numbers m and b in the equation of a line. You will need these skills when you do the Chapter Project, and the following projects in the Project Book.

- Hair Products Research
- Scuba-Diving Tours

COMMUNICATING THE IDEAS

In the 17th century, François Blondel proposed the ideal staircase: the measurements of the run (y) plus twice the rise (x) equalled 620 mm (i.e., $y + 2x = 620$). Explain what information about the graph can be gained by writing the equation in the form $y = mx + b$.

TUTORIAL
6.3 Applications of Linear Functions

Many relationships in business, industry, science, and medicine can be represented by linear functions. Depending on the situation, the slope and the intercepts can represent different things. Often, variables other than x and y are used in the equation of the function to show what they represent.

Example 1 Interpreting a linear function

The cost, C, in dollars, of a banquet depends on the number, n, of people attending. A formula that relates these variables is given below.

$$C = 25n + 1000$$

a) Draw a graph of the function.

b) Determine the slope and C-intercept of the graph.

c) One method of finding the slope is to draw a right triangle and use the formula Slope $= \frac{\text{Rise}}{\text{Run}}$

What do rise and run represent here?

d) What does slope represent? What are its units?

e) What does the C-intercept represent in this model?

SOLUTION

a) Use a graphing calculator. Rename n as x and C as y. We must first choose a suitable window. The number of people attending the banquet is represented by n, so the domain of the function is the whole numbers and the minimum value for x is 0.

Try 100 as a reasonable maximum value for x. A scale of 10 should produce reasonable points.

The equation has constant term 1000, so reasonable settings for y are minimum 0, scale 1000, and maximum 4000. If these settings do not produce a useful graph, they must be adjusted using trial and error.

The window and graph are shown below.

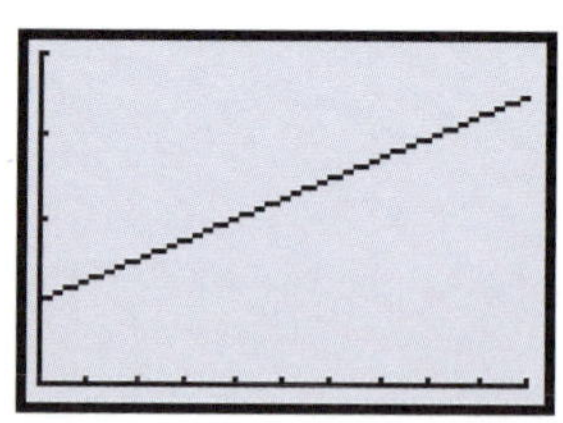

b) Compare the equation $C = 25n + 1000$ with $y = mx + b$, where $m = 25$ and $b = 1000$. The slope is 25 and the C-intercept is 1000.

c) Rise equals the change in cost. Run equals the change in the number of people attending the banquet.

d) Slope represents how much the cost increases when one more person attends. The units are dollars per person.

e) The C-intercept represents the cost when 0 people attend the banquet. This is the *fixed cost*, such as the hall rental.

Example 2 **Interpretation of a linear equation**

A car is travelling south toward Hay River. The distance in kilometres that the car is north of Hay River is represented by d. The distance, d, is related to the time travelled, t hours, by the equation $d = -80t + 240$. The driver starts his clock at 0 when he is 240 km north of Hay River.

a) Graph the function defined by the equation.

b) What are the domain and range of the function?

c) Determine the slope and intercepts.

d) What does the slope represent, and what are its units?

e) What does the intercept with the d-axis represent?

f) What does the intercept with the t-axis represent?

SOLUTION

a) Use a graphing calculator. The details that follow refer to the TI-83 calculator. If your model is different, refer to the owner's manual.

Enter the equation in the Y= list, renaming d as y and t as x. Using the standard window settings, the screen is blank. Examine the equation.

Time is measured in hours and measured from the start of the journey, so the minimum value for x is 0, and we can try 4 as the maximum value, with scale 1. The constant term in the equation is 240 and y represents the distance from Hay River, where the journey will end. Use 0 as the minimum value and 250 as the maximum value, with a scale of 50 to produce a reasonable number of divisions. (If this window did not produce a reasonable graph, we would adjust these settings.)

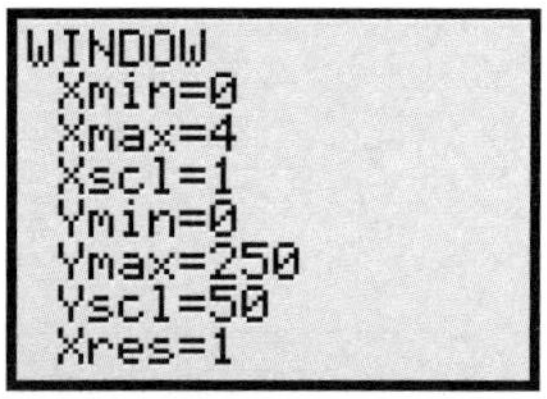

The graph is drawn.

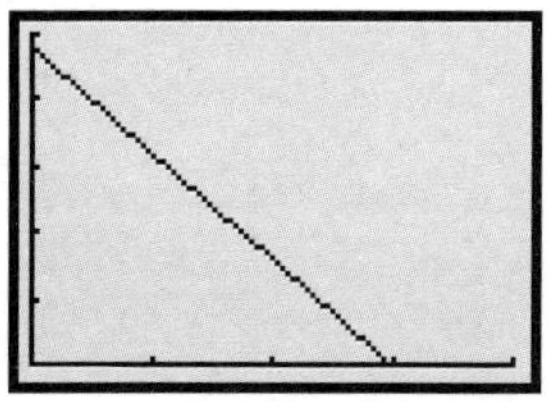

b) It is often convenient to start measuring time at the start of a journey. This is represented by t. The journey ends when the car reaches Hay River and $d = 0$. This occurs when $t = 3$. Thus, the domain is all real numbers from 0 to 3. Using the graph, the range is all real numbers from 0 to 240.

c) The slope and d-intercept are found using the equation

$d = -80t + 240$.

The slope is -80 and the d-intercept is 240.

To find the t-intercept, substitute $d = 0$ into the equation.

$0 = -80t + 240$

$t = 3$

The t-intercept is 3.

d) The slope represents the rate at which distance is changing with respect to time, and its units are kilometres per hour. This is speed. Since distance is measured toward the north and the car is travelling in the opposite direction (south), the slope is negative.

e) The d-intercept represents the starting distance from Hay River.

f) The t-intercept represents the time when the car is 0 km away from Hay River. This is the journey time, in hours.

Example 3 Direct variation

The formula for the circumference, C, of a circle with diameter, d, is given by the equation $C = \pi d$.

a) Graph the function.

b) What is the slope and the vertical intercept?

c) What does the slope represent? Is there a unit for the slope?

d) What does the vertical intercept represent?

e) What happens to C if d is doubled? What happens if it is tripled?

SOLUTION

a) Use a graphing calculator. Choose a suitable window by looking at the equation to be graphed. Rename C as y and d as x. Both variables represent lengths and so cannot be negative. The minimum value for each should be 0. Choose the maximum value for x to be 4, with scale 1. Choose 15 for the maximum value of y with scale 5, since the approximate value of π is 3. A suitable window setting and the graph of the function are shown below.

```
WINDOW
 Xmin=0
 Xmax=4
 Xscl=1
 Ymin=0
 Ymax=15
 Yscl=5
 Xres=1
```

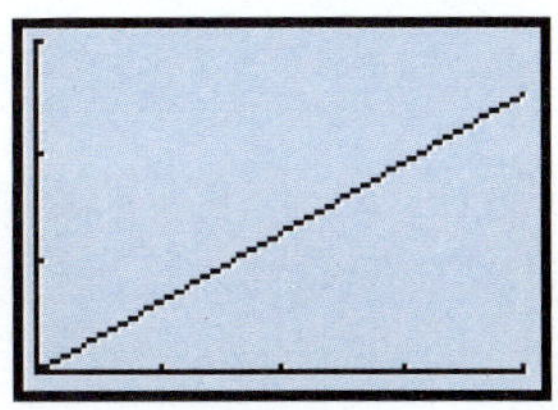

b) The slope is π and the vertical intercept is 0.

c) The slope represents the ratio circumference:diameter. The unit for slope is obtained by considering $\frac{\text{Units of rise}}{\text{Units of run}} = \frac{\text{cm}}{\text{cm}} = 1$
The slope has no units.

d) The vertical intercept is the circumference of a circle with diameter 0.

e) From the graph, if d is doubled, C is doubled. If d is tripled, then C also triples.

In relationships such as this, we say that C *varies directly* as d.

The graph of a direct variation relationship is a straight line through the origin, and the equation of the function is of the form $y = mx$, or, in this case, $C(d) = md$.

Example 4 Direct variation

Sam sells computers and earns straight commission on the value of his sales. His commission, C, varies directly with his sales S. C depends on S, therefore C is the dependent variable, S is independent. He earned a commission of $150 for sales valued at $3000. Create a table of values for the relation and draw its graph. Use the graph to determine Sam's commission on $8000 worth of sales. If Sam earns $200 in commission, what is the value of his sales?

SOLUTION

C varies directly as S, so when $S = 0$, $C = 0$.

S ($)	C ($)
0	0
3000	150

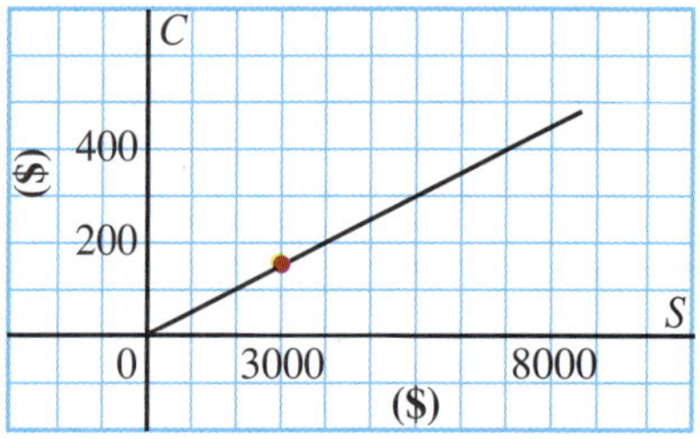

Use your graph, extending the line if necessary. This process of finding values outside the given range is called *extrapolation*.

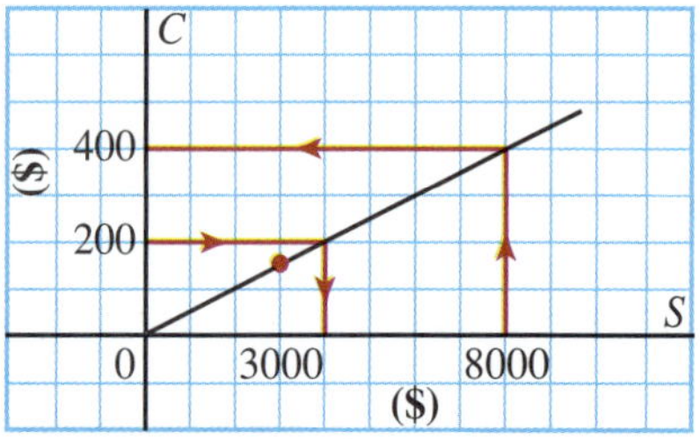

When $S = 8000$, $C = 400$. Sam earns $400 commission on sales of $8000.

If $C = 200$, $S = 4000$. Sam sells goods for $4000 to earn a commission of $200.

DISCUSSING THE IDEAS

1. The slope of a line shows the rate at which one quantity is changing with respect to the other. How do we obtain a unit for slope?

2. In *Example 2*, explain the significance of the negative slope. What would the equation for the car's motion be if the car started at the same place, but travelled north at 80 km/h? What would it be if the car started its journey 240 km south of Hay River and travelled north at 80 km/h?

3. What needs to be considered when finding domain and range?

4. P varies directly as t. What equation can you write down that relates P and t? Describe the graph of the equation.

5. When is a linear function an example of direct variation?

EXERCISES

Checking Your Skills

1. A helicopter is travelling at maximum speed toward a boat in distress. The equation that relates its distance, D, in nautical miles, away from the boat to the time travelled, t, in minutes, is $D = -0.5t + 23$.

   a) Draw a graph of the function. Should the points be connected? A suitable window setting is shown below.

```
WINDOW
 Xmin=0
 Xmax=50
 Xscl=2
 Ymin=0
 Ymax=30
 Yscl=2
 Xres=1
```

   b) What is the domain and range of the function?

   c) Determine the slope and D-intercept. What are the units for slope?

   d) What do the slope and vertical intercept represent? Why is the slope negative?

   e) Determine the horizontal intercept. What does it represent?

2. A local promoter is organizing an outdoor summer music concert in the park. The profit, P dollars, is a function of the number of tickets, T, sold. The equation is $P = 25T - 12\ 000$.

   a) Draw a graph of this function. Should the points be connected?

   b) What is the price of each ticket?

c) What are the promoter's fixed costs for the concert?

d) How many tickets must be sold for the promoter to break even?

e) What is the most money that the promoter can make if the permit for the park allows a maximum of 5000 people?

3. The boiling point, T°C, of water depends upon the height, H metres, above sea level. A formula that relates these two variables is $T = -0.0034H + 100$.

a) Graph the function. Explain why the points should be connected.

b) Determine the slope and vertical intercept of the line.

c) What do the slope and vertical intercept represent in this application? What are the units for slope?

d) What does the horizontal intercept represent in this equation? Do you think this is possible? Explain.

e) The highest mountain in the world is Mt. Everest at 8848 m. Use the TABLE feature on your calculator to determine the temperature at which water boils at the top of Mt. Everest.

UTILITY

How to use the TABLE feature on the TI-83 is described in Utility 9.

4. A tanker truck drives on a weigh scale and is then filled with crude oil. The mass, M kilograms, of the truck and the volume, V barrels, of crude oil are related by the formula below.

$M = 180V + 14\,000$

a) Use the graphing calculator to graph this equation for values of V between 0 and 500.

b) Determine the slope and interpret it. What are the units for slope?

STUDENT REFERENCE

Refer to the Student Reference to review "density."

c) Determine the M-intercept. What does it represent?

d) What is the domain of this function?

e) What is the range of this function?

5. The stopping distance, d, of a supertanker varies directly as its speed, s. It takes 3 km for a supertanker travelling at 15 km/h to stop.

   a) Create a table of values and graph this function.

   b) If a supertanker is initially travelling at 25 km/h, how far will it go before it comes to a complete stop?

   c) How fast would a supertanker be travelling if it needed 1 km to stop?

6. There is often a delay between seeing lightning and hearing the thunder. This time delay can be used to estimate the distance you are away from the storm. The distance from the storm, d km, varies directly as the time delay, t s.

   Emily saw a flash of lightning and counted a 10-s delay before hearing the thunder. She found out later that a barn 3.5 km away had been struck by lightning in that storm.

   a) Graph the function.

   b) Emily's friends Rivka and Miriam saw the same storm and counted a 6-s delay. How far away from the storm were Miriam and Rivka?

7. A hydrologist studied the relationship between the pressure on an object and its depth of submersion in a liquid. The following graph was sketched.

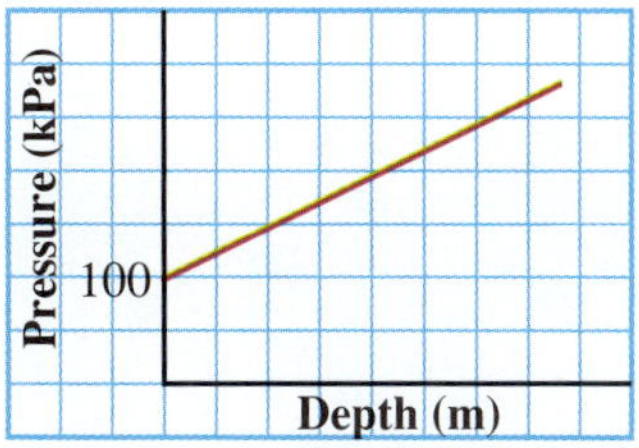

   Draw conclusions based upon the sketch.

Extending Your Thinking

8. Using a TI CBR unit or a CBL with a motion detector, do Activity 1 "Match the graph" of the TI booklet, *Getting Started with CBR*.

9. a) The graph below represents the journey of a car. Give a description of the car's journey in words. Include where it starts, how fast it goes, how long it travels for, and where it ends its journey.

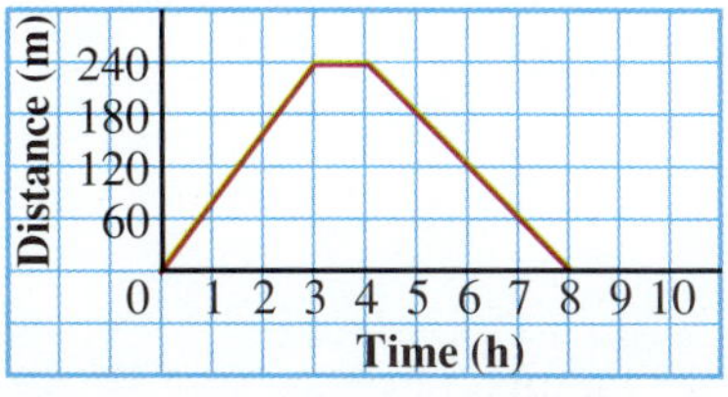

b) Graph the following journey. A motorist starts at a town 40 km away from Saskatoon. Her route takes her away from Saskatoon. She drives at 90 km/h for 3 h. After a meal break lasting 2 h, she travels directly home to Saskatoon. How fast must she travel to reach home in 2.5 h?

PROJECTS

In this Tutorial you interpreted linear functions. You will need these skills when you do the Chapter Project, and for the following projects in the Project Book.

- Hair Products Research
- Scuba-Diving Tours

COMMUNICATING THE IDEAS

Explain why all examples of direct variation are examples of linear functions, but not all linear functions are examples of direct variation. Use examples in your explanation.

TUTORIAL 6.4

Applications of Number Patterns

You will now investigate a number pattern graphically by creating a scatterplot, and a table on your graphing calculator. You will explore the relationship between the position of the term in the pattern and its value.

Investigation 1 Number Patterns

The following patterns show different arrangements of metal "struts" used in the bridge construction.

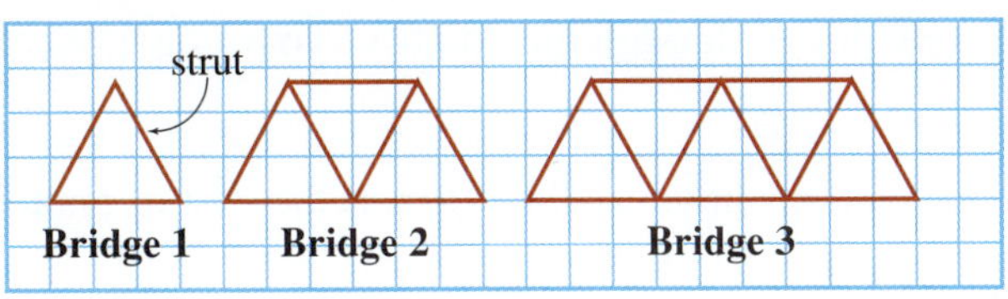

1. Draw bridge 4 and bridge 5 in your notebook to continue the pattern.

2. Create a table to record the number of the bridge and the total number of struts in each bridge. You can create these lists in your graphing calculator.

UTILITY

To review creating tables on the graphing calculator, see Utility 7.

3. Draw a graph of the relation. Represent the number of the bridge on the horizontal axis and the number of struts on the vertical axis.

4. Should the points be connected? Explain.

5. Look at the patterns in the table. Describe how to get the next three entries in the table without drawing the bridges.

6. What is the domain of the function?

7. If a line were drawn through the points in your graph, what would be the slope of the line? What is the relation between this value and the rule you described in exercise 5?

8. Create another table recording the number of the bridge and the number of triangles in each bridge.

9. Repeat exercises 3 to 7 for the table of values created in exercise 8.

Investigation 2 shows you how patterns that have similar characteristics can occur in many different contexts. In this Investigation you will determine the equation of the function defined by the table.

Investigation 2 Photocopying Costs

1. Photocopying costs 8 cents per copy. Create a table showing costs for up to 10 copies.

2. What is the domain of the function?

3. Graph the function.

4. Should the points be connected? Explain your answer.

5. If a line were drawn through the points of your graph, what would be the slope?

6. Look at the patterns in your table. How is the cost of photocopying n sheets obtained from the cost of photocopying $n - 1$ sheets?

7. What is the relationship between the slope you determined in exercise 5 and the rule you wrote in exercise 6?

8. Write an equation for the cost, C cents, of photocopying n sheets.

In each number pattern you investigated, the domain of the function was a set of natural numbers. The graphs you drew were sets of points, all of which lay on a straight line whose slope was the difference between successive terms. Such linear functions are called arithmetic sequences.

> An *arithmetic sequence* is a linear function whose domain is the set of natural numbers. The slope of the line is the difference between successive terms.

DISCUSSING THE IDEAS

1. Using the bridge structures described in *Investigation 1*, another table could be created, listing the number of triangles in the bridge and the number of struts. Would this table represent an arithmetic sequence? Why or why not?

2. Explain how to generate an arithmetic sequence relating a number of triangles to struts in *Investigation 1*. What would be the slope of its graph? What would be the common difference between any two successive terms?

3. In *Investigation 2*, describe a relation between one value of the function and the next.

4. The value of the linear function $f(x)$ when $x = 1$ is called the first term of the sequence. What would be a reasonable name for the y-intercept of the function?

Example

Use an arithmetic sequence to solve a problem

A person who evaluates computer programs charges a fee based on the number of days required to evaluate a given program. His fee structure for the first 5 d is given below.

Day (d)	1	2	3	4	5
Fee (F) ($)	500	800	1100	1400	1700

a) Graph the function.

b) On which day will the evaluator earn $3500 for that day's work?

c) Use the graph to find her daily earnings on the 15th day of evaluating a given program.

SOLUTION

a) Use grid paper. Look at the table. The domain of the function is the natural numbers. The fee for each day after the first is found by adding $300 to the previous day's fee. The table represents an arithmetic sequence, so the graph will be a straight line. The slope of the line is the common difference between successive values, which is 300. Draw coordinate axes and plot the points as shown on page 278.

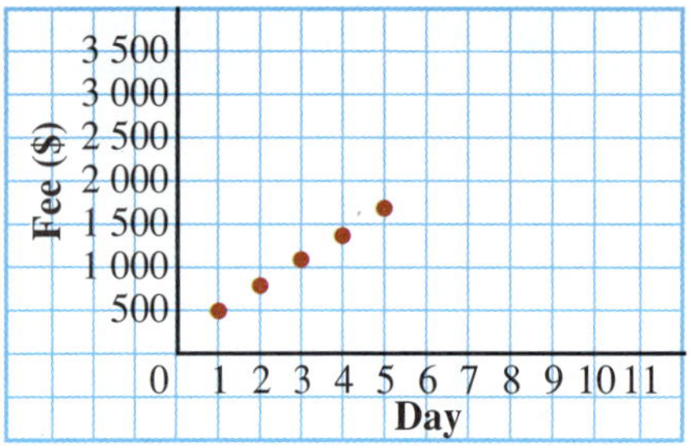

b) Use the graph. Draw a line through the points.

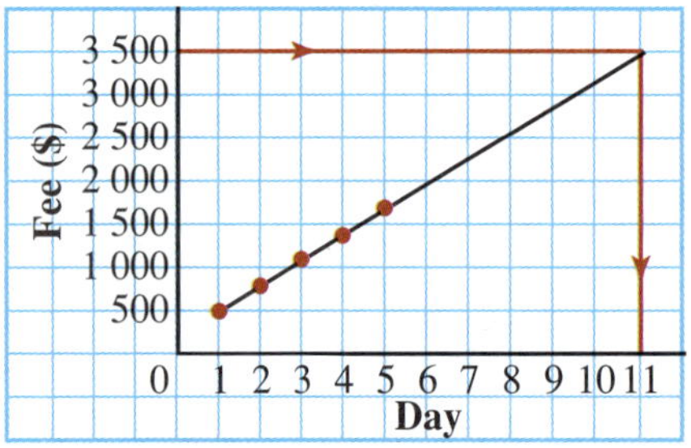

If F = \$3500, d = 11

The evaluator will earn \$3500 on the 11th day of an evaluation.

c) Use the graph. Extend the line.

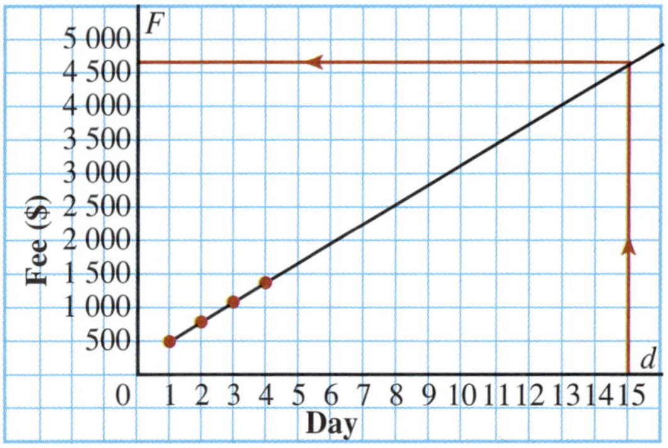

The evaluator will earn \$4700 on the 15th day of an evaluation.

EXERCISES

Checking Your Skills

1. Quenchables Soft Drinks Inc. has been increasing its production each day, as shown in the table on page 279. Its aim is to produce 10 000 cans daily. The number of cans produced, C, is a function of the number of days, d, of production.

Day (d)	Number of cans produced (C)
1	4000
2	4200
3	4400
4	4600
5	4800

a) Graph this function.

b) How many cans will be produced on day 10?

c) If the trend continues, on what day will they produce 10 000 cans?

2. Here is the method of costing the production of Orca Yearbooks. It costs \$8000 to set up the proofs and press. Each yearbook then costs \$4 to print and bind. The company only prints yearbooks in batches of 50.

a) Create a table relating the number of books printed and the cost.

b) Graph the function with the number of books as the independent variable. Should the points be connected? Why or why not?

c) Use the graph to find the cost for 900 yearbooks.

d) Determine the slope and vertical intercept (the dependent variable). What do they represent?

e) Describe the domain and range of the function.

f) If the printing and binding cost for each copy were reduced to \$3, and the initial set-up costs were increased to \$8400, visualize the graph this would produce. Describe the changes from the original graph.

3. The number of metres, L, of cable required for an elevator depends on the number of storeys, f, in the building it serves. The formula used is $L = 12 + 20f$ for buildings with no more than 30 storeys.

a) Create a table.

b) Graph the function. Should the points be connected?

c) What is the domain of the function?

d) Determine the vertical intercept. What does this represent?

4. The amount of pancake batter required varies directly with the number of people who come to breakfast. It takes 4 cups of batter to serve 6 people.

a) Create a table of values and graph the relation.

b) What is the domain of the function?

c) How many cups must you prepare for 30 people?

d) How many people can you serve with 12 cups of batter?

5. A video game operator gives all her change in quarters. From a $20 bill, she gives 56 quarters as change for a $6 purchase. She gives 8 quarters as change from a $20 bill for an $18 purchase. Purchases are always multiples of $0.25 and never more than $20.

a) Create a table.

b) Graph the number of quarters given as change, N, on the vertical axis and the amount of the purchase, P, on the horizontal axis. Assume that a $20 bill was given.

c) What are the domain and range of the function?

d) How would the graph change if a $10 bill were used?

6. Use toothpicks to create a pattern of squares that illustrates an arithmetic sequence. Draw pictures of the toothpick patterns and create the table of values for the sequence.

Extending Your Thinking

7. The yearbook club wants to choose a company to print the school yearbooks. Blue Heron Yearbooks charges $8000 for set up and $4 per copy, and Miles Ahead Yearbooks charges $8400 and $3 per copy.

a) Graph the functions representing the costs for each company on the same grid.

b) Where do the lines cross? What does this point represent?

c) If 300 yearbooks are printed, which company would be cheaper? If 800 yearbooks are printed, which company would be cheaper? Explain your answers.

PROJECTS

In this Tutorial you investigated arithmetic sequences. You will need these skills when you return to the Chapter Project, and for the following project in the Project Book.

- Scuba-Diving Tours

COMMUNICATING THE IDEAS

Your friend missed class today. Write her a message to explain the work she missed. Include examples so that she can try her homework.

TUTORIAL 6.5 The Equation of a Linear Function

When we model a situation in mathematics, we often use a function. To use the function, it is helpful to know its equation. To write the equation of a linear function we must determine the value of the slope, m, and vertical intercept, b. In many applications these values can be found from the graph, or calculated using algebra.

Example 1 The equation of a line given the slope and y-intercept

Fuel consumption is measured in L/100 km. This means that a car with a fuel consumption of 8 L/100 km uses 8 L of fuel to travel 100 km.

The graph of the number of litres of gas remaining in the tank, G, for a Mercedes-Benz C230, related to the distance travelled, d, measured in hundreds of kilometres, is provided.

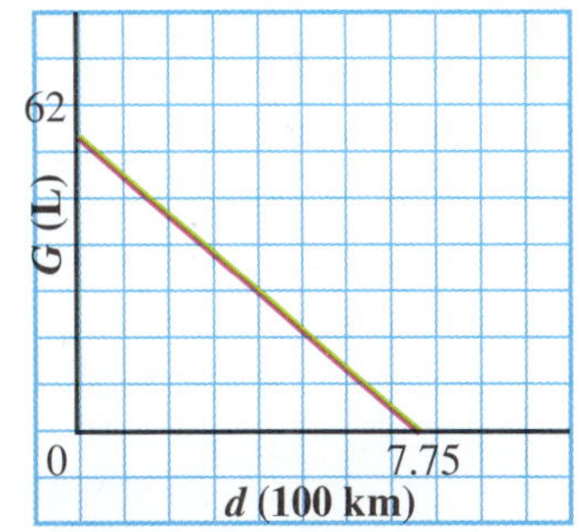

a) What is the slope, m, of the line?
What is the G-intercept of the graph?

b) What is the equation of the linear function?

c) How far can you drive on a tank of gas in a Mercedes-Benz C230?

SOLUTION

a) Use the triangle created by the line and the axes to find slope.

$$m = \frac{\text{Rise}}{\text{Run}}$$
$$= \frac{-62}{7.75}$$
$$= -8$$

The slope is -8. The G-intercept is 62.

b) Use the slope y-intercept form of the equation of a line and the values determined in a.

The equation is $G = -8d + 62$.

c) The tank is empty when $G = 0$. This gives the horizontal intercept.

$d = 7.75$ hundred kilometres
$= 775$ km

Example 2 The equation of a linear function given the slope and one point

The graph below shows the distance of a car from Winnipeg as it drives west, away from St. Eustache, at 90 km/h. After 2 h the driver sees a sign in his rear-view mirror indicating that he is 230 km away from Winnipeg. Find the equation of the linear function represented by the graph.

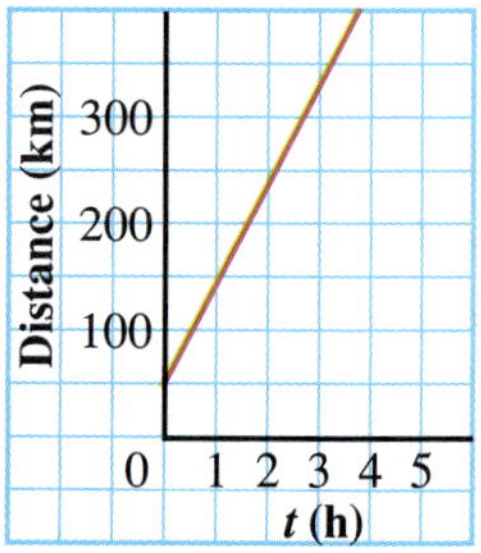

SOLUTION

The graph relating distance to time is a straight line, so the equation of the function is $d = vt + b$, where v and b are constants. The rate of change of distance with time is velocity, so the slope of the line must be his velocity of 90 km/h.

$$v = 90$$

and so $d = 90t + b$

He sees that he is 230 km away from Winnipeg after 2 h, so the point (2, 230) must lie on the graph.

Substitute $t = 2$ and $d = 230$ into the above equation to get the following equation.

$$230 = 90(2) + b$$

Now solve for b.

$$\begin{aligned} 230 &= 180 + b \\ 230 - 180 &= 180 + b - 180 \\ 50 &= b \end{aligned}$$

The equation of the function is $d = 90t + 50$.

Example 3 **The equation of a line given two points on it**

For men, shoe size is a linear function of the length of the foot. A man with a 9-inch foot has a shoe size 5. A man with an 11-inch foot has a shoe size 11. Determine the equation of the linear function relating shoe size to the length of a man's foot.

SOLUTION

The relation between length, h inches, and shoe size, s, is linear, so

$s = mh + b$, for numbers m and b.

We are told that the ordered pairs (9, 5) and (11, 11) belong to the function and so satisfy the equation of the function. The points must lie on the line that is the graph of the function.

To find the slope of the line, we can use the slope formula for the line segment joining these 2 points.

$$\begin{aligned} m &= \frac{11-5}{11-9} \\ &= \frac{6}{2} \\ &= 3 \end{aligned}$$

The equation is $s = 3h + b$.

To find b, we can proceed as in *Example* 2. Substitute the coordinates of a point on the line. Use the point (9, 5).

$$5 = 3(9) + b$$

Solve for b.

$$\begin{aligned} b &= 5 - 27 \\ b &= -22 \end{aligned}$$

The equation of the function is $s = 3h - 22$.

DISCUSSING THE IDEAS

1. In *Example 2*, explain why the slope is 90. How far from Winnipeg did the car start its journey?

2. Explain why you can use any point on the line in order to find b.

3. Units are very important when using linear functions. In *Example 2*, explain how the units used for the two quantities relate to the slope of the line.

4. When you finish solving a problem, you should check to see if your answer is reasonable. How can you do this in *Example 3*?

PROJECTS

In this Tutorial you developed the equation of a line, given sufficient information. You will need these skills when you do the Chapter Project, and for the following projects in the Project Book.

- Hair Products Research
- Scuba-Diving Tours

EXERCISES

Checking Your Skills

1. A motorist starts a journey at Portage la Prairie, 87 km west of Winnipeg. He drives west at a steady speed of 75 km/h.
   a) Create a table showing the motorist's distance from Winnipeg related to the time travelled.
   b) Draw a graph of the first four hours of the motorist's journey. Use time as the independent variable.
   c) What is the slope of the line? What is the y-intercept?
   d) What is the equation of the linear function?

2. Louise Green can read her history textbook at a steady rate of 0.75 pages/min. She still has 35 pages to be read after she has been reading steadily for 10 min. The graph shown relates the number of pages to the number of minutes of reading the history text.

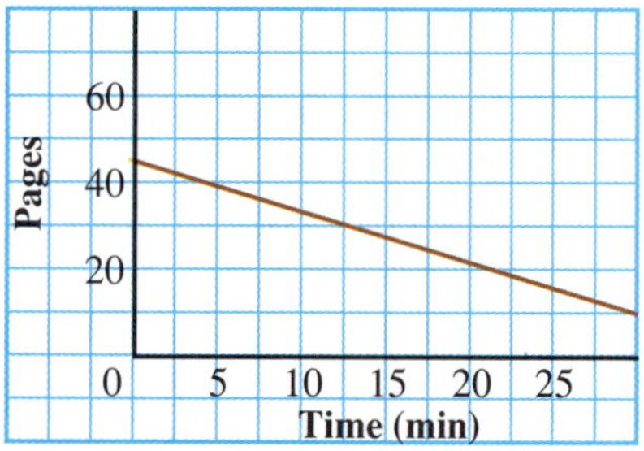

   Determine the equation of the linear function.

3. A car starts outside Winnipeg and travels west away from Winnipeg along a highway at a steady speed of 100 km/h. After 1 h, the driver sees a sign in his rearview mirror that indicates he is 120 km from Winnipeg.

a) How far from Winnipeg does the journey start?

b) Draw a graph showing the relation between distance from Winnipeg and time. What is the slope of the graph? State the coordinates of one point on the graph.

c) Determine the equation of the function.

4. A jet ski rental operation at Lake Okanagan charges a fixed insurance premium, plus an hourly rate. The total cost for 2 h is \$50, and \$110 for 5 h.

a) Graph the relation.

b) Find the fixed insurance premium and the hourly rate to rent the jet ski.

5. Simple interest varies directly with the amount borrowed.

a) If \$100 is borrowed, the interest is \$5. If \$325 is borrowed, what interest is charged?

b) Create a table of values.

c) Graph the relation and write the equation of the graph.

6. When you exercise, your heartbeat increases. There is a recommended safe maximum rate that a person's heartbeat should not exceed. This maximum rate depends on age. The chart shows the maximum recommended heart rates for different ages.

Age (in years)	Maximum Heart Rate (beats/min)
30	194
40	182
50	170

a) Draw a graph to show the maximum recommended heartbeat as a function of age.

b) Determine the equation of the function.

c) Use the equation to calculate the recommended safe maximum heart rates for a 20-year-old, a 70-year-old, and a 35-year-old person.

d) What is your own recommended maximum rate?

e) Is it reasonable to extrapolate beyond 70 years or before 20 years? Explain why or why not.

f) If realistic data for ages greater than 70 is graphed, explain how you think this will affect the equation of the function and the extrapolation.

7. Given the distance-time graph shown here, answer the following questions.

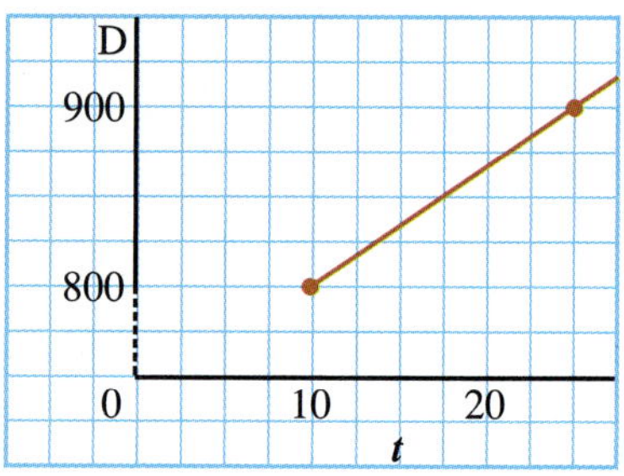

a) If $D = 850$ km, what is t?

b) If $t = 25$ h, what is D?

c) If $D = 1500$ km, what is t?

d) What is the equation of the function?

e) Verify the accuracy of your estimate in a, b, and c using the equation of the function.

8. Given the data in the table, predict the fuel consumption for the following engines.

Engine size (L)	Consumption (L/100 km)
2.2	6.4
3.0	7.5
3.8	8.6
4.6	9.7

a) 2.5 L

b) 5.0 L

c) Determine the equation of the function and use it to verify your estimates in a and b.

Extending Your Thinking

9. Musicians receive royalties on the total number of their CDs sold. They also receive a basic payment before any sales occur. A record company negotiates with a band and agrees to a basic payment of $20 000, with 3% royalties on the total sales of their CDs. The band's earnings, E, are a function of the total sales, S.

a) What is the equation of the function?

b) If a million copies of their CD are sold at an average manufacturer's price of $5, how much does the band earn?

c) The band considers a new contract that has a basic payment of $50 000 and a 2.5% royalty on CD sales. Which is the better contract?

10. High mountains have snow on them all year round, since temperature decreases as elevation above sea level increases. For every 1 km of height gain, the temperature drops approximately 6.5°C. On April 24th, the temperature in the mountains at an altitude of 6 km was –24°C.

a) Graph the function and determine its equation.

b) Use this equation to find the temperature at sea level on April 24th.

c) Determine the temperature at the summit of Mt. Logan (altitude 5951 m) on April 24th.

d) At what altitude is the temperature zero on April 24th?

e) Describe the domain and range of this graph.

f) The temperature at sea level on May 13th was 20°C. Sketch the graph of the new function on the same axes you have been using. What would be the equation of this function?

COMMUNICATING THE IDEAS

A friend has called you for help with his math homework. He has to find the equation of a line joining two points with known coordinates. Write a list of the steps he could follow.

TUTORIAL 6.6

The Equation of a Line of Best Fit

When we collect data, one way to display the results is to create a scatterplot. To analyze the results, we try to find a function whose graph passes through, or almost passes through, the points of the scatterplot. When most of the data points lie close to a line this function is linear. To use the function, we need its equation.

In these *Investigations*, you will collect data and analyze them graphically. Complete two of the following three Investigations. Work with a partner.

Investigation 1

The Spring

You will need a spring, or a new, thick elastic band, and a set of 5 or more known masses for this *Investigation*.

1. Attach the spring securely to a surface so that it hangs freely, or hang it from a hook. Measure and record the length of the spring.
2. Attach a known mass to the end of the spring and allow it to hang freely. Allow the spring to come to rest. Measure and record the mass and the new length of the spring holding the attached mass. Do not include the mass in the measurement of length.
3. Repeat exercise 2 using at least 4 more known masses.
4. Draw a scatterplot of the data.
5. Draw an estimated line of best fit. Determine the slope of the line. What does the vertical intercept represent?
6. Choose appropriate letters to represent length and mass. Write the equation of the line of best fit.

Investigation 2 The Candle

For this *Investigation* you will need a small birthday candle 6- to 8-cm high, plasticine, a clock or watch, and a ruler.

1. Set the candle firmly in plasticine so that it is as vertical as possible. BEFORE you light it, measure the length of the candle from the edge of the plasticine to the end of the wax.
2. Carefully light the candle and start timing. Try not to disturb the flame. Measure and record the height of the candle every 2 min. After 10 min, quickly blow out the candle and measure its height. Do not let the candle burn down completely.
3. Create a scatterplot of the data, with height represented on the vertical axis and time on the horizontal axis.
4. Draw an estimated line of best fit for the data. Determine the slope.
5. What is the equation of this line?
6. Use the equation to predict how long it would take to burn the candle down to the plasticine.

Investigation 3 The Bouncing Ball

This *Investigation* may be done using a CBR unit or CBL and motion detector, or it can be "eyeballed." Complete exercises A 1 to 3 if you do not have a CBR, or exercises B 1 to 3 if you do. Then do exercises 4 to 8.

Without technology

A You will need a ball that bounces easily, such as a golf ball, a ping pong ball, or a basketball.

1. If you are working without technology, tape 2- or 3-m sticks, one above the other against a wall so that you can measure the height from the floor.
2. Hold the ball near the metre sticks so that the bottom of the ball is at a known height. Drop the ball. Measure the height of the bottom of the ball at the first bounce. Record the drop height and the bounce height in a table. Repeat the same drop 3 times and work out the average height of first bounce for that drop height.
3. Repeat exercise 2 for 6 more known drop heights.

With technology

B If you are using a CBR, use a ball about the size of a volleyball or basketball.

1. Follow the instructions for the Bouncing Ball Lab given in the booklet *Getting Started with CBR*. Allow the ball to bounce up and down only once for each drop height.
2. Follow the instructions under *Explorations* to find the vertex of the bounce. The y-value of the vertex is the height the ball bounced for each drop height. Record the results.
3. Repeat for 6 more drop heights.
4. Draw a scatterplot representing drop height on the horizontal axis, and bounce height on the vertical axis.
5. Which point must be on the graph?
6. Draw an estimated line of best fit for the data. Determine the slope.
7. Write the equation of the line.
8. If the same ball were to be dropped from a height of 5 m, how high would you expect it to bounce?

DISCUSSING THE IDEAS

1. In each of the *Investigations* you did, how close were the points on your scatterplot to lying on a straight line?
2. Would all students' lines of best fit be exactly the same? Explain.
3. In each *Investigation*, what do the slope and intercepts represent?
4. In *Investigation 2*, if a different candle, made of the same type of wax but with a bigger diameter, were used, would the slope change? What would be the effect of using a candle with different wax?
5. In *Investigation 3*, the line must go through the point (0, 0). Explain why this is so.
6. In these *Investigations*, the vertical intercept was easy to find. How could the equation of the estimated line of best fit be determined if this were not so.

7. An empty cylindrical can, a calibrated cylinder, and water are available. Describe a simple experiment to show that the volume of water in the can is linearly related to the height of the water. Explain how your experiment could be used to find an approximate value for π.

PROJECTS

In this Tutorial you determined the equation of an estimated line of best fit. You will need these skills when you do the Chapter Project, and for the following projects in the Project Book.

- Hair Products Research
- Scuba-Diving Tours
- Anthropology

COMMUNICATING THE IDEAS

A friend has completed an experiment that, when graphed on a scatterplot, produced data points which were close to a line. He is unsure how to find the equation of his estimated line of best fit. Write a paragraph explaining to him what to do.

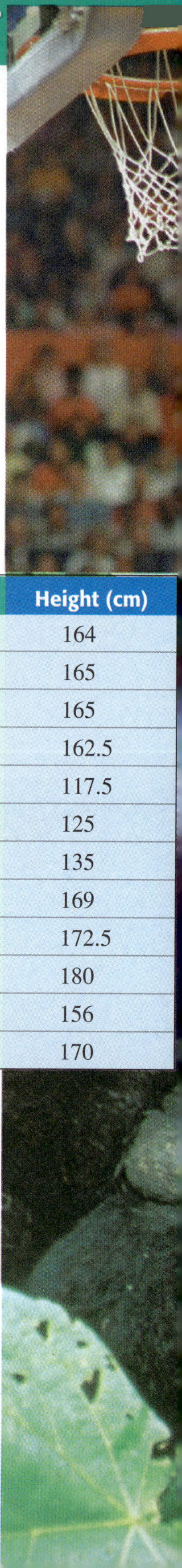

Height/Arm-Span Relationship

At the start of this project, on page 254 you considered the behaviour of gorillas. In *Tutorial* 6.1 you collected and graphed data relating arm span and height of humans. To try to relate characteristics of a species, you must consider the same quantities. The table below gives data for gorillas from several zoos in North America.

- Graph this data as a scatterplot. Represent arm span on the horizontal axis, and height on the vertical axis.
- Draw an estimated line of best fit through the data.
- Determine the equation of the line of best fit.
- Use the equation of the line of best fit for gorillas. Determine the expected arm spans of Koko and Ndume.
- Use the scatterplot and estimated line of best fit for humans from *Tutorial 6.1*. Determine the equation of the line.
- Use the equation for humans to estimate the arm spans of:

  Michael Jordan: 6 feet 6 inches
  Theoren Fleury: 5 feet 6 inches
  Silken Laumann: 5 feet 11 inches

Name of Gorilla	Arm Span (cm)	Height (cm)
Pete	234	164
Kiki	243	165
King Tut	275	165
Hatari	245	162.5
Mahari	180	117.5
Katherine	188	125
Timbo	215	135
Sara	260	169
Koko	?	172.5
Ndume	?	180
Kakinga	250	156
Tuffy	265	170

CHAPTER PROJECT

To complete this Chapter Project, you need to obtain lines of best fit that give a better match with the data. Complete *Tutorials 6.7* and *6.8* to develop an understanding of systematic methods of determining lines of best fit. You will need these skills when you return to the Chapter Project on page 310.

Career Skills

People who work in forensic science use previously gathered data to enable them to make predictions when some part of the information is missing. They use an equation generated by fitting a known function to the data points. Plan to include your estimated lines of best fit for the two sets of data as part of the presentation of your project.

TUTORIAL

6.7 The Equation of a Median-Median Line of Best Fit

In *Tutorials 6.1* and *6.6* you estimated a line of best fit, probably using a clear ruler. When you compared your line to that of other members of your class, you probably found that the lines varied somewhat. A more systematic method is needed so that we obtain a line that comes as close as possible to the points.

The median-median method was devised to handle large sets of data before electronic calculators became available. It is now often programmed into a graphing calculator. The following *Investigation* will help you understand the mathematics of the median-median method.

Investigation

The Median-Median Line of Best Fit

Use the data on the age and diameter of the Red Pine tree given below.

Age x (years)	Diameter y (cm)
8	9
19	12
11	10
4	1
16	19
18	9
12	6
22	15
5	5

1. Rearrange the data points in order, from smallest to largest, based on the values of the x-coordinates. Be sure to keep the y-value with the x-value.

2. Graph the data on a grid.

3. Try to split the data into three groups of equal size. In cases where there is one extra point when dividing by three, give the middle group the extra point. If there are two extra points, then give the first and last groups each one extra point. Here, the data can be equally divided.

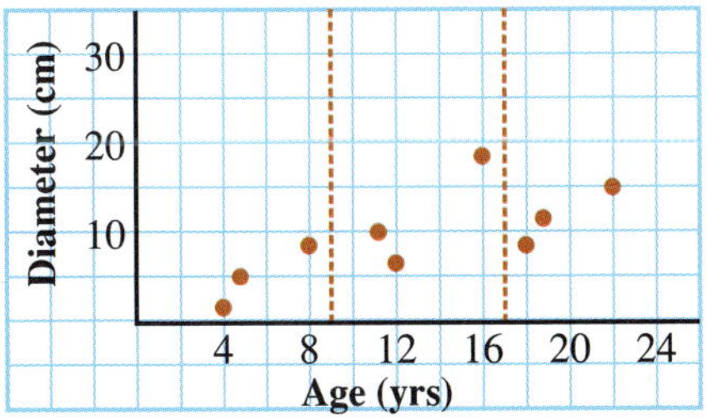

4. Find the median of the x-values and the y-values for each group to get three summary points. Record the coordinates of these points.

To review how to find the "median" of a set of numbers, refer to the Student Reference.

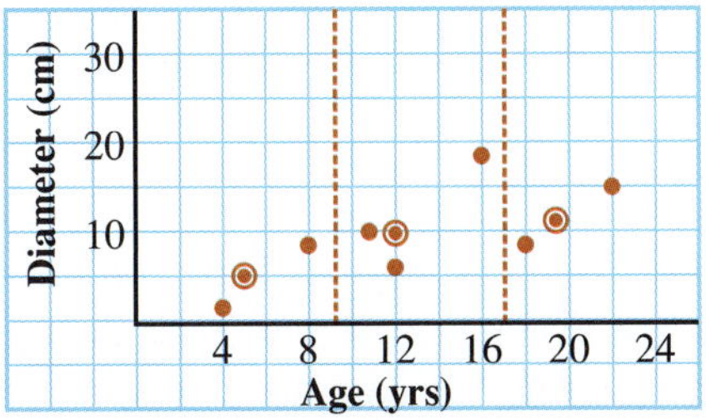

5. Plot and label the three summary points on the graph. Draw a line passing through the two outer points.

6. Determine the equation of this line.

Some people use this line with equation $y = \frac{1}{2}x + \frac{5}{2}$ as a line of best fit.

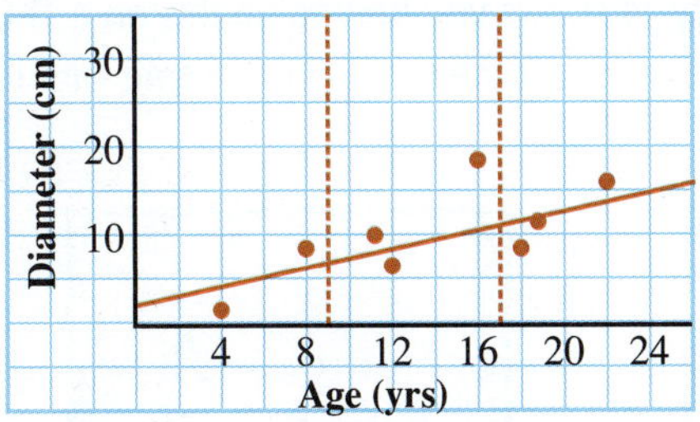

The median-median line of best fit is found by drawing a line parallel to the line drawn, but $\frac{1}{3}$ of the vertical distance toward the middle summary point.

7. Calculate the y-coordinate of the point on the line joining the outer two summary points, vertically below the middle summary point. You can do this by substituting the x-coordinate of the middle summary point into the equation of the line.

8. Determine the vertical distance between the two points. Determine coordinates of the point that is $\frac{1}{3}$ of the vertical distance toward the middle summary point.

9. Use your knowledge of parallel line segments to find the equation of the new line of best fit.

Check that your equation is $y = \frac{1}{2}x + 3$.

This is one method used by some graphing calculators. Other graphing calculators use different methods to split the data into thirds. This results in slightly different equations.

Example **Use technology to determine the median-median line of best fit for a data set**

A technician discovered that when compiling the data for the red pine tree used in the Investigation, one piece of information had been omitted accidentally from the table. A red pine tree aged 25 years had been growing in a very unfavourable place and had a diameter of 5 cm. Use technology to find the new median-median line of best fit for the complete set of data.

SOLUTION

Enter the data into Lists L1 and L2. Be sure to include the extra data point (25, 5).

UTILITY

If you have never found the equation of a median-median line of best fit using a graphing calculator, Utility 14 shows you how to do this on a TI-83. If you have a different graphing calculator, check the manual that came with it.

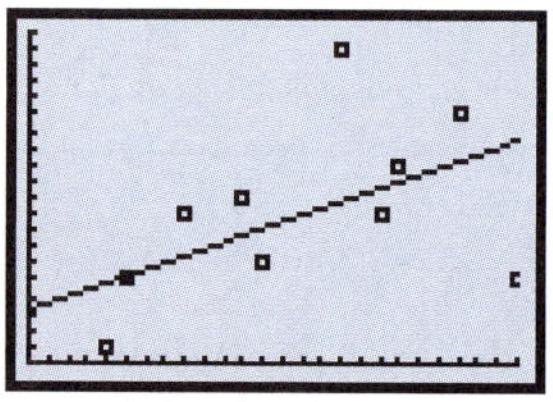

You should have found that the new equation of the median-median line of best fit is:

$$Y = 0.4117647059x + 3.205882353$$

DISCUSSING THE IDEAS

1. Explain why you think an estimated line of best fit is still used initially when analyzing data.

2. When using technology, when do you think you might use the median-median method? Why may it produce an equation that is easier to work with?

3. In the Example, what was the effect on the median-median line of best fit of an additional outlier data point?

PROJECTS

In this Tutorial you determined the equation of a line of best fit using technology. You will need these skills when you do the Chapter Project, and for the following projects in the Project Book.

- Hair Products Research
- Scuba-Diving Tours
- Anthropology

EXERCISES

Checking Your Skills

1. Below are the heights, in metres, and masses, in kilograms, of 13 students.

Height	**1.50**	**1.51**	**1.52**	**1.54**	**1.56**	**1.58**	**1.60**	**1.61**	**1.64**	**1.65**	**1.66**	**1.70**	**1.72**
Weight	**51**	**56**	**54**	**58**	**56**	**62**	**91**	**65**	**66**	**70**	**71**	**74**	**74**

Plot the data and determine lines of best fit, using the following methods.

a) estimation

b) median-median method

2. The table below shows the winning times (in seconds) for the men's Olympic 100-m dash. Donovan Bailey won the gold medal for Canada in Atlanta with a world record time of 9.84 s.

a) Use the median-median method to find the equation of a line of best fit. Predict the winning time for the 100-m dash in 2004.

Atlanta 1996	Donovan Bailey	Canada	9.84 s
Barcelona 1992	Linford Christie	Great Britain	9.96 s
Seoul 1988	Carl Lewis	U.S.A.	9.92 s
Los Angeles 1984	Carl Lewis	U.S.A.	9.99 s
Moscow 1980	Allen Wells	Great Britain	10.25 s
Montreal 1976	Hasely Crawford	Trinidad and Tobago	10.06 s
Munich 1972	Valeri Borzov	Soviet Union	10.14 s
Mexico City 1968	Jim Hines	U.S.A.	9.95 s
Tokyo 1964	Bob Hayes	U.S.A.	10.0 s
Rome 1960	Armin Hary	West Germany	10.2 s

b) This exercise assumes that the relationship is linear. What are the implications of this assumption?

3. An obstetrician checks the measurements of various parts of a fetus using ultrasound technology. She is able to determine whether the baby is developing at a healthy rate by checking her measurements in a table that shows average sizes for particular stages of development. The table below shows a portion of the doctor's chart.

Age (weeks)	Head Circumference (cm)
12	7.1
16	12.4
20	17.5
24	22.1
28	26.2
32	29.7
36	32.5
40	34.5

a) Use technology to graph a scatterplot of head circumference as a function of age and find the equation of a line of best fit.

b) Use the equation to estimate an average measurement of head circumference for a fetus aged 30 weeks.

c) A pregnant woman visits her doctor and an ultrasound finds that the head circumference of the fetus is 20.6 cm. What age in weeks does the doctor predict for the fetus?

Extending Your Thinking

4. Research population data for your own province. You may wish to use the Internet and start your search at the Addison Wesley site. Plot the data and determine a line of best fit using a computing tool. Can you predict the population for the year 2000 based on the graph? How reliable would the prediction be? Explain.

5. Use your results from exercise 3. A growth rate that is ahead, or behind, by more than two weeks gives a doctor reason for concern. If a woman is 33 weeks pregnant and the fetal head circumference measures 28.3 cm, will the doctor be concerned? Explain.

COMMUNICATING THE IDEAS

Write a short summary of the sequence of the steps needed to find and graph the equation of the line of best fit for the model of calculator that you are using. Create a troubleshooting poster to display in the classroom.

TUTORIAL 6.8

The Equation of a Line of Best Fit Using the Least Squares Method and Technology

One of the most widely used methods of determining the straight line that best fits a given set of data points is the method of least squares.

You know already that some of the data points usually lie above the line of best fit and some below it. The least square method considers the vertical distance of each point from the line. This vertical distance is called a *residual*.

For example, consider the data set below with scatterplot and line of best fit.

Course Mark	Entrance Mark
63	29
67	17
70	26
72	30
74	30
77	22
81	32

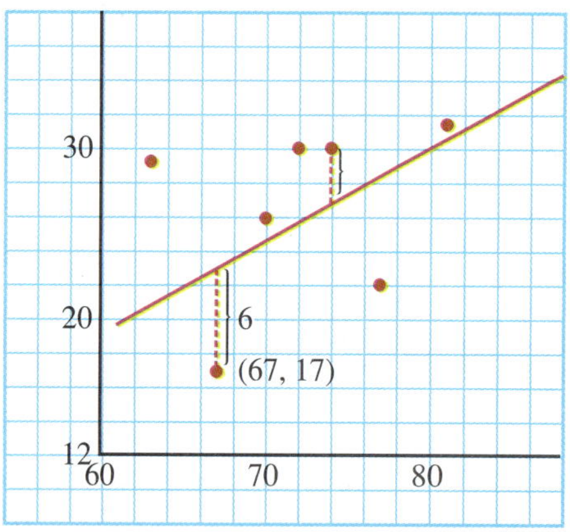

The residuals of some of the points are shown. The point (67, 17) has a residual of 6. The square of this residual is 36, and the method of least squares requires that the sum of all such squares should be a minimum.

The calculation involved in this method is substantial. The method has been programmed into the graphing calculator, spreadsheet programs, and many scientific calculators. Some programs require that the squares of the perpendicular distance of the point from the line should be a minimum.

The following Investigation shows you how to find the equation using a graphing calculator.

Investigation 1 Least Squares Method for Finding the Equation of the Line of Best Fit

Use the data for the Red Pine tree given in the Investigation in *Tutorial 6.7*. Have a graphing calculator beside you as you work through this Investigation.

1. If you have not already done so, enter the data in the list editor. Enter the ages in the first list and the diameter in the second list.

If you need to review entering data into lists, see Utility 7.

2. Define the viewing window. Choose values so that the data will appear on the screen.

3. Define a statistical plot. You must identify the list for each axis and the type of graph you want.

If you need to review this skill, see Utility 7.

4. Graph the data. Make sure that the screen is clear and press [GRAPH].

5. Determine the equation of the line of best fit. Press [STAT] then right arrow key to highlight CALC. Press [4] to choose LinReg(ax+b): Linear Regression that uses the least squares method to find the equation. Press [ENTER] to get the results. The screen should look like the one below.

6. Graph the line of best fit. Press [Y=] then [VARS] 5 to select Statistics. Press right arrow key twice to select EQ. EQ and 1: RegEQ should be highlighted. Press [ENTER] [GRAPH] to display the scatterplot and the line of best fit. Your screen should look like the one below.

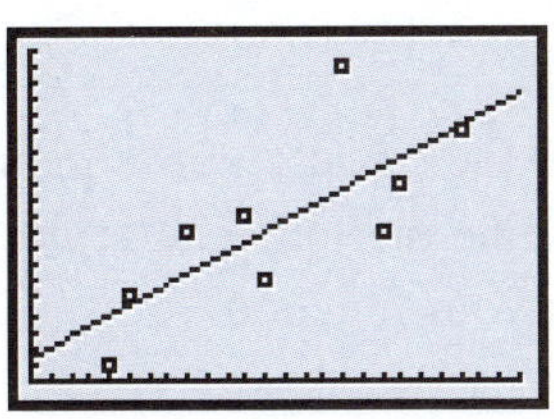

In the Investigation that follows you will compare the three methods of obtaining a line of best fit.

Investigation 2 Compare the Lines of Best Fit Obtained Using Different Methods

A student was investigating the resistance (R, ohms) in an electrical circuit in the science laboratory by measuring the voltage (V, volts) when a current (A, amperes) was passing through the circuit. The data below were collected.

Current (A)	Voltage (V)
0.5	5.0
1.0	10.3
1.5	15.2
2.0	20.4
2.5	25.5
3.0	30.5
3.5	35.8
4.0	4.7
4.5	46.0

1. Draw a scatterplot of the data on a coordinate grid. If you can print from your calculator, you could enter the data into list L1 and L2 and draw the scatterplot on your calculator. Plot the current on the horizontal axis and the voltage on the vertical axis.

2. Use a clear ruler. Draw an estimated line of best fit.

3. Determine the equation of the estimated line of best fit.

4. Enter the data into list L1 and L2 of your graphing calculator. Create a scatterplot of the data and determine the equation of the line of best fit using the median-median method. Draw the line on your scatterplot. Record the equation in your notebook.

5. Use your calculator to determine the equation of a line of best fit using the least squares method. Draw this line on your scatterplot. Record the equation of the line of best fit in your notebook.

6. Which of the three methods do you think gives the most appropriate line of best fit for this data set? Why?

Discussing the Ideas

1. What is the effect of an outlier such as (4.0, 4.7) in *Investigation* 2 on the line of best fit obtained using technology?
2. The data used in *Investigation* 2 have all the points except for one that is very nearly collinear. How could you account for the outlier?
3. Explain why you should always look at the scatterplot of a data set before deciding which method to use to determine a line of best fit.
4. Why is it important when using technology to estimate the domain and range of the data?
5. The graphing calculator only follows instructions. When a graph does not appear, or if there is an error message, it is important to be able to troubleshoot. Describe how the following situations might be remedied.
   a) The graph does not appear.
   b) The graph appears, but is located close to the edge of the window.
   c) The graph on the screen is different from those of other students.
6. How can the graph obtained using technology be used to find the coordinates of points on the line?

PROJECTS

In this Tutorial you determined the equation of a line of best fit using technology. You will need these skills when you do the Chapter Project, and for the following projects in the Project Book.

- Hair Products Research
- Scuba-Diving Tours
- Anthropology

Exercises

Checking Your Skills

Redo the exercises of *Tutorial 6.7*, using the Least Squares Method for finding a line of best fit.

Communicating the Ideas

Write a paragraph comparing the various methods for determining an equation of a line of best fit.

TUTORIAL 6.9

The Correlation Coefficient

In the scatterplots that were graphed in previous *Tutorials*, some sets of data gave graphs that were very close to being linear. Other sets of data showed a linear trend in the points, but not as strongly.

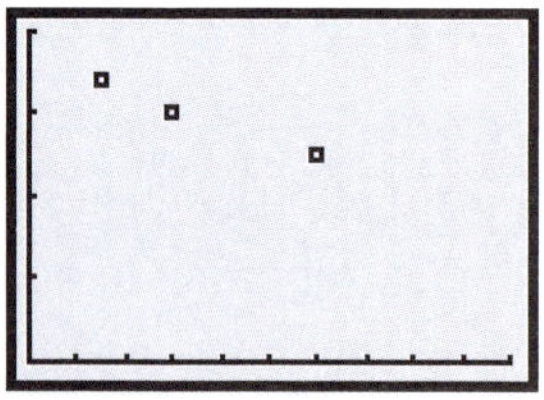

The graph above shows data points that are very close to a line. The graph below shows points with a linear trend.

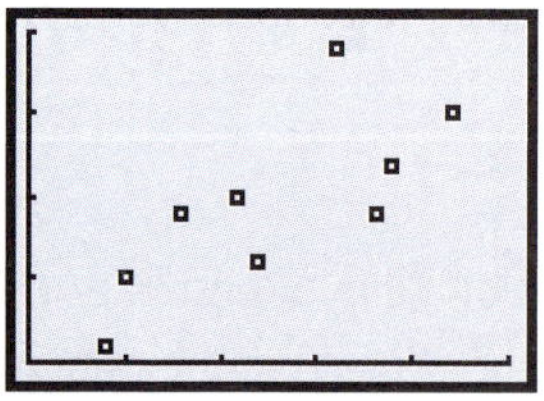

Statisticians assign a number to indicate how close the points in a scatterplot are to forming a line. This is the *correlation coefficient*, r.

Some graphing calculators determine r when they find the equation of the line of best fit using the least squares method. To display the correlation coefficient with the equation of the line of best fit, you must turn on the diagnostic feature. This is done before the data are entered and the window is set, by pressing [2nd] [CATALOG], then scrolling down the list using the down arrow until Diagnostic On is reached. Press [ENTER] [ENTER]. When the equation for the line of best fit is displayed, the value for r appears at the bottom of the display.

If you are using a different graphing calculator, or a scientific calculator, consult the manual that came with it to find the appropriate steps to determine r.

In the Investigation that follows, you will determine the correlation coefficient for various data sets. You will investigate the effect of outliers on the correlation coefficient. Work in groups of 5 to complete this *Investigation*.

Investigation

The Correlation Coefficient

In this *Investigation* the x-values and y-values are all in the range from 0 to 10. If you are using a graphing calculator, set the window accordingly.

1. Enter each of the sets of data below into a computing tool and find the correlation coefficient, r, for each set. Draw a scatterplot of each data set in your notebooks and print the value of r underneath each. Each member of the group should do 2 parts of this question.

a)

x	1	2	4	5	8	8	10
y	2	2	3	5	6	8	10

b)

x	0	1	2	3	5	6	6
y	0	2	4	6.5	8	9	10

c)

x	1	2	3	4	7	8	10
y	1	3	6	2	9	6	7

d)

x	1	1.5	2	2.5	4	4.5	5
y	2	3	4	5	8	9	10

e)

x	1	3	4	5	7	8	10
y	9	8	6	5.5	6	3	2

f)

x	1	2	4	6	7	9	10
y	1	2	4.5	6	7.5	1	10

g)

x	1	1	3	4	7	8	10
y	5	8	2	6	5	2	1

h)

x	1	2	4	5	5	8	8
y	1	6	5	7	2	5	8

i)

x	0	1	2	3	6	8	10
y	8	7.5	7	6.5	5	4	3

j)

x	2	2	3	5	5	8	10
y	2	7	4	2	8	7	1

2. For each of the graphs you plotted, draw an estimated line of best fit, if possible. If it is not possible, then write "not possible."

3. For each of the graphs, describe, in words, how closely the points fit the line. Use the following terms: exactly, very closely, somewhat closely, weakly, not at all.

4. Share your work with the other members of your group.

5. Compare the descriptions in exercise 3 to the value of r for each graph. What is the connection between how close a set of points is to being linear and its correlation coefficient?

6. Which of the lines have a negative slope, and which have a positive slope? What is the connection between the sign of r and the slope of the line of best fit?

DISCUSSING THE IDEAS

1. Between what two numbers does the correlation coefficient lie?

2. Describe the relationship between the value of r and the shape of the scatterplots.

3. In graph f, if the point with coordinates (9, 1) were changed to the point (9, 9.5), what would be the new correlation coefficient?

4. Explain why a scatterplot with only two data points will always have an r value of 1, or -1, or undefined.

5. Describe how exercise 1 f illustrates the limitations of only using a calculator and the correlation coefficient to determine how close a data set is to a linear function.

EXERCISES

Checking Your Skills

1. Sketch possible graphs of scatterplots that have approximately the following correlation coefficients.

a) $r = -0.95$ **b)** $r = 1$ **c)** $r = 0.25$ **d)** $r = 0.65$

2. For each of the following graphs, estimate the value of r.

a)

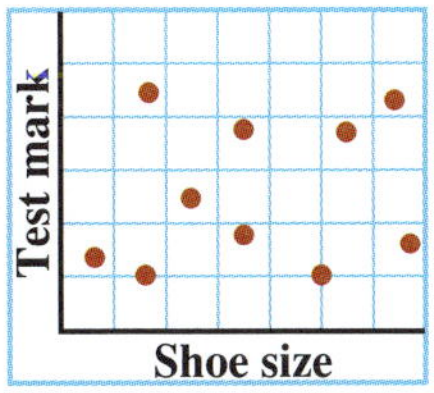

b)

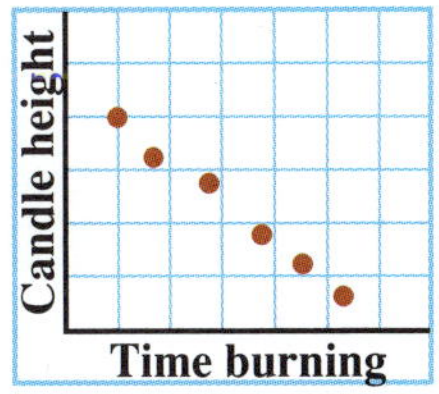

c)

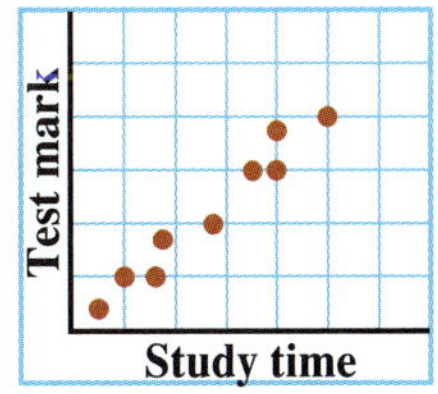

d)

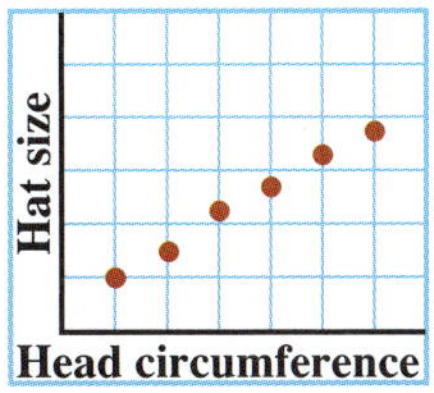

e)

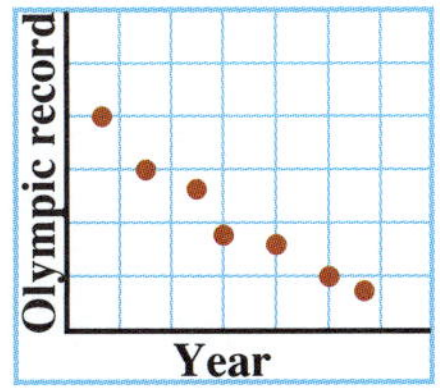

3. The following table gives data on top scoring players from the N.H.L. in 1998.

Sweater #	Name	Shots	Goals
68	JAGR	235	32
99	GRETZKY	184	20
96	BURE	290	45
10	LECLAIR	266	44
14	FLEURY	251	26
77	OATES	109	16
88	LINDROS	186	28
8	RECCHI	192	30
13	SUNDIN	195	29
39	WEIGHT	177	25
19	YASHIN	259	30
16	PALFFY	239	37

a) Which of the following relations would you expect to most closely fit a linear model?

i) goals scored versus sweater number

ii) goals scored versus attempted shots

b) Predict a correlation coefficient for each of i and ii, then use technology to find the correlation coefficient for each function. Comment on how close your predictions were.

4. The following shows a patient's temperature taken over a period of 14 h.

Time	Temperature (°C)
08:00	39
10:00	39.5
12:00	39.5
14:00	40
16:00	40.5
18:00	38
20:00	37.5
22:00	38

a) Graph the temperature as a function of time. Predict a value for the correlation coefficient.

b) Use the graphics calculator to find the equation of a line of best fit and the correlation coefficient r.

c) Explain why it would not be wise to use the equation you have found to predict the patient's temperature at midnight.

5. a)

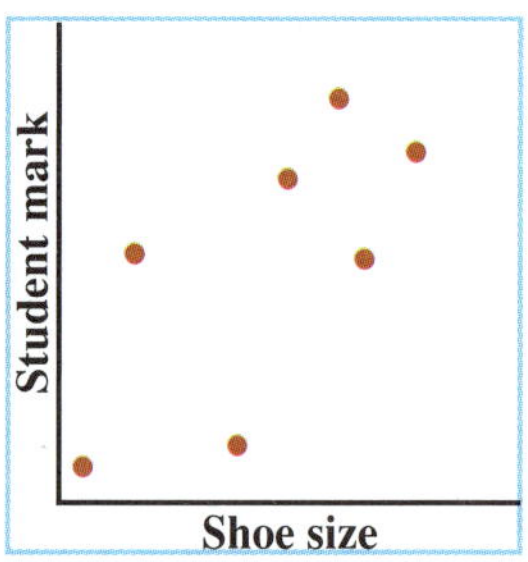

b)

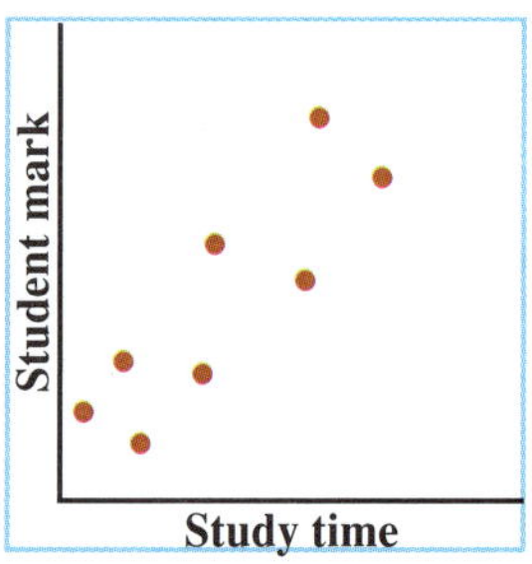

Scatterplot (a) is a plot of student marks on the last test against their shoe size. The value for r was calculated to be 0.2. Scatterplot (b) is the plot of student marks on the last test against the time spent studying. The value for r was calculated to be 0.8. Describe the relationship between the values for r and the shape of the scatterplots.

Extending Your Thinking

6. Gina is doing a science report on the effectiveness of sunscreen as indicated by its sunscreen protection factor (SPF). She has found out that the percentage of the sun's ultraviolet light that passes through the sunscreen can be calculated using the SPF number. She created a table showing her data, but did not get the percentage for SPF 2 or for SPF 45. She decides to make a guess, and to put in 15 for SPF 2 and 0.1 for SPF 45. Graphing a scatterplot and using her calculator, she finds the equation for the line of best fit, and the correlation coefficient.

Sunscreen Protection Factor (SPF)	Percentage of ultraviolet light passing through
2	?
5	20
8	12.5
15	6.7
25	4.0
45	?

a) What are Gina's results for the equation and for the correlation coefficient r?

b) Can she safely assume that the equation she found is correct?

c) She later checks up on her research and finds that in fact the true percentage for SPF 2 is 50, and that for SPF 45 is 2.2. She decides to use the calculator again to find the equation and the correlation coefficient. What results does she get?

d) Explain how Gina's two sets of results (one false, one true) show the limitations of the correlation coefficient.

There are many different types of functions, as you saw in Chapter 3: inverse, quadratic, exponential, and so on. This example illustrates the need to look at the scatterplot to help you decide whether the relationship is linear or not.

PROJECTS

In this Tutorial you were introduced to the correlation coefficient. You will need this skill when you complete the Chapter Project, and for the following projects in the Project Book.

- Hair Products Research
- Scuba-Diving Tours
- Anthropology

COMMUNICATING THE IDEAS

Explain the meaning of the term "correlation coefficient." Describe the relationship between values of r and the shape of scatterplots. Use diagrams in your explanation.

CHAPTER PROJECT

Gorillas and Humans: Contrasting the Species

You have now determined the estimated line of best fit. The data can now be analyzed using technology.

- Use a graphing calculator to determine the equation of a line of best fit, and the correlation coefficient for the human data you collected in *Tutorial 6.1, Investigation 1*. Note the equation and value of r in your notebook. Draw the scatterplot and line of best fit for the data. If the technology is available, print out the graphs.
- Repeat the first exercise for the data relating to gorillas, given in the Chapter Project on page 292.
- Compare each equation to the estimated lines of best fit obtained in the Chapter Project on page 292.
- Which set of data has the highest value of r?
- Give an interpretation of the slope for each graph.
- Consider the relationship between structure and behaviour. Suggest reasons why the slope of the graphs you drew for gorillas is different from the slope for humans.

Career Skills

People who work in the field of science and technology collect, graph, and analyze data. When exploring the possible relationship between two quantities, people first check for a linear relationship. The equation of a line of best fit and its interpretation are essential skills.

CONSOLIDATING YOUR SKILLS

What Do I Need To Know?

Tutorial	Skills and Concepts	Important Results and Formulas
6.1	• Investigate the equation of a linear function • Determine the intercepts of a linear function	• The equation of a linear function is $y = mx + b$. • The x-intercept is the x-coordinate of the point where the line intersects the x-axis. • The y-intercept is the y-coordinate of the point where the line intersects the y-axis.
6.2	• Investigate the equation of a line; interpret the constants m and b • Investigate the equations of vertical lines and horizontal lines	• The graph of the equation $y = mx + b$ is a line with slope m and y-intercept b. • The slope y-intercept equation of a line is $Y = mx + b$. • The equation of a vertical line is $x = a$. • The equation of a horizontal line is $y = b$.
6.3	• Apply and interpret linear functions to solve problems • Understand direct variation	• Y varies directly as x if $y = mx$. • The graph of a direct variation relationship is a straight line through the origin.
6.4	• Investigate number patterns • Understand what is an arithmetic sequence • Understand the relationship between the common difference between terms and the slope of the graph	• An arithmetic sequence of terms is a linear function whose domain is the natural numbers. • The common difference between terms of an arithmetic sequence is the slope of the graph of the function.
6.5	• Determine the equation of a line, given the slope and y-intercept • Determine the equation of a line, given the slope and one point on the line • Determine the equation of a line, given two points on the line	
6.6	• Determine the equation of an estimated line of best fit	
6.7	• Determine the equation of a line of best fit using the median-median method	
6.8	• Determine the equation of a line of best fit using the least squares method and technology	
6.9	• Investigate the correlation coefficient	

What Should I Be Able To Do?

When you have worked through the *Tutorials* and exercises in this chapter, you should be able to solve the following problems. Part A is investigative. Refer to the *Tutorials*, *Utilities*, and *Student Reference* as required when you do these exercises.

Part A

You will need grid paper, a clear ruler, and a measuring tape or ribbon if you collect your own data.

You will investigate the relationship between the size of a person's wrist and the size of that person's neck. Your teacher will indicate whether you will use data collected from your class or if you should use the data provided here.

An applied mathematics class measured the circumference of their wrists and necks. The resulting data are given in the table.

Wrist (cm)	Neck (cm)
14.5	30.5
15	32
15.5	31.5
15.7	34.2
16	33
16.1	34.5
16.5	37.2
16.7	35.4
17	33.4
17.1	32
17.1	36
17.2	37.1
17.7	34.5
18	37
18.4	37.5
18.7	39.5
19	36
19.5	37.5
19.5	39.9
20.5	39

1. Draw a scatterplot of the data on page 313 on grid paper.

2. Draw an estimated line of best fit and determine its equation.

3. Enter the data into list L1 and L2 of your graphing calculator. Determine the equation of the line of best fit using the least squares method, and the correlation coefficient.

4. Is it reasonable to say that there is an approximately linear relationship between the wrist size and the neck size for these students? Explain.

5. Use the equation of a line of best fit to predict the neck size of a student whose wrist size is 18.2 cm.

6. Measure your own wrist size. Predict your neck size. Check your prediction by measurement.

Part B

7. Determine the intercepts of the lines below.

a) $y = 2x - 8$ **b)** $3x + 4y + 24 = 0$

8. Determine the slope and y-intercept of each line.

a) $-2x + 3y + 10 = 0$ **b)** $4x - 3y - 6 = -6$

9. The cost, C dollars, for a school basketball team to play in a tournament is given by the formula $C = 300 + 20n$, where n is the numbers of players.

a) What is the domain of the function $C(n)$?

b) Draw a graph of the function.

c) What is the slope of the graph? What are its units? What does it represent?

d) What is the C-intercept of the graph? What does it represent?

10. A supertanker travelling at 25 km/h needs 5 km to come to a complete stop. Suppose stopping distance varies directly as speed.

a) Draw a graph of stopping distance as a function of speed. Use speed as the independent variable.

b) Determine the stopping distance for a supertanker travelling at 12 km/h.

c) Use your graph. The stopping distance for a supertanker is 3.5 km. At what speed was it travelling before it began to slow down?

11. A taxi company sets its fares using the following scheme. It charges $2.50 when you enter the cab and an additional $0.10 for every 12 s after the meter has started.

a) Create a table that shows the total fare after 0, 1, 2, 3, 4, 5, and 6 min in the cab.

b) What type of sequence do the fares in the table form?

c) Graph the function defined by your table.

d) Write an equation to represent the function.

e) Use your graph. Determine the fare for a 10-min taxi ride. Use the equation to check your answer.

12. The following data on used cars were collected from the classified section of a newspaper.

Age of car (years)	Asking price ($)
6	7000
1	15 000
9	1500
3	13 500
5	11 900
4	6900

a) Use grid paper. Create a scatterplot of the data.

b) Determine the median-median line of best fit for the data.

c) How well does a linear function describe these data?

d) Use technology to check your answer to exercise c, and to determine the correlation coefficient.

e) A person is asking $6000 for a car that is 6 years old. Is this asking price reasonable? Explain.

Part C

The Chapter Project combines many skills and concepts in a single problem. Here is a sampling of possible student work at various stages of the project. Review these samples to gain insight into your own project.

13. Here are the graphs plotted by one student.

- Look at the graph. Has the student chosen scales that display the data well?
- Are the data plotted correctly?
- Compare the student's estimated line of best fit for the gorilla data with yours. How closely do you agree?

Write a summary of your assessment of this students' work.

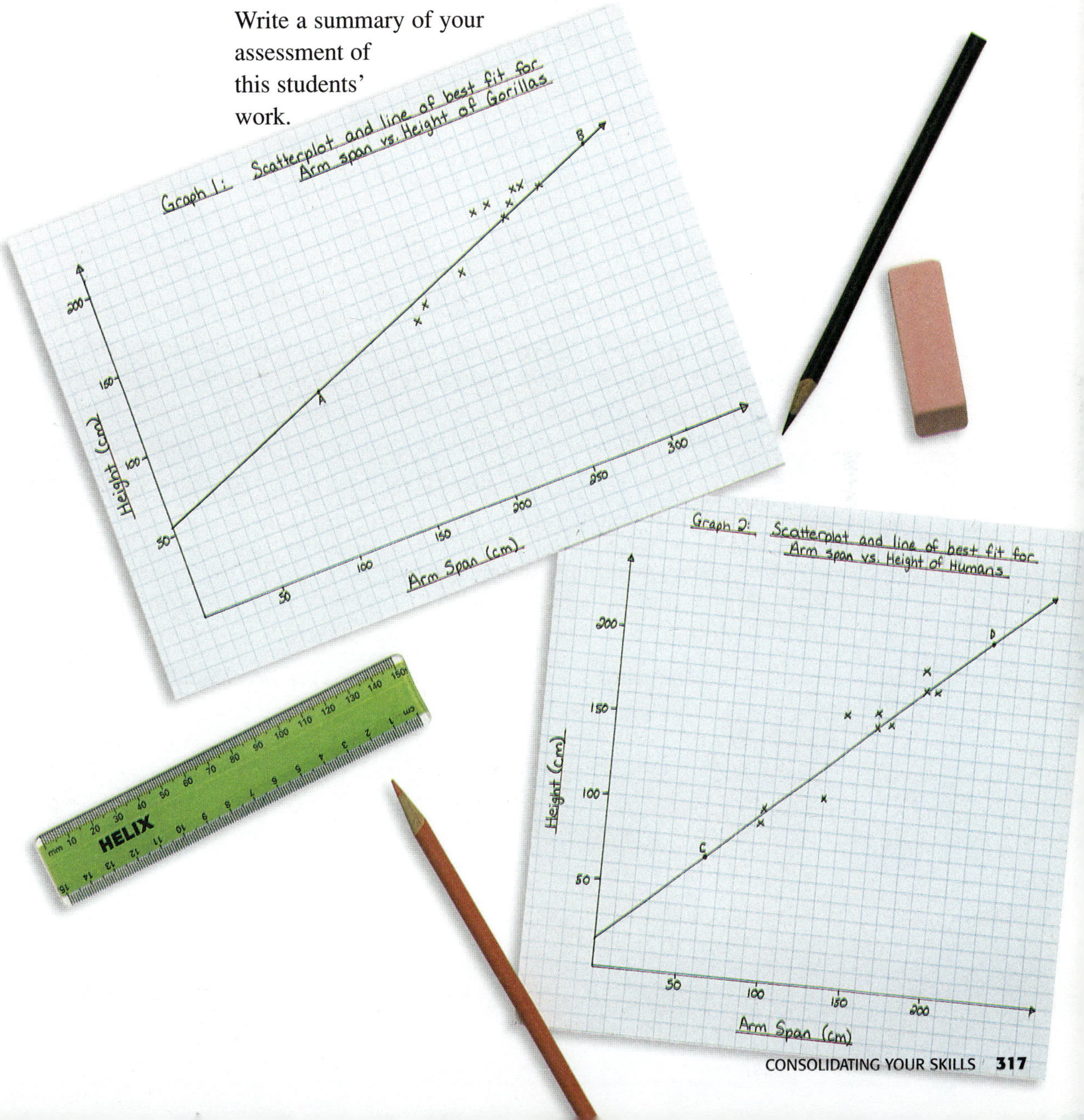

14. The student estimates the slope of his line of best fit for the gorilla data to be approximately 0.4. The student used the point with coordinates (110, 100) on the line of best fit and calculated the equation to be $y = 0.4x + 56$.

Using this equation, the student estimated the arm span of Koko and Ndume to be 291 cm and 310 cm respectively.

- Did the student calculate the equation for this line of best fit correctly?
- Are the student's figures for the missing arm spans correct?
- Did you get approximately the same results?

Write a summary of your assessment of this student's work.

15. When analyzing the results for the Project, a student wrote:

My estimated line of best fit for the gorilla data was really close to the one I got on my calculator, especially for the slope. My estimated line of best fit for the human data was very close to the slope obtained with the calculator, but not close for the vertical intercept.

The correlation coefficients for both sets of data are close to 1, so I think linear models are appropriate. When I looked at the graph for the gorilla data, I noticed that it is a bit scattered for gorillas with heights in the 160 to 170 cm range. The overall graph can still use a linear model.

The slope represents height to arm-span ratio. It does not have units. The slope for gorillas is smaller than that for humans, which means that the ratio of height to arm span is smaller. This is because gorillas have really long arms compared to their body length. For humans, the slope is close to 1. This means that the height and arm span for a human is almost the same.

- Has the student interpreted the data in a way that makes sense to you?
- Is there anything the student has missed considering?

Write a summary of this student's work.

7 Trigonometry

Overview

PROJECT

You should do at least one project that uses the skills you learn in this chapter. The recommended projects in the Project Book are:

- Jet Propulsion
- Reach for the Top
- Remote Sensing

CHAPTER PROJECT

Land Surveying

A land survey is a study of an area of land to determine its exact boundaries and contours by measuring distances and angles. Surveyors use instruments such as a clinometer and transit.

In this Chapter Project you will survey your school property, or an assigned area of your community. You will use your survey and those of your classmates to create a model of the school property or the designated community area.

Here are some initial questions to consider.

- When surveying a property, what information is important?
- How are distances measured?
- How are angles measured?
- What instruments does a surveyor use? What does each instrument measure?
- What instrument or measuring tools do you need for your survey?

Research land surveying on the Internet or at a library.

CHAPTER PROJECT

To do this Chapter Project, you will need a clinometer and a transit. You will return to the Chapter Project on page 328.

FYI Visit: www.awl.com/canada/school/connections/

You can start your research from our Internet site: Click on MATHLINKS, followed by the *Applied Mathematics 10* logo. Then select a topic under Land Surveying.

TUTORIAL
7.1
Indirect Measurement

In an earlier grade you were introduced to trigonometry. The word means "triangle measurement." Using trigonometry, you can calculate the angles of a triangle and the lengths of its sides, provided you have sufficient information to draw the triangle.

Trigonometry is used to determine the height of tall objects from a distance.

Practise Your Prior Skills

In the work that follows, you will determine the lengths of sides and measures of angles in right triangles.

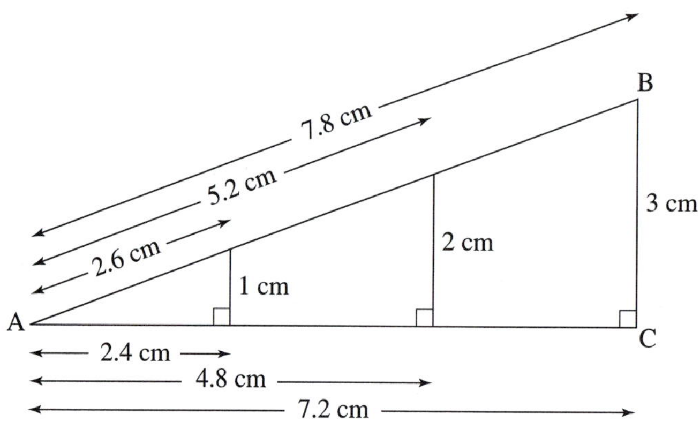

If ∠A is an acute angle in a right triangle, then

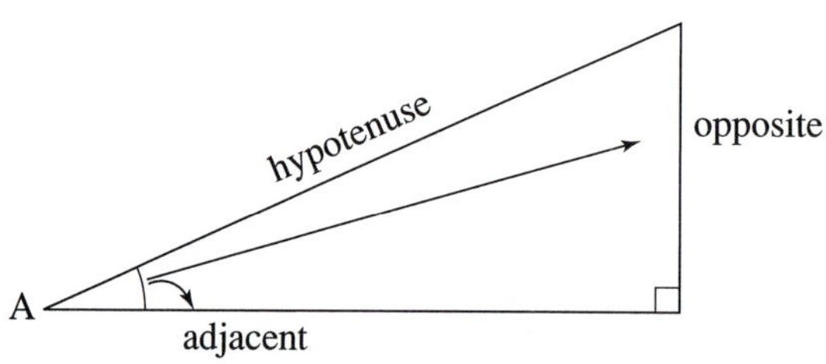

$$\text{Tan A} = \frac{\text{Length of side opposite } \angle A}{\text{Length of side adjacent to } \angle A}$$

$$\text{Sin A} = \frac{\text{Length of side opposite } \angle A}{\text{Length of hypotenuse}}$$

$$\text{Cos A} = \frac{\text{Length of side adjacent to} \angle A}{\text{Length of hypotenuse}}$$

STUDENT REFERENCE

If you would like to look at some worked examples using the trigonometric ratios to determine the lengths of unknown sides and measures of angles, look in the Student Reference under "tangent," "sine," and "cosine."

Try these exercises with your calculator set in degree mode. To check this, press MODE. The screen below will appear.

The unit of measurement for angles is displayed on the third line. If Degree is not highlighted as shown, move the curser to this word and press ENTER.

1. In right △ABC, calculate tan A, ∠A, and the length of side AC to the nearest centimetre.

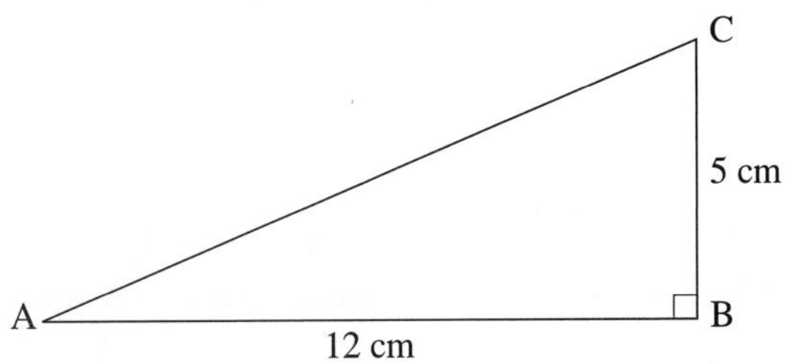

2. In right △PQR, calculate sin R, ∠R, and the length of QR to the nearest centimetre.

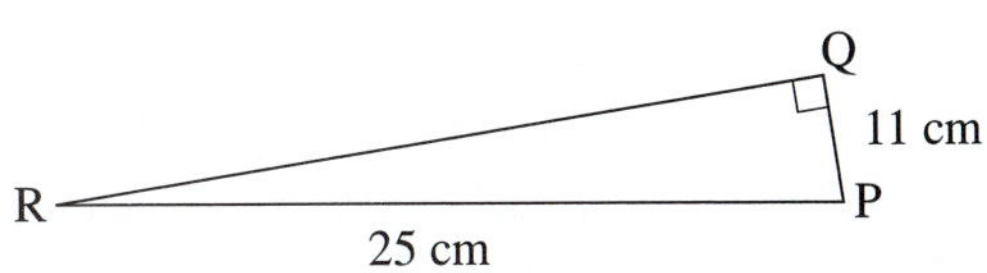

3. In the right △XYZ, determine the lengths of XZ and XY to the nearest millimetre.

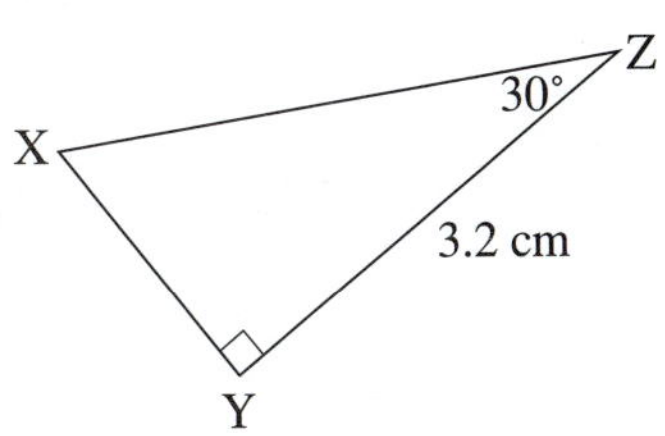

Trigonometry is a powerful tool for determining distances that cannot easily be measured directly.

Investigation 1 **Indirect Measurement**

You will need a metre stick and an empty carton (such as an empty photocopy paper box).

In this *Investigation* you will use your knowledge of right angle trigonometry to determine the angle of inclination of a metre stick leaning against a wall and its height. Both you and your partner should make each measurement three times.

1. Measure the dimensions of the carton.

2. Place the stick inside the carton as shown in the diagram below left. Use your measurements and your knowledge of trigonometry to determine the angle of inclination of the stick.

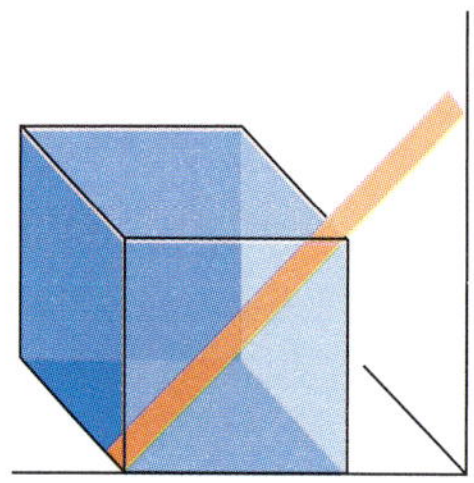

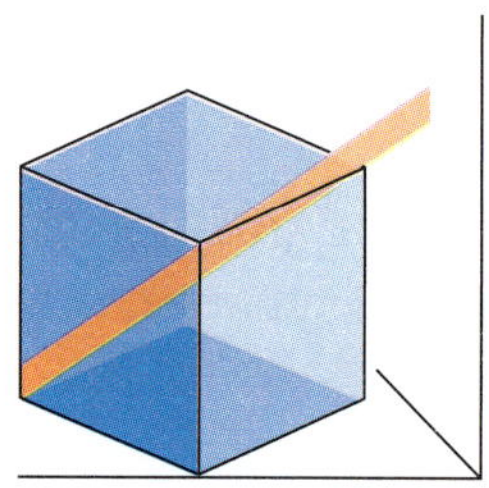

3. Place the carton on the floor near the wall, with the top of the metre stick just touching the corners of the box and the wall. Use the length of the stick and your answer to exercise 2 to calculate how far up the wall the stick reaches.

4. Check your answer to exercise 3 by measurement. Comment on the results. Which answer do you think is more accurate?

5. Move the carton away from the wall. Place the metre stick along the main diagonal of the carton, as shown in the diagram above right. What additional measurements or calculations must you make to calculate the angle of inclination of the metre stick? Determine the angle of inclination.

6. Place the carton on the floor near the wall so that the metre stick just touches the wall and the corners of the box. Calculate how high up the wall the stick reaches.

7. Check your answer by measuring. Comment on the accuracy of the results.

8. Explain why the angle of inclination you found in exercise 5 is less than the angle of inclination you found in exercise 2.

Example 1 **Determine the height of a kite**

A boy flying a kite lets out 200 m of string. The string is taut and makes an angle of 72° with the horizontal. If the boy's hand is 1.42 m above the ground, how high is the kite?

SOLUTION

Sketch the boy and kite from the side. The string is the hypotenuse of a right triangle.

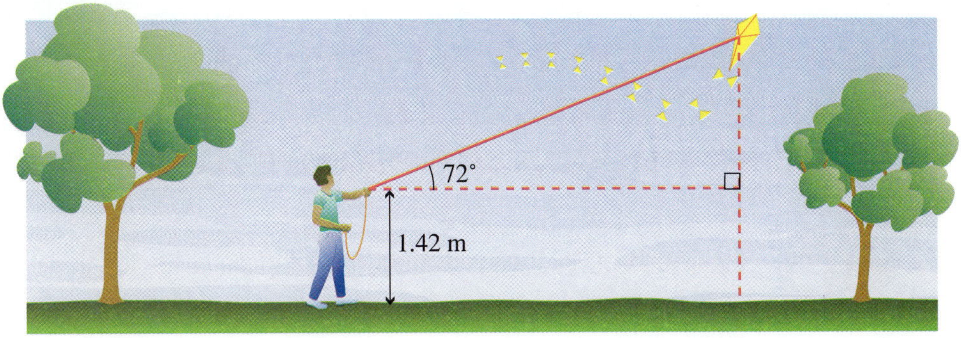

Note: this diagram is not drawn to scale.

Draw a diagram of the right triangle. Let the height of the kite above hand height be x m.

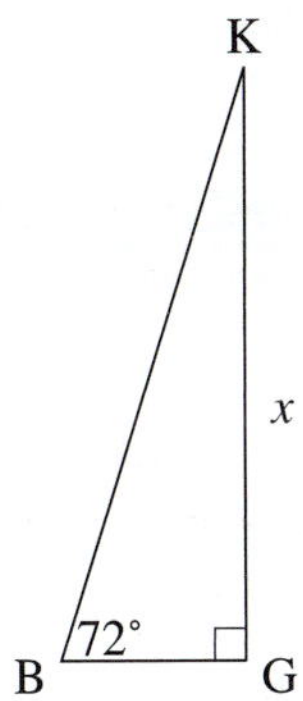

From the diagram, the side opposite the 72° angle is x m, and the length of the hypotenuse is 200 m. Use the sine ratio.

$$\begin{aligned}\text{Sin } 72^\circ &= \frac{\text{Length of the opposite side}}{\text{Length of the hypotenuse}} \\ &= \frac{x}{200}\end{aligned}$$

Clear the fraction and isolate x by multiplying both sides of the equation by 200.

$$200 \times \sin 72^\circ = x$$

Press **200** [×] [SIN] **72** [ENTER]

$$x \doteq 190.21 \text{ m}$$

To determine the height of the kite, we must now add the boy's hand height to the value for x.

$$\text{Height of the kite} \doteq 1.42\,\text{m} + 190.21\,\text{m}$$
$$\doteq 191.63\,\text{m}$$

The kite is $\doteq$ 191.63 m high.

DISCUSSING THE IDEAS

1. What is the importance of drawing diagrams?

2. In *Investigation 1*, will the accuracy of your measurements affect your results? Will the precision of your instruments affect your results?

PROJECTS

In this Tutorial you used your knowledge of trigonometry to calculate heights. You will need these skills to complete the Chapter Project and for the following projects in the Project Book.

- Reach for the Top
- Remote Sensing
- Jet Propulsion

EXERCISES

Checking Your Skills

1. A ladder is 15 m long. The top rests against the wall of a house, and the foot rests on level ground 2 m from the wall. Draw a diagram to illustrate the situation. Calculate the angle between the ladder and the ground.

2. The longest slide in the world is in Vermont, U.S.A. It drops 213 m in a horizontal distance of 1200 m.

a) How long is the slide?

b) What is its angle of inclination?

3. The angle of elevation of the sun is 68° when a tree casts a shadow 14.3 m long. How tall is the tree?

4. A tightrope walker attaches a cable to the roofs of two adjacent buildings. The cable is 21.5 m long. The angle of inclination of the cable is 12°. The buildings are 21.0 m apart. The shorter building is 10.0 m high. What is the height of the taller building?

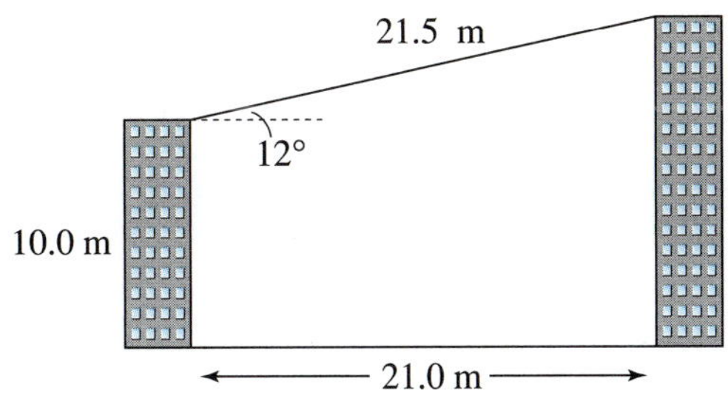

5. An architect plans to build a wheelchair ramp with a rise of 0.6 m. Safety standards indicate that the ramp may have an angle of inclination of 8°. How long must the ramp be?

6. An airplane is flying at an altitude of 6000 m over the ocean directly toward the coastline. At a certain time, the angle of depression to the coastline from the airplane is 14°. How much farther does the airplane have to fly before it reaches the coastline?

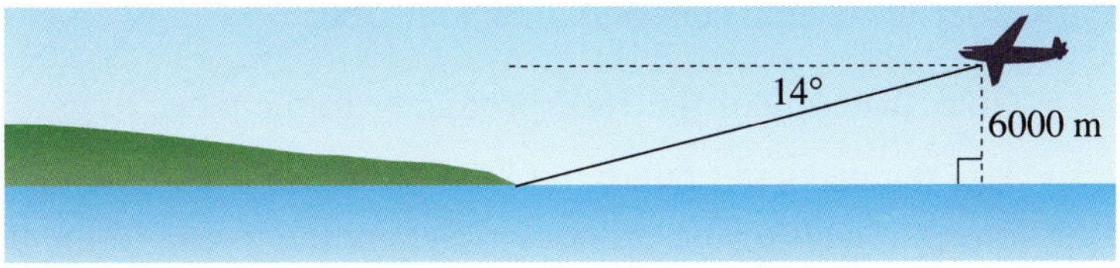

Extending Your Thinking

7. A cylindrical oil tank is 55.3 m high and 28.4 m in diameter. The top of the tank is reached by a spiral stairway that circles the tank exactly once. Calculate the angle of inclination of the stairway.

   (You may find it helpful to visualize the oil tank as a cardboard tube and the stairway as a line drawn on the tube. If the cylinder was cut open along the length of the cylinder from the top of the stairway to the bottom, how would you describe the line of the stairway?)

COMMUNICATING THE IDEAS

Given a flagpole, describe one strategy using direct measurement and one strategy using indirect measurement to determine its height. List the advantages and disadvantages of each strategy.

Making and Using a Clinometer and a Transit

Surveyors use a clinometer to measure angles of elevation or depression. Work with a partner to make a simple clinometer for use in your surveys.

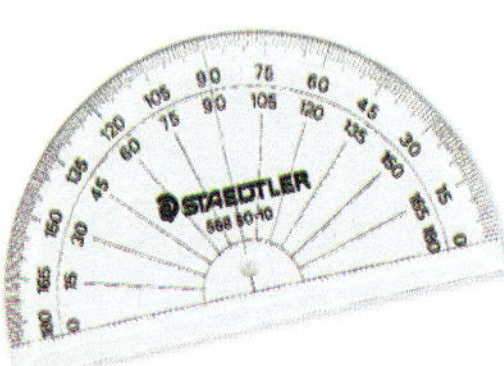

You need an enlarged photocopy of a 180° protractor, a rectangular piece of heavy cardboard, a straw, a needle, strong thread, a small washer or weight, scissors, glue, and tape.

- Stick the copy of the 180° protractor to the piece of cardboard.
- Use the needle to pull the thread through the cardboard at the cross-threads of the protractor. Secure the thread to the back of the cardboard with tape. Attach the small washer or weight to the other end of the thread.
- Tape a straw to use as a sighting tube along the top edge of the protractor.

CHAPTER PROJECT

When you return to the Chapter Project on page 376, you will make your survey. *Tutorials* 7.2 to 7.5 will help you develop the relevant skills.

To use the clinometer, work with a partner. One of you will hold the clinometer in front of you with the weight hanging down in front of the protractor. Look along the straw to the object whose angle of elevation or depression you wish to find. Your partner should read the scale of the protractor using the thread as the indicator.

A transit is used to measure horizontal angles.

You need cardboard, a straw, a photocopy of a 360° protractor, scissors, a paper fastener, a tripod, glue, and tape. You can use a dowel that has one pointed end to secure it in the ground in place of the tripod.

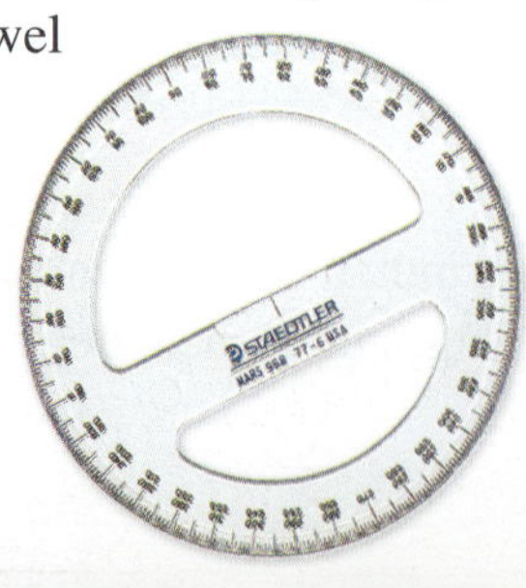

- Cut out the copy of the 360° protractor and stick it on the cardboard.
- Use the needle to pull the thread through the cardboard at the centre of the protractor. Secure the thread to the back of the cardboard with tape. Insert the thread through the straw and attach the washer or weight to end of the thread.
- Attach the cardboard to the tripod or dowel.

To use the transit, place the straw so that one end of the straw is at the cross-threads and the weight is hanging freely. Position the transit so that the sighting straw, 0° on the protractor, and the first object are all lined up. Move the sighting straw round so that the second object is in sight. Read the angle. Use the outer scale if the straw was rotated counter clockwise, and the inner scale if the straw was rotated clockwise.

Start work on your survey with a partner. Sketch your area.

Whether your class will create a model of the school or an area of your community, you will need to measure the height of buildings and other tall features such as trees and flagpoles.

Work with a partner. You will need a tape measure, a clinometer, and a transit. Both of you should take each measurement 3 times.

- Choose the tall object in your chosen area that you must measure. It could be a tree, or a flagpole, or an apartment building or school building.
- Mark a convenient spot A in the school yard or home area.
- From that place, use your clinometer to measure the angle of elevation to the top of the object. Record your measurements.
- Use the transit. Turn through an angle of 90° from the line of sight to the object. Use the tape to measure a distance of 10 m of the tape in this perpendicular direction. Mark this new position B.
- Use the transit from position B. Measure and record the horizontal angle between the line you measured in the schoolyard and the base of the object. You have now completed the outdoor measurements for this activity.
- Determine the average of each set of measures. Use the average in your calculations.
- Copy the diagram below into your notebook. Mark all right angles. Write the measurements on this diagram.

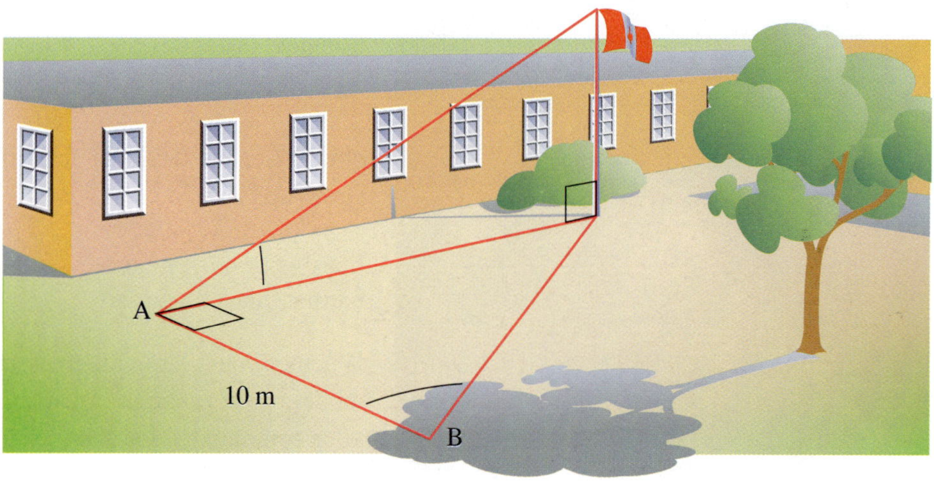

- Use your knowledge of trigonometry to determine the distance to the base of your object. Mark this on your diagram.
- Use your result from the previous exercise to determine the height of the object. Remember to add the height to eye level.

You will use your clinometer and transit to complete your land survey. Store them, and your results, carefully.

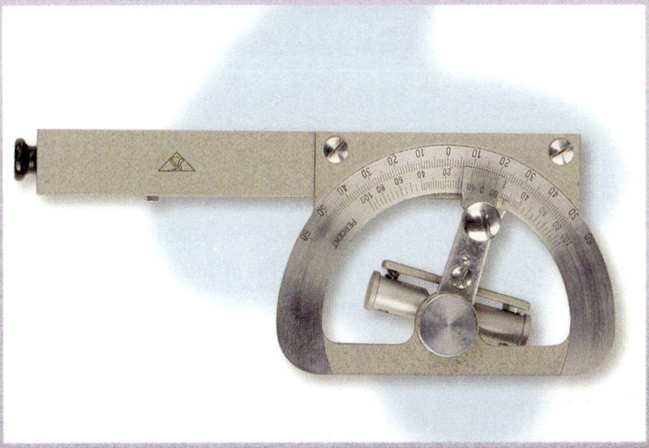

Career Skills

Surveyors make detailed plans before beginning a survey. They must decide what measurements they need to take to meet the needs of their client. Then they must choose the appropriate measuring tools to take these measurements.

Think about the area you are going to survey. What land forms and structures do you need to measure? What measuring tools do you need to use?

TUTORIAL

7.2 Solving Problems Using More Than One Right Triangle

Trigonometry was originally developed to solve navigation problems. Today, it is a powerful tool used to solve many problems.

Most problems in the real world are presented in words. Once you have understood the problem, a first step in solving it is to draw a diagram to illustrate the situation. We always assume that buildings are vertical and the ground horizontal.

Example 1 Comparing heights using indirect measurement

Two trees are 100 m apart. From a point midway between them, the angles of elevation to their tops are 8° and 13°. How much taller is one tree than the other? Answer to the nearest centimetre.

SOLUTION

Visualize the trees and the angles of elevation. Draw a diagram to model the situation. Label the vertices of the triangles as shown below.

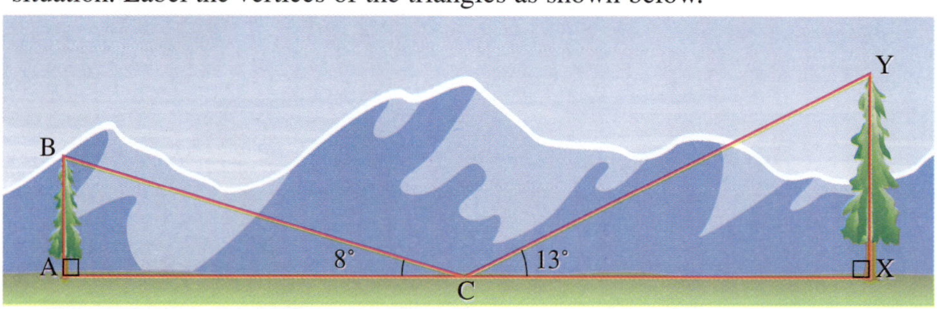

Note: this diagram is not drawn to scale.

To compare the heights, we must calculate the heights of the triangles, AB and XY. The point C is midway between the trees, so

CA = CX = 50 m.

Label the diagram.

Label the sides of each triangle opposite, adjacent, and hypotenuse in terms of the angles of elevations at C, as shown below.

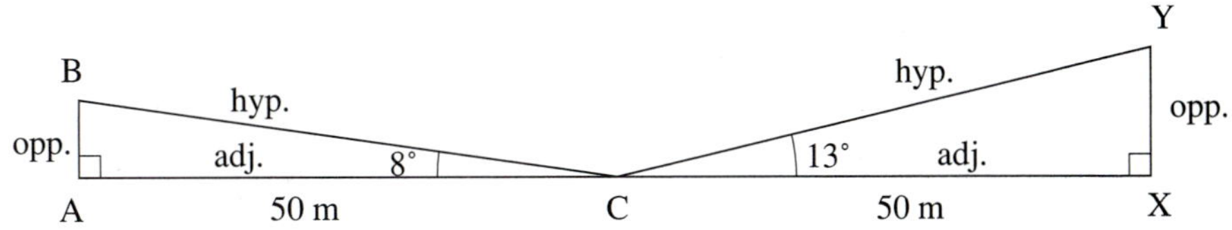

Choose the appropriate trigonometric ratio to use. In each triangle we know the length of the adjacent side and wish to find the opposite side to the known angle. Use the tangent ratio.

In triangle ABC,

$$\begin{aligned}\text{Tan } 8^\circ &= \frac{\text{Opposite}}{\text{Adjacent}} \\ &= \frac{AB}{50}\end{aligned}$$

Solve for AB.

$$\begin{aligned}50(\tan 8^\circ) &= AB \\ AB &\doteq 7.03\end{aligned}$$

Similarly, in right triangle CXY,

$$\begin{aligned}\text{Tan } 12^\circ &= \frac{\text{Opposite}}{\text{Adjacent}} \\ &= \frac{XY}{50}\end{aligned}$$

Solve for XY.

$$\begin{aligned}50(\tan 12^\circ) &= XY \\ XY &\doteq 10.63\end{aligned}$$

The trees are approximately 7.03 m and 10.63 m high respectively. Thus, one tree is about 3.60 m taller than the other.

Example 2 **Using right triangles in the same plane**

The 8th floor of an apartment building is 25 m above the ground. From the 8th floor, the angle of elevation to the top of another taller building is 50°. The angle of depression to the base of the taller building is 34°. Determine the height of the taller building.

SOLUTION

Draw a diagram to illustrate the buildings. Draw a side view. The connection between the two right triangles is their common side, which represents the distance between the buildings.

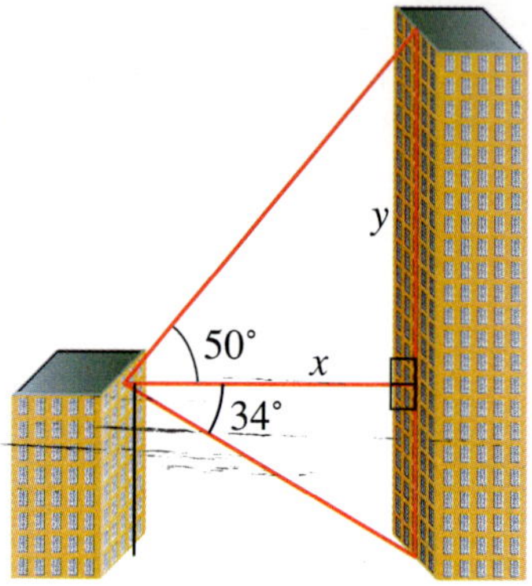

Let x metres represent the distance between the buildings.

Let y metres represent the height of the taller building above the 8th floor.

To determine x, use the lower right triangle. We are given the length of the side opposite to the known angle, and we must determine the length of the side opposite the known angle. Use the tangent ratio.

$$\text{Tan } 34^\circ = \frac{\text{Length of the opposite side}}{\text{Length of the adjacent side}}$$
$$= \frac{25}{x}$$

Multiply both sides of the equation by x to clear the fraction:

$$x \tan 34^\circ = 25$$

Divide both sides by $\tan 34^\circ$ to isolate x:

$$x = \frac{25}{\tan 34^\circ}$$
$$\doteq 37.06$$

To calculate the height of the taller building above the 8th floor, we can now work in the upper right triangle. We have just calculated the side adjacent to the known angle and have to calculate the side opposite the known angle. Use the tangent ratio.

$$\tan 50^\circ = \frac{y}{x}$$

Isolate y by multiplying both sides by 37.06.

$$37.06 \times \tan 50^\circ = y$$
$$y \doteq 44.17$$

The height of the taller building $\doteq 25\text{ m} + y\text{ m}$
$\doteq 69.17\text{ m}$

The taller building is $\doteq$ 69 m high.

Example 3 Using right triangles in different planes

A climbing club plans to scale a cliff overlooking a river. To prepare for the climb, a surveyor visited the site and took some measurements to calculate the height of the cliff. From a point R on the shore directly across the river, the angle of elevation to the top of the cliff is $\angle TRB = 43°$. From a point S, 30 m down the river, $\angle BSR = 69°$. How high is the cliff? Express the answer to the nearest metre.

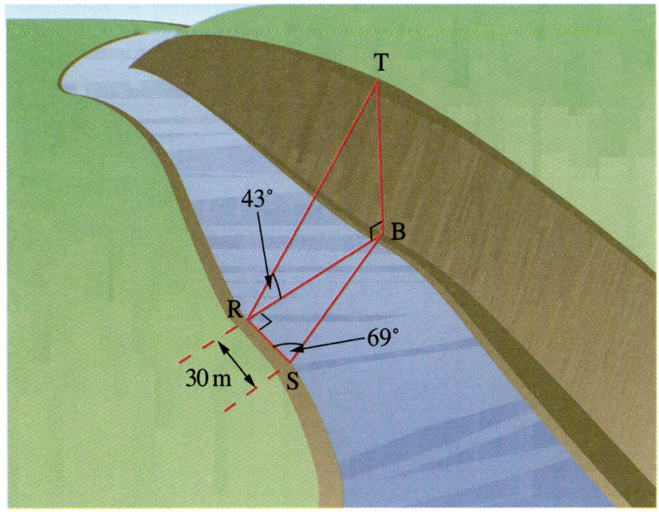

SOLUTION

Triangle TRB is in a vertical plane and $\triangle RBS$ is in a horizontal plane.

Think of a plan.

The height of the cliff is TB. To determine this height, we need to know the length of one side of $\triangle TRB$.

RB is a side of both triangles. We can find its length using $\triangle RBS$ and then use it in $\triangle TRB$.

Draw $\triangle RBS$. Mark the length of RS and label the sides in terms of $\angle S$.

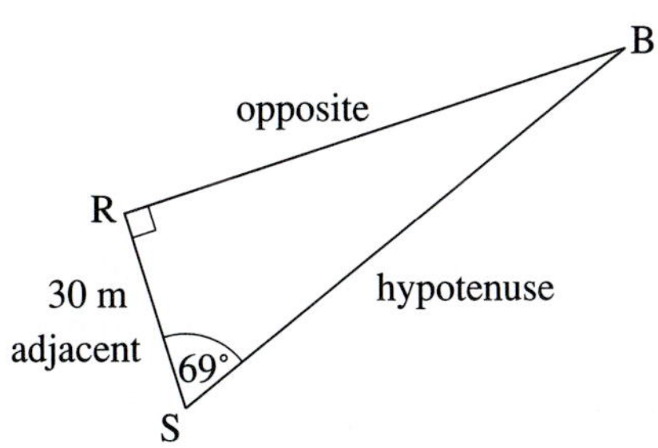

Use the tangent ratio.

$$\text{Tan } 69° = \frac{\text{Opposite}}{\text{Adjacent}}$$
$$= \frac{RB}{30}$$

Solve for RB.

$$30(\tan 69°) = RB$$
$$RB \doteq 78.15$$

Now draw ∠TRB. Mark the length of RB, ∠R, and label the sides in terms of ∠R.

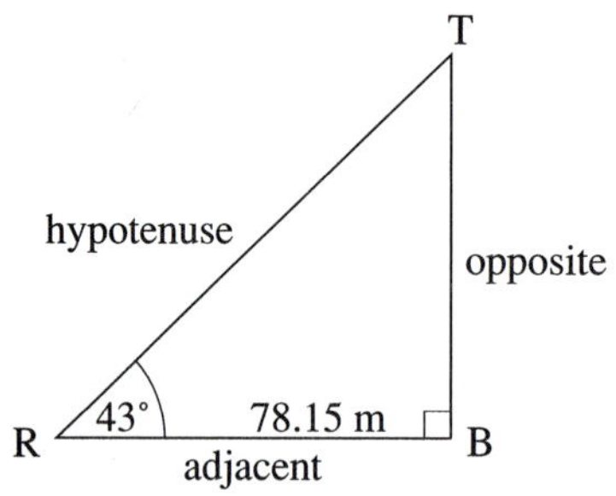

Use the tangent ratio to find TB.

$$\text{Tan } 43° = \frac{\text{Opposite}}{\text{Adjacent}}$$
$$= \frac{TB}{78.15}$$

Solve for TB.

$$78.15(\tan 43°) = TB$$
$$TB \doteq 72.88$$

The height of the cliff is about 73 m.

DISCUSSING THE IDEAS

1. Why is it important to mark all right angles when drawing a diagram to model a 3-dimensional problem?

2. At what stage in the problem-solving process should you try to think of a plan?

3. In *Example 3*, each triangle being used was drawn out. Why was this important when we used side RB that was common to both triangles?

PROJECTS

In this Tutorial you learned to solve complex problems that involved more than one right triangle. You will use these skills in the following projects in the Project Book.

- Reach for the Top
- Remote Sensing
- Jet Propulsion

EXERCISES

Checking Your Skills

1. The diagram below shows a roof truss for a model of a house. Calculate the length of BC.

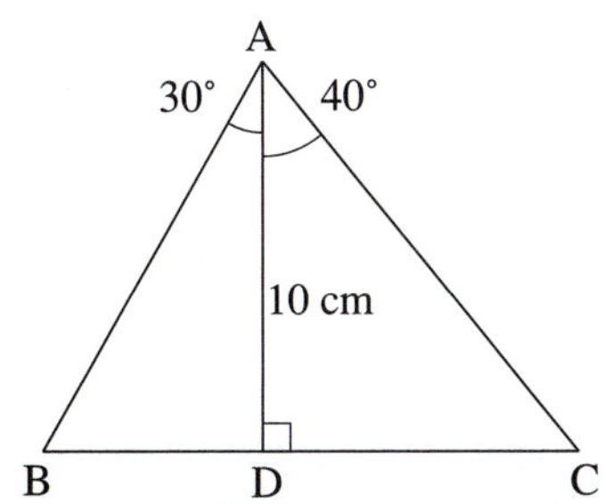

2. A plot of land in the shape of right triangle ABD is to be subdivided by the line BC as shown in the diagram below. Calculate the measure of $\angle ABC$.

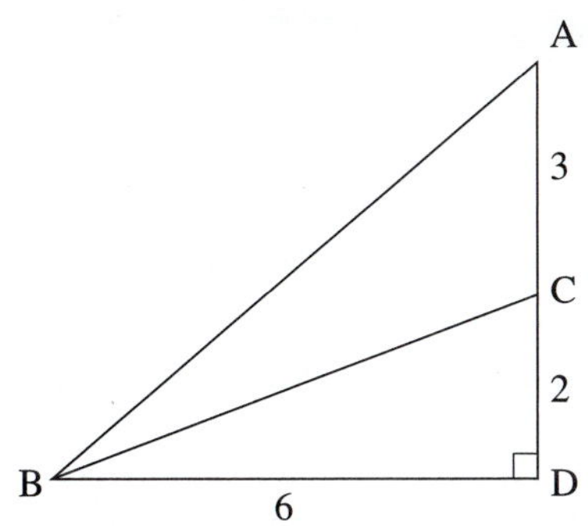

3. Two trees of the same species are grown 32 m apart in a tree nursery, but are given different nutrients. A biologist wishes to compare the trees' heights. From a point halfway between the trees, she measures the angles of elevation to the tops of the trees to be 52° and 43° respectively.

a) Draw a diagram to illustrate the situation.

b) Calculate the height of each tree.

c) What is the height difference as a percentage of the shorter tree?

4. Two buildings are 31.7 m apart. From the 12th floor of the shorter building, the angle of elevation to the top of the taller building is 27.5°. The angle of depression to the base of the taller building is 48.2°. What is the height of the taller building? Express the answer to the nearest tenth of a metre.

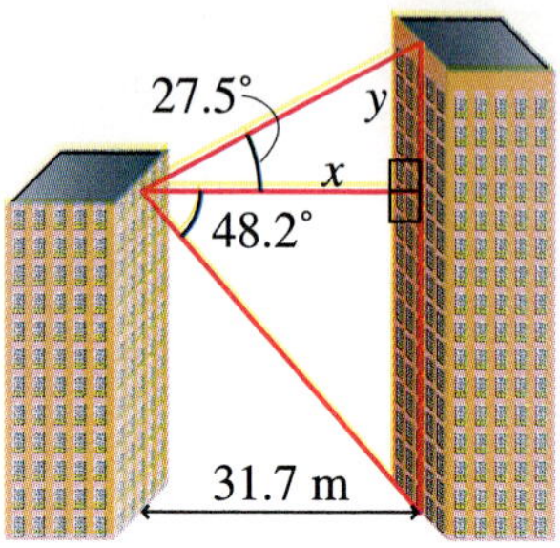

5. A microwave tower is supported by a series of guy wires. The anchor point of one guy wire is 9.8 m from the base of the tower. The angle of inclination of this wire is 37°. The angle of elevation from this anchor point to the top of the tower is 58°. How tall is the tower? How far from the top of the tower is the guy wire attached to the tower? Express the answers to the nearest tenth of a metre.

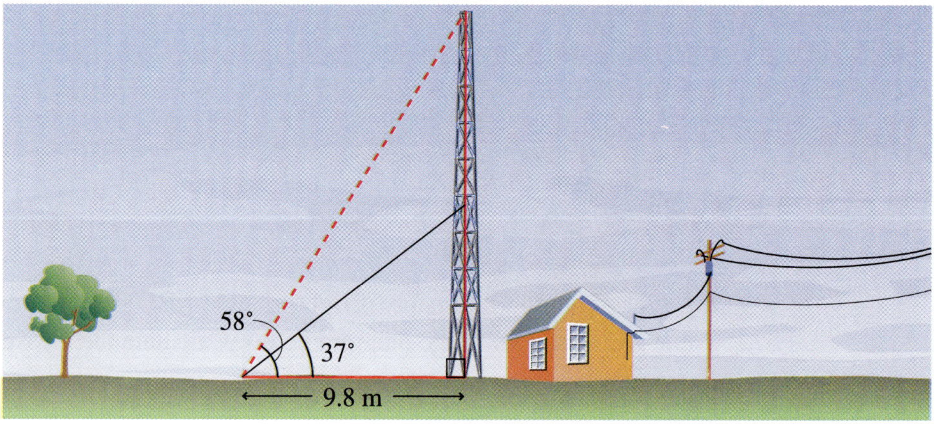

6. The angle of elevation from an observer to the top of a building located 210 feet from the observer is 28°. The angle of elevation to the top of a radio tower on top of the building is 38°. What is the height of the radio tower?

7. From the top of a 100-m fire tower, a fire ranger observes two fires, one at an angle of depression of 5° and the other at an angle of depression of 2°. Assuming that the fires and the tower are in a straight line, determine the distance between the fires for the following:

a) when the fires are on the same side of the tower

b) when the fires are on opposite sides of the tower

8. One of the world's longest suspension bridges crosses the Humber Estuary in England. The towers of the bridge reach about 135 m above the level of the bridge. The angles of elevation of the towers measured from the centre of the bridge and either end are 10.80° and 18.65° respectively. How long is the bridge?

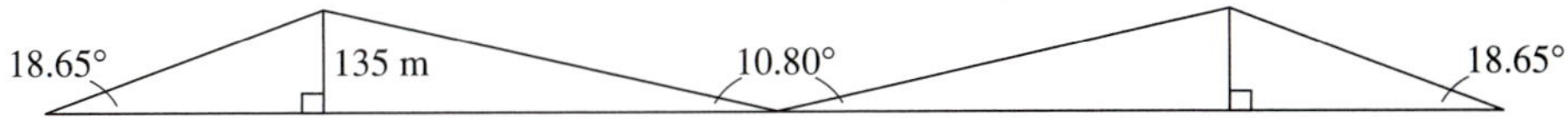

9. Calculate the height of the cliff in the diagram below.

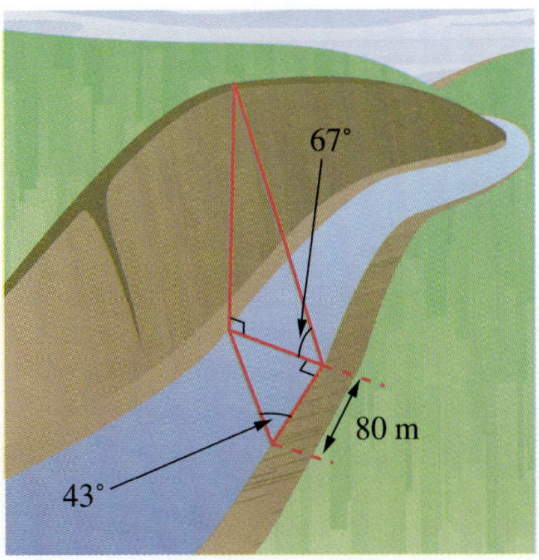

10. The triangles ABC and BCD have right angles at B and C respectively.

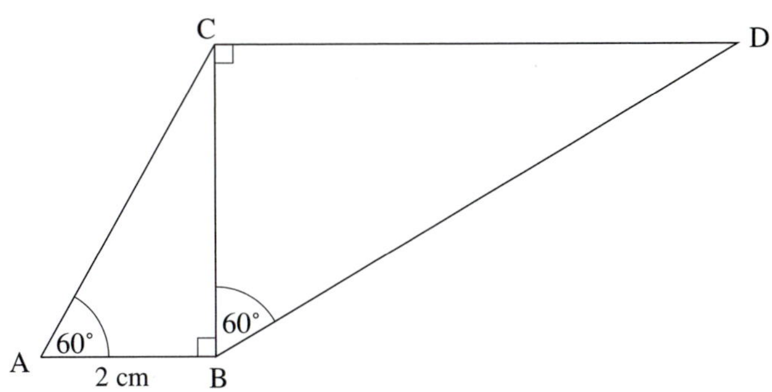

a) Calculate the length of BC and CA. Answer to one decimal place.

b) Calculate the length of side CD, and state the ratio of length BD to length AC. Answer to one decimal place.

c) What ratio in $\triangle ABC$ is equivalent to the ratio $\frac{DC}{DB}$ in $\triangle BCD$?

Extending Your Thinking

11. You work in an office tower down the street from a church. Daydreaming, you wonder how tall is the church. You estimate your height above the ground to be about 21 m, the angle of depression to the top of the church to be 15°, and that to base of the church to be about 48°. What is the approximate height of the church?

12. From the top of a 120-m fire tower, a fire ranger observes smoke in two locations both with angles of depression of 4°. The ranger notes the horizontal angle between the fires is 75°. What is the distance between the fires? What is the distance from each fire and the tower?

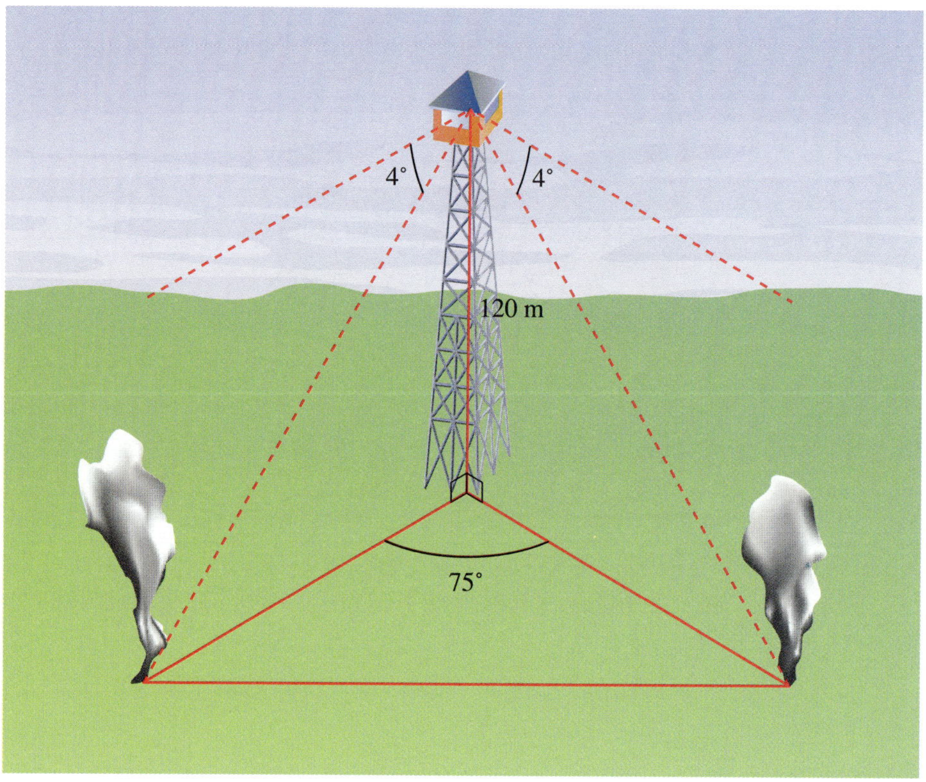

Note: this diagram is not drawn to scale.

COMMUNICATING THE IDEAS

Make a list of the steps you would follow to solve a problem using trigonometry.

TUTORIAL **7.3**

Extending the Concepts of Sine and Cosine for Angles from 0° to 180°

Our present definitions of the sine, cosine, and tangent of an acute angle use the lengths of the sides of a right triangle. Not all angles are acute. Visualize: can an angle of 100° be an angle of a right triangle? Can our present definitions for trigonometric ratios work for obtuse angles?

Triangles that do not contain a right angle are called oblique triangles. These triangles may contain an obtuse angle.

The instructions in the following Investigations are for a graphing calculator set in degree mode. To check this, press [MODE]. The screen below will appear.

```
Normal Sci Eng
Float 0123456789
Radian Degree
Func Par Pol Seq
Connected Dot
Sequential Simul
Real a+bi re^θi
Full Horiz G-T
```

The unit of measurement for angles is displayed on the third line. If Degree is not highlighted as shown above, move the cursor to this word and press [ENTER].

Investigation 1 Extend the Concept of Sine for Angles between 0° and 180°

1. Press [SIN] 30 [ENTER] to display 0.5. Hence
$\sin 30° = 0.5$.

2. Press [SIN] 150 [ENTER] to display 0.5. Hence
$\sin 150° = 0.5$. So, the sine of an obtuse angle *does* exist.

3. Your calculator will graph a picture that represents the trigonometric ratio of any angle. In this *Investigation* we are only concerned with angles between 0° and 180°. Change the window to the setting shown below.

```
WINDOW
 Xmin=-4
 Xmax=184
 Xscl=1
 Ymin=-1.5
 Ymax=1.5
 Yscl=1
 Xres=1
```

UTILITY

If you need to review changing the window setting, refer to Utility 7.

4. To graph $y = \sin x$, press Y= SIN X,T,θ,n GRAPH to display the screen below.

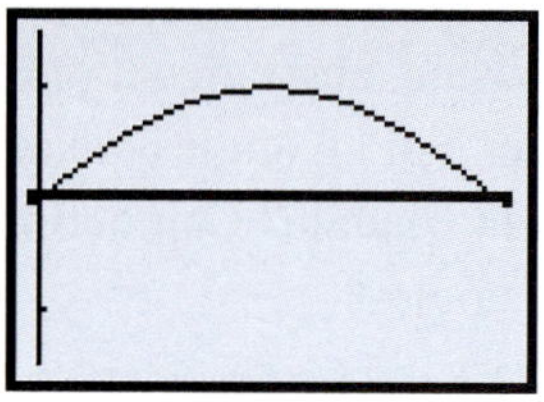

5. Copy this table into your notebook.

Angle x	$y = \sin x$	Another value for x with the same value for y
2		
10		
28		
32		
46		
58		
62		
80		
88		

6. Use the TRACE feature of the calculator to complete the second and then the third columns of the table.

7. What is the relationship between the first and last columns in the table?

8. Use the relationship you described in exercise 5. Complete the following equations. The first one is done for you.

$\sin 2^\circ = \sin 178^\circ$

$\sin 10^\circ =$

$\sin 38^\circ =$

$\sin 66^\circ =$

$\sin 146^\circ =$

$\sin 154^\circ =$

$\sin 160^\circ =$

$\sin 178^\circ =$

Investigation 2 Extend the Concept of Cosine for Angles between 0° and 180°

1. Repeat *Investigation 1*, replacing $\sin x$ with $\cos x$. In exercise 5, adjust the 3rd column heading to read "value for x that results in the negative value of y."

Discussing the Ideas

1. Look again at the graph of $y = \sin x$ you drew on your calculator in *Investigation 1*. What symmetry does the graph have? What is the maximum value of $\sin x$?

2. Look again at the graph of $y = \cos x$ you worked with in *Investigation 2*. Redraw the graph on your calculator if you need to. Does this graph have any symmetry? Explain.

3. Describe the relationship between the sines of *supplementary angles*. Write an equation relating $\sin (180 - x)^\circ$ to $\sin x^\circ$, for any x between 0 and 180.

4. Describe the relationship between the cosines of supplementary angles.

5. *Complementary angles* add to 90°. Look at the tables you completed in the Investigations. What relationship exists between the sine and cosine of complementary angles?

Exercises

Checking Your Skills

1. Without using a calculator, state the angles that are supplementary to:

a) 20° **b)** 100° **c)** 47° **d)** 118°

2. Without using a calculator, find the angle supplementary to the one given and state its sine or cosine.

a) $\sin 10^\circ = 0.1736$ **b)** $\cos 123^\circ = -0.5446$

c) $\sin 174^\circ = 0.1045$ **d)** $\cos 72^\circ = 0.3090$

3. Determine the sine and cosine of each of the following angles. Write your answer correct to four decimal places.

a) 50° **b)** 130° **c)** 127° **d)** 140°

e) 92° **f)** 40° **g)** 88° **h)** 31°

i) 53° **j)** 149°

4. Without using a calculator, what do you know about the measure of $\angle A$ if $\cos A = -0.1234$ and $0^\circ \leq A \leq 180^\circ$?

5. Calculate the value(s) for $\angle A(0^\circ \leq A \leq 180^\circ)$ that satisfy each of the equations listed. Give your answer to the nearest degree.

a) $\sin A = \sin 130^\circ$

b) $\sin A = \sin 127^\circ$

c) $\sin A = \sin 47^\circ$

d) $\sin A = 0.5736$

e) $\sin A = 0.9205$

f) $\sin A = \frac{1}{2}$

g) $\cos A = 0.8910$

h) $\cos A = -0.5879$

i) $\cos A = -\frac{1}{2}$

Extending Your Thinking

6. Copy the diagram below into your notebook.

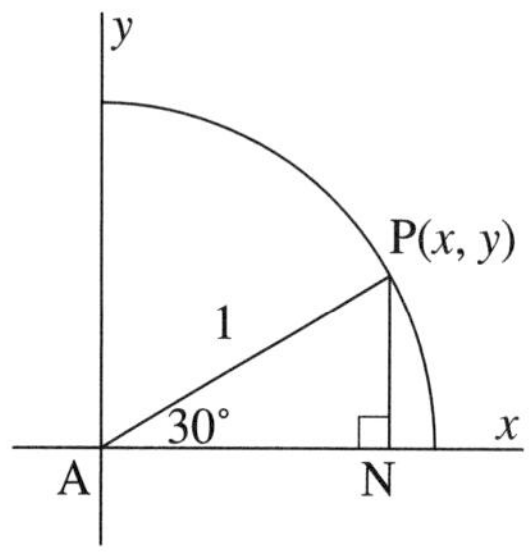

a) AN is the x-coordinate of P. What is the length of AN, to two decimal places?

b) NP is the y-coordinate of P. What is the length of NP, to two decimal places?

c) Visualize the triangle changing, as $\angle PAN$ increases to 90°. Create a table similar to the one on the opposite page. Extend the table for 5 more lines. For each $\angle A$, determine the sine and cosine to two decimal places. Use them to write the coordinates of P.

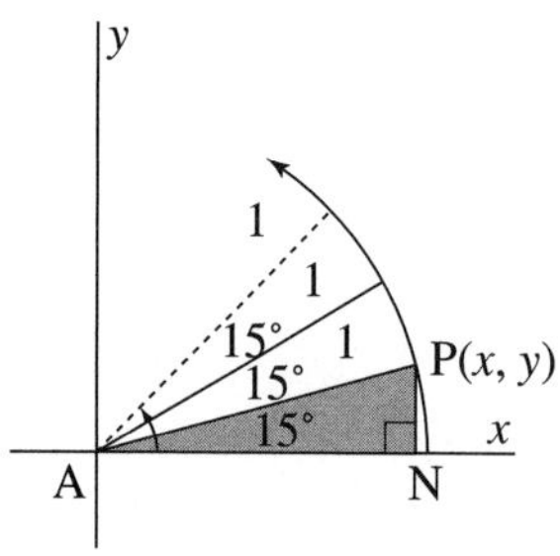

∠A	Cos A	Sin A	P(x, y)
15°			
30°			
45°			
60°			
75°			

d) Look at the patterns in the table. Visualize the line segment rotating past the y-axis toward the negative x-axis. Extend the patterns in your table to predict the coordinates of P.

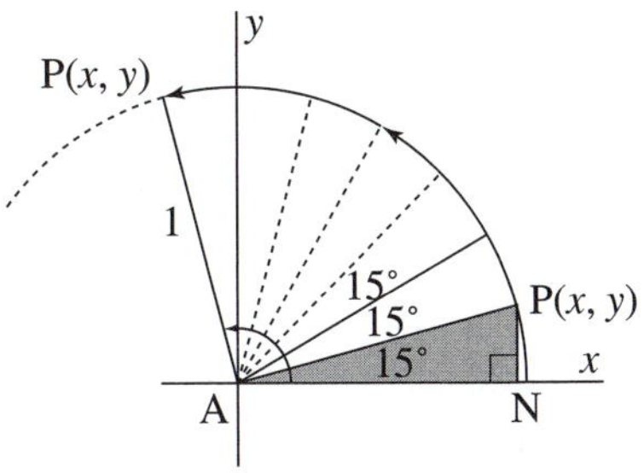

∠A	Cos A	Sin A	P(x, y)
105°			
120°			
135°			
150°			
165°			

e) In the first quadrant $P(x, y)$ corresponds to $P(\cos A, \sin A)$. Assume this relationship can be extended into the second quadrant. Enter appropriate numbers for the cos A and sin A in the extra lines of the table. Confirm your results using your calculator.

CHAPTER PROJECT

In this Tutorial you extended the concept of sine and cosine to obtuse angles. You will use this knowledge when you return to the Chapter Project on page 376.

COMMUNICATING THE IDEAS

Explain the relationship between the cosine of an acute angle and the cosine of its supplement. Include diagrams with your explanation.

TUTORIAL 7.4

The Sine Law

A bridge must be built to cross a river from point A to point B on the opposite bank.

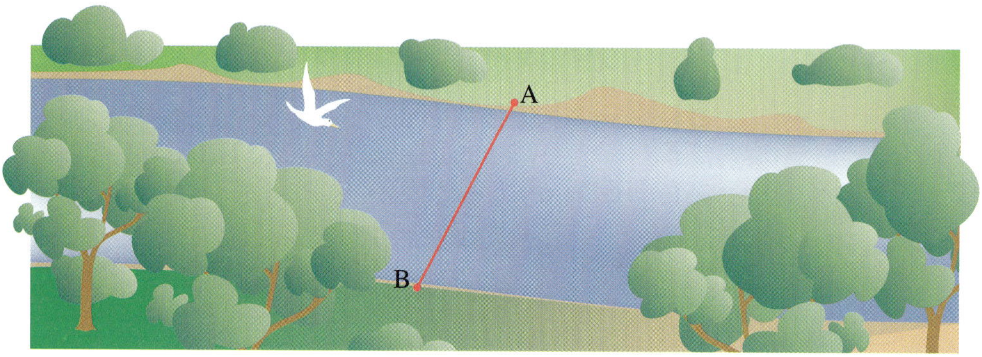

The surveyor must determine the length of the proposed bridge, but cannot take direct measurements or use right triangles because of the terrain. The surveyor marks a line 9.5 m long on the ground from point B to point C.

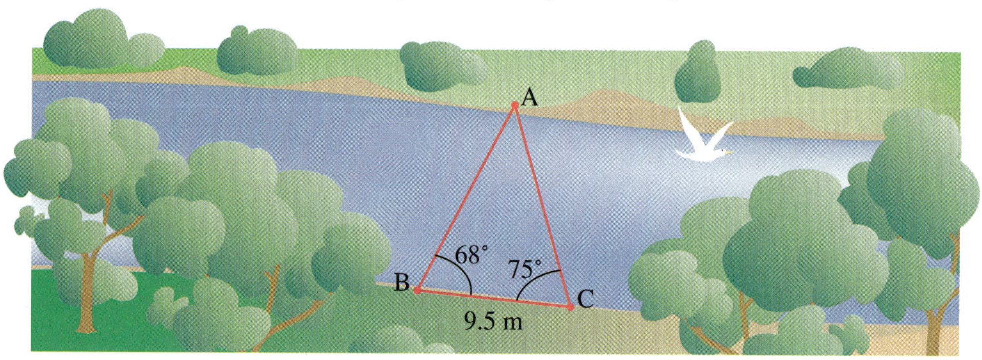

Note: this diagram is not drawn to scale.

This line will represent the base of a triangle. From each end of this line, BC, the surveyor measures the angle to point A on the opposite bank. The angles are 68° and 75° respectively, as shown in the diagram above. The surveyor could make a scale drawing of the situation, but a more accurate method is to calculate the length of AB.

Solving this problem using right triangle trigonometry will be difficult. The solution can be found more easily, however, once we learn to use trigonometry to solve oblique triangles. We will return to this problem in *Investigation 3*.

It is convenient to name the lengths of the sides of a triangle in terms of the vertices. The side of length a is opposite angle A, the side of length b is opposite angle B, and the side of length c is opposite angle C, as shown in the diagram on page 347.

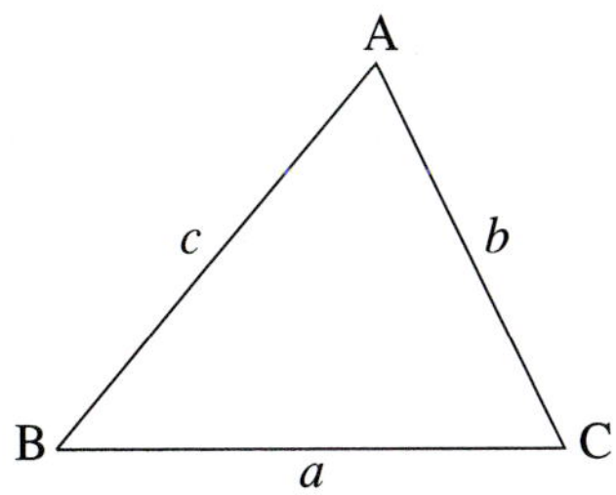

In the Investigation that follows, you will look for relationships between the lengths of sides and the sines of the angles of a triangle.

Do either *Investigation 1* if you are using paper and pencil, or *Investigation 2* if you have access to a computer with spreadsheet software and a dynamic geometry package such as Geometer's Sketchpad.

Investigation 1

The Sine Law

You will need a ruler and a protractor.

1. Use a ruler and pencil to draw 4 large triangles in your notebook. Make all the sides of the triangles long so that you can measure the angles easily with your protractor. Label the vertices of each triangle A, B, and C. Label the triangles 1, 2, 3, and 4.

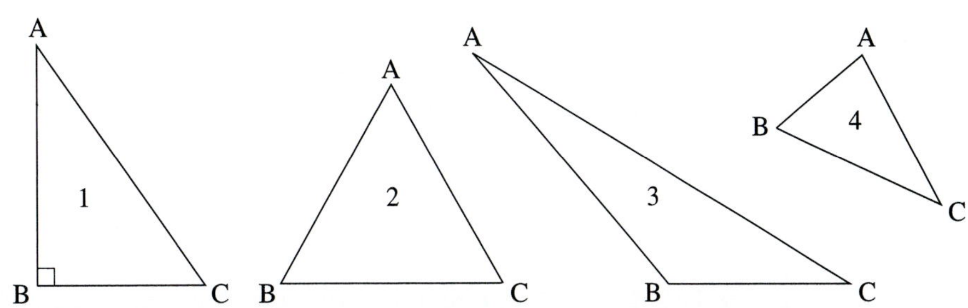

2. Set up a table as shown below.

△	a	b	c	A	B	C	$\frac{a}{\sin A}$	$\frac{b}{\sin B}$	$\frac{c}{\sin C}$	$\frac{\sin A}{a}$	$\frac{\sin B}{b}$	$\frac{\sin C}{c}$
1												
2												
3												
4												

3. Use your ruler and protractor to measure accurately the sides and angles of each triangle. Enter the data in the appropriate place in the table.

4. Calculate the entries for the remaining columns of the table. Round your answers to 2 decimal places.

5. Describe any patterns that you see between the columns of data in your table.

UTILITY

The graphing calculator can be used as a spreadsheet. Utility 15 shows you how to do this on a TI-83 calculator. The calculator has only 6 lists available, so the table above cannot be entered directly.

Investigation 2 The Sine Law Using Technology

You will need access to a computer with spreadsheet and dynamic geometry software.

1. Use the geometry software to draw 4 triangles. Follow the instruction in the manual that came with the software.

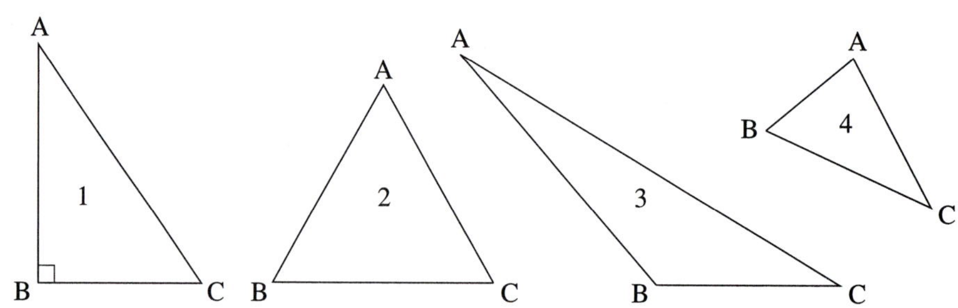

2. Use the measure tool to measure the sides and angles of each triangle.

3. Set up a spreadsheet with column headings as shown below.

	A	B	C	D	E	F	G	H	I	J	K	L	M
1	Δ	a	b	c	A	B	C	$\frac{a}{\sin A}$	$\frac{b}{\sin B}$	$\frac{c}{\sin C}$	$\frac{\sin A}{a}$	$\frac{\sin B}{b}$	$\frac{\sin C}{c}$

Note: When entering a formula that has a trigonometric ratio into a spreadsheet in Microsoft Works, you must include "*PI()/180" after the angle; in ClarisWorks and Excel, include RADIANS before the angle. For example, the formula to enter in cell H2 for the 7th column is =B2/sin(E2*PI()/180) or =B2/sin(RADIANS(E2)). The formula can be dragged to I2 and J2.

4. Enter the data for each triangle in the appropriate place in the spreadsheet. Drag the formulas in columns H to M down the columns.

5. Compare columns H, J, and K. Compare columns K, L, and M. What do you notice? You should have found the following:

$$\frac{a}{\sin A} = \frac{b}{\sin B} = \frac{c}{\sin C} \quad \text{and} \quad \frac{\sin A}{a} = \frac{\sin B}{b} = \frac{\sin C}{c}$$

These results are true for *any* triangle. This is the *Sine Law*. It was first written about in A.D. 150 by Ptolemy of Alexandria and should be used in oblique triangles when two angles and one side are known.

Investigation 3 Using the Sine Law

1. Copy the diagram into your notebook. This diagram models the problem posed at the start of the Tutorial.

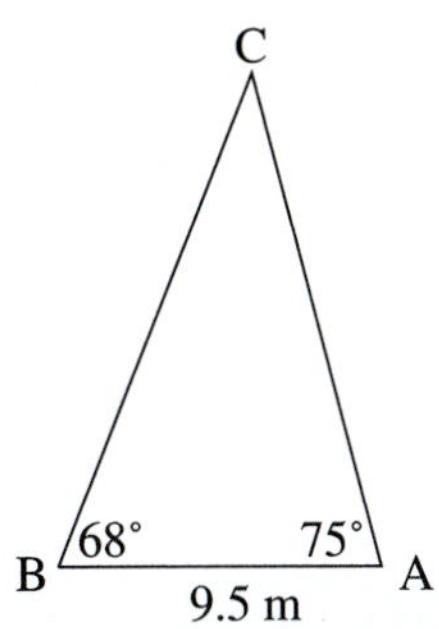

2. Label the sides of the triangles a, b, and c, according to the rules given earlier in this Tutorial.

3. The sum of the angles of a triangle is 180°. Determine the measure of ∠C.

4. Use the Sine Law to find a. Choose the pair of equal ratios involving a, where the other 3 values are known.

$$\frac{a}{\sin A} = \frac{c}{\sin C}$$

Substitute the values for c, ∠C, ∠A.

$$\frac{a}{\sin 75^\circ} = \frac{9.5}{\sin 37^\circ}$$

5. Solve for a. Did you determine that the bridge will be about 15.2 m long?

DISCUSSING THE IDEAS

1. Rewrite the Sine Law for △XYZ.

2. How many equations can you make from each version of the Sine Law? For one of the versions, write all the equations.

3. What determines which of the equations you will use?

4. When is it easier to use $\frac{a}{\sin A} = \frac{b}{\sin B} = \frac{c}{\sin C}$, rather than the other version of the Sine Law?

5. What information must you have to use the Sine Law?

PROJECTS

In this Tutorial you learned the Sine Law. You will use this law for the Chapter Project and for the folowing projects in the Project Book.

- Reach for the Top
- Remote Sensing

COMMUNICATING THE IDEAS

Write a paragraph to explain why we must know one complete pair, such as ∠A and a, together with one other fact, in order to use the Sine Law in △ABC.

TUTORIAL

7.5 Solving Problems Using the Sine Law

The Sine Law provides a short method of solving many problems.

Example 1 Applying the Sine Law

The diagram below shows 3 roads in a certain town. What is the angle between Scarborough Avenue and Cornwall Drive? Express your answer to the nearest tenth of a degree.

SOLUTION

Draw a working copy of the diagram. Label the triangle BCS as shown below.

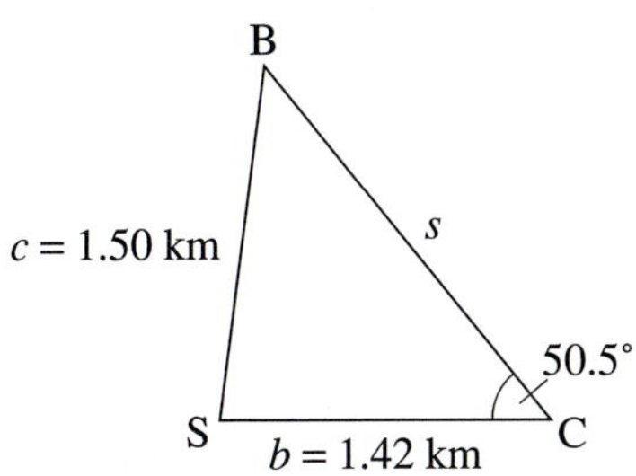

Think of a plan.

We must find the ∠B. Use the Sine Law in △BCS.

$$\frac{\sin B}{b} = \frac{\sin C}{c} = \frac{\sin S}{s}$$

Choose the equation in which we know 3 of the 4 quantities.

$$\frac{\sin B}{b} = \frac{\sin C}{c}$$

Substitute the values.

$$\frac{\sin B}{1.42} = \frac{\sin 50.5°}{1.50}$$

Solve for sin B.

$$\sin B = 1.42 \times \frac{\sin 50.5°}{1.50}$$
$$= 0.730\ 471\ 272\ 3$$

This decimal represents the sine of ∠B. To complete the solution and determine ∠B, we must use the inverse function on the calculator.

On the TI-83, press [2nd] [SIN] [2nd] [-] [ENTER] to obtain 46.925 917 03.

$$\angle B \doteq 46.9°$$

The angle between Scarborough Avenue and Cornwall Drive is about 46.9°.

Example 2 **Using the Sine Law**

When a plane is coming in to land at a 2510-m runway, the angles of depression to the ends of the runway are 10° and 13° respectively. How far is the plane from the near end of the runway? Answer correct to the nearest metre.

SOLUTION

Draw a diagram to model the problem. Label the triangle PNF and mark in the angles and length known, as shown below.

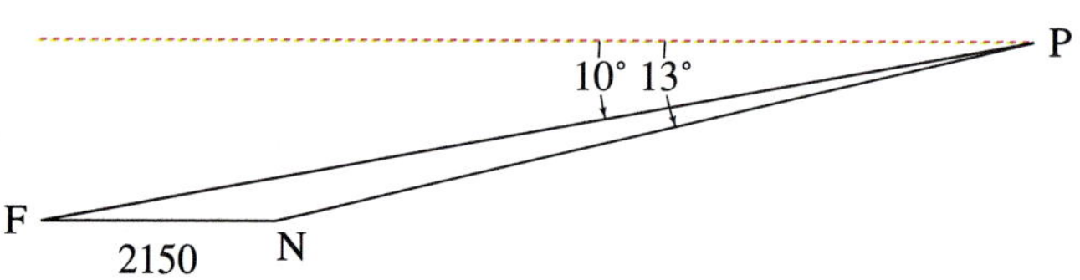

Think of a plan.

In △PFN we know p. We must find the length of PN, which is f. To use the Sine Law we must find two of the angles in the triangle.

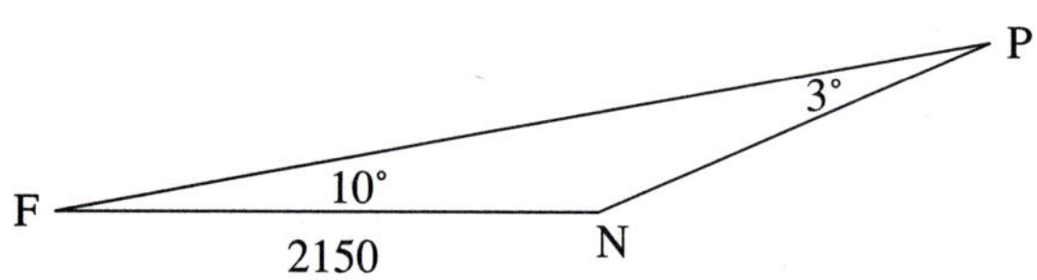

We can determine $\angle P$ by subtracting the angles of depression.

$$\angle P = 13^\circ - 10^\circ = 3^\circ$$

Since the runway is horizontal, the angle of depression to the far end of the runway and $\angle F$ are alternate angles, so, $\angle F = 10^\circ$.

STUDENT REFERENCE

If you need to review "alternate angles," refer to the Student Reference.

The Sine Law for $\triangle PFN$ is:

$$\frac{p}{\sin P} = \frac{f}{\sin F} = \frac{n}{\sin N}$$

The equation to use to find f is:

$$\frac{p}{\sin P} = \frac{f}{\sin F}$$

Substituting the values gives the following:

$$\frac{2510}{\sin 3^\circ} = \frac{f}{\sin 10^\circ}$$

Solve for f.

$$(\sin 10^\circ)\frac{2510}{\sin 3^\circ} = f$$

$$f = 8328.058\ 896$$

The plane is about 8328 m from the near end of the runway.

Example 3 Determine an angle in an obtuse triangle

Boats are anchored at positions A, B, and C on a lake. Boats A and B are 70 m apart and A and C are 100 m apart. The angle between the lines of sight from B to A and from B to C is 120°. What is the angle between the lines of sight from A to B and C?

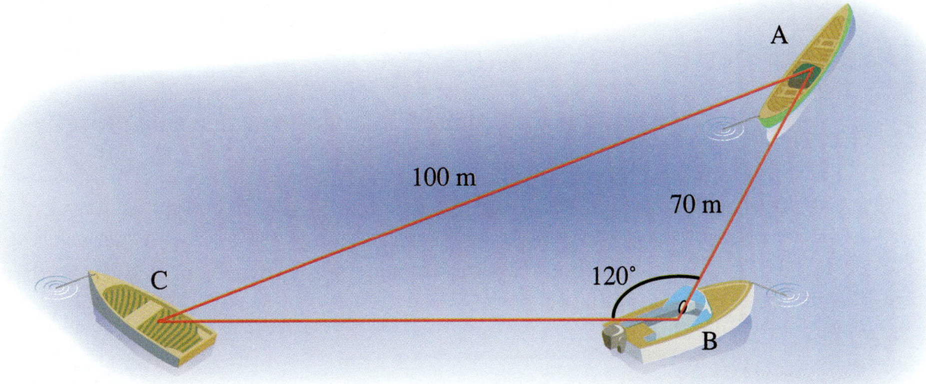

SOLUTION

Make a working drawing of the diagram showing only △ABC. Label the sides.

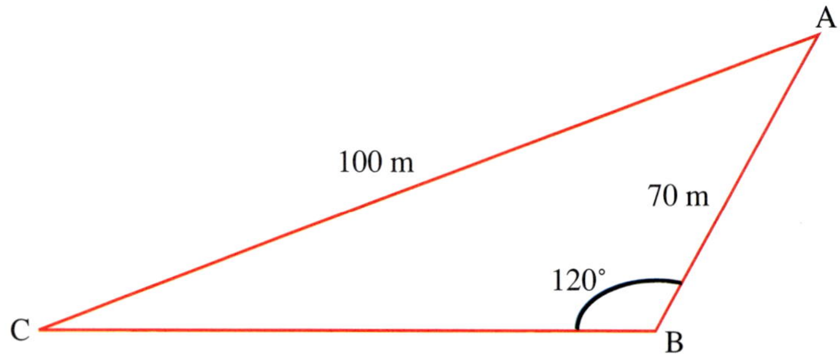

Think of a plan. We know the pair ∠B and b, together with c. Use the Sine Law in △ABC to find ∠C. Then use the angle sum property to determine ∠A.

Choose to use the version of the Sine Law that has the lengths in the denominator of the fractions.

$$\frac{\sin A}{a} = \frac{\sin B}{b} = \frac{\sin C}{c}$$

Choose the pair of ratios where we know 3 of the 4 quantities.

$$\frac{\sin B}{b} = \frac{\sin C}{c}$$

Substitute the known values.

$$\frac{\sin 120^\circ}{100} = \frac{\sin C}{70}$$

Isolate the unknown by multiplying both sides by 70.

$$\begin{aligned}\sin C &= \frac{70 \sin 120^\circ}{100}\\ &= 0.606\ 217\ 782\ 6\end{aligned}$$

Complete the solution by using the inverse sine on the calculator.

$$C \doteq 37.3^\circ$$

To determine the required ∠A, use the angle sum property of the triangle.

$$\begin{aligned}\angle A + 120^\circ + 37.3^\circ &= 180^\circ\\ \angle A &= 22.7^\circ\end{aligned}$$

The angle between the lines of sight from boat A to boats B and C is approximately 22.7°.

Discussing the Ideas

1. In *Example 1*, why did we use that particular version of the Sine Law?

2. It is always appropriate to use the Sine Law to find the other sides when two angles and one side of a triangle are known. What other combinations of sides and angles might work also?

Exercises

Checking Your Skills

1. Calculate the length of c in each triangle.

a)

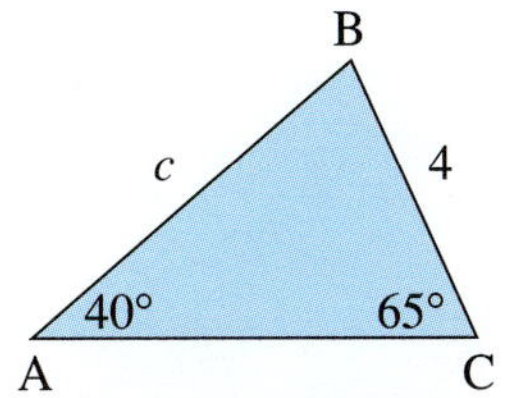

b)

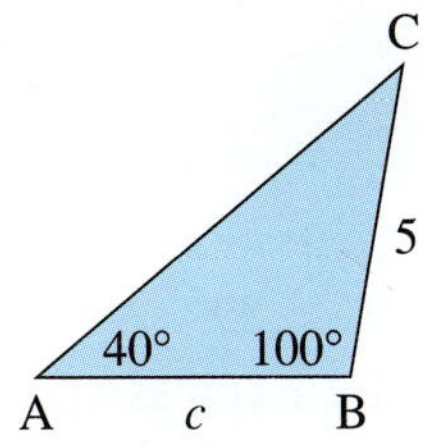

2. Calculate the measure of $\angle C$ in each triangle.

a)

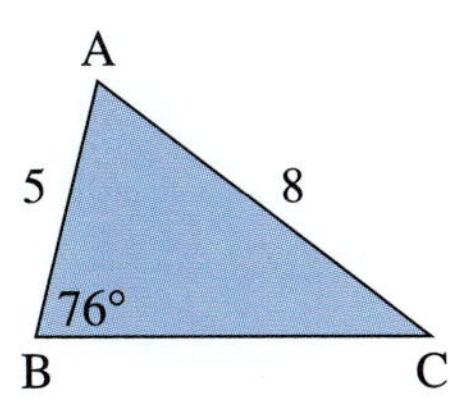

b)

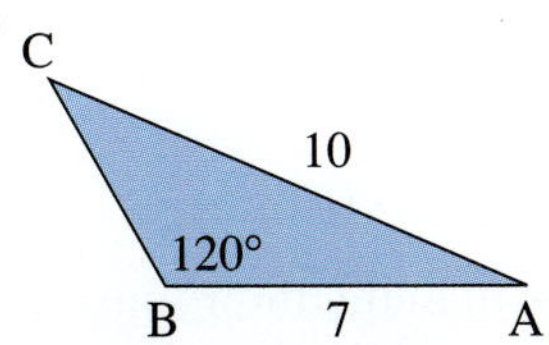

3. The diagram below represents two ships that are 21.4 km apart. Angle P is 68° and angle Q is 42°. How far is each ship from a lighthouse at R?

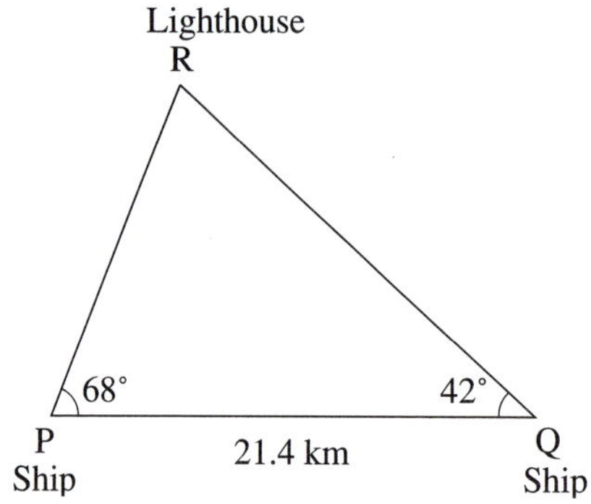

4. A bridge will be built across a river to connect two streets from point A to point B.

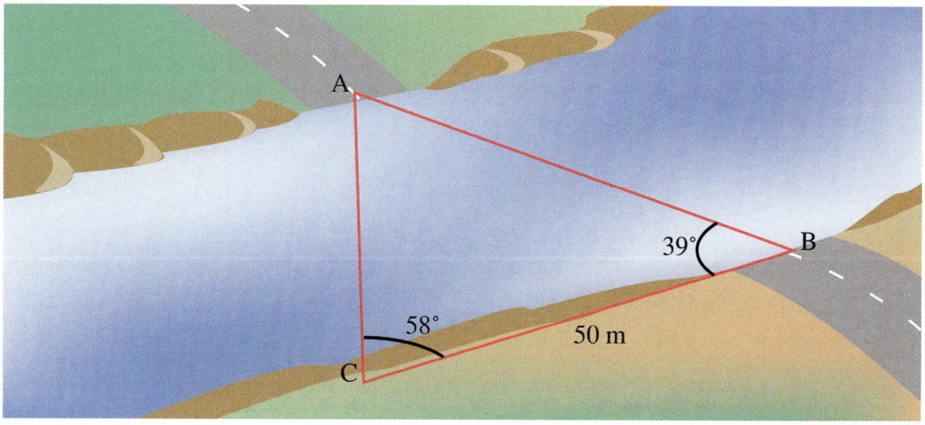

The engineer walks 50 m along the shore in a line from point B to point C. He measures ∠ACB = 58° and ∠ABC = 39°. What is the length of the bridge if it spans the river from A to B? Express your answer to the nearest tenth of a metre.

5. A house has been designed with non standard roof trusses. They have the following measurements.

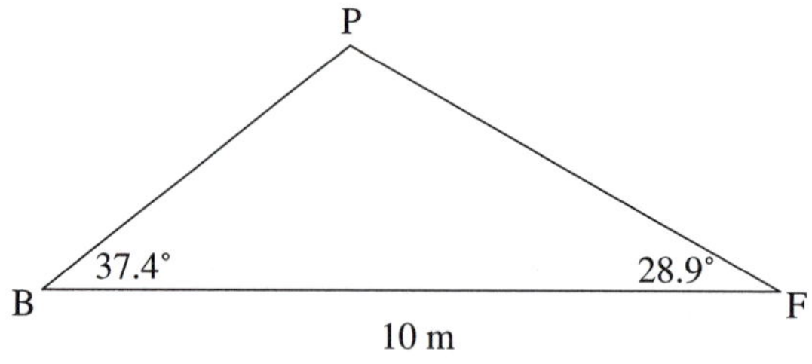

∠PBF = 37.4°, ∠PFB = 28.9°, BF = 10 m

Before building the trusses, the manufacturer must determine the lengths of BP and FP. Do the calculations required.

6. The longer two sides of a triangular park measure 251.0 m and 208.2 m respectively. The angle between the longest and the shortest side is 56.0°.

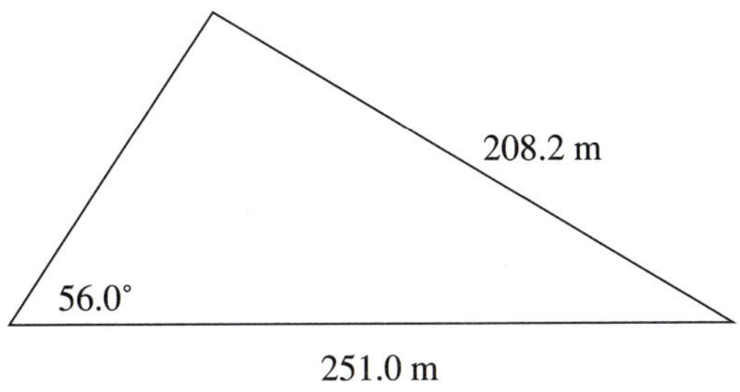

a) What is the angle between the shorter two sides of the park?

b) How long is the shortest side?

7. In navigation, direction is often represented using a bearing. This is the angle between the north line and the direction, measured in a clockwise direction and expressed using 3 digits. The directions for bearings 215° and 025° are shown below.

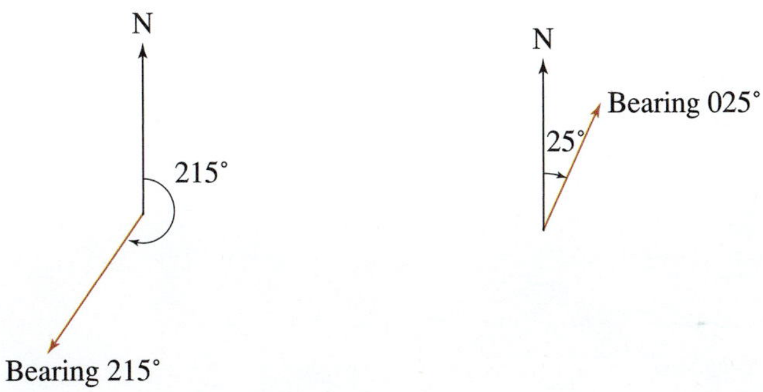

A boat is travelling on a bearing of 045° at 12 kn (nautical miles per hour). At 3 o'clock the captain sights a navigation buoy at 020°. An hour and a quarter later he sights the buoy at 230°. The situation is illustrated on page 358. How far has the boat travelled (in nautical miles) in an hour and a quarter? How many nautical miles is the boat from the buoy at the later time?

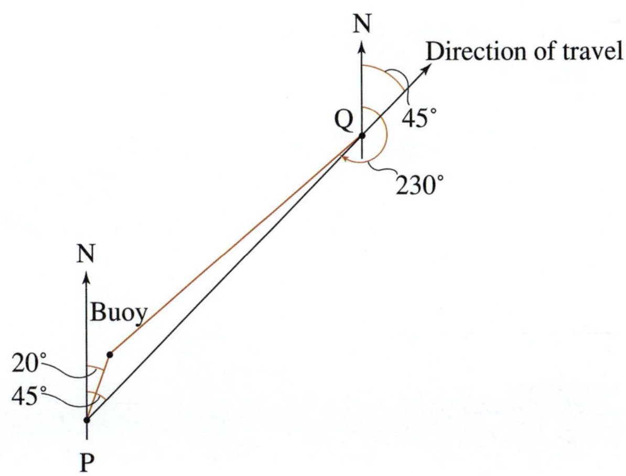

8. Cattle Point is part of Victoria, BC. Maynard Cove is 2.4 km from Cattle Point, on a bearing of 053°. A sailboat leaves Cattle Point on a bearing of 079°. After sailing for 1.8 km, the boat turns and heads directly to Maynard Cove, on a bearing of 008°.

a) What is the bearing of Cattle Point from Maynard Cove?

b) Calculate the total distance the boat travels to get to Maynard Cove.

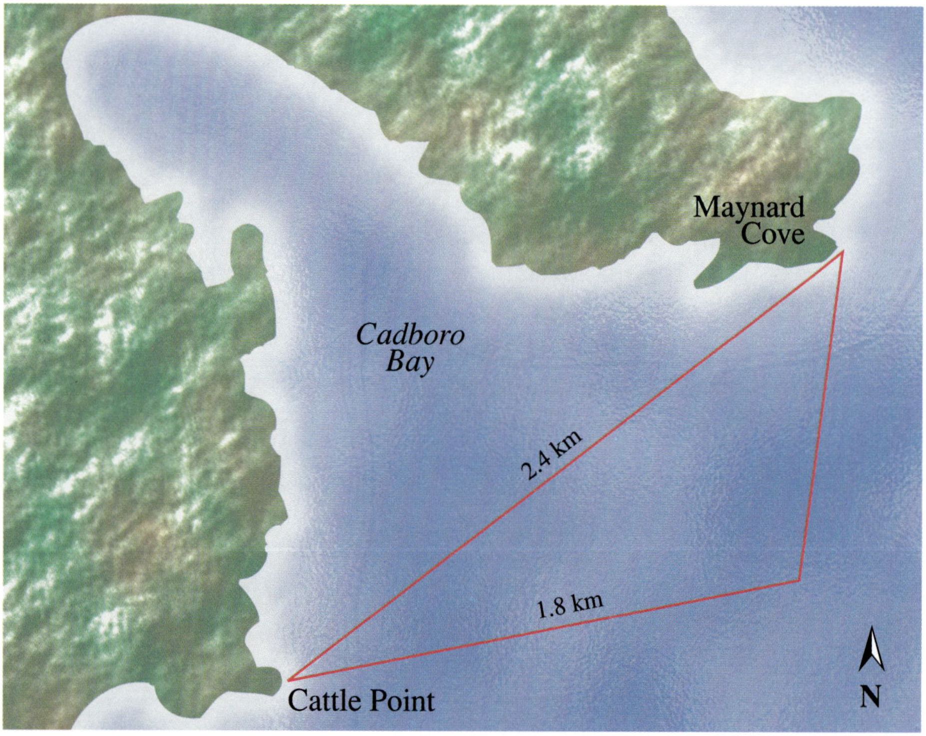

Extending Your Thinking

9. Two cabins are located 500 m apart on the same side of a river. A boathouse is located across the river as shown in the diagram below. Use the measurements to find the width of the river, to the nearest tenth of a metre.

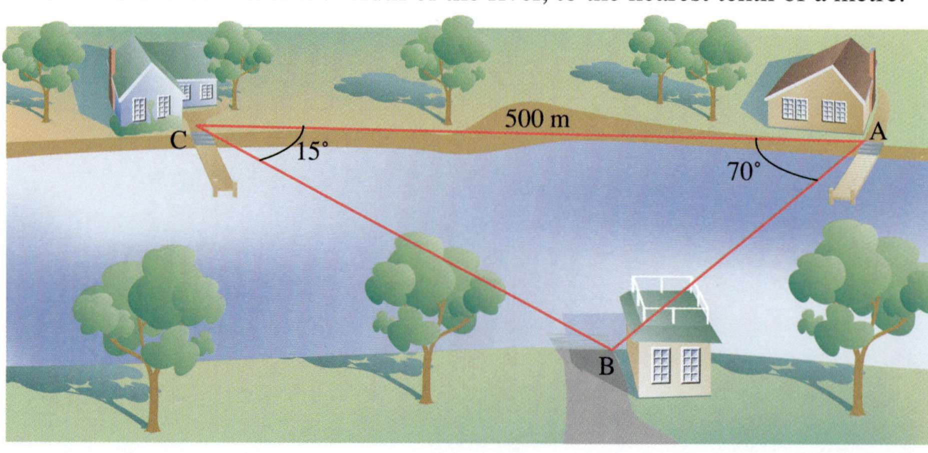

10. A 7-m electrical pole makes an angle of 88° with the ground.

a) Using a spreadsheet or a graphing calculator, find the length of the shadow for at least 10 different angles of elevation of the sun.

b) Plot the angle of elevation on the horizontal axis and the length of the shadow on the vertical axis.

c) Describe in words how the length of the shadow changes as the sun's angle of elevation changes.

PROJECTS

In this Tutorial you used the Sine Law to solve problems. You will use the Sine Law in the Chapter Project to make calculations before you draw an accurate plan. You will also use this law for the following projects in the Project Book.

- **Reach for the Top**
- **Remote Sensing**

COMMUNICATING THE IDEAS

You are responsible for summarizing the Sine Law for the mathematics page on your school's web site. Write your submission.

TUTORIAL

7.6 The Cosine Law

In *Tutorial 7.4*, the Sine Law was developed to help solve certain types of oblique triangles. It cannot be used to solve all well-defined oblique triangles, as illustrated below.

Example 1

Determine the third side of a triangle

A radar station is tracking two ships. At noon, the ships are 5 km and 8 km away from the radar station. The angle between the lines of sight to the ships is 70°. How far apart are the ships at noon? Express your answer to the nearest kilometre.

SOLUTION

Draw a diagram to model the situation.

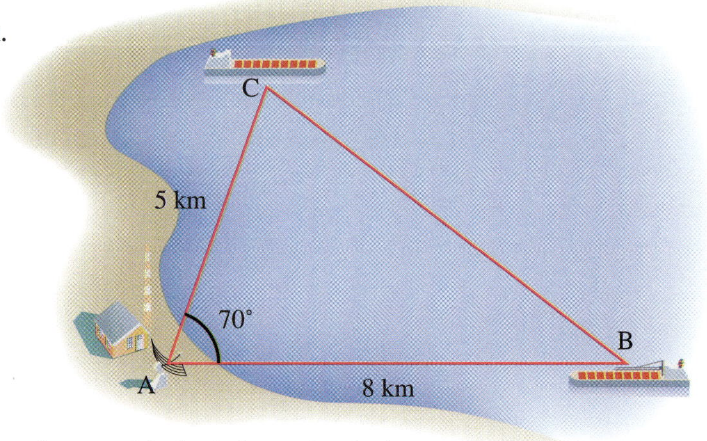

Label the diagram as shown with the information below.

$b = 5$ km $\quad c = 8$ km $\quad \angle A = 70°$

Think of a plan.

Triangle ABC is oblique — try the Sine Law.

$$\frac{a}{\sin A} = \frac{b}{\sin B} = \frac{c}{\sin C}$$

We cannot pick out a proportion where we know 3 of the quantities, and so we cannot use this law.

There is another law, called the Cosine Law, that can be used to solve this problem. It was first described by François Viète (1540-1603), a lawyer at the court of Henri IV of France.

The Cosine Law

In any triangle ABC the following relationships exist.

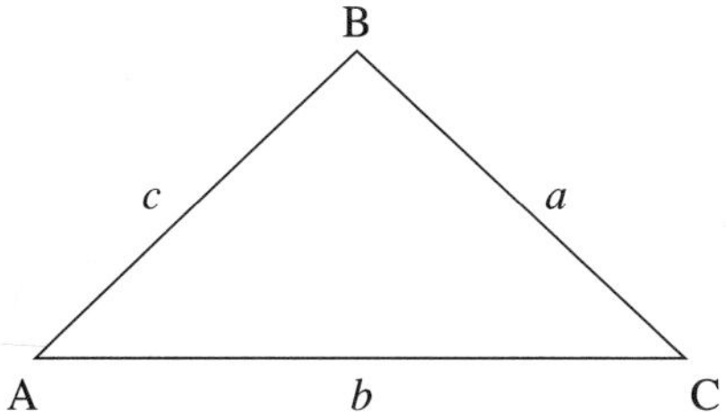

$a^2 = b^2 + c^2 - 2bc \cos A$
$b^2 = a^2 + c^2 - 2ac \cos B$
$c^2 = a^2 + b^2 - 2ab \cos C$

Look at the patterns. The isolated side is the side opposite the given angle. If angle A is given, side a is squared and by itself. The other two sides are squared, then added; the last term consists of the product of the other 2 sides and the cosine of the given angle. It is more effective to understand the pattern in the formulas than to memorize the three different formulas!

Return to the opening *Example 1*.

We know the value for b, c, and $\angle A$, and wish to determine a.

Substitute the values in the Cosine Law.

$$\begin{aligned} a^2 &= b^2 + c^2 - 2bc \cos A \\ &= 5^2 + 8^2 - 2 \times 5 \times 8 \times \cos 70° \\ &= 61.638\,388\,53 \\ a &\doteq 7.85 \end{aligned}$$

The ships are approximately 8 km apart at noon.

The Cosine Law worked well in this problem where we knew two sides and the included angle.

Example 2 Use the Cosine Law to find the length of a side of a triangle

A roof truss spans 8.2 m. One arm of the truss is 6.8 m long. It is set at an angle of 35°, as shown in the diagram below. Calculate the length of the other arm of the truss.

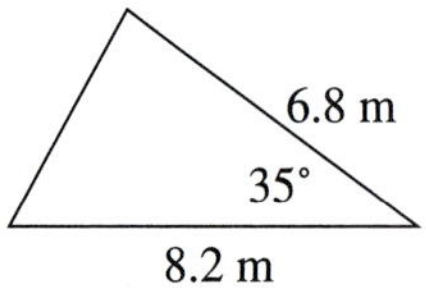

SOLUTION

Make a working copy of the diagram. Label the vertices of the triangle and the unknown side as shown below.

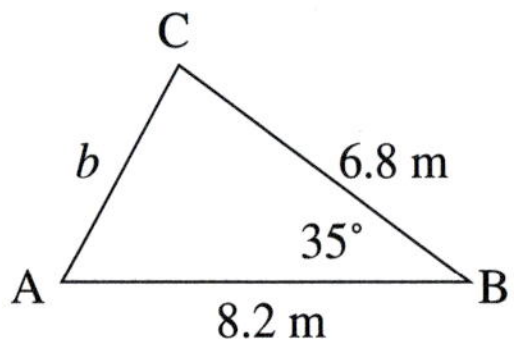

We are given 2 sides and the included angle. Use the Cosine Law with side b isolated.

$$b^2 = a^2 + c^2 - 2ac \cos B$$

Substituting the known values, we get the following.

$$b^2 = 6.8^2 + 8.2^2 - 2 \times 6.8 \times 8.2 \times \cos 35°$$

Enter the right side into a graphing calculator exactly as it is written.

Press [CLEAR] 6.8 [x^2] [+] 8.2 [x^2] −2 [×] 6.8 [×] 8.2 [×] [COS] 35 [ENTER]

$$b^2 = 22.128\ 164\ 02$$
$$b \doteq 4.70$$

The other arm of the truss is about 4.7 m long.

The Cosine Law can be used to find an angle of a triangle.

Example 3 **Use the Cosine Law to determine an angle of a triangle**

An efficient walker has a narrow trackway and a step angle approaching 180°. This means that if you drew the footprints of an efficient walker you would see a diagram resembling the one shown here.

Analysis of the walking pattern is useful when training athletes. A race walker's stride and pace are measured and found to be 117 cm and 59 cm respectively. What is the race walker's step angle?

SOLUTION

Draw a diagram and label the triangle ABC as shown below.

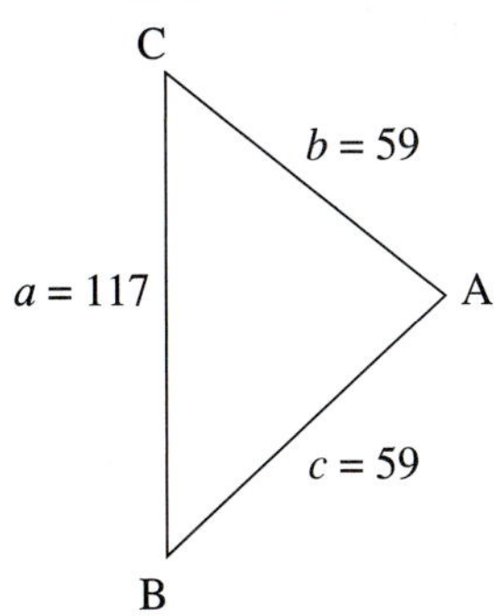

In the pattern of the Cosine Law, the isolated side is opposite the angle used.

The side opposite the step angle represents stride, the other sides pace.

Use the Cosine Law.

$$a^2 = b^2 + c^2 - 2bc \cos A$$

Substitute for the known values.

$$117^2 = 59^2 + 59^2 - 2 \times 59 \times 59 \times \cos A$$

Isolate the term containing the unknown.

$$117^2 - 59^2 - 59^2 = -2 \times 59 \times 59 \times \cos A$$

Solve for cos A.

$$\frac{117^2 - 59^2 - 59^2}{-2 \times 59 \times 59} = \cos A$$

Use your calculator to find the angle A whose cosine is the number on the left side. Using a graphing calculator, press:

[( ] 117 [x^2] [–] 59 [x^2] [–] 59 [x^2] [ )] [÷] [( ] [(–)] 2 [×] 59 [×] 59 [ )] [ENTER]

You should arrive at –0.966 245 331 8.

This is the cosine of ∠A. To calculate A, on the TI-83, press [2nd] [COS] [2nd] [–] [ENTER]

$$\angle A \doteq 165°$$

The walker's step angle is about 165°.

DISCUSSING THE IDEAS

1. Rewrite the Cosine Law for △PQR.
2. What information must you know about a triangle to be able to use the Cosine Law to determine a side?
3. What information must you know about a triangle to be able to use the Cosine Law to determine an angle?
4. To assist in the verification of answers to problems, it is often useful to know which is the smallest angle of a triangle. Given the lengths of all three sides of a triangle, how can you determine which is the smallest angle without any calculation?
5. In *Example 2*, after we have found the length of the other arm of the truss, what else could we calculate? Describe two different ways to do this.
6. Most students only use the Cosine Law when they cannot use the Sine Law. Can you suggest a reason for this?

PROJECTS

This Tutorial introduced you to the Cosine Law. You will use the Cosine Law in the Chapter Project to make calculations before you draw an accurate plan. You will also use this law for the follwing projects in the Project Book.

- Reach for the Top
- Remote Sensing

EXERCISES

Checking Your Skills

1. Calculate the length of AC in each triangle.

a)

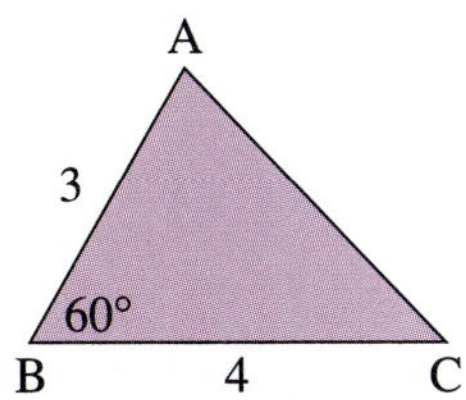

b)

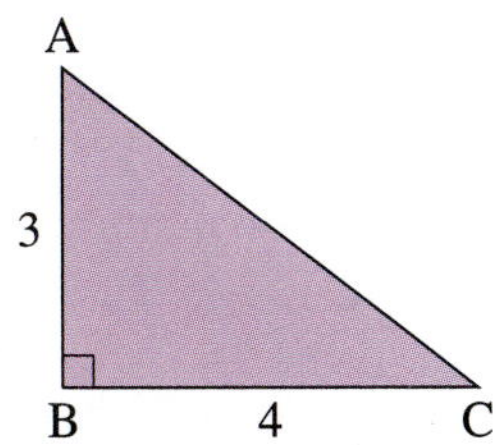

c)

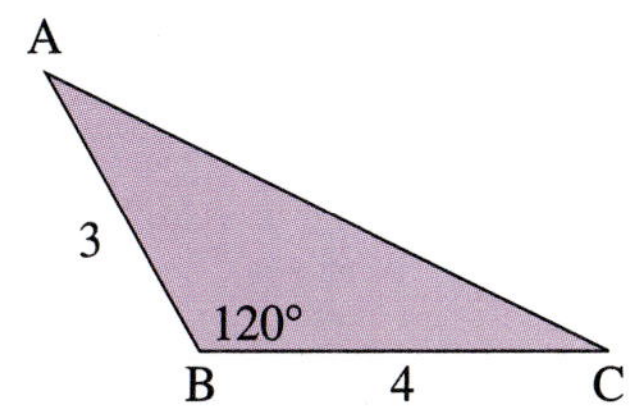

2. Calculate the measure of ∠A in each triangle.

a)

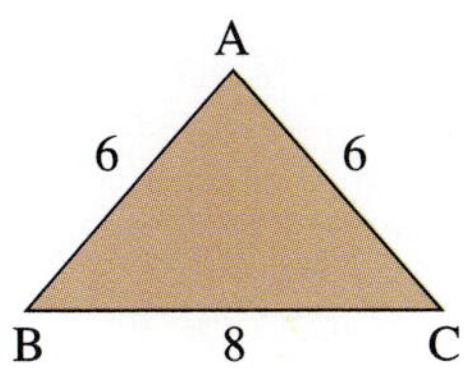

b)

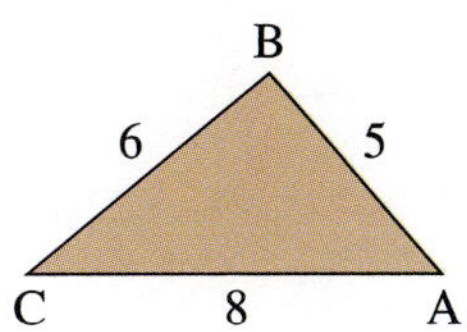

3. An electric transmission line must cross directly over a pond. Poles A and B will support the power line. To determine the length of wire required, a surveyor must determine the distance AB across the pond. She locates a convenient position C and measures the distance BC as 580 m, the distance AC as 337 m, and ∠BCA as 105.3°. What is the distance between poles A and B?

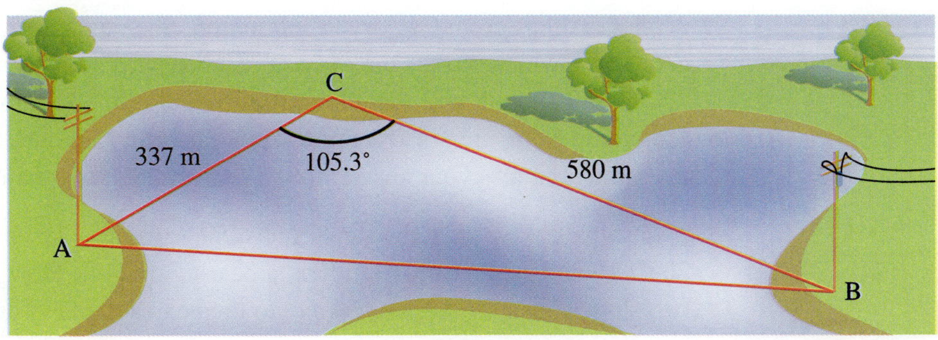

4. Refer to *Example 3* on page 363. Faustina runs through a puddle on the track and keeps on running. Her stride is 129 cm and her pace is 67 cm. What is Faustina's stride angle? Answer to the nearest tenth of a degree.

5. When engineers design buildings they must determine the forces acting on the components of the building. To calculate these forces, the engineer must know the lengths and angles of each component.

   A homeowner wants the roof to slope down gently at the back of her house, but more steeply at the front of the house. The rough measurements are shown in the diagram below.

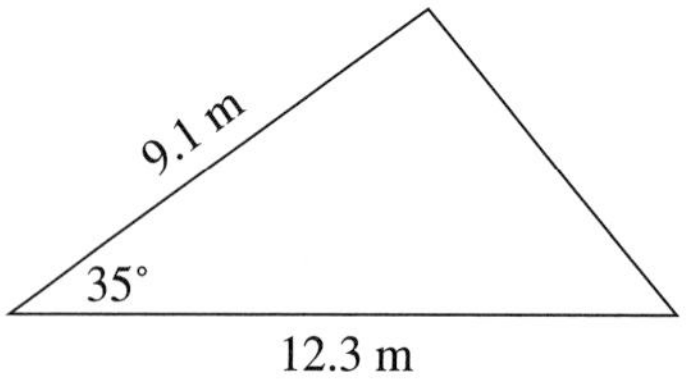

   Calculate the unknown angles and the length of this truss. Express your answers to one decimal place.

6. A hiking trail has been marked out. The map maker wants to supply bearings for the leaflet that describes the trail. What are the measures of the angles between the paths? Answer to one decimal place.

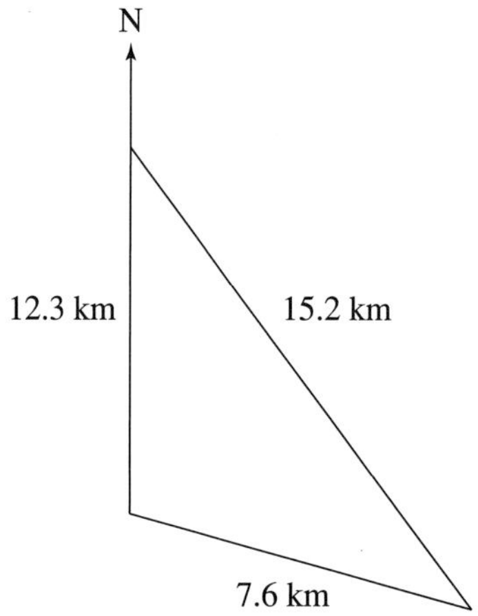

7. A pilot is flying from Calgary to Edmonton. She neglects to account for a crosswind, which pushes the plane 7° off course. The plane can fly at 120 mph. After 30 min, the pilot discovers her error. The distance from Calgary to Edmonton is 183 miles. How far from Edmonton is the plane at that time? Express your answer to the nearest tenth of a mile.

8. Two ships leave port at the same time. One sails at 17 km/h on a bearing of 205°. The other sails at 21 km/h on a bearing of 243°. How far apart are the two ships after 2 h? Answer correct to the nearest tenth of a kilometre.

9. A boat leaves port and sails 20 km in the direction 180° to a fishing spot. After fishing for a while, the boat heads off on a bearing of 165°. After 12 km, the boat stops to fish again. The time is 1:30 P.M. The boat can travel at 13 km/h. How many minutes can the boat fish at this location if it must return to port before dark at 6:00 P.M.?

10. When describing molecules, the distance between the nuclei of the atoms and the bond angles are used.

The distance between the nuclei of the oxygen and hydrogen atoms in the water molecule is 9.6 nm.

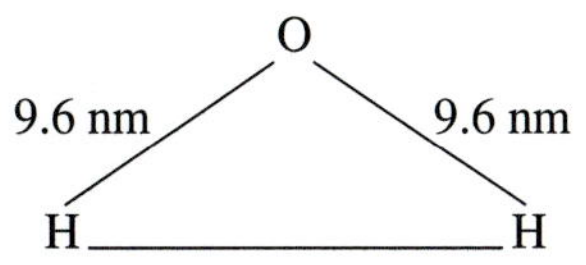

The distance between the nuclei of the hydrogen atoms is 15.2 nm. What is the bond angle of the water molecule? (Note: 1 nanometre = 10^{-9} cm). Express your answer to the nearest hundredth of a degree.

Extending Your Thinking

11. Laser trabeculoplasty is a procedure used to treat glaucoma, a disease of the eye. The machine used by the ophthalmologist must have the laser aligned with respect to the lens of the machine and the eye of the patient. It is programmed to accept data.

Develop the formula that will allow the machine to calculate the angle that the laser must make with the lens of the machine and the eye of the patient.

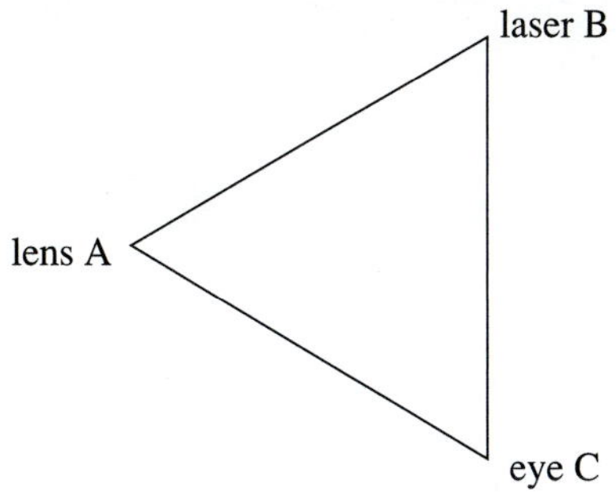

The data input to the machine are angle A, side b, and side c.

Manipulate the Cosine Law (twice) to find a formula that will find angle B.

COMMUNICATING THE IDEAS

Refer to exercise 1. Explain why the Cosine Law can be thought of as a generalization of the Pythagorean Theorem.

TUTORIAL 7.7

Selecting a Strategy

When solving a problem that involves an oblique triangle, you must decide which law to use. A combination of laws and right triangle trigonometry are needed for some problems.

Example 1

Solve a problem using a combination of oblique and right triangle trigonometry

The angles of elevation to a weather balloon from 2 different tracking stations, aligned on the same side of the balloon, are 17° and 72°. The tracking stations are 39 km apart. Ignoring Earth's curvature, which is negligible at this distance, what is the altitude of the balloon? Express the answer to the nearest tenth of a kilometre.

SOLUTION

Draw the diagram below to model the problem.

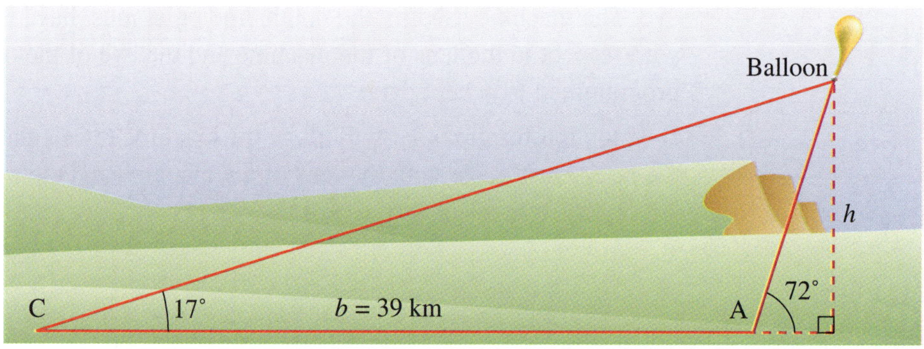

Think of a plan.

To find the height, h, you could use right triangle trigonometry, but do you have sufficient information to do this? First, you should calculate either c or a. Choose c.

Which law should you use to solve the oblique triangle for c? Look at the given information marked on your diagram. The obtuse angle at A can be found. It is the supplement of 72°.

The Sine Law is used whenever two angles are known. Use the Sine Law to determine c.

Calculate the third angle in the triangle using the angle sum property. $\angle B = 55°$.

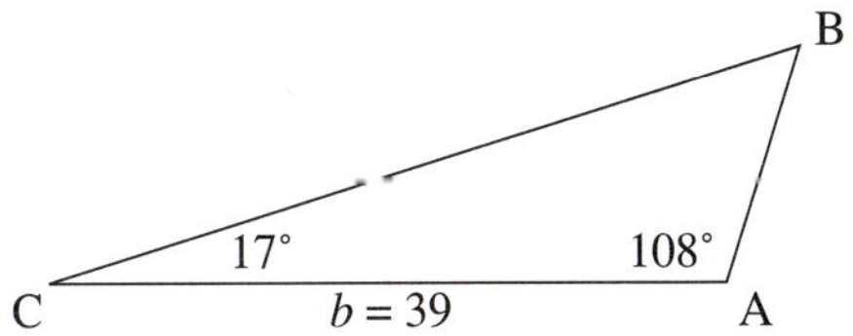

Use the Sine Law in △ABC to determine c. Choose the equation where 3 values are known.

$$\frac{c}{\sin C} = \frac{b}{\sin B}$$

Substitute.

$$\frac{c}{\sin 17^\circ} = \frac{39}{\sin 55^\circ}$$

Solve for c.

$$c = \frac{39}{\sin 55^\circ} \times \sin 17^\circ$$
$$c \doteq 13.919\ 877\ 96$$

Since c will be used in future calculations, **do not round at this stage**.

Using right triangle trigonometry,

$$\sin 72^\circ = \frac{h}{c}$$

Solve for h.

$$c \sin 72^\circ = h$$

Substitute the value for c.

$$h = 13.919\ 877\ 96 \times \sin 72^\circ$$
$$h \doteq 13.2$$

The altitude of the balloon is about 13.2 km.

Example 1 gives a model for an alternative method for determining the height of inaccessible objects, such as a flagpole or tree.

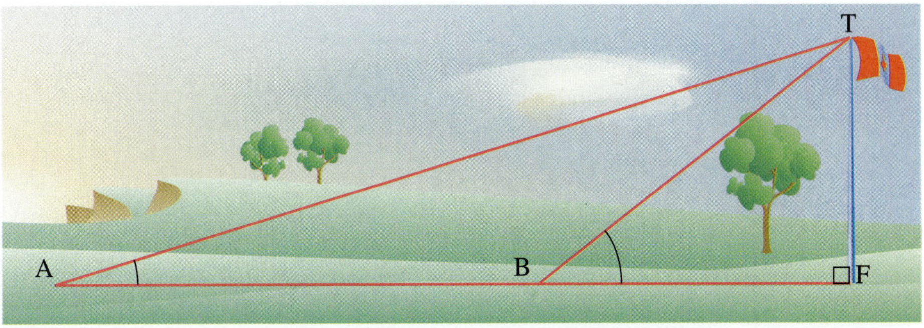

- Choose a position where the top of the object can be seen, and measure the angle of elevation of the top of the object from this position A.
- Move a measured distance toward the object to position B and measure the angle of elevation from this point.
- The height of the object can be determined using the same method as *Example 1*.

Example 2 Using a combination of laws to solve an oblique triangle

An engineering contractor plans to dig a tunnel through a mountain to connect points B and C with a straight line.

It will be faster to dig the tunnel from both sides. How could the engineer determine which direction to dig?

Line BC represents the extended line of the tunnel. Point A is chosen to be visible from both points B and C. Measurements are taken and show $\angle A = 72°$, $AB = 3.2$ km, and $AC = 4.1$ km. Find $\angle B$ and $\angle C$ to the nearest hundredth of a degree.

SOLUTION

Draw a working copy of the diagram. Label the sides and angles as shown.

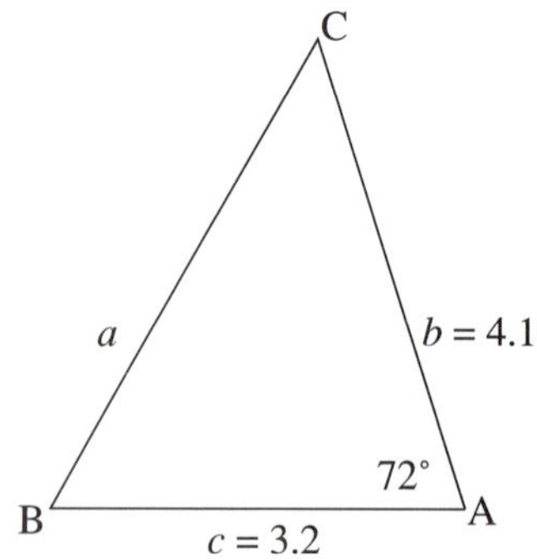

Think of a plan.

To find an angle in an oblique triangle, all three sides must be known, or two angles and one side must be known. We know only two sides and the included angle. Begin by finding the third side, *a*, using the Cosine Law. Once we have all three sides we can use the Cosine Law again, or the Sine Law, to obtain the second angle. The angle sum of a triangle property will determine the remaining angle.

Write the Cosine Law with side *a* isolated.

$$a^2 = b^2 + c^2 - 2bc \cos \text{A}$$

Substitute the given values $b = 4.1$, $c = 3.2$, and $\angle\text{B} = 72^\circ$.

$$a^2 = (4.1)^2 + (3.2)^2 - 2 \times 4.1 \times 3.2 \times \cos 72^\circ$$
$$a = \sqrt{(4.1)^2 + (3.2)^2 - 2 \times 4.1 \times 3.2 \times \cos 72^\circ}$$

Use your calculator to obtain *a*.

$$a \doteq 4.352\ 171\ 19$$

Use the Cosine Law again to find $\angle$B. Write the version that has *b* isolated.

$$b^2 = a^2 + c^2 - 2ac \cos \text{B}$$

Substitute the values for *a*, *b*, and *c*.

$$(4.1)^2 = (4.352\ 171\ 19)^2 + (3.2)^2 - 2(4.352\ 171\ 19)(3.2) \cos \text{B}$$

Isolate the term containing the unknown B.

$$(4.1)^2 - (4.352\ 171\ 19)^2 - (3.2)^2 = -2(4.352\ 171\ 19)(3.2) \cos \text{B}$$
$$\frac{(4.1)^2 - (4.352\ 171\ 19)^2 - (3.2)^2}{-2(4.352\ 171\ 19)(3.2)} = \cos \text{B}$$
$$\angle\text{B} \doteq 63.63^\circ$$

Use the property that angles in a triangle add to 180°.

$$\angle\text{C} \doteq 180^\circ - (72^\circ + 63.63^\circ)$$
$$\doteq 44.37^\circ$$

Angle B measures about 63.63° and $\angle$C measures about 44.37°.

DISCUSSING THE IDEAS

1. When you are solving problems involving triangles, how can you tell whether to use the Sine Law or Cosine Law?

2. When solving a problem, how do you know that more than one step will be involved?

3. What should you remember about the use of units in application questions?

4. Discuss another method you can use to solve *Example 2*.

EXERCISES

Checking Your Skills

1. To measure the height of a hill, a surveyor measures the angle of elevation to the summit of the hill and finds it to be 34°. The surveyor walks 320 m horizontally toward the hill and then finds the angle of elevation to be 57°. What is the height of the hill, to the nearest tenth of a metre?

2. The highest waterfall in Canada is the Della Falls on Vancouver Island. From a certain point the angle of elevation to the top of the falls is 58°. At a point 41 m closer to the falls, the angle of elevation is 62°. Calculate the height of Della Falls.

3. A farmer has a triangular field. From one corner, it is 530 m to the second corner and 750 m to the third corner. The angle between the lines of sight to the second and to the third corners is 53°. Find the perimeter and area of the field. Express your answers correct to the nearest metre or square metres.

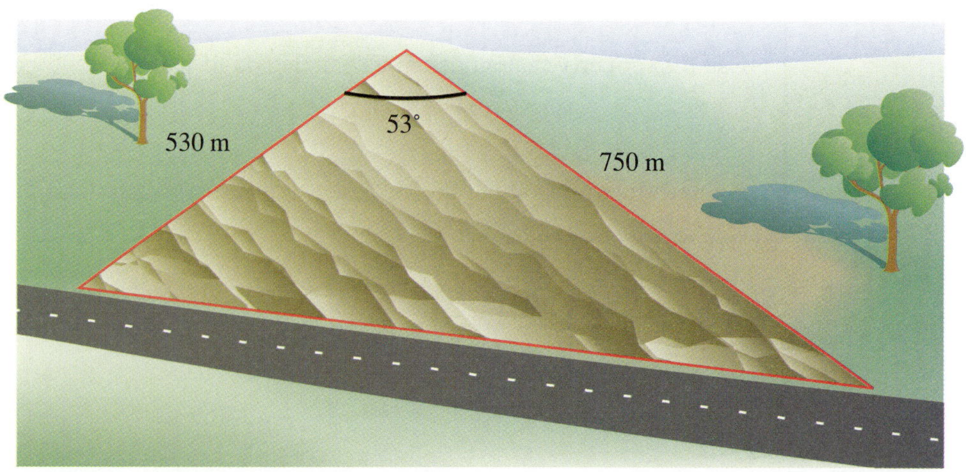

Note: this diagram is not drawn to scale.

If you need to review area of a triangle, refer to the Student Reference.

STUDENT REFERENCE

4. When flying, it is necessary to know the height of the clouds for visibility. The pilot's licence, VFR (Visual Flight Regulations), requires the pilot to be able to see the ground at all times, fly no higher than 1000 feet, and have 3 miles of visibility. At night the cloud height is determined by shining a light on the clouds and having an observer, a certain distance from the light source, measure the angle of elevation of the light reflecting from the clouds. Given the following scenario, what is the height of the clouds? Answer to the nearest foot.

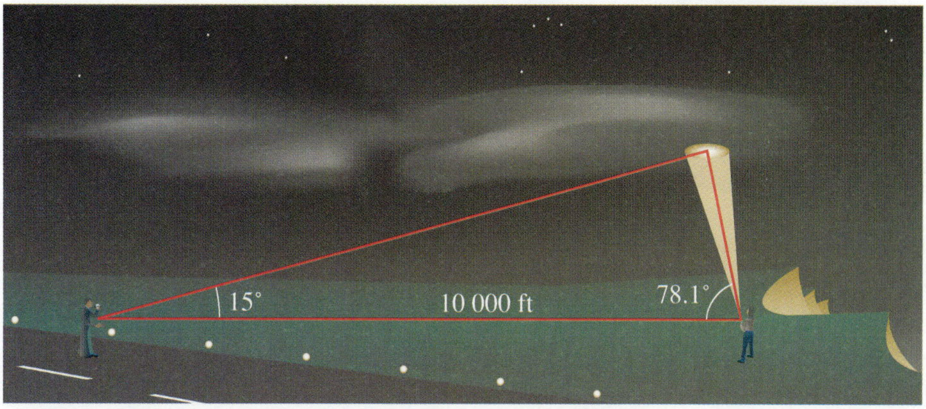

5. A forest ranger takes measurements of the heights of trees and plots this data on a growth chart, much like a doctor does with a child. On May 15th, the ranger stands and records the angles of elevation of three collinear trees to be 32.4° (tree 12A), 30.9° (tree 50F), and 32.8° (tree 17D). The ranger then moves 10 m closer to the line of trees and measures the angles of elevation now to be 58.7° (tree 12A), 56.1° (tree 50F), and 59.3° (tree 17D).

a) Copy and complete the table (all measurements are in centimetres).

	Feb. 15	Mar. 15	Apr. 15	May 15
tree 12 A	1026	1027	1029	
tree 50 F	987	992	997	
tree 17 D	1032	1034	1037	

b) Plot this data on a grid. Use different colours to represent the different trees. Which tree is growing best?

6. A real estate agent is selling a parcel of land but needs to calculate its area. The agent takes the following measurements and sketches the following diagram.

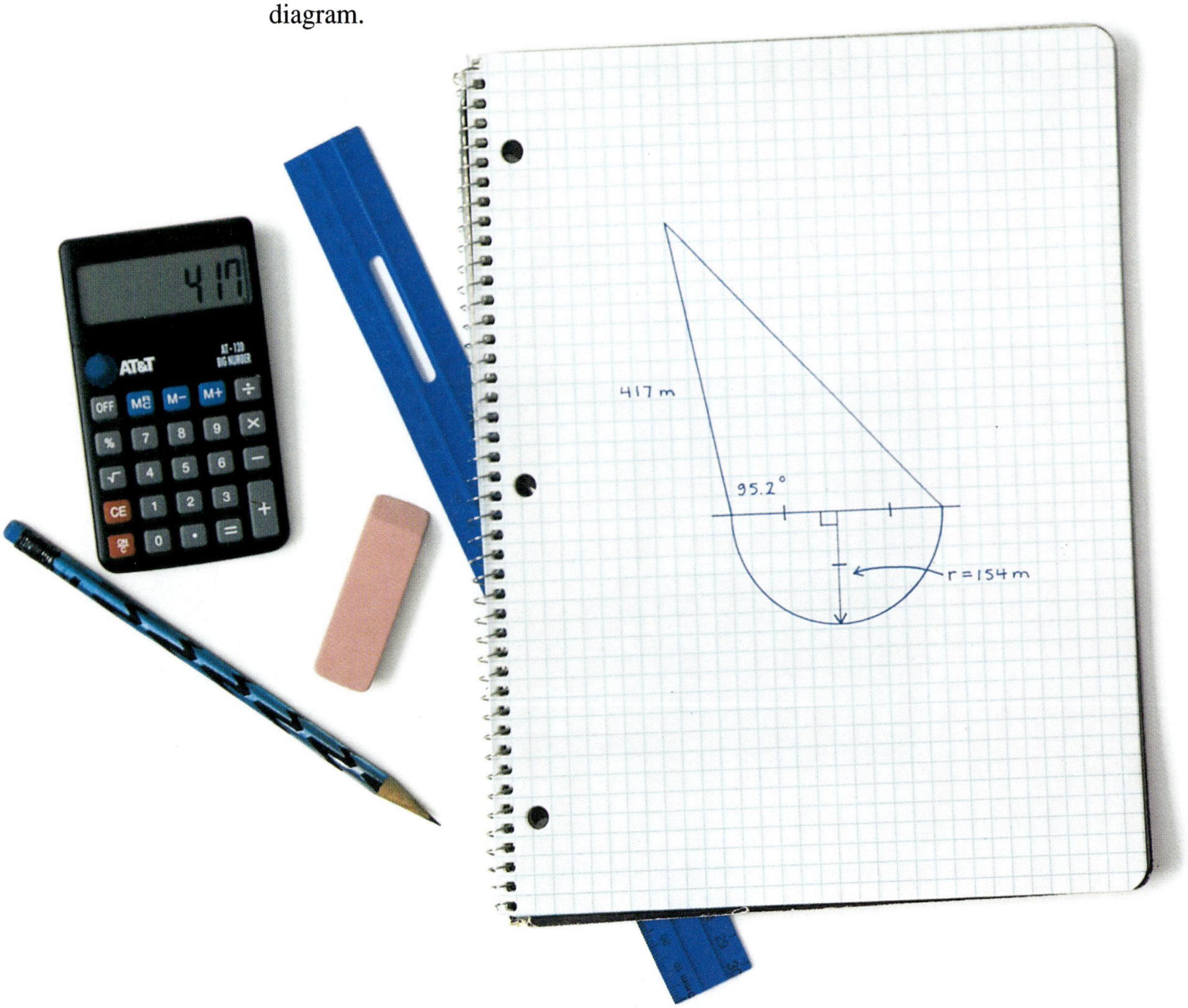

a) Estimate the area of the parcel of land. Explain and justify the method you used.

b) Calculate the area of this parcel of land.

7. A designer is creating a geometric design for fabric. He draws the diagram shown here. To place the basic shape on the fabric he must calculate the length marked h. What was his answer?

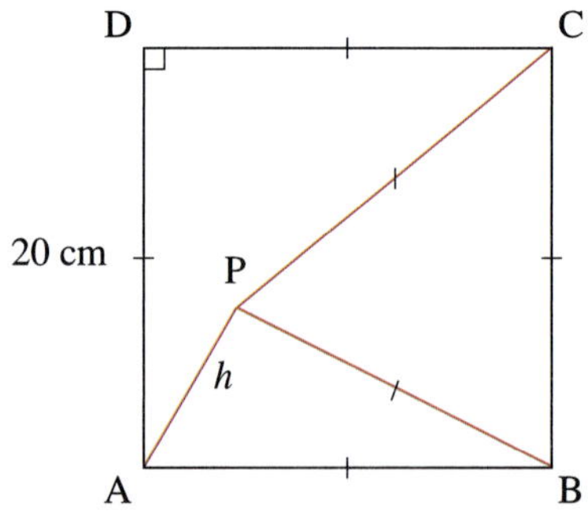

Extending Your Thinking

8. You are at a tracking station at the North Pole and wish to transmit a beam to intersect with a satellite at 6:15 P.M. The satellite is in a circular orbit 1587 km above Earth, and will be directly over the tracking station at 6:10 P.M. The satellite takes 1 h and 58 min to orbit the earth. The radius of Earth is approximately 6378 km.

a) Through what angle does the line of sight to the satellite from the tracking station turn between 6:10 P.M. and 6:15 P.M.?

b) At what angle above the horizon should the antenna be pointed so that its beam will intercept the satellite at 6:15 P.M.?

CHAPTER PROJECT

In this Tutorial you solved problems that involve the different trigonometric ratios and rules you learned in this chapter. You will use your trigonometric skills to do your survey and draw scale diagrams in the Chapter Project.

COMMUNICATING THE IDEAS

Your mom had to upgrade her math in order to get a promotion at work. Explain, in writing, a possible approach to the questions of the type seen in this section.

The Survey

You and your partner will complete the survey of your area.

- Look back at the sketch you made in your earlier work.
- Decide what measurements you can take directly and what you will have to use indirect methods for. Remember that you can set up a baseline, and determine long distances using your transit and the Sine Law or Cosine Law.
- Take measurements and do the necessary calculations. Label your sketch.
- Draw detailed diagrams showing different views of the area. Label the angles of elevation and depression and all the other measurements you took and calculated.
- Put your work together with that of your classmates. Work cooperatively to create a model of the designated area.

Career Skills

Professional surveyors and architects present their work as scale diagrams, illustrations, or models. Precision and accuracy are extremely important. Engineers and builders may use the survey to plan the location of a structure or to build the structure. Any errors in measurement can have serious consequences.

CONSOLIDATING YOUR SKILLS

What Do I Need To Know?

Tutorial	Skills and Concepts	Important Results and Formulas
7.1	• Use right triangle trigonometry to make indirect measurements	$\sin A = \frac{\text{Length of opposite side}}{\text{Length of hypotenuse}}$ $\cos A = \frac{\text{Length of adjacent side}}{\text{Length of hypotenuse}}$ $\tan A = \frac{\text{Length of opposite side}}{\text{Length of adjacent side}}$
7.2	• Use 2 right triangles to solve problems in both 2 and 3 dimensions	
7.3	• Understand how to determine the sine and cosine of obtuse angles • Investigate the relationship between the sines and cosines of supplementary angles	$\sin (180 - A)^\circ = \sin A^\circ$ $\cos (180 - A)^\circ = -\cos A^\circ$
7.4	• Investigate the Sine Law	In $\triangle ABC$, $\frac{\sin A}{a} = \frac{\sin B}{b} = \frac{\sin C}{c}$
7.5	• Use the Sine Law to solve problems • Understand when the Sine Law is applicable	
7.6	• Use the Cosine Law to solve problems	In $\triangle ABC$, $a^2 = b^2 + c^2 - 2bc \cos A$ $b^2 = a^2 + c^2 - 2ac \cos B$ $c^2 = b^2 + c^2 - 2ac \cos C$
7.7	• Use combinations of right triangle trigonometry, the Sine Law, and the Cosine Law to solve problems	

What Should I Be Able To Do?

After completing the work of the chapter, you should be able to answer the following questions. Use any source of information you need.

Part A

An irregular plot of land in the shape of quadrilateral ABCD is to be fenced at a cost of \$40/m. A land survey produced the following information.

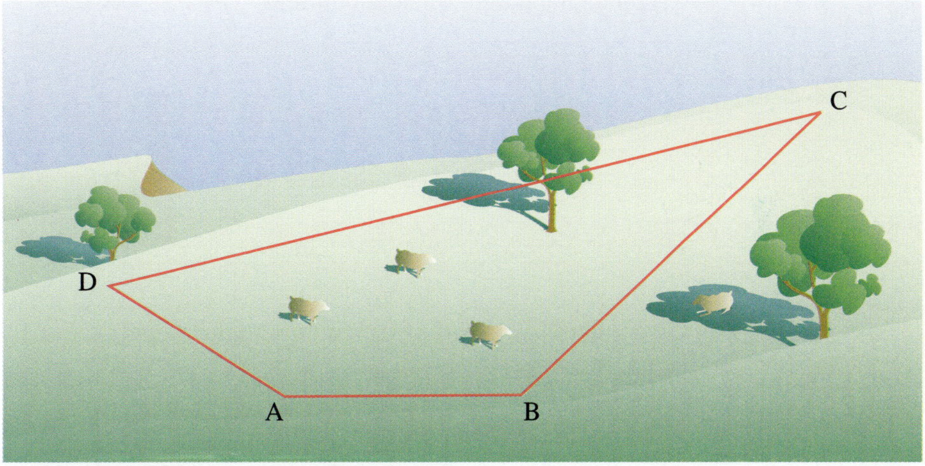

Note: this diagram is not drawn to scale.

AB = 54.0 m $\quad\angle ABC = 90°$ $\quad\angle BAC = 73°$ $\quad\angle ABD = 30°$ $\quad\angle BAD = 134°$

Investigate the cost of fencing the land by completing the exercises below.

1. Make a working sketch of the quadrilateral in your notebook. Mark the given angles and length.
2. Determine the length of BC and enter it on your diagram.
3. Identify a triangle you can use to determine AD. Calculate the length of AD and mark the result on your diagram.
4. Identify a triangle you might use to determine DC. If there is insufficient information in this triangle, calculate the additional length or angle you need.
5. Calculate DC and enter the result on your diagram.
6. Calculate the perimeter of the quadrilateral ABCD.
7. Calculate the cost of fencing the plot of land.

Part B

8. The escalator in a department store rises 4.5 m for every 5.0-m horizontal run. Calculate the angle of inclination of the escalator.

9. Two apartment buildings are 42.5 m apart. From the top of the taller building the angle of depression to the top of the shorter building is 27.5°. The angle of depression to the base of the shorter building is 72.6°. Calculate the height of each building.

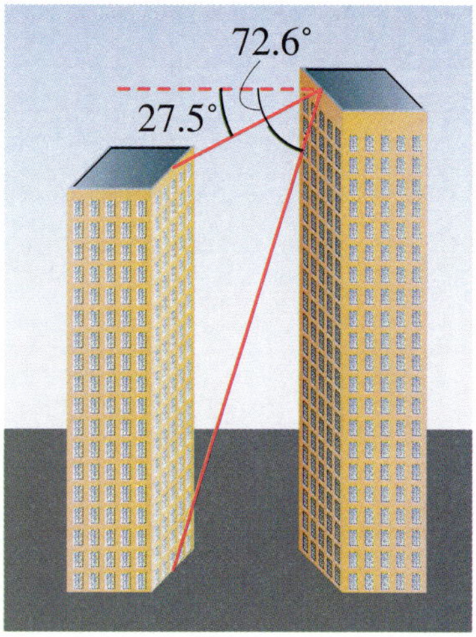

10. Given that $0° \le \angle A \le 180°$, determine the value(s) of $\angle A$.

a) $\sin A = 0.7071$ **b)** $\cos A = -1$ **c)** $\cos A = 0.75$

11. Two friends are 42 m apart at points A and B on the same side of a canyon when they spot a bird at point C on the opposite side. They determine that $\angle BAC$ is 72° and $\angle ABC$ is 53°. Which friend is closer to the bird?

12. In major league baseball, the 4 bases form a square with sides of length 90 feet. The pitcher's mound is on the diagonal of the square with the front edge 60.5 feet from home plate. Find the distance from the front edge of the pitcher's mound to the first base.

13. A kite is made in the shape ABCP below. ABCD is a square of length 0.3 m. Point P is such that $\angle PAD = \angle PCD = 30°$.

a) Calculate the length of PD to one decimal place.

b) Calculate the length of PC to one decimal place.

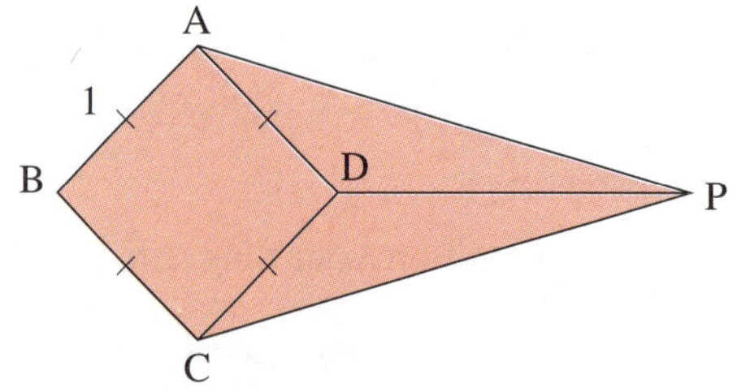

14. A hot air balloon is seen over Campbell River simultaneously by two observers at points A and B. Assume that the observers and the balloon are in the same vertical plane. The angle of elevation of the balloon from point A is 28° and from point B is 37°. A and B are on opposite sides of the balloon and 2.32 miles apart. Assume that the balloon and observers are in the same vertical plane, as shown below. How high is the balloon?

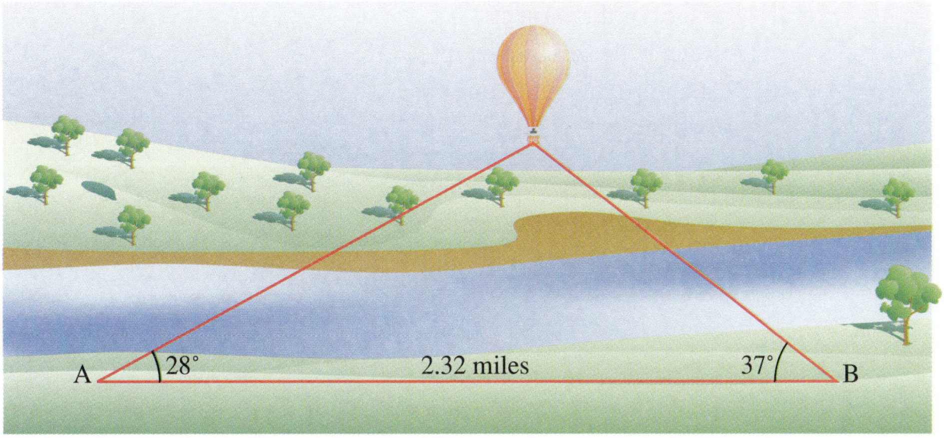

15. A market gardener has to fertilize a triangular field that has side lengths of 90 m, 45 m, and 65 m. The fertilizer is spread so that 1 kg covers 10 m^2. One bag of fertilizer has a mass of 9.1 kg. How much fertilizer will be needed?

Part C

The Chapter Project combines many skills and concepts in a single problem. Here is a sampling of possible student work from different stages of the project. Review these samples to gain insights into your own project work.

16. Here are two clinometers made by two students.

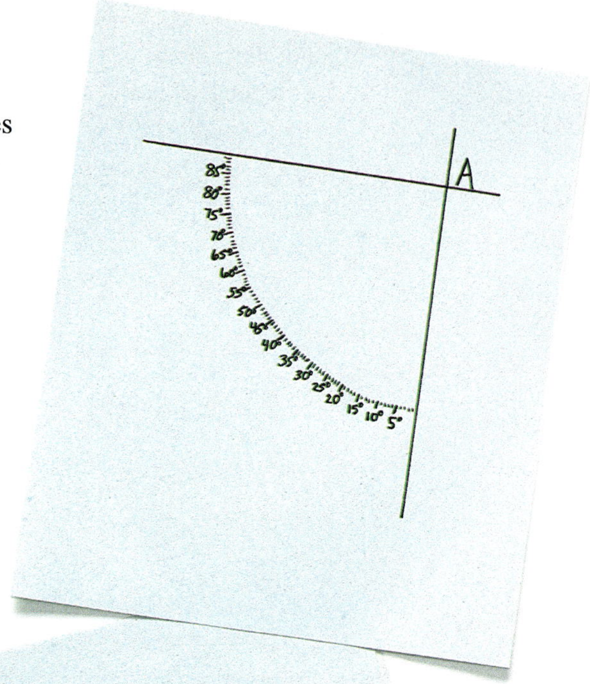

- Examine the clinometer on the left. Are the angles accurate?
- Compare the precision of the clinometers.
- Which clinometer do you think takes more accurate measurements? Why?

Write a summary of your assessment of these students' work.

17. Here are the measurements taken by the same two students and the scale diagrams they drew.

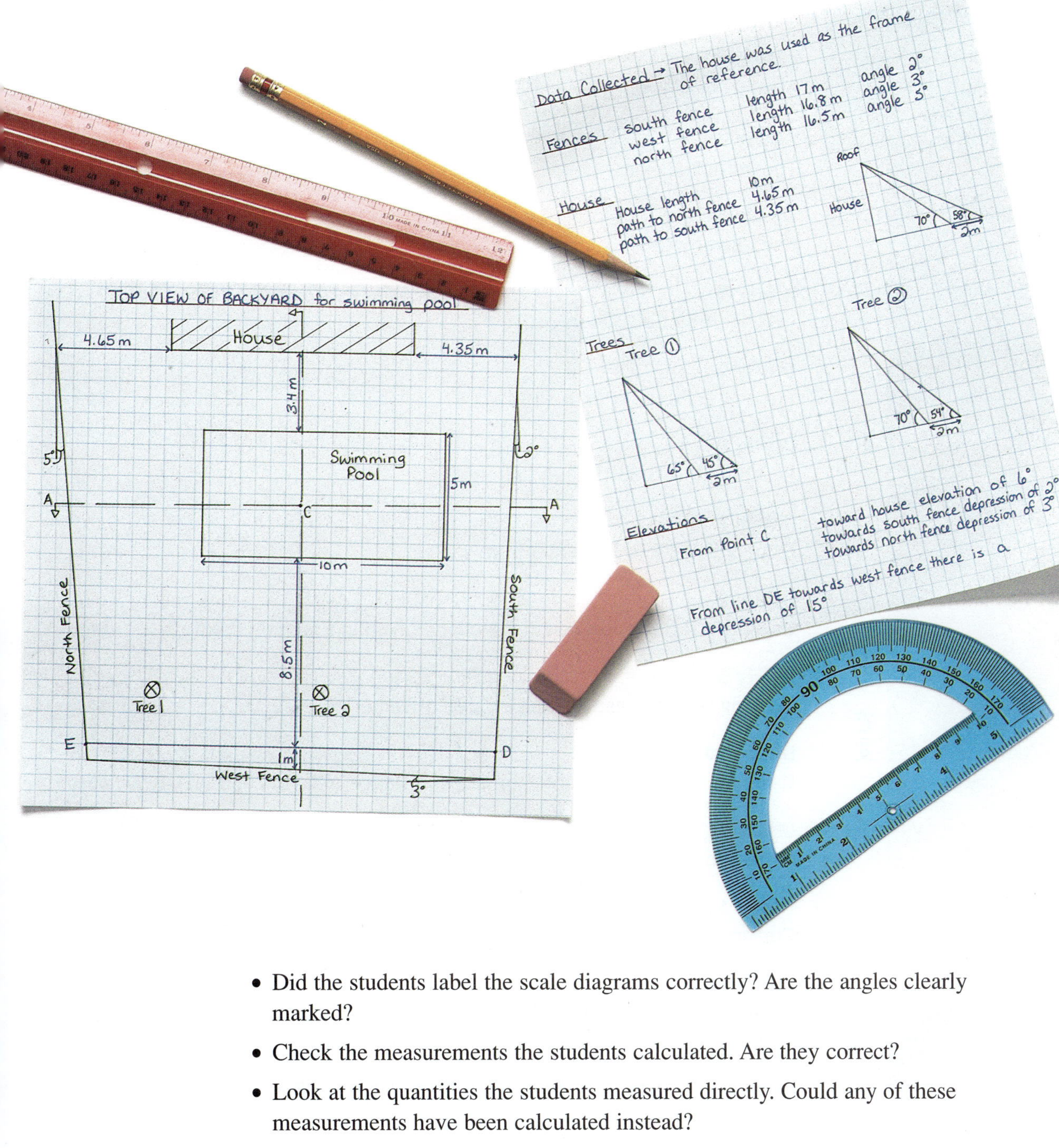

- Did the students label the scale diagrams correctly? Are the angles clearly marked?
- Check the measurements the students calculated. Are they correct?
- Look at the quantities the students measured directly. Could any of these measurements have been calculated instead?
- Are there any measurements the students missed? Should these measurements be measured directly or calculated?

Write a summary of your assessment of these students' work.

CONTENTS

Utilities

How to Search the World Wide Web

The World Wide Web (or just "the Web," as it is commonly known) consists of millions of pages of information, spread across hundreds of thousands of Web "sites." Not only is the quantity of information incredibly vast, it is dynamic — thousands of pages of information are added each day while other pages "disappear" or become unavailable as they are deleted or taken off-line. So how do you find the information that you are looking for? Fortunately, there are tools on the Web to help you with your search — sites containing indexes, directories, and search "engines." The key to using the Web for research is knowing how these tools work, and how to use them effectively.

The Web Browser Search Button: A Good Starting Point

Most modern Web browsers have a Search button on their toolbar, or in their pull-down menus. Usually, the browser manufacturer has formed alliances with a number of search sites, and the Web page linked to the Search button presents you with a list of choices. Some feature the "search engine of the day" along with alternatives. As you become more familiar with these tools, you may want to bookmark them or add them to your "favourites" folder. At right is a sample screen-shot of what Internet Explorer 4 displayed when the Search button was clicked. A search entry screen for Infoseek was presented, but links to other search engines are also available.

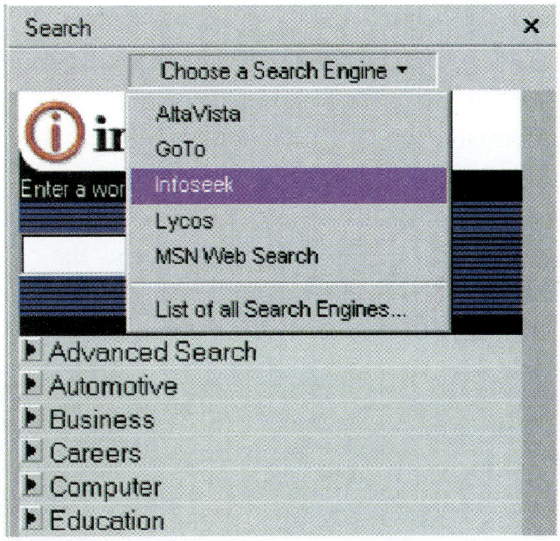

Search Sites, Search Engines, and Other Tools

Search sites present you with one or more tools to look for information on the Internet. One of the tools might be an index of Web sites, organized by subject area. You "drill down" through the choices to narrow your search. For example, using a popular search site index (www.yahoo.ca) to find information about gorillas, you would click on Science to begin with, then Biology, then Zoology. Here you would find Animals, Insects, and Pets among the choices, but Primatology would be a better choice. Under Primatology is Apes, and under Apes is Gorillas. Today, there are 11 sites listed.

A more efficient tool is the search "engine." To use this tool, you enter "keywords" into a form. The search engine (a computer program) then looks through all the Web pages in its database for those that match your keywords, and presents them to you.

Entering **gorillas** into the search engine of Yahoo! yields 64 sites today. Why so many more "hits" (matches)? This search not only brought up the sites that were found under Science/Biology/Zoology/Primatology/Apes/Gorillas, it also lists sites that contain information about gorilla dolls, a baseball team called The Gorillas, a musical group called Gorilla Biscuits, and other sites that aren't relevant. You can usually narrow the search results by providing more keywords to either include or exclude from the search. How you go about this will depend entirely on the search site you are using.

More Advanced Searches: Learning the Tools of the Site

Let's take our gorillas example. Entering just **gorillas** at www.yahoo.ca yields 64 sites. Suppose you enter **gorillas primates** into the search box, in order to further focus your search. At Yahoo!, your new search yields 11 sites, all of which have both the word gorillas and the word primates somewhere in their content. At another search site, www.excite.ca, entering **gorillas** yields 4441 hits today (these are links to individual pages, not just site addresses). Entering **gorillas primates** yields 13 602 hits. What's going on? The search engine at Excite brought up any Web pages

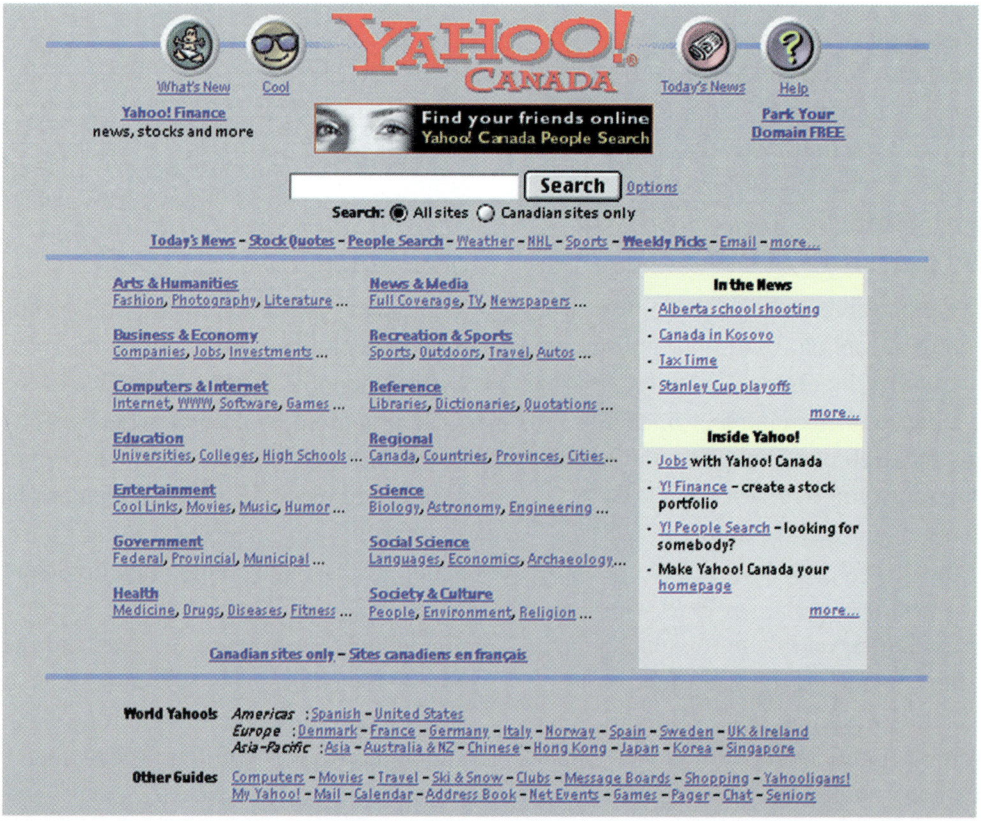

that had the word gorillas or the word primates somewhere in their content. In other words, Yahoo! interpreted your search as gorillas AND primates (both must be present for a match), whereas Excite interpreted the search as gorillas OR primates (either word may be present for a match).

Fortunately, Excite and many other search engines "weight" their results. Although the second search (gorillas primates) brought up many more sites at Excite, the ones where both words appeared together were listed first. In fact, even these are weighted by the number of times each word appears in the document. The more times the keywords appear, the higher in the list the Web page is shown by Excite. Excite, and most other search engines, also allow you to enter Boolean operators into their search query box. Boolean operators are connecting words, like AND and OR, that vary the engine's searching method. For example, entering **gorillas AND primates** yields just 615 hits today. Remember, different search sites and engines work differently. Before you use a search site, read any information or tips about how to use the site, or how to do advanced searches.

Where Can You Get To from Here?

The great thing about the Web is that it is incredibly interlinked. Find one site on gorillas, and it may have several valuable links to other gorilla sites, some of which may not have shown up in your search site's hits. Occasionally, your search discovers a site that is dedicated to providing links to other sites about a particular topic. These sites can be very useful, because someone has already gone to a lot of trouble to research and provide "quality" links to sites and pages. Be aware, however, that you may be looking at a list that has been compiled and edited by someone who is not an expert in the field.

Finding Canadian Information

Entering **Canada** as one of the keywords for your search may help narrow your hits to Canadian information (especially if you use the Boolean **AND Canada**). Some search sites provide additional "regionalized" conditions that you can apply to a search. Yahoo! Canada (www.yahoo.ca) has a button choice for All sites or Canadian sites only.

The MetaSearch: Using Multiple Search Engines

Another tool that appears on the Web is the MetaSearch site. These sites submit your keywords to multiple search engines at the same time. Why are there so many search sites and different search engines? Each search site does things a little bit differently. Some boast that they have the largest number of Web pages indexed in their database. Some place their emphasis on making searches easier for the user. Some provide unique resources in their database, or specifically avoid certain Internet resources (usenet group information, for example). The terrific thing about these sites is that they are all competing for you to use them, mostly free of charge! They do contain some advertising (which is how they make their money).

To Use the World Wide Web Effectively

- Be prepared to spend some time to learn the ins and outs of a particular search site.
- Hone your search skills. You may have to try a number of sites to find one that works well for you. You may also find that certain sites are better than others for certain types of searches.
- If you are having difficulty finding what you want, try different key words. Use a thesaurus to look for synonyms. Sometimes the information is really there, but the words you are using aren't quite right.

Search Site List

Here is a list of some of the more common search sites available today.

Internet Search Sites			
AltaVista *altavista.digital.com*	Excite *www.excite.com*	HotBot *www.hotbot.com*	Infoseek *www.infoseek.com*
LookSmart *www.looksmart.com*	Lycos *www.lycos.com*	Northern Lights *www.nlsearch.com*	Open Text Index *index.opentext.net*
PlanetSearch *www.planetsearch.com*	Search *www.search.com*	WebCrawler *www.webcrawler.com*	Yahoo! Canada *www.yahoo.ca*
Internet MetaSearch Sites			
1Blink *www.1blink.com 2Q*	QuickQuest *www.2q.to*	Cyber411 *www.cyber411.com*	Dogpile *www.dogpile.com*
Highway 61 *www.highway61.com*	Internet Sleuth *www.isleuth.com*	MetaCrawler *www.metacrawler.com*	Surfy *www.surfy.com*

The Vernier Caliper

The vernier caliper is a precision measurement tool that has several functions. It can usually be used to measure outside dimensions and inside dimensions, as shown in the diagram below. Most vernier calipers have a “tail” that extends beyond the main arm of the caliper and can be used to measure depth.

Calipers may have different scales and precisions. The one shown below has an inch scale and a centimetre scale. The precision of this instrument is 0.01 inch or 0.01 cm. Some calipers show inch scales with a precision of $\frac{1}{128}$ inch.

Always close (or open for inside measurements) the caliper using the thumb wheel. This ensures an even pressure on the object each time you take a measurement. This means that the object is not deformed by the instrument and the measurement should be reproducible.

Reading a Vernier Caliper

1. First decide which units are needed: inches or centimetres.

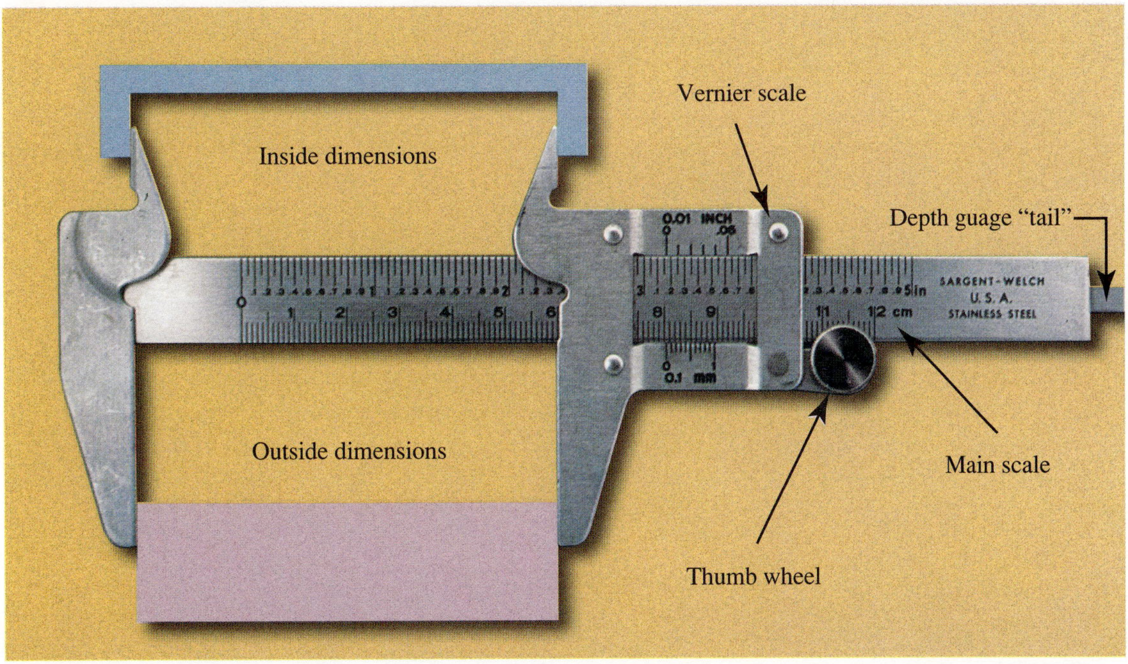

2. Notice the position of the zero or far left line on the vernier (the sliding scale). You can get a coarse reading by taking the value of the first mark on the main scale to the left of the vernier 0.

In the diagram below, the coarse reading is 3.35 inches, or 8.5 cm.

3. To refine the reading, find the one line on the vernier that best matches any line on the main scale.

In the diagram below, this is the 2nd line on the inch vernier scale and the 6th line on the metric vernier scale.

4. Add the value of the matching vernier line to the coarse reading to get the caliper reading. If the vernier line 0 is the best match, add the value 0.00.

In the diagram below, each division on the inch vernier represents 0.01 inches, so the vernier line has a value of 0.02 inches and the caliper reading is
3.35 inches + 0.02 inches, or 3.37 inches.
Each division on the metric vernier represents 0.1 mm, or 0.01 cm, so the vernier line has a value of 0.06 cm and the caliper reading is
8.5 cm + 0.06 cm, or 8.56 cm.

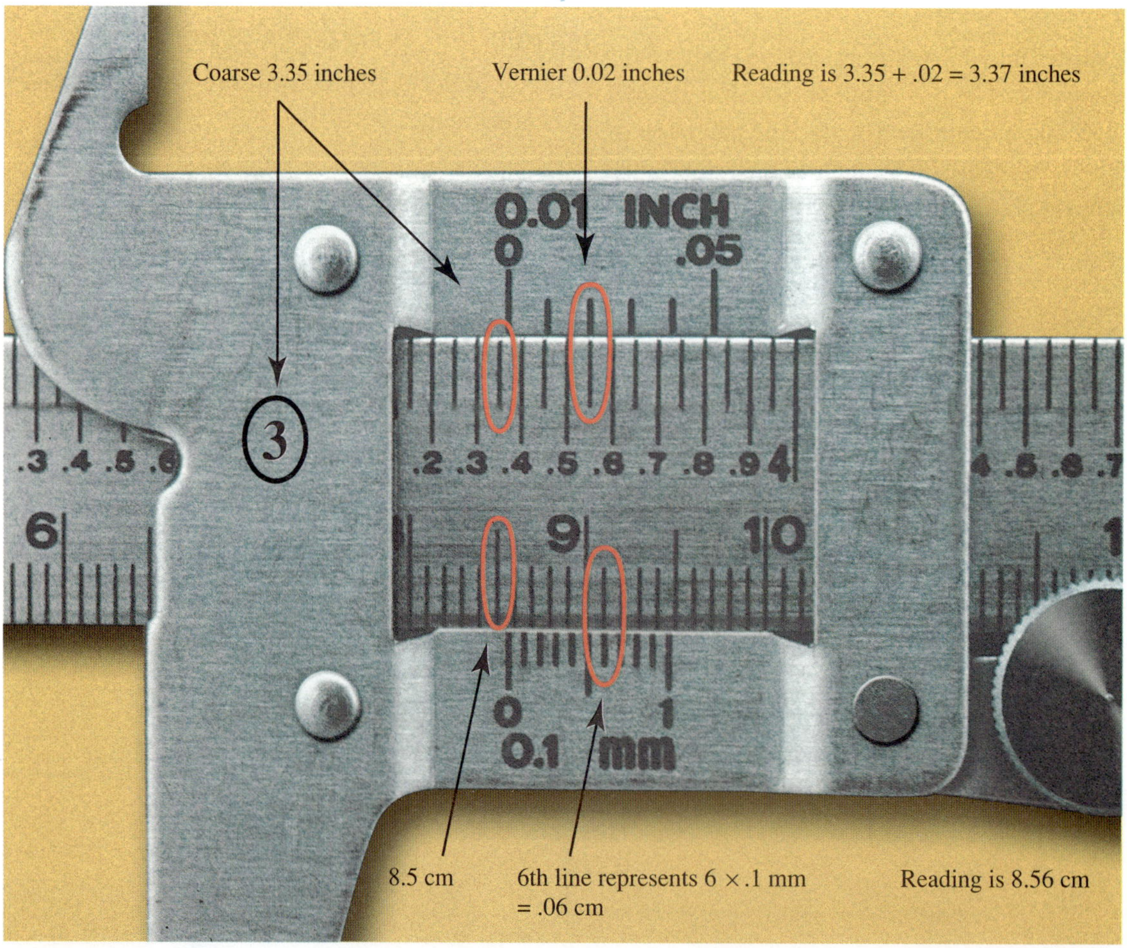

Check your skill at reading a vernier caliper by reading the diagrams below in both inches and centimetres. The answers are given in the Answer Key.

1.

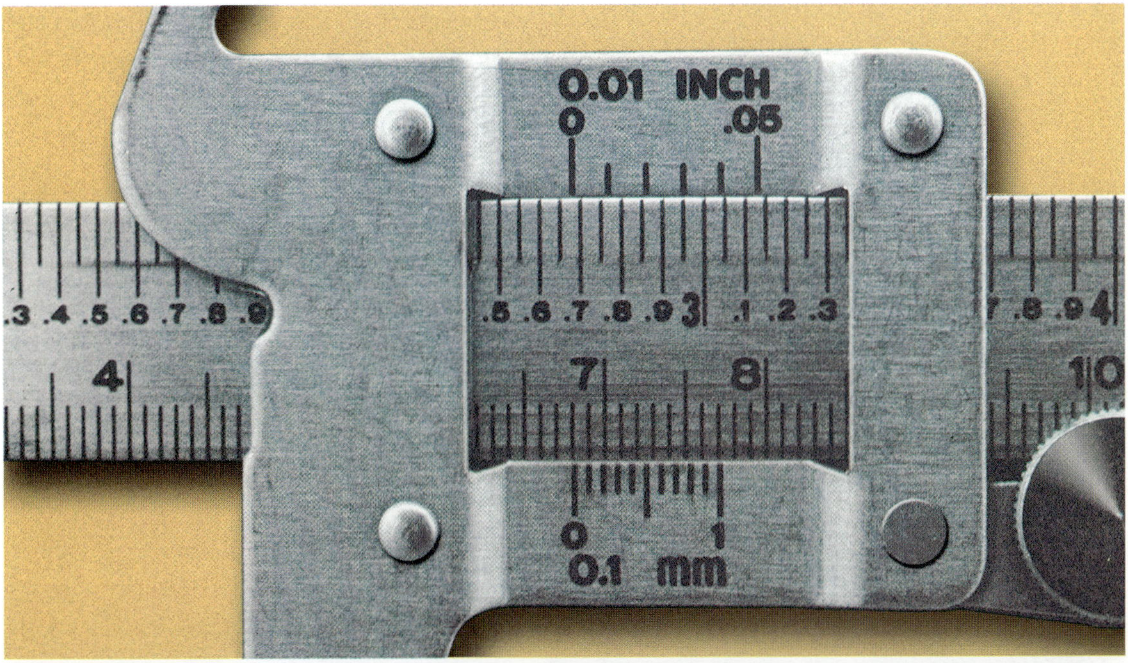

2.

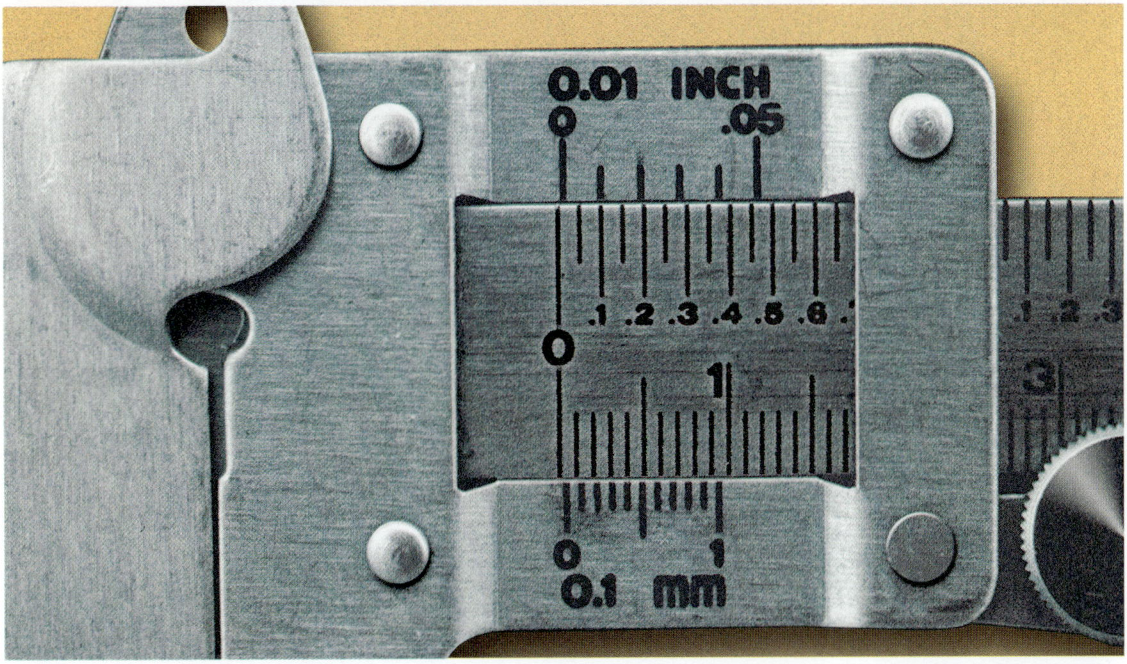

UTILITY 2

In the case of a vernier caliper with divisions of an inch given as common fractions, you read it in a similar way, but you obtain the final reading by adding fractions. The diagram below shows you how to read such a caliper.

The scale on the main arm is divided into $\frac{1}{16}$ inches. The coarse reading is $2\frac{5}{16}$ inches. Since there are 8 divisions on the vernier scale, each one represents $\frac{1}{8}$ of $\frac{1}{16}$ of an inch, or $\frac{1}{128}$ inch. The vernier scale shows that an extra $\frac{6}{128}$ inch must be added to the coarse reading.

$$\begin{aligned}\text{The caliper reading is } & 2\tfrac{5}{16} + \tfrac{6}{128} \\ &= 2\tfrac{5}{16} + \tfrac{3}{64} \\ &= 2\tfrac{20}{64} + \tfrac{3}{64} \\ &= 2\tfrac{23}{64} \text{ inches.}\end{aligned}$$

The Micrometer

The micrometer is a precision device used to measure the outside dimensions of small objects. The micrometer shown below can measure lengths up to 2.5 cm and has a precision of 0.01 mm or 0.001 cm.

Always close the micrometer using the thumb screw. This ensures an even pressure on the object each time you take a measurement. It also means that the measurement should be reproducible, or precise.

Each time the thimble makes one complete turn, it moves along the sleeve a distance of 0.5 mm. The sleeve scale is marked in 0.5-mm increments. The barrel scale is divided into 50 divisions, so a complete turn (0.5 mm) can be measured in 50 parts. Each division on the barrel scale represents $\frac{0.5\text{ mm}}{50} = 0.01\text{ mm}$. The instrument allows you to measure within 0.001 mm if you use estimation. This is a micrometer (1 μm).

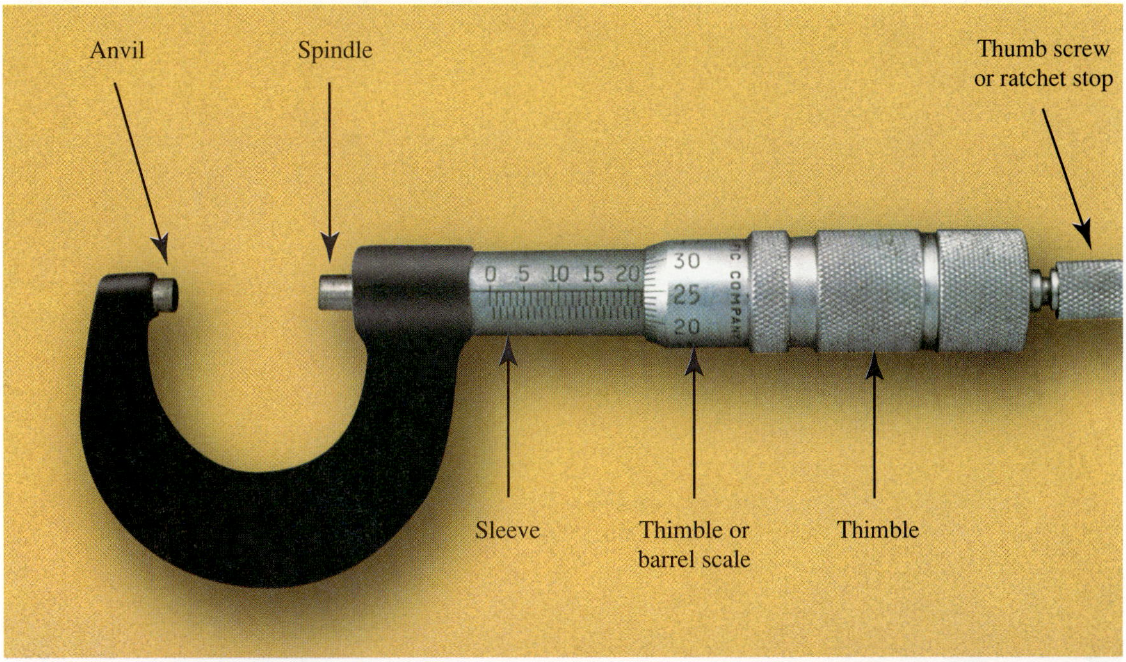

To Read a Micrometer

1. Note the value of the last fully visible line shown on the sleeve. This is the coarse reading.

On the diagram below the coarse reading is 2.5 mm.

2. Determine the value of the line on the barrel scale that best matches up with the reference line that runs the length of the sleeve.

On the diagram below the line representing 36 best matches the reference line.

3. Add the value of the line on the barrel scale to the coarse reading to obtain the micrometer reading.

The value of the line on the barrel scale is 36×0.01 mm $= 0.36$ mm, so the micrometer reading is 2.5 mm $+ 0.36$ mm $= 2.86$ mm.

4. Always make sure that the reading you have taken makes sense.

The 3-mm line is partially visible on the barrel, so our reading of 2.86 mm, which is close to 3 mm seems about right, whereas if we had reported a reading of, say, 3.36 mm this would be too big.

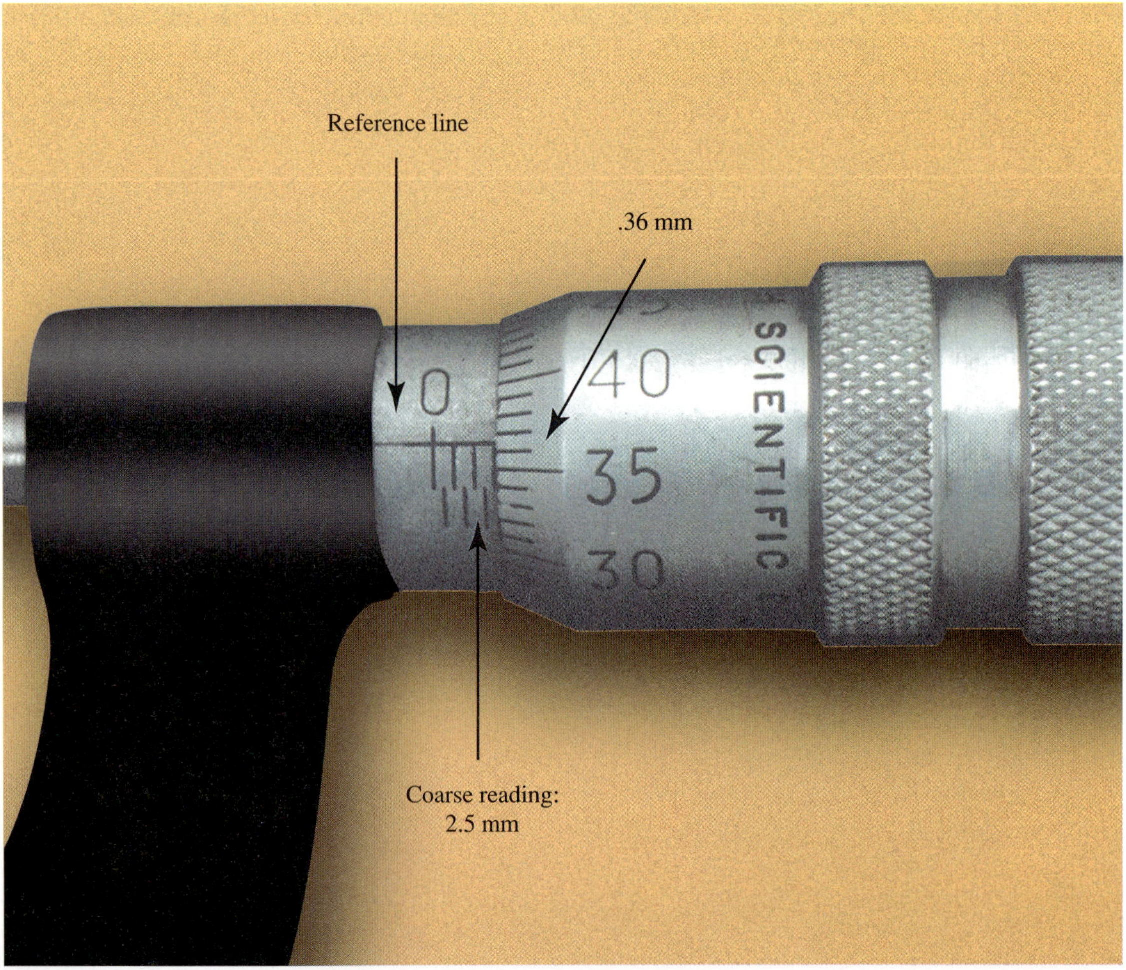

Check your skill by reading the micrometers shown below. The answers appear in the Answer Key.

1.

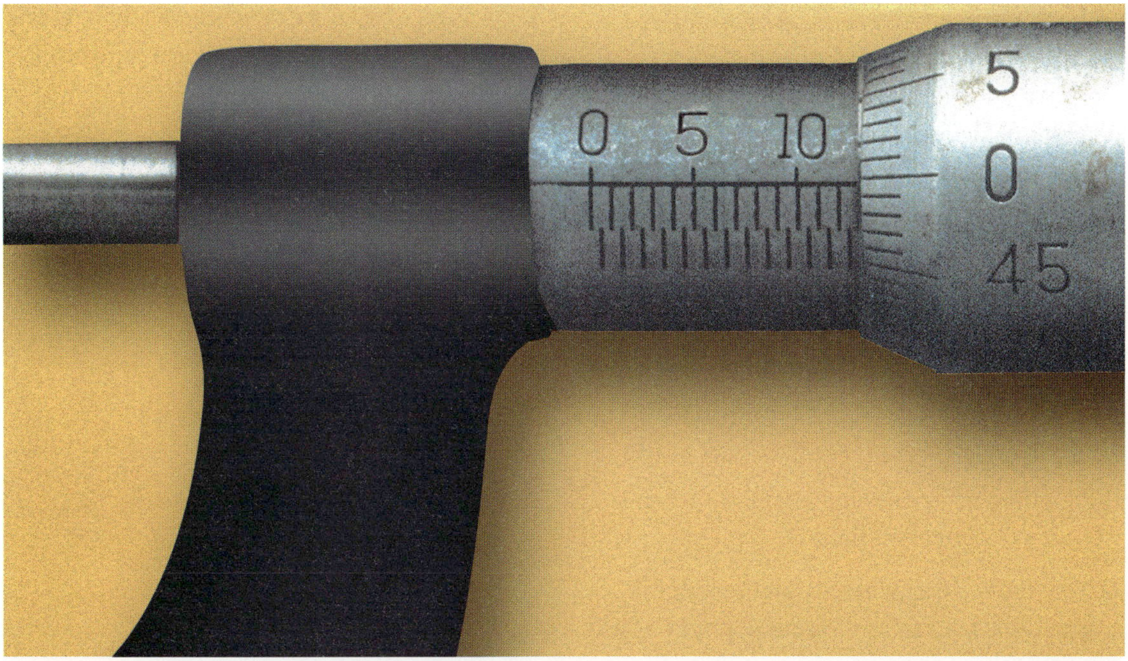

2.

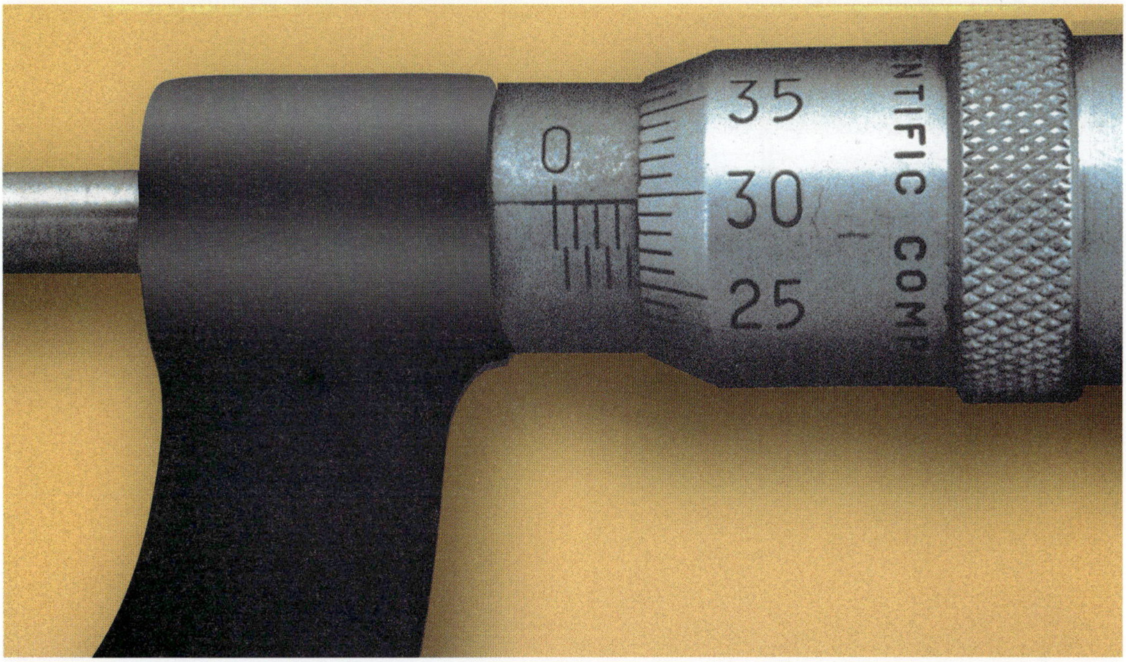

Zero Correction

The micrometer is a sensitive instrument. To use it properly and obtain good accuracy, the micrometer should be zero-corrected each time it is used. When the micrometer is closed, it should read 0.00, as shown in the diagram below.

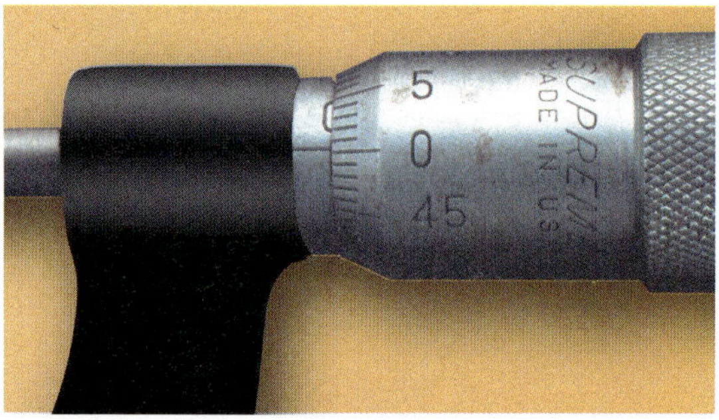

If the micrometer does not read 0.00 when it is closed, a correction must be applied.

1. Note the reading when the micrometer is closed. This reading is the zero correction. It can be positive or negative, but it will always be subtracted from the reading.

2. If the closed micrometer reads some positive value, it is reading too much, and the zero correction is positive.

In the diagram below, the closed micrometer is reading 0.02 mm. The zero correction is +0.02 mm.
When the micrometer is tightened on a small ball bearing, the reading is 3.57 mm. The corrected reading is 3.57 mm – (+0.02) mm = 3.55 mm.

Zero correction = +0.02 mm

3. If the closed micrometer reads some value below zero, it is reading too little, and the zero correction is negative.

In the diagram below, the closed micrometer is reading 0.47 mm, or 0.03 mm below 0. The zero correction is –0.03mm.

When the micrometer is closed on a small ball bearing, the reading is 4.32 mm. The corrected reading is

4.32 mm – (–0.03) mm

= 4.32 mm + 0.03 mm

= 4.35 mm.

Zero correction = –0.03 mm

Linking TI-83 Calculators

Using the LINK feature and the cable that is provided with each calculator, programs, lists, defined matrices, window settings, and basically anything that has been saved in the memory of one calculator can be transferred to the memory of another. Although this Utility will concentrate on transferring programs between calculators, other types of data can be transferred using the same process.

To begin, connect the two calculators using the cable provided. Ensure that the cable is pushed firmly into each calculator. In this process, one calculator will send the data and the other will receive it.

To Receive Data

- Press [2nd] [X,T,θ,n] to select the LINK function.
- Use your arrow key to move the cursor over to RECEIVE.
- Press [ENTER] and the receiving calculator is now ready to receive data (the message "Waiting" will be in the display). The sending calculator should then transmit the data. If the transmission is successful, the program name and the word "Done" will be in your display.

If the data being received already exist in your calculator, the screen below will appear. You can choose to Rename the program, Overwrite the program that is currently in your calculator (this means the current program in the receiving calculator will be lost), Omit the program, or Quit the transmission.

To Send Data

- Press [2nd] [X,T,θ,n] to select the LINK function.

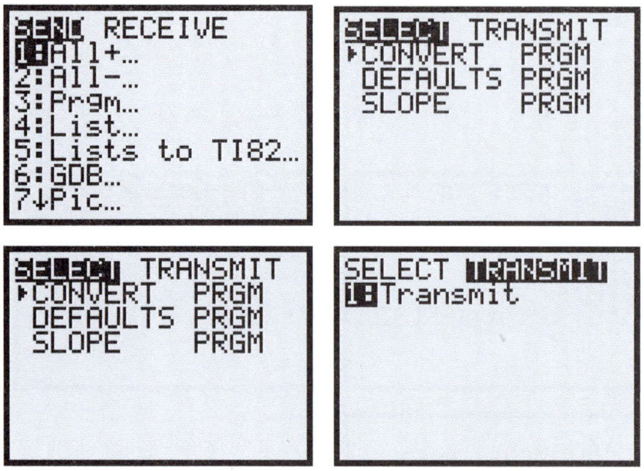

- In this case, since we wish to send a program, select 3:Prgm.... This allows us to choose from any of the programs in the memory we wish to transfer.

Note: These are examples only. These programs may not be in your calculator.

- Select the items you wish to transmit to another calculator using the arrow and [ENTER] keys. When an item has been selected, it is marked with a black box in front of it. To deselect a program, press [ENTER] again.
- To transmit the selected items, use your arrow key and move over to TRANSMIT. Once the second calculator is prepared to receive the data, press [ENTER] and the data will be transferred. Remember: the second calculator must be prepared to receive the data before the first calculator begins transmitting it.

If the cable is not making a good connection with one of the calculators, an error message will appear. Ensure that the cable is properly connected to both calculators and try to send the program again. Once all the data have been sent, the screen should indicate what data have been transmitted and that the transfer is done.

Here is a list of the other functions on the LINK screen.

1: All+... allows you to select individual items, with all items selected initially.

2: All–... allows you to select individual items, with all items deselected initially.

3: Prgm... displays programs only, with no programs selected initially.

4: List... displays list names only, with no lists selected initially.

5: Lists to TI82... displays lists L1 to L6, with no lists selected initially.

6: GDB... displays graph databases only, with no databases selected initially.

7: Pic... displays all picture data types only, with none selected initially.

8: Matrix... displays matrices only, with no matrices selected initially.

9: Real... displays all real variables only, with no variables selected initially.

0:Complex... displays all complex variables only, with no variables selected initially.

A:Y-Vars... displays all Y= variables only, with no variables selected initially.

B:String... displays all string variables only, with no variables selected initially.

C:Backup... selects everything for backup to the TI-83.

Running a Program on a TI-83

Using the TI-83, three things can be done to a program. First, you can EXECute or run a program. Second, if a program that has been entered into the calculator is not protected, you can EDIT or make changes to it. Third, you can create a NEW program for the TI-83. Refer to the manual for instructions on programming.

To Run a Program

- Press PRGM.
- Select the program to be run using either the arrow keys and ENTER, or by pressing the appropriate number or letter.
- The program name should appear on the home screen. To run the program press ENTER.

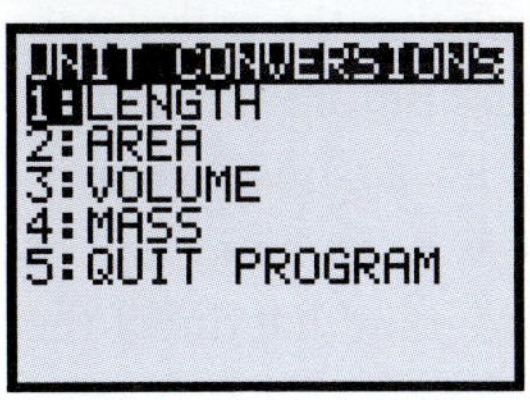

Note: This is an example only. The program may not be in your calculator.

If a command (or partial command) that was on the home screen has not been executed, you might receive the Error message shown below right. In this case you would choose **2** and delete all of the characters that appear prior to the program name, and then press ENTER to begin the program.

To Interrupt a Program

- ON will break the program. Select **1:Quit** or ENTER to return to the home screen.

Note: If the program being executed is not protected, a second option, 2:Goto, will appear on the screen. If this option is selected, the calculator will return to the place within the program where the program was interrupted. To leave the program, press 2nd MODE. If any other keystroke is selected, the program will be altered.

Resetting the TI-83 Default Settings

Have you ever picked up a calculator to solve a problem, only to find that the settings have been changed? This Utility will explain how to restore a calculator to its default settings. Default settings are set at the factory when the calculator is manufactured. The calculator will always revert to its default settings in the absence of other instructions.

The TI-83 has an easy way of returning the MODE, WINDOW, FORMAT, and STAT PLOT menus to their default settings. The default settings for these menus are shown below.

MODE MENU

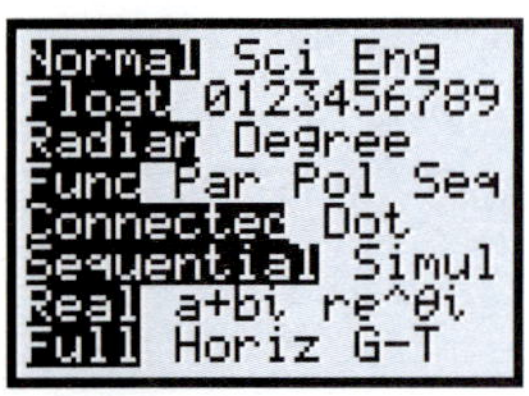

WINDOW MENU

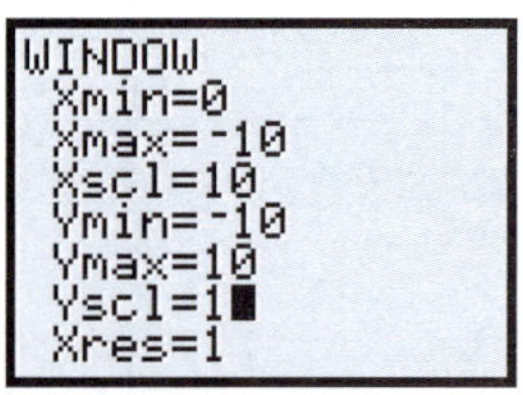

FORMAT MENU

STAT PLOT MENU

Follow these instructions carefully. If you press the wrong buttons you may erase your programs.

1. Display the Memory menu. Press [2nd] [+]. The screen should look like the one shown.

2. Press **5** to select Reset. The screen should look like the one shown.

3. Press **2** to select Defaults. The screen should look like the one shown.

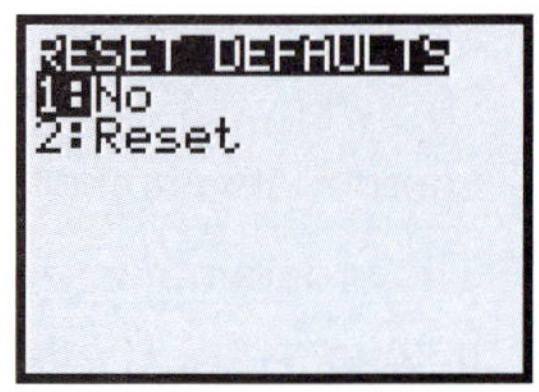

4. Press **2** to select Reset. The screen should look like the one shown.

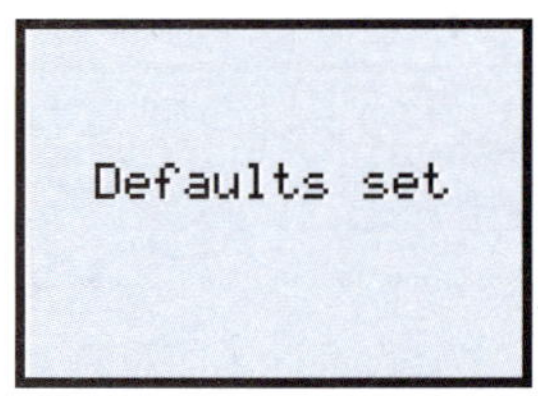

5. Press [ENTER] and you are done! The default settings are once again in use.

Most programmers assume that the calculator is using its default settings. Before running any program, you should always reset your calculator. An alternative is to include steps at the beginning of every program that direct the calculator to reset the defaults. Although this second choice is not difficult, it is a little more time consuming than resetting using the above steps.

Using the TI-83 to Plot Data from Tables

The TI-83 can display a scatterplot using data you input.

Here is a table of data for you to graph in this Utility. Have a TI-83 beside you as you follow the instructions below.

Women in the Saskatchewan Legislature

Year	Percent of Women in Saskatchewan's Provincial Legislature
1975	3.3
1980	1.6
1984	7.8
1988	7.8
1993	18.2

1. First go to the data list screen to clear any previously entered data. Press STAT. Press **1** to select Edit.... You should see a screen like the one below.

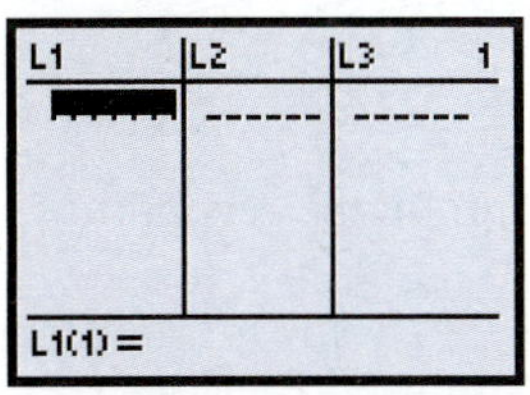

Are there data in column L1? Press the up arrow key to highlight the column heading L1; this selects the complete column L1. Then press CLEAR ENTER.

Now look at column L2. If it contains data, use the arrow keys to move to the column, and clear the data. You only need columns L1 and L2, so you do not have to clear data in any other lists. Stay in this screen.

2. Enter the data on the percent of women in the Saskatchewan legislature. Follow the steps below.

Move the cursor back to column L1. Enter all the dates from the first column of the table. Press ENTER after keying in each date.

Move the cursor to column L2. Enter all the percents from the second column of the table. Press ENTER after keying each percent.

This Utility enters all the data in list L1 before the data in list L2. You have the option of entering each ordered pair, L1 then L2, for each entry. This can be useful if the lists of data are long, and one missed entry can be hard to find.

You are now finished working in this screen. Select QUIT to leave the screen: press 2nd MODE.

3. Set up your calculator to graph a scatterplot. Clear any functions in the Y= list. Press [Y=]. If there is an expression on the first line, press [CLEAR]. Use the down arrow and [CLEAR] to remove any other expressions in the list.

You need to access the STAT PLOT feature. Press [2nd] [Y=] [ENTER] to display the screen below.

The cursor needs to be on the word On. If it isn't, move it using the arrow keys. Then press [ENTER].

Ensure other statplots are off. Choose the type of graph you need—in this case, a scatterplot. If the icon of the scatterplot is darkened, it is already selected. If it is not darkened, move your cursor so that it is flashing on the picture of the scatterplot, and press [ENTER].

You are finished working in this screen. Select QUIT to leave the screen.

4. The TI-83 allows you to adjust the graphing window to reflect the data. Press [WINDOW].

The cursor should be flashing on the value for Xmin. This is the smallest value that will be represented on the horizontal, or x-axis. Press **1970** [ENTER].

The cursor moves to Xmax. This is the largest number represented on the horizontal axis. Press **1995** [ENTER].

The cursor moves to Xscl. This is the scale to be used for the x-axis. Tick marks will appear at each scale mark on the x-axis. Press **1** for Xscl.

Continue by selecting the range of values to be represented on the vertical, or y-axis, and a suitable scale.

Enter **0** for Ymin, **20** for Ymax, and **1** for Yscl.

Select QUIT to leave the screen.

5. Your calculator is ready to graph the scatterplot. Press [GRAPH]. When you are finished, select QUIT.

6. Sometimes you can improve the readability of the graph by modifying the scales.

Try changing the scales you used for your graph.

Press [WINDOW]. Use the down arrow to move the cursor until the Xscl is highlighted. Press **5** [ENTER].

Use the down arrow to move the cursor until Yscl is highlighted. Press **2** [ENTER].

Press [GRAPH] to produce the scatterplot with different scales marked.

Using the TI-83 to Represent Functions Given in Equation Form

The TI-83 can display functions from their equations.

Exercises 1 to 4 demonstrate how to display the graph of $y = 3x^2 + 2$, and the corresponding table of values. Have a TI-83 beside you as you read this Utility.

1. Press [Y=] to display a screen like the one below. You will see a flashing cursor to the right of the first = sign.

You can store up to 10 functions and graph one or more functions at once.

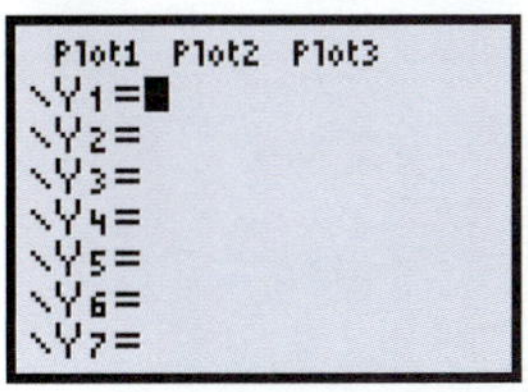

If there is an expression on the first line, press [CLEAR]. Use the down arrow and [CLEAR] to remove any other expressions on the list.

To enter the expression $3x^2 + 2$, press **3** [X,T,θ,n] [x^2] [+] **2** [ENTER].

2. Before graphing, make sure the calculator window reflects appropriate endpoints for the x-axis and y-axis. The standard-size window has endpoints –10 and 10 for both axes. Since the calculator screen is not square, though, this standard size distorts the graph of the function. Endpoints of +9 and –9 for the x-axis, and +6 and –6 for the y-axis, or an approximate ratio of 3:2 for the range in values of x compared to the range in values of y, will display graphs that are in proportion.

3. Press [GRAPH] to display the graph below.

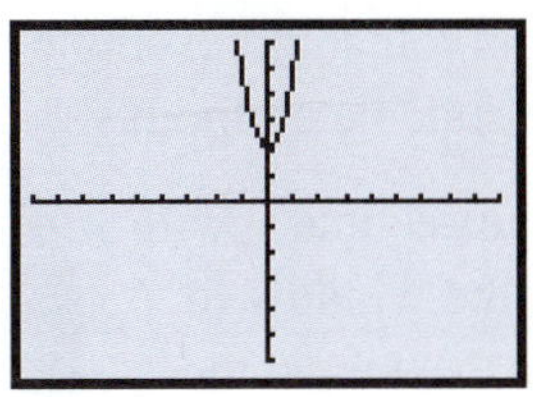

4. Another way to represent the function you defined for Y1 is in a table of values. First, define the x-values you want in the table. Press [2nd] [WINDOW] to access the TABLE SETUP feature. The cursor should be flashing on the line for TblStart: press **0** [ENTER] to start the x-values at 0. On the line ΔTbl, press **1** [ENTER] to have the x-values increase by 1. Your screen display should match the one below left.

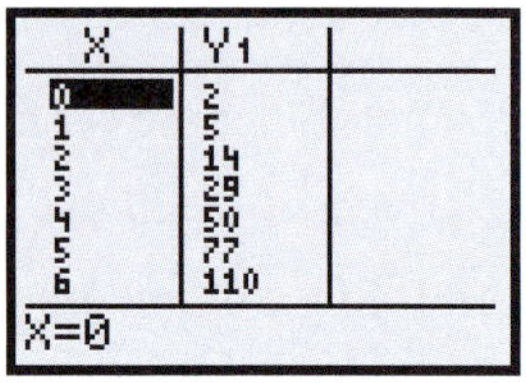

To access the TABLE view, press [2nd] [GRAPH]. Your screen display should match the one above right. Use the arrow keys to scroll up and down the table as far as you wish.

Try the following exercises to practise graphing other equations of functions.

5. Enter the equation $y = x^2 + 12$, and press [GRAPH].
The display shows the axes only, which tells you that you must resize the window. You could use trial and error, or you could examine the equation to determine suitable endpoints.

From the equation, you can see that y will always be at least 12. Set the window to display y-values from 0 to 20. Leave the x-values as they are. Press [GRAPH].

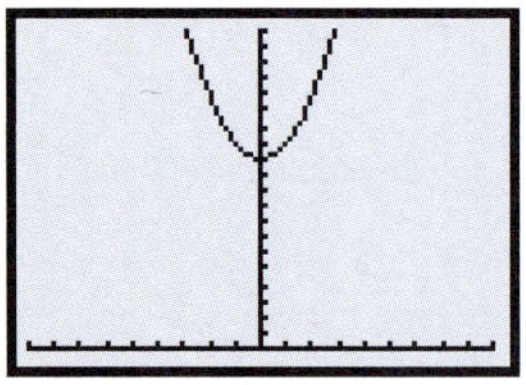

6. To graph an equation on the TI-83, it must be in the form $y =$ (an expression in x).

To graph $3y + 6x + 15 = 0$, first rearrange the equation with y on the left side: $y = -2x - 5$. Proceed as in exercise 1.

7. The letters we use as variables are not always x and y. To graph the equation $A = \pi r^2$, treat A as y, since it is isolated, and treat r as x. Rewrite the equation as $y = \pi x^2$ and graph this.

Working with Tables: Viewing a Table of Values

- Enter a function in the Y= screen. In the example below, the function $y = -0.0034x + 100$ has been defined as Y_1.
- To view a table of values for a specified function, press [2nd] [GRAPH]. By using the up and down arrow keys the table can be scrolled up or down. The x-values used in the table can be adjusted by changing the table setup.

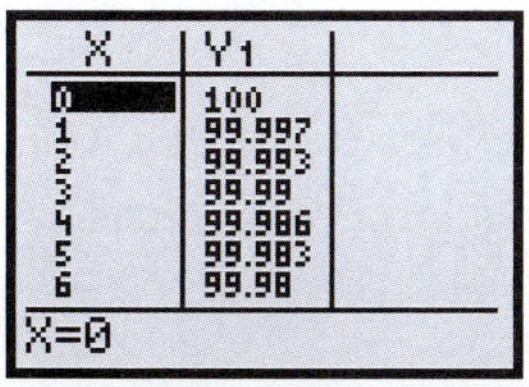

Changing the Table Setup

For the table shown above, the x-values start at 0 and change in increments of 1.

The table can be adjusted so that it starts at a specified value of x and changes using any given increment. To change the table setup, do the following.

- Press [2nd] [WINDOW].
- To change the x-value that you want the table to start with, enter this number as the TblStart value and press [ENTER].
- To change the increment that you want the x-values to change by, enter this number as the ΔTbl value and press [ENTER].

In order for the x- and y-values to be generated automatically, both the Indpnt and Depend variables must be set to Auto as shown below.

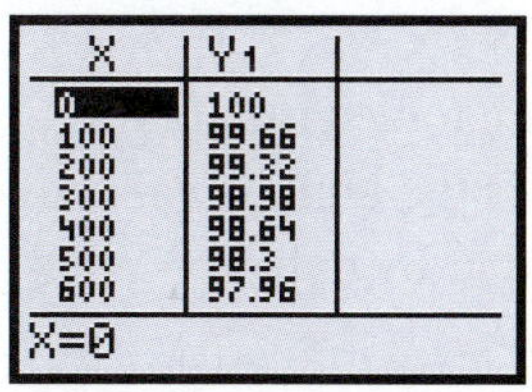

By having the table start at zero and the x-values change by increments of 100, the above table was generated. To find the value of y at a specific value of x, such as $x = 8848$, the start of the table could be changed accordingly.

Using the TI-83 to Find the Domain and Range of a Function

In this Utility you will use the TRACE and TABLES features of the calculator to find the domain and range of a function.

1. Graph $y = 2x^2 + 1$.

If the graph of a function goes to the edge of the screen, it often means that the graph continues in a similar way forever.

2. Press [TRACE]. The equation appears at the top of the screen; a point is flashing on the graph, and the x-value and y-value for that point appear at the bottom of the screen.

3. Use the right arrow key to move the flashing point along the curve to the right. Notice that the x-value and y-value change accordingly. Move the flashing point back using the left arrow key.

4. Use the TRACE feature to determine the lowest value of y. What is the highest value of y? What is the lowest value x can have? What is the highest?

What do you think are the domain and range for this function?

5. Use the TRACE feature to find the domain and range of the function $y = \sqrt{x^2 + 2}$.

6. Enter $y = \frac{1}{x+2}$ in the Y= list.

Press [2nd] [GRAPH] to obtain a table of values for the function. Which value of x is not permitted? What is the domain of this function?

7. To find the range of the function $y = \frac{1}{x+2}$, obtain the table of values as before. Scroll up or down this table using the up and down arrow keys.

8. Think of other possible uses for the TRACE and TABLE features. Check out your ideas.

Generating Random Numbers on a TI-83

The TI-83, like many computers, is able to generate random numbers using a factory installed program. The list of numbers generated depends on an initial value, called a *seed value*, stored in the calculator. The factory-set seed value is 0. Every calculator will generate the same sequence of numbers given the same seed value, since all of the calculators have the same program.

To change the seed value, a new value must be stored.

- Enter any non-zero number and press [ENTER].
- Press [STO►] [MATH] [◄] [ENTER].
- Press [ENTER] to display the seed value you entered.

In the screens below, a seed value of 8 was entered.

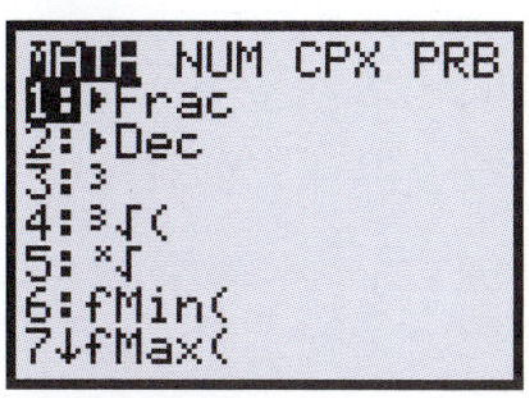

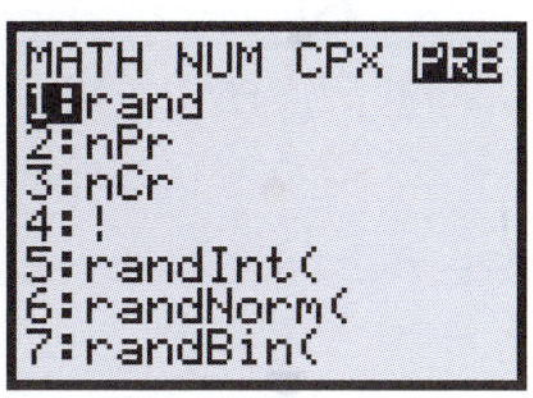

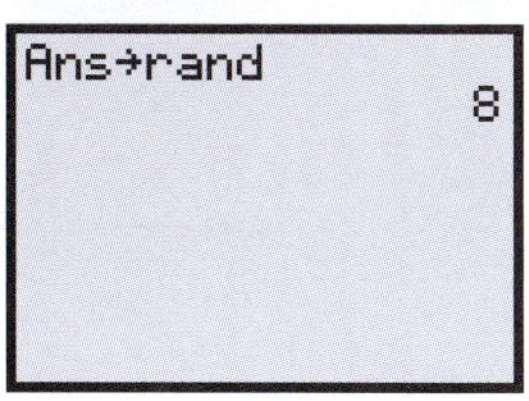

To Generate Random Numbers between 0 and 1

1. Press [MATH] [◄] [ENTER] [ENTER] to generate one random number between 0 and 1. To obtain additional random numbers, press [ENTER] repeatedly.

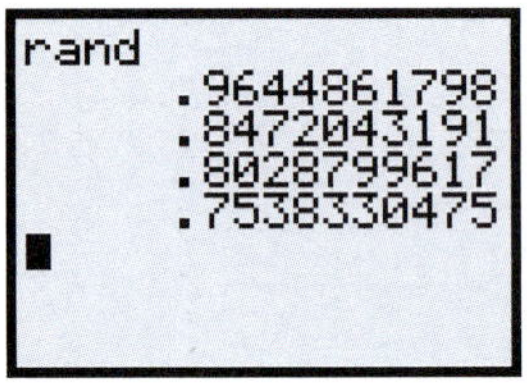

2. To generate two or more random numbers at the same time, enter the number you wish to generate within parentheses, after the rand command has been entered.

For example, to generate random numbers 2 at a time, press [MATH] [◄] [ENTER] [(] 2 [)] [ENTER]. To see the second number completely, press the right arrow key until the entire number is displayed.

To Generate Random Integers between Two Given Numbers

1. Use the randInt command. For example, to choose an integer between 1 and 6, enter [MATH] [◄] **5 1** [,] **6** [)] [ENTER]. This command requires that you use the format randInt (lower number, upper number). Press [ENTER] repeatedly to obtain more than one random number.

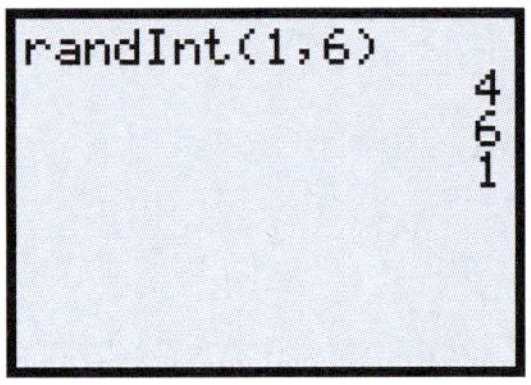

2. If you wish to generate more than one number at a time, for example, if you wish to simulate rolling two dice, the command format is randInt (lower number, upper number, number of trials).

For example, press [MATH] [◄] **5 1** [,] **6** [,] **2** [)] [ENTER] to obtain the screen below. The last two entries were obtained by pressing [ENTER] two more times.

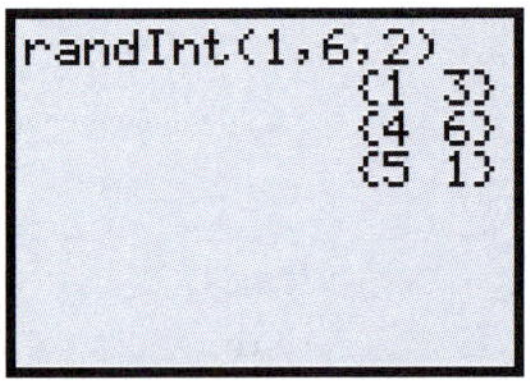

Creating Alphabetic Characters on the TI-83

Almost every key on the TI-83 keypad has more than one use. Pressing the key produces the number, symbol, or action stated on the key itself. To perform the function indicated in yellow on the top left of the key, you first press [2nd], the yellow button, and then the key itself.

Letters can be produced in the display. These are shown in green on the top right of the key. To produce the letter shown, you must first press [ALPHA], the green button, followed by the appropriate key.

- To produce the letter A in the display, press [ALPHA] [MATH]. Notice the green A above MATH.

If you wish to enter a word, [ALPHA] must precede each key. This is time consuming. As a short cut, when many letters are being entered, lock the keys onto the green alpha-symbolic functions by selecting A-LOCK. Press [2nd] [ALPHA]. The cursor changes to a flashing rectangle with the letter A in the middle. This is to remind you that the keys are in alphabetic mode.

- Produce the word SLOPE. Press [2nd] [ALPHA] [LN] [ )] **7 8** [SIN].
- Practise using the green alphabetic function keys. Write

THIS IS FUN

- To produce a space, press **0** if you are in alphabetic mode, or [ALPHA] **0** if you are not. A space is represented by the green [ALPHA] above 0.
- Remember to remove the A-LOCK when you need to use other sets of key functions.

Write (D – B) / (C – A) in the display. Remember that the / sign indicates division, so you will enter this using [÷].

- Write your name and address in the display.

Programming a TI-83 Calculator

TI-83 calculators are programmable. From *Tutorial 5.2*, the slope of the line segment joining (a, b) and (c, d) is

$$\text{Slope} = \frac{\text{Rise}}{\text{Run}} = \frac{d - b}{c - a}$$

In this Utility, you will write a program that will allow you to input the x- and y-coordinates of each point and then calculate the slope.

1. Set up your calculator to accept a new program.

Press [PRGM], then move the cursor to NEW. Press [ENTER]. You should see this screen.

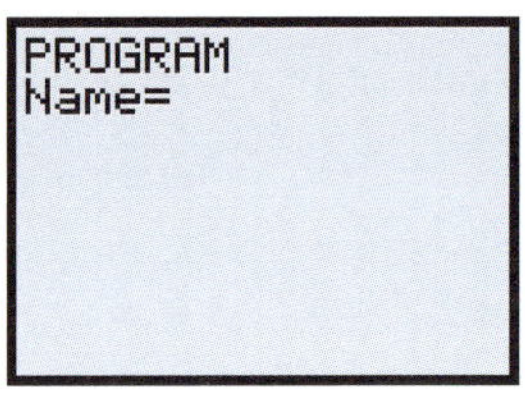

2. Type in the name of the new program.

If you need help on how to input letters on the TI-83, refer to Utility 12.

Enter S L O P E. Press [ENTER].

3. Program the steps for inputting the coordinates of two points.

Your calculator is now ready for you to type the program. When using the program, you need to enter the values of the x- and y-coordinates of the points. In order to do this, you must program the calculator to request these. Two commands will be used, Disp and Prompt.

a) When the calculator sees the command Disp, it will display on the calculator screen whatever is in quotation marks after the command Disp, or it will display the result of a requested calculation.

We want (A, B) (C, D) to be displayed on the calculator screen.

Press [PRGM]. Move the cursor to I/O and select 3:Disp. Press [ENTER].

Enter the coordinates of the points. (Recall from Utility 12, to produce quotation marks you must press [ALPHA] [+].) Press "[(]A[,]B[)][(]C[,]D[)]" [ENTER]. Your screen should look like the one shown.

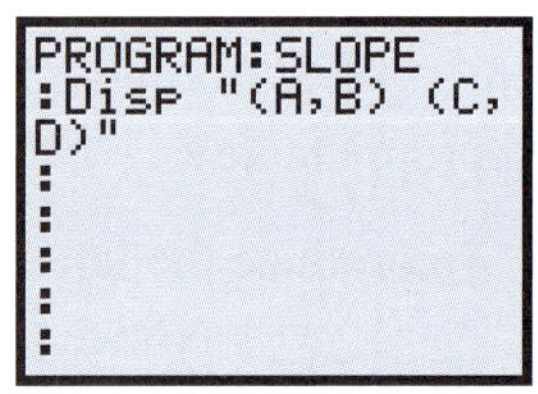

This command will display (A, B) (C, D) when the program is running.

b) When the calculator sees the word Prompt, it will ask the user to input a number for a specific variable.

In this case, you want to be asked for the numbers represented by A, B, C, and D.

Press [PRGM]. Move the cursor to I/O and select 2:Prompt. Press A [ENTER].

Repeat this step to prompt B, C, and D. After you have done this, your screen should look like the one below.

```
PROGRAM:SLOPE
:Disp "(A,B) (C,
D)"
:Prompt A
:Prompt B
:Prompt C
:Prompt D
:
```

This will prompt you to enter values for A, B, C, and D, one at a time, when the program is running.

4. Program the steps to input the formula.

The slope formula is

$$\text{Slope} = \frac{D - B}{C - A}$$

The calculator must save this expression as another variable. We will call the variable S. Press [( ] D [–] B [ )] [÷] [( ] C [–] A [ )] [STO►] S [ENTER]. Your screen should look like the one below.

```
PROGRAM:SLOPE
D)"
:Prompt A
:Prompt B
:Prompt C
:Prompt D
:(D-B)/(C-A)→S
:
```

5. Program the steps to display the word SLOPE.

Press [PRGM], move the cursor to I/O and select 3:Disp.

Press " **S L O P E** " [ENTER]. Your screen will now look like the one below.

```
PROGRAM:SLOPE
:Prompt A
:Prompt B
:Prompt C
:Prompt D
:(D-B)/(C-A)→S
:Disp "SLOPE"
:
```

6. Program the steps to display the value of the slope.

Slope is $\frac{\text{rise}}{\text{run}}$ which is represented in this program by S.

Press [PRGM]. Move the cursor to I/O and select 3:Disp. Press [ENTER] S [ENTER]. Your screen should look like the one below.

```
PROGRAM:SLOPE
:Prompt B
:Prompt C
:Prompt D
:(D-B)/(C-A)→S
:Disp "SLOPE"
:Disp S
:
```

7. Program the steps to tell the calculator to quit the program.

Press [PRGM], move the cursor to F:Stop (off the screen at the bottom), then press [ENTER]. Your screen should look like the one below.

```
PROGRAM:SLOPE
:Prompt B
:Prompt C
:Prompt D
:(D-B)/(C-A)→S
:Disp "SLOPE"
:Disp S
:Stop
```

Press [2nd] [MODE] to quit the programming mode. The program SLOPE is automatically stored in memory.

8. Does the program work?

a) Using the SLOPE program, determine the slope of line segment EF, where E is (4, 7) and F is (5, 16).

Press PRGM and move the cursor to the program SLOPE. Press ENTER ENTER. Follow the screen prompts. Press ENTER after every number you input.

b) Check the result using the slope formula (*Tutorial* 5.2).

Use the example as a guide as you write your programs. Consider each of the steps in the example. Ask yourself if the step remains the same for your new program or if it needs to be modified.

9. Write a program that allows the user to input the coordinates of two points and determine the distance between the points. Include a set of instructions that will lead the user through entering the program into the calculator. Test the program with at least two sets of points.

10. Write a program that allows a user to input the coordinates of two points and determine the midpoint of the line segment joining two points. Include a set of instructions that will lead the user through entering the program into the calculator. Test the program with at least two sets of points.

Using the TI-83 to Find the Median-Median Line of Best Fit

In this Utility you will use the data for the Red Pine tree given in *Tutorial* 6.7. For convenience, this is reproduced below.

AGE x (Years)	Diameter y (cm)
8	9
19	12
11	10
4	1
16	19
18	9
12	6
22	15
5	5

1. Access the list editor by pressing [STAT] [ENTER]. Clear any data entered in list L1 and list L2. Use the arrow keys to highlight L1, and then press [CLEAR] [ENTER]. Use the right arrow key to move to L2 and repeat. Enter the data from the table above in the list editor. Enter the ages in the first list and the diameters in the second list. Remember to press [ENTER] after keying in each number.

2. To graph the data as a scatterplot, press [2nd] [Y=] [ENTER]. Highlight On and press [ENTER]. Remember to turn functions and other statplots off. Define a suitable display window. Press [WINDOW]. Change the entries to the ones shown.

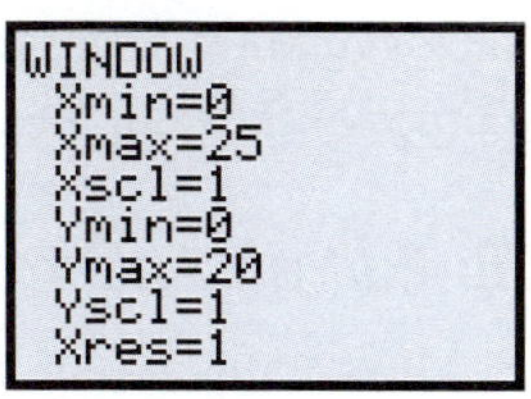

3. Press [STAT] [►]. The screen should be as shown below.

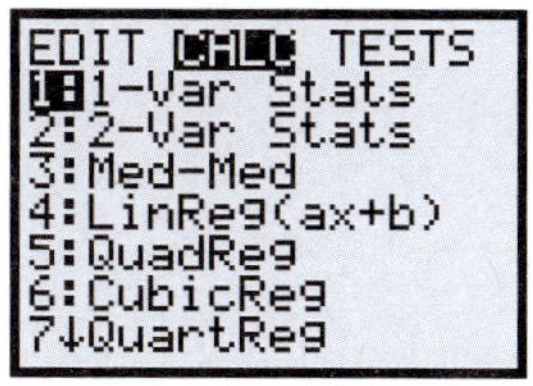

Press **3** to select the median-median line of best fit. Press [ENTER] to display the equation of the median-median line of best fit for the data. Your display should be similar to the one shown.

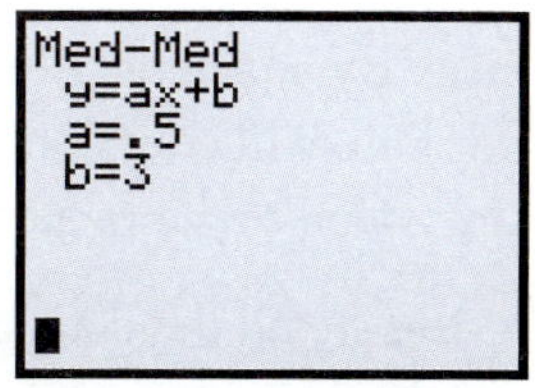

4. To graph the scatterplot and the line of best fit on the same screen, press [Y=] [VARS] **5.** Use the right arrow to highlight EQ. The screen should be similar to the one shown.

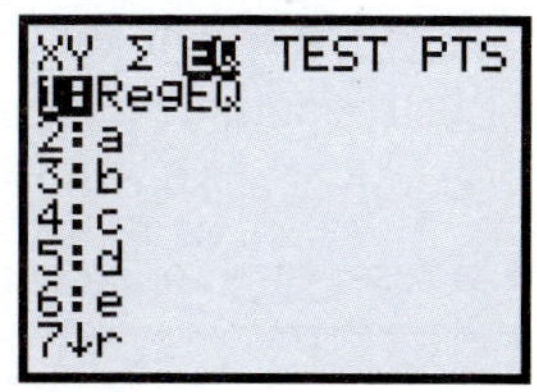

Press [ENTER].

Press [GRAPH] to display the graph.

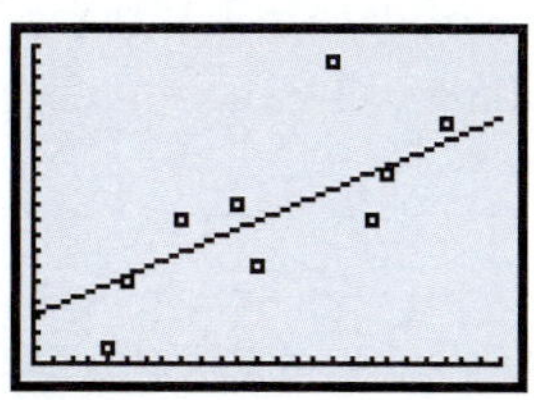

Attaching a Formula to a List

The TI-83 can be used as a spreadsheet provided the rows within the spreadsheet are not related recursively. In order to use the TI-83 in this way, we must attach a formula to a list.

When a formula is used to define a list, each element in the list will be calculated using the formula and data that presently exist in related lists. By attaching a formula to a list, the formula will continue to be applied when data are added to the related list.

- Ensure all the data are cleared out of the lists that you wish to use. To do this, press [STAT] and then choose 4:ClrList. The lists must now be specified. Press [2nd] 1 [,] [2nd] 2. If you are clearing more than two lists, continue naming lists separated by a comma, as shown below.
- Press [ENTER] to execute the command.

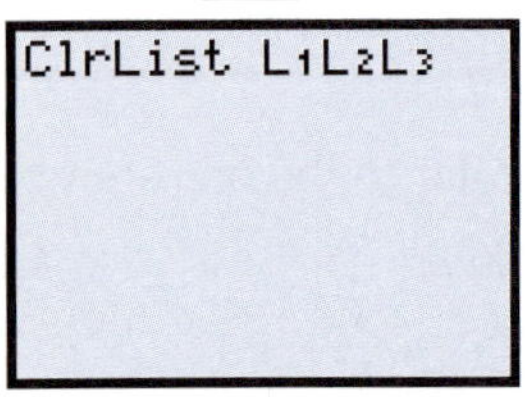

- Enter at least one piece of data in L1. Press [STAT] [ENTER]. Enter the data using the numeric and [ENTER] keys.

To Attach a Formula to a List

- Move the cursor to the top of the list that is to have the formula attached to it.
- To indicate that a formula is being attached, quotation marks must be placed around the formula. Press [ALPHA] [+]. Enter the formula and then press [ENTER]. The formula will calculate the appropriate value in L2 using the value from L1. If additional values are entered in L1, corresponding values will automatically be calculated in L2.

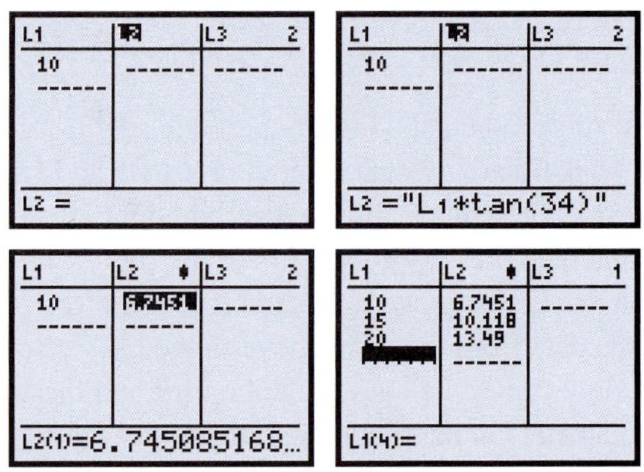

Once a formula has been attached to a list, a lock symbol will appear in the top right hand corner of the column.

To Edit an Attached Formula

- Move to the top of the list to access the formula.
- Press [ENTER] and the cursor should appear in the editing bar.

- Make the changes to the formula. As soon as you press ENTER the values in the list will be recalculated using the new formula.

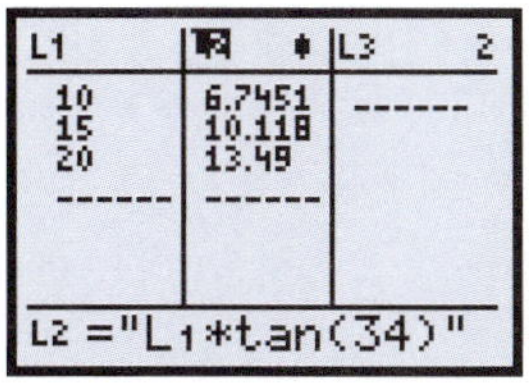

To Detach (Clear) an Attached Formula

- This can be done using the ClrList command mentioned at the beginning of this Utility. To clear the list without leaving the list screen, follow these steps.
- Move to the top of the list to be cleared so that the formula appears. Press ENTER so that the formula can be edited. Press CLEAR and then ENTER. Notice the formula is no longer attached, although the data still remain in the list.
- To clear the data in the list, move to the top of the list and press CLEAR ENTER.

Storing Window Settings into Memory

The standard window settings for the TI-83 are shown below left. Although these values are convenient, when the TRACE feature is used, the *x*- and *y*-values generated may be difficult to use. The function $y = 2x + 3$ has been graphed, below right, using this window setting. The values produced by using TRACE are inconvenient.

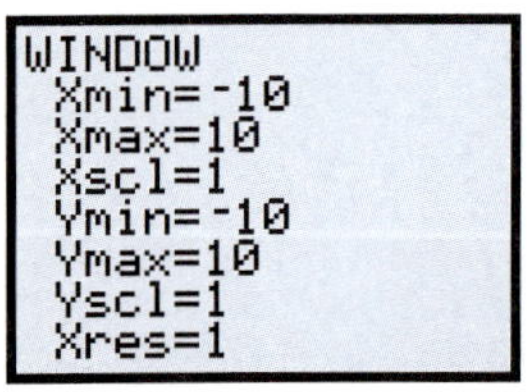

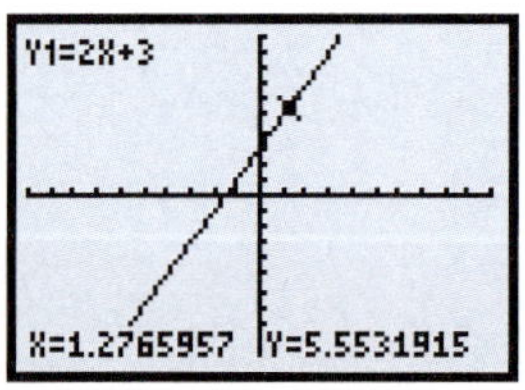

Given the width of the screen of the TI-83, if the difference between the Xmin and Xmax values is a multiple of 18.8 (such as 9.4, 37.6), the TRACE feature will provide more useful *x*- and *y*-values. The window settings shown below left will be referred to as the "user friendly window." The values produced using TRACE are more convenient, as shown by the two graphs below.

This window setting can be stored in the memory of the calculator so that it can be quickly and easily recalled.

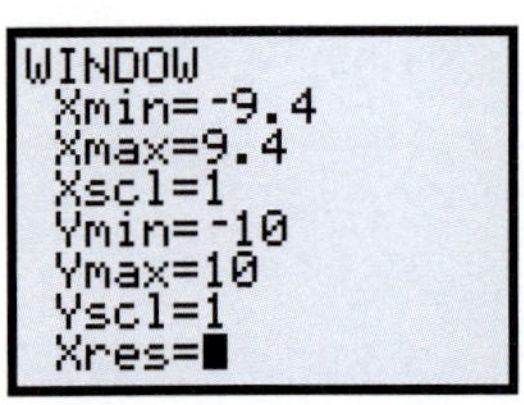

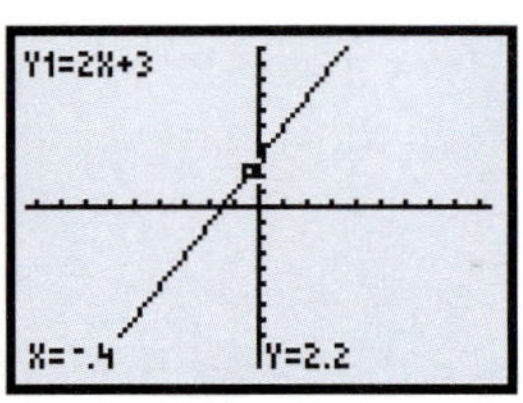

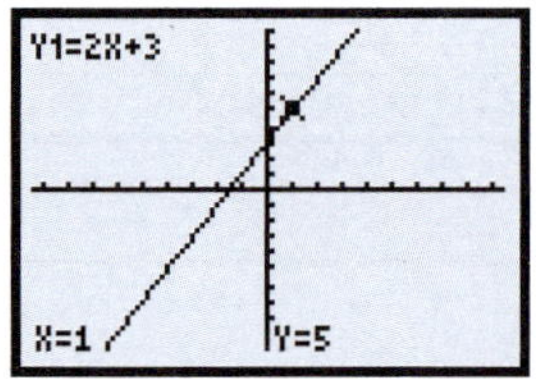

To Store Window Settings into Memory

- Press WINDOW and then enter the window settings you wish to store in the memory.
- Press ZOOM and then move the cursor over to MEMORY using the right arrow key.
- Choose 2:ZoomSto to store these values into memory.

To Recall These Window Settings

- Press ZOOM and then move the cursor over to MEMORY using the right arrow key.
- Choose 3:ZoomRcl to recall the stored window settings.

absolute cell reference: in a spreadsheet formula, a reference to one particular cell of the spreadsheet that will not change when the formula is moved to a different cell

$B$3 indicates that the value or expression contained in cell B3 is to be used in the formula.

accuracy: when referring to a measurement, it indicates how close the measurement comes to its true value; refer to *Tutorial 1.4*, for additional information

active cell: the cell of a spreadsheet into which an item of data is placed when you start to type; see *Tutorial 2.2*

acute angle: an angle whose measure is less than 90°

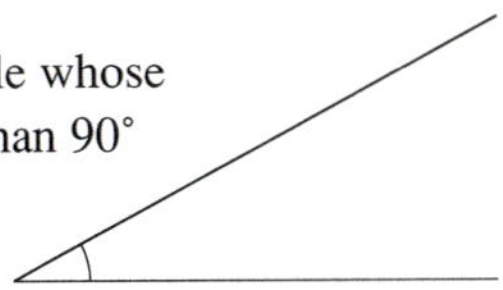

adjacent side: in a right triangle, the side next to the named angle that is not the hypotenuse

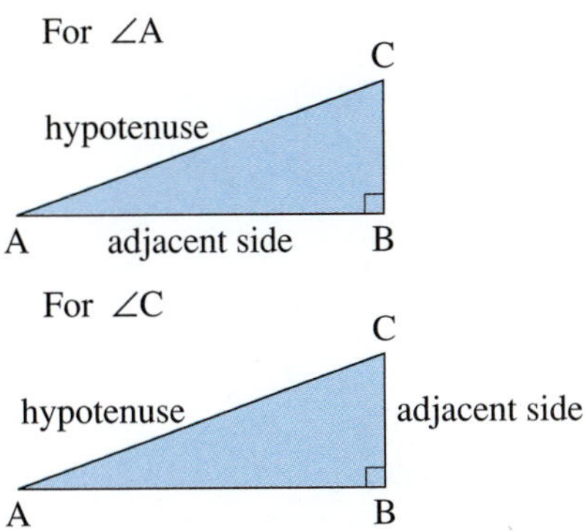

algebraic expression: a mathematical expression that contains at least one variable

$6x + 4$ is an algebraic expression.

alternate interior angles: a pair of angles that are between two lines, but are on opposite sides of a transversal that cuts the two lines; see *parallel lines*

Angles 1 and 2 are alternate angles.

Angles 3 and 4 are alternate angles.

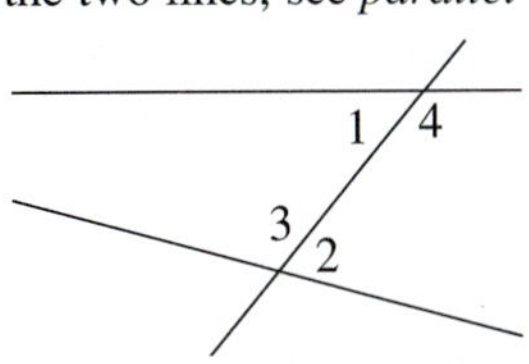

altitude: the perpendicular distance from the base of a figure to the opposite side or vertex; the height of an aircraft above the ground

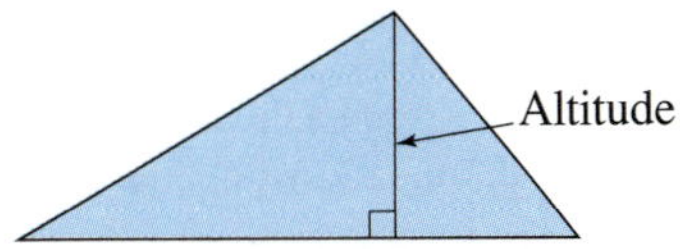

angle: the geometric figure formed by two rays that have the same endpoint

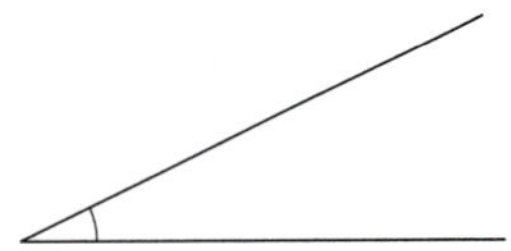

angle of depression: the angle between the horizontal and the oblique line joining the observer's eye to a point lower than eye level

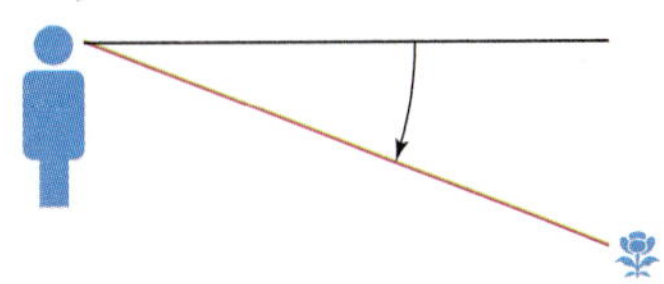

angle of elevation: the angle between the horizontal and the oblique line from the observer's eye to some object above eye level

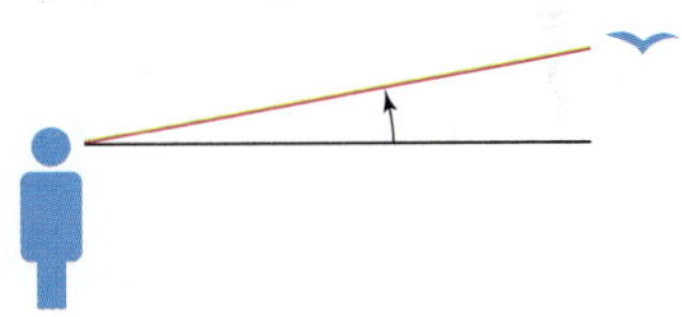

angle of inclination of a line segment: the acute angle, measured from the horizontal to the line segment

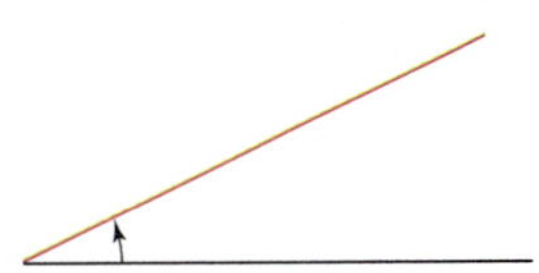

anthropology: the science that deals with the origin, development, and customs of people

approximation: a number close to the exact value of a quantity or an expression; the symbols $\doteq$ and $\approx$ mean "is approximately equal to"

3.14 is an approximation for π.

area: the number of square units needed to cover a surface; common units used to express area include cm^2, m^2, and hectares; see *circle*, *rectangle*, *square*, and *triangle*

arithmetic sequence: a sequence of numbers in which each term after the first is formed by adding a constant to the preceding term

The numbers 1, 4, 7, 10 … form an arithmetic sequence, since each term after the first is formed by adding 3 to the previous number.

average: a single number that is used to represent a set of numbers; to find the average, all the numbers in the data set are added together and the sum is divided by the number of entries in the data set; see *mean*

The data set 1, 3, 4, 7, 7, 8 has 6 entries.

$$\text{Average} = \frac{1+3+4+7+7+8}{6} = 5$$

average speed: the speed that, if the object travelled at that speed constantly, would result in the same total distance being travelled in the same total time; to calculate average speed, the total distance travelled during the given time period is divided by the total time

In one hour a car travels 100 km. The car stops for 0.5 h and then travels 80 km in the next hour. Find the average speed of the car.

The total distance travelled is 180 km and the time required to travel this distance includes the stopping time of 0.5 h.

$$\text{Average speed} = \frac{\text{Distance}}{\text{Time}}$$

$$v = \frac{d}{t} = \frac{180\text{ km}}{2.5\text{ h}} = 72\text{ km/h}$$

bar graph: a graph that displays data by using horizontal or vertical bars whose lengths are proportional to the number they represent

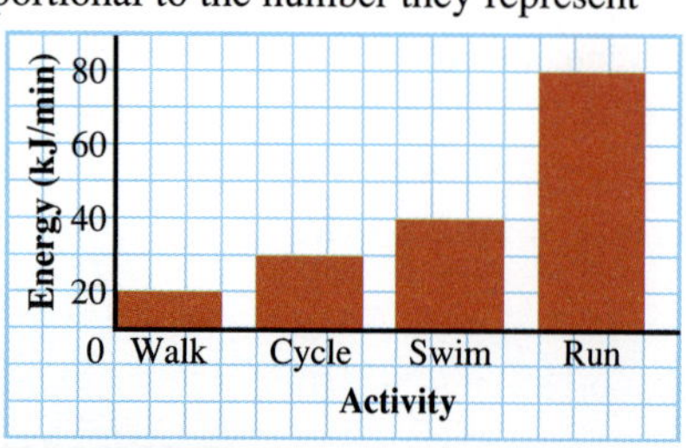

base: the side of a polygon, or the face of a solid, from which the height is measured; also, the factor repeated in a power

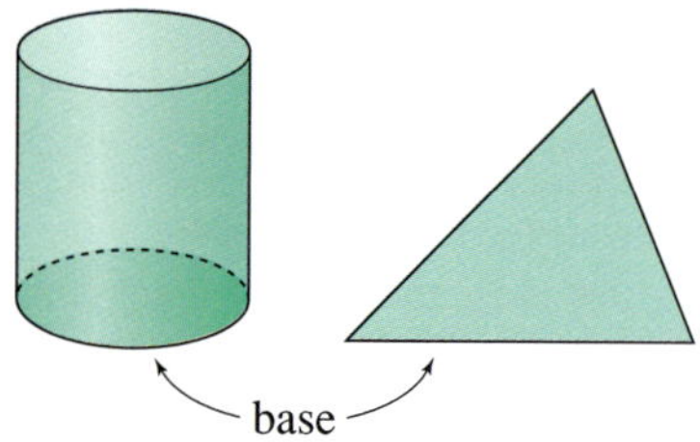

In the expression 5^3, 5 is the base.

bearing: the 3-digit angle, measured in a clockwise direction, between the north line and a given direction

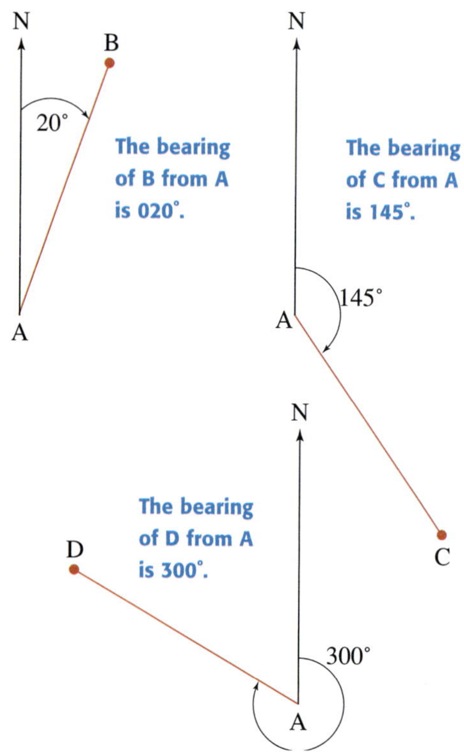

bias: an emphasis on characteristics that are not typical of the entire population; see *Tutorial 4.2*

biased sample: a sample containing members of the population that are not representative

broken-line graph: a graph that displays data by using points that are joined by line segments

broken-line graph: a graph that displays data by using points that are joined by line segments

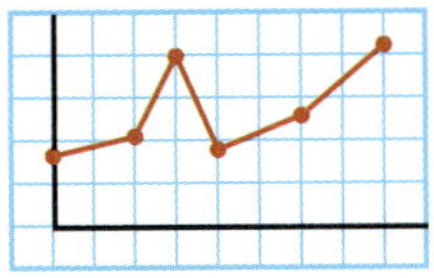

cell: a rectangle in a spreadsheet into which data may be entered

cell reference: the name of a cell in a spreadsheet, given by indicating the column and row to which it belongs

Cell B3 is the cell in column B and row 3 of the spreadsheet document.

census: an official count of the people of a country or district; see *Tutorial 4.1*

circle: the set of points in a plane that are a given distance from a fixed point (the centre)

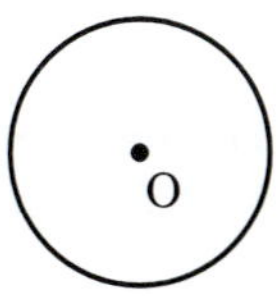

The area of a circle is:

$A = \pi r^2$, **where** r **is the radius**

$= \frac{\pi d^2}{4}$, **where** d **is the diameter**

The circumference of a circle is:

$C = 2\pi r$, **where** r **is the radius**

$= \pi d$, **where** d **is the diameter**

The area of a circle with radius 5 cm is:

$$A = \pi(5\text{ cm})^2$$
$$= \pi(25\text{ cm}^2)$$
$$\doteq 79\text{ cm}^2$$

The circumference of a circle whose radius is 5 cm is:

$$C = 2\pi(5\text{ cm})$$
$$\doteq 31\text{ cm}$$

circumference: the distance around a circle; the boundary of any region whose boundary is a simple closed curve

clinometer: a device used by surveyors to measure angles of elevation and depression; see *angle of depression*, and *angle of elevation*; see also *Project, Chapter 7*

cluster sample: a sample in which every member of a randomly chosen section of the population is selected; see *Tutorial 4.3*

collinear points: points that lie on the same line

common difference: the number obtained by subtracting any term from the next term in an arithmetic sequence

For the arithmetic sequence: 1, −5, −11, −17, … , the common difference = (−5) − 1

= −6

complementary angles: two angles whose measures add up to 90°

∠ABC and ∠CBD are complementary angles.

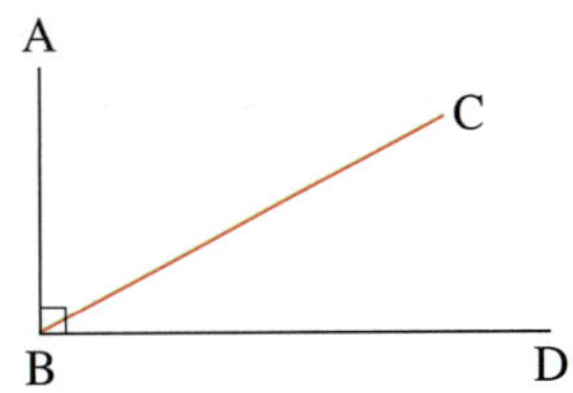

compound interest: when the interest due is added to the original amount invested and thereafter earns interest; see *Tutorial 2.4*

cone: a solid that is formed by a region (the base of the cone) and all the line segments joining points on the boundary of the region to a point not on the region

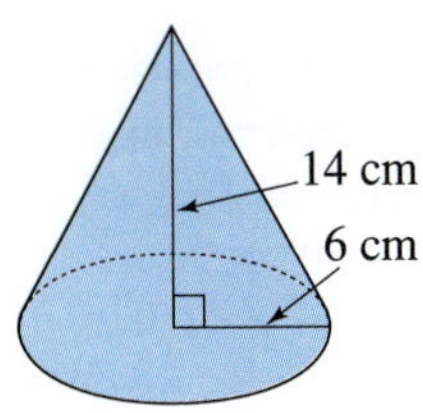

The volume of a cone can be found using the formula:

Volume $= \frac{1}{3}$ (Base area)(Height)

$= \frac{1}{3}(\pi r^2)(h)$, where the circular base has radius r, and the height of the cone is h.

The volume of a cone whose circular base has a radius of 6 cm and a height 14 cm is:

$V = \frac{1}{3}(\pi \times (6 \text{ cm})^2)(14 \text{ cm})$

$\doteq 528 \text{ cm}^3$

congruent: figures that have the same size and shape, but not necessarily the same orientation

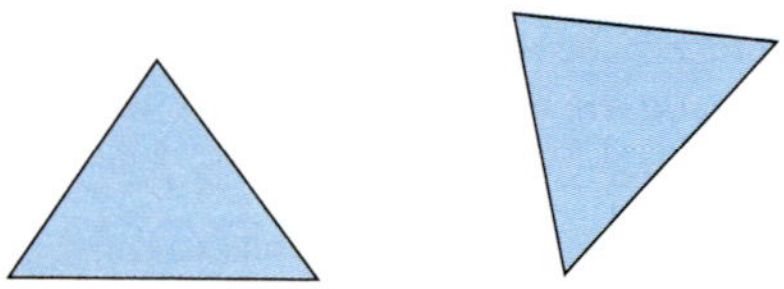

consecutive integers: integers that come one after the other without any integers missing

34, 35, 36 are consecutive integers, so are –2, –1, 0, 1.

constant: a particular number

constant term: a number

convenience sample: a sample whose members are selected based on convenience; refer to *Tutorial 4.3*

coordinate axes: the horizontal and vertical number lines on a grid that represents a plane

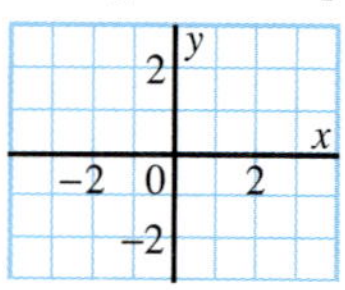

coordinate plane: a two-dimensional surface on which a coordinate system has been set up

coordinates: also called Cartesian coordinates; the numbers in an ordered pair that locate a point in the coordinate plane

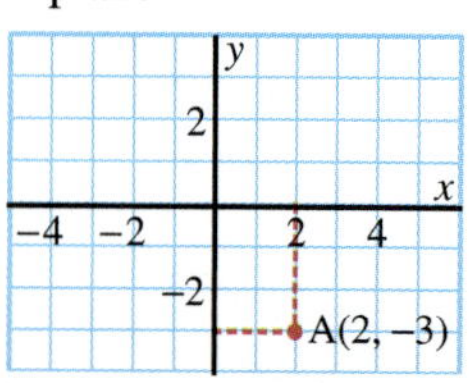

The coordinates of point A are (2, –3).

correlation coefficient: a measure of how closely data can be described by a certain type of function; the closer the value of the correlation coefficient to 1 or –1, the closer the data fit the function; see *Tutorial 6.8*

corresponding angles: angles that are on the same side of a transversal that cuts through two lines and on the same side of each line.

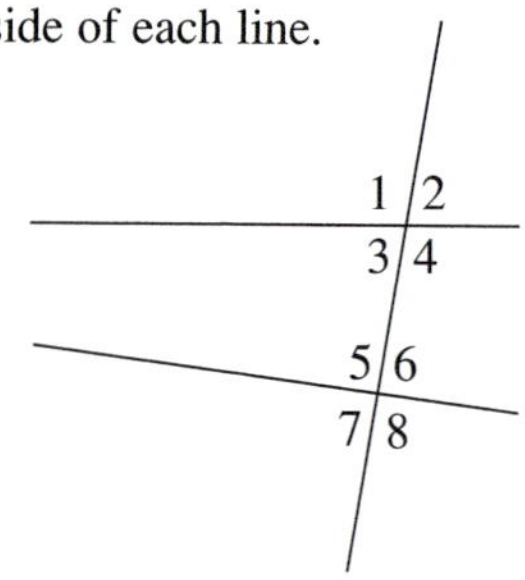

Angles 1 and 5 are corresponding angles.

Angles 2 and 6 are corresponding angles.

Angles 3 and 7 are corresponding angles.

Angles 4 and 8 are corresponding angles.

corresponding angles in similar triangles: two angles, one in each triangle, that are equal

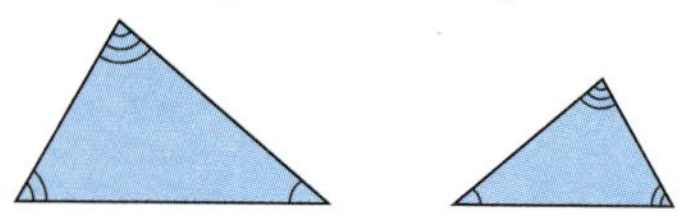

cosine: for an acute angle in a right triangle, the ratio of the length of the side adjacent to the angle to the length of the hypotenuse

cosine of $\angle A = \dfrac{\text{Length of the adjacent side}}{\text{Length of the hypotenuse}}$

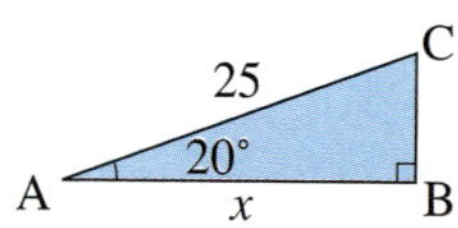

To determine AB in the diagram above:

$\cos \angle A = \dfrac{\text{Length of the adjacent side}}{\text{Length of the hypotenuse}}$ Substitute the known quantities.

$\cos 20^\circ = \frac{x}{25}$ Use a calculator to determine cos 20°.

$0.9397 \doteq \frac{x}{25}$ Multiply both sides by 25.

$23.5 \doteq x$

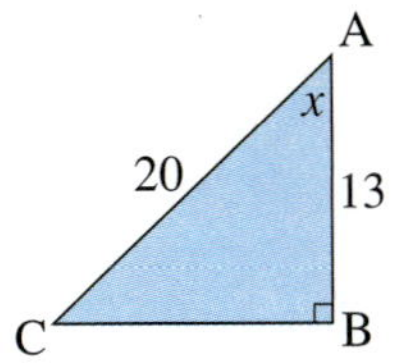

To determine ∠A in the diagram above:

$\cos \angle A = \frac{\text{Length of the adjacent side}}{\text{Length of the hypotenuse}}$ **Substitute the known quantities.**

$\cos x^\circ = \frac{13}{20}$ **Convert the fraction into a decimal.**

$\cos x^\circ = 0.65$ **Use the $\cos^{-1}$ ("the angle whose cosine is") function on the calculator.**

$x \doteq 49.5^\circ$

Cosine Law: a trigonometric law used to solve triangles that are not right triangles; see *Tutorial 7.6*

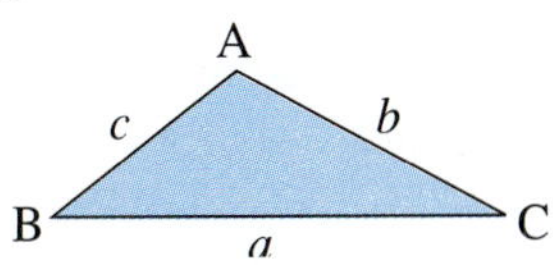

In any △ABC,

$a^2 = b^2 + c^2 - 2bc \cos A$, so $\cos A = \frac{b^2 + c^2 - a^2}{2bc}$

$b^2 = a^2 + c^2 - 2ac \cos B$, so $\cos B = \frac{a^2 + c^2 - b^2}{2ac}$

$c^2 = a^2 + b^2 - 2ab \cos C$, so $\cos C = \frac{a^2 + b^2 - c^2}{2ab}$

Use the Cosine Law to solve problems when you know all 3 sides of a triangle and wish to find an angle, or 2 sides and the included angle and wish to find the other side.

cost price: the price paid by a retailer to purchase an item for resale

cube: a rectangular solid whose length, width, and height are all equal

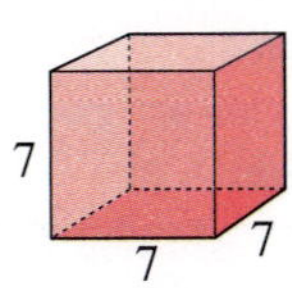

For a cube with sides of length s, the surface area of the cube is calculated by $S = 6s^2$; the volume of the cube is $V = s^3$.

If s = 7 cm

Surface area $= 6(7)^2 \text{ cm}^2$

$= 294 \text{ cm}^2$ **and**

Volume $= (7)^3 \text{ cm}^3$

$= 343 \text{ cm}^3$

cube root: a number that, when raised to the power 3, results in the given number

$\sqrt[3]{8} = 2$, since $2^3 = 8$

cubic units: units that measure volume; common cubic units include cm^3 and m^3

cylinder: a solid with two parallel, congruent, circular bases

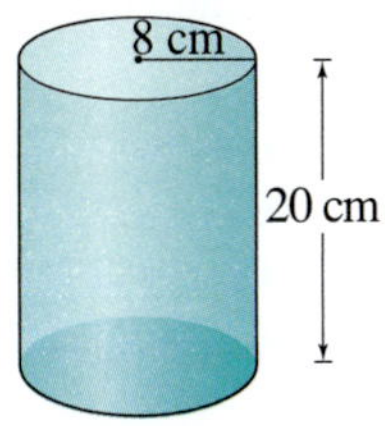

Surface area $= 2\pi rh + 2\pi r^2$

$= 2\pi(8)(20) + 2\pi(8)^2$

$\doteq 1005.3 + 402.1$

$\doteq 1407 \text{ cm}^2$

Volume $= \pi r^2 h$

$= \pi(8)^2(20)$

$\doteq 4021 \text{ cm}^3$

data: numeric or non-numeric facts or information

density: the mass of a unit volume of a substance; common units for measuring the density of a substance include g/cm^3, kg/m^3, g/mL, or kg/L

Find the density of an object that has a mass of 577.8 g and a volume of 214 cm^3.

Density $= \frac{\text{Mass}}{\text{Volume}}$

$= \frac{577.8 \text{ g}}{214 \text{ cm}^3}$

$= 2.7 \text{g/cm}^3$

dependent variable: the output of a relation, often denoted y; also called the responding variable

diagonal: a line that joins two vertices of a figure, but is not a side

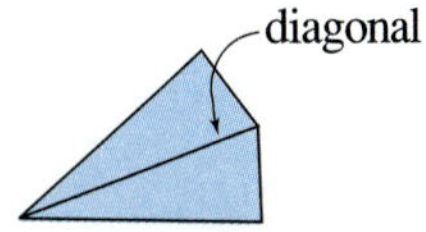

diameter: a line segment that joins two points on a circle (or sphere) and passes through its centre; the diameter of a circle is twice the length of the radius; see *circle*

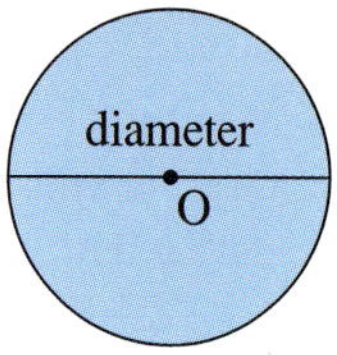

direct variation: when the ratio of two variable quantities remains constant

If y varies directly as x, the equation that relates y to x is $y = mx$, where m is a constant; the graph of a direct variation is a straight line that passes through the origin; see *Tutorial 6.3*

distance: the space between two points; also, the distance travelled by an object that is moving at a constant speed for a time is determined from the relation Distance = Speed × Time, where a consistent set of units must be used

If an object travels at a constant speed of 20 m/s for 2 min, the distance travelled is

$$d = (20 \text{ m/s})(120 \text{ s})$$
$$= 2400 \text{ m}$$

distance formula: a formula used to determine the distance between two points whose coordinates are known; see *Tutorial 5.1*

If $A(x_A, y_A)$ and $B(x_B, y_B)$, then

$$AB = \sqrt{(x_B - x_A)^2 + (y_B - y_A)^2}$$

domain of a relation or function: the set of all possible x-values (or valid input values) represented by the graph or equation; see *Tutorial 3.5*

equation: a mathematical statement indicating that two expressions are equal

$2x + 5y = -4$

equation of a line: an equation that gives the relationship between the coordinates of every point on the line; see *Tutorial 6.2*

The common forms for the equation of a line are:

The slope-intercept form: $y = mx + b$, where m is the slope of the line and b is the y-intercept of the line

The standard form: $Ax + By + C = 0$, where A, B, and C are numbers

equidistant: the same distance apart

Points A and B are equidistant from the y-axis since they are both 3 units from the y-axis.

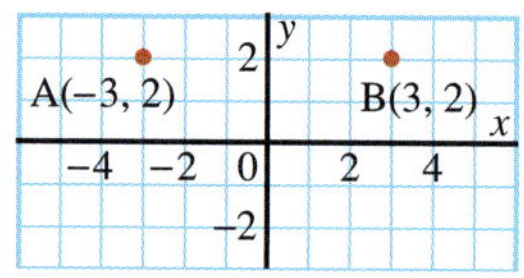

evaluate an expression: substitute a value for each variable in the expression, then work out the resulting arithmetic expression applying the order of operations rules

Evaluate $2x^2 + 3y - 4$, if $x = -3$ and $y = 5$.

Replace the letters by their value, placing each number in a bracket to prevent errors with signs.

$$\begin{aligned}2x^2 + 3y - 4 &= 2(-3)^2 + 3(5) - 4\\ &= 2(9) + 3(5) - 4\\ &= 18 + 15 - 4\\ &= 29\end{aligned}$$

experiment: a procedure, carried out under controlled conditions, that is used to test a hypothesis

exponent: a number, shown in a smaller size and raised, that tells us how many times the number before it is used as a factor

2 is the exponent in 6^2.
The laws of exponents are given below left, with examples to the right.

$a^m \cdot a^n = a^{m+n}$	$x^3 \cdot x^5 = x^{3+5} = x^8$
$(a^m)^n = a^{mn}$	$(x^3)^4 = x^{3 \cdot 4} = x^{12}$
$(ab)^m = a^m b^m$	$(4x)^3 = 4^3 \cdot x^3 = 64x^3$
$\left(\frac{a}{b}\right)^m = \frac{a^m}{b^m}$	$\left(\frac{x}{2}\right)^4 = \frac{x^4}{2^4} = \frac{x^4}{16}$
$\frac{a^m}{a^n} = a^{m-n}$	$\frac{x^8}{x^2} = x^{8-2} = x^6$
$a^{-m} = \frac{1}{a^m}$	$2^{-4} = \frac{1}{2^4} = \frac{1}{16}$
$a^0 = 1$	$7x^0 = 7 \cdot 1 = 7$

extrapolate: estimate a value beyond the known values

Using the graph below to estimate the distance travelled after 10 h requires extrapolation; the last known value occurs when the time is 8 h.

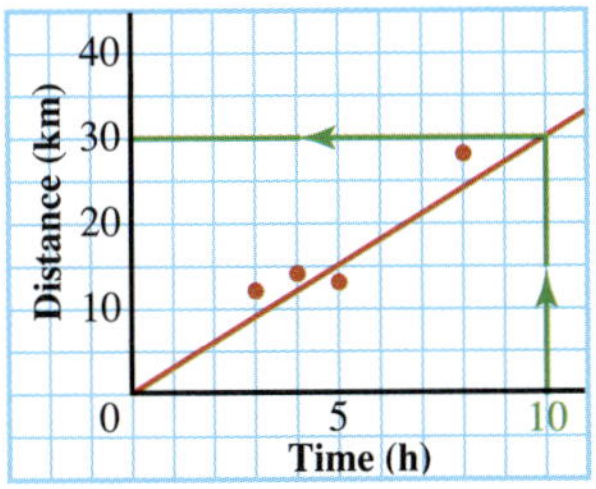

extremes: the highest and lowest values in a set of numbers

fixed cost: a cost, such as rent, that remains constant over a time period

force: a push or a pull on an object in a certain direction

A force of 1 Newton (N) will cause a 1-kg object to accelerate at a rate of 1 m/s.

formula: an equation that is used to describe the relationship between two or more quantities

The formula that describes how the volume, V, of a sphere is related to its radius, r, is $V = \frac{4}{3}\pi r^3$.

formula rearrangement: changing a formula to an equivalent form using the rules of equality

1. **Rearrange the equation $y = mx + b$ to isolate x.**

   $y = mx + b$

   Subtract b from both sides of the equation.

   $y - b = mx + b - b$

   $y - b = mx$

   Divide by m to isolate x.

   $\frac{y-b}{m} = \frac{mx}{m}$

   $\frac{y-b}{m} = x$

2. **Make d the subject of the formula $F = \frac{12\text{ g}}{d^2}$.**

   $F = \frac{12\text{ g}}{d^2}$

   Clear the fraction by multiplying both sides of the equation by d^2.

   $Fd^2 = 12\text{ g}$

   Divide both sides of the equation by F to isolate d^2.

   $\frac{Fd^2}{F} = \frac{12\text{ g}}{F}$

   $d^2 = \frac{12\text{ g}}{F}$

   Take the square root of both sides of the equation to isolate d.

   $d = \pm\sqrt{\frac{12\text{ g}}{F}}$

frequency: the number of times an event occurs in an experiment; the number of times that something occurs in a given time; a common unit is the Herz (Hz), which is the number of cycles that occur in 1 s

If you eat breakfast, lunch, and dinner every day, your meal frequency is 3 times a day. If a pendulum swings back and forth 10 times in 5 s, its frequency would be 10 cycles/5 s = 2 cycles/s = 2 Hz.

function: a rule that gives a single output number for each input number; see *Tutorial 3.4*

function notation: the use of the function name, such as *f*, to indicate the output value for a particular input; see *Tutorial 3.6*

gross pay: the total amount paid to someone before any deductions are made

gross profit: the difference between the cost price and selling price of an item; also called the *markup*

Lori's fashions buys a coat for $29.00 and sells it for $49.99.

The gross profit on the coat is $(49.99 – 29.00), or $20.99.

hectare: a metric unit used for land area; the area of a square of side 100 m, so 1 ha = 10 000 m^2

hemisphere: half of a sphere

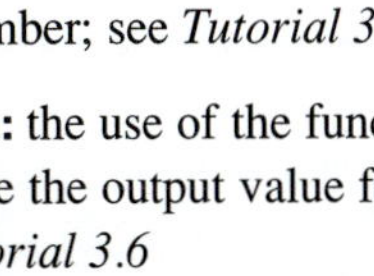

horizontal intercept: the horizontal coordinate of the points(s) where the graph of the line or function intersects the horizontal axis

hydrologist: a person who studies the properties and distribution of water

hypotenuse: the side opposite the right angle in a right triangle

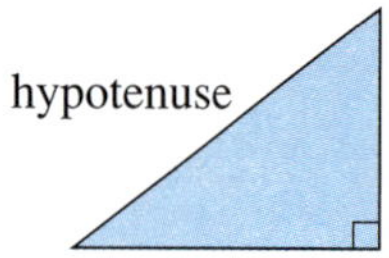

imperial system: a system of measures that was used in Canada prior to 1976 and a variant is still used in the U.S.A.; measuring devices using this system often have each unit subdivided by halving, then halving the subdivisions; see *Tutorial 1.2*

The smallest subdivision represents $\frac{1}{2}$ of $\frac{1}{2}$ of $\frac{1}{2}$ of $\frac{1}{2}$ an inch, or $\frac{1}{16}$ inch.

The relationship between some common imperial units and their relationship to metric units are given in the chart below.

Relationship between common imperial units	Relationship between common imperial units and SI units
Length	
1 mile = 1760 yards	1 mile = 1.609 km
1 yards = 3 feet	1 yard = 0.9144 m
1 foot = 12 inches	1 inch = 2.54 cm
Capacity (Volume)	
1 gallon = 4 quarts	1 gallon = 4.546 L
1 quart = 2 pints	
Mass (Weight)	
1 ton = 2000 pounds	1 pound = 0.454 kg
1 pound = 16 ounces	1 ounce = 28.35 g

independent variable: the input variable in a relation, often called x; also called the manipulated variable

inference: a conclusion about a population that is based on data collected from a sampling of the population; see *Tutorial 4.5*

integers: the set of numbers that contains all positive and negative whole numbers, together with zero; see *number systems*

… −3, −2, −1, 0, 1, 2, 3 … is the set of integers.

intercepts: the horizontal and vertical coordinates of the points at which a graph crosses the horizontal and vertical axis

interest (simple): money paid for the use of money, usually at a predetermined percent. If P is the amount invested or borrowed, r, the rate of interest per annum, and t, the time in years, then I, the interest, is given by the formula $I = Prt$.

Juanita purchased a \$500 bond at an interest rate of 6.5% per annum. After 6 months, she received the following interest:

$$\begin{aligned} I &= \$500 \times 6.5\% \times \frac{6}{12} \\ &= \$500 \times 0.065 \times 0.5 \\ &= \$16.25 \end{aligned}$$

interpolate: estimate a value that lies between known values; see *Tutorial 6.3*

irrational numbers: the set of numbers that cannot be written in the form $\frac{m}{n}$, where m and n are integers and $n \neq 0$; see *number systems*

π and $\sqrt{2}$ are irrational numbers.

least squares method: for a set of data, a method of determining a line of best fit that is used by many calculators and computers; see *Tutorial 6.8*

line of best fit: a line that passes as close as possible to a set of plotted points; it can be estimated by eye, or determined using the median-median method, or the least square method; see *Tutorials 6.6* to *6.8*

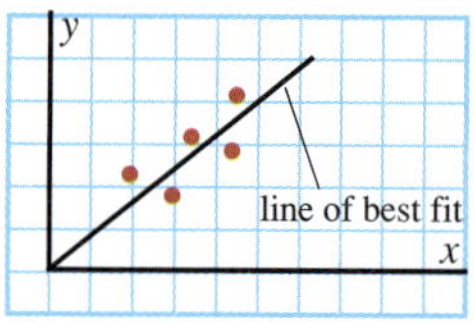

line segment: the part of a line between two points on the line, including the two points

linear equation: an equation that represents a line; see *Tutorial 6.2*

$3x + 4y + 7 = 0$ is a linear equation.

linear function: a function whose equation can be written in the form $y = mx + b$, and whose graph is a non-vertical line; see *Tutorial 6.1*

mapping diagram: a visual representation of a relation, where each input number is connected by an arrow to its corresponding output number(s)

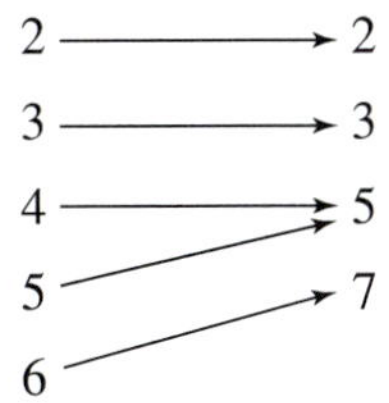

markup: the difference between the cost price and the selling price of an item; also called *gross profit*

mass: a measure of the amount of material in an object; common units are grams or kilograms

mean: the average of a set of numbers; see *average*

measurement error: see *uncertainty of measurement*

median: the middle number of a set of numbers arranged in numerical order; if there are two middle numbers, their average is the median of the data set

For the data 2, 4, 8, 9, and 11 the median is 8.

For the data 2, 4, 6, 8, 9, and 11 the median is 7, since $\frac{6+8}{2} = 7$.

median-median line of best fit: the line of best fit for a set of data points determined using the median-median method; see *Tutorial 6.7*

metric system: also called the *SI system*; based on a decimal system, with each unit subdivided into tenths and prefixes showing the relation of a unit to the base unit; commonly used base units are:

Metre (m) for length Gram (g) for mass
Litre (L) for capacity Second (s) for time

Prefix	Multiplying Factor	Symbol
mega	1 000 000	M
kilo	1 000	k
hecto	100	h
deca	10	da
	1	
deci	0.1	d
centi	0.01	c
milli	0.001	m
micro	0.000 001	µ
nano	0.000 000 001	n

Note: 1 L = 1000 cm^3, so 1 mL = 1 cm^3

1 tonne (sometimes called a metric ton) is used for mass: 1 t = 1000 kg

Convert 43.6 cm to m:

from the table above, 1 cm = 0.01 m

$$34.6 \times 1\text{ cm} = 34.6 \times 0.01\text{ m}$$
$$34.6\text{ cm} = 0.346\text{ m}$$

Convert 246 cm^2 to mm^2:

from the table above, 1 cm = 10mm

$$(1\text{ cm})^2 = (10\text{ mm})^2$$
$$1\text{ cm}^2 = 100\text{ mm}^2$$
$$246 \times 1\text{ cm}^2 = 246 \times 100\text{ mm}^2$$
$$246\text{ cm}^2 = 24\ 600\text{ mm}^2$$

Convert 35 mL to L:

from the table above, 1 mL = 0.001 L

$$35 \times 1\text{ mL} = 35 \times 0.001\text{ L}$$
$$35\text{ mL} = 0.035\text{ L}$$

micrometer: a measuring device that can be used to measure small objects to the nearest 0.01 mm; see *Utility 3*

midpoint: the point that divides a line segment into two equal parts; see *Tutorial 5.5*

On a coordinate grid, if the endpoints are A(x_A, y_A) and B(x_B, y_B), the coordinates of M are:

$$x_M = \frac{x_A + x_B}{2} \qquad y_M = \frac{y_A + y_B}{2}$$

natural numbers: the set of counting numbers 1, 2, 3, 4, …; see *number systems*

negative number: a number less than 0

net of a rectangular box: a figure drawn on a plane that can be folded to create a rectangular box

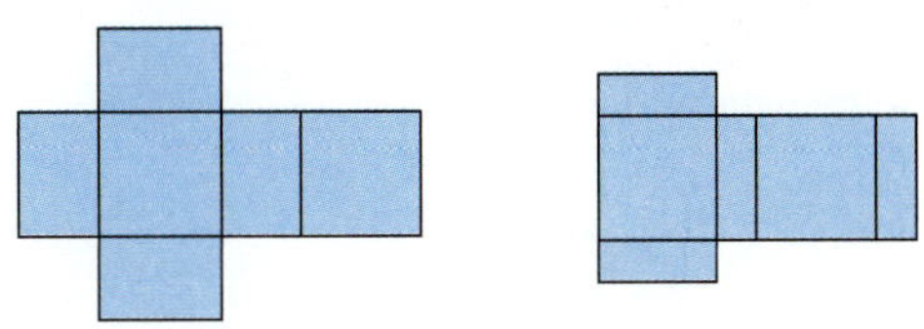

number systems:

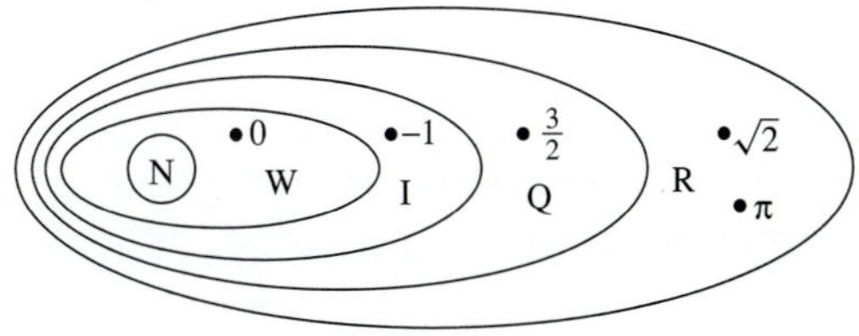

The *Natural numbers*, N, also called the counting numbers, are 1, 2, 3, 4, 5, …. If the number 0 is included, we get the *Whole numbers*, W: 0, 1, 2, 3, 4, 5, ….

The *Integers*, I, contain all of the whole numbers and all of their negatives: …, –3, –2, –1, 0, 1, 2, 3, ….

The *Rational numbers*, Q, consist of all numbers that can be expressed as fractions, with the denominator not equal to zero. Every integer is also a rational number, since every integer can be expressed as a fraction with denominator 1. All terminating or repeating decimals are rational numbers also.

Numbers such as $\sqrt{2}$ and π cannot be expressed as fractions involving integers. They are called *Irrational numbers.*

The number system that consists of all rational numbers together with all irrational numbers is called the *Real number* system, R. It can be represented by all positions on a number line.

oblique triangle: a triangle that does not contain a 90° angle

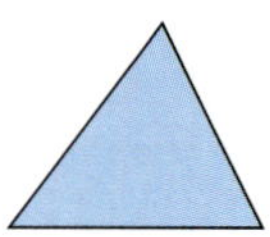

obtuse angle: an angle greater than 90° but less than 180°

obtuse triangle: a triangle with one obtuse angle

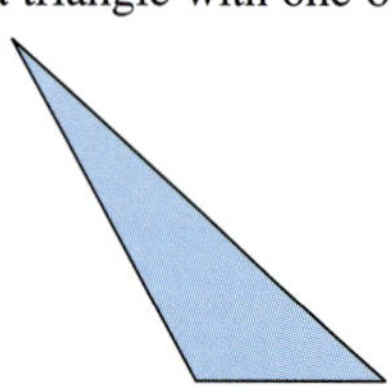

ophthalmologist: a medical doctor specializing in the structure, function, and diseases of the eye

opposite side: the side opposite a given angle in a right triangle

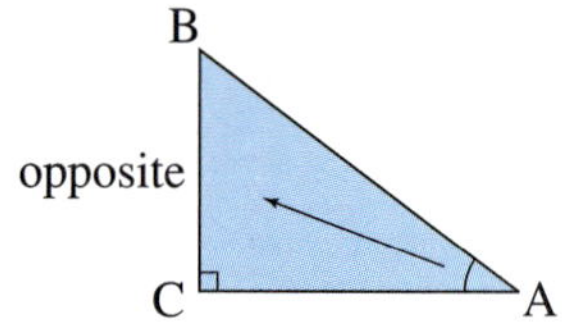

order of operations: the rules that are followed when simplifying or evaluating an expression:

Complete all operations within brackets following the order of operations.

Evaluate all exponents.

Complete all multiplication and division in the order they appear from left to right.

Complete all addition and subtraction in the order they appear from left to right.

Evaluate the following:

$5 - 2(4 + 2^3 \div 4)$	Begin with the exponent within the brackets.
$= 5 - 2(4 + 8 \div 4)$	Complete the division within the brackets.
$= 5 - 2(4 + 2)$	Complete the addition within the brackets.
$= 5 - 2(6)$	Complete the multiplication.
$= 5 - 12$	Finish by completing the subtraction.
$= -7$	

ordered pair: a pair of numbers, written as (x, y), that represents a point on the coordinate plane; see *coordinates*

outcome: a possible result of an experiment; a possible answer to a survey question

For the experiment of tossing a six-sided die, the possible outcomes are rolling a 1, 2, 3, 4, 5, or 6.

outlier: an observed value that differs markedly from the pattern established by most of the data

parallel lines: lines in the same plane that do not intersect

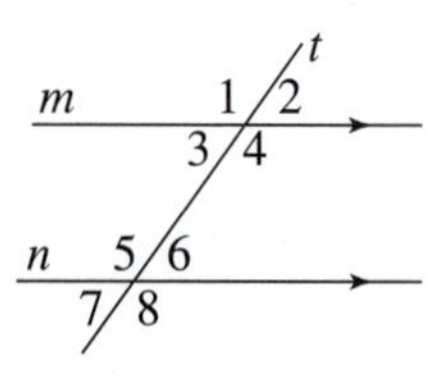

Lines *m* and *n* are parallel with a transversal, *t*. If two lines are parallel and cut by a transversal, then the following will be true:

The alternate interior angles will have equal measures (congruent).

$\angle 3 = \angle 6$ and $\angle 4 = \angle 5$

The corresponding angles will have equal measures (congruent).

$\angle 1 = \angle 5$ and $\angle 2 = \angle 6$ $\quad \angle 3 = \angle 7$ and $\angle 4 = \angle 8$

The same-side interior angles add up to 180° (supplementary).

$\angle 3 + \angle 5 = 180°$ and $\angle 4 + \angle 6 = 180°$

If any one of these conditions is true then the lines must be parallel. Lines that are parallel will have the same slope.

parallelogram: a quadrilateral with opposite sides parallel

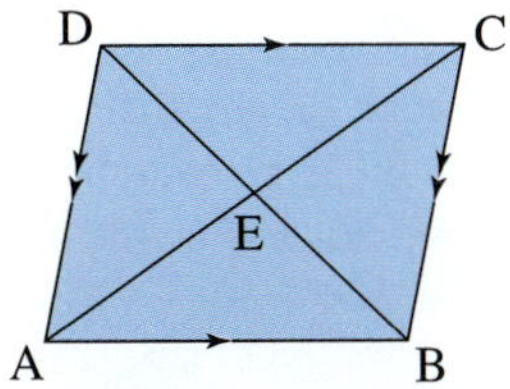

A parallelogram has the following properties:

The opposite sides have equal lengths. AB = CD and AD = BC

The opposite angles have equal measures (congruent).

$\angle A = \angle C$ and $\angle B = \angle D$

The diagonals bisect each other (cut each other into equal lengths).

AE = EC and DE = EB

percent: means "out of 100"; symbolized by %

A percent can be written as a fraction with denominator 100, or as a decimal.

$$45\% = \frac{45}{100} = 0.45 \text{ and } 150\% = \frac{150}{100} = 1.50$$

1. What percent is 33 out of 48? We must determine x, where $\frac{33}{48} = \frac{x}{100}$.

   To isolate x, multiply both sides by 100.

   $$100 \times \frac{33}{48} = 100 \times \frac{x}{100}$$
   $$68.75 = x$$

   33 out of 48 is 68.75%.

2. Find 7% of 45.95.

   7% of $45.95 = 0.07 \times 45.95$, changing the percent to its decimal form

   $= 3.2165$

   7% of 45.95 is 3.2165.

3. 7.5 is 20% of what number?

   Let the unknown number be x and write the question as:

   $$7.5 = 20\% \text{ of } x$$

   Use the decimal form of the percent.

   $$7.5 = 0.20 \times x$$

   Solve for x by dividing both sides of the equation by 0.20.

   $$\frac{7.5}{0.20} = \frac{0.20x}{0.20}$$
   $$37.5 = x$$

   Thus 7.5 is 20% of 37.5.

perimeter: the distance around a closed figure; see *square*, *rectangle*, *triangle*, and *circle*

perpendicular: intersecting at right angles

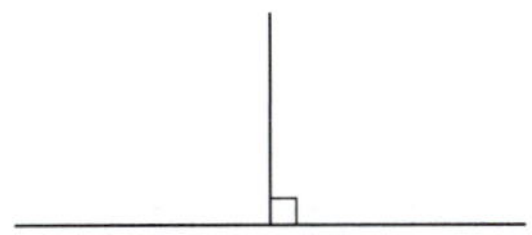

Two lines are perpendicular if their slopes are negative reciprocals of one another; see *Tutorial 5.4*

pi (π): the ratio of the circumference of a circle and its diameter; $\pi \doteq 3.1416$

polygon: a closed figure that consists of line segments that only intersect at their endpoints

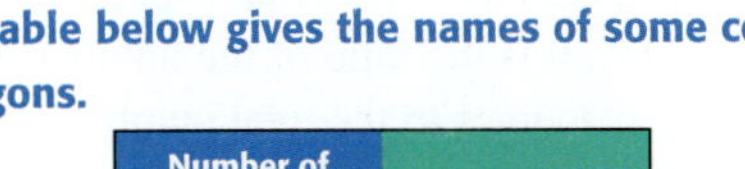

The above figures are polygons.

These figures are not polygons.

The table below gives the names of some common polygons.

Number of sides	Polygon
3	Triangle
4	Quadrilateral
5	Pentagon
6	Hexagon
8	Octagon
10	Decagon
n	n-gon

population: the entire set of objects, people, or processes being studied; see *Tutorial 4.1*

positive number: a number greater than 0

power: see *exponent*

precision: an indication of how close a set of measurements are to one another; the smallest scale division of a measuring instrument

pressure: a measure of the amount of force acting on a unit area of a surface; calculated by dividing the force acting on a surface by the area of the surface

If a force of 20 Newtons is acting on a surface whose area is 4 m², what is the pressure on the surface?

$$\text{Pressure} = \text{Force/Area}$$
$$P = 20\text{ N}/4\text{ m}^2$$
$$= 5\text{ N/m}^2$$

principal: the amount of money invested or borrowed

prism: a solid with two congruent and parallel faces (bases), all other faces are parallelograms

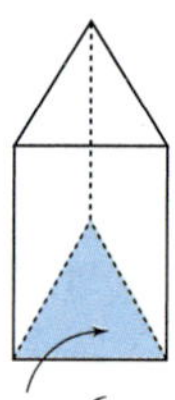

The volume of a prism is the area of the base multiplied by the height.

$$\text{Volume} = (\text{Area of base})(\text{Height})$$
$$V = A \times h$$
$$= (6\text{ cm}^2)(10\text{ cm})$$
$$= 60\text{ cm}^3$$

probability: an indication of the likelihood of an event occurring; if the outcomes of an experiment are equally likely, it is the ratio of the number of favourable outcomes to the total number of outcomes

proportion: a statement that two ratios are equal

To solve for an unknown quantity within a proportion, first clear the fraction by multiplication.

$$\frac{x}{12} = \frac{2}{5}$$
$$12 \times \frac{x}{12} = 12 \times \frac{2}{5}$$
$$x = 4.8$$

$$\frac{3}{x} = \frac{4}{5}$$
$$5x \times \frac{3}{x} = 5x \times \frac{4}{5}$$
$$3 = 4x$$
$$\frac{3}{4} = \frac{4x}{4}$$
$$0.75 = x$$

pyramid: a solid with one face that is a polygon (base) and other faces that are triangles with a common vertex

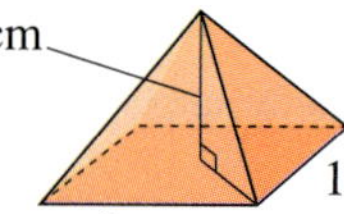

The formula to calculate the volume, *V*, of a pyramid is:

$$\text{Volume} = \frac{1}{3}(\text{Base area})(\text{Height})$$

For the pyramid shown:

$$V = \frac{1}{3}(8\text{ cm} \times 10\text{ cm})(12\text{ cm})$$
$$= 320\text{ cm}^3$$

Pythagorean Theorem: for any right triangle, the area of the square on the hypotenuse is equal to the sum of the areas of the squares on the other two sides

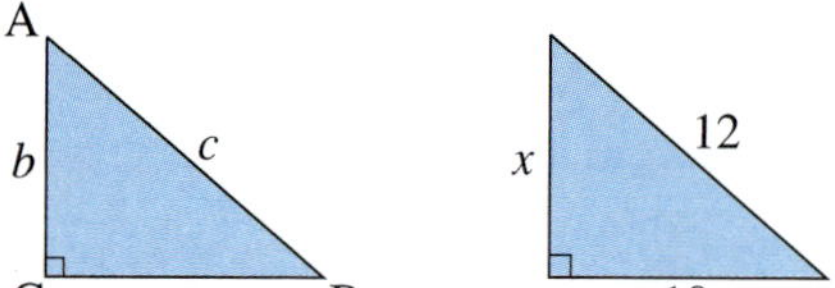

In right triangle ABC: $a^2 + b^2 = c^2$

Using the values for the right triangle shown, substitute into the above formula.

$10^2 + x^2 = 12^2$	**Simplify each side.**
$100 + x^2 = 144$	**Isolate the unknown.**
$100 + x^2 - 100 = 144 - 100$	
$x^2 = 44$	**To solve, take the square**
$x \doteq 6.6$	**root of both sides.**

quadrant: one of the four regions into which the coordinate axes divide the plane, usually numbered as shown in the diagram

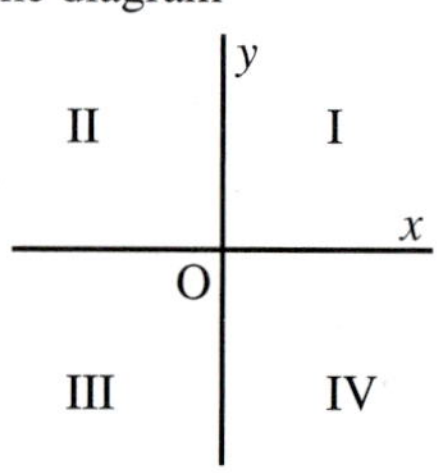

quadrilateral: a four-sided polygon; see *polygon*

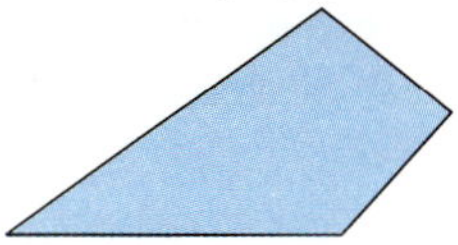

radical: the root of a number

$\sqrt{5}$, $\sqrt[3]{5}$, $\sqrt{2.6}$

radius: the distance from the centre of a circle to any point on the circumference; also, a line segment joining the centre of a circle to any point on the circumference

The radius of a circle is half the length of its diameter.

random sample: a sampling in which all members of the population have an equal chance of being selected; see *Tutorial 4.4*

range: the difference between the highest and lowest values in a set of data

range of a function or a relation: the set of output numbers of a function or a relation; see *Tutorial 3.5*

rate: a certain quantity of one thing considered in relation to one unit of another

Speed is the rate at which distance travelled changes in relation to one unit of time.

The slope of a line is the rate at which the line rises for one unit of horizontal run.

ratio: a comparison of two or more quantities with the same unit

A rectangular box has length 18 cm, width 5 cm, and height 8 mm. To give the ratio of the lengths of its sides, first change all lengths to the same units, mm, then reduce by dividing by common factors:

180:50:8 = 90:25:4

rational numbers: the set of numbers that can be written in the form $\frac{m}{n}$, where m and n are integers and $n \neq 0$; see *number systems*

real numbers: the set of numbers that includes both rational and irrational numbers; that is, all numbers that can be expressed as decimals; see *number systems*

rectangle: a quadrilateral with right angles

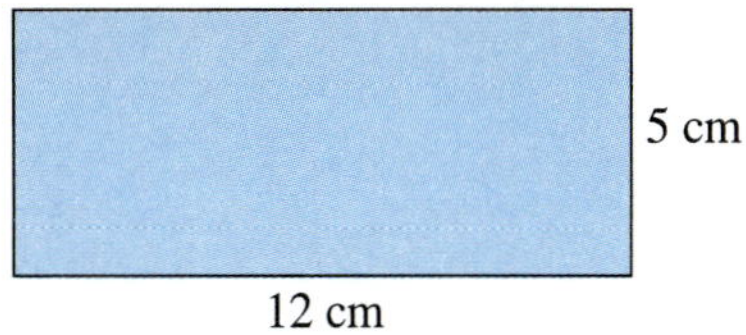

Perimeter = 2 × Length + 2 × Width

$P = 2l + 2w$

Area = Length × Width

$A = lw$

For the rectangle shown:

$P = 2(12\text{ cm}) + 2(5\text{ cm})$
$= 24\text{ cm} + 10\text{ cm}$
$= 34\text{ cm}$

$A = (12\text{ cm})(5\text{ cm})$
$= 60\text{ cm}^2$

recursive relation: a rule where a number in a list, other than the first number, is specified in terms of some of the numbers that come before it

The list 3, 6, 12, 24 is recursive, since each successive term after the first is twice the previous one.

regular polygon: a polygon with all sides and all angles equal

The polygons below are regular polygons.

relation: a rule that produces one or more output number for every valid input number; see *Chapter 3*

reliability: for a sample statistic, if nearly the same result is obtained in subsequent studies; for a test, if, when repeated, the test results are nearly the same; see *Tutorial 4.2*

residual: the vertical distance between a plotted point and a line of best fit; see *Tutorial 6.8*

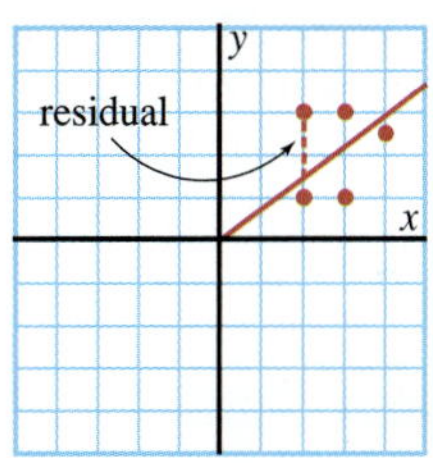

retail price: the price paid by consumers

revenue: money brought in from the sale of goods or services

The sale of 158 tickets for a show costing $20 each produces a revenue of $3160.

rhombus: a parallelogram with four equal sides

right angle: a 90° angle

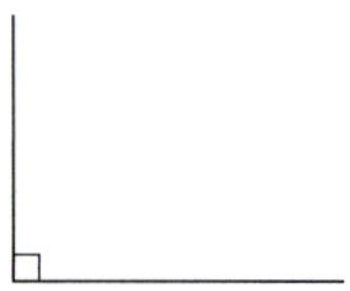

right triangle: a triangle with one right angle

rise: the vertical distance between two points; see *Tutorial 5.2* and *slope*

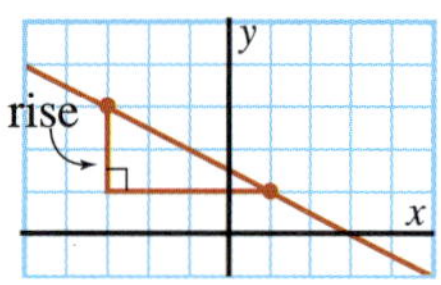

run: the horizontal distance between two points; see *Tutorial 5.2* and *slope*

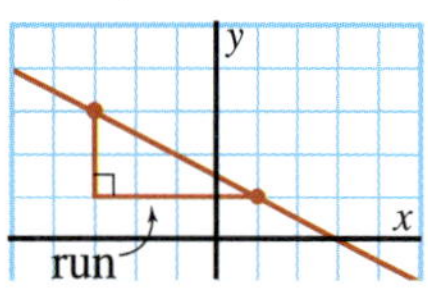

sample: part of a population chosen to represent the total population in a study; see *Tutorials 4.1* to *4.3*

sample statistic: a numerical value that is used to describe a sample, such as the *mean*

sampling: the process used to choose part of a population to represent the total population in a study

scale: for a map, model, or diagram, the ratio of the distance between two points to the distance between the actual locations; also the numbers on the coordinate axes

scale factor: the ratio of corresponding sides on similar figures

The triangles in the diagram are similar. To find the scale factor, find the ratio of the corresponding sides.

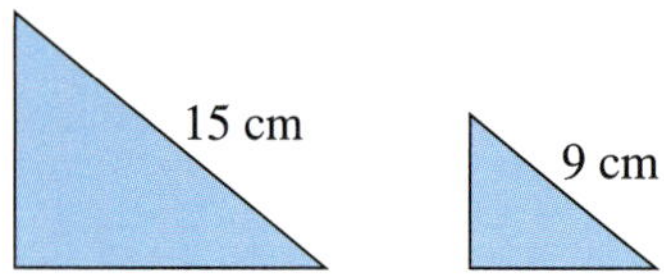

Scale factor $= \frac{9 \text{ cm}}{15 \text{ cm}}$

$= \frac{3}{5}$, **dividing by the common factor 3**

$= 0.6$

scatterplot: a graph of data that are a series of points

Height (cm)	154	162	172	178
Mass (kg)	56.3	60.1	72.2	64.3

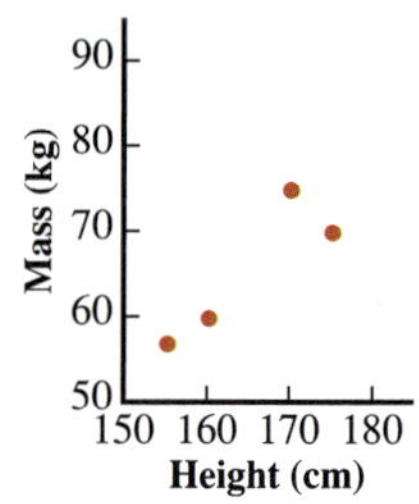

scientific notation: a number expressed as the product of a number greater than −10 and less than −1, or greater than 1 and less than 10, and a power of 10; used to express very large and very small numbers

$47\ 000 = 4.7 \times 10^4$, **and** $-26 = -2.6 \times 10^1$

seed value: a number used to start a calculation or process

self-selected sample: a sample in which only interested members of the population will participate; see *Tutorial 4.3*

semicircle: half a circle

SI system: see *metric system*; SI stands for Système Internationale des unités

similar figures: figures that have the same shape but not necessarily the same size

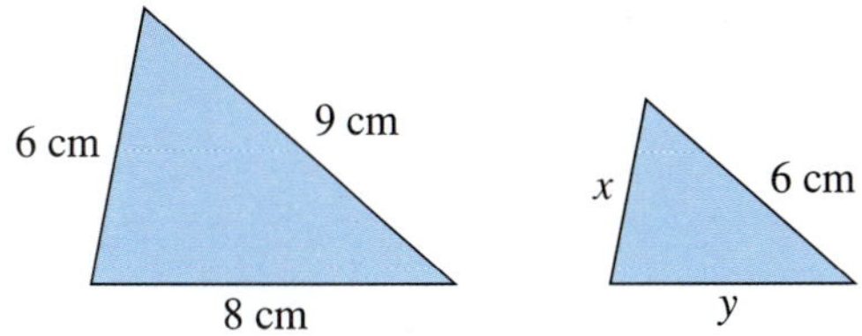

When two figures are similar, their corresponding angles will have equal measures, and their corresponding sides are in proportion (all have the same scale factor). The symbol ~ is used to indicate two figures are similar.

To find an unknown side of one similar figure, use a proportion.

$$\frac{9}{6} = \frac{8}{y} = \frac{6}{x}$$

$$\text{Scale factor} = \frac{9}{6} = \frac{3}{2} = 3{:}2$$

To find x, solve the following proportion.

$$\frac{3}{2} = \frac{6}{x}$$
$$2x \times \frac{3}{2} = 2x \times \frac{6}{x}$$
$$3x = 12$$
$$x = 4$$

To find y, solve the following proportion.

$$\frac{3}{2} = \frac{8}{y}$$
$$2y \times \frac{3}{2} = 2y \times \frac{8}{y}$$
$$3y = 16$$
$$y \doteq 5.33$$

similar objects: objects that have the same shape but not necessarily the same size

All the corresponding angles will have equal measures and all dimensions will be proportional.

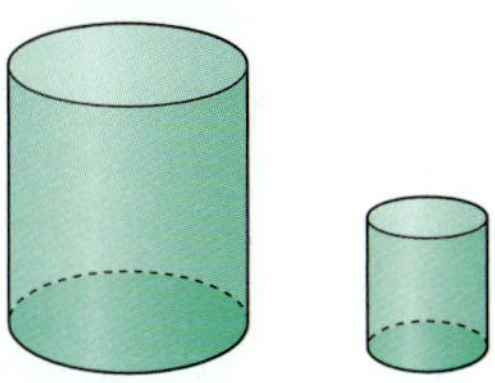

simple random sample: see *random sample*

sine: for an acute ∠A in a right triangle, the ratio of the length of the opposite side to the length of the hypotenuse

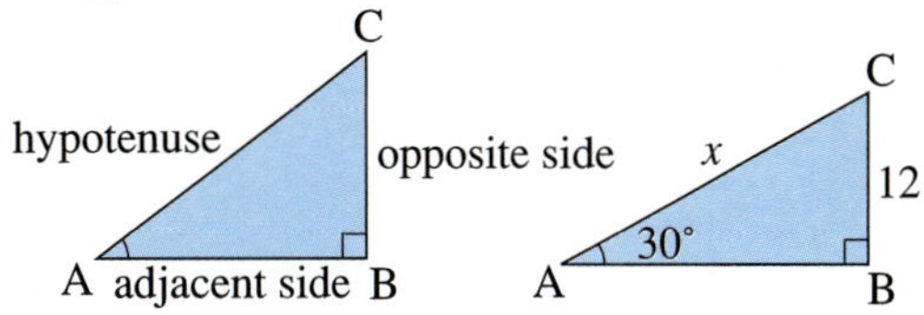

$\sin \angle A = \frac{\text{opp}}{\text{hyp}}$	**Substitute in the known quantities.**
$\sin 30° = \frac{12}{x}$	**Use a calculator to determine the sine ratio.**
$0.5 = \frac{12}{x}$	**Multiply to clear the fraction.**
$x \times 0.5 = x \times \frac{12}{x}$	
$x \times 0.5 = 12$	**Divide to isolate x.**
$\frac{x \times 0.5}{0.5} = \frac{12}{0.5}$	
$x = 24$	

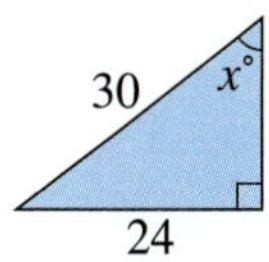

$\sin \angle A = \frac{\text{opp}}{\text{hyp}}$	**Substitute in the known quantities.**
$\sin x° = \frac{24}{30}$	**Convert the fraction into an equivalent decimal.**
$= 0.8$	**Use $\sin^{-1}$ (the angle whose sine is a function).**
$x \doteq 53.1°$	

Sine Law: a trigonometric law used to solve triangles; see *Tutorials 7.4* and *7.5*

Use the Sine Law in an oblique triangle where 2 angles and one side are known.

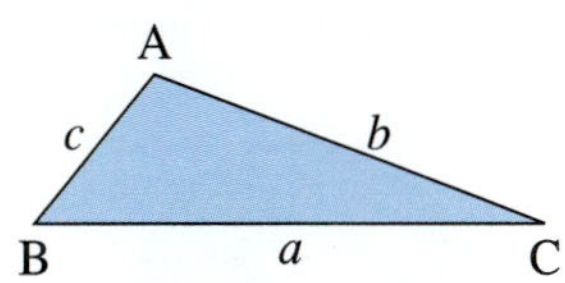

In any triangle ABC: $\frac{\sin A}{a} = \frac{\sin B}{b} = \frac{\sin C}{c}$ **and** $\frac{a}{\sin A} = \frac{b}{\sin B} = \frac{c}{\sin C}$

slope: a measure of the steepness of a line; see *Tutorial 5.2*; the tangent of the angle made by the line with the x-axis

The slope of a line segment joining $A(x_A, y_A)$ and $B(x_B, y_B)$ is:

$$\text{Slope} = \frac{\text{rise}}{\text{run}} = \frac{y_A - y_B}{x_A - x_B}$$

slope, *y*-intercept form: the equation of a line in the form $y = mx + b$, where m is the slope of the line and b is the y-intercept of the line

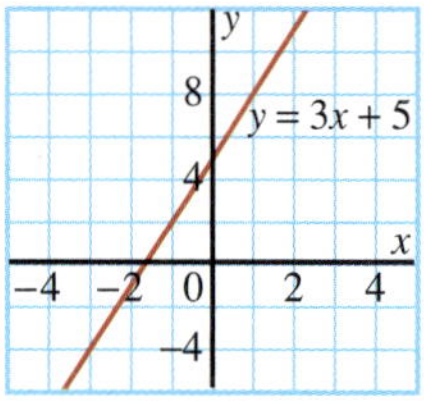

The equation $y = 3x + 5$ is that of a line with a slope of 3 and a y-intercept of 5.

solve an equation: determining the value of the unknown that, when substituted for the unknown in the equation, results in a true statement

Solve the equation $3x + 5 = 5x - 4$.
Use inverse operations to move all the terms in the variable to one side of the equation.

$3x + 5 - 3x = 5x - 4 - 3x$	Subtract $3x$ from both sides.
$3x - 3x + 5 = 5x - 3x - 4$	Rearrange to collect like terms.
$5 = 2x - 4$	Simplify.
$5 + 4 = 2x - 4 + 4$	Isolate the term in x; add 4 to both sides.
$9 = 2x$	Simplify.
$\frac{9}{2} = \frac{2x}{2}$	Isolate x; divide both sides by 2.
$4.5 = x$	

speed: see *average speed*

sphere: the set of points in space that are a given distance (radius) from a fixed point (centre); see *Tutorials 1.5* and *1.6*

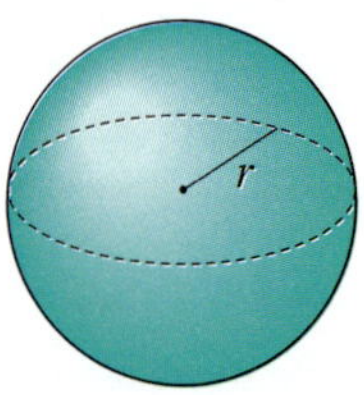

Surface Area, $S = 4\pi r^2 = \pi d^2$ Volume, $V = \frac{4}{3}\pi r^3 = \frac{\pi d^3}{6}$

spreadsheet: a computer-generated arrangement of data in rows and columns, where a change in one value can result in appropriate calculated changes in the other values

square: a rectangle with four equal sides

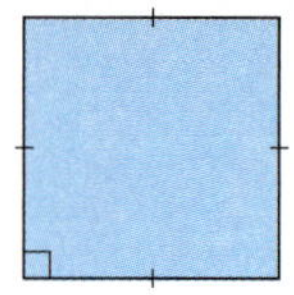

Perimeter = 4 × Length of side
$P = 4s$
Area = (Length of side)^2
$A = s^2$

For the square shown:
$P = 4(11 \text{ cm}) = 44 \text{ cm}$ $A = (11 \text{ cm})^2 = 121 \text{ cm}^2$

square root: a number which, when multiplied by itself, results in the given number

5 and −5 are the square roots of 25, since $5^2 = 25$ and $(-5)^2 = 25$. The notation $\sqrt{25}$ is reserved for the positive square root only.

standard form: for the equation of a line, the standard form is

$Ax + By + C = 0$, where A, B, and C are integers; see *equation of a line*

statistics: the branch of mathematics that deals with the collection, organization, and interpretation of data

strata: the non-overlapping subgroup obtained when a population is separated into sub-populations

stratified random sample: a sample in which all members of different segments of the population have an equal chance of being selected; see *Tutorial 4.4*

substituting into an expression: in an algebraic expression, replacing the letters with the indicated numbers or expressions each time they occur and simplifying according to the order of operations

Substitute $r = 4.5$ and $t = 3v$ into the expression $8r^2 - 2t$.

$$8r^2 - 2t = 8(4.5)^2 - 2(3v) = 8(20.25) - 6v = 162 - 6v$$

supplementary angles: two angles whose sum is 180°

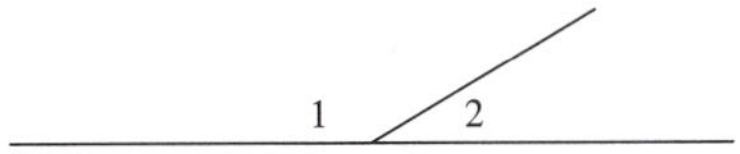

∠1 and ∠2 are supplementary.

surface area: a measure of the area on the surface of a three-dimensional object; see *cube*, *cylinder*, and *sphere*

survey: an investigation of a topic to find out people's views

systematic sample: a sample in which every *n*th member of a population is selected; see *Tutorial 4.3*

tangent: for an acute ∠A in a right triangle, the ratio of the length of the opposite side to the length of the adjacent side

1.

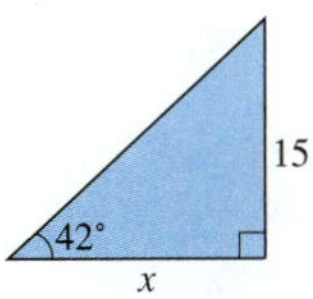

2.

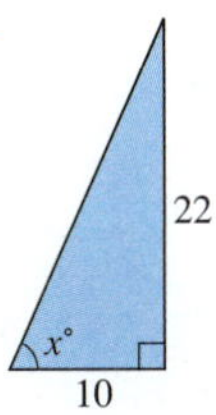

1. In the triangle shown above left, $\tan \angle A = \frac{opp}{adj}$.
Substitute the known value.

$\tan 42^\circ = \frac{x}{15}$	**Use a calculator to obtain the value of tan 42°.**
$0.9004 = \frac{x}{15}$	**Clear the fraction.**
$0.9004 \times 15 = 15 \times \frac{x}{15}$	
$13.5 = x$	

2. In the triangle shown above right, $\tan \angle A = \frac{opp}{adj}$.
Substitute in the known values.

$\tan x^\circ = \frac{22}{10}$	**Convert the fraction into an equivalent decimal.**
$= 2.2$	**Use $\tan^{-1}$ (the "angle whose tangent is" function).**
$x \doteq 65.6^\circ$	

ticketed price: the price placed on an item that is offered for sale

transit: a device used by surveyors for measuring a horizontal angle; see *Project*, *Chapter 7*

transversal: a line that crosses two or more lines at different points

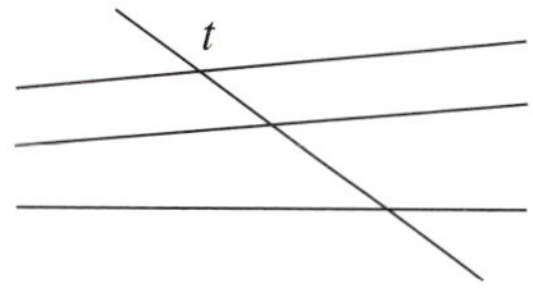

Line *t* is a transversal.

triangle: a three-sided polygon

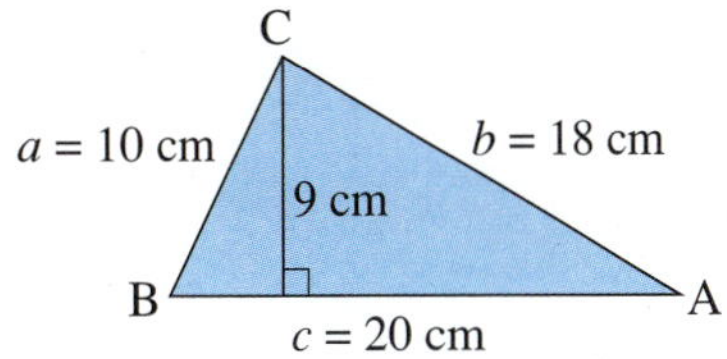

Perimeter = Sum of the three sides

$$= a + b + c$$
$$= 10 \text{ cm} + 18 \text{ cm} + 20 \text{ cm}$$
$$= 48 \text{ cm}$$

$$\text{Area} = \frac{1}{2}(\text{Base})(\text{Height})$$
$$= \frac{1}{2}bh$$
$$= \frac{1}{2}(20 \text{ cm})(9 \text{ cm})$$
$$= 90 \text{ cm}^2$$

An alternate formula, known as Heron's formula, is useful for finding the area of a triangle when the lengths of the three sides are known but the height is not.

Area = $\sqrt{s(s-a)(s-b)(s-c)}$, where $s = \frac{1}{2}(a+b+c)$

For the triangle shown:

$$s = \frac{1}{2}(10 \text{ cm} + 18 \text{ cm} + 20 \text{ cm})$$
$$= \frac{1}{2}(48 \text{ cm})$$
$$= 24 \text{ cm}$$

$$A = \sqrt{24 \text{ cm}(24 \text{ cm} - 10 \text{ cm})(24 \text{ cm} - 18 \text{ cm})(24 \text{ cm} - 20 \text{ cm})}$$
$$= \sqrt{24 \text{ cm}(14 \text{ cm})(6 \text{ cm})(4 \text{ cm})}$$
$$= \sqrt{8064 \text{ cm}^4}$$
$$\doteq 90 \text{ cm}^2$$

The interior angles in any triangle add up to 180°. If the measures of two angles within a triangle are known, the third can be calculated by adding the measures of the two known angles and subtracting this from 180°.

If ∠A = 35° and ∠B = 48°

then $\angle C = 180^\circ - (35^\circ + 48^\circ)$

$$= 97^\circ$$

trigonometric ratios: see *cosine*, *sine*, and *tangent*

uncertainty of measurement: for any measurement, the uncertainty is equal to one-half of the smallest scale division of the instrument; also called *measurement error*; see *Tutorial 1.4*

For a millimetre ruler, the uncertainty in any measurement would be ±0.5 mm.

validity: an indicator of how well a test really measures what it is supposed to measure; a sample statistic is valid if it closely approximates the quantity for the population; see *Tutorial 4.2*

variable: a letter or symbol used to represent a quantity that can vary

vary directly: see *direct variation*

vernier caliper: an instrument that can be used to measure an object to the nearest 0.01 cm; see *Utility 2*

vertex: the corner of a figure or solid

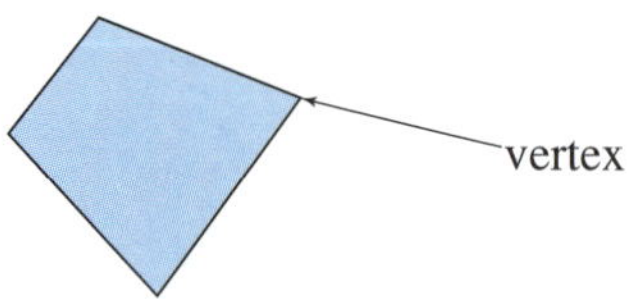

vertical intercept: the vertical coordinate of the point at which the graph of the line or function intersects the vertical

whole numbers: the set of numbers 0, 1, 2, 3, ...; see *number systems*

wholesale price: see *cost price*

x-axis: the horizontal number line on a coordinate grid

x-intercept: the x-coordinate where the graph of a line or function intersects the x-axis; see *horizontal intercept*; see *Tutorial 6.1*

y-axis: the vertical number line on a coordinate grid

y-intercept: the y-coordinate where the graph of a line or function intersects the y-axis; see *vertical intercept*; see *Tutorial 6.1*

Answers

CHAPTER 1 MEASUREMENT

TUTORIAL 1.1

Practise Your Prior Skills, page 4

1. 42 **2.** 108.6

Investigation 1, page 5

1. Answers may vary. For example, 49.6 cm
2. Answers may vary. For example, External Diameter 1.80 cm, Internal Diameter 1.38 cm
3. Answers may vary. For example, 126.22 cm^3
4. Answers may vary. For example, 74.19 cm^3
5. Answers may vary. For example, 52.03 cm^3

Investigation 2, page 6

1. Length = 27.9 cm; width = 21.6 cm
2., 3., 4., 5. Answers may vary.

TUTORIAL 1.2

Investigation 1, page 10

Answers may vary.

Investigation 2, page 11

1. a) Feet and inches **b)** Inches and square inches
c) Miles **d)** Yards
e) Inches and square inches **f)** Inches

2. a) Centimetres, or metres and centimetres
b) Centimetres and square centimetres
c) Kilometres
d) Metres
e) Centimetres and square centimetres
f) Millimetres or centimetres, depending on thickness of book

3. Answers may vary.

4.

Imperial Units	Conversion	Approximate Metric Convsersion
1 inch	2.5 cm	2.5 cm
1 foot = 12 inches	2.5 × 12	30.0 cm
1 yard = 36 inches	2.5 × 36	90.0 m = 0.9 m
1 mile = 1760 yards	0.9 × 1760	1584 m = 1.6 km

Investigation 3, page 11

Answers may vary.

Investigation 4, page 12

2. Side length = 100 cm; 1 m^2 = 10 000 cm^2

4. A little less than 11 square feet in 1 m^2; about 1.2 square yards in 1 m^2; 9 square feet in 1 square yard

5., 6. Answers may vary.

TUTORIAL 1.3

Practise Your Prior Skills, page 14

1. 654 cm **2.** 0.038 54 **3.** 25 000 cm^2

Investigation 1, page 15

1.

Yards	Feet
1	3
2	6
3	9
4	12
10	30
56	168
180	540

2. Number of feet = number of yards × 3

3.

Inches	Feet
12	1
24	2
36	3
48	4
180	15
540	45
1800	150

4. Number of feet = number of inches ÷ 12

5. Answers may vary.
Possible rule: Number of ounces = number of pounds × 16

Investigation 2, page 16

1. 8800 yards

2.

Miles	Yards
5	8 800
10	17 600
15	26 400
20	35 200
25	44 000
30	52 800

3. Number of yards = number of miles × 1760

4. Answers may vary.
Conversion Number of metres = number of feet × 0.3048
Number of feet = number of metres × 3.2808

EXERCISES, page 20

Checking Your Skills

1.

Celebrity Height				
	Feet, Inches	a) inches	m	b) Passport information (m)
Wayne Gretsky	6, 0	72	1.8288	1.83
Silken Laumann	5, 11	71	1.8034	1.80
Joanne Malar	5, 8	68	1.7272	1.73
Michael J. Fox	5, 4	64	1.6256	1.63
Theoren Fleury	5, 6	66	1.6764	1.68
Celine Dion	5, 7	67	1.7018	1.70

2. 7.24 m

3. The 100-m dash is farther by 9.36 yards or 8.56 m.

4. a) 577 778 square yards **b)** 483 096 m^2

5. 1227.99 km/h using CONVERT program
1227.73 km/h using conversion 1 mile = 1.609 km

Extending Your Thinking

6. a) b) c) Using conversion 1 mile = 1.609 km

Miles per Gallon	Kilometres per Litre	Litres per 100 km
5	2.125	47.048
10	4.251	23.524
20	8.502	11.762
30	12.753	7.841
40	17.004	5.881
50	21.255	4.705

e) 26 miles per gallon

f) 7 L/100 km from graph; 6.7 L/100 km from calculation

g) Answers may vary.

TUTORIAL 1.4

EXERCISES, page 26

Checking Your Skills

1. Answers may vary.

a) Appropriate **b)** Not appropriate
c) Appropriate **d)** Not appropriate
e) Appropriate **f)** Not appropriate
g) Not appropriate

2. a) Accuracy is important. It determines the length to be bought.
b) Different tools may give different measurements, depending on accuracy.

3. Diagram c represents the best precision and accuracy.

4. Answers may vary.

5. Answers may vary. The significance of the error depends on whether the mass of the object is large or small.

6. A ruler divided into millimetres; explanations may vary.

Extending Your Thinking

7. a) Micrometer 0.01 mm; ruler 0.1 cm
b) The measurement of length with error of less than 1% is more accurate than the measurement of thickness with error of 10%.

TUTORIAL 1.5

Investigation, page 30

1., 2., 3. Answers may vary.

4. The volume of water equals the volume of the ball.

5. At the end of exercise 3, the can was $\frac{2}{3}$ full.

6. The volume of the sphere is $\frac{2}{3}$ the volume of the cylinder.

7. Answers may vary.

8. Answers may vary.

9. Volume of can = $2\pi r^3$; volume of sphere = $\frac{4}{3}\pi r^3$

Practise Your Prior Skills, page 32

1. 1.25×10^6 **2.** 30 780

EXERCISES, page 34

Checking Your Skills

1. a) 41.6 cm^3 **b)** 4780.1 cm^3
c) 26.52 cm^3 **d)** 33.5 cm^3

2. 1.412×10^{18} km^3

3. a) 12.096 cm **b)** 7413 cm^3

4. 27 times

5. a) 25 460 km **b)** 6.91×10^{13} km^3

Extending Your Thinking

6. 3139 **7.** About 5:4

TUTORIAL 1.6

Investigation, page 36

1., 2., 3., 4., 5. Answers may vary.

6. The ratio of the surface area of a sphere to the square of its diameter equals π.

7. Surface area $A = \pi d^2$ **8.** $A = 4\pi r^2$

Practise Your Prior Skills, page 38

1. 294.7 **2.** 35¢

EXERCISES, page 39

Checking Your Skills

1. a) 58.1 cm^2 **b)** 1372.3 cm^2
c) 43.01 cm^2 **d)** 50.3 cm^2

2. 1839.8 cm^2 **3.** 168 cm^2

4. a) 509 million km^2 **b)** 112 million km^2
c) 8.2%

5. a) 460 million km^2 **b)** 92 million km^2

6. a) 314 m^2 **b)** About $11 288.30
c) About $22 774.33

7. The surface area of the moon is twice as large as the area of the circle it appears to be.

Extending Your Thinking

8. Surface area A = $\frac{C^2}{\pi}$ **9.** Answers may vary.

TUTORIAL 1.7

Practise Your Prior Skills, page 41

1. 3.162 **2.** 5

3. $(25)^{\frac{1}{2}} = 5$ **4.** 2^6

5. a) 1 **b)** 4

Investigation, page 41

1. Answers may vary; $r \doteq 3$ cm

2. Answers may vary; $r \doteq 6$ cm

3. Answers may vary.

EXERCISES, page 44

Checking Your Skills

1. a) 1.59 **b)** 0.27

2. 1.5 cm

3. 2.9 cm

4. 4.2 m

5. 20 cm

6. 10 cm^3

7. a) 4.4 cm **b)** 60.27 cm^2

Extending Your Thinking

8. a) 4.95 m **b)** 63.51 m^3 **c)** 76.98 m^2

TUTORIAL 1.8

Investigation 1, page 46

1.

Rectangle	Length (cm)	Width (cm)	Perimeter (cm)	Area (cm^2)
A	1	3	8	3
B	2	6	16	12
C	5	12	40	75

2.

Rectangle	Scale Factor	Ratio of Permeters	Ratio of Areas
B to A	2:1 = 2	16:8 = 2	12:3 = 4
C to A	5:1 = 5	40:8 = 5	75:3 = 25
C to B	5:2 = 2.5	40:16 = 2.5	75:12 = 6.25

3. a) The scale factor and the ratio of the perimeters are equal.

b) The ratio of the areas is the square of the scale factor.

Investigation 2, page 47

1.

Sphere	Radius (cm)	Surface Area (cm^2)	Volume (cm^3)
A	1	12.57	4.19
B	3	113.10	113.10
C	5	314.16	523.60

2.

Sphere	Scale Factor	Ratio of Surface Areas	Ratio of Volumes
B to A	3:1 = 3	113.1:12.57 = 9	113.1:4.19 = 27
C to A	5:1 = 5	314.16:12.57 = 25	523.6:4.19 = 125
C to B	$5:3 = 1\bar{6}$	$314.16:113.10 = 2.\bar{7}$ or $\frac{25}{9}$	523.6:113.1 = 4.63 or $(1.\bar{6})^3$

3. a) The ratio of the surface areas of the spheres equals the square of the scale factor.

b) The ratio of the volumes of the spheres equals the cube of the scale factor.

4. a) 452.40 cm^2 **b)** 904.80 cm^3

5.

Cylinder	Radius (inches)	Height (inches)	Surface Area (square inches)	Volume (cubic inches)
A	1	3	25.13	9.42
B	2	6	100.53	75.40
C	5	15	628.32	1178.10

6.

Cylinder	Scale Factor	Ratio of Surface Areas	Ratio of Volumes
B to A	2:1 = 2	4:1 = 4	8:1 = 8
C to A	5:1 = 5	25:1 = 25	125:1 = 125
C to B	5:2 = 2.5	25:4 = 6.25 or 2.5^2	125:8 = 15.625 or $(2.5)^3$

7. a) The ratio of the surface areas of two similar cylinders equals the square of the scale factor.

b) The ratio of the volumes of two similar cylinders equals the cube of the scale factor.

c) They are the same.

8. a) 226.17 square inches **b)** 254.34 cubic inches

9. The ratio of the surface areas of two cubes is the square of their scale factor. The ratio of the volumes of two cubes is the cube of their scale factor.

10. a) $k^2 : 1 = k^2$ **b)** $k^3 : 1 = k^3$

EXERCISES, page 50

Checking Your Skills

1. a) 3 cm **b)** $0.000\ 1\bar{3}$

2. Moon's volume is $\frac{1}{64}$ or 0.015 625 that of Earth.

3. 16 times larger

4.

Scale Factor	Ratio of Edges	Ratio of Surface Areas	Ratio of Volumes
2:5	2:5	4:25	8:125
4:3	4:3	16:9	64:27
1:4	1:4	1:16	1:64
5:6	5:6	25:36	125:216
3:2	3:2	9:4	27:8
5:3	5:3	25:9	125:27
4:7	4:7	16:49	64:343
1:6	1:6	1:36	1:216
3:5	3:5	9:25	27:125

5. Answers may vary. Although the heights of the bars are in a 2:1 ratio, their areas are in a 4:1 ratio. Since we often make quick comparisons of figures based on area rather than height, we might be misled into thinking that Rapid Realty's sales are 4 times as large as their competitors' sales. The graph can be improved by making the bars the same width. Then the height and the area are both in a 2:1 ratio.

6. a) 4 **b)** 1.732

7. a) 10 m **b)** 45 m^2 **c)** 15.75 m^3

8. a) 2:3 **b)** 4:9 **c)** 8:27

d) The ball with the 15-cm diameter is the better buy.

9. Answers may vary.

CONSOLIDATING YOUR SKILLS

What Should I Be Able To Do?, page 57

1. a) to **f)** Answers may vary.

g) The sphere

h) Heat loss is a function of surface area. The ball (sphere) has the smallest surface area for a given volume.

2. a) Vernier caliper **b)** Tape or trundle wheel

c) Vernier caliper **d)** Micrometer

3. a) 21.232 mm with precision of 0.001 mm

b) 21.2 cm; because the other two measurements agree (about 2.1 cm)

c) 2.12 cm; vernier
21.232 mm; micrometer
21.2 cm; ruler

4. 12 496.8 m

5. 6

6. a) 4.19 cubic feet **b)** 12.57 square feet

7. 1.716 788 672 or 1.72

8. a) 4.12 mm b) 101.91 mm^2
c) The length of the side increases to 5.19 mm, a scale factor of 1.26. Ratio 5:4
The surface area increases to 161.77 mm^2, a factor of 1.59 or $(1.26)^2$.

9. 144 inches or 12 feet
22 400 inches or 155.6 square feet

CHAPTER 2 NUMBER PATTERNS IN TABLES

TUTORIAL 2.1

Investigation, page 64

1. Newfoundland, Nova Scotia, Quebec, Alberta
2. Ontario, Manitoba, Saskatchewan, Alberta, British Columbia
3. Overall, adolescents spend less time watching TV than any other age group in Canada. In Nova Scotia, children 2–11 years old spend the same amount of time watching TV, on average, as adolescents in that province. In English-speaking Quebec and Alberta, children spend fewer hours watching TV than adolescents.
4. 20.8; 22.7. The averages are not the same because the number of people in each category is not the same. For instance, the total number of men and women 18 years old or older (who spend more time watching TV, on average, than other groups) is much greater than the number of adolescents (who spend fewer hours watching TV, on average, than other groups).
5. Album-oriented rock, Contemporary, Dance, and U. S. Stations
6. Easy Listening and Sports
7. Answers may vary. Some possibilities include ethnic music, jazz, and classical.
8. Adolescents: 100; Men: 100.2; Women: 99.9. The columns for men and women do not total 100 as a result of rounding the individual entries in the columns.
9. No. If the male teacher in Yellowknife listened to CBC for the national average percentage of time, he would have listened for 1.62 h (18 × .09). However, individual listening habits are not necessarily the same as the averages. There are many adult males who would not have listened to CBC at all.

Practise Your Prior Skills, page 67

1. a) About 14 percent of Canadians are under 5 years old.
b) The area of Africa is about 20 percent of the world's total land area.
c) 80% of students in a class had an A grade.

2. 0.06 3. 15 kg

EXERCISES, page 68

Checking Your Skills

1. a) $2x + y = n$ where n = total points
b) The standings have changed. Anaheim and Phoenix now have the same point total, but Anaheim was ahead of Phoenix. Also, Phoenix and St. Louis were tied, but now Phoenix is ahead; Edmonton and Chicago were tied, but now Edmonton is ahead.

	Points Per:	3	0	1		
Teams	Games Played	Wins	Losses	Ties	"New" Points	"Old" Points
Colorado	82	49	24	9	156	107
Dallas	82	48	26	8	152	104
Detroit	82	38	26	18	132	94
Anaheim	82	36	33	13	121	85
Phoenix	82	38	37	7	121	83
St. Louis	82	36	35	11	119	83
Edmonton	82	36	37	9	117	81
Chicago	82	34	35	13	115	81
Vancouver	82	35	40	7	112	77
Calgary	82	32	41	9	105	73
Toronto	82	30	44	8	98	68
Los Angeles	82	28	43	11	95	67
San Jose	82	27	47	8	89	62

c) The standings do not change.

	Points Per:	1	–1	0		
Teams	Games Played	Wins	Losses	Ties	"New" Points	"Old" Points
Colorado	82	49	24	9	25	107
Dallas	82	48	26	8	22	104
Detroit	82	38	26	18	12	94
Anaheim	82	36	33	13	3	85
Phoenix	82	38	37	7	1	83
St. Louis	82	36	35	11	1	83
Edmonton	82	36	37	9	–1	81
Chicago	82	34	35	13	–1	81
Vancouver	82	35	40	7	–5	77
Calgary	82	32	41	9	–9	73
Toronto	82	30	44	8	–14	68
Los Angeles	82	28	43	11	–15	67
San Jose	82	27	47	8	–20	62

2. a) 133.75 b) 143.75

Price ($)	7% Discount ($)	Discounted Price ($)	PST ($)	GST ($)	Total Price ($)
100.00	7.00	93.00	6.51	6.51	106.02

3. a) 107.00
b) No. The price without GST is $107.00. The price using the store method is $106.02.

4. a) The rate of GST for all provinces is 7%. It is calculated by multiplying the price by 0.07: GST = Price × 0.07. Therefore, $80 \times 0.07 = 5.60$ and $124.75 \times .07 = 8.73$.
b) The effective rate of PST is 10.7% of the original price $(8.56 \div 80.00 \times 100)$. But PST is actually calculated here by charging PST of 10% on the sum of the original price and the GST:
Let x represent the price. PST $= (x + 0.07x) \times 0.10$;
PST $= 1.07x \times 0.10$; PST $= 0.107x$
c) Prince Edward Island

5. a) Let x represent the price. Total $= x + 0.07x$; Total $= 1.07x$
b) Total $= x + 0.07x + 0.08x$; Total $= 1.15x$
c) Total $= x + 0.07x + ((x + 0.07x)) \times 0.10)$;
Total $= x + 0.07x + 0.107x$; Total = Price × 1.177
d) Total $= x + 0.07x + ((x + 0.07x)) \times 0.065)$;
Total $= x + 0.07x + 0.06955x$; Total $= 1.13955x$

6. **a)** The total stopping distance is the sum of the reaction time distance and the braking distance.
   b) 66 feet or 20.1 m
   c) 64 km/h or 40 mph **d)** 41.1 m

7. **a)** **i)** 73.14 US dollars **ii)** 124.16 German marks
   iii) 8 865 Japanese yen
   b) **i)** 329.13 US dollars **ii)** 203.45 British pounds
   iii) 557 622 Italian lira
   c) **i)** 112.80 Canadian dollars **ii)** 472.76 French francs
   iii) 140.05 German marks

8. **a)** Step 1: Find the currency you require in the first row of the table. Step 2: In that column, find the "foreign" currency that you wish to convert to the "required" currency, and note the conversion value. Step 3: Multiply the amount of the required currency by the value found in Step 2.
   b) **i)** 90.42 British pounds **ii)** 838.22 French francs
   iii) 17 730 Japanese yen
   c) **i)** 341.80 Canadian dollars **ii)** 424.38 German marks
   iii) 423 545 Italian lira
   d) **i)** 1 105.85 Canadian dollars
   ii) 808.85 US dollars **iii)** 98 035 Japanese yen

Extending Your Thinking

9. **a)**

	Price ($)	Discount ($)	Price after Discount ($)	GST ($)	PST ($)	Final Price ($)
CD1	15.99	3.20	12.79	0.90	0.90	14.59
CD2	12.99	2.60	10.39	0.73	0.73	11.85
Totals	28.98	5.80	23.18	1.63	1.63	26.44

b)

	Price ($)	GST ($)	PST ($)	Price after Taxes ($)	Discount ($)	Final Price ($)
CD1	15.99	1.12	1.12	18.23	3.64	14.59
CD2	12.99	0.91	0.91	14.81	2.96	11.85
Totals	28.98	2.03	2.03	33.04	6.60	26.44

   c) The multiplication operations required for calculating GST, PST, and discount can be done in any order and still produce the same result. Price × 0.8 (the discount) × 1.14 (to add PST and GST), is the same as Price × 1.14 (to add GST and PST) × 0.8 (the discount).
   d) No. The store receives the amount the customer pays, minus the taxes it remits to Federal and Provincial governments. When the store discounts the items before applying tax, there is less tax to remit, and the store keeps more money.
   e) No. For CD1, governments receive $1.80 tax when the discount is applied before taxes, and $2.24 when the discount is applied after taxes.

10. The customer pays the same price:
    $0.8x \times 1.14 = 1.14x \times 0.8$; $0.912x = 0.912x$
    The tax paid is different:
    $0.8x \times 0.14 < x \times 0.14$; $0.112x < 0.14x$

TUTORIAL 2.2

Computer Lab, page 74

1. **a)** 2
   b) The formula told the spreadsheet to take the value of cell A1, add 1 to it, and display the result in cell A2.
   c) The spreadsheet displays the text **A1+1** and does not perform the calculation.

2. **a)** The numbers 1 to 15 in order from cell A1 to A15
   b) The cell reference in the formula of each filled cell changed so that it always references the cell directly above.
   c) When the number in cell A1 is changed to 10, the spreadsheet recalculates the other cells. This results in cells A2 through A15 displaying the numbers 11 through 24 respectively.
   d) The formulas in cells A3 to A15 do not automatically change when the formula in A2 is changed. To change the formulas so that the first 15 odd numbers are displayed in column A, highlight cells A2 through A15 and use **Fill**, or **Fill Down**, from the spreadsheet's menus.

3. **a)** To display numbers from 2 to 15 in cells A3 to A16: Enter **=A2+1** in cell A3. Highlight cells A3 through A16 and use **Fill**, or **Fill Down**, from the spreadsheet's menus.
   d) In column B, the formula in each cell displays the sum of the cell in column A from the same row, and the cell B1. In column C, the formula in each cell displays the sum of the cell in column A from the same row, and the cell in column B from the row immediately above.

4. The numbers in column B increase by 5s.
   a) =A2*3
   b) The numbers in column D increase by 8s. This is because column B multiplies column A by 5, and column C multiplies column A by 3 : $5x + 3x = 8x$

EXERCISES, page 77

Checking Your Skills

1. Rows are labelled with numbers from the top down. Columns are labelled with letters, beginning with A on the left.
2. Cell Reference gives the position of the cell in the spreadsheet. Cell D6 means column D, row 6.
3. Where the cursor is, or the cell currently selected
4. Numbers, text, or formulas
5. Press Enter, Return, or Tab.
6. The equals sign =
7. Numbers, cell names, and mathematical operators or functions
8. Click on the cell and look at the data entry bar.
9. An absolute cell reference contains a $ sign (for example, $B$2). This indicates that the value is fixed. In the fill down process, this fixed value is used in all operations.
10. A relative cell reference is a cell reference without a $ sign. In the fill down process, the formula and data number in the cell changes to match the row number.
11. The number pattern increases by multiples of 5.
12. In cell B2, enter =A2*A2. Fill down to create square numbers in column B. Answers may vary. In C2, enter =A2*B2. Fill down to create cubic numbers in column C.

Extending Your Thinking

13. a) In cell A3, type =A2+1. Fill down to A13.

b) In cell C1, type =B1+1. Fill right to M1.

c) Answers may vary. For example: To fill column B — In B2, type =$B$1*A2 and fill down. To fill column C — In C2, type =$C$1*A2 and fill down. Continue the process to column M.

TUTORIAL 2.3

Investigation 1, page 79

1. a) $0.01 **b)** $0.01 **c)** $0.07 **d)** $0.08 **e)** $0.08

2. Round to the nearest cent

3. $0.08

4. For example, 7% tax is $0.08 for both $1.09 and $1.12. This is due to rounding.

5.

Cost Range	7% Tax
0.01 – 0.07	0.00
0.08 – 0.21	0.01
0.22 – 0.35	0.02
0.36 – 0.49	0.03
0.50 – 0.64	0.04
0.65 – 0.78	0.05
0.79 – 0.92	0.06
0.93 – 1.00	0.07

6. Tax on $1.00 is $0.07. Tax on $0.66 is $0.05.
Total tax = $0.07 + $0.05 = $0.12

7.

Cost Range	8% Tax
0.01 – 0.06	0.00
0.07 – 0.18	0.01
0.19 – 0.31	0.02
0.32 – 0.43	0.03
0.44 – 0.56	0.04
0.57 – 0.68	0.05
0.69 – 0.81	0.06
0.82 – 0.93	0.07
0.94 – 1.00	0.08

Investigation 2, page 80

3.

Year	Opening Value of the Bond ($)	Annual Interest Rate (%)	Interest Payments ($)	Closing Value of the Bond ($)
1998	1000.00	3.00	30.00	1000.00
1999	1000.00	4.00	40.00	1000.00
2000	1000.00	5.00	50.00	1000.00

4. The bond value does not change because the interest is paid to the owner.

5. Yes. The calculation in the third row is not dependent on prior calculations in the table.

6. The total interest earned by this bond is the sum of the values in the **Interest Payments ($)** column: 30 + 40 + 50 = 120

EXERCISES, page 82

Checking Your Skills

1. a)

Year	Opening Value of the Bond ($)	Annual Interest Rate (%)	Interest Payments ($)	Closing Value of the Bond ($)
1998	5000.00	3.00	150.00	5000.00
1999	5000.00	4.00	200.00	5000.00
2000	5000.00	5.00	250.00	5000.00
			600.00	

b) The interest earned by the $5000 bond is 5 times greater than the interest earned by the $1000 bond.

c) The total interest on a comparable bond of any value can be calculated as the Opening Bond Value × the sum of Annual Interest Rates. If x represents Opening Bond Value, then Total Interest = $0.12x$.

2. a)

Item	Price ($)	GST ($)	PST ($)	Total ($)
Cassette Tape	5.99	0.42	0.48	6.89
CD	16.75	1.17	1.34	19.26

b) Let x represent Price: GST = $0.07x$; PST = $0.08x$
Total = $x + 0.07x + 0.08x = 1.15x$

c)

Item	Price ($)	GST ($)	PST ($)	Total ($)
Cassette Tape	5.99	0.42	0.42	6.83
CD	16.75	1.17	1.17	19.09

3. a) The effective rate of PST is 10.7% of the original price (12.84 ÷ 120.00). But PST is actually calculated here by charging PST of 10% on the sum of the original price and the GST:
Let x represent Price. PST = $(x + 0.07x) \times 0.10$;
PST = $1.07x \times 0.10$; PST = $0.107x$

b) Table altered to reflect 6.5% PST, charged on price before taxes

Price ($)	GST ($)	PST ($)	Total ($)
120.00	8.40	7.80	136.20
275.00	19.25	17.88	312.13

c) 8%

4.

Chai Kim	Su	M	Tu	W	Th	F	Sa	Total Hours
	5.00	8.50	7.25	8.75	8.25	3.50	0.00	41.25
Regular Hourly Rate			Reg. Earnings ($)		OT Earnings ($)		Total Earnings ($)	
		8.50		340.00		21.25		361.25

Extending Your Thinking

5.

Ben Singh	Su	M	Tu	W	Th	F	Sa	Total Hours
Total Hours	0.00	9.50	7.00	10.75	4.50	8.75	0.00	40.50
Reg. Hours	0.00	8.00	7.00	8.00	4.50	8.00	0.00	35.50
OT Hours	0.00	1.50	0.00	2.75	0.00	0.75	0.00	5.00
Regular Hourly Rate			Reg. Earnings ($)		OT Earnings ($)		Total Earnings ($)	
		7.80		276.90		58.50		335.40

6. a) Total OT Hours/day = Total Hours – 8
Use only positive values.
Find the total number of regular hours and the total number of OT hours.
Total earnings = (Total reg.)(7.80) + (Total OT)(7.80)(1.5)

b)

Ben Singh	M	Tu	W	Th	F	Total
Total Hours	9.50	7.00	10.75	4.50	8.75	40.50
Reg. $7.80/h	8.00	7.00	8.00	4.50	8.00	35.50
OT $11.70/h	1.50	—	2.75	—	0.75	5.00
Earnings	Reg. hours	276.90	OT hours	58.50	Total	335.40

TUTORIAL 2.4

Investigation 1, page 85

1. Answers may vary. For the purposes of these solutions, let each page be 0.1 mm thick.

2.

Number of Cuts	Number of Layers	Thickness (mm)
0	1	0.1
1	2	0.2
2	4	0.4
3	8	0.8
4	16	1.6
5	32	3.2

3. For each cut the number of layers and the thickness doubles. Predicting three more folds:

Number of Cuts	Number of Layers	Thickness (mm)
6	64	6.4
7	128	12.8
8	256	25.6

4. a) The number of layers is double the number of layers in the previous row.

b) Let n represent the number of folds.
Layers $= 2^n$

5. Doubling the layers in the previous row is a recursive method.

6. Let n represent the number of folds.
Layers $= 2^n$
Thickness (mm) $= 2^n \times 0.1$

7. Answers may vary.

Investigation 2, page 86

3. The closing value of the bond is the sum of the opening value plus the interest payments.

4.

Year	Opening Value of the Bond ($)	Annual Interest Rate (%)	Interest Payments ($)	Closing Value of the Bond ($)
1998	1000.00	3.00	30.00	1030.00
1999	1030.00	4.00	41.20	1071.20
2000	1071.20	5.00	53.56	1124.76

5. No, since the third row of the table depends on the closing value of the bond in the second row.

6. Solution 1: Calculate the interest payments for each year and add them together.
Solution 2: Use the interest rates compounded yearly to calculate the final closing value of the bond. To find the interest paid, subtract the opening value. Let x represent the opening value.
Interest Payments $= 1.03x \times 1.04x \times 1.05x - x$
Interest Payments $= 1.12476x - x$
Interest Payments $= 1124.76 - 1000$, or 124.76

7. Compound interest savings bonds

8. Regular interest savings bonds pay the interest to the owner yearly, rather than at the end of the term.

Practise Your Prior Skills, page 88

1. 0.4 **2.** 3534

EXERCISES, page 89

Checking Your Skills

1. a) c)

Month	Units Sold in Month
Apr 97	28 000
May 97	56 000
Jun 97	112 000
Jul 97	224 000
Aug 97	448 000
Sep 97	896 000
Oct 97	1 792 000
Nov 97	3 584 000
Dec 97	7 168 000
Jan 98	4 300 800
Feb 98	2 580 480
Mar 98	1 548 288

b) 7 168 000 **c)** 22 737 568

d) Yes. However, at some point it will be impossible for sales to drop to exactly 60% of the previous month's sales, since this would involve fractions of a sale.

2. a)

Year	Previous Year's Salary ($)	Increase Rate (%)	Pay Increase ($)	Salary for the Year ($)
1	38 750.00	2.00	775.00	39 525.00
2	39 525.00	3.00	1185.75	40 710.75
3	40 710.75	1.00	407.11	41 117.86

b) Yes, the rows are related recursively. In each row, the pay increase cannot be calculated unless the previous year's salary has been calculated in the previous row.

c)

Year	Previous Year's Salary ($)	Increase Rate (%)	Pay Increase ($)	Salary for the Year ($)
1	38 750.00	2.00	775.00	39 525.00
2	39 525.00	2.00	790.50	40 315.50
3	40 315.50	2.00	806.31	41 121.81

3. a)

Year	Opening Value of the Bond ($)	Annual Interest Rate (%)	Interest Payments ($)	Closing Value of the Bond ($)
1997	5000.00	3.00	150.00	5150.00
1998	5150.00	4.00	206.00	5356.00
1999	5356.00	5.00	267.80	5623.80
			623.80	

b) Answers may vary.

4. a)

Year	Opening Balance ($)	Annual Interest Rate (%)	Interest Earned ($)	Closing Balance ($)
1	1000.00	4.00	40.00	1040.00
2	1040.00	4.00	41.60	1081.60
3	1081.60	4.00	43.26	1124.86
			124.86	

b) $1124.86 **c)** $124.86

5. a) Answers may vary. A common prediction might be that the interest earned would double.

b)

Year	Opening Balance ($)	Annual Interest Rate (%)	Interest Earned ($)	Closing Balance ($)
1	1000.00	8.00	80.00	1080.00
2	1080.00	8.00	86.40	1166.40
3	1166.40	8.00	93.31	1259.71
			259.71	

c) $259.71. The final interest earned at 8% is more than double the final interest earned at 4%.

6. a) To calculate the interest earned in each year, multiply the opening balance by the annual interest rate:
$1000 \times 0.04 = 40$

b) The opening balance of each row is the value of the closing balance in the row above.

7. a)

Year	Cost of Item Jan. 31 ($)	Inflation Rate (%)	Price Increase ($)	Cost of Item Dec. 31 ($)
1989	500.00	4.02	20.10	520.10
1990	520.10	4.82	25.07	545.17
1991	545.17	5.61	30.58	575.75
			75.75	

b)

Year	Cost of Item Jan. 31 ($)	Inflation Rate (%)	Price Increase ($)	Cost of Item Dec. 31 ($)
1989	80 000.00	4.02	3216.00	83 216.00
1990	83 216.00	4.82	4011.01	87 227.01
1991	87 227.01	5.61	4893.44	92 120.45
			12 120.45	

c) $4.03

Year	Cost of Item Jan. 31 ($)	Inflation Rate (%)	Price Increase ($)	Cost of Item Dec. 31 ($)
1989	3.50	4.02	0.14	3.64
1990	3.64	4.82	0.18	3.82
1991	3.82	5.61	0.21	4.03

8. a)

Day	Cost at Start of Day ($)	Discount ($)	Cost at End of Day ($)
1	249.00	24.90	224.10
2	224.10	22.41	201.69
3	201.69	20.17	181.52
4	181.52	18.15	163.37
5	163.37	16.34	147.03

b) No. The discount is not 10% of the original amount each day, but 10% of the previous day's amount, which is smaller than the original amount. Thus, the amount that is discounted decreases each day.

9.

Day	Distance Remaining at Start of day (m)	Distance Travelled Up (m)	Distance Remaining at End of day (m)	Distance Slid Back at Night (m)
1	30.00	3.00	27.00	1.00
2	28.00	3.00	25.00	1.00
3	26.00	3.00	23.00	1.00
4	24.00	3.00	21.00	1.00
5	22.00	3.00	19.00	1.00
6	20.00	3.00	17.00	1.00
7	18.00	3.00	15.00	1.00
8	16.00	3.00	13.00	1.00
9	14.00	3.00	11.00	1.00
10	12.00	3.00	9.00	1.00
11	10.00	3.00	7.00	1.00
12	8.00	3.00	5.00	1.00
13	6.00	3.00	3.00	1.00
14	4.00	3.00	1.00	1.00
15	2.00	2.00	0	0

Extending Your Thinking

10. a) The value of a regular bond always remains the same. The interest earned is paid out to the owner each year rather than added to the original amount of the bond.

c) For a regular interest bond, the interest earned in each year is calculated by multiplying the original value of the bond times the annual rate of interest. While the rate of interest can change, the value of the bond does not. For a compound interest bond, the value of the bond increases as interest is added to it. The interest earned in each year is calculated by multiplying the value of the bond at the end of the previous year by the annual rate of interest.

d) The formula **=Sum(D6:D12)** totals the interest earned each year on the regular bond, as calculated in cells D6 through D12.

e) The regular bond earned $3600.00 interest. The compound interest bond earned $4199.28 interest in the same period. The difference is $599.28.

f) The regular bond pays out its earned interest each year. The compound interest bond does not pay out any interest until the end of the full term of the bond. However, the compound interest bond earns more interest overall.

11. a)

Square	Wheat Grains	Square	Wheat Grains
1	1	32	2,147,483,648
2	2	33	4,294,967,296
3	4	34	8,589,934,592
4	8	35	17,179,869,184
5	16	36	34,359,738,368
6	32	37	68,719,476,736
7	64	38	137,438,953,472
8	128	39	274,877,906,944
9	256	40	549,755,813,888
10	512	41	1,099,511,627,776
11	1,024	42	2,199,023,255,552
12	2,048	43	4,398,046,511,104
13	4,096	44	8,796,093,022,208
14	8,192	45	17,592,186,044,416
15	16,384	46	35,184,372,088,832
16	32,768	47	70,368,744,177,664
17	65,536	48	140,737,488,355,328
18	131,072	49	281,474,976,710,656
19	262,144	50	562,949,953,421,312
20	524,288	51	1,125,899,906,842,620
21	1,048,576	52	2,251,799,813,685,250
22	2,097,152	53	4,503,599,627,370,500
23	4,194,304	54	9,007,199,254,740,990
24	8,388,608	55	18,014,398,509,482,000
25	16,777,216	56	36,028,797,018,964,000
26	33,554,432	57	72,057,594,037,927,900
27	67,108,864	58	144,115,188,075,856,000
28	134,217,728	59	288,230,376,151,712,000
29	268,435,456	60	576,460,752,303,423,000
30	536,870,912	61	1,152,921,504,606,850,000
31	1,073,741,824	62	2,305,843,009,213,690,000
32	2,147,483,648	63	4,611,686,018,427,390,000
33	4,294,967,296	64	9,223,372,036,854,780,000

b) Answers may vary. To increase the accuracy of measurement, use a larger number of grains of wheat (100, for instance) and divide the total mass by the quantity.

c), d), e), f) Answers may vary.

TUTORIAL 2.5

Computer Lab, page 96

1.

Year	Opening Balance ($)	Interest Rate (%)	Interest Charged ($)	Regular Payments ($)	Closing Balance ($)
1	25 000.00	9.00	2250.00	6427.31	20 822.69
2	20 822.69	9.00	1874.04	6427.31	16 269.42
3	16 269.42	9.00	1464.25	6427.31	11 306.36
4	11 306.36	9.00	1017.57	6427.31	5 896.62
5	5 896.62	9.00	530.70	6427.31	0.01
			7136.56		

a) Closing balance = Opening Balance + Interest Charged – Regular Payments

d) The total interest paid on the loan is $7136.56.

e) The total interest on the loan may be calculated by totaling the interest charged in each year, or by multiplying the regular payments by the number of years in the loan, and subtracting the opening balance. In this case: $6427.31 \times 5 - 25\ 000$. The second method assumes that the regular payments have been calculated to fully pay off the loan at the end of the term.

2. a) The annual payment would double to $12 854.62.
   b) The interest paid over five years would also be double: $14 273.12.

3. a) Over the longer term of the loan, there are five more instances when interest is charged. There is more total interest charged. Therefore, the annual payments must be larger to pay off the loan at the end of the term.
   b) Over ten years, there would be $13 955.03 interest paid.
   c) There is $6818.47 more interest paid for the 10-year loan than for the 5-year loan.

4. a) The annual payment is less: $3559.44.
   b) The annual payment is more: $4516.86.

5. a) The annual payment is $1203.17.
   b) The annual payment is $5288.45.

6. a) The annual payment is $2545.16.
   b) The annual payment is $10 375.44.

7. a) The total interest paid is $38 628.68.
   b) The total interest paid is $107 508.68.

8. b) The total payment made reduces from $38 955.03 to $38 127.00.
   c) The total interest paid reduces from $13 955.03 to $13 127.00.

9. a) $24 032.44 b) $15 786.82

EXERCISES, page 100

Checking Your Skills

1. a) 8 years
   b) The amount of annual payment is $17 072.70.
   c) The annual interest rate is 7.5%.

2. a)

Year	Opening Balance ($)	Interest Rate (%)	Interest Charged ($)	Regular Payments ($)	Closing Balance ($)
6	44 398.00	7.50	3329.85	17 072.70	30 655.15
7	30 655.15	7.50	2299.14	17 072.70	15 881.59
8	15 881.59	7.50	1191.12	17 072.70	0.01

   b) The total amount paid is $136 581.60.
   c) The interest paid is $36 581.60.

3. a) 43.9% b) 39.7% c) 25.1%

4. a) $277.95
   b) Closing balance = opening balance + opening balance × interest rate − annual payment
   Closing balance = 15 881.60 + 15 881.60 × 0.0925 − 17 072.70
   Closing balance = 15 881.60 + 1469.05 − 17 072.70
   Closing balance = 277.95

5. a)

Year	Opening Balance ($)	Interest Rate (%)	Interest Charged ($)	Regular Payments ($)	Extra Payments	Closing Balance ($)
1	100 000.00	7.50	7500.00	17 072.70		90 427.30
2	90 427.30	7.50	6782.05	17 072.70		80 136.65
3	80 136.65	7.50	6010.25	17 072.70		69 074.20
4	69 074.20	7.50	5180.56	17 072.70	20 000.00	37 182.06
5	37 182.06	7.50	2788.65	17 072.70		22 898.02
6	22 898.02	7.50	1717.35	17 072.70		7 542.67
7	7 542.67	7.50	565.70	8 108.37		0

5. b) $30 544.57 c) $6 037.03

6. a) $11 892.15 b) $24 676.20 c) $38 419.05

7. a) $12 522.82, $12 614.10
   b) $7451.47, $24 514.70 c) $5841.48, $37 622.20
   d) $5092.61, $51 852.20 e) $4683.94, $67 098.50
   f) As the term increases, the annual payment decreases, but the total interest paid increases.

8. a) $12 329.09, $23 290.90 b) $13 586.80, $35 868.00
   c) $14 902.95, $49 029.50 d) $17 698.42, $76 984.20
   e) $20 690.11, $106 901.10

Extending Your Thinking

9. a) Extra $4000 payment is made at end of year 16. Loan is paid off in year 20. Total interest decreases from $82 963.45 to $81 521.49.
   b) Extra $4000 payment is made at end of year 10. Loan is paid off in year 19. Total interest decreases from | $82 963.45 to $78 363.87.
   c) Extra $4000 payment is made at end of year 4. Loan is paid off in year 19. Total interest decreases from $82 963.45 to $73 671.22.
   d) Extra $4000 payment is made at end of year 1. Loan is paid off in year 18. Total interest decreases from $82 963.45 to $70 397.40.
   e) When an extra payment is made on a loan, it has the greatest effect when paid in early years. An extra payment reduces the amount of money on which interest is paid for all succeeding years. A payment in year 1 of a 20-year loan reduces the interest charged in the following 19 years. A payment in year 8 of a 20-year loan reduces the interest charged in only the following 12 years.

CONSOLIDATING YOUR SKILLS

What Should I Be Able To Do?, page 105

1. a) C3 b) C4 c) C5

2. a) 7791.00 b) 2788.37 c) 3228.05

3. 35 867.94
   74 369.04. The interest for 20 years is slightly more than double that for 10 years.

4. a) 191.08 b) 639.58

5. a) 7% c) 12.5%

8) The pricing method used in Exercise 8b results in a better return for the store.

CHAPTER 3 RELATIONS AND FUNCTIONS

TUTORIAL 3.1

EXERCISES, page 115

Checking Your Skills

1. a) Graph 2 or 3
   b) Graph 1 (or Graph 4 if we are looking at a short time interval)
   c) Graph 2, 3, or 4 d) Graph 4

2. Answers may vary.
   a) A ball thrown into the air: The ball reaches a maximum height and then falls to the ground.

b) The cost of mailing several packages: The postal rate increases in steps, depending on the weight of the package. For example, 0 g to 25 g costs $1.00, 25.1 g to 50.0 g costs $2.00, and 50.1 g to 75.0 g costs $3.00.

c) The electric charge stored by a battery as time passes: As the battery is used, the amount of charge it contains decreases.

d) The effect of the tide on water level at a particular location: The graph begins with mean sea level, rises to a maximum at high tide, falls through mean sea level to a minimum at low tide, then returns to mean sea level and the cycle begins again.

3. Answers may vary.

4. Answers may vary. The walk includes two stops.

5. Answers may vary.

6. Answers may vary.

Extending Your Thinking

7. Answers may vary.

TUTORIAL 3.2

Investigation 1, page 117

1., 2.

Length (cm)	Time for 5 cycles (s)
100	10.0
80	9.0
60	7.8
40	6.3
20	4.5

4. Yes. The pendulum can be any length over 0 cm.

5. 7.1 s; period 1.4 s

6. From the graph, the time for 5 cycles is about 7.1 s. Therefore the frequency of a pendulum that is 50 cm long is 0.7 cycles per second.

7. Find the length of 50 cm on the horizontal axis. Draw a vertical line from 50 cm upward to meet the graph. Then draw a horizontal line from this point on the graph to the vertical axis. The point where the horizontal line meets the vertical axis is the time for 5 cycles. Divide the time by 5 to get the time for one cycle. Then take the reciprocal of this number to get the frequency. The frequency for other pendulum lengths can be predicted using the same method.

Investigation 2, page 118

1., 2., 3. Answers may vary.

4. No. Each point represents the measurement for one person.

5., 6. Answers may vary.

Investigation 3, page 119

1. 2, 3, 4, 5, 6, 7, 8, 9, 10, 11, 12

2., 3., 4. Answers may vary.

5. No. The points should not be connected because only whole number results are possible.

6. The chance of getting the middle sums is greater because there are more ways to get them.

Investigation 4, page 120

1., 2. Answers may vary.

3. It is appropriate to represent the situation with a smooth curve because the time can be any value and there is a temperature at each time.

4. Answers may vary.

5. The drink might have cooled more slowly. The difference in the temperature from 0 min to 20 min would have been less.

TUTORIAL 3.3

EXERCISES, page 127

Checking Your Skills

2. b) $100. Answers may vary.
c) $600

3. a) The highest power of x is 1.
b) Powers of x are greater than 1.
c) There is only one value of y for each value of x.

4. a) The distance increases from zero until the object reaches the ground.
b) From 20 m, 2.0 s; from 30 m, 2.5 s
c) On a planet with no air, the speed at which an object falls does not depend on its mass. On Earth, air resistance affects the motion of objects. Thus the speed at which an object falls on Earth does depend on factors such as its mass, size, shape, and its smoothness.

5. a) The salesperson's earnings increase in a straight line from the basic salary of $2083.33. For every $1000 in merchandise she sells, her earnings increase by $30.
b) From the graph, approximately $14 000; from the formula, $13 889
c) $41 666.67 per month; approximately $500 000 for the year. Answers may vary.
d) Answers may vary.

Extending Your Thinking

6. a) Answers may vary. You can modify the formulas as follows to give the answers in units of billions:
$P = 6(1.01)^x$, $P = 6(1.03)^x$, $P = 6(1.005)^x$

b)

Average annual population increase (%)	Predicted population in billions, 2010	Predicted population in billions, 2050
1	7.035	10.475
3	9.628	31.408
0.5	6.498	7.933

c) For 0.5% annual increase, 2132; for 1% annual increase, 2063; for 3% annual increase, 2017;

d) Answers may vary.

TUTORIAL 3.4

EXERCISES, page 132

Checking Your Skills

1. i)

A	B
1	–1
2	0
3	1
4	2
5	3
6	4

ii)

H	K
–4	–8
–1	–2
0	0
3	6
5	10
9	18

iii)

J	J + 2
–6	–4
–2	0
0	2
1	3
2	4
3	7

iv)

R	R^2
–3	9
–1	1
0	0
1	1
2	4
6	36

b) They all represent functions. For each input, there is only one output.

c) i) Subtract 2 from the input. **ii)** Multiply the input by 2. **iii)** Add 2 to the input. **iv)** Square the input.

d) i) $y = x - 2$ **ii)** $y = 2x$

2. a)

Months	Cost
1	400
2	800
4	1600
8	3200
12	4800
16	6400
20	8000
24	9600

c) $C = 400n$

3. a)

Time (in min)	0	1	10	20	29	30	40	50	59	60
Cost (in $)	0	2	2	2	2	4	4	4	4	6

b) The cost of parking is $2.00 for every half hour or part thereof.

4. Answers may vary.

5. a)

Time (in hours)	0	1	2	3	4	5	6	7	8
Total area lost (acres)	0	240	480	720	960	1200	1440	1680	1920

c) $A = 240t$

Extending Your Thinking

6. Answers may vary.

TUTORIAL 3.5

Investigation, page 138

1.–5. Answers may vary.

6. No. Each trial is a discrete event. You cannot have part of a trial.

7. The natural numbers from 1 up to the last trial, after which no candies remain

8. The whole numbers from 0 to 100

EXERCISES, page 143

Checking Your Skills

1. Domain; all real numbers between –2 and 2
Range; all real numbers between zero and 2

2. a) Domain; all real numbers greater than or equal to 0.5
$x \geq 0.5$
Range; all real numbers greater than or equal to zero
$y \geq 0$

b) 0.5 min Answers may vary. May be lag time for machine

3. a)

Speed (km/h)	40	50	64	80	100
Time (h)	2	1.6	1.25	1	0.8

b) Yes. The speed can be any value between 40 and 100 km/h.

c) Any value between 40 and 100, including 40 and 100. The domain of the function

d) Any value between 0.8 and 2. The range of the function

4. b) The domain of the graph is 0 to 6. Madison is paid for at least half an hour once the job begins. No job is longer than 6 h. The range is 1.5, 3.0, 4.5, 6.0, 7.5, 9.0, 10.5, 12.0, 13.5, 15.0, 16.5, 18.0.

5. a)

Term of the sequence	1	2	3	4	5	6	7	8	9	10	11
Value of the term	2	4	8	16	32	64	128	256	512	1024	2048
Units digit of the term	2	4	8	6	2	4	8	6	2	4	8

b) No. The points represent unconnected measurements.

c) The domain is 2, 4, 8, 16, 32, 64, 128, 256, 512, 1024, 2048. The range is 2, 4, 6, 8.

d) The units digit repeats every 4 terms: 2, 4, 8, 6, 2, 4, 8, 6, ...

e) 2^{113} is the first term in round 29 of the sequence. The units digit will be 2.

6. The domain of the circle is 0 to 8. The range of the circle is 0 to 8.

Extending Your Thinking

7. Using the Pythagorean Theorem, $5^2 = x^2 + y^2$. Therefore x and y can be any values such that the sum of their squares equals 25.

TUTORIAL 3.6

EXERCISES, page 150

Checking Your Skills

1. a) 50°F equals 10°C.

b) Freezing temperature is 32°F. Boiling temperature is 212°F.

c) 356°F **d)** 218°C

2. a) Answers may vary. The number of animals in the population is a function of the time since the study began.

b) $N(0) = 50$; $N(1) = 54.2$; $N(-1) = 46.2$. Explanations may vary.

3. a) Answers may vary. **b)** 4

4. $y = 11 - 2x$ Domain; all real numbers. Range; all real numbers.

5. a) 2 **b)** 6 **c)** Answers may vary.

Extending Your Thinking

6. a) b) c)

Functions Group A

Equation	$y = x$	$y = 2x + 3$	$x + 3y = 6$	$y = 2$
Domain	$x \in R$	$x \in R$	$x \in R$	$x \in R$
Range	$y \in R$	$y \in R$	$y \in R$	$y \in 2$
Similarities of graphs	All the graphs are straight lines.			
Similarities of equations	In each equation, the highest power of x is 1.			

Functions Group B

Equation	$y = x^2$	$x^2 + y = 3$	$2x^2 - y - 5 = 0$	$y = x(x - 2)$
Domain	$x \in R$	$x \in R$	$x \in R$	$x \in R$
Range	$y \geq 0$	$y \leq 3$	$y \geq 5$	$y \geq -1$
Similarities of graphs	All the graphs are U-shaped.			
Similarities of equations	In each equation, the highest power of x is 2.			

Functions Group C

Equation	$y = x^3$	$y = x^3 - 2$	$y = 0.5x^3 + 3$	$y = x(x - 2)^2$
Domain	$x \in R$	$x \in R$	$x \in R$	$x \in R$
Range	$y \in R$	$y \in R$	$y \in R$	$y \in R$
Similarities of graphs	All the graphs rise steeply the farther from the origin you go. The first three graphs rise gradually near the origin. The fourth graph dips near the origin.			
Similarities of equations	In each equation, the highest power of x is 3.			

Functions Group D

Equation	$y = 2^x$	$y = 1.5^x$	$y = 1.5^{3x}$	$y = 4^{-3x}$
Domain	$x \in R$	$x \in R$	$x \in R$	$x \in R$
Range	$y > 0$	$y > 0$	$y > 0$	$y > 0$
Similarities of graphs	All the graphs have a zone of gentle rise or descent and a zone of very steep rise or descent.			
Similarities of equations	All the equations have x as an exponent.			

Consolidating Your Skills

What Should I Be Able To Do?, page 157

1. a) 5

Number of Layer	Pyramidal Number
1	1
2	5
3	14
4	30
5	55

One represents the topmost layer in any square-based pyramid.
$1^2 = 1$

b) No. Each layer is discrete. You cannot have part of a layer.

c) $P_n = P_{(n-1)} + n^2$

d) Domain: All positive integers
Range: Positive integers which result as output from $P_n = P_{(n-1)} + n^2$

e) There is only one output for each input.

f) $P_6 = 1^2 + 2^2 + 3^2 + 4^2 + 5^2 + 6^2$

2. a) Answers may vary. **b)** Answers may vary.

3. a) Time; temperature **b)** Answers may vary.

4. No. There are two output values for the input of 9.

5. b) $y = 4x$ $y = x^2 - 1$ $y = 2x - 1$

6. b) Domain: All integers greater than or equal to zero
Range: All real numbers greater than or equal to 35

c) 65.00 **d)** Cost of 250 newsletters

7. a) $d = \sqrt{100^2 + h^2}$

c) Domain: All real numbers greater than or equal to zero, but less than or equal to 2000
$0 \leq h \leq 2000$
Range: All real numbers greater than or equal to 100, but less than or equal to 2002
$100 \leq d \leq 2002$

d) The distance when the height is 50 m

CHAPTER 4 SAMPLING

TUTORIAL 4.1

Investigation 1, page 166

1., 2. Answers may vary.

3. Answers may vary. The percentage of "only children" in the small sample probably does not compare well to the actual percentage in the class.

4., 5. Answers may vary.

Investigation 2, page 167

Answers may vary.

EXERCISES, page 168

Checking Your Skills

1. Answers may vary.
a) Random sample of population of city
b)–e) Random sample of Canadians

2. Answers may vary.
a) Students over the legal age for driving
b) All students and staff
c) All students

3. Answers may vary.
a) You are deciding what to wear for a special occasion, so you ask some family members for their opinions.
b) You are deciding what school club to join, so you ask some of your friends what clubs they are going to join.
c) The boss wants to know how her employees are feeling about the company lately, so she asks the opinions of a few of them.
d) A small quantity of your blood is taken for a blood test.

4. It is extremely expensive to gather information about all of a large population. As well, it is difficult to be sure that all of the population has been located. Finally, unless the information is gathered quickly, the population may change while it is being studied.

5.,6.,7. Answers may vary.

Extending Your Thinking

8., 9. Larger samples usually give better results than smaller ones, provided that they are still representative of the population.

TUTORIAL 4.2

Investigation 1, page 171

Answers may vary.

Investigation 2, page 172

1. Yes

2.–5. Answers may vary.

6. Only if the agreement was very strong

EXERCISES, page 174

Checking Your Skills

1. a), b) Answers may vary.

c) The result may not be valid because one class in a Canadian high school is not a representative sample of world opinion.

2. Validity depends on what the population is. If the population is the magazine's readers, then the results may be valid. If the population is all the people in the country, then the results may not be valid, since the respondents to the survey may not be a representative sample. The results are not likely to be reliable, but that can only be determined by repeating the survey a few times.

3. The results are not likely to be valid since the sample that voted is not likely to be representative of the whole population. Whether the results are likely to be reliable is debatable; perhaps only the most motivated people vote during a snowstorm, so roughly the same people might vote again if another storm occurred. However, if a storm hits a different part of the community, perhaps different people would be able to vote.

4. The advertisers want us to conclude that 75% of all dentists prefer their product, but they don't tell us anything about the sample size or whether the sample was representative. Maybe the sample size was only 4, and the 3 who preferred their product were paid large sums of money to say so!

5. This depends on the population, what kind of sample was taken, and how large the school is.

6. Answers may vary.

7. The key question to consider is whether a fire fighter needs to be tall and strong in order to do a good job.

8. Answers may vary.

Extending Your Thinking

9. Answers may vary.

TUTORIAL 4.3

EXERCISES, page 178

Checking Your Skills

1. This is a self-selected sample; it is not representative of the population so reliability will probably be low.

2. Answers may vary. The voters are a self-selected sample drawn from the readers who are a biased sample of the population as a whole. Reliability will be low.

3. Answers may vary. This is a convenience sampling to find tasters. Voters are a self-selected sample from among the tasters. The sampling of the recipes is not random. Reliability will be low.

4. Answers may vary.

5. The sample may be biased, considering the population as a whole. The method may be appropriate, however, since the population that the station is interested in is the viewers of the station.

6. Workers may not produce items of the same quality at different times of the day. Thus, selecting items made at different times of the day is likely to produce more valid results.

Extending Your Thinking

7. Answers may vary. The most popular players are not necessarily the best players. Also, selectors usually are more knowledgeable about local players than those who are far away or play for teams from smaller cities. Thus, there is a bias toward selecting players on teams from larger cities, since teams from larger cities are likely to have more fans than those from smaller cities.

TUTORIAL 4.4

EXERCISES, page 184

Checking Your Skills

1. This sample is not random, since only viewers of the television program will respond. Thus, not all members of the population have an equal chance of being in the sample. Furthermore, the sample is self-selected; only those viewers who wish to respond will respond.

2. Systematic sampling

3. Answers may vary.

a) Assign a number to every student and then choose the numbers randomly, using, for example, the telephone-book method.

b) You could select the 5th car in each row.

c) You could select all residents who have certain postal codes, or all residents who have certain digits for the first 3 digits of their telephone numbers.

d) You could select a certain number of strawberries from each plant.

4., 5., 6. Answers may vary.

7. Answers may vary. A systematic sample would involve testing every 20th item, for example, or testing an item from the production line at regular intervals, say every 15 min.

Extending Your Thinking

8. Answers may vary. For a stratified random sample: Sample a number of students from each grade level in proportion to the size of each grade level. This would involve 6 from grade 8, 8 from grade 9, 9 from grade 10 and so on.

TUTORIAL 4.5

EXERCISES, page 189

Checking Your Skills

1., 2. Answers may vary.

Extending Your Thinking

3. Answers may vary.

CONSOLIDATING YOUR SKILLS

What Should I Be Able To Do?, page 193

1., 2., 3., 4. Answers may vary.

5. Answers may vary.
- **a)** Those who have strong opinions in favour or against the new course.
- **b)** The results may not be valid, since the respondents may not represent the population of grade 10–12 math teachers as a whole.
- **c)** Self-selected

6., 7. Answers may vary.

CHAPTER 5 LINE SEGMENTS

TUTORIAL 5.1

Practise Your Prior Skills, page 200

1. A(3, 2); B(–5, –3); C(0, 4)

2. The coordinates of all points in quadrant IV will be positive for x and negative for y.

Investigation 1, page 201

1. 150 m

2. Subtract 800 from 950.

3. Subtract 800 from 950.

4. Yes. Explanations may vary.
The order is important because we want to find the magnitude of the number not the direction, 'down' being negative.

5. Subtract the smaller y-coordinate from the larger one.

6. Subtract the smaller x-coordinate from the larger one.

Practise Your Prior Skills, page 202

1. 14.6
2. 3.9

Investigation 2, page 202

3. AC = 5; BC = 7

4. $AB^2 = AC^2 + CB^2$

5. AB = 8.6

EXERCISES, page 207

Checking Your Skills

1. 11

2. Along roads 360 m
Direct path 268.3 m

3. a) 8.5
b) i) 38 **ii)** 35.0

4. 2200 units

5. a) FS = 322 nautical miles; FC = 286 nautical miles; C is closer.
b) Answers may vary. Tide direction, water currents, rocks

6. 5.5 units No. Explanations may vary.

7. Answers may vary.
10.8 m + 20.1 m + 30.1 + 10.0 m+30.0 m = 101 m

Extending Your Thinking

8. a) AB = 21.1 km, BC = 25.1 km, CA = 32.8 km
b) 264.2 km^2

9. b) ii) The x-coordinate increases and the y-coordinate stays the same.
d) 71.13
e) iii) They are all 120°. **iv)** 30°, 60°, 90°
f) i) CD = 50, BD = 28.9, BC = 57.7
ii) $\frac{BD}{BC} = \frac{1}{2}$
iii) $\frac{CD}{BD} = \sqrt{3} = 1.73$

TUTORIAL 5.2

Investigation 2, page 214

2. b), c)

Time (h)	Distance from Ici (km)
0	0
1	60
2	120
3	180
4	240

f) 60 km/h; slope of graph is speed of car.
g) Answers may vary. Speed would probably not be held constant.

3. b), c)

Time (h)	Distance from Ici (km)
0	30
1	130
2	230
3	330
4	430

f) 100 km/h; slope of graph = speed of car

4. b), c)

Time (h)	Distance from Ici (km) for model car A	Distance from Ici (km) for model car B
0	0	40
1	50	70
2	100	100
3	150	130
4	200	160

f) 50 km/h, 30 km/h; slope of graph = speed of car
g) This is the place where Car A overtakes Car B.

Investigation 4, page 217

4. AC = 13

5. BC = 10

x-coordinate of A	y-coordinate of A	x-coordinate of B	y-coordinate of B	Rise	Run	Slope of AB
–2	–3	11	7	10	13	$\frac{10}{13}$
1	4	9	–15	–19	8	–2.375

9. Rise = y-coordinate of B – y-coordinate of A
Run = x-coordinate of B – x-coordinate of A

10. slope = $\frac{y\text{-coordinate of B} - y\text{-coordinate of A}}{x\text{-coordinate of B} - x\text{-coordinate of A}}$

TUTORIAL 5.3

EXERCISES, page 224

Checking Your Skills

1. $-\frac{5}{3}$ or -1.67

2.

Line Segment	Slope
AB	1.5
BC	undefined
CD	–1.5
DE	0
EF	1.5
FG	undefined
GH	–1.5
HA	0

3. $\frac{1}{3}$

4. $k = -1$

5. a) Diagrams will vary. The roller coaster climbs from A to B and from E to F; it drops from C to D and from G to H.
b) Hill BC, 12 m; hill FG, 8 m
c) AB has the steeper climb, since it has slope = 1. EF has slope = 0.8.
d) GH has the same slope as CD. Both have slope = 1.
e) They have different runs.
f) A steeper track means a faster ride.

6. 0.4, –0.9

7. b) 0.2 cm/day = $\frac{1}{5}$ cm/day
c) 0.2 cm/day; 1.4 cm/week
d) The answers are the same. The slope of the line is the rate of change of the height of the plant.

8. Answers will vary.

9. b) 1 m/s, 2 m/s, 3 m/s, 5 m/s, 4 m/s; these slopes represent average speeds for the car during the corresponding time intervals.
d) 1 m/s^2, 1 m/s^2, 1 m/s^2, 2 m/s^2, –1 m/s^2; these slopes represent the average rates of change of speed for the car during the corresponding time intervals. The common word for this is acceleration.
e) Positive acceleration means that the car is speeding up, and negative acceleration means that the car is slowing down.

10. a) 0.13, –0.02, –0.17, –0.025
b) In all but the second section

Extending Your Thinking

11. Coordinates (17, 4), (22, 10), (25, 8), (30, 6), (31, 2), (37,1)
Length
i) 15.6 m **ii)** 10.6 m **iii)** 7.8 m **iv)** 3.6 m
v) 5.4 m **vi)** 4.1 m **vii)** 6.1 m

12. a) Answers may vary.
b) 3.5 m **c)** 3.75 m

TUTORIAL 5.4

Investigation 1, page 232

3., 4., 5. Slopes are the same, unless both lines are vertical, in which case neither has a slope.

6. Parallel line segments have the same slope, unless they are both vertical, in which case neither has a slope.

7. Answers may vary. The rule makes sense because parallel lines have the same rise and run.

Investigation 2, page 233

1., 2., 3. Answers may vary.

4., 5., 6. Each slope is the negative reciprocal of the other, unless one line is horizontal and the other is vertical, in which case one slope is zero and the other does not exist.

7. The slopes of perpendicular line segments are negative reciprocals of each other, unless one is horizontal and the other is vertical, in which case one slope is zero and the other does not exist.

8. Answers may vary.

Investigation 4, page 235

3.–7. Answers may vary.

EXERCISES, page 236

Checking Your Skills

1. a) AB and CD are parallel.

2. a) $-\frac{3}{2}$ **b)** $-\frac{8}{5}$ **c)** 3 **d)** $\frac{1}{2}$

3. Line segments JK and LM are perpendicular
Slope JK$\frac{4}{3}$; Slope LM $-\frac{3}{4}$

Extending Your Thinking

4. b) Slope OD 10.16
The slope represents distance per second; Bailey's speed.
c) Slope OM 10.35
The slope represents distance per second; Johnson's speed.
d) Michael Johnson covers a greater distance per second. Johnson is faster.
e) Answers may vary.
f) 0.36 s

TUTORIAL 5.5

Investigation 1, page 238

5. (3, 1)

8. The x-coordinate of the midpoint is the average of the x-coordinates of the two endpoints.

9. The y-coordinate of the midpoint is the average of the y-coordinates of the two endpoints.

10. If the endpoints are (a, b) and (c, d), then the coordinates of the midpoint are $\left(\frac{a+c}{2}, \frac{b+d}{2}\right)$.

11. (6, 4)

12. (0, 5.5), (1.5, –6.5), (–2.5, 3.5)

Investigation 2, page 239

13. The x-coordinate of the midpoint is the average of the x-coordinates of the two endpoints.

14. The y-coordinate of the midpoint is the average of the y-coordinates of the two endpoints.

15. If the endpoints are (a, b) and (c, d), then the coordinates of the midpoint are $\left(\frac{a+c}{2}, \frac{b+d}{2}\right)$.

Investigation 3, page 241

All answers are approximate in this investigation.

3. (10.0, 7.0)

4. (7.2, 5.5)

5. (7.2, 4.7), (7.2, 4.8), (7.2, 4.5)

EXERCISES, page 244

Checking Your Skills

1. The highway is perpendicular to the line segment joining the two towns and passes through the midpoint of the line segment joining the towns, (7807, 3003).

2. False.

3. (5.5, 8.05); $330 816.82

4. (500, 500), (1500, 800), (3500, 800), (6000, 500)

5. a) Diagrams may vary.

d) Opposite sides of the new quadrilateral have the same length and slope.

e) The figure formed by joining the midpoints of the sides of any quadrilateral is a parallelogram.

6. a) Diagrams may vary.

e), f) The line joining the midpoints of two sides of a triangle has half of the length of the third side and is parallel to the third side.

Extending Your Thinking

7. (6, 6.1)

CONSOLIDATING YOUR SKILLS

What Should I Be Able To Do?, page 249

1.–4. Answers may vary.

5. 220; slope 1

6. Answers may vary.

7. a) 10 including direct paths only

b) 150 m by direct routes

c) 108.17 m

8. $\frac{2}{5}$

9. a), b), c)

Line	Slope	Midpoint	Line	Slope	Relation to $\triangle ABC$
AB	–1	P(–1, 1)	RQ	–1	parallel to AB
BC	4	Q(3, 2)	RP	4	parallel to BC
CA	$\frac{1}{4}$	R(0, 5)	PQ	$\frac{1}{4}$	parallel to CA

10. Diagonals PR, slope 1; QS, slope –1. PR and QS are perpendicular.

11. a) (0, 13), (7, 0), (7, 13) **b)** 1.84 m

12. Answers may vary. (0, 6.5), (3.4, 13), (4.75, 0), (7, 4)

13. Four. The shortest path is by (7, 4).

CHAPTER 6 LINEAR FUNCTIONS

TUTORIAL 6.1

Investigation 1, page 256

Answers may vary.

Practise Your Prior Skills, page 257

1. $y = 5x - 6$

2. $y = -3x + 1$

3. $y = 5x - 3$

4. $y = \frac{1}{2} - \frac{3}{2}x$

Investigation 2, page 257

3. $y = 2x + 3$, $y - 3 = 2x$, $y = -x + 3$, $y + 5 = x$, $y = 0.75x + 4$

4. All of the terms in these equations are terms that have degree 1 or zero. Thus there are no powers greater than 1, and x and y are not multiplied or divided by one another. Furthermore, there are no square roots or other more complicated radicals.

Investigation 3, page 258

2. (0, 4) **3.** (–0.8, 0)

4.

Equation	x-intercept	y-intercept
$y = x - 3$	(3, 0)	(0, ⁻3)
$y = 5x + 6$	$\left(-\frac{6}{5}, 0\right)$	(0, 6)
$y = 3x + 4$	$\left(-\frac{4}{3}, 0\right)$	(0, 4)
$y - 2x = 1$	(–0.5, 0)	(0, 1)
$2y + x = 2$	(2, 0)	(0, 1)

5. $x = 0$; $x = 0$ for all points on the y-axis

6. $y = 0$; $y = 0$ for all points on the x-axis

TUTORIAL 6.2

Investigation 1, page 260

3. All of the graphs pass through the point (0, 2).

4. All of the equations are of the form y = (a term involving x) + (a constant term). In each equation, the constant term is 2.

5. Each graph has a different slope.

6. The coefficient of x is different in each equation.

7. 2

8. The graph pivots about the point (0, 2). As m increases, the line pivots counterclockwise. As m decreases, the line pivots clockwise.

9. m represents the slope of the line.

Investigation 2, page 261

3. The graphs all have the same slope; in other words, the lines are all parallel.

4. The coefficient of x is 2 in each equation.

5. The intercepts of each graph are different.

6. The constant term is different in each equation.

7. As b increases, the line moves up the page, remaining parallel to the original line. As b decreases, the line moves down the page, remaining parallel to the original line.

8. b represents the y-intercept of the graph.

Investigation 3, page 261

3.

Graph	Slope	y-intercept
$y=5$	0	5
$y=2$	0	2
$y=-4$	0	−4

4. As b increases, the line moves up the page, remaining parallel to the original line. As b decreases, the line moves down the page, remaining parallel to the original line. The line $y = b$ has slope 0 and y-intercept b.

5. The graph of the equation $x = 3$ is a vertical line through the point (3, 0). Graphing calculators can only graph functions, and this equation does not represent a function.

6. The line $x = 3$ has no slope; an attempt to calculate its slope yields division by zero, which makes no sense. Since the line does not intersect the y-axis, it has no y-intercept.

7. As a increases, the line moves to the right, remaining parallel to the original line. As a decreases, the line moves to the left, remaining parallel to the original line.

8. The line $x = a$ has no slope; an attempt to calculate its slope yields division by zero, which makes no sense. Since the line does not intersect the y-axis, it has no y-intercept.

EXERCISES, page 264

Checking Your Skills

1.

Equation	Slope	y-intercept
$y=2x+3$	2	3
$y=-x+5$	−1	5
$y=\frac{3}{2}x+3$	$\frac{3}{2}$	3

2. a) $m = 1$; the slope is 1.
   b) $b = 0$; The x-intercept and the y-intercept are both zero at the point (0, 0).

3.

	Equation	Slope	y-intercept
a)	$y=-4x+2$	−4	2
b)	$y=-2x+8$	−2	8
c)	$y=\frac{5}{2}x+\frac{7}{2}$	$\frac{5}{2}$	$\frac{7}{2}$
d)	$y=-\frac{5}{3}x-\frac{1}{3}$	$-\frac{5}{3}$	$\frac{1}{3}$
e)	$y=-\frac{3}{5}x-6$	$-\frac{3}{5}$	−6
f)	$y=\frac{x}{3}-\frac{5}{3}$	$\frac{1}{3}$	$-\frac{5}{3}$

4.

	x-intercept	y-intercept	Slope	Domain	Range
a)	0	0	$\frac{1}{3}$	R	R
b)	none	3	0	R	3
c)	4	none	none	4	R
d)	−15	5	$\frac{1}{3}$	R	R

6. $y = -2$; x is a real number between −2 and 2.
   $y = 2$; x is a real number between −2 and 2.
   $x = -2$; y is a real number between −2 and 2.
   $x = 2$; y is a real number between −2 and 2.

7.

	x-intercept	y-intercept	Slope	Domain	Range
a)	0	0	2	0, 1, 2, 3, 4, 5, 6	0, 2, 4, 6, 8, 10, 12
b)	0	0	−1	−3, −2, −1, 0, 1, 2, 3	−3, −2, −1, 0, 1, 2, 3

Extending Your Thinking

8. $y = -\frac{A}{B}x - \frac{C}{B}$, provided that B does not equal 0. Note that $m = -\frac{A}{B}$ (provided that $B \neq 0$), the x-intercept is $-\frac{C}{A}$ (provided that $A \neq 0$), and the y-intercept is $-\frac{C}{B}$ (provided that $B \neq 0$).

TUTORIAL 6.3

EXERCISES, page 271

Checking Your Skills

1. a) Yes. The function is continuous. You can find distance for fractions of a minute travelled.
   b) Domain: all times between 0 and 46; range: all distances between 0 and 23
   c) Slope is −0.5 nautical miles/minute. Vertical intercept is 23 nautical miles.
   d) The slope represents the rate at which the distance between the helicopter and the boat is changing. Because the distance is decreasing the slope is negative. The magnitude of the slope, 0.5 nautical miles/minute, is the speed of the helicopter, assuming that the boat is at rest. The vertical intercept represents the distance from the helicopter to the boat at time $t = 0$.
   e) The horizontal intercept is 46 min. It represents the time when the helicopter reaches the boat.

2. a) No. The function is not continuous. You cannot sell fractions of a ticket.
   b) \$25
   c) \$12 000
   d) 480
   e) \$113 000

3. a) It is a continuous function. The boiling point T°C, can be found for any height in fractions of a metre.
   b) −0.0034, 100
   c) The slope represents the rate of change of the boiling point of water; thus, the boiling point of water decreases by 0.0034°C for every metre that the height increases. The vertical intercept represents the boiling point of water at sea level.
   d) The horizontal intercept represents the height above sea level at which the boiling point of water is 0°C. This seems strange, since 0°C is the freezing point of water at sea level! No doubt the formula is valid only up to a certain height.
   e) 69.92°C

4. b) 180 kg/barrel; the slope represents the density of the oil (each barrel of oil has a mass of 180 kg).
   c) 14 000 kg; the vertical intercept represents the mass of the truck when it has no oil in it.

d) $0 \le V \le 500$

e) $14\ 000 \le M \le 104\ 000$

5. a) Tables may vary.

s	*d*
0	0
15	3

b) 5 km **c)** 5 km/h

6. b) 2.1 km

7. Even when the object is not touching the fluid (depth = 0), there is still some pressure. This is due to the air pressing on the object. (Air pressure depends on altitude and weather conditions, but is approximately 100 kPa at sea level.) The deeper the object is submerged, the greater the pressure on the object.

Extending Your Thinking

8. See your calculator manual.

9. a) The car starts at position 0 and travels for 3 h at a speed of 80 km/h, reaching a distance of 240 km away from the starting position. Then the car stops and remains motionless for 1 h. Then the car goes back to its starting position, travelling at a speed of 60 km/h, and reaching the starting position in 4 more hours. The total travel time is 8 h.

b) 124 km/h

TUTORIAL 6.4

Investigation 1, page 275

2.

Bridge	Struts
1	3
2	7
3	11
4	15
5	19

4. The points should not be connected because there are only whole numbers for the number of bridges.

5. Add one to the number of bridges and four to the number of struts.

6. The natural numbers

7. The slope is 4. For every addition to the number of the bridge the number of struts increases by four. This corresponds to a slope of four.

8.

Bridge	Triangles
1	1
2	3
3	5
4	7
5	9

9. No. The points should not be connected because there are only whole numbers of triangles. Add one to the number of bridges and two to the number of triangles. The domain is the natural numbers. The slope is 2. For every addition to the number of bridges, the number of triangles increases by two. This corresponds to a slope of two.

Investigation 2, page 276

1.

Copies	Cost (cents)
1	8
2	16
3	24
4	32
5	40
6	48
7	56
8	64
9	72
10	80

2. Natural numbers from 1 to 10 inclusive

4. No. It only makes sense to make a whole number of copies.

5. The slope is 8.

6. $Cost_n = Cost_{(n-1)} + 8$

7. For every increase by one sheet, the cost increases by 8 cents; this is the same as a slope of 8.

8. $C = 8n$

EXERCISES, page 278

Checking Your Skills

1. b) 5800 **c)** 31

2. a) Tables may vary.

Books	Cost ($)
50	8 200
100	8 400
150	8 600
200	8 800
250	9 000
500	10 000
750	11 000
1000	12 000

b) The points should not be connected because the number of books increases in batches of 50. The function is not continuous.

c) $11 600

d) Slope = 4; vertical intercept = 8000. The slope represents the cost per yearbook, not taking into account the initial set-up charges. The vertical intercept represents the initial set-up charges.

e) Domain: natural numbers divisible by 50; range: 8200, 8400, 8600, 8800, ...

f) The graph would be similar to the one drawn in part b. The slope of the new graph would be less (3 instead of 4), and the vertical intercept would be more (8400 instead of 8000).

3. a) Tables may vary.

Number of storeys	Length of cable
1	32
5	112
10	212
15	312
20	412
25	512
30	612

b) No. A building has a whole number of storeys.

c) The natural numbers 1, 2, 3, ...

d) 12; this is the number of metres of cable required in addition to the amount of cable per storey

4. a) Tables may vary.

People	Batter (cups)
0	0
6	4
12	8

b) The natural numbers 1, 2, 3, ..., since we can have only a whole number of people

c) 20

d) 18

5. a) Tables may vary.

Amount of Purchase	Number of Quarters in Change
2	72
6	56
10	40
14	12
18	8

c) Domain: multiples of 0.25 between 0.25 and 20 inclusive; range: whole numbers between 0 and 79 inclusive

d) Domain: multiples of 0.25 between 0.25 and 10 inclusive; range: whole numbers between 0 and 39 inclusive

6. Answers may vary.

Extending Your Thinking

7. b) The lines cross at (400, 9600). This point represents the number of yearbooks for which the cost is the same for each company. For 400 yearbooks ordered, each company charges $9600.

c) As you can see from the graph, for fewer than 400 yearbooks, Blue Heron is cheaper. For more than 400 yearbooks, Miles Ahead is cheaper.

TUTORIAL 6.5

EXERCISES, page 284

Checking Your Skills

1. a)

Time Travelled	Distance from Winnipeg (km)
0	87
1	162
2	237
3	312
4	387

c) The slope is 75. The y-intercept is 87.

d) $y = 75x + 87$

2. $y = -0.75x + 42.5$

3. a) 20 km

b) Slope = 100 (slope could be −100 for some graphs) Answers may vary.

c) $y = 100x + 20$

4. b) Fixed insurance is $10. Hourly rate is $20/h.

5. a) $16.25

b) Tables may vary.

Amount Borrowed	Interest
1	0.05
50	2.50
100	5.00
150	7.50
200	10.00
250	12.50
300	15.00
325	16.25

c) $y = 0.05x$

6. b) $y = 230 - 1.2x$

c) 206 beats/min, 146 beats/min, 188 beats/min

d) Remember that the equation in this exercise represents a generalization that is valid for most people who are in good health. If you have a particular health problem then your recommended maximum heart rate may be lower than the one predicted by the equation.

e) No. People under 20 may not be fully grown, and those over 70 may have special health concerns. In either case, it would be unwise to apply a general formula to them. Also, there is a normal operating range for human hearts, and the relationship between maximum heart rate and age is not likely to continue to be approximately linear near the edges of that range.

f) The maximum heart rate will probably decrease faster than would be predicted by the equation in part b. If we were to try to encompass all of the data with a linear equation, the slope of the line of best fit would probably be less than −1.2. Even with a wider range of data, it would still be unwise to extrapolate beyond the data range in this case.

7. a) 1517.57

b) 790

c) 80

d) $D = 10t + 700$

e) Answers may vary.

8. a) 6.8 L/100 km

b) 10.25 L/100 km

c) $y = \frac{11x + 27}{8}$

Extending Your Thinking

9. a) $E = 20\,000 + 0.03S$

b) $170 000

c) They would make $175 000 with the new contract, so the new contract is better.

10. a) $T = 15 - 6.5x$

b) 15°C

c) −23.68°C

d) 2.3 km

e) No doubt the equation is valid only up to a certain height. (Without doing some research, it's not possible to say what this maximum height is.) Thus, the domain is all real numbers between 0 and whatever the maximum height is. The range is all real numbers between $15 - 6.5H$ and 15, where H is the maximum height.

f) $T = 20 - 6.5x$

TUTORIAL 6.6

Investigations 1, 2, 3, page 288

Answers may vary.

TUTORIAL 6.7

Investigation, page 294

1. (4, 1), (5, 5), (8, 9), (11, 10), (12, 6), (16, 19), (18, 9), (19, 12), (22, 15)

3. (4, 1), (5, 5), (8, 9); (11, 10), (12, 6), (16, 19); (18, 9), (19, 12), (22, 15)

4. (5, 5), (12, 10), (19, 12)

6. $y = \frac{1}{2}x + \frac{5}{2}$

7. 8.5

8. (12, 9)

9. $y = \frac{1}{2}x + 3$

EXERCISES, page 297

Checking Your Skills

1. **a)** Estimated lines of best fit may vary.
2. **a)** $y = -0.00286x + 15.6581$; 9.93 s
   b) Since the slope is negative, the line will eventually intersect the x-axis (about the year 5400); in that year the predicted time is zero! After that, the predicted time is negative! This is absolutely unrealistic, so the line of best fit cannot be a good approximation forever. This should lead us to question whether a linear model is appropriate for this data.
3. **a)** $y = 1.005x - 3.113$ **b)** 27.04 cm
   c) 23.6 weeks

Extending Your Thinking

4. Answers may vary.
5. No. A measurement of 28.3 cm is predicted for a fetus of 31.3 weeks. Since the fetus is 33 weeks old, the discrepancy is 1.7 weeks, which is less than 2 weeks.

TUTORIAL 6.8

Investigation 1, page 301

Answers may vary.

Investigation 2, page 302

1., 2., 3. Answers may vary. $y = 10.5x$

4. $y = 8.5x + 2.617$
5. $y = 6.617x + 4.9472$
6. Answers may vary.

EXERCISES, page 303

Checking Your Skills

1. **a)** Estimated lines of best fit may vary.
2. **a)** $y = -0.00595x + 21.8091$; 9.89 s
   b) Since the slope is negative, the line will eventually intersect the x-axis (about the year 3663); in that year the predicted time is zero! After that, the predicted time is negative! This is absolutely unrealistic, so the line of best fit cannot be a good approximation forever. This should lead us to question whether a linear model is appropriate for this data.
3. **a)** $y = 0.991x - 3.018$
   b) 26.7 cm **c)** 23.83 weeks

Extending Your Thinking

4. Answers may vary.
5. No. A measurement of 28.3 cm is predicted for a fetus of 31.6 weeks. Since the fetus is 33 weeks old, the discrepancy is 1.4 weeks, which is less than 2 weeks.

TUTORIAL 6.9

Investigation, page 305

1. **a)** $r = 0.96$ **b)** $r = 0.98$
   c) $r = 0.75$ **d)** $r = 1$
   e) $r = -0.95$ **f)** $r = 0.59$
   g) $r = -0.68$ **h)** $r = 0.53$
   i) $r = -1$ **j)** $r = -0.17$
2. The least-squares lines of best fit have the following equations:
   a) $y = 0.88x + 0.37$ **b)** $y = 1.52x + 0.66$
   c) $y = 0.65x + 1.62$ **d)** $y = 2x$
   e) $y = -0.76x + 9.77$ **f)** $y = 0.61x + 1.20$
   g) $y = -0.49x + 6.53$ **h)** $y = 0.5x + 2.5$
   i) $y = -0.5x + 8$ **j)** $y = -0.16x + 5.23$
3. Answers may vary.
   a) Very closely **b)** Very closely
   c) Somewhat closely **d)** Exactly
   e) Very closely **f)** Somewhat closely
   g) Somewhat closely **h)** Somewhat closely
   i) Exactly **j)** Not at all
4. Answers may vary.
5. If the correlation coefficient is ± 1, then the data lie exactly on a line. If r is nearly 1 or -1, then the data lie nearly on a line. The closer to 0 that r is, the harder it is to draw a line of best fit, and the more scattered away from the line the data are.
6. Positive slope: a, b, c, d, f, h; negative slope: e, g, i, j. The sign of r is the same as the sign of the slope.

EXERCISES, page 306

Checking Your Skills

1. Sketches may vary.
2. Estimates may vary.
   a) $r = 0.1$ **b)** $r = -0.8$ **c)** $r = 0.97$
   d) $r = 0.99$ **e)** $r = -0.97$
3. **a)** ii
   b) **i)** $r = -0.22$ **ii)** $r = 0.83$
4. **b)** $y = -0.125x + 40.875$; $r = -0.57$
   c) There is no reason to expect the data to be linear. Thus, using a linear model to make predictions makes no sense. This is supported by the correlation coefficient, which is not close to 1. Furthermore, experience tells us that if a high fever has dropped and remained low for the past 4 hours, it is likely to remain low.
5. Scatterplot 2 has a greater r value and its points cluster more closely to a line that the points in scatterplot 1.

Extending Your Thinking

6 **a)** $y = -0.41x + 16.59$; $r = -0.90$
   b) No, because it's not clear whether the data should satisfy a linear model. Furthermore, even if the model is linear, if her guesses were quite wrong, the equation would be changed significantly.
   c) $y = -0.76x + 28.59$; $r = -0.68$

d) Just because the correlation coefficient is close to 1 or –1 does not mean that either the data or the linear model should be considered correct.

CONSOLIDATING YOUR SKILLS

What Should I Be Able To Do?, page 313

2. Answers may vary.

3. 1.405 69 + 11.087 62; $r = 0.83$

4. Yes. A correlation coefficient of 0.83 suggests moderately close agreement to a linear relationship.

5. 36.7 cm

6. Answers may vary.

7. a) x-intercept, (4, 0); y-intercept, (0, –8)
   b) x-intercept, (–8, 0); y-intercept, (0, –6)

8. a) Slope, $\frac{2}{3}$; y-intercept $\left(0, -\frac{10}{3}\right)$
   b) Slope, $\frac{4}{3}$; y-intercept (0, 0)

9. a) The domain is all positive integers, including zero.
   c) Slope, 20; units are cost per unit player. The slope represents the cost to the club for each additional player.
   d) $300. It represents the fixed costs which would be payable even if there were no players.

10. b) 2.4 km   c) 17.5 km/h

11. b) An arithmetic sequence
   d) $y = 0.5x + 2.5$ e) $7.50

12. b) $y = -1818x + 17\ 784.8$
   c) A linear function describes these data very well.
   d) By the method of least squares:
   $y = -1668.75x + 17\ 088, r = -0.9$
   e) Yes, $6000 is a reasonable price. By the median-median method the appropriate asking price is $6877, and by the method of least squares the appropriate asking price is $7075.

CHAPTER 7 TRIGONOMETRY

TUTORIAL 7.1

Practise Your Prior Skills, page 322

1. tan A = 0.4167; ∠A = 23°; AC = 13 cm

2. sin R = 0.44; ∠R = 26.1°; QR = 22 cm

3. XZ = 37 mm; YZ = 18 mm

Investigation 1, page 324

Answers may vary.

EXERCISES, page 326

Checking Your Skills

1. 82°

2. a) 1219 m   b) 10°

3. 35.4 m

4. 14.5 m

5. 4.3 m

6. 24 km

Extending Your Thinking

7. 32°

TUTORIAL 7.2

EXERCISES, page 337

Checking Your Skills

1. 14 cm

2. 21°

3. b) 5.6 m   c) 37%

4. 52.0 m

5. 15.7 m; 8.3 m

6. 52 ft

7. a) 1721 m   b) 4007 m

8. 2215 m

9. 176 m

10. a) BC = 3.5 cm; CA = 4.0 cm
   b) CD = 6; $\frac{BD}{AC} = \sqrt{3} = 1.7$ c) $\frac{BC}{AC}$

Extending Your Thinking

11. 15.9 m

12. 2089 m; 1716 m

TUTORIAL 7.3

Investigation 1, page 341

5.

x	y	Another value of x with the same value for y
2°	0.0349	178°
10°	0.1736	170°
28°	0.4695	152°
32°	0.5299	148°
46°	0.7193	134°
58°	0.8480	122°
62°	0.8829	118°
80°	0.9848	100°
88°	0.9994	92°

7. The numbers add up to 180°.

8. sin 2° = sin 178°
   sin 10° = sin 170°
   sin 38° = sin 142°
   sin 66° = sin 114°
   sin 146° = sin 34°
   sin 154° = sin 26°
   sin 160° = sin 20°
   sin 178° = sin 2°

Investigation 2, page 342

5.

x	y	Another value of x that results in the negative value of y
2°	0.9994	178°
10°	0.9848	170°
28°	0.8829	152°
32°	0.8480	148°
46°	0.6947	134°
58°	0.5299	122°
62°	0.4695	118°
80°	0.1736	100°
88°	0.0349	92°

7. The numbers add up to 180°.

8. cos 2° = −cos 178°
cos 10° = −cos 170°
cos 38° = −cos 142°
cos 66° = −cos 114°
cos 146° = −cos 34°
cos 154° = −cos 26°
cos 160° = −cos 20°
cos 178° = −cos 2°

EXERCISES, page 343

Checking Your Skills

1. a) 160° b) 80°
c) 133° d) 62°

2. a) sin 170° = 0.1736 b) cos 57° = 0.5446
c) sin 6° = 0.1045 d) cos 108° = 0.3090

3. a) sin 50° = 0.7660, cos 50° = 0.6428
b) sin 130° = 0.7660, cos 130° = −0.6428
c) sin 127° = 0.7986, cos 127° = −0.6018
d) sin 140° = 0.6428, cos 140° = −0.7660
e) sin 92° = 0.9994, cos 92° = −0.0349
f) sin 40° = 0.6428, cos 40° = 0.7660
g) sin 88° = 0.9994, cos 88° = 0.0349
h) sin 31° = 0.5150, cos 31° = 0.8572
i) sin 53° = 0.7986, cos 53° = 0.6018
j) sin 149° = 0.5150, cos 149° = −0.8572

4. $90° \le A \le 180°$

5. a) 50°, 130° b) 53°, 127° c) 47°, 133°
d) 35°, 145° e) 67°, 113° f) 30°, 150°
g) 27° h) 126° i) 120°

Extending Your Thinking

6. a) 0.87 b) 0.50

c)

A	cos A	sin A	P(x, y)
15°	0.97	0.26	(0.97, 0.26)
30°	0.87	0.50	(0.87, 0.50)
45°	0.71	0.71	(0.71, 0.71)
60°	0.50	0.87	(0.50, 0.87)
75°	0.26	0.97	(0.26, 0.97)

d), e)

A	cos A	sin A	P(x, y)
90°	0	1	(0, 1)
105°	−0.26	0.97	(−0.26, 0.97)
120°	−0.50	0.87	(−0.50, 0.87)
135°	−0.71	0.71	(−0.71, 0.71)
150°	−0.87	0.50	(−0.87, 0.50)
165°	−0.97	0.26	(−0.97, 0.26)
180°	−1	0	(−1, 0)

TUTORIAL 7.4

Investigation 1, page 347

Answers may vary.

Investigation 3, page 349

3. 37°

5. 15.2 m

TUTORIAL 7.5

EXERCISES, page 355

Checking Your Skills

1. a) 5.6 b) 5

2. a) 37° b) 37°

3. 15.2 km, 21.1 km

4. 42.7 m

5. BP = 5.3 m, FP = 6.6 m

6. a) 88.1° b) 147.3 m

7. 12.7 km

8. a) 233° b) 2.9 km

Extending Your Thinking

9. 122.1 m

10. Answers may vary.

TUTORIAL 7.6

EXERCISES, page 365

Checking Your Skills

1. a) 3.6 b) 5.0 c) 6.1

2. a) 48.5° b) 46.6°

3. 744 m

4. 148.6°

5. 12.9 m, 48.5°, 96.5°

6. angles in triangle: 53.5°, 29.8°, 96.7°;
bearings: 126.5°, 96.7°, 180°

7. 123.7 miles

8. 25.9 km

9. 123.5 min

10. 104.68°

Extending Your Thinking

11. $\cos B = \dfrac{c - b\cos A}{\sqrt{b^2 + c^2 - 2bc\cos A}}$

TUTORIAL 7.7

EXERCISES, page 372

Checking Your Skills

1. 384.1 m

2. 440 m

3. 1884 m; 158 729 m^2

4. 2536 feet

5. a) tree 12A: 1033 cm; tree 50F:1001 cm;
tree 17D: 1044 cm

6. a) Explanations may vary. b) 101 207 m^2

7. 10.4 cm

Extending Your Thinking

8. a) 61.3° b) 28.7°

Consolidating Your Skills

What Should I Be Able To Do?, page 379

2. BC = 176.6 m

3. AD = 98.0 m

5. DC = 161.8 m

6. 490.4 m

7. $19 616

8. 42°

9. Height of the taller building 135.6 m; height of the shorter building 113.5 m

10. **a)** 45° **b)** 180° **c)** 41.4°

11. The person at A is closer. AC = 41 m; BC = 49 m

12. 63.7 feet

13. **a)** 0.6 m **b)** 0.8 m

14. H = 0.72 miles

15. 16 bags for the area of 1387 m^2

UTILITY 2 THE VERNIER CALIPER

Reading a Vernier Caliper, page 391

1. 2.68 inches; 6.81 cm

2. 0.01 inches; 0.04 cm

UTILITY 3 THE MICROMETER

To Read a Micrometer, page 395

1. 13.49 mm

2. 3.80 mm

Index

R

S

T

U

V

W

X

Y

Z

PHOTO CREDITS AND ACKNOWLEDGMENTS

The publisher wishes to thank the following sources for photographs, illustrations, articles, and other materials used in this book. Care has been taken to determine and locate ownership of copyright material used in the text. We will gladly receive information enabling us to rectify any errors or omissions in credits.

PHOTOS

p. 1, 2–3 Dave Starrett; **p. 4** PhotoDisc, Inc.; **p. 6, 7, 8** Dave Starrett; **p. 9** (left) Canapress Picture Archives, (right) Canapress Picture Archives (Canadian Press CP); **p. 10, 12, 14, 18** (top) Dave Starrett, (bottom) Canapress Picture Archives (Associated Press AP); **p. 19** PhotoDisc, Inc.; **p. 20** Canapress Picture Archives (Associated Press AP); **p. 22, 25, 28–29, 30, 32, 35** Dave Starrett; **p. 36** (top) PhotoDisc, Inc., (bottom) Dave Starrett; **p. 38** Dave Starrett; **p. 39–45** PhotoDisc, Inc.; **p. 46** Dave Starrett; **p. 49, 52** PhotoDisc, Inc.; **p. 53** The Everett Collection, Inc.; **p. 54** (left) Dave Starrett; **p. 55, 59, 60** Dave Starrett; **p. 61** (left) PhotoDisc, Inc., (right) Dave Starrett; **p. 62** (left) Dave Starrett; **p. 62–63** (top) Jeff Zaruba/Tony Stone Images, **p. 63** (bottom left) Dave Starrett; **p. 68** Canapress Picture Archives (Canadian Press CP); **p. 71, 72** PhotoDisc, Inc.; **p. 76, 77** Eyewire, Inc.; **p. 81** Dave Starrett; **p. 83** (top) John Henley/First Light, (bottom-clock) Thierry Dosogne/Image Bank; **p. 84** Dave Starrett; **p. 86** Canapress Picture Archives (Canadian Press CP); **p. 87** Maria Stenzel/National Geographic Society Image Collection; **p. 89** Eyewire, Inc.; **p. 91, 93** PhotoDisc, Inc.; **p. 94** (left) Dave Starrett; **p. 94–95** (top) Gary Gladstone/Image Bank, (bottom right) Mahaux Photo/Image Bank; **p. 96, 100** PhotoDisc, Inc.; **p. 102** (left) Dave Starrett; **p. 102–103** (top bkgd) John Banagan/Image Bank, (top middle) Dave Starrett, (bottom) Paul Austring/First Light; **p. 107, 108** Dave Starrett; **p. 109** (left) Dave Starrett, (right) PhotoDisc, Inc.; **p. 110** (left) Dave Starrett, (right) PhotoDisc, Inc.; **p. 111** (top left) Dave Starrett, (bottom, and right), PhotoDisc, Inc.; **p. 112** L. Klove/NonStock/First Light; **p. 114** (top) Marten Bot/Mach 2 Stock Exchange, (bottom) Mach 2 Stock Exchange; **p. 117** Dave Starrett; **p. 125** PhotoDisc, Inc.; **p. 127** First Light; **p. 128** Dave Starrett; **p. 129** PhotoDisc, Inc.; **p. 130, 133**, Dave Starrett; **p. 135** PhotoDisc, Inc.; **p. 136** (left) Dave Starrett, (right) PhotoDisc, Inc.; **p. 137** (top left and top right) PhotoDisc, Inc., (bottom) Dave Starrett; **p. 138** Dave Starrett; **p. 140** PhotoDisc, Inc.; **p. 141** BSIP Krassovsky/Publiphoto; **p. 143** CORBIS/Jacques M. Chenet; **p. 144** Dave Starrett; **p. 146** Ole Tenold/Mach 2 Stock Exchange; **p. 150** (bottom) John Agnone/National Geographic Society Image Collection; **p. 154** (top left, bottom left) Dave Starrett, (middle left) PhotoDisc, Inc., (bottom right) PhotoDisc, Inc.; **p. 155** (top) CORBIS/Ed Young, (bottom) PhotoDisc, Inc.; **p. 158–160** PhotoDisc, Inc.; **p. 161–162** Dave Starrett; **p. 163** (top left) Dave Starrett, (top right) Canapress Picture Archives (Canadian Press AP); **p. 164–165** PhotoDisc, Inc.; **p. 166** Dave Starrett; **p. 169** PhotoDisc, Inc:; **p. 171** Dave Starrett; **p. 172** Thad Samuels Abell II/National Geographic Society Image Collection; **p. 173** Canapress Picture Archives (Associated Press AP); **p. 174** Canapress Picture Archives (Canadian Press CP); **p. 176** Chuck Savage/First Light; **p. 177** Canapress Picture Archives; **p. 179** Canapress Picture Archives (Associated Press AP); **p. 180, 183, 185** Dave Starrett; **p. 190** PhotoDisc, Inc.; **p. 191** (top left) Dave Starrett, (top right and bottom) PhotoDisc, Inc.; **p. 196** PhotoDisc, Inc.; **p. 197** (left) Detlef Schnepel, (right) George Mobley/National Geographic Society Image Collection; **p. 198** (left) Detlef Schnepel; **p. 198–199** (bkgd) Jodi Cobb/National Geographic Society Image Collection, **p. 199** (inset) Canapress Picture Archives (Canadian Press OTTS), (bottom right) Jodi Cobb/National Geographic Society Image Collection; **p. 209** The City of Calgary; **p. 210** John Heseltine/S.P.L./Photo Researchers; **p. 213** Detlef Schnepel; **p. 216** Rob Waymen; **p. 221, 222** (top) L. J. Lozano; **p. 225** George Mobley/National Geographic Society Image Collection; **p. 226** PhotoDisc, Inc.; **p. 228** Ron Watts/First Light; **p. 230** (left) Detlef Schnepel; **p. 230–231** (top) Jodi Cobb/National Geographic Society Image Collection, (bottom) Detlef Schnepel; **p. 231** (bottom right) Canapress Picture Archives (Canadian Press MCTN); **p. 232** Dave Starrett; **p. 237** (left and right) Canapress Picture Archives (Associated Press AP); **p. 238, 246** (left) Detlef Schnepel; **p. 246–247** (top) Eyewire, Inc.; **p. 247** (top right) Jodi Cobb/National Geographic Society Image Collection, (bottom right) Detlef Schnepel; **p. 250–252** Dave Starrett; **p. 253** (left) Canapress Picture Archives (Associated Press AP), (right) Detlef Schnepel; **p. 254** (top left) Detlef Schnepel, (bottom) PhotoDisc, Inc.; **p. 255** (top left) Detlef Schnepel, (right) PhotoDisc, Inc.; **p. 256, 260**, Detlef Schnepel; **p. 267** Victoria Hurst/First Light; **p. 270, 272** Dave Starrett; **p. 280** Detlef Schnepel; **p. 282** Rob Waymen; **p. 285** Canapress Picture Archives (Associated Press AP); **p. 288, 291, 292** (left) Detlef Schnepel; **p. 292–293** (top) Canapress Picture Archives (Associated Press AP), (bottom) Geer T. - WWF/Publiphoto; **p. 293** (top middle) Canapress Picture Archives (Canadian Press CP), (top right) Canapress Picture Archives (Associated Press AP), (bottom right) Detlef Schnepel; **p. 294** George Mobley/National Geographic Society Image Collection; **p. 298** Canapress Picture Archives (Associated Press AP); **p. 302, 304, 310** (top left) Detlef Schnepel; **p. 310** (bottom) Gerard Lacz - Sunset/Publiphoto; **p. 311** (top left) Stephen Homer/First Light, (top right) Detlef Schnepel, (bottom) Gerard Lacz/Publiphoto; **p. 313** Detlef Schnepel; **p. 314–316** PhotoDisc, Inc.; **p. 317** Dave Starrett; **p. 319** (top left) Detlef Schnepel, (top right and bottom) Rob Waymen; **p. 320** Rob Waymen; **p. 321** (top) First Light, (bottom) Rob Waymen; **p. 322** Detlef Schnepel; **p. 328** (top left) Rob Waymen, (middle left and bottom) Dave Starrett; **p. 328–329** (top) PhotoDisc, Inc., (bottom) Rob Waymen; **p. 330** (top left) Rob Waymen; **p. 331** (left) Chris Cheadle/First Light, (bottom right) Rob Waymen; **p. 332** (top) Raymond Gehman/National Geographic Society Image Collection; **p. 347** Detlef Schnepel; **p.360** (top) Maria Stenzel/National Geographic Society Image Collection; **p. 361** Corbis/Bettmann; **p. 368** (top) Richard Olsenius/National Geographic Society Image Collection; **p. 374** Dave Starrett; **376–377** (top) Rob Waymen, (bottom) PhotoDisc, Inc.; **p. 381** (bottom) PhotoDisc, Inc.; **p. 382–383** Dave Starrett; **p. 389–397** Paul Williams/Red Deer College/Red Deer, Alberta **p. 397** Dave Starrett; **p. 401–403** Detlef Schnepel; **p. 404–407** L. J. Lozano; **p. 409** Detlef Schnepel; **p. 409** Detlef Schnepel; **p. 412** L. J. Lozano; **p. 415** Detlef Schnepel

ILLUSTRATIONS

Michael Herman: 54 (middle), 119–121, 145, 150 (top), 163 (bottom), 170, 184, 193, 275, 363, 370, 375
Margo Davies Leclair: 175, 188, 207, 283
Dave McKay: 208, 222 (bottom), 241, 242, 249, 325, 327, 330, 332 (bottom), 334–346, 351–358, 360 (bottom), 365, 368 (bottom), 369, 372–373, 379–380, 381 (top)
Jack McMaster: 26, 51
Jun Park: 116, 202
Pronk&Associates: 157
Rose Zgodzinski: 79, 201, 205, 297, 309